HISTORY OF THE JEWISH NATION

HISTORY

OF

THE JEWISH NATION

*AFTER THE DESTRUCTION OF JERUSALEM
UNDER TITUS*

BY

ALFRED EDERSHEIM

Revised by
HENRY A. WHITE

With a Preface by
WILLIAM SANDAY

BAKER BOOK HOUSE
Grand Rapids, Michigan

Paperback edition issued January 1979
by Baker Book House Company

ISBN: 0-8010-3335-7

PHOTOLITHOPRINTED BY CUSHING - MALLOY, INC.
ANN ARBOR, MICHIGAN, UNITED STATES OF AMERICA
1 9 7 9

PREFACE TO THE THIRD EDITION

THE years which have elapsed since the death of Dr. Edersheim have served to enhance rather than to diminish the sense of his loss. He had more than one contemporary who was, like himself, at once Jew and Christian, and, like himself, had command of the common ground of both. In particular, there was a group gathered round the great Franz Delitzsch,—Dr. Ferdinand Weber, whose *System der altsynagogalen palästinischen Theologie*, published posthumously under the editorship of Delitzsch and Schnedermann, is a work of the highest utility, and Dr. J. H. R. Biesenthal, who left behind an edition of the Epistle to the Hebrews, which contains some information not accessible to everyone. At Christiania there was Dr. C. P. Caspari, a giant of learning, whose field of labour was, however, less characteristic of his origin. In England we had also here and there a Christian Rabbi. But now all these—or nearly all—are gone; and though there still remain some distinguished Jewish scholars who treat of things Christian, and some distinguished Christian scholars who treat of things Jewish, I know not where we could point either to the Jew whose Christian profession opened to him the secret of the New Testament, or to the Christian whose Jewish birth gave him the almost indispensable key to the stores of the Talmud.

For these reasons, every work of Dr. Edersheim's is invested with peculiar value; and it will, I think, be felt that this applies in a high degree to the work which is now once more offered to the public. The first edition appeared in 1856, and was quickly followed by a second. The book was written some ten years after the author's admission to the Scottish Free Church, and when he was engaged in active parochial work at Old Aberdeen. A brief account of this period is given in the Memoir prefixed to the collection of Thoughts and Aphorisms published after his death under the title *Tohu-va-Vohu* (Longmans, 1890). As the work of a young man of thirty, whose career had been broken by the struggles and sacrifices consequent upon his conversion to Christianity, it is indeed remarkable.

In preparing a new edition, two objects had to be kept in view. It was of course essential to go through Dr. Edersheim's own later work, so as to take account of every modification or development of opinion in the author himself; and it was also desirable to check the results by comparison with the collateral literature which has appeared since 1856, and especially with the great work of Schürer, *Geschichte der jüdischen Volkes im Zeitalter Jesu Christi*, now translated into English (first edition, 1874; second edition, 1886–1890; Eng. translation, 1885–1890). Dr. Schürer and Dr. Edersheim may be said to be the complements of each other: with the one the centre of gravity rests in the Greek and Roman sources, and in the balanced judgment of the trained Western philologist; with the other, in the Talmud and the inborn imaginative sympathy with every side of Jewish life. I hope and believe that something of these double excellences will be found in this new edition as it has been prepared by Mr. H. A. White, to whose loyalty and care I gladly bear witness.

Thanks are also due to the publishers, who, although they had acquired possession of the stereotyped plates, liberally consented to forego the use of these, and to issue the work in a form which is altogether improved, and, in its present shape, a fitting memorial to its author.

W. SANDAY.

OXFORD, *November* 1895.

AUTHOR'S PREFACE

FOR many years have I cherished the desire of writing a History of the Jewish Nation. It is remarkable, that a work apparently of such interest and importance to the Christian student should not long ere this have been supplied. It is my deliberate conviction that Jewish History casts much light on the evangelical accounts in the Gospels, on the Book of Acts, and on later Ecclesiastical History, both in its records of the spread of Christianity, and of the origin and development of heretical sects.

The illustrations which Jewish History affords of the New Testament are not confined to a description of the circumstances, social relations, and religious opinions which are there assumed as well known. It is impossible to read even a single page in the Gospels without being struck with the contrast between the spiritual tendency and direction of the Old Testament, as there brought to light, and the formalism and literalism of the Synagogue. A simple and impartial account of Judaism on the one hand, and a perusal of the Gospels on the other, constitutes one of the most convincing proofs of the Divine origin of the Christian religion, and of its organic connection with that of the Old Testament. Again, it is impossible to read the Gospel narrative in the light of Jewish history without feeling that the notions and circumstances to which it alludes, are exactly those of the time in which Jesus Christ lived and taught on earth. They apply to that period, and to that period only. The notions, the modes of speaking, the opposition and its very manner, to which the New Testament refers, are exactly those of that period. If a copy of the Gospels were put into the hands of an impartial Jewish historian, he could not fail to discover that the events there chronicled must have taken place exactly at the time when, according to Christian belief, Jesus walked amongst men. The Gospels, historically speaking, cannot be an after-production. However, as it was my purpose not so much to illustrate the New Testament as rather to give an account of the Jewish nation, I have, in this book, almost entirely omitted direct references to its statements.

In the course of this history I have sometimes indicated the bearing of Jewish upon Ecclesiastical History, and especially on the origin of Gnosticism. Without entering on the common causes of all mysticism, every student must have felt some difficulty in accounting for the sudden rise of the Gnostic sects, and for the apparent extravagancies of their systems, the more so as coming so soon after the promulgation of Christian truth. But if it be true that these sects found their prototype in Jewish mysticism, their origin and spread is explained. In general, it may be desirable to trace back every heresy or misbelief to its source and origin, and to connect it, as far as possible, with the erroneous tendency in the Church from which it sprung, and to which it claims kindred. It is thus only that Ecclesiastical History, in its facts, development, and contests, can be satisfactorily presented. To these considerations it is unnecessary to add anything regarding the interest which must attach to the history of the Jewish nation in the minds of those who take a proper view of their past, their present, and their future.

In preparing my materials for this volume, I have freely availed myself of the labours of any, Jews or Christians, historians or antiquarians, whose productions were within reach, or could be of use. This general acknowledgment must be taken instead of detailed references in every case to special sources of information, which would needlessly have encumbered the book. To have mentioned once a work or a section to which I was indebted, must be held to imply that I availed myself as frequently and fully of its aid as I felt requisite. The researches, of which this volume is the result, have been laborious and conscientious. They have been unremittingly prosecuted during four years, so far as ministerial and other engagements have permitted. I can only add, that I have attempted to write fairly and impartially, and, although thoroughly convinced of the truth of Christianity, and cordially attached to my nation, have not allowed either the one or the other to bias me in the representation of facts.

The information which this volume is intended to communicate has hitherto lain scattered over a large number of books and pamphlets, and been partly buried in ancient and neglected records. Amongst ourselves, later Jewish History has been almost entirely neglected. With all respect for the writers, it can scarcely be maintained that in the existing manuals the History of the Jews, after the destruction of Jerusalem, has ever been satisfactorily written in the English language. Even the minute investigations of the Germans have produced a large variety of treatises rather than a connected history. The first and the most impartial of modern German Jewish historians was Dr. Jost of Frankfort, whose history, extending over ten volumes, opened the way. The work of Dr. Grätz (of which only one volume has as yet appeared) contains later, and in many respects more accurate information, but is disfigured by violent partisanship, and an uncompromising enmity to Christianity, which often does violence to plain historical facts. The short sketch in Ersch's Encyclopedia, by Selig Cassel, who, I am glad to know from his later writings, has since become a convert to Christianity, is, as all the writings of that author, replete with sound sense, and contains most extensive and accurate information. To these historians I have been deeply indebted, as well as to the researches of Prideaux, Lightfoot, Selden, Buxtorf, Bartolocci, Wolfius, and the classical labours of Winer, Delitzsch, Zunz, Frankel, Hirschfeld, Dukes, Franck, Dähne, Ideler, Gfrörer, Forbiger, Hartmann, Schwartz, etc. Basnage is not always accurate, and adds little to one's stock of information ; but he was one of the first in the field. The works of Eisenmenger, Wagenseil, and others of the same stamp, are disfigured by their violent hatred of Judaism and the Jews. Of the works of Christian Fathers and of ecclesiastical writers I have availed myself so far as requisite.

It was the peculiar object of this History, not only to give an impartial account of *facts*, but especially to describe the state of society, of trades, commerce, agriculture, arts, sciences,

theology, etc., during the first centuries of our era.   In this
respect I beg to refer the reader more especially to Chapters
IX., X., and XI., which have probably cost more labour and
involved more research than any other part of the book.   Too
often, in the narrative of events, it has been necessary to
indicate that some Jewish accounts were apparently more or
less legendary or exaggerated,—a circumstance which could
perhaps scarcely be avoided in the then state of science, and
by writers who composed their accounts very much in the
spirit of religious partisanship.

The materials for it being ready, I hope that the second
volume, in which I intend to bring down this History *to our
own days*, will shortly appear.

Any disproportion between the period over which this
volume extends, and that which the next is to describe, can
readily be explained.   Many previous facts of Jewish History
which could not be taken for granted, had to be introduced in
the first volume, and in general the commencement of the
Christian era seemed to require a more elaborate record.
Besides, in deference to the judgment of those in whom I
have full confidence, I resolved to condense in *one* volume
what had originally been meant to extend over *two*.   In
acknowledging my obligations to others, I have specially to
thank the authorities of King's College, Aberdeen, for the
liberal use which they have allowed me to make of its library;
Dr. Jost of Frankfort, for his advice, as also the Rev. Dr.
Hanna of Edinburgh for the encouragment given by him.
My friend the Rev. Walter Wood, of Elie, has rendered me
most valuable assistance, both during the composition of the
manuscript and the revision of the proofs, by the suggestions
which his extensive reading and elegant taste have prompted.

In bringing these labours to a close, I may perhaps be
allowed to plead the extent and difficulty of the undertaking,
in extenuation of any imperfections which may be pointed out.
Still, I am thankful and glad that these, the "first-fruits"
of my studies in Ecclesiastical History, should be devoted
to a cause and service which I have so deeply at heart.

OLD ABERDEEN, *3rd May* 1856.

EDITORIAL NOTE

A FEW words of explanation must be given with regard to
the additions and alterations introduced into the present
edition of the *History of the Jewish Nation*. Where small
changes or obvious corrections were required, they have been
made without acknowledgment. Larger alterations, on the
other hand, are enclosed within square brackets, except where
the editor had the express authority of any of Dr. Edersheim's
more recent writings. It did not, however, seem to be
necessary to mark in any special way passages which have
been simply abridged, or passages in which a quotation has
been corrected by a comparison with the words of the original
author. It has not been possible to be quite consistent in
indicating the fresh matter, for which the present editor is
alone responsible; but the endeavour has been made, in no
case to seem to attribute to Dr. Edersheim opinions which
he perhaps would not have himself endorsed. In the preparation of this edition the valuable library of Dr. Edersheim,
which was presented after his death to Exeter College, has
been of the greatest service.

References to the Mishna are given according to the
edition of Surenhusius, but in the tractate *Pirke Aboth*
according to the edition of Strack (Berlin, 1888). In Philo

the pages cited are those of Mangey. In quotations from the Talmud and Midrashim, use has generally been made of the translations of Wünsche, where available. Below will be found a list of the complete titles of certain works, which are frequently referred to in the footnotes in an abbreviated form.

H. A. W.

Life and Times, . *The Life and Times of Jesus the Messiah*, by Dr. Edersheim, 6th ed., 1891.

SCHÜRER . . . *The Jewish People in the Time of Jesus Christ.* English Translation (T. & T. Clark), 1885–90.

BACHER, *Tann.* . *Die Agada der Tannaiten*, vol. i. 1884; vol. ii. 1890.

BACHER, *Pal. Amor.* *Die Agada der palästinensischen Amoräer*, vol. i. 1892.

DERENBOURG . *Histoire de la Palestine*, 1867.

Dict. Chr. Biog. . Smith and Wace, *Dictionary of Christian Biography*, 1877–87.

GRÄTZ . . . . *Geschichte der Juden*, vol. iii. 4th ed., 1888; vol. iv. 2nd ed.

HAMBURGER . . *Real-Encyclopädie für Bibel und Talmud*, 1883; Supplementband i., 1886.

LEVY, *NHWB* . *Neuhebräisches Wörterbuch*, 1871–89.

MOMMSEN . . . *The Provinces of the Roman Empire.* English Translation, 1886.

NEUBAUER . . . *La Géographie du Talmud*, 1868.

WEBER . . . . *System der altsynagogalen palästinischen Theologie*, 1880.

ZUNZ . . . . . *Die Gottesdienstlichen Vorträge der Juden*, 2nd ed., 1892.

CONTENTS

———

APPENDIX

HISTORY OF THE JEWISH NATION

CHAPTER I

THE HEBREW COMMONWEALTH

In the Divine dispensation, Israel was destined to sustain the highest and most important part that can be assigned to any nation. Originally chosen to be the depositary of spiritual truth, and separated from all other nations in order to fulfil this mission, it was preserved till the Divine purposes were accomplished. These purposes seem to have been, to serve as the channel and as the exemplification of Divine truth, and to afford a medium by which the fulness of Divine truth, and of Divine fact, might become embodied in the person of the Lord Jesus Christ.

If every nation is the representative, and its history the embodiment, of *some* truth, this applies in a special manner, or at least becomes specially manifest, in the case of Israel Israel was meant to be a *theocracy*. Not only in its ecclesiastical, but in its political constitution also, was it to show forth the supremacy, the authority, and the continued presence of Jehovah with His Covenant people. If this truth was to be exhibited in the world, it became necessary to fix upon and to separate from the rest one nation. But though in the *preparatory* stage national, these were spiritual facts and truths, which ultimately could not belong, and were not meant to be confined to any *one* race. These realities are necessarily universal; they are designed for and apply to all, both to those who are afar off, and to those who are nigh.

Another, and a kindred feature, of the preparatory dispensation, was its *typical* character. Israel, its history, its ordinances, its prophecies, all were not only so many present realities, they pointed also to something future, to which they stood in the relationship of shadows. The grand end and meaning of the preparatory stage was to show the need of, and to open the way for, the advent of the Saviour. With His coming, what was typical gave place to what is real—what was preparatory ceased. " Grace and truth have been brought to light by the Gospel."

The truths which the Old Testament dispensation and history embodied, were chiefly these,—that Jehovah is the *living*, and that He is the *true* God. In opposition to heathenism, it exhibited the unity, the personality, the character, and the purposes of the Deity. We do not deny that certain traditions, containing some portions of spiritual truth, circulated amongst the heathen, nor that the spirit of God who moved over that chaotic deep awakened amongst them aspirations after, and ultimately produced a general preparedness for, the coming of the kingdom. But we hold that the pre-Christian history of the world only exemplified the experience contained in the Book of Ecclesiastes, and may be summed up in the words of an Apostle,—" The world by wisdom knew not God." Here all the different tendencies of thought, of morals, and of fact, were allowed to ripen into maturity, and in turn proved that, in the highest and only true aim, man left to himself is as unprofitable, and hence must, in the righteous dispensation of his Lord, meet with the same doom as did the unfruitful fig-tree which Jesus cursed. The Jewish nation also, notwithstanding the eternal seed in the midst of it, misunderstood its mission, and, when finally left to its own development, only exhibited by its judgments the truths which at one time it had, and is again designed to declare and to enjoy.

The misunderstandings of the Jews reached their climax in the national rejection of the Saviour, and after this the downfall of Jerusalem was not long delayed. Yet even after the destruction of the temple and city, they eagerly followed out the same religious tendency which had led to that catastrophe, and developed the formalism of true religion to its utmost, until their religion became only a recollection of the past. Still, Israel was to have a future history, and it could not be destroyed. They wandered, but could not be lost. However, in none of their undertakings could they prosper. It was vain for them, once and again, to renew the unequal contest for national restoration, although they achieved deeds of valour unsurpassed by those of any other nation. They thought and laboured in their colleges; they prayed and fasted in their synagogues; they wrought and gained in their temporal pursuits. But their researches were fruitless for good; they did not benefit the world by their religious ardour; nor were they even allowed to enjoy the advantages of their activity and commerce. *Ichabod* was written upon all their undertakings, for the glory had departed. Israel and its history are typical; yet will they, as such, meet with a blessed realisation.

Viewed in this light, the history of the Jews gains additional interest and importance. Their past importance can scarcely be overstated; they gave to the world a Bible and a Saviour. Their present importance is indicated by their almost miraculous national preservation, and the fact of their being scattered by the Divine hand broadcast over the fields of the world and of its history, as so many seeds of spiritual truths. Their future importance lies in this, that they are seeds which are yet to take root, to spring up and to bear fruit; and that their future is connected with the last and brightest events of coming history. Israel and its history are inseparably connected with Scripture. We meet them everywhere; and everywhere their past, their present, and their future are full of the deepest meaning. And so shall it continue to be, till their bringing in prove "as life from the dead."

During the period of the Judges, the nation of Israel was gradually gaining in unity and strength, and it enjoyed its greatest prosperity in a political point of view under the reign of David. The splendour of Solomon's reign only concealed for a while the corruption of the social and religious life of the nation which then commenced. The introduction of foreign luxury and foreign customs soon produced its natural result. From that period we may date the commencement of the peculiar pre-Babylonian form of religious apostasy. It had, indeed, appeared even before that event; but now it rapidly developed, and finally assumed gigantic proportions. In this stage the idolatry of Israel consisted not so much in the rejection of the truth, as in its admixture with and neutralisation by foreign elements. The worship of Jehovah was not wholly set aside, but He was only looked upon as their national Deity; and along with Him other national Deities were more or less avowedly made objects of worship. The sad consequences of this made themselves felt in the series of national judgments, which terminated in the deportation of Israel, and then of Judah to Babylon. Israel without its God, became Israel without its country. This judgment had so far its effects, that the spiritual degeneracy of Israel never afterwards appeared again in the form of idolatry. There were some who, in the school of affliction, had in Babylon sought after the Lord God of Israel. But side by side with them were those who, while willing to acknowledge their former national sins, and desirous of returning to the land of their fathers, expressed their repentance by simply going to the opposite extreme of an exclusively Jewish formalism. And now Jehovah was still only a national Deity, although *the only* national Deity,—just as the Jews were the only nation; all others had neither meaning nor purpose. Judaism as such, in its national and typical state, was the sole and the highest truth.

Such, in its religious aspects, was the Jewish nation when the captives returned to the land of their fathers. It will readily be conceived that this event encouraged and strengthened the peculiar *national* tendencies to which we have already alluded. In fact, the second or *post-Babylonian* form of spiritual degeneracy had now been entered upon. It consisted in laying an extreme value upon the form and letter as such, and developing it alone. In room of the priest came the teacher or Rabbi; in room of experience, knowledge; in room of the spirit and reality of the Bible, its letter and form. So much was this the case, that even when the temple was at last destroyed, and the Old Testament economy had thereby become impossible, the change was only felt in a national, not in a religious point of view. It was this tendency which opposed itself to the spirituality of the Gospel, and led to the rejection of the Son of God. That event must not be looked upon as an isolated fact. The contest between the Pharisees and the Lord was in reality that of opposing religions; as far as the Scribes were concerned, it was a life and death struggle. The synagogue contended for continued existence in its peculiar form. It overcame, because it could make use of carnal weapons; but from that moment the doom of Israel was sealed. Before the coming of Christ, two parties might co-exist within the Jewish nation and the synagogue. A contest was still possible. But His advent closed it by bringing it to the issue of a battle. After His death, and before the destruction of Jerusalem, a mistake was still possible. But the latter event made any misunderstanding for ever impossible. With His own hand God took down the tabernacle, and closed the temple doors: He put His seal to the termination of the Old Testament dispensation.

But we have so far anticipated certain points in the religious history of the Jews, to which we shall have to recur more fully in the sequel. We return to sketch their political history. After their return from Babylon, the Jews continued subject to the kings of Persia, and under the administration of their own high priests. But when Alexander the Great on his march of conquest subdued Syria, Judea also fell into his power. A Jewish tradition[1] relates that, when the high priest Jaddua refused to pay to him in future the customary tribute, on the plea of his oath of allegiance to the Persian monarch, Alexander advanced against Jerusalem. But at no great distance from the city he was met by a solemn procession, with the high priest at its head, who had come to welcome the conquerer, in obedience to a command given to Jaddua in a vision. It is added that Alexander had

[1] Jos. *Ant.* xi. 8. 3-5; comp. Joma 69*a*.

seen a similar vision, and, in accordance with its injunction,
now received the deputation most graciously, not only spared
their city and temple, but even offered sacrifices there, and
accorded great privileges to the Jewish nation. This narrative,
whatever may be its historical value, and the numerous other
stories about Alexander which Jewish legend has to record,
prove at least the deep impression which his appearance
made ; and certainly ever afterwards the Jews remained
attached to his interests. It is well known that Alexander
succeeded in his enterprises, that he conquered Persia, and at
last died in the midst of his prosperity at Babylon.

After his decease, his former generals, who obtained
possession of the various provinces which had constituted his
empire, became speedily involved in mutual hostilities. The
first consequence of these disturbances, so far as Judea was
concerned, was that Ptolemy Lagus, to whom Egypt had been
assigned, along with it seized upon Palestine.[1] The reign of
that prince was very prosperous. Mild and humane, he not
only confirmed the privileges which Alexander had conferred
on the Jews, but encouraged their settlement in the city of
Alexandria, and in the province of Cyrene. But when his
rival Antigonus, whose ambition was equalled by his courage,
possessed himself for a time of Syria, Phœnicia, and Palestine,
the latter country became the theatre of war. This circumstance must have contributed to swell the number of Jewish
emigrants into Egypt. But a victory gained over his
antagonist at Gaza soon restored Palestine to Ptolemy. At
the same time the allies of Ptolemy attempted to make a
diversion in the East against Antigonus. Seleucus, a general
who shared the enlightened policy of Ptolemy, was encouraged
to endeavour there to found an empire for himself. Babylonia
gladly welcomed him. He became the first of a dynasty.
His accession was hailed in the East as the commencement of
a new era. Men reckoned after it, and the so-called "Seleucian
Era " dates from the period of his gaining firm possession of
the above province (about 312 B.C.).[2] Soon afterwards,

---

[1] Jos. *Ant.* xii. 1. 1.   On what follows compare generally *Life and Times*, ii.
App. iv.   [2] Ideler, *Chronologie*, i. 450-453.

Antigonus, who had gained some successes against the Arabs and in Greece, attempted an invasion of Egypt, but was completely repulsed. The ambitious plans of that restless monarch, together, perhaps, with a growing desire on the part of Seleucus, who had now firmly established his power in the East, to possess himself of the dominions of Antigonus, led to a grand combined attack against the latter, in which Seleucus took the lead. Antigonus was beaten, and fell in battle; and Seleucus received Syria, Asia Minor, and the provinces east of the Euphrates, as his share in the common spoil. Seleucus prosecuted the same liberal policy in his new dominions, which had secured for him the attachment of his Babylonian subjects. He built a number of large cities, amongst them Antioch and Laodicea in Syria, and encouraged the influx of wealthy, industrious, and loyal Jewish settlers, by according them privileges similar to those which their brethren enjoyed in Egypt.[1] These not only constituted them citizens, but made them in some respects independent, by placing them under the government of rulers of their own. Meantime the Jewish high priest Jaddua had been succeeded by Onias I. (about 321 B.C.), and the latter, by Simon the Just (about 300 B.C.), to whom tradition ascribes an extensive and import-ant part in the religious history of the Jews.

But the successors of the kings of Syria and Egypt did not inherit the moderation of their fathers. They became embroiled in mutual jealousies and in hostilities, which led to no decisive result in favour of either party, but enabled the disaffected subjects of Antiochus II., on the eastern banks of the Tigris, to found what afterwards grew into the formidable Parthian Empire. The war between the monarchs of Syria and Egypt was at last terminated by the marriage of Antiochus with the daughter of Ptolemy II. But on the death of the latter monarch, his daughter, the Syrian queen, was re-pudiated. Antiochus recalled in her stead a former wife of his, who, dreading the fickleness of her lover, murdered him, and placed her son Seleucus on the throne. Ptolemy III. now marched upon Syria, in order to avenge the disgrace and

[1] Jos. *Ant.* xii. 3. 1.

the murder of his sister, who had fallen a victim to her
former rival.   The queen-mother was killed, and Seleucus
obtained from Ptolemy a ten years' truce.   He was defeated
by the Parthians, who thus secured their independence, and,
dying after a reign of twenty-one years, was succeeded by his
son, Seleucus III., and, after the murder of the latter, by
Antiochus III.   Meanwhile the inhabitants of Palestine had
continued to enjoy the favour of the Egyptian monarchs, to
whom they were tributary.   The successors of the high priest
Simon the Just were Eleazar, Manasseh, and Onias II. (about
250 B.C.).[1]   All these priests farmed the revenues of Palestine
for a certain sum, which they undertook annually to pay to
the king of Egypt.   In return, they exercised a kind of
sovereignty in Palestine, where they administered affairs
according to the Divine law.   But Onias had, for a considerable time, omitted to pay this tribute,—a course which, but
for the timely interposition of his nephew Joseph, would have
led to serious circumstances.   It is about this time that the
political leanings of a certain party of the Jews towards Syria,
and the moral deterioration by the introduction of Grecian
manners and modes of thinking, led to the formation of a Hellenising party.   The influence of the Syrians became daily greater.

The Egyptian king, Ptolemy III., had been succeeded by
his son, Ptolemy IV., who abandoned himself to every vice.
Encouraged by the inactivity of the Egyptians, Antiochus
III. of Syria overran and took Phenicia and Palestine.   But
Ptolemy at last roused himself from his drunken revels, met
and overcame his antagonist near Raphia (217 B.C.), and
recovered his ancient possessions.   The Greek romance known
as the Third Book of the Maccabees records the persecutions
which the Jews are said to have suffered at the hands of
Ptolemy upon his return to Egypt.[2]   We are told that after
his victory the king visited Jerusalem.   There he attempted
to penetrate into the Holiest of all, against the advice of the
high priest, Simon II. (who had succeeded Onias II.), and was
struck down by the hand of the Lord.   On his return to
Egypt he meant to vent his resentment upon the Jews of

[1] Jos. *Ant.* xii. 4. 1–5.   [2] Comp. Schürer, II. iii. 216–219.

Alexandria, whom he deprived of their privileges, and even resolved to exterminate. For this purpose he caused them to be shut up in the arena and exposed to elephants. But when these animals only turned against the assembled spectators instead of the Jews, and other portents appeared, the superstitious king as suddenly changed, and restored to the Jews their former privileges. [Josephus [1] relates this story in a simpler and probably more original form, but he refers the events to the reign of Ptolemy VII.]

Ptolemy IV. was succeeded by his infant son, Ptolemy V. Antiochus III. of Syria availed himself of the period of helplessness of the Egyptian monarch, to regain Cœle-Syria and Palestine. In this undertaking he was encouraged by a party amongst the Jews. At last a peace was concluded between the two monarchs, on condition of a marriage between Cleopatra, the daughter of Antiochus, and young Ptolemy, and on the understanding that Cleopatra should receive the disputed provinces as her dowry. This treaty left Antiochus at liberty to encounter other and much more powerful opponents, in the coming masters of the world—the Romans. But he was unsuccessful, and was obliged to conclude a very disadvantageous peace, and to give hostages, amongst them his son, Antiochus Epiphanes. Soon afterwards he was slain in Persia, and succeeded by his son, Seleucus IV.

Meanwhile the times were becoming more troublous in Palestine, which had never been surrendered to the Egyptian monarch. A dispute arose between Onias III., the son and successor of Simon II., and a certain Simon, a captain of the temple guard, who belonged to the Hellenising party. Simon appealed to the cupidity of the Syrians by referring to the untold treasures deposited in the temple. Probably it was only superstition which arrested the Syrian general at that time, but a well-known legend [2] relates how the treasurer Heliodorus was struck down by a supernatural apparition when he attempted to plunder the temple. Onias appealed to Seleucus against Simon, and for the rest of his reign that king seems to have been favourable to the Jews.

[1] *Against Apion*, ii. 5. [2] 2 Macc. iii.

But a period of severe persecution commenced after the murder of Seleucus by Heliodorus, when Antiochus IV., surnamed Epiphanes, who had just returned from Rome, succeeded his brother on the throne of Syria (175 B.C.). First, Onias III. was superseded by his brother Jason, who had bribed the king, and obtained not only the priesthood, but leave to erect a gymnasium at Jerusalem.[1] This institution proved a source of very great temptation to the Jewish youth, by leading them to conform to Grecian manners. Under that wicked priest the Grecian party became almost dominant. Jason was in turn superseded by a new rival, Menelaus, who had promised a larger sum to Antiochus than that which had been paid by his predecessor. In order to raise it, he plundered the temple treasury, and then incited his accomplices to the murder of Onias, who from his exile had protested against the sacrilege. It was in vain the Jews appealed for redress to Antiochus; their deputies were only slaughtered. Meantime, Ptolemy V. had died, and the executors of his children claimed from Antiochus the provinces which had been promised to their father. On the refusal of Antiochus, both parties prepared for war, and the Syrian monarch soon possessed himself of Egypt. During the confusion, the priest Jason returned to Jerusalem, and forced Menelaus to seek refuge in the castle of the Syrian garrison attached to the city.[2] But Antiochus soon marched upon the Jewish capital, and not only obliged Jason to retire, but, regarding the resistance to his nominee as rebellion against himself, he took a fearful vengeance, by slaughter of the inhabitants of Jerusalem and plunder of the temple.[3] Two years later (168 B.C.), Antiochus again invaded Egypt, when the Roman Senate peremptorily ordered him to withdraw. He sullenly obeyed, but vented his anger upon the Jews. He despatched Apollonius, his chief collector of tribute, with 22,000 men to Jerusalem, where the inhabitants received them cheerfully, not surmising any evil. Then the Syrian soldiery was let loose upon the Jews. The men were slaughtered, and

[1] 2 Macc. iv. 7–50; Jos. *Ant.* xii. 5. 1.   [2] 2 Macc. v. 1–10.
[3] 1 Macc. i. 20–28; 2 Macc. v. 11–21; Jos. *Ant.* xii. 5. 3.

the women and children sold into slavery. Whoever was able escaped from the city ; the sanctuary was deserted, and the daily worship ceased. Jerusalem was henceforth to be a Greek city ; and the better to ensure this result, the old walls were broken down, and the citadel in the neighbourhood of the temple was newly fortified and occupied by a Syrian garrison.[1]

And now began an unprecedented persecution, for the Syrian king had resolved on nothing short of an extinction of the Jewish faith.[2] For that purpose he converted the temple at Jerusalem into one dedicated to Jupiter Olympius. A small heathen altar was reared on the great altar of burnt offering, and on the 25th Chislev (December) the first sacrifice was offered upon it. Circumcision, the keeping of the Sabbath, and every outward observance of the law, were made capital crimes. Every copy of the law was to be surrendered to the authorities and destroyed ; every Jew in Palestine was to be obliged to apostatise. In the persecutions which now ensued, many noble instances of a preference of death to blasphemy occurred. At last, Mattathias, a priest, and the head of the Asmonean family, raised the standard of resistance to the Syrian tyranny, and called upon all the faithful in Israel to arm in defence of their lives and laws.[3] The mountains of Judea afforded the little band a secure retreat and meeting-place. Gradually the number of armed patriots increased into a little army. The first important step they took was to agree that it should be considered lawful to defend themselves on Sabbath-days—a resolution of great practical moment, as it protected the Jews from hostile attacks, which frequently were planned in the belief that they would not be resisted on the day of rest. The aged Mattathias soon died, but was succeeded by his vigorous and youthful son, Judas Maccabæus.[4] Notwithstanding their great disparity in numbers, Judas routed and slew Apollonius, the Syrian general. To obtain means for

[1] 1 Macc. i. 29–40 ; 2 Macc. v. 23–26 ; Jos. *Ant.* xii. 5. 4.
[2] 1 Macc. i. 41–64 ; 2 Macc. vi. vii. Comp. Schürer, I. i. 206 ff.
[3] 1 Macc. ii. 15–70 ; Jos. *Ant.* xii. 6. 2–4.
[4] 1 Macc. iii. iv. ; 2 Macc. viii. ; Jos. *Ant.* xii. 7.

carrying on the Jewish and other campaigns, King Antiochus proceeded eastwards, in the hope of replenishing his exhausted treasury by the spoil of temples and cities.   Meanwhile the governor Lysias, to whose charge the king had committed his infant son, was to continue the Jewish war.   So confident were the Syrians of success, that a large number of slave merchants thronged their camp, preparing to purchase the expected Jewish captives.   A Syrian detachment, considerably superior to that of Judas, was sent to meet the Jews.   But the latter eluding them, managed to surprise the Syrian camp, routed the panic-stricken soldiers, killed many, took others captive, and got an immense booty.   When the Syrian detachment which had been sent to meet Judas returned from its unsuccessful expedition, and discovered the camp in flames, terror seized them, and they also fled precipitately.   A second campaign, undertaken the following year, terminated as disadvantageously for the Syrians ; and Judas, advancing to Jerusalem, purified the temple, and solemnly rededicated it, exactly three years after its desecration.

During the next two years the Syrian government was fully occupied by events elsewhere.   Antiochus Epiphanes died towards the close of the year 164,[1] and Lysias administered the kingdom during the minority of his successor, Antiochus v.   Judas meantime was engaged in fortifying strong positions in Judea, and chastising the hostile heathen border tribes.   But when he laid siege to the citadel of Jerusalem, some of the Syrian garrison who had escaped, together with representatives of the Grecian party among the Jews, appealed to Lysias for help.   He invaded Judea with a powerful army, and forced Judas to seek safety behind the fortifications of Jerusalem.   The prospect was becoming hopeless, when troubles at home recalled the Syrian army, and led to a treaty of peace, in which the Jews acknowledged Syrian supremacy, but were secured liberty of conscience and worship.   After his retreat Lysias is said to have put to death the apostate high priest Menelaus.   It was probably a few years later that the son of the murdered Onias, who had

[1] 1 Macc. vi.; Jos. *Ant.* xii. 9 ; xiii. 3.

taken refuge in Egypt, seeing no prospect of ever receiving his priestly inheritance, founded a rival temple at Heliopolis.

Judas Maccabæus was now practically at the head of the Jewish people, and from this point a new period commences.[1] Since the Syrian monarch's rule had ceased to be oppressive, the original cause for the struggle no longer existed, while the Grecian party in Judea felt themselves endangered by the measures of Judas. Demetrius, son of Seleucus IV., who had been murdered by Heliodorus, was now on the throne of Syria. When, therefore, in answer to the complaints of the Grecian party, he appointed Alcimus their leader as high priest, the *Chasidim,* or strict Jewish party, were at first disposed to support him, in spite of the opposition of Judas. Soon, however, fresh troubles arose. Judas once more took the lead in resisting the intruder and his allies, and the Syrian army was completely routed, and their general Nicanor slain. Still, the prospect was far from reassuring, and division had already appeared in the ranks of the Jews. Judas took therefore the bold step of appealing for help to Rome.[2] But before aid could be granted, he succumbed to superior numbers, and fell in an engagement, together with the greater part of his adherents.

The command now devolved on his brother *Jonathan.*[3] The new commander retired to Jordan, where he successfully defended himself. The Syrian general, after taking measures for the complete subjugation of Judea, and establishing strong Syrian garrisons in the country, withdrew once more. An interval of peace ensued, which Jonathan assiduously employed in strengthening his party. On the return of the Syrians to Palestine two years later, the Jewish leader was so successful in the almost passive resistance which he offered, that the Syrian Bacchides was wearied out, and a treaty of peace was made. In the period which followed, the Jewish parties appear to have made terms with one another, and the power

---

[1] 1 Macc. vii. ; 2 Macc. xiv. xv. ; Jos. *Ant.* xii. 10.; Comp. Schürer, I. i. 227 ff.

[2] 1 Macc. viii. ix. 1-22 ; Jos. *Ant.* xii. 10. 6 ; 11.

[3] 1 Macc. ix. 23-73 ; Jos. *Ant.* xiii. 1.

of the Asmoneans steadily increased. The views of the
national party had enlarged during these campaigns. They
now sought not only religious but political independence also,
and circumstances soon occurred which furthered their designs.[1]
A rival to King Demetrius had been set up in Syria, and both
parties contended for the powerful co-operation of Jonathan,
by attempting to outbid one another in promises. The Jews
espoused the cause of the pretender, and, on his accession to
the Syrian throne, Jonathan was declared Meridarch, or
commander in Judea. But his predecessor's misfortunes did
not teach the new Syrian monarch to eschew his vices.
Accordingly, Demetrius II., the son of Demetrius, was soon
welcomed back by his subjects, and regained his father's
throne. Although the Jews had formerly supported his
opponent, they obtained from him a confirmation of their
privileges, on condition of rendering him aid against his rebel
subjects. But the ingratitude of Demetrius II. alienated all
hearts from him, and enabled Tryphon, the guardian of the
young son of the pretender, once again to bring about a
change of dynasty, by procuring the throne of Syria for his
ward. The latter, who assumed the title of Antiochus VI.,
was only a puppet in the hands of Tryphon, who desired
ultimately to gain the crown for himself. To attain this
purpose, he first sought to get rid of Jonathan, who had given
in his adherence to the new government. In this he succeeded
by treachery, as also in accomplishing the murder of his
young master.

The government of Judea now devolved on *Simon*, the
last surviving brother of Judas and Jonathan.[2] Simon prosecuted the same line of policy as his predecessors, and, like
them, endeavoured to secure the sympathy of the Romans.
By espousing the cause of those who could be of use to them,
and, laying hold of every opportunity for extending their
sway, the Maccabees had gradually obtained all but the title
of kings. To further his objects, Simon now made overtures
of reconciliation to the dethroned Demetrius II., whom his

[1] 1 Macc. x. xii. ; Jos. *Ant.* xiii. 2–6.
[2] 1 Macc. xiii.–xvi. ; Jos. *Ant.* xiii. 6. 7 ; 7.

brother had forsaken for Antiochus VI. By a treaty, the Jews were no longer obliged to pay tribute; Simon was made hereditary prince ; and, indeed, such terms were obtained from the fallen monarch, that the Jews ever afterwards dated from this year as the first of their liberation (143 B.C.). Still the cause of Demetrius seemed hopeless, and in an expedition against Parthia he was taken prisoner. He was, however, kindly treated by the Parthian king, whose daughter he married. His brother, Antiochus VII., now took up the struggle against Tryphon. While his success remained doubtful, Antiochus courted the favour of Simon, but no sooner had he gained a decided advantage than he changed his attitude towards the Jews, and refused to acknowledge their claims to independence. He marched an army into Palestine, which was repulsed by John Hyrcanus, the son of Simon. But when *Hyrcanus* became high priest and governor[1] (135 B.C.), his father and brothers having fallen victims to a foul conspiracy, Antiochus again invaded Palestine. Jerusalem was besieged, and Hyrcanus was obliged to sue for peace, which the Syrian monarch granted on reasonable terms. Soon after, Antiochus VII. fell in an expedition against the Parthians, and his brother, Demetrius II., who had escaped from the captivity in which he had been kept by the Parthian court, which only used him as a tool, reascended the throne of Syria. John Hyrcanus meantime extended his sway in Palestine ; he subdued the Samaritans, and also conquered the Idumeans, whom he forced to become Jewish proselytes. But Demetrius II. did not long retain the Syrian crown. After the brief reign of a pretender, he was succeeded by his son, Antiochus VIII.

The reign of the high priest Hyrcanus is marked by the first public contest between the two great Jewish parties,[2] which seem to have made their appearance about the time of the high priest Jonathan. The Pharisees, the representatives of the earlier Chasidim, were the more strictly religious party, while the Sadducees consisted of the more moderate men, who sympathised with the later tendencies of the Maccabees, and their endeavours to secure national power and independence

---

[1] Jos. *Ant.* xiii. 8–10 ; *Wars,* i. 2.   [2] Comp. Schürer, I i. 286 ff.

By tradition and necessity, Hyrcanus belonged to the sect of the Pharisees, but there was too much of the ambitious warrior about him to suit the tastes of the stricter Jews, nor were they pleased with the innovations introduced by him in religious matters. Ultimately an open quarrel broke out between this party and Hyrcanus, and decided him to join the Sadducees. The subsequent history of the Maccabees presents a picture of rapid declension. At his death (105 B.C.), Hyrcanus left the principality to his wife; but their eldest son, *Aristobulus*,[1] deposed his mother, and she soon afterwards perished in prison, as the story went, by hunger. His favourite brother Antigonus also fell a victim to his jealous suspicions, and after a reign of only one year Aristobulus died of a painful disease. He was succeeded by his third brother, *Alexander Jannœus*,[2] probably the most warlike, as he was the most cruel and least popular of the Asmoneans. His ambitious projects were not attended with success, and as, besides, he was a professed Sadducee, the public discontent broke, on two distinct occasions, into open rebellion. These insurrections were indeed quelled, but not without much bloodshed.

Alexander left the kingdom to his wife,[3] with directions that, after his death, she should join the party of the Pharisees, whose adherence to her rule was thereby procured. After her decease, Hyrcanus, her elder son, a weak prince, would have seized the crown, but found a rival in his younger and more energetic brother, *Aristobulus*[4] (69 B.C.). Hyrcanus, indeed, resigned the crown in his favour, but by the advice of one Antipater, an Idumean, who had acquired considerable influence, betook himself for assistance to Aretas, king of Arabia, who gladly espoused his cause. Judea now became the scene of a civil war between the rival brothers. Hyrcanus advanced with an army, and shut up Aristobulus in Jerusalem. Meantime the Roman general Pompey had penetrated victoriously into Syria, and both brothers hastened to submit their claims to him for arbitration and assistance. Though

[1] Jos. *Ant.* xiii. 11 ; *Wars*, i. 3.　　[2] *Ib.* xiii. 12–15 ; *ib.* i. 4.
[3] *Ib.* xiii. 16 ; *ib.* i. 5.　　[4] *Ib.* xiv. 1–4 ; *ib.* i. 6–7.

the Roman chief delayed his decision, he was clearly disposed to favour the weak Hyrcanus as more likely to be serviceable to himself, and Aristobulus resolved to fight for the crown. He at first attempted to defend Jerusalem, but surrendered on the approach of Pompey. His adherents retired to the temple, which, after a three months' siege, was taken by assault on a Sabbath day. *Hyrcanus*[1] was now confirmed in his dignity as high priest, but he was deprived of the crown, and became tributary to Rome. Aristobulus and his children (with the exception of Alexander, who escaped by the way) followed Pompey as captives (63 B.C.).

It was in vain that Alexander, and afterwards Aristobulus, endeavoured again to raise the standard of rebellion in Palestine. The watchful and energetic Romans, who were now virtually masters of the country, specially Mark Antony, defeated all their plans. At the same time, Antipater succeeded in ingratiating himself with the new lords of the soil. The war between Cæsar and Pompey seemed at first to hold out new prospects to the party of Aristobulus, as Antipater had espoused the cause of Pompey; but the adherents of the latter killed Aristobulus and his son, while Antipater himself seasonably changed sides, and compensated for his former opposition by rendering such effective assistance to Cæsar, that he obtained even greater privileges than he had before possessed, being nominated Roman procurator in Judea. The national party was naturally jealous of the unbounded influence which the Idumean Antipater and his sons (of whom Herod was the most promising) were acquiring in Palestine. But, though Antipater was poisoned, the influence of his sons remained unshaken, and they preserved their power in spite of all the revolutions which at this period took place throughout the Roman world. Cæsar had been slain, and the short-lived republic was succeeded by the triumvirate. The affairs of the East were now confided to Mark Antony, a friend of Antipater; and Herod, though he had previously given assistance to the republican party, soon gained his favour.

[1] Jos. *Ant.* xiv. 5–13 ; *Wars*, i. 8–12.

In vain did the Jews send successive deputations to complain
of the exactions of the sons of Antipater. The latter were
confirmed in the government of Judea under Hyrcanus, and
their power was still further established by the betrothal of
Herod with the beautiful Mariamne, the grand-daughter of
the high priest. Soon afterwards Mark Antony was
captivated by the charms of Cleopatra.

Antony's inactivity and exactions exposed his provinces
to the inroads of the Parthians, who soon possessed themselves of Syria; but the threatening aspect of affairs in Italy
obliged Antony to return immediately to Rome, where he
happily effected a temporary reconciliation with his colleagues.
During his absence from the East, *Antigonus*, a son of the
late Aristobulus, had secured from the Parthians the recognition of his claims upon the Jewish throne[1] (40 B.C.). By
treachery, both the aged high priest Hyrcanus and the
brother of Herod were made captives and put in chains; but
Herod himself had managed to escape to Masada, where he
placed his friends in safety, and then departed for Rome.
Meanwhile Herod's brother had committed suicide in prison, and
Antigonus had cut off the ears of Hyrcanus, in order to unfit
him for the priesthood. Herod had originally gone to Rome,
for the purpose of procuring the government of Judea for Aristobulus, the brother of Mariamne, under whom he hoped to act
as Antipater had done under Hyrcanus; but, when there, he
succeeded in obtaining his own elevation to the Jewish throne.

Herod returned to Palestine to conquer his new kingdom
by help of the Romans, and, after a two years' struggle
(37 B.C.), recovered the country. Antigonus was executed,
and Herod reigned undisturbed. One by one he removed his
dangerous rivals of the family of the Asmoneans out of the
way. The first victim was young Aristobulus, his brother-in-
law, who was far too great a favourite with the people to be
allowed to live. Next followed the aged Hyrcanus, who had
inconsiderately returned to Palestine from his asylum in
Parthia. By and by none of the Asmoneans remained.
While ridding himself of every possible rival, Herod also

[1] Jos. *Ant.* xiv. 13–16 ; *Wars*, i. 13–18.

knew how to conciliate the favour not only of Antony, but, after his fall, of Octavius.   In this brief sketch we cannot refer more fully to the eventful reign of Herod.   Cunning, ambitious, bold, and energetic, he was equally hated and feared by his subjects.   The two distinguishing features of his character and government were the most unrelenting cruelty, which sacrificed even those nearest to him to the slightest suspicion, and a magnificence which induced him everywhere to raise lasting monuments to himself.   Signal instances of the former occurred, when he caused not only his wife, but even his sons and other near relatives, to be executed.   Of the latter, the rebuilding of the temple of Jerusalem, and the foundation of new cities, such as Cæsarea Stratonis, are examples.   But to no monument does Herod owe the preservation of his memory so much as to the fact that towards the close of his reign Jesus was born in Bethlehem.[1]

The last act of Herod's life is sufficiently indicative of his character.   The loathsome disease, which at last cut him off, had for some time preyed on his vitals.   When he felt his end approaching, he summoned the principal men amongst the Jews, and ordered them to be shut up and to be killed immediately after his decease, in order to secure (as he said) that his decease should occasion a general mourning throughout the land.[2]   Happily this cruel behest was not obeyed. The possessions of Herod were divided by the emperor between his three sons.[3]   Archelaus was made ethnarch of Judea, Samaria, and Idumea, but soon afterwards banished to Gaul; Herod Antipas (the Herod of the Gospels) obtained Galilee and Perea; and Philip, the northern district on the eastern bank of Jordan.   On the banishment of Archelaus, Judea was brought directly under Roman rule, and placed under a procurator, who was to some extent subordinate to the imperial legate of Syria.   The Jewish hatred of foreign rule, and the inability of the Romans to understand the

---

[1] [On the census of Cyrenius or Quirinius, see *Life and Times*, i. pp. 181–183.   There is a full discussion of the question in Schürer, I. ii. 105–143, where, however, a different conclusion is reached.]

[2] Jos. *Ant.* xvii. 6. 5 ; *Wars*, i. 33. 6.

[3] *Ib.* xvii. 11. 4–5 ; *ib.* ii. 6. 3.

prejudices of the nation, would in any case have rendered difficult the administration of the province.   But, in fact, the breach between the Romans and the Jews was made continually wider, owing to the rapacity and cruelty with which almost all the governors of Judea exercised their office.   The most noted of these procurators was Pontius Pilate, under whose administration the Lord Jesus, being delivered by the Jews into the hands of the Romans, " offered Himself by the Eternal Spirit unto the Father."   But Pilate's tyranny was too great to be long tolerated.   When, on another occasion, he caused a number of unoffending Samaritans to be slaughtered, he was sent to Rome by Vitellius, the legate of Syria, in order to answer for his conduct before the Emperor Tiberius (37 A.D.).[1] The Roman legates and procurators imitated the conduct of Herod in frequently changing the occupants of the high priesthood, to gratify their own avarice or caprice.   [Nevertheless the high priests retained considerable power down to the fall of Jerusalem.   They were almost always chosen from among a few favoured families, who formed an influential aristocracy, and strengthened the power of the high priest.] Even Jewish authorities represent these priests as morally and religiously so degraded as by their sins to have called down the Divine vengeance upon the people.[2]

Once more, ere its final extinction, a brief prospect of comparative independence was held out to the Jewish nation.[3]   Herod Agrippa, a grandson of Herod by one of those sons whom he had ordered to be executed, had been educated at Rome.   There he had gained the favour of Caligula, who, on his accession to the empire, gave him the tetrarchy of Philip, who had died in the interval, together with that of Abilene, and bestowed on him the title of king. This unexpected elevation of Herod Agrippa (the Herod of the Book of Acts) excited the envy of his uncle, Herod Antipas.   He applied to the emperor for similar honours, but was banished, and his tetrarchy of Galilee and Perea given to Herod Agrippa.   After the assassination of Caligula,

---

[1] Jos. *Ant.* xviii. 4. 1-2.　　　[2] Pes. 57*a* ; comp. Derenbourg, p. 232 ff.
[3] Jos. *Ant.* xviii. 6 ; xix. 5-9 ; *Wars,* ii. 9-11.

Claudius obtained the purple, partly through the influence of Herod Agrippa. In acknowledgment of these services, Herod now received Judea, Samaria, and Idumea, so that his kingdom was actually more extensive even than that of his grandfather Herod,—an instance this (we may observe by the way) of historical justice to the descendant of the murdered son of Mariamne, from whom he had sprung.

Agrippa was thoroughly Roman in his habits and modes of thinking, though in a certain way attached to the national religion. By his influence with the emperor, he had already succeeded in averting one and another storm of persecution from his subjects, whose favour he courted by an apparent zeal for the synagogue. From such motives he caused James, the brother of John, to be killed, and imprisoned Peter. The signal judgment which put an end at the same time to his presumption and his life, is well known to the readers of the New Testament. Although the Jews had cause to deplore the death of Herod Agrippa, who may be designated as the last native prince who held authority in Palestine, the Greek inhabitants, and even the Roman soldiers in Cæsarea, publicly exhibited their joy at his decease in so indecent a manner, as to induce Claudius to resolve on removing these cohorts from Judea. Cæsarea was one of those places in which the contentions, which now became very general, between the Jewish and the Gentile inhabitants of Palestine were most continuous and bitter. Although built by Herod the Great and with Jewish money, it was, on various grounds, claimed by the Greeks as a heathen city. Being the seat of the Roman government and of their principal garrison in Palestine, the collisions were frequent between the heathens, who were numerous and influential, and the Jews, and their contentions for supremacy in the town peculiarly obstinate. It was here that the spark fell which ultimately enveloped Judea in the flames of a great national war.

Herod Agrippa II. (the King Agrippa of the Acts) was ultimately appointed king of Chalcis, and superintendent of the temple.[1] Palestine itself remained, ever after the death

---

[1] Jos. *Ant.* xx. 1. 3 ; 5. 2.

of Herod Agrippa I., a Roman province.   In the year 48 A.D.,
Cumanus [1] was appointed procurator of Palestine.   Under his
administration, the discontent which had long prevailed in
the public mind, manifested itself, for the first time, in acts
of open resistance.   The first outbreak occurred during the
celebration of the passover of that year.   In order to preserve
order amongst the multitudes who thronged the capital at the
great feasts, a guard of Roman soldiers was placed in the
corridors surrounding the temple.   Some idea of the numbers
usually present at these festivities may be conceived, from the
fact that, about twenty years afterwards, the inhabitants of
Jerusalem, during that period, were computed to amount to
nearly three millions.   The grossly outrageous conduct on
this occasion of one of the Roman soldiers, who was not
brought to justice for it, excited a popular tumult, which was
quelled only after a considerable loss of life.   This indignity
was soon followed by other acts of lawless oppression and of
outrage upon the Jewish faith.   The Samaritans were not
slow to avail themselves of the growing anti-Jewish feeling on
the part of the authorities.   Some pilgrims coming from
Galilee were murdered in a Samaritan village.   If the Romans
did not connive at it, the Samaritans at least escaped un-
punished.   As usual, before the outbreak of a revolution,
numbers of the national party now formed themselves into
bands of *guerillas*, and resorted to the mountains of Judea,
where all who were disaffected joined them.   This plan had
been the commencement of a successful resistance to foreign
tyranny under the Maccabees, and the land of Judea offered
peculiar facilities for it.   At last, Agrippa, who instead of
Chalcis received the former tetrarchy of Philip, successfully
pleaded the Jewish cause with the emperor, and obtained from
him the recall of Cumanus, in room of whom *Felix* was appointed (probably 52 A.D.).   This governor, who speedily
became the husband of Drusilla, one of King Agrippa's sisters,
was as tyrannical and corrupt as his predecessor.

When Felix was at length recalled, Nero, who succeeded
Claudius in the empire, appointed *Festus* procurator (*circ.*

[1] Jos. *Ant.* xx. 5. 3–6. 3 ; *Wars,* ii. 12.

60 A.D.).[1] The latter was, on the whole, a much better governor than any of his predecessors; but he only lived to administer Jewish affairs for about two years, and was followed by *Albinus*, a man whose covetousness made every attempt at administering justice impossible. In 64 A.D. he was recalled, and *Gessius Florus*, in many respects the worst governor whom Judea had ever seen, was appointed in his place.[2] The historian Josephus charges him with almost every crime. It is certain that his mal-administration converted the public excitement into the utmost state of frenzy. In 66 A.D., Cestius Gallus, the governor of Syria, and the superior of Florus, attended at the paschal festivities at Jerusalem. In vain did the Jews prefer their complaint against Florus; they were put off with promises, while the procurator stood by laughing. Events were now hastening to a crisis. The last and decisive provocation was given at Cæsarea, which was adjudicated by Nero to belong to the heathens, who were in future to hold first rank as citizens in that town. Dissensions soon arose, and acts of provocation on the part of the heathens drove the Jews into an open rebellion, which speedily extended to Jerusalem. It was in vain that King Agrippa, and the more moderate party, besought the people to abstain from entering on so unequal a combat. Eleazar, the president of the temple, refused to offer sacrifices for the prosperity of the Roman empire; and one, Menahem, a son of Judas of Galilee, openly took up arms against Rome. But although he and most of his adherents were murdered by Eleazar, who in turn assumed authority, the insurrection was not quelled. Cestius now marched against Jerusalem, and took and burnt one of the suburbs.[3] He then proceeded to attack the temple mount, but, after six days, when a part of the northern wall had been already undermined, he most unaccountably withdrew. The Jews followed him, and routed the Romans with great slaughter. Many of their military engines fell into the hands of the Jews, who afterwards employed them against the Romans.

[1] Comp. Schürer, I. ii. 182 ff.   [2] Jos. *Ant.* xx. 11 ; *Wars,* ii. 14 ff.
[3] Jos. *Wars,* ii. 19.

This event changed a partial rebellion into a general rising, and invested it with the character of a national war. The most moderate amongst the Jews now felt that they had entered on a struggle which the Romans would feel in honour bound to prosecute to the end, and in which they would indiscriminately take vengeance on all prominent persons in the nation. The only chance of safety now lay in successful resistance; and if death by Roman hands were ultimately to fall to their lot, it was at least desirable to meet it in honourable defence of their liberty and faith. Accordingly, however unwilling they might formerly have felt, all now entered cordially into plans which were too hastily conceived, and imperfectly carried out. To Josephus, a Jewish general, the defence of Galilee was entrusted. Against him Vespasian, Nero's ablest general, had been despatched. Successful in every engagement, he took city after city. At last Josephus surrendered to him—an event which threw the leaders of the national party in Jerusalem into the utmost consternation. In that doomed city, instead of harmony, strife and contention had reigned; instead of uniting against the common foe, they were engaged in an internecine war. Three parties fought for supremacy in Jerusalem. They sought only to destroy one another and the stores which were so necessary for a protracted defence of the city, and at last killed every wealthy and peaceably disposed person. In the interval, Vespasian succeeded to the Roman empire, and left the command of the army to his son Titus, who appeared before Jerusalem in April 70. The garrison soon felt the combined horrors of famine and pestilence, of the reign of terror within, and the presence of a relentless enemy without the city walls. The siege lasted altogether four months, and was attended with varying success. We purposely abstain from giving any of the details connected with it. The Jews displayed the greatest valour, and an enthusiasm which almost bordered on madness. They fought under the conviction that some deliverance must at last be wrought for them, since God could not give up His city, people, and temple. But Titus, who, in order to prevent any escape from the city, had caused it to be completely surrounded with a stone wall, made continuous though slow progress. Gradually he penetrated into the city, until, on the 10th Ab (August), the temple was burnt,[1] and, on the 8th Elul (September), the upper city destroyed.[2] Titus had to the last been most desirous to spare at least the temple, but a torch thrown into it by a soldier quickly enveloped it in flames, which could not be suppressed.[3]

Thus perished the proud and beautiful city, which " would not have this man reign over it." With it perished the last remainder of the typical dispensation, and of the Jewish state. A new era now commences. Israel is again cast forth as a wanderer, but this time without a home in view—without a tabernacle in which to worship—and without the cloud by day, or the guiding pillar of fire by night. Yet can we learn many a lesson as we trace the footmarks in the sand of time. And these footmarks they have left on *every* shore, as they have inscribed their name on *every* page of history. A nation without a country—a religion which, historically speaking, belongs to the past, and has become impossible in the present—a people persecuted yet not exterminated, driven from every place yet always reappearing, and who, without having a present, bear in their past the seed of future greatness—such is the picture now presented to us. Israel can be neither transformed nor subdued by the hand of *man*. *They belong to God.* Since the destruction of Jerusalem, a continual miracle, kept as a testimony to the God of the Bible before the eyes of an unbelieving world, and as the harbinger of future blessings in the prayers of an expectant Church, both they and their history are unaccountable by an ordinary mode of reasoning, and can only be understood when viewed in the light of scriptural statement and prediction.

[1] Jos. *Wars*, vi. 4. [According to Rabbinical tradition, the temple was destroyed on the evening of the Sabbath (Taan. 29*a*). With this agrees the statement of Dio Cassius, lxvi. 7. Comp. Derenbourg, p. 291.]

[2] *Ut supra*, vi. 8. 4–5.

[3] [On the ground of a statement of Sulpicius Severus (*Chronicon* ii. 30), which is probably taken from a lost book of Tacitus, it has been disputed whether Titus really wished to spare the temple, Comp. Schürer, I. ii. 244 f.]

CHAPTER II

CLOSING SCENES OF THE JEWISH WAR OF INDEPENDENCE.

THE last embers of the conflagration had died out at Jerusalem, and silence reigned in her deserted streets, save that the hollow tread of the Roman guard betokened the presence of the conqueror. The streams of blood which had flowed down the steep streets of Mount Zion to the valley of the Son of Hinnom, were dried up; the groans of the dying, the lamentations of the bereaved and the captives, were hushed. Of the beautiful and proud city nothing remained but three towers, left to indicate the strength of a place which, after so protracted a defence, could not resist Roman prowess; a portion of the old wall, to serve as defence to the garrison; and a few houses here and there, where the aged, the feeble, and, in general, those from whom nothing could be apprehended, found a shelter.[1]

Before marching against the capital of Judea, the Roman generals had wisely resolved to subdue the whole country. By this plan Jerusalem was isolated, the defenders of Jewish nationality were ultimately shut up in it, all supplies cut off, while the fall of the city necessarily put a period to farther resistance. This plan of operations, and the fact that the siege of Jerusalem overtook the Jews during the celebration of the Passover, when multitudes came to worship in the temple, will also account for the large number of captives taken in that city. When it is said that these amounted to not less than 97,000, that 1,100,000 had fallen since the commencement of the war,[2] while multitudes escaped from

[1] Jos. *Wars*, vii. 1. 1 ; Epiph. *Mens et Pond*. 14.
[2] *Ut supra*, vi. 9. 3.

the city during its protracted siege, it will be understood what
gigantic proportions the war had assumed. All the captive
Jews were ranged on the summit of the temple-mountain,
to have their respective sentences awarded by a Roman captain named Fronto, and a freedman of Titus, to whom their
adjudication had in the first place been committed.[1] Influence with the victors secured the release of many. Amongst
others, the historian Josephus, before his surrender to the
Romans one of the Jewish generals, obtained a free pardon
for 190 of his personal friends. Others bought their liberty
by pointing out to the Romans places were articles of value
had been concealed by the besieged. The rest of the prisoners
were sentenced by court-martial either to death or to servitude in the mines of Egypt. This fate befell all above seven-
teen years of age ; those of more tender years were sold into
slavery.

It need scarce be mentioned that the Romans eagerly
ransacked the city in search of plunder, the more so as fabulous accounts of the wealth stored up in Jerusalem had previously been circulated. Amongst other places, the subterranean
vaults which intersected Jerusalem in all directions, almost
like streets, were carefully examined. There a number of
Jews had found a brief respite. The two principal actors in
the defence of Jerusalem, John of Giscala and Simon Gioras,
had fled to these hiding-places. If John and his friends had
ever hoped to be able to remain in concealment till the lapse
of time induced a relaxation of vigilance on the part of the
Roman guards, they soon felt constrained to relinquish these
expectations. Hunger obliged them to surrender to the
enemy. Simon Gioras had chosen apparently more promising
means of securing safety.[2] When, with a small party of
friends, he retreated to the vaults, they took with them provisions, pickaxes and other tools, with which they hoped to
work their way underground to some place of safety. They
penetrated as far as the vaults extended, but the labour of
excavation was impeded by the ruined state of the city and
the stench of putrefying bodies, which in some places almost

---

[1] Jos. *Wars*, vi. 9. 2-4 ; *Life*, 75.   [2] Jos. *Wars*, vii. 2.

filled the vaults.   At the same time their means of subsistence began to fail, notwithstanding the care with which they
had from the first been husbanded.   Although constrained
to desist from this attempt, Simon was not the man to perish
underground.   Hoping to take advantage of the superstitious
fears of the Roman soldiers, he stripped one of the bodies, and
arrayed himself in a white tunic, over which he then arranged
a costly purple cloak.   Thus attired, he surprised the guard
stationed near the temple.   As he had hoped, terror struck
the bystanders at the sudden and strange apparition, but they
soon recovered from their alarm and arrested his progress,
demanding his name.   Some strange fancy, or a desire not to
surrender to an inferior—perhaps a hope to move the pity of
an equal, or to secure his interest—induced Simon to demand
to be brought before the general of the garrison.   When
Terentius appeared, Simon threw back his cloak and surrendered himself.   He was sent in chains to Cæsarea, there
to expect the arrival of Titus.

Before leaving Jerusalem, Titus had addressed his soldiers
in language highly commendatory of their bravery and fidelity,
and distributed amongst them valuable gifts.[1]   Some acknowledgment of their services the soldiers had indeed deserved, for
their courage, endurance, and manifest attachment to the person
of the young Cæsar.   When at last the Roman standards had
been planted on the east gate of the temple, their enthusiasm
could no longer be restrained, and they proclaimed Titus
Imperator.[2]   The war being virtually at an end, the auxiliaries
were then dismissed to their respective countries, and the
legions transported to other battlefields.   The 12th legion,
which at the beginning of the war had suffered so ignominious
a defeat from the Jews, was sent to Melitene in Cappadocia,
near the Euphrates.   The 10th, entrusted to the command
of Terentius Rufus, was left as garrison in Jerusalem ; the
5th and 15th legions, which were to be sent to the banks of
the Danube, accompanied Titus to Cæsarea, whence he intended to set sail for Egypt.[3]   But before finally leaving the

[1] Jos. *Wars*, vii. 1.   [2] *Ut supra*, vi. 6. 1–2.
[3] *Ut supra*, vii. 1. 3 ; 5. 3.

soil of Palestine, he visited Cæsarea Philippi (Paneas), the city of King Agrippa and of Bernice.[1] Wherever the victor appeared—at Paneas, Berytus (Beyroot), and in other Syrian towns—festivities were celebrated in honour of himself, of the Emperor Vespasian (Titus's father), and of Domitian (his brother). As usual on similar occasions, thousands of Jewish captives had to contend in the arena, either with each other or with wild beasts, for the amusement of the spectators. On his return, Titus passed once more through what had been Jerusalem. It is said that the sight of the ruins filled with sorrow and awe the conqueror, in whose character (according to the statement of contemporaries)[2] good and evil strangely alternated.

A Jewish legend[3] has embellished this circumstance, by describing in the most fabulous terms certain tortures which Titus had to endure in punishment for the destruction of Jerusalem and the temple. On his voyage from Egypt to Italy (so goes the story), Titus was overtaken by a storm, which threatened to destroy the vessel that bore him. Conscious of the righteous anger of the God of Israel whom he had offended, Titus broke forth in blasphemies against Him, as if His power were limited to the sea in which He had once destroyed Pharaoh, and now threatened his own safety, while He was unable successfully to contend against him upon land. A voice from on high rebuked the blasphemy. The storm was hushed; but no sooner had Titus landed than he felt excruciating pains in his head, occasioned, as it afterwards turned out, by an insect gnawing on his brain, which, according to the Divine threatening, was to continue his tormentor through life. Only once, and for a short time, the noise from a blacksmith's shop caused the insect to desist. On his deathbed, Titus ordered the physicians, after his decease, to open his skull, in order to ascertain the occasion of this ceaseless agony. To their astonishment they discovered in it an animal, which had grown to the size of a swallow, two talents in weight, with metal bill and claws, which had gnawed at the emperor's brain. So far the tradition, by which Jewish

---

[1] *Jos. Wars*, vii. 2. 1 ; 3. 1.   [2] Dio, *In Vespas.* lxvi. 18.   [3] Gitt. 56*a*.

hatred sought to avenge itself on the destroyer of Jerusalem. We have mentioned it in order to indicate how firm the conviction which the Jews entertained, that God had not forsaken them, but would avenge their cause; and also to show what extraordinary fables could pass current on such subjects.

During Titus's absence in the East, a report had spread, perhaps partly on the ground of his largesses to the soldiers, that he intended to found in the East an empire independent of his father Vespasian. The circulation of such rumours, to which a reported attempt on the part of his brother Domitian to excite the Germanic legions to rebellion, may have lent the appearance of likelihood, had induced Titus to hasten his return to Rome. On his approach, his imperial father, the senate and magistracy, hastened to meet him. Titus threw himself into the arms of his parent, warmly exclaiming, perhaps with reference to the above-mentioned reports, " I have come, my father, I have come."[1] Rome greeted the victorious Vespasian and Titus with a triumph, in which the envious Domitian took an unwilling part, following the victors' car, mounted on a white charger. The captive Jews who were to grace the triumphal entry, had already arrived. They consisted of seven hundred of the noblest and fairest of the youth of Palestine, and of the two leaders of the insurrection, Simon Gioras and John of Giscala. The sacred roll of the law, the table of shewbread, the golden candlestick, and other parts of the temple furniture, were exhibited in the triumph, and then deposited amongst the spoils. The procession ascended the Capitol, where, according to usage, it halted till the leader of the rebellion had been scourged and executed. The senate adjudged this punishment to Simon Gioras. John of Giscala was sentenced to perpetual imprisonment; and the rest of the captives were employed in various public works.[2] Amongst others, the Colosseum, built by Vespasian, was, according to a late Christian tradition, mostly reared by Jewish labour.

Very different from the fate of the generality of the actors in this melancholy drama, was that of three who had more or less openly sided with the enemies of their nation.

[1] Sueton. *In Titum*, § 5.   [2] Jos. *Wars*, vii. 5. 5–6.

At one time, indeed, King Agrippa and his fair sister Bernice seemed deeply interested in the welfare of their countrymen. But where principle of any kind is wanting—where selfishness and the love of sin are dominant—mere ebullitions of generosity are at best transient, and all such manifestations of kindness only capricious. Queen Bernice soon descended to become the paramour of Titus. Report accused her even of incest with her brother.[1] At the termination of the war, Agrippa and Bernice enjoyed, as reward for the part they had taken in it, all the pleasures which wealth could procure or the ingenuity of luxury devise. Bernice was also honoured with the special confidence of the emperor, and was even allowed to sit as judge on a certain occasion, when Quintilian pleaded her cause before her.[2] The attachment between her and Titus was so great, that nothing but the general outcry of the Romans against an alliance with a Jewess, could induce the heir-presumptive of the empire to repudiate one whom it was generally believed he had secretly espoused. Although this step caused deep sorrow to both parties,[3] it seems doubtful whether Bernice had at any time been faithful to her imperial lover. At least, Caecina, a man of consular dignity, had to expiate with his life her supposed favours.[4] Up to the period of her repudiation, Bernice had lived in the palace, and in every way acted as the future empress,[5] while her brother had been elevated to the rank of praetor. Afterwards she left Rome about the year 75, and though she returned after the death of Vespasian, she came no more to court.

The part sustained by the historian Josephus had been even less honourable than that of Agrippa and Bernice. Unfortunately we only possess his own version of his conduct and of Jewish affairs generally. Yet, on comparing his *Jewish Wars* with the *Account of his Life*, drawn up twenty years after the former work, in reply to the elegant and telling history of his opponent, Justus of Tiberias, start-

---

[1] Juvenal, *Sat.* vi. 157 f.
[2] Quint. *Inst. Orat.* iv. 1.
[3] Sueton. *In Titum*, § 7.
[4] Aur. Victor, *Epit. in Tit.* x. 4.
[5] Dio, *In Vespas.* lxvi. 15, 18.

ling incongruities and damaging admissions become apparent. It is not our present purpose to discuss the conduct of Josephus; but where gross exaggerations, vanity, and bitterness against those with whom he had formerly acted, are prominent features, we have fair grounds for suspecting the honesty and good faith of the writer. If Josephus was not from the first a traitor, his *conduct*, at least, appears sufficiently treasonable, and seems to have early roused the suspicions of his colleagues. Perhaps Josephus speedily perceived that the cause of Israel was in a desperate state, while he did not see his way, or else did not choose, to relinquish the command which had been entrusted to him in Galilee. Unfortunately, his was of all the most important position, which might have been longest held, and ought to have been most strenuously defended. It certainly seems strange that Josephus should not only have at first accepted, but afterwards so tenaciously clung to his appointment, when it clearly appears that if he did not throughout play into the hands of the Romans, he neglected most obvious duty, was ever anxious to propitiate Rome, her friends and her allies, and careful to prepare a way for his own safety.

After his surrender to the enemy, Josephus proved in various ways most helpful to the Roman cause, and was at last richly rewarded by Titus, whom he accompanied on his return to Rome.[1] He received from the emperor possessions in lieu of those which he had held near Jerusalem. He was made a Roman citizen, and had a pension assigned to him; and, notwithstanding the intrigues of his enemies, retained the full confidence of the court. It must be allowed that, except when private interests or a thirst for revenge actuated him, he used his influence in favour of his countrymen. Josephus had, by the order of Vespasian, married in Cæsarea a captive Jewess, in spite of the Jewish law which interdicted connections between priests and captives, but he soon separated from her. He was subsequently married a second time, during his stay at Alexandria, and had three sons, of whom, however, the youngest only attained to maturity.

[1] Jos. *Life*, 75, 76.

Finally, having repudiated his second wife, with whose conduct he was dissatisfied, he united himself to a wealthy, talented, and noble Jewess from Crete, who shared his happy retreat at Rome. His third wife made him father of two sons, Justus and Simonides Agrippa. From the moment that he betrayed his country's cause, he was as violently hated and persecuted as he had before been respected by the Jews. Nor did the intrigues of his enemies cease with the Jewish war. In Rome, various attempts were made to undermine his influence and position; but these proved ineffectual, and he remained to the end a favourite with Vespasian, Titus, and Domitian, and specially enjoyed the good graces of the Empress Domitia. Among his principal opponents was one Jonathan, a Zealot, who had fled from Judea and excited a rebellion in Cyrene. We shall by and by refer more particularly to his intrigues. Suffice it in the meantime that his accusations against Josephus were found false, and Jonathan was scourged and condemned to the stake. Even one of Josephus' eunuchs, to whom he had confided the training of his sons, conspired against him; but he also met with deserved punishment. Domitian exempted Josephus from all taxes. He must have survived beyond the year 100 A.D., the date of the death of Agrippa II., to which in his *Autobiography* he alludes.[1]

In the absence of other historical documents, the writings of Josephus must always remain a most valuable source of information, both of the events which befell and the views which were entertained by the Jewish nation. After making due allowance for exaggerations, we may accept his *relations of facts* as substantially correct, though his mode of representing them, and the inferences which he draws, are often calculated to give a wrong impression. It must be borne in mind, that confessedly he not only surrendered to the Romans, but tried to promote that cause against which he had formerly led the armies of Judea. Naturally, then, he would attempt to represent himself as first ardently patriotic, and ready to fight his country's battles against those whom he believed its

[1] *Life*, 65.

enemies. But his nation's crimes had called down the Divine judgment, and he now felt it his duty to espouse the cause of Judea's enemies as warmly, and from the same convictions, which had induced him formerly to embrace that of the national party. If, besides, we take into account the egotism and vanity which constitute such prominent characteristics of our author, it will be understood on what grounds he presented his country's struggle and his nation's sins in the light in which he attempted to place them. A representation of his own importance and sufferings in the cause of the Romans, which he had only reluctantly embraced from a conviction of its rightness, would also secure the gratitude of his protectors, while an exaggerated account of the crimes of the Jews and the virtues of the Romans, would serve as an apology both for the invaders of Judea and for his own conduct. The Romans could not but appreciate the surrender of one in whom the Jews had reposed such confidence. His attachment to the national cause (till driven from it), his bravery, and yet his entire devotedness to the conquerors, served to recommend him; while his acquaintance with the country, the language, the habits and resources of the Jews, must have been of signal service to them.

It will readily be conceived what impression the tidings of his treachery made upon his countrymen. A party more zealous, or more discerning than the rest, had long suspected him; but, by his cunning and violence, Josephus had managed to elude their vigilance.[1] After his surrender, their policy seemed the only safe one; and when at last the most unwilling and incredulous became convinced of the general's treachery, a feeling of general distrust possessed the minds of the community, and prepared the way for the reign of terror inaugurated by the violent Zealots. The chiefs of the moderate party in Jerusalem were slain, without respect of age, character, or station; and those fearful scenes were enacted which preceded, and in measure made the capture and destruction of the city possible. It will be understood how hateful even his appearance must afterwards have been to the

[1] Jos. *Wars*, ii. 21; *Life*, 13-18, 26-30.

brave defenders of their country; and, accordingly, whenever he addressed them in favour of the Romans, in language which we can scarcely call aught but canting and hypocritical, the Zealots were often roused to sheer frenzy, and the Romanising Jew narrowly escaped with his life. Unfortunately, the important history of the Jewish war by Justus of Tiberias has been lost. Josephus composed his *Autobiography* in reply to it. Some passages in this work throw a light on events detailed in the *Jewish Wars*, different from that in which the author had intended to present them.

Besides the *Jewish Wars* and his *Autobiography*, we possess from the pen of Josephus a *Reply to the Misrepresentations of Apion concerning the Jews;* but· the small treatise on the *Power of Reason*, in which the martyrdom of seven youths during the time of the Maccabees is described, though from early times attributed to Josephus, is doubtless not of his composition. His largest work is one on the *Antiquities of the Jews.* This book contains many inaccuracies and liberties with the text of Scripture, but is valuable on account of some of the explanations which it offers, and the insight it affords into Jewish manners and modes of thinking. The substantial accuracy of Josephus' description of the last Jewish war was confirmed by Titus, who received the work into his collection of books.[1] In conclusion, we may notice the strange mixture of religious elements which combined to make up the creed of Josephus. He was truly an eclectic Jew. The Pharisees, the Sadducees, the Essenes, and the Grecians, might equally claim him by turns. When such a stage of religious consciousness becomes general among the educated, it always marks a period of decadence. The Jews, at a much later period, added to the genuine writings of Josephus those of another Josephon, or Josippon ben Gorion, which contain a treatise on Jewish history, written in elegant Hebrew, but full of the grossest anachronisms.[2]

Two memorials of the destruction of Jerusalem, each

[1] Jos. *Life*, 65; *Against Apion*, i. 9.
[2] It has appeared with a Latin translation by J. F. Breithaupt, 1707.

characteristic in its own way, remain to our days.[1]   Rome
erected a triumphal arch, on which the seven-branched
candlestick and other principal spoils of the war are
represented. Israel has marked the day of desolation by a
national fast. By a strange coincidence, that same day, the
9th of the Jewish month Ab (Tisha-be-Ab), commemorates
at the same time the threefold loss of Jewish independence—
that under Nebuchadnezzar, that under Titus, and again, at a
later period, that under Hadrian. In the plaintive strains of
the religious services for that day, Jerusalem is likened to a
sorrowing dove ; yet confession and mourning are mingled
with ardent and high aspirations after an anticipated and
complete deliverance.[2]

After the fall of Jerusalem, Judea was formed into a
province entirely independent of Syria. The first governor
appointed after the departure of Titus was Cerealis, who was
at the same time the commander of the garrison. Though
three fortresses—Herodion, Machærus, and Masada—were
still held by desperate Zealots, belonging to the national
party, Cerealis took no steps to drive them out of these last
strongholds. He was succeeded, only a year after his
appointment, by Lucilius Bassus, who immediately addressed
himself to the task which Cerealis had neglected.[3]   Herodion,
so named after Herod, its builder, and situated near
Jerusalem, surrendered without attempting a defence. Not
so Machærus, a strong citadel, reared on the eastern shore of
the Dead Sea. It dated from the time of the Asmoneans,
who destined it as a bulwark against the inroads of the
Arabians. Situated on an inaccessible rock, and surrounded
on all sides by deep valleys, it was, in truth, one of the

---

[1] [Coins were struck by Vespasian, Titus, and Domitian, commemorating the
capture of Jerusalem. Many of them bear a figure representing the mourning
captive Judea, with the inscriptions *Judœa capta, Judœa devicta,* and the like.
See Madden, *Coins of the Jews,* pp. 207–229.]

[2] See the prayers for Tisha-be-Ab. [According to the express statement of
Josephus (*Wars,* vi. 4. 5), the temple was destroyed on the 10th of Loos or Ab.
The Rabbinical tradition, however (see Mishna, Taan. iv. 6), always speaks of
the 9th of Ab as the day of the destruction of the temple, *i.e.* the day on
which, according to Josephus, fire was laid to the gates.]

[3] Jos. *Wars,* vii. 6.

strongest places in Palestine. Gabinius, the legate of Pompey, had, indeed, once destroyed it; but Herod I. restored it, and built a palace there, encompassed by strong walls, and protected by impregnable towers. A small town, likewise surrounded by walls, had sprung up around the citadel. Such was the appearance of Machærus when Bassus commenced operations against it, selecting as his base a valley to the east of the fort, which was less deep than the others. But the place seemed capable of enduring a long siege. The town derived its supplies of water from one of the many streams which passed through the valleys, while the fort was well supplied by a large number of cisterns. This place, which has been identified with certainty as the modern Mkaur, was, according to Pliny, a fortress second only to Jerusalem in importance. There was no lack of provisions or of arms, and the garrison was brave and resolute. The population of the town consisted originally of Syrians and of Jews. On the approach of the Romans, the latter retreated into the citadel, leaving the foreign part of the population in the lower town. The Jews of Machærus were under the command of Eleazar, a young man of noble birth and of great courage. The defenders, however, differed considerably from the Zealots of Jerusalem; for, though firmly attached to the national cause, they seem from the outset to have considered the possibility of saving their lives, if need be, by surrendering their citadel.

However, at first everything seemed to be favourable to the Jews. Their frequent sallies interrupted or destroyed the siege-works of the Romans, and harassed them incessantly. Eleazar was always foremost in the sallies. Unfortunately, on some such occasion, the youth, whether from bravado or inadvertency, lingered behind his comrades, conversing with a soldier on the rampart. The Romans perceived their advantage, and one of them, Rufus, rushed forward, seized the youth, and carried him off to the camp. Rightly judging it the best means for subduing Eleazar and inducing his friends to surrender, Bassus caused him to be stripped and scourged in sight of his soldiers, who raised a loud wailing.

A cross was next erected in a conspicuous place, and preparations made for the execution of Eleazar. These indications upset the courage of the young man. His own lamentations and the affection of his followers—who, perhaps, had never been very sanguine of ultimate success against the Romans—induced them to capitulate, on condition of freedom to their general, and a safe-conduct to themselves. The Syrians were not prepared for such a termination. Whether they had not been included in the agreement, or had even been actually betrayed to their enemies, certain it is that, under the impression of treachery, they attempted to escape from the city. Their example and influence prevailed on some of the others to follow them. But the Romans were not willing to allow their prey thus to escape. Only a part of the fugitives succeeded in leaving Machærus, the rest were seized—the men slaughtered, the women and children condemned to slavery. Meantime, about three thousand fugitives had sought safety in a dense wood, on the road from Machærus to Jerusalem. Bassus caused the wood to be surrounded by his cavalry. Felling the trees before them, they advanced, till at last nothing was left for the fugitives but to cut their way through the Romans. In this hopeless attempt all perished. After this victory—if so it may be styled—Bassus returned. He died soon afterwards, and was succeeded by Flavius Silva, to whom the termination of the Jewish war was reserved.

Masada, the strongest Jewish fortress, was also the last to hold out against the common enemy.[1] It would scarcely have been possible to have chosen a better site, or to have added more judiciously to the defences of nature by the appliances of art and military science. For between three and four miles, one approach to Masada—called, from its narrow windings, " the Serpent "—led over steep and otherwise inaccessible rocks, and along fearful precipices. The nearer the fortress was approached, the more difficult became the way to it. At last, however, a fertile plateau was

[1] Jos. *Wars*, vii. 8, 9. Comp. G. A. Smith, *Historical Geography of the Holy Land*, p. 512 ff.

reached. Its well-cultivated fields were intended to supply sufficient support to the garrison. This plateau was surrounded by a wall, eighteen feet high and twelve feet broad, and defended by thirty-seven towers, each seventy-five feet in height. On the east, the fort was also protected by the Dead Sea; on the west, a second rocky way to it was commanded by a high tower. Such was the place which Herod I. had designed for a retreat in cases of extreme danger, and where, according to his usual practice, he had reared a palace, which in splendour rivalled that of Jerusalem. A resolute garrison might have been able to hold the place for any number of years. A large number of cisterns contained an abundant supply of water, irrespective of that which was derived from the valley; great stores of oil and corn had been laid up, sufficient for the wants of many years; and the arsenal was replenished with ammunition of every kind. When Silva marched against Masada, it was held by a party of those Zealots who, in their fastnesses, had so long dreamed of victory and liberty. Their commander was Eleazar, a man well fitted to sustain the part assigned to him in the last harrowing scene of the war. A competent authority has declared this siege—both in the attack and defence of Masada—unequalled by anything in modern warfare. However memorable the former sieges of Jotapata and of Jerusalem had been, this surpassed them in some respects, as in the horrors of its termination, so in the skill and determination displayed by both parties.

The first object of Silva's care was to protect the siege-works, about to be constructed, from the sorties of the enemy. Accordingly he first surrounded the place of his operations with a wall. He chose as his point of attack, a rock on the west side of the fort, and immediately beyond the tower which commanded the approach. Though four hundred and fifty feet lower than Masada, it was really the only possible point of attack. On this rock he reared a mound three hundred feet high, and upon it a platform of stone seventy-five feet in height, and as much in width. Thus the besiegers were only seventy-five feet from the top of the fortress. To complete his preparations, a tower with iron gratings was placed on the stone wall above described. The various machines now hurled stones and darts against the defenders of the fort, while a tremendous battering-ram was employed to effect a breach in the wall. They soon succeeded in this; but with rare ingenuity the defenders had reared an inner wall, which bade defiance to the battering-ram. It was constructed partly of wood and partly of earth. The framework of wood was supported by earth, with which also its interstices were filled up. Of course the projectiles hurled by the enemy had no other effect than that of strengthening and consolidating this defence. Silva ordered burning arrows and pieces of wood to be thrown upon it, in order, if possible, to set it on fire. He succeeded. At first, indeed, an adverse wind threatened to carry the flames against the Roman tower and machines. But the wind veered round, and speedily the last hope of the defenders was removed. The wooden wall and part of the palace were now in flames. At this sight the Romans raised a shout of joy ; and, having taken every precaution against the possible escape of the garrison, they retired to their camp, intending on the morrow to storm the dismantled fort.

Evening with its calm and silence settled on the scene around. The stars twinkled, just as they had done in happier days, over the burning walls of Masada. Beneath rolled heavily the Dead Sea—the monument of former wrath and woe ; in the distance, as far as the eye could reach, the desolate landscape bore the marks of the oppressor. Before them was the camp of the Roman, who watched with eager anxiety for his prey and the morrow. All was silent in Masada. Defence now seemed impossible, and certain death stared the devoted garrison in the face. Despair settled on the stoutest heart, deepened by the presence and the well-known fate of the women and children. Nought was heard but the crackling of burning timbers, and the ill-suppressed moans of the wives and children of the garrison. Then for the last time Eleazar summoned his warriors. In language such as fierce despair alone could have inspired on his, or brooked on their part, he reminded them of their solemn oath —to gain freedom or to die. One of these alternatives alone remained for them—to die. The men of war around him had not quailed before any enemy, yet they shrank from the proposal of their leader. A low murmur betokened their disapprobation. Then flashed Eleazar's eye. Pointing over the burning rampart to the enemy, and in the distance towards Jerusalem, he related with fearful truthfulness the fate which awaited them on the morrow,—to be slain by the enemy, or to be reserved for the arena ; to have their wives devoted in their sight to shame, and their children to torture and slavery. Were they to choose this alternative, or a glorious death, and with it liberty—a death in obedience to their oath, in devotedness to their God, and to their country ? The appeal had its effect. It was not sudden madness, nor a momentary frenzy, which seized these men, when they brought forth, to immolate them on the altar of their liberty, their wives, their children, their chattels, and ranged themselves each by the side of all that had been dear to him in the world. The last glimmer of hope had died out, and with the determination of despair the last defenders of Judea prepared to perish in the flames which enveloped its last fortress. First, each heaped together his household gear, associated with the pleasures of other days, and set fire to it. Again they pressed to their hearts their wives and children. Bitter were the tears wrung from these iron men ; yet the sacrifice was made unshrinkingly, and each plunged his sword into the hearts of his wife and children. Then they laid themselves down beside them, and locked them in tender embrace—now the embrace of death. Cheerfully they presented their breasts to ten of their number, chosen by lot to put the rest of their brethren to death. Of these ten, one had again been fixed upon to slay the remaining nine. Having finished his bloody work, he looked around to see whether any of the band yet required his service. But all was silent. The last survivor then approached as closely as possible to his own family, and fell upon his sword. Nine hundred bodies covered the ground.

Morning dawned upon Masada, and the Romans eagerly

approached its walls; but within was the silence of death.
A feint was apprehended, and the soldiers advanced cautiously,
raising a shout, as if the defenders on the wall implored the
help of their brethren.   Then two women, who, with five
children, had concealed themselves in vaults during the
murderous scene of the preceding evening, came forth from
their retreat to tell the Romans the sad story.   So fearfully
strange did it sound, that their statements were scarcely
credited.   Slowly the Romans advanced; then, rushing through
the flames, they penetrated into the court of the palace.
There lay the lifeless bodies of the garrison and their families.
It was not a day of triumph even to the enemy, but one of
awe and admiration.   They buried the dead and withdrew,
leaving a garrison.   " O Jerusalem, Jerusalem, thou that killest
the prophets, and stonest them which are sent to thee; how
often would I have gathered thy children, as a hen gathereth
her chickens, but ye would not!   Therefore, behold, your
house is left unto you desolate."

Thus terminated the war of Jewish nationality.   Various
causes conspired to make this contest one of the most obstinate
ever witnessed.   The Roman legions were led by the ablest
generals of the empire, and instigated by the recollection of
the shameful defeat which they had sustained at the commencement of the war, and by the obstinate resistance now
made by a small and unwarlike race, whom they had long
affected to despise.   Nor was the issue of the struggle unimportant to the Roman State.   Defeat under any circumstances
would have been the first step in the decadence of the empire,
which was now only delayed by the able administration of the
early emperors.   On the other hand, the Jews contended for
all that is dear to a people.   They fought for national
existence, for political and religious liberty, for their lives, for
their hearths and homes.   Flushed at first by victory, relying
on the zeal and enthusiasm of the whole nation, and defending
themselves in their own country and amongst its fastnesses
against the foreign invaders, the Jews fought with the despair
of men who knew what awaited them in case of defeat.   Nor
was this contest merely one for national independence; it was

essentially also a religious war. Jerusalem was not only a political, but also a religious capital. In fighting for their country, the Jews fought also for their religion, which, indeed, was almost inseparable from the soil of Palestine, and hence, as they thought, for the name and cause of their God. Were it requisite, proofs could readily be adduced of this. Even after they had been defeated, it was stated by the theological expositors of popular sentiment, that since the day of the destruction of the temple, God had mourned for the fate of His people, and that joy had become a stranger in the celestial mansions. Hence they confidently reckoned all along on the Divine assistance. The Maccabees had in former times, with a mere handful of men, defied the Syrian hosts, and why should not similar success be vouchsafed to them under more advantageous circumstances? And even if it turned out otherwise, surely it could only happen in judgment, and for a season, that their God had left His covenant-people, His special favourites, for whose sakes even heaven and earth had been created, and who alone fulfilled the end of their being by glorifying their Maker. Whatever, then, might be their divinely-appointed fate, to conquer or to die, the Zealots were ready to meet it in such a cause. Nor were the expectations entertained about that time of the sudden appearance of a Messiah, who would suddenly come forth to deliver His people from the enemies which threatened them, without their effect on the minds of the people. Though the life and death of the blessed Saviour had too lately taken place for the leaders of the people lightly to risk the safety of the synagogue, by bringing Messianic views prominently forward, as they did at an after-period in the war under Bar-Cochab, in order to inflame the zeal of their followers, such considerations must, no doubt, have had some influence. At times these hopes seemed about to be realised. More than once were the Roman generals in imminent danger—the Roman engines destroyed—the Jews successful—the legions panic-struck or dispirited. Yet the sceptre passed finally and irrevocably from Judah by the same Hand which had at first placed it there. True it is that " the history of the world is the judgment of the world";[1] and the people, which, in its national existence, had exhibited the right relationship between religion and life, even to its climax in the Incarnation of the Son of God, sank when it had misunderstood and perverted that truth, and confounded the type with the reality. The grave could no longer contain true religion— the living was no longer to be found amongst the dead—it rose on the morning of the resurrection, and went forth to animate and to regenerate the world. The lifeless form of the nation, which had misunderstood and neglected its task, lies in the valley of the slain. In judgment are they dead as a nation, yet alive as individuals. Still even now mercy is mixed with judgment, for we may yet witness that soul returning, and Judea arising to embody the full idea of a Christian theocracy. Israel is not dead, it but sleepeth!

About the same time that the Jewish war terminated, Rome attained the climax of her grandeur. Hostile movements had taken place in other provinces, but these had now been suppressed, and Vespasian closed once again the temple of Janus. But this prosperity was of short duration. We do not mean to connect the destruction of Jerusalem and the decline of the Roman Empire as cause and effect; but it is certain that the former immediately preceded the latter event.[2] The insurrections in the northern parts of the empire were only quelled for a while,—the fire still smouldered under the ashes,—in due time it burst forth anew, and destroyed that mighty engine with which the Lord had, in fulfilment of prophecy, punished His people. So has it ever been: the rod of His vengeance, after having served its purpose, has always been speedily broken in pieces.

---

[1] Schiller.

[2] Comp. Gibbon's *Decline and Fall*—the preface ; Schlosser, *Gesch.* iv. 264.

CHAPTER III

THE DISPERSED OF ISRAEL

CONSIDERING the large number of Israelites dispersed over the various parts of the world, who, by their annual contributions, and the delegation of parties to offer vicarious sacrifices, had been wont to acknowledge Jerusalem as their political and religious capital, it may at first appear strange that some attempt should not have been made by them to assist their brethren in the common national contest. Although the Jews who had settled in other lands had in some cases departed from the pious observances of their co-religionists in Palestine, theirs was the exception, and not the rule, as even the successful zeal of so many to win proselytes to Judaism amply attested. Their apathy on this occasion has been ascribed by some to the liberty of conscience which they enjoyed in the lands of their dispersion,—to the feelings of patriotic attachment which they consequently entertained towards those countries, —and to the political ·alienation from Palestine which had thereby been induced. But we must not lay too much stress upon such motives. It is true that, while we hear of attempts made by means of embassies to rouse the Babylonian Jews,[1] the only aid actually given to the insurgents in Palestine was that rendered by the proselyte princes of Adiabene.[2] But the fact that the rising in Palestine took place before any plan had been properly preconcerted, and that the war itself had been prematurely hastened on by the actings of a party, besides the confusion arising from the want of *one* recognised leader, would have rendered any regular co-operation extremely difficult. The distance, also, between the various lands of

[1] Jos. *Wars,* vi. 6. 2.   [2] *Ut sup.* ii. 19. 2 ; vi. 6. 4.

the dispersion, and the peculiar circumstances of their Jewish inhabitants, go far to account for their inactivity. A rapid survey, not so much of the history of their migrations, as of their state in the countries which they inhabited, will place both this matter and their condition generally more clearly before our minds.

According to the narrative in the Book of Acts,[1] Parthians, Medes, Elamites, dwellers in Mesopotamia, inhabitants of Cappadocia, Pontus, Asia (*i.e.* Ionia, the Roman province of Asia), Phrygia, and Pamphylia, as well as Jews who had settled in Egypt, Cyrene, Crete, and even in Arabia, were amongst the worshippers at Jerusalem to whom Peter addressed his memorable discourse. The mention of these countries sufficiently indicates the wide extent of territory over which we have to follow the dispersed of Israel. For convenience' sake, we may classify them as Asiatic, African, and European Jews. Of these the most important branch were the Asiatic Jews, and, among them, those who inhabited the *Parthian* Empire. Their history lies in the main outside our present subject, and we relate only what is absolutely necessary to be known.

A considerable number of the Jews, who had at first been transported by their enemies to Babylon, by and by came to prefer the quiet and comfortable settlements in that wealthy empire to a return to the land of their fathers. The disturbed state of Palestine at later periods increased the number of these settlers, and when at last the Babylonian seats of learning even excelled the schools of Palestine, the pride of the exiles found expression in a vaunting claim of superiority, the more arrogantly preferred that Palestine still continued to claim the spiritual allegiance of all her scattered descendants. Thus it was asserted in Babylon, that when the Jews returned from Exile, the best portion had remained behind. While, with reference to their purity of descent (their non-admixture with Gentile and other interdicted elements), the Hebrew population of Judea claimed to stand in the same relation to their brethren, scattered throughout the various provinces of the Roman Empire, as " pure flour to

[1] Acts ii, 9–11.

mixed dough," the Jews of Babylon in turn characterised their brethren of Palestine [1] as only like " dough," when compared with their claims to purity. Without doubt the various distinctive elements of the synagogue, traditionalism and mysticism, had originated during the stay of the nation in Babylon. Always afterwards a numerous and wealthy class in that empire, they prosecuted not only commerce and agriculture, but also the study of the law, and of science in general. In fact, in the latter the Babylonians greatly excelled their brethren of Palestine. Besides, some of the leading theologians of Judea were of Babylonian extraction, although they had been principally educated in Palestine. Thus, to go no farther, the grand founder of Jewish theology, Hillel, who flourished shortly before the time of our Lord, was of Babylonian origin.[2] But, till the decay of the schools in Judea, those of Babylon were subject to the former in all authoritative interpretations of matters of faith and practice. The patriarch and the Sanhedrin of Judea continued the supreme court of decision and of appeal. Thus all decrees concerning things declared lawful or unlawful, and the important function of fixing the beginning of every new month, on which the arrangement of the festivals depended, originated in Judea and were communicated to Babylon——the latter by a kind of telegraph by means of watchfires. The Jews of Babylon were indeed for a long period under the rule of a Prince of the Captivity, who claimed descent from the house of David; but, until the extinction of the patriarchate in Palestine, his government was rather secular than spiritual, and he himself confessedly subject to his colleague of Judea.[3] This relationship is easily accounted for by the former position of Palestine in religious matters, and by the continuation of the Jewish schools, which claimed to be the lawful substitutes for the authorities of the temple, after its destruction had

---

[1] Kidd. 71a.   [2] Succa 20a.

[3] [The Babylonians claimed for their own prince the higher dignity, but it was allowed that to the patriarch of Judea belonged the right of giving laws for Israel. It was said " that the former held the sceptre ; the latter was the lawgiver." San. 5a ; Hor. 11b, cf. jer. Kil. ix. 4.]

virtually put an end to the Old Testament economy. Of course the Jews of Babylon managed the affairs of their own synagogues, and their spiritual authorities taught and administered their laws throughout the land.

At the time when the Romans suppressed the rebellion, and brought the Jewish war to a successful termination, the greater portion of what had formerly constituted the Persian monarchy owned the sway of the Parthians. Indeed, the Romans and Parthians met in Syria, the western part of which was held by the former, and the eastern by the latter power. The Parthians were semi-barbarous and wild, and the authority of the king was often disputed by his nobles. But they were uncompromising enemies of the Romans. Under their government the Jews enjoyed not only liberty and peace, but even a kind of independence. This is the more remarkable, as the same benefits were not extended to their Greek and Syrian subjects. Perhaps their common hatred of, and resistance to the Romans, may, in some measure, account for this distinction. Some towns in Parthia were almost wholly held by Jews. Thus the cities of Nahardea and Nisibis— afterwards so celebrated for their colleges—were fortified and almost exclusively occupied by Jews, who there deposited the annual tribute for the temple, which was sent to Jerusalem under a strong escort.[1]   It was asserted that King Jeconiah had been deported to Nahardea (600 years before Christ), and that he had built there a synagogue, partly with materials taken from the temple at Jerusalem. The synagogue of Shafjatib, as it was termed, was in consequence of this deemed so peculiarly sacred, that, as tradition expresses it, even the Shechinah might dwell there.[2]   Near this place was also the synagogue of Hozal, reputed equally sacred with the former, and by tradition traced to Ezra, who was said to have founded a theological school there.[3]

[1] Jos. *Ant.* xviii. 9. 1.   Nisibis was not upon the banks of the Euphrates, as Josephus has it, but of the Mygdonius, a tributary of the Chaboras, or Khabur, which flows into the Euphrates at Carchemish.   Nahardea was at the junction of the Euphrates and the Grand Canal.

[2] Rosh ha-Shanah 24b.   *Vide* Fürst's *Kultur-Geschichte*, p. 8.

[3] Fürst, *ut sup.*

Besides these two principal cities, there were other Jewish towns which alternated in rank and importance according to the lore and celebrity of the teachers resident in them. A few miles to the south of Nahardea, and fifty miles from Ctesiphon, lay Phirus Shabor (afterwards Anbar, the Pirisabora of Ammianus), which numbered no less than 90,000 Jewish inhabitants. Not far from it, and on one of the many canals formed by the Euphrates, was Pumbaditha,[1] a beautiful and strong city, which was generally considered the commercial capital of the dispersed. Its inhabitants were deemed very clever, but equally unprincipled. Accordingly a common proverb advised—" If a person from Pumbaditha journeys along with you by the road, see to it that you quickly change your quarters."[2] Following the course of the Euphrates southward to where it forms the lake Surah, the city of Sura was reached,[3] a place inhabited partly by Jews and partly by heathens. Not far from Sura was Mata-Mechasia.[4] Owing to the yearly inundations of the Euphrates, the whole of that neighbourhood was reputed to have been as fruitful as the valley of the Nile.[5] The inhabitants were exceedingly simple and honest. Hence the common saying[6]—" It were better to live on a dunghill in Mechasia, than in one of the palaces of Pumbaditha."

On the banks of the Tigris, and near to the termination of the royal canal (the Nahar-Malka), lay the city of Machuza, situated only a few miles from Ctesiphon, the capital of the Parthian Empire. Close by it was the fortress of Coché, which commanded Ctesiphon. So thoroughly Jewish were these important places, that a later Rabbi expressed his astonishment[7] at not finding, according to Jewish wont, at the entrance to Machuza, that portion of the law affixed which is always conspicuous over the doors and gate-posts of Jewish houses and cities.[8] It was asserted that the majority

[1] Rosh ha-Shanah 23*b*. [Pumbaditha was probably situated at the mouth of a canal, Baditha, which is not otherwise known. See Neubauer, *Géog. du Talm.* p. 349.]

[2] Chulin 127*a*.   [3] M. Kat. 24*b*.

[4] [These two places are often wrongly identified. See Neubauer, *ut sup.* p. 344.]

[5] *Ut sup.* p. 333.   [6] Ker. 6*a*.   [7] Joma 11*a*.   [8] Called the " Mezuzah."

of the Jewish inhabitants of Machuza were not pure Hebrews, but had descended from proselytes.[1]   Their worldliness, lightness, and frivolity procured for them the common appellation of " Candidates of hell." [2]   The men were but little engaged in mercantile pursuits, and were much given to luxury ; the women were famed for their idleness and vanity. In proof of this, it was related that when the Sanhedrin in Palestine allowed Jewish females to wear on Sabbaths golden or jewelled frontlets, only twenty-four females in all Nahardea availed themselves of this privilege, while one quarter alone of Machuza sent forth no less than eighteen ladies arrayed with the most gorgeous head-dresses.[3]   Many Jews also lived in Ctesiphon and in Ardshir.   That district of the country was plentifully supplied with water, and so fair and fertile as to present the appearance of a garden.   To this productiveness of the soil, and to the vicinity of the capital, with its attendant luxury, the general corruption of manners, and the religious indifferentism of the inhabitants, were ascribed. Hence the common saying—" A basket of dates for a cent— and let the inhabitants forbear from studying the law."

Besides the above mentioned, from twenty to thirty other Jewish cities, referred to in Talmudical writings, have been identified.[4]   A glance at the map of Asia will convince the reader how extensive were the Jewish settlements in those regions.   On the east bounded by the Zagras mountains, on the west by the Euphrates, they extended southward as far as the Persian Gulf, and included Southern Armenia, Mesopotamia, Chaldea, Mesene ; and east of the Tigris, Cordyene, Assyria, Adiabene, Susiana, and Chusistan.   The settlement of Jews in a part of Ispahan, which bears to this day the designation of " Jehudia," dates from the third century of our era.   From biblical and other sources we also know that Jews had settled in Elymais, Media, Corbiene, etc.[5]   That they had enjoyed peace in Susiana, is apparent from the fact

---

[1] Kidd. 73a.   [2] Rosh haSh. 17a.   [3] Shab. 59b.
[4] Comp. Ersch's *Encycl.* xxvii. 186 ; Grätz, *Gesch.* iv. 270 ff.; Fürst's *Kultur-Gesch.*, and Neubauer, *Géog. du Talm.* pp. 320–368.
[5] Comp. Ersch's *Encycl.* xxvii. 173.

recorded by Jewish tradition,[1] that a representation of Susa was placed above one of the gates of Jerusalem, to remind its inhabitants of the favours there received.

But even the above-mentioned boundaries did not confine the Jews. As already mentioned, a distinction was made between the Jewish inhabitants of various provinces, some of whom had intermarried, or otherwise become mixed up with their heathen neighbours. The latter were denounced and despised as having become impure. A kind of scale of the degrees of purity and impurity existed, showing how tenaciously the Jews of the dispersion clung to their religious nationality, and to the usages of the synagogue. The district most favoured in respect of purity was that included between the Euphrates and the Tigris, and extending probably no farther north than the 34th degree of latitude. It was pre-eminently the "land of Babylon" of the Jews, and even received from the members of the synagogue there resident the designation of "the land of Israel."[2] Its inhabitants had preserved them-selves pure from Gentile admixture, and were hence character-ised as "healthy." On the contrary, in this respect Media was said to be "sickly"; Elymais "in the last gasps"; and Mesene to be "dead."[3]

For a long time after their deportation into Babylonia, the Jews lived there unmolested in the enjoyment of liberty and happiness. They inhabited all the fruitful districts beyond the Euphrates, except a small portion of the neighbourhood of Babylon.[4] But, some twenty or thirty years after the birth of our Lord, circumstances occurred which put an end to this state of prosperity.[5] At that time Artabanus III. (or Arsaces XIX.) occupied the throne of Parthia. His reign was disturbed by internal dissensions and insurrections. The immediate occasion of the persecution of the Jews was the following occurrence :—In Nahardea lived a poor widow, whose two sons, Asineus and Anileus, early deprived of their father, supported themselves and their mother by the same trade which St. Paul exercised—tent-weaving. Some trifling

[1] Midd. i. 3.   [2] Genesis Rabba, c. 16.   [3] Kidd. 71*b*.
[4] *Vide* Philo, *Legat. ad Cajum*, ii. 587 (ed. Mangey).   [5] Jos. *Ant.* xviii. 9.

cause led to a dispute between the youths and their employer, in which the latter maltreated them.   Bent on revenge, they seized the arms in the house, and, with a few like-minded companions, fled to the neighbourhood of Babylon.   There they built a small citadel, in a position easily defended. Gradually, as they were allowed to plunder unresisted, their followers increased in number, until, like the feudal lords in the Middle Ages, they levied regular contributions from all around, in return for which they afforded protection to the inhabitants.   At last the satrap of the province marched against them at the head of a considerable force.   He had hoped to surprise them on the Sabbath, perhaps unarmed, or at least otherwise occupied, expecting that the religious pre-judices of his enemies would obviate the necessity of engaging them.   But the scouts of Asineus had brought him timely notice of the plan.   The Jewish leader accordingly went to meet the satrap, slew the greater part of his followers, and put the rest to flight.

The party of Asineus acquired such celebrity and influence by this exploit, that the Parthian king courted their alliance, in the hope of availing himself of their services against his own rebellious nobles.   Accordingly, upon his invitation, Anileus repaired to court, with a large retinue and rich presents for the king.   Asineus, who had at first distrusted the Parthian monarch, soon followed his brother.   He was nominated governor of a considerable portion of Mesopotamia, and continued in authority for fifteen years.   Of these two brothers, both equally brave, the elder, Asineus, was small and delicate,—the younger, Anileus, tall and noble-looking. Unfortunately, a Parthian noble was appointed to preside over the province adjoining that of the Jewish brothers.   The beautiful wife of the Parthian captivated the heart of Anileus. The lady seems to have encouraged his advances.   Anileus surprised and killed her husband, and married the widow. But the Parthian wife brought with her the Parthian idols, and, to the sorrow and disappointment of her husband's followers, she introduced their worship.   At last growing dissatisfaction forced Asineus, who had always been most indulgent towards his brother, to remonstrate with him on this subject. As might have been expected, he was unsuccessful, and the Parthian lady soon afterwards got rid of the troublesome monitor by poisoning him.

Anileus now reigned alone. But, carried away by self-confidence, love of plunder, and military fame, he undertook an expedition against the province of Mithridates, one of the noblest satraps, and son-in-law of the Parthian king. Mithridates was routed and taken prisoner; but, instead of using his victory with moderation, Anileus caused the captive satrap to be conducted naked, and riding on an ass, through the Jewish camp,—a treatment viewed by the Parthians as inflicting the greatest insult. At last, fear of the king procured the liberation of Mithridates, who returned to concert measures of revenge. To this he was still more incited by his proud wife, who refused to own him as her husband till he had wiped off, in Jewish blood, his late disgrace. Thus the antagonists met once again, though not under the same circumstances. Anileus had gradually lost his veteran soldiers, partly in battle, and partly in consequence of his idolatrous practices. The reinforcements which had joined his standard consisted mostly of untrained recruits; hence, though numerically superior, he was in reality inferior to his opponent. The Jews were beaten, and obliged to flee to the woods, whence they continued to make marauding expeditions into the plains of Babylon. The inhabitants naturally became exasperated, and demanded that Nahardea should surrender its chief. Compliance with this demand was impossible, as Anileus was not in their power; but Nahardea concluded a separate peace, and a deputation, consisting of Jews and Babylonians, was sent to induce Anileus to come to terms. The Babylonian ambassadors finding that, under the impression that the war was virtually at an end, Anileus had yielded to security, brought back tidings of this. Their companions hastened to avail themselves of the unprotected state of their enemies, surprised them, and killed all, Anileus amongst the rest.

Far from allaying the passions of the populace, this success only incited them to a general persecution. Finding the Jews dispirited and defenceless, they rose everywhere against the unsuspecting Hebrew inhabitants of the different towns, slew all on whom they could lay hands, and forced the rest to seek safety in flight. Most of the latter took refuge in Seleucia, on the banks of the Tigris. That city seemed to offer peculiar advantages, being at that time almost an independent State. It had originally been destined by its builder, Seleucus I., a celebrated general of Alexander the Great, to become the capital of the new Græcio-Syrian Empire, which extended from the shores of the Mediterranean to beyond the Indus. Afterwards, however, the seat of that government had been transferred to Antioch, a city on the Orontes. The distance of that capital from the provinces beyond the Euphrates enabled the Parthians to drive the Greeks from the eastern banks of that river. At the period to which we refer, Seleucia was no longer held by the Greeks, though not yet formally occupied by the Parthians, while, happily for the fugitive Jews, it was inhabited by native Syrians and by Greeks, who lived in continual jealousy and enmity. When the Jews arrived in Seleucia, they made common cause with the Syrians against the Greeks. Soon afterwards, a pestilence, which broke out on the banks of the Euphrates, drove great numbers to Seleucia, and this seems to have produced a change in the state of parties. Certainly the Syrians began to feel that they had more interests in common with the Greeks than with the Jews, and they succeeded in coming to terms with their former opponents. Disturbances broke out in the city, which, as frequently under similar circumstances, were in the last instance entirely directed against the Jews. A fearful carnage ensued, in which no less than 50,000 Jews fell. Flight alone prevented their complete extermination. The fugitive Jews found in part a resting-place in Nahardea and in Nisibis. But, notwithstanding those popular risings, which to a greater or less extent occurred throughout the whole land, the number of Jews in Babylonia continued very considerable.[1]

It is probable that during those persecutions many Jews

[1] Jos. *Ant.* xviii. 9. 8–9.

betook themselves to Adiabene, a province of Assyria lying east of the Tigris, and between the greater and lesser Zeeb. Jewish settlers seem to have lived in Adiabene so early as the time of the captivity of the ten tribes. The throne of Adiabene was at the period to which our record refers occupied by Izates, a Jewish proselyte. The history of the conversion of that royal family is too interesting to be omitted.[1] The father of Izates, King Monabazus, had a son by his sister Helena, to whom he was afterwards united in wedlock. Informed in a dream that his first son (after the marriage with Helena) should enjoy the special favour of the gods, he preferred him to all his other children, even to his elder brother Monabazus. This favourite son was Izates. Under the apprehension that the jealousy of the princes might endanger the safety of Izates, his father sent him, laden with rich presents, to the court of Abennerig, king of Charax, whose capital lay in Mesene, an island formed by the Pasitigris and the Eulæus, which was also known by the name of Spasini Charax and Characene.[2] Izates married the daughter of the king, and received with her a small province as dowry. At the royal court a Jewish merchant of the name of Ananias exercised considerable influence. He succeeded in converting not only some of the noble ladies, but in convincing even the heir of Adiabene of the truth of Judaism. Strange to say, about the same time, Helena, Izates' mother, had undergone at home a similar change. Soon afterwards, Monabazus, feeling his end approaching, recalled Izates, and assigned to him the administration of a beautiful tract of the country, where he continued to reside during the remainder of his father's life.

At the time of the decease of Monabazus, neither Izates nor Helena had publicly professed Judaism. But the latter was so far influenced by its principles, as to refuse her consent to the proposal of the nobles to follow up the proclamation of

[1] Jos. *Ant.* xx. 2.

[2] Mesene means a tract lying between two rivers. The Mesene mentioned in the text is that of which Trajan afterwards took possession. It must not be confounded with the Mesene lying between the Pasitigris and the canal of Bassorah, or with the Mesene above the modern Bagdad, formed between the Tigris and Dujeel or Little Tigris.

Izates by a wholesale murder of all the other princes.   They
were, however, confined to prison, there to await the arrival
of Izates.   Only Monabazus, Helena's eldest son, who in the
meantime was to administer the government, was allowed to
retain his liberty.   On his arrival, Izates immediately liberated
the captive princes, but sent them as hostages partly to Rome
and partly to Artabanus, king of Parthia.   The time had now
arrived when Izates proposed by circumcision to make an
open profession of Judaism.   But Helena, who dreaded a
popular rising in consequence, and Ananias, who apprehended
that the fury of the populace might vent itself on the religious
adviser of the king, tried to persuade Izates that this observance was not binding on him.   But the neophyte, who had
more spiritual and less temporal anxiety than his advisers,
could not be so easily satisfied.   Another teacher from
Galilee, Eleazar, was now sent for.   On his arrival he found
the king engaged in the study of the law.   This circumstance
afforded the zealous teacher an opportunity of urging the duty
of immediate compliance with *all* its requirements.   His
representations were successful, and the sacred rite was performed before the queen-mother or Ananias had even been informed of his intention.   Happily this bold step had no evil
consequences.   To express her gratitude for what was looked
upon as a Divine interposition, Helena undertook a pilgrimage
to Jerusalem.   Izates accompanied her part of the way, and
added his largesses to the rich presents which she carried to
the temple.   She found the inhabitants of the Holy City hardly
pressed by a famine.[1]   To relieve their wants, she sent for corn to
Alexandria and Cyprus, and caused it to be distributed amongst
the poor.   In these largesses Izates followed her example.

Shortly after these events, the ruler of Adiabene had
occasion to show kindness to his liege lord, the king of the
Parthians.[2]   Artabanus, the then reigning monarch, being driven

---

[1] It was to provide against the same famine that Paul and Barnabas collected
and brought to Jerusalem the offerings of the Church at Antioch.   To this con-
currence the reports of Helena's conversion to Christianity may be due.   Comp.
Burton's *Lect.* i. 142.

[2] Jos. *Ant.* xx. 3-4.

from his throne, sought safety with Izates. The unhappy
fugitive met Izates returning on horseback to his capital.
According to Eastern custom, Artabanus threw himself on
the ground, and implored protection and assistance. But no
sooner had Izates heard the tale of the fugitive, than, displaying a conduct vastly different from that of other governors,
he immediately dismounted to assign the place of honour to
Artabanus, proposing to walk on foot beside him. The friendly
dispute which ensued about this mark of respect, terminated
in the two monarchs entering the capital side by side. But the
friendly offices of Izates did not exhaust themselves in marks
of attention. He prevailed upon the Parthians to restore
Artabanus to his throne. In token of gratitude, Izates received
great privileges from Artabanus. Amongst others, he got possession of the town of Nisibis, which was chiefly inhabited by his
co-religionists. Izates sent five of his sons to be educated at
Jerusalem. Monabazus and the rest of the king's relatives by
and by also embraced Judaism. These multipled defections
to a foreign and despised creed at last incited the nobles to
discontent and rebellion. The insurgents, who had secured
the assistance of Abia, the king of Arabia, were successful
in the first engagement, owing to treachery amongst Izates'
troops ; but in a second battle the king defeated the rebels,
and Abia escaped capture only by falling on his sword.

However, soon afterwards another insurrection broke
out. This time the malcontents had, by representing Izates
as being generally unpopular, prevailed on the Parthian king,
Vologeses, the third [1] on the throne since Artabanus, to deprive
Izates of his former privileges, and even to declare war
against him. Izates could not have resisted the whole force
of the Parthian Empire, but tidings of an insurrection within
his own dominions obliged Vologeses to return. From that
time Izates enjoyed undisturbed peace. Helena continued in
Jerusalem during the lifetime of her son ; after his decease
she returned to Adiabene, but soon died. Monabazus succeeded
Izates, having been selected in preference to the children of

---

[1] So Josephus, *Ant.* xx. 3. 4. [According to Tacitus, *Ann.* xi. 8–10, xii. 14,
he was the fourth successor to Artabanus.]

the latter. He caused the bodies of his mother and brother to be interred in Jerusalem, and erected a splendid sepulchre, which is still pointed out as the best preserved, and in some respects the finest, monument in the neighbourhood of that city.[1] Orosius (a later ecclesiastical writer) speaks of the conversion of the royal house of Adiabene to Christianity; but his account is historically and internally unsupported. After this period we lose sight of this royal family, except that two of its members, Izates and Monabazus, were in Jerusalem during the last war. Titus showed great attention and kindness to these princes. They seem to have encouraged the Jews to look for help to the East. Without doubt, although the Parthians were prevented by their king from rendering active assistance to the Jews in their struggle, much sympathy was felt for them, and many of the fugitives found a ready welcome on the Parthian territory.

Besides their settlements in that province, the Jews seem to have spread over the whole of that portion of Asia. They were specially numerous in Armenia, where, as in Adiabene, they had settled from a very early period, and many of them claimed to be descended from the *ten* tribes of Northern Israel. Without entering into particulars which properly belong to the history of a previous period, we may mention that the Talmud interprets the *Chabor* of the Bible, not as the river Chaboras, but as the country of Adiabene.[2] Elsewhere, we are told that the ten tribes travelled along the road to Armenia;[3] while other accounts speak of them as dwelling in Phrygia, in Media as far as the Caucasus, in Africa, and in the mountains of Seloug.[4] [These varying accounts imply that the exiles of Israel were already lost among the native tribes with whom they dwelt; but it is probable that a small portion of them still survived in the Jewish population of the Caucasus. Of recent years numerous attempts have been made to rediscover the lost ten tribes in the Afghans, the Chinese Jews, and elsewhere. The most

---

[1] For particulars, compare Robinson's *Palestine*, i. 528.
[2] Kidd. 72*a*.   [3] Midrash, Lam. Rab. i. 14.
[4] Neubauer, *Géog. du Talm.* p. 372.

successful attempt of this kind was that of Dr. Asahel Grant, who believed that he had discovered the lost tribes among the Nestorians, in the mountains north of old Nineveh. The argument, however, derived from similarity of customs, is generally insufficient; for in many cases the customs appealed to are common to many Oriental peoples, and the features of the Nestorians are by no means of an exclusively Jewish type. Even if these people are really of Jewish origin, as they boast, we cannot be certain that they are descended from the ten tribes.

Large masses of Jews undoubtedly settled in Armenia at an early date; but it is uncertain what circumstance led to their settlement in the country. We first hear of direct relations between the Jews and Armenians in the later Asmonean times, when Tigranes, king of Armenia, had made himself master of Syria (about 75 B.C.[1]). Towards the close of the reign of Queen Alexandra, Tigranes assumed a threatening attitude towards Palestine; but the queen was able to pacify him with presents, and shortly afterwards the advance of Lucullus against Armenia compelled Tigranes to retire. It has been supposed that on this occasion there was a large removal of Jewish families to Armenia. Our principal authority for Armenian history is the work of Moses of Khorene, based largely upon popular ballads and legends of the country; but the historical value of the book is much less than was once supposed. Up till the third century of our era, it is proved by contemporary Greek and Roman annals to be quite untrustworthy. Moses of Khorene describes the honours bestowed upon the noble Jewish family of the Pacarduni,[2] and he also records the persecutions which the same family endured at different times on account of its faith.[3] Another noble family claiming to be of ancient Jewish origin, was that of the Pagratides, who gained the supreme power in North and Central Armenia in the year 743 A.D., and established a dynasty which lasted for more

[1] Josephus, *Ant.* xiii. 16. 4.
[2] See Moïse de Khórene, *Hist. d'Arménie* (Ven. 1841), vol. ii. chs. 7 and 8.
[3] Moïse de Khórene, *ut sup.* ii. pp. 19, 24.

than three hundred years.] We have only to add, that Christianity found at a very early period disciples among the Jewish descendants and proselytes who inhabited the ancient provinces of Armenia and Adiabene.

Still more interesting, at least at the period which we now describe, are the settlements of the Jews in Syria. The proximity of that country to Palestine, and the privileges conferred on the Jews resident there, caused such an influx of settlers, that some of the rural districts, and most of the larger cities, were extensively inhabited by Jews. A very close connection was maintained between Antioch and Jerusalem. The Jews of Antioch transmitted regularly their annual contributions to the temple treasury; they had synagogues, and were subject to their own independent rulers or archons; the study of theology was not neglected, and the Jewish law was administered very much as in Palestine. But Grecian culture, or at least its deleterious moral consequences, had spread into Syria, and made sad havoc amongst a people naturally inclined to luxurious habits. It is well known how detrimental the introduction of Syrian manners and modes of thinking had proved even in Palestine at a former period. It is, then, scarce to be wondered at that the Syrian Jews did not escape the contamination. When the king of Syria had despoiled the temple of Jerusalem, the synagogue of Antioch did not hesitate to receive from his successors and to retain the articles abstracted. On other occasions, however, the Syrian Jews pleaded for exemption from military service on pretence of religious duties. But although they enjoyed a long period of peace and prosperity, and even gained many proselytes, they were despised and hated by most of the natives.

An opportunity at last occurred for manifesting the popular feeling.[1] Strange as it may appear, as if all Israel's political troubles were to befall the generation which rejected the Saviour, the persecutions which we are about to describe, like those of Parthia, occurred during that period. The story is the more sad, that it stands connected with one of the few

[1] Jos. *Wars*, vii. 3. 3–4.

examples of filial ingratitude recorded in Jewish history. From motives not well ascertained, Antiochus, the son of a Jewish ruler, had resolved to destroy the leading men of his nation, and with them his own father. At an assemblage in the theatre, he disclosed a pretended plan hatched by the Jews, under the direction of his father, the object of which was stated to have been the destruction of Antioch by fire. The improbability of a story rarely prevents its reception by the populace, especially if their prejudices or their passions are in any way in favour of it. Without further inquiry, the accused Jews were committed to the flames. But even this summary punishment did not allay the popular excitement. Antiochus, who had in the meantine apostatised, kept up the irritation, and proposed, as a test of their innocency, to call upon the Jews to violate the Sabbath, and to sacrifice to the gods. Only a few bought their lives at such a price. The apostate now put himself at the head of the populace. The synagogue was destroyed, and a dreadful carnage ensued amongst the Jews. No sooner had the storm abated a little, than a fire really broke out in the city, and spread with alarming rapidity. A later investigation proved, indeed, that it had been the work of some hardly-pressed debtors, who hoped to escape their obligations by a destruction of the public records. But the mob laid the whole blame upon the Jews. A fresh slaughter took place, which doubtless would have only ended with the extermination of all the Jews, had not the Romans interposed. Though the innocence of the Jews was soon afterwards fully established, the Antiochians were not easily satisfied; and when Titus made his entrance after the destruction of Jerusalem, they mingled with their shouts of welcome clamorous demands for the expulsion of the Jews.[1] On Titus's second visit to that city, the inhabitants again requested him to consent to the destruction of the brass tablets on which the civic rights of the Jews were re-corded, as well as to the expulsion of the hated race. But the Roman general refused, on the ground that it was impossible to banish from the lands of their dispersion those whose

[1] Jos. *Wars*, vii. 5. 2.

country had now been rendered desolate. After this the Syrian Jews enjoyed unbroken peace under the protection of the Roman emperors.

Another scene of horror enacted in Asia remains to be told. From a very early period Jews had settled in Damascus. Their number was very great at the time when the Jews of Palestine rose to shake off the Roman yoke. Many of the heathens—indeed, almost the whole female population of Damascus—had also embraced Judaism. The tidings of the rising in Palestine caused considerable uneasiness in Damascus.[1] By way of precaution, a large number of Jews were shut up in the arena. When the news arrived of the first and brilliant success of the insurgents, and that Cestius Gallus had been routed, the Damascenes, whether in revenge or by way of protecting themselves, fell upon the Jews, and in one hour killed no less than 10,000 of them.

The Jews in Asia Minor shared in the general degeneracy of its inhabitants. There the Romans encountered no longer the spirit of valour and independence which had once distinguished its people. The same causes which had led to the decline of the native rulers, also operated, as in Syria, detrimentally upon the Jewish settlers. Mostly engaged in trade, they had accumulated wealth, which excited the cupidity, while their refusal to engage in military service, on the plea of religious scruples, called forth the indignation, of the populace. By and by the annual exportation of large sums as contributions to the temple treasury was denounced as involving a public loss, and gave rise to bitter complaints. Under the partial administration of corrupt Roman governors, several attempts were made to prevent or to alienate these contributions.[2] The Jewish inhabitants of the isle of Delos appealed for protection to Julius Cæsar, who bore a grateful remembrance of the valuable aid afforded him by the Jews in Egypt.[3] Their prayer was granted, and a special decree secured their freedom. After the murder of Cæsar, the opportunity seemed favourable to renew former hostile

---

[1] Jos. *Wars*, ii. 20. 2.   [2] Cicero, *Pro Flacco*, 28.
[3] Jos. *Ant.* xiv. 10. 8–26.

attempts against the Jews—this time on the plea of their resistance to military service. Hyrcanus the Asmonean, however, advocated their cause in Rome, and succeeded the more readily that the troubled state of the empire did not admit of argument with distant provinces. After the defeat of Brutus and Cassius, renewed disputes were again settled in favour of the Jews. Still the Jews were not free from occasional interferences, and when Herod accompanied Agrippa through that province, they publicly complained of their grievances.[1] Nicolaus of Damascus represented their case, and they obtained immediate relief. They now increased rapidly in numbers and influence. We find them in Crete, Cyprus, Phrygia, Lydia, Mysia, in Cappadocia, with its capital Mesheg, and in Cilicia, with its capital Tarsus. Philo gives a glowing account[2] of their state and prosperity. Indeed, from the time when Antiochus the Great had transplanted 2000 Jewish families into Phrygia and Lydia, in order to serve as a counterpoise to the rebellious native population, they seem to have rapidly multiplied and spread into Pamphylia, Galatia, and Mysia.[3] They enjoyed at first considerable privileges; amongst others, they were exempted for ten years from all taxation.[4] Finally, references in the New Testament and in the writings of Philo prove that Jews early penetrated into Greece Proper, and spread over the whole of the Peleponnesus.

Turning our steps again towards the East, we come upon the important Jewish settlements in Arabia. By the ancients that country was commonly divided into three districts or provinces, called respectively Arabia Petræa, Deserta, and Felix (the Stony, the Desert, and the Happy). The plains and mountains round the coast are in part barren, in part susceptible of cultivation. The high central plateau is tolerably fertile, but is separated from the coast region by a broad strip of desert waste. The south-western portion, close by the Red Sea, is the most fertile, and is well known in history as the kingdom of Saba, of Yemen, of the Joctanites, or of the

---

[1] Jos. *Ant.* xvi. 2. 3–4. [2] Philo, *Legat. ad Cajum*, ii. 582, 587.
[3] Acts ii. 9, 10. [4] Jos. *Ant.* xii. 3. 4.

Homerites. This diversity of names proves that the country
was peopled by different tribes. [The discovery of inscriptions
has greatly increased our knowledge of the Sabeans, whose
language is proved to have been closely allied to the Arabic.]
It is impossible to determine at what time Judaism found its
way into this country, and whether it came from Palestine
across the desert, from Ethiopia across the Red Sea, or from the
east (Persia, etc.) across the Gulf. Probably at different
periods Jewish wanderers found their way into Arabia from
all these directions. The intimate relations which subsisted
between Arabia Petræa and Judea belong to an earlier period,
that of the later Asmonean princes. We cannot dwell on
them, and only gather the most interesting particulars connected with the history of the other two provinces of Arabia.

Tradition speaks of a very early connection between the
Jews and the native Arabian tribes. From the time of Mohammed it was even maintained that the Caaba, or ancient
temple of Mecca, had been originally dedicated to the God of
Abraham. Under the reign of Solomon, Jewish merchants
traded to Saba, probably exporting thence the products of
Arabia Felix. The visit of the Queen of Sheba to King
Solomon affords proof of a further connection between Arabia
and the Jews. More than one of the kings of Judah afterwards attempted to reopen the trade with Arabia by the
Red Sea, but with only partial success. The intercourse
between the nations continued to be carried on mainly by
land along the regular caravan routes. As troubles at home
and abroad obliged the Hebrews to seek shelter in more distant regions, the number of Jews in Arabia increased. Their
comparatively settled mode of living, their cultivation and
wealth, must have secured for them a peculiar influence
among the nomadic tribes of that country. No doubt they
improved their position, amongst other ways, in attempting to
gain proselytes. At a later period, many Jews passed with
Gallus across the Red Sea into Arabia in his unsuccessful
expedition against the Sabeans.[1] The Talmud mentions the

[1] Jos. *Ant.* xv. 9. 3 ; Strabo, xvi. 4. 23. Comp. Mommsen, *Provinces*, ii.
290–293.

Jewish settlements in Arabia, and records some ordinances referring to them.[1] After the fall of Jerusalem, many Jews doubtless retreated to Arabia. When the oasis of Yathrib or Medina first appears in history, it was mainly occupied by Jews; and Jewish settlements were also numerous and ancient in the district of Cheibar, four or five days' journey from Medina. There warlike Jewish tribes had reared and held fastnesses. They adopted many customs from the Arab races around them; and the testimony of the Talmud shows that heathen customs and the peculiar forms of idolatry and immorality common in those districts were well known to Jewish authorities.

But Judaism was not merely tolerated—in South Arabia it became dominant for a short period. [The first Jewish king of the Homerites, Abu-Cariba-Asad, flourished about the year 500 A.D., though legend has fixed his reign several centuries earlier. His conversion is accounted for in the following manner :[2]—Abu-Cariba, a brave and warlike sovereign, while on an expedition against Persia and the northern parts of Arabia, occupied Medina, and left his son there as governor of the province. The inhabitants rose in rebellion, and slew their governor; and to avenge this deed, and quell the insurrection, the king turned back with his army to Medina. The population of this town was partly of Arabian and partly of Jewish origin, but all united to make a brave defence against the besiegers. The siege was prolonged, and the Homerite king began to suffer from want of water. This circumstance disposed him to peace, and two Jewish teachers in the town sought and obtained an interview with Abu-Cariba. The Jewish sages were able to interest the king in Judaism; he himself adopted their religion, and compelled his army to do the same. Some of the neighbouring princes also became converts to Judaism. Abu-Cariba did not long survive his conversion. Two of his sons, who were both Jews, succeeded to the throne in turn; and after the brief reign of a usurper, the youngest son, Zorah or Dhu-Nowas, obtained the crown. But the zeal displayed by Dhu-Nowas for the creed which he had

[1] Shab. 65*a*.   [2] Comp. Grätz, *Gesch.* v. 77 ff.

adopted led to the downfall of his power.   In retaliation for
the persecutions, which the Jews had to suffer about this
time in the Byzantine Empire, Dhu-Nowas began to oppress
the Christians of Yemen.   The Christians appealed for help
to the Ethiopian king Elesbaan,[1] who at once prepared for
war.   He invaded Yemen, drove Dhu-Nowas from the throne,
and established a viceroy in the country (*circ.* 519 A.D.).   A
few years later, Dhu-Nowas recovered his power and renewed
his persecutions.   Elesbaan thereupon fitted out another expedition, which was completely successful.   Dhu-Nowas was
killed, his kingdom fell into the hands of the invaders, and an
Axumite dynasty ruled Yemen for seventy years.

But the wanderings of the Jews extended much farther,
and at some unknown date many penetrated eastwards as far
as China.   In the old Jewish temple at Kae-fung-foo, there is an
inscription, claiming to have been erected in 1488 A.D., which
states that the first synagogue there was built in the year
1166 A.D.   Another inscription states that the Jewish religion
entered China during the Han dynasty (205 B.C. to 226 A.D.).
Copies of the Scriptures which have been obtained from Kae-
fung-foo are written according to the Rabbinical principles,
and contain no variations of importance from the text of our
Hebrew Bibles.   From the occurrence of Persian words in
the inscriptions and in certain manuscripts, it seems probable
that these settlers came originally from Persia ; but their early
history is involved in obscurity.   The Chinese Jews have now,
through long isolation, forgotten the Hebrew language and
Jewish rites.][2]

From an early period the relations between the Jews and
Egyptians were very intimate.   Many instances of this are
met with even in biblical times.   But these occurrences, their
settlement in the city which Alexander the Great built and

---

[1] Comp. Grätz, *ut supra ; Dict. of Chr. Biog.* ii. " Elesbaan."

[2] [See J. Finn, *The Orphan Colony of the Jews in China ;* and Dr. Neubauer,
in *Jewish Quarterly Review,* Oct. 1888, pp. 23, 28.] In Delitzsch's *Jüd. Poesie,*
pp. 59, etc. ; Jost, *Geschichte,* vol. ix. Index, may be found many particulars
collected from the writings of the missionaries Gozani (1700 A.D.) and Kögler
(1715–1746 A.D.).   [Gozani knew no Hebrew, and many of his statements are
open to suspicion.]

called after his name, as well as their subsequent history, and
the rearing of the rival temple in Heliopolis, to which the
passage Isa. xix. 18, 19 was applied, belong to a former
period of our history. The Jews of Egypt enjoyed considerable privileges, and for a long time, on the whole, a greater
amount of liberty and safety than did their brethren in other
countries. They were under a chief or ethnarch of their
own, whose place after the time of Augustus was taken by a
Sanhedrin.[1] The temple of Heliopolis, built by the fugitive
high priest Onias, was to have rivalled, not only in importance,
but in beauty, that of Jerusalem. It was built in the form
of a tower, ninety feet high, and the altar at the entrance of
it was similar to that of Jerusalem. Instead of the golden
candlestick which graced the temple of Judea, a golden lamp
was suspended in front of the veil. The temple of Heliopolis
was destroyed by Vespasian.[2] The Jews had also many other
synagogues throughout Egypt. The most magnificent of
these was in Alexandria. Tradition describes its splendour
in almost fabulous terms, and declares that the person who
had not worshipped there, had not witnessed the glory of
Israel.[3] It rose like a large basilica, and was said sometimes
to have contained a number of worshippers twice as great as
that which Moses led out of Egypt. Seventy golden chairs,
richly studded with gems, were placed in it for the members
of the Sanhedrin. In the middle of the synagogue was the
wooden platform occupied by the person who led the devotions.
As one rose to read in the law or during prayers, an officer
waved a flag, and the vast congregation responded from all
parts of the building. The worshippers did not sit pro-
miscuously, but were arranged according to trades or guilds,
so that a stranger might be able at once to join himself to
his own craft. The synagogue at Alexandria seems to have
been destroyed in the time of Trajan.

The Egyptian Jews continued in the enjoyment of peace
under Roman domination till the time of Caius Caligula,
about the year 38 of our era. But the readiness with which

[1] Philo, *In Flaccum*, ii. 527.   [2] Jos. *Wars*, vii. 10. 2–4.
[3] Jer. Succa v. 1 ; b. Succ. 51*b*.

the Gentiles then rose against the Hebrews, proves that the
public mind must have been long excited against them.   Nor
is it difficult to understand the cause of this.   Egypt was no
longer what it once had been.   Its Jewish inhabitants were
now, if not the most learned, yet the most industrious and
wealthy in the land.   Their number, privileges, thriving
condition, and the advantages accruing from their constant
connection with their brethren in other countries, were a
continual source of annoyance to the Egyptians.   The first
opportunity which presented itself for displaying their feelings was eagerly seized.[1]   During a visit to Alexandria, the
Jewish king Agrippa was exposed to the open scorn of the
Alexandrian mob.   Flaccus Avillius, the Roman governor,
tolerated if he did not connive at this conduct.   Encouraged
by this, the populace soon increased in violence.   The
Emperor Caius, of whose reign it would be difficult to say
whether madness or wickedness was its most prominent
characteristic, had taken the fancy of insisting upon the
universal adoration of his statue.   On pretence of showing
respect to the emperor, the Alexandrians attempted to place
the idol in the various synagogues.   The Jews resisted, and
in the contest some of their sanctuaries were burnt down,
others violated, and statues of the emperor set up in them.
The occasion seemed favourable, and Flaccus, instead of interfering to restore order, permitted, and indeed encouraged, the
erection of statues in the synagogues.   He next proceeded to
revoke by a proclamation the privileges of the Jews, and to
sanction an organised persecution.

The populace now rose against the Jews in various
districts of the city, profaned their synagogues, and practised
all manner of cruelties upon them.   In Alexandria, the Jews
had, not from necessity, but from choice, inhabited two
separate quarters of the city.   They were now shut up in one
of these.   Many were obliged to remain in the streets, exposed to hunger and the inclemency of the weather.   Meanwhile the mob pillaged and burnt their dwellings.   All

<hr />

[1] Philo, *In Flaccum*, ii. 521–525.
[2] *Ut supra*, ii. 525–532 ; comp. *Legat. ad Cajum*, ii. 563–565.

business was at a stand, and everywhere the shops were shut. Many Jews perished from want, others from overcrowding; others were brutally murdered by the populace, who hurried them off to the market-place, burnt them alive, trampled them under foot, and even dragged them along the streets till their mangled members covered the pavement. Neither sex, age, nor dignity were respected. Of the members of the Sanhedrin, thirty-eight were, by order of Flaccus, publicly scourged, and some of them died in consequence; three were deprived of their property, and chastised; others were cruci- fied. The Jewish females were ordered to eat pork: in case of refusal, they were at once given up to torture. During the whole time that these infamous deeds were perpetrated, the populace feasted and made merry with games and rioting. The Jews had probably at first attempted to resist these un- provoked attacks; at any rate, the plea of a search after weapons, and of disarming the Jews, afforded pretext for continual acts of violence. Meanwhile, the chiefs of the congregation had resolved on appealing to the emperor. Un- fortunately, they entrusted the petition to Flaccus, who did not transmit it to Rome. The Jews then applied to their countryman, King Agrippa, who was a favourite with the emperor. He forwarded their petition, together with an account of the conduct and motives of Flaccus. Caligula immediately sent Bassus to depose and punish the pre- sumptuous governor.[1] Flaccus was enjoying the pleasures of the table when the imperial envoy appeared to lead him in chains to the isle of Andros. A year afterwards, he was put to death, by order of the emperor. No sooner did tidings of this unexpected deliverance reach the Jewish quarter, than a general burst of thanksgiving rose from every Jewish home.

But the change of governor did not bring the hoped-for relief. The mob had learnt to indulge unchecked in its hatred of the Jews. Insult and licentiousness had not only been tolerated, but a way discovered by which to procure money more easily than by industry. Accordingly, the disturbances were soon renewed. At last a deputation was

[1] Philo, *In Flaccum*, ii. 533–544.

despatched to the emperor, to induce him to revoke the
privileges which the law had hitherto accorded to the Jews.[1]
At the head of this deputation was Apion, well known in
Alexandria as the author of an Egyptian history, a work
none the less popular that in its pages the shafts of bitter
irony were so frequently directed against the Jews.   The
Jews met this measure by a counter-deputation, at the head of
which was the brother of the Alabarch, Philo, the celebrated
eclectic Jewish philosopher.[2]   The Jews secured in Rome the
friendly offices of Agrippa, who providentially was in the
capital at the time.   The Egyptians gained for their cause
Helicon, a special favourite of the emperor.   Thus prepared,
both parties awaited the arrival of the emperor in Rome.
But though their petitions were handed to Caligula, their
cause was not immediately heard.   The ambassadors accordingly followed the emperor to Puteoli, where, to their dismay,
the Jews learned of the attempt to set up the emperor's
statue in the temple at Jerusalem.   Still they persisted, and
at last, in Rome, an audience was granted, which painfully
illustrates the state of the empire at the time.[3]   While both
parties were each urging its cause, the emperor went through
one of his palaces ordering improvements, etc., and only occasionally accosting the deputies in his own peculiar way.
Caligula reproached the Jews as being the only people who
refused to own his claims to divinity.   At this the Alexandrians shouted assent, and accused their opponents of even
refusing to offer sacrifices for the emperor's welfare.   It was
in vain that the Jews denied the latter charge.   The emperor
retorted, that it did not matter though they offered *for* him,
if they refused to sacrifice *to* him.   This altercation was
intermixed with some of the emperor's wonted follies, and
with blasphemies against the God of Israel.   Silence now
ensued, during which the emperor continued his tour of
inspection, the ambassadors following him.   Of a sudden he
turned round to ask the Jews why they refused to eat pork.

[1] Jos. *Ant.* xviii. 8. 1.

[2] Philo, *Legat. ad Cajum*, ii. 570–573.

[3] *Ut supra*, ii. 597–600.   Comp. Schürer, I. ii. 97 f.

Shouts of laughter greeted this query. In vain the Jews urged, that every people had its peculiar customs. It was evident the emperor was only in a mood to deride them. At last, when questioned as to their claims for civic rights, they referred to documents. The emperor then refused to continue the audience, and dismissed them with the remark that, after all, these people were not so wicked, but rather to be pitied for not discovering that he really was a god. Philo and his friends returned without having succeeded. At Agrippa's intercession, Palestine was indeed exempted from adoring the Roman god, but their co-religionists in Alexandria remained exposed to the fury of the rabble. Happily the world was soon freed from Caligula, and his successor Claudius restored to the Jews their ancient privileges.

Five-and-twenty years had elapsed since the above events had taken place, and the Jews of Alexandria were beginning to recover their former prosperity, when the storm broke out afresh.[1] The former dissensions had left a feeling of mutual distrust and bitterness, and the Jews and Gentiles kept almost entirely aloof from each other. But a popular assembly had been convoked to consult about some embassy to Nero, at which, unfortunately, some Jews made their appearance. This was the signal for an outbreak. A cry of treason was raised. The mob attacked the Jews. Some were killed while fleeing, others flew to arms, and soon all Alexandria was in commotion. The Jews attempted to set fire to the amphitheatre, and thus to destroy the multitude there assembled; but the governor, Tiberius Alexander, an apostate Jew, marched down the Roman garrison, with leave not only to kill the resisting, but to plunder and burn down the Jewish quarter. A desperate struggle now ensued, and blood literally flowed down the streets of the Delta, as the principal quarter of the Jews was termed. The steady onset of the regular and well-disciplined troops overcame the desperate courage of the Jews. A carnage commenced, in which, without distinction, old and young, male and female, were cut down. The glare of the burning houses lit up that night of

[1] Jos. *Wars*, ii. 18. 7–8.

horror, and discovered a multitude of bodies covering the streets. Thousands had already fallen, and probably the whole Jewish population would have been exterminated if they had not implored quarter.

Once again, after the destruction of Jerusalem, a number of Jewish Zealots, who escaped to Africa, had almost involved their countrymen there in fresh troubles.[1] The recollection of their past sufferings induced the Jews of Alexandria to resist the solicitations of the fugitives to rise against the Gentiles. The ringleaders and many of their confederates, in all 600 persons, were delivered to the Roman authorities; but some fled to Thebais. An attempt at resistance proved vain, and the captives chose to undergo the most exquisite tortures rather than own fealty to the emperor. Thus perished the remainder of that resolute band.

From Egypt the Jews had, since their first settlement, spread towards the west, and occupied Lybia and Cyrene. Indeed, Ptolemy Soter, the Egyptian king, had transported them into these districts, and accorded them great privileges.[2] They seem to have been a turbulent community, and they took a prominent part in the disturbances which broke out in Cyrene in 86 B.C.[3] So thoroughly did the Jews remain separate from the other inhabitants, that in describing the population, Strabo enumerates them as a distinct class.[4] The materials for their history are but scanty. We know that a Cyrenian Jew, Jason, wrote a work on the victory of the Maccabees, part of which is preserved in the second of the two apocryphal books which bears that name. In Berenice, one of the five principal cities of Cyrene, the Jews must have possessed considerable influence, as is indicated by an inscription, dating probably from the year 13 B.C. From this source we learn that the Jews formed a separate community under nine rulers of their own.[5] After a long period of undisturbed prosperity, they seem, during the reign of Augustus, to have been obstructed in the exercise of their religion, and

[1] Jos. *Wars*, vii. 10, 1.   [2] Jos. *Against Apion*, ii. 4.
[3] Comp. Plutarch, *Lucull.* 2.   [4] Comp. Jos. *Ant.* xiv. 7. 2.
[5] *Corp. Inscr. Græc.* iii. 5361.

specially to have been prevented from sending their usual contributions to Jerusalem.[1] An application to Rome brought them relief from this interference.

Thus matters continued prosperously till after the destruction of Jerusalem, when one of the fugitive Zealots, Jonathan, endeavoured, by the practice of magic, to rally followers round his standard.[2] The peaceably disposed amongst the Jews denounced the plot to Catullus, the Roman governor, ere it had time to develop. The yet unarmed followers of the impostor were surprised, and many of them slain. At last Jonathan himself was captured. In revenge, he denounced the noblest of the Jews and all his personal opponents as secret accomplices in the plot. Apparently glad of the excuse, Catullus cruelly slew about 3000 Jews, and confiscated their goods. To give an appearance of justice to these proceedings, he resorted to the fiction of a widely-spread conspiracy, in which fortunately some of the most respected persons, such as the historian Josephus, were said to have been implicated. A strict investigation proved the groundlessness of this charge. Catullus died soon afterwards in contempt and obscurity. About the same time, and probably in connection with these disturbances, the Jewish temple of Heliopolis, in Egypt, was closed by order of Vespasian, and during the governorship of Lupus.[3] Paulinus, his successor in Alexandria, despoiled it of all its treasures. It had stood altogether for about 230 years.

The writings of the New Testament and the statements of Philo confirm other accounts, which detail the spread of Judaism and of Jews throughout Egypt, Cyrene, Lybia, and even Ethiopia. Philo computes the number of his countrymen in Egypt at a million of souls.[4] Recent investigations have brought to light a number of interesting particulars connected with the Jews of Ethiopia.[5] Until lately various rumours had been current about them. Thus it was asserted

---

[1] Jos. *Ant.* xvi. 6. 1. [2] Jos. *Wars*, vii. 11.
[3] Jos. *Wars*, vii. 10. 2–4. [4] Philo, *In Flaccum*, ii. 523.
[5] Comp. an interesting paper in Frankel's *Monatsschrift*, Nov. 1853, p. 423.

by some that Minilek, a son of King Solomon and the Queen of Sheba, had there founded a Jewish dynasty. At all events, an Ethiopian chronicle mentions a Jewish queen, Sague, who, in the beginning of the tenth century, drove a Christian king, Deland, from his throne, and founded a dynasty, which reigned for three and a half centuries. Travellers record that up to the close of the sixteenth century, the mountainous districts of Ethiopia were inhabited by Jews. Their posterity, forced to abandon their religion, are said to be still easily recognised by the features peculiar to the Jewish race. In Gondar, the principal city of Abyssinia, there is still a Jewish quarter inhabited by about sixty families. The Jews are called by the nations "Falasha," or wanderers; but they repudiate that name. From the peculiar contents of their sacred canon, it may be inferred that they came originally from Egypt, not earlier than the close of the second century before our era; while the absence of a fast to commemorate the destruction of the second temple supplies perhaps the latest date possible for their emigration. Their present customs indicate a strange mixture of corrupt Judaism and of equally corrupt Christianity. Amongst other superstitious rites, they celebrate on the twelfth of every month a feast in honour of St. Michael. They divide the year into lunar months, and intercalate a month of thirty days at regular intervals of four years. Fifty days after the Passover, they have the Feast of Marar, in commemoration of the giving of the Law. On the fifteenth day of every month they celebrate the Feast of Tabernacles. The fourth Sabbath of the month is deemed peculiarly solemn. The Feast of Drums (of Trumpets, or the New Year?) takes place on the first of the seventh month. Ten days after it is the Feast of Astary, or of the appearance of God to Jacob. On that day the sins of the past year are supposed to be forgiven. This is also commemorated on the tenth day of every month. On the thirteenth day of the seventh month is the Feast of Booths. Amato-so is a feast on which prayer is offered on the top of the mountains. They observe a great number of fasts, said, variously, to have been instituted by kings and prophets—some lasting six, ten,

and even eleven days. Generally they fast three times every
week, on Mondays, Thursdays, and Fridays. Their canonical
books, which are in the language of the country, contain also some
of the Apocrypha. They also possess some non-canonical writings. They have a kind of order of monks established amongst
them, and suppose that some of the Old Testament saints practised celibacy. A person who touches a dead body has to be
purified on the third day with the ashes of a red goat which had
been offered up by a priest. The Ethiopian Jews are ignorant
of Hebrew. The accounts which they give of the occasion and
the course of their wanderings are manifestly fabulous.

Having briefly traced the dispersion of Israel to the
farthest limits of Asia and Africa, we return to inquire into
their condition in Italy. Passing over the legend which
traces the origin of Rome to a grandson of Esau,—a fable
possibly due to the Jewish identification of that empire with
Edom,—we first hear definitely of the Jews in Rome in the
time of the Maccabees. Judas Maccabæus, shortly before his
death, sent an embassy in order to form an alliance with the
Romans,[1] and from this time onwards the Jews came more
and more in contact with the masters of the world. Under
Pompey, Jews were sold in Rome as slaves. They soon, however, gained their liberty, for their adherence to their national
customs rendered them inconvenient servants in a heathen
household.[2] Many received the privileges of Roman citizen-
ship; and Julius Cæsar was so great a patron of the Jews,
that after his murder their lamentations rent the air.[3]
Augustus was generally an enemy to all foreign religions, and
even praised Caius, the son of Agrippa, for not having sacrificed in Jerusalem.[4] But he showed unvarying favour towards the Jewish people, and even ordered that sacrifices for
his welfare should be offered in the Jewish temple.[5] Under
his reign the Jews attained to a high degree of importance.
Even Horace, with all his contempt for the race, bears testimony to the extent of their influence.[6] The kindly feelings

[1] 1 Macc. viii. 17–32.   [2] Philo, *Legat. ad Cajum*, ii. 568.
[3] Sueton. *In Julium*, 84.   [4] Sueton. *In Octav.* 93.
[5] Philo, *Legat. ad Cajum*, ii. 569, 592.   [6] Hor. *Sat.* i. 9. 71 f.

of Augustus towards the Jews were no doubt increased by his
private friendship for Herod, and the many tokens of fidelity
and attachment which that monarch had given.   The religion
of the Jews was at that time not only tolerated, but every
facility was given them for the exercise of their rites.   Thus
it was arranged that, when the distribution of corn and money
(to a certain class of citizens, according to ancient custom)
fell on a Sabbath, the Jews received their portion on the
following day.[1]

But the exclusiveness and the isolation of the Jews at
Rome raised against them popular prejudice.   The Romans,
who were indeed willing to assign some place to the national
Deity of the Jews, could not understand on what grounds the
Jews kept so much aloof, nor why they despised them and
their worship, as if the gods of an empire which had overcome and was virtually reigning over the Jews, were to yield
to a deity of a conquered country.   Their practices also
excited popular suspicion.   Even the better informed gave
way to prejudices.   Thus Cicero bitterly inveighed against
their practice of sending large annual contributions to the
temple.   He dreaded their number and influence in the
popular assemblies, and even denounced their creed, attempting to prove how little acceptable to the gods that nation
must be whose country had been subdued.[2]   However,
Cicero's political opinions may in some measure account for
this aversion.   But even these denunciations prove that the
Jews were at the time numerous and influential in Rome.

As Judaism became better known, and the political state
of Palestine one of increasing subjection to Rome, this
contempt and hatred increased.   Rome tolerated, indeed, all
religions, but only because there was a bond of affinity, both
in religion and in practice, between all kinds of polytheism.
All readily admitted of being incorporated in the Roman
body politic, and soon became integral parts of it.   Not so
the religion of the Jews.   Not that the Jewish rites were so
poor, empty, and meaningless,[3] for they possessed at least the

[1] Philo, *Legat. ad Cajum*, ii. 569.   [2] Cicero, *Pro Flacco*, c. 28.
[3] Tacit. *Hist.* v. 5.

powerful charm of mysteriousness; but as in both cases religion and life were so closely intertwined, while their fundamental principles were antagonistic, Romans and Jews lived side by side, but always remained strangers to, and entirely separate from, each other. Besides, the continual recurrence of Sabbaths, of feasts, of circumcision—their manifest attachment to those of their own nation, and their equally manifest contempt of heathenism, if not of heathens —contributed to embitter the public mind.[1]

The grossest misapprehensions prevailed among *all* classes, as to the origin, history, and creed of the Jews. Thus even Tacitus (90 A.D.), recounting the current traditions of their origin, in which most other heathen historians agree,[2] relates that the Jews derived their name from Mount Ida (Idæi, Judæi); that they had at one time been expelled from Crete; that Jerusalem had been called after Hierosolymus, who, with Judah, was the leader of their wanderings; that they had found their way into Egypt, whence they were expelled on account of their leprosy. They had left that country under the leadership of Moses. A troop of wild asses had conducted them to a spring, when they were almost perishing from thirst. On this account they ever afterwards adored the golden head of an ass, which was kept in their innermost sanctuary. Their abstinence from swine's flesh was accounted for, either on the ground that they adored that animal,[3] or else because swine were peculiarly liable to leprosy. Their observance of the Sabbath was variously traced to the service of Saturn (to whom the Romans had dedicated that day), the supposed god of the Ideans, or else to the superiority of the star of that name. Some reported that the Jews fasted on Sabbaths,[4] others that they spent the day in idleness[5] and feastings. It was also suggested that the Jews observed the Sabbath, as being the day on which they got possession of Palestine. They were described as

---

[1] Juvenal, *Sat.* xiv. 96–106.   [2] Tacit. *Hist.* v. 2 ff.
[3] Petron. *Sat.*, Frag. ed. Burm. p. 683; cf. Plutarch, *Symp.* iv. 5.
[4] Petron. *ut supra;* Sueton. *In Octav.* 76.
[5] Cl. Rutil. *Itiner.* i. 391 f.

exceedingly dangerous to the State, on account of their contempt for the religion of the Romans, and their hatred of all but their co-religionists.[1]   Their rites were said to be contemptible, and their whole creed empty and unmeaning. Circumcision formed a theme of never-failing scorn,[2] and was stated by some to have been derived from the Egyptians.[3] Various opinions prevailed as to the origin of the city and name of Jerusalem (Hierosolyma).   One party traced it to the people of Solymi, celebrated in Homeric verse.   Again, the blowing of trumpets, the use of branches in some of the feasts, and the name of Levites (supposed to be derived from Evius), were taken as indications of their service of Bacchus.[4] On the other hand, some accused them either of Atheism, or else of the adoration of an invisible god, or even of the sky and of the clouds.[5] The Jewish hatred of the Romans is described to have been such, that they would not point out the road to a stranger, or conduct the thirsty to a well.[6] However, the superstitious Romans imitated their rites, and many of them were even circumcised.[7]   Jews were frequently resorted to for soothsaying and the preparation of charms, or consulted as to the future.[8]

In Rome the Jews engaged in all kinds of trade.   The poorer classes are ridiculed as vendors of matches and similar trifles;[9] others are characterised as beggars, as in abject poverty, or as renting the ground where Numa had been wont to meet his friendly nymph.   They seem to have inhabited separate quarters of the city, the region where they first settled being the district beyond the river and the Tiber island.   As in other countries, they had rulers or archons, who, as far as was practicable, administered the Jewish law. They also maintained a continual intercourse with Palestine.[10] Under the reign of Augustus, 8000 Roman Jews are said to

---

[1] Tacitus et Juvenalis, *ut supra*.

[2] Hor. *Sat.* i. 9. 70 ; Martial, vii. *Ep.* 30, 35 ; Petron. et Juven. *ut supra*.

[3] Herodot. ii. 104.

[4] Plutarch, *Symp.* iv. 6.

[5] Juven. *Sat.* xiv. 96 f.

[6] Juven. *ut supra*, 103, 104.

[7] Juven. *ut supra*, 99.

[8] Juven. *Sat.* vi. 542–547.

[9] Mart. i. 42 ; xii. 57.

[10] Acts xxviii. 21.

have joined a deputation from Palestine.[1] Their number at
that time is calculated to have amounted to 40,000. The
first direct persecution of the Jews occurred under the reign
of Tiberius, who sent 4000 Jewish youths against the robbers
of Sardinia, purposely exposing them to the inclemencies of
the climate, and who banished all the others from Rome.[2]
The ground of this decree is stated to have been the
- emperor's desire to suppress all foreign superstitions, more
especially the Jewish, which numbered many proselytes.
Josephus explains that a certain Jewish impostor, who acted
as a Rabbi in Rome, had, in concert with three other Jews,
succeeded in proselytising Fulvia, a noble Roman lady. On
pretence of collecting for the temple, they received from her
large sums, which they appropriated to their own purposes.[3]
The fraud was detected, and Sejanus, who at that time was
high in the emperor's confidence, used the opportunity for
inciting his master to a general persecution of the Jews.[4]
After the death of Sejanus, the Jews were allowed to return
to Rome. Of the mad attempts of Caligula to be adored by
them, we have already spoken. Claudius (41–54 A.D.) again
decreed the expulsion of the Jews from Rome, probably on
account of the disputations and tumults excited by them in
consequence of the spread of Christianity; [it appears, however, that the edict was never fully carried out].[5] Nero, who
persecuted the Christians, had apparently not molested the
Jews; and, indeed, the Empress Poppæa seems to have had
a leaning towards Judaism.[6] Such was the chequered history
of the dispersed of Israel during the period which ends with
the destruction of Jerusalem. The events which befell them
in the Roman Empire and elsewhere, will form the subject
of subsequent history.

[1] Jos. *Ant.* xvii. 11. 1 ; *Wars,* ii. 6. 1.
[2] Tacit. *Annal.* ii. 85 ; Sueton. *In Tiber.* 36.
[3] Jos. *Ant.* xviii. 3. 5.
[4] Euseb. *Hist. Eccl.* ii. 5 ; Philo, *Legat. ad Cajum,* ii. 569.
[5] Comp. Dio Cassius, lx. 6, with Acts xviii. 2 ; Sueton. *In Claud.* 25. See
also Schürer, II. ii. 236 f.
[6] Jos. *Ant.* xx. 8. 11 ; *Life,* 3.

CHAPTER IV

POLITICAL AND RELIGIOUS STATE OF THE JEWS AFTER THE
DESTRUCTION OF JERUSALEM

THE destruction of Jerusalem, and the final subjugation of
the land of Israel, do not seem to have permanently affected
the condition of the Jews either in or out of Palestine.
Immediately after the taking of the capital, Vespasian is said
to have instituted an inquiry after the descendants of the
house of David.[1] This investigation was the signal for a fresh
persecution. But the search could not have been very
extensive or long continued, as certain Rabbins could at a
later period claim kindred with the royal family. At all
events, the Christian Jews, who, in accordance with the Lord's
injunction, had left Jerusalem and fled beyond Jordan, escaped
unmolested. Two Roman ordinances were promulgated, meant
to indicate the entire subjugation of Palestine and of the
whole Jewish people;[2] [otherwise the political rights of the
Jews were respected by Vespasian]. The first of these
enjoined that the annual contribution hitherto paid by all
Jews to Jerusalem should in future be rendered to the temple
of Jupiter Capitolinus at Rome. The second assigned the
whole country to the emperor as his private possession.
Grants of land were, however, made to favoured individuals,
such as Josephus; and 800 discharged veterans were settled
at the village of Emmaus, near Jerusalem. The first of these
measures, though not really involving any additional pecuniary
payment, was yet a continual national and religious affront.
The inhabitants of Palestine had previously groaned under
the burden of an excessive taxation; all property was

[1] Euseb. *Hist. Eccl.* iii. 12.   [2] Dio Cass. lxvi. 7; Jos. *Wars*, vii. 6. 6.

subject to a land tax; every individual had to pay a kind of poll-money; agriculture and commerce were hampered by the exaction of excessive customs and duties. In addition to all these imposts, the Roman government now claimed the temple-didrachm or half-shekel (about one and threepence of our money). It will readily be conceived that this forced diversion of a religious contribution to the support of a hated idolatry must have been felt to be peculiarly galling.

[The inhabitants of Palestine were terribly impoverished by the long struggle, and even after the end of the war a general feeling of insecurity prevailed. When lands were offered for sale, which had been violently taken from their original owners by freebooters (*sicarii*), or by the Roman government, the Jews hesitated to purchase, fearing that the original owners might establish a claim to their property. To enable the Jews to settle again in their own country, the Sanhedrin, or highest religious tribunal, decreed that all sales of land in Judea made after the destruction of Jerusalem were to be held valid, provided that the original proprietors had previous to the sale given their consent to the transaction. This decree was subsequently modified, and it was determined that the purchaser must give to the original owner one quarter of the price which he paid for the land.][1]

Vespasian died on the 23rd June, A.D. 79, much as he had lived, proud and unconcerned. When he felt his end approaching, he observed, in ironical allusion to the deification of his predecessors, " I suppose I am becoming a god." At his express request, he was lifted from his bed, as he wished to die *standing*, as became a Roman emperor.[2]

Titus was about thirty-nine years old when he succeeded

---

[1] M. Gittin, v. 6 ; jer. *ib.* v. 47*b* ; bab. *ib.* 55*b* ; Tosifta, *ib.* c. iii. [On the *Din Sicaricon*, or law of the Sicarii, see Derenb. pp. 294, 475–478 ; Grätz, iv. 24, 422 f.; Levy, *Neuhebr. Wörterb.* iii. p. 518*b*. According to Derenbourg, the term Sicaricon was applied to the general principle which allowed an original owner to make good his claim against a purchaser ; Grätz understands the term of an exceptional measure suspending this right. Schürer (I. ii. 179) refers the Sicaricon to the time after the war of Hadrian ; and Derenbourg (p. 478) allows that there are reasons which support this view.]

[2] Sueton. *In Vespas.* 23, 24.

Vespasian. His brother Domitian, envious of his merit and honours, accused him of having forged the title to the succession. The former connections of Titus sufficiently indicated that the present occupants of the throne had risen from comparatively humble circumstances. His first wife, Arrecina, had been the daughter of a Roman knight. After her decease, he married Marcia Furnilla, of whom he had a daughter. In Palestine he formed a connection with the Jewish queen Bernice, and probably on her account repudiated his wife. Nature and art seem to have combined in favouring Titus.[1] His face was handsome, and his figure, though not tall, commanding. With these natural advantages he combined gallantry, excellent horsemanship, grace of deportment, and great muscular power. Considerable attention had also been paid to his education. He possessed accomplishments which were highly esteemed at that time. He was a beautiful and rapid writer, a good musician, an engaging companion, well versed in Roman and Greek literature, and even an author.[2] After Vespasian's accession to the purple, Titus was made prefect of the prætorian guard. But in this situation he not only disappointed the hopes of his friends, but excited the lively apprehensions of all. The dark rumours which were current regarding his licentiousness, avarice, and cruelty painfully recalled the reign of Nero.[3] Happily Titus did not realise these fears; or his reign, at least, was of too short duration to display the dark side of his character. It only lasted two and a half years, during which some severe disasters befell the empire. Thus, a fearful eruption of Mount Vesuvius buried the cities of Herculaneum and Pompeii. In this catastrophe perished Agrippa, son of Drusilla, and nephew of the last Jewish King Agrippa,—the last member of the Jewish royal family whose death history records.[4] Then a pestilence ravaged Italy [5] with such virulence, that, according to one account, for several days its daily victims in Rome and its neighbourhood amounted to 10,000.[6]

---

[1] Tacit. *Hist.* ii. 5.
[2] Sueton. *In Titum*, 3, etc.
[3] Sueton. *ut supra*, 6, 7.
[4] Jos. *Ant.* xx. 7. 2.
[5] Sueton. *In Titum*, 8.
[6] Euseb. *Chronicon* (Schœne), ii. 158 f.

Again, a dreadful fire destroyed, during three days and nights, many of the principal buildings in Rome, and seemed specially to direct its fury against the Capitol. The Jews naturally viewed these visitations in the light of national judgments, in consequence of the destruction of Jerusalem and of the sanctuary. The reign of Titus is often represented as that of the kindliest and wisest monarch ; and, in confirmation, his well-known saying is cited when he had spent a day without having done some good, " Friends, I have lost a day." It is not difficult to decide whether such unqualified praise is justly due to his brief reign.

His successor, Domitian, displayed, at the beginning of his reign, a moderation and care for justice which had been quite unexpected ; but after a few years any dreams of the return of a golden age were speedily dissipated. It was suspected, and perhaps not unjustly, that Domitian had poisoned his brother. His subsequent conduct, amongst others, to Julia, Titus's daughter, confirmed this rumour, which in part arose from his well-known jealousy and hatred of his brother. Julia's husband was put to death ; she herself was made the mistress of her uncle, and afterwards forced to use means for procuring abortion, under which she died. But this crime was not a solitary instance of Domitian's debauchery and cruelty. Not only Jews and Christians, but Gentiles of all classes, fell victims to his suspicions, to his whims, or to his cupidity after their possessions. One historian alleges that, from the frequency of these executions, it was at last found desirable or necessary to discontinue their registration.[1] In the rhetorical language of an eyewitness, " the sea was covered with the banished, and the rocks reddened with the blood of those who had been exposed on them." [2] The system of regularly employing spies and denouncers (which had been discountenanced by the emperor in the earlier part of his reign) was now fully carried out, and any person who had either private or public opponents, or a fortune, was no longer safe from public prosecution. To the general avarice of his ancestors, and of

---

[1] Dio, *In Dom.* lxvii. 11.   [2] Tacitus, *Hist.* i. 2.

the Flavian family generally, pressing requirements were added, as the dissipation of Domitian had ruined his fortunes, while his unbridled passions always led to fresh demands. In order to have an excuse for confiscating properties and legacies, new crimes were invented; and the most unsatisfactory testimony was held sufficient to ensure conviction.

Under the reign of Domitian, ecclesiastical history chronicles the second general persecution of Christians. During its course, amongst other sufferers, the Apostle John was banished to Patmos. Nor did the Jews escape unmolested. The oppressive character and the peculiar mode of levying the taxes which were specially exacted from them, induced some either to conceal their origin, or at least not publicly to declare themselves Jews. Notwithstanding the energetic remonstrances of the spiritual authorities, others— amongst them, perhaps, some who had abandoned Judaism— even submitted to a painful operation to efface the bodily mark of their descent.[1]   As thereby some might have succeeded in evading payment of the *Jewish tax*, denouncers were employed to bring the offenders to justice. A Roman author [2] speaks of the disgust with which, when young, he had witnessed a public examination instituted upon the body of a man ninety years of age, for the purpose of discovering his Jewish descent. As many members of the Church were of Jewish extraction, the Christians were often molested in this manner. Indeed, although the authorities had learned to distinguish between the two parties,[3] and were ready to persecute Christians as such, it sometimes served their purpose to confound the Church with the synagogue. An administration such as that of Domitian was necessarily detested, and the tyrant was kept in continual apprehension for his safety. It was under the influence of such feelings that, when informed that some of the maternal relatives of Jesus Christ were still in Palestine, he summoned the grandchildren of Judas, the Lord's brother, to Rome. But theirs

---

[1] Tosifta, Shab. c. 16. Comp. Grätz, iv. 79.   [2] Sueton. *In Dom.* 12.

[3] Ramsay, *The Church in the Roman Empire*, pp. 264–268.

was not a worldly ambition or earthly grandeur. Their humble appearance, and the marks of hard manual labour which they bore, convinced even Domitian of the groundlessness of his suspicions. They were accordingly dismissed.[1] Jewish authorities record that, at the same time, commissioners were appointed to inquire into the character of the distinctive doctrines of the synagogue. The result was favourable to the Jews. They reported, however, against the restrictions which prevented a fuller intercourse between Jews and heathens, and that, in their opinion, the property of heathens was not so jealously respected by the Jewish law as that of Israelites. The latter suggestion was immediately attended to, and the Jewish patriarch published an ordinance, by which the properties of Jew and Gentile were placed on the same footing.[2]

If Domitian persecuted Jews and Christians, it will readily be believed that *proselytes* were objects of his special rigour. The number of converts to Christianity was continuously and largely increasing. Some of these had, no doubt, as at the first, passed from heathenism to Christianity through the preparatory stage of Judaism. To distinguish those who remained, or even who had first become Jewish proselytes, from those who, from the first, or ultimately, joined the Church, is often extremely difficult. Heathen authorities vaguely allude to charges of Atheism,[3] or of devotion to foreign superstitions; while ecclesiastical writers and Jewish authors each claim for their own party the sufferers for conscience' sake. Under these circumstances we can only balance the probabilities. It is, however, certain that many Romans, and amongst them persons of rank, had at that time either adopted Jewish practices, or wholly joined the synagogue. From Dio we learn that many who had gone astray after the manners of the Jews were executed, others

---

[1] Euseb. *Hist. Eccl.* iii. 20.

[2] Baba Kama 38*a*; jer. *ib.* iv. 4*b*. Comp. Grätz, iv. 119; Derenbourg, p. 322.

[3] [It is doubtful whether the charge of Atheism would apply to the Jews; Judaism was a religion recognised by law. Comp. Lightfoot, *Clement of Rome*, i. 34.]

were banished, and their property confiscated.[1]   Some historians would include amongst them *Flavius Clemens* and *Domitilla* his wife; [but Domitilla was certainly a Christian, and it is now generally admitted that her husband was also.][2] Clemens was a noble Roman, closely related to Domitian. He had formerly shared with the emperor the consular dignity, and it was supposed that his children might even succeed to the empire.   But Clemens was denounced for attachment to Jewish customs and for Atheism or sacrilege. His rank and circumstances did not protect him : he was executed, and Domitilla banished to one of the small islands, Pontia,[3] or Pandateria,[4] where she remained till after the death of Domitian.   Another sufferer of note, claimed on somewhat doubtful grounds as a Christian,[5] was Glabrio, a man of high rank.   He was exposed to wild beasts, but overcame and killed the lion which had been let loose upon him.   This circumstance, however, did not preserve his life.

Jewish authorities record the persecution of one Onkelos bar Kleonimos, or Kleonicos, a nephew of Titus, who was a proselyte.[6]   In connection with his history, we may mention certain Jewish traditions, without warranting their truth in all particulars.[7]   Tidings of some impending danger had caused great alarm in Judea.   Although the season was unfavourable,[8] the patriarch, in company with three of the leading Rabbins, hastened to Rome, if possible to avert the calamity.   The fact of this journey seems sufficiently attested, though several of its details exhibit marks of traditional ornaments.   When the Rabbins reached the neighbourhood of Rome, the noise of the yet distant capital so forcibly brought before their minds the sad contrast beween the busy

---

[1] Dio Cassius (*ex epit. Xiphil.*), *In Dom.* lxvii. 14.

[2] See Lightfoot, *ut sup.* 33–39 ; Ramsay, *ut sup.* 261 ; Schürer, II. ii. 239, 309.

[3] Euseb. *Hist. Eccl.* iii. 18.   [4] Dio Cassius, *l.c.*

[5] Ramsay (pp. 261–263) asserts, Lightfoot (i. 81 f.) denies, that Glabrio was a Christian.

[6] Aboda Sara, 11*a* ; Gittin 56*b*.

[7] Comp. Grätz, iv. 121 f. ; Derenbourg, pp. 334–340.

[8] Succa 23*a*, 41*b* ; jer. Succ. ii. 52*d*.

capital of the West and their own desolate Zion, that they
could not refrain from bursting into tears. Only one of their
number, Rabbi Akiba, retained his composure, and suggested
to his friends, by way of comfort, that if God had thus
mercifully dealt by His enemies, the portion reserved for His
children would certainly at last prove much more glorious.[1]
The part sustained by that Rabbi in a subsequent Jewish
war but too painfully exhibited the sincerity of these hopes.
Arrived at Rome, the Rabbins learnt that the Senate had
passed a decree ordering a wholesale slaughter of all the Jews
in the Roman Empire at the end of thirty days. This
tidings was given to them by a senator who secretly favoured
their cause. The senator's wife, herself a proselyte also,
nobly suggested a plan by which to ensure the safety of her
co-religionists, although at the sacrifice of her husband's life.
The story apparently presupposes that it was a practice in
Rome to declare a decree void if one of the senators had died
between its enactment and its execution. To take advantage
of this provision, the lady suggested that her husband should
empty the poisonous contents of the ring which he wore.
It is said that the senator followed the advice, after having
undergone circumcision.[2] Another account relates how a
Roman noble—called by the Jews *Ktia bar Shalom*—pleaded
successfully before Domitian in favour of the Jews, but fell
a victim to his zeal. It is added that he left his extensive
property to Rabbi Akiba and his friends.[3] Certain it is that
if any such decree as that to which we have alluded ever
existed, it was not carried into execution.[4]

Notwithstanding the rigour of the law, conversions to
Judaism must have been numerous during the reign of
Domitian. Thus a tombstone has been discovered, which
records in bad Latin the good deeds of a Roman lady, who,
at the age of seventy, had become a proselyte, and is
described as " mother " (probably builder or chief supporter)

---

[1] Maccoth 24a.   [2] Deut. Rabba, c. 2 (on iii. 25).   [3] Aboda Sara 10b.
[4] Grätz (*Gesch.* iv. 121) refers this history to the time of Domitian ; Jost
(*Gesch.* iii. 237), to that of Hadrian. The chronology of these traditions is often
involved in great difficulties, [and many particulars seem to be quite legendary].

of various synagogues.[1]   This lady, called on the tombstone
Beturia, has been identified by some with the proselytes
Beruzia and Beluria, who are mentioned in Jewish writings.
We are informed that before Beruzia was formally admitted
into the synagogue, she had administered the baptism by which
proselytes were initiated to some of her slaves.   According
to the patriarch's decision in the case, these slaves obtained
thereby immediately their freedom, as, according to Hebrew
law, a heathen could not possess Jewish slaves.   The lady
herself, and all her household, soon afterwards became Jews.[2]
Beluria is said to have been well versed in the Scriptures,
and in cases of difficulty to have applied directly to the patriarch [3] for advice.

The empire was at last relieved of the tyranny of
Domitian by his assassination [4] on the 18th September 96.
The Empress Domitia, so notorious for her boundless passion
for the pantomime Paris, was privy to the plot.   She had
accidentally seen a list of parties proscribed, and, amongst
others, descried her own name on the fatal list.   To anticipate
her fate, she immediately entered into negotiations with some
of the chamberlains whose names were also amongst those
about to be killed.   At the head of the conspirators was
Stephen, the steward of Domitian's niece.   He had been
charged with misappropriation of some funds, and was now
prepared and allowed to seek this mode of safety and revenge.
To disarm all suspicion, Stephen, who undertook the lead in

---

[1] The inscription (Orelli, 2522 ; *Corp. Inscr. Grœc.* iv. 9905) reads as follows :—

Beturia . Pau .
lla . F. Domi .
Heterne . quos .
Tituta . que . bi
Xit . An. lxxxvi., Meses. vi.
Proselyta . An. xvi.
Nomine . Sara . Mater .
Synagogarum . Campi .
Et Bolumni .
En . Irenæ . Ai .
Kymysis Ay . . . . . .

[2] Masech. Gerim.   [3] Rosh ha-Shanah 17*b*.
[4] Dio Cassius, *ut sup.* 15 ; Suet. *In Dom.* 17 ; Philostr. *Vit. Apollon.* viii. 25.

executing the plot, appeared with his arm bandaged, and in a sling, as if suffering from some injury. At the appointed hour he presented to Domitian a memorial, purporting to divulge the particulars of a conspiracy which Stephen had discovered. While the emperor was greedily poring over the contents of the memorial, Stephen wounded him in the abdomen with a dagger which he had concealed within his bandage. Domitian, who was endowed with great bodily strength, immediately precipitated himself on his assailant, and succeeded in throwing him to the ground. A child who never left his chamber was now ordered to bring the emperor a sword which hung over his bed; but this emergency had been provided against, and only the hilt stuck in the empty scabbard. The child ran to call the guards; but every door had been locked. A fearful struggle for life or death now ensued. While Domitian held down Stephen, he sought to wrest the dagger from him, and with his bleeding fingers made for the eyes of Stephen; but the other conspirators hastened to the spot, and the emperor was despatched.

It is strange that Domitian should have so much disappointed the expectations of the people. Before his elevation he cultivated letters, and the first years of his reign were characterised by such liberality and love of justice, that a writer [1] remarks that Roman judges had never before been less accessible to corruption; but as Domitian gradually imitated the vices of Tiberius and Caligula, his cruelty increased like theirs. At last it became almost a passion. It seemed his chief occupation to invent new torments; it was his delight first to excite false hopes in his victims, and then to witness their sufferings. When wearied with tormenting men, he would busy himself for hours tormenting flies. The Senate equally hated and dreaded Domitian. Not so the populace, who did not feel the effects of his cruelty, and were amused by the frequent games which he celebrated, and gratified by the splendid buildings which he reared. Domitian was a special favourite of the soldiers, whose pay he raised by one-fourth. So much were the guards attached to him, that when his

---

[1] Suetonius, *ut supra*, 8.

successor, who probably had been privy to the plot, refused to hand over the conspirators to justice, they took summary vengeance on them.

Nerva, an old and respected senator, was proclaimed Domitian's successor. It is matter of regret that the reign of an emperor equally distinguished for wisdom and modera- tion should have been so short, and have occurred under peculiarly unfavourable circumstances. Nerva endeavoured as much as possible to retrieve the disastrous consequences of his predecessor's reign. He opened the prisons and recalled the banished. The adoption of Judaism or of Christianity was no longer punished as a crime.[1] One of the reforms instituted which proved most grateful to the Jews, was the modification of the special tax which his predecessors had imposed on them. In acknowledgment of this relief, a medal was struck to commemorate the removal " of the calumny of the Jewish impost." It bears on the reverse a palm-tree, with fruits depending, and the inscription, " Fisci Judaici calumnia sublata." [2] It will readily be understood that a mild reformer such as Nerva could not be popular in those degenerate times. The crimes of Domitian had not injured the populace, nor had his vices shocked them, as they bore no greater proportion to theirs than did his rank and means. On the other hand, he had spent immense sums—partly raised by unjust procedure against rich persons—in public amuse- ments. Nerva had neither the inclination nor the means of following the same course. His endeavours lay rather in the direction of curtailing the public expenditure. Accordingly, his popularity declined, and attempts were even made upon his life. The soldiers, who might have ensured his safety, could but ill brook the government of an old and immartial senator. To put an end to the discontent, the emperor wisely resolved to conjoin with himself in the empire Ulpius Trajanus,

---

[1] Dio, lxviii. 1.

[2] [This probably implies that the tax was now exacted in a form less likely to offend the religious feelings of the Jews. Perhaps the money was no longer devoted to the temple of Jupiter Capitolinus. The tax certainly existed at a much later period (see Origen, *Ep. ad Afr*. 14). Comp. Schürer, II. ii. 267.]

a Spaniard by birth, whose victorious exploits had procured him both popular favour and the support of the legions.

Soon afterwards Nerva died, having held the reins of government for a period less than two years, and was succeeded by Trajan.

It is not our delightful task to trace the spread of Christianity under the above-mentioned emperors, nor our province to record the struggles and the trials which attended its progress. Yet should we fail to give an accurate sketch of the history of the Hebrew nation, did we not, even at this stage, chronicle the progress of Christianity amongst the Jews since the destruction of Jerusalem.[1] It has already been mentioned that, in obedience to the warning given by our Lord, the Christian Israelites, on the approach of the Romans, retired from Jerusalem beyond Jordan, to Pella and its neighbourhood.[2] From the then existing relations between the Jews and Christians, the latter, however averse to Roman domination, or favourable to Jewish nationality, could not have taken part in the last war, even although they had not been directly warned to separate themselves from their guilty brethren. At first the Christians had no doubt been only considered as a Jewish sect, and had continued to frequent the temple and the synagogue, and to take part in such of the Mosaic rites as were either partly national, or else had not yet been wholly accomplished. Such observances gave them ready access to their countrymen without violating their consciences. But in the providence of God the separation became daily more decided. Partly the increasing admissions of heathens and proselytes into the Church, partly the increasing hatred and persecutions of the synagogue, as the distinctive dogmas of the gospel became better known and the zeal and piety of its disciples extended its sway, and partly providential circumstances, by degrees forced Jewish believers to stand more apart from their unconverted brethren. Even the historical portions of the New Testament bring the operation of these causes to light.

---

[1] For some particulars connected with it, compare also the succeeding chapters.

[2] Euseb. *Hist. Eccl.* iii. 5 ; Epiph. *Hær.* 29. 7 ; *Mens. et Pond.* 15.

This gradual separation between the Jews and the Christians was completed by the removal of the Church from Jerusalem to Pella beyond Jordan.[1]   Only the first fifteen bishops of Judea were of Jewish descent.   The decided estrangement in doctrine and life which afterwards took place between them, led to the formation of an intermediate party of professing Christians, who still kept either part or the whole of the law, and entertained opinions more or less unsound on the person of Christ and on other subjects.   This party, which separated equally from the Church and from the synagogue, split again into sects more or less orthodox, which were known as the Nazarenes, Ebionites, etc.   At the same time, the general disposition of the Church and the tone of ecclesiastical writers became gradually more hostile, not to Judaism, but to the Jews, and Christians took increasing care not to identify themselves with the synagogue.   The synagogue naturally manifested in return its bitterness and enmity. Not only were believers denounced in the synagogues and expelled, but the Jews frequently tried to stir up the multitude against them, and some of the fiercest persecutions were encouraged by the Jews.   They are also charged with circulating accusations of an atrocious character against Christians.   Thus the calumny, afterwards so fearfully retaliated upon themselves, that in their feasts the Christians used human blood and indulged in disgraceful orgies, was said to have originated with the Jews.[2]

However, Christianity had from the first taken a deep hold on Jewish society.   Even the many ordinances passed by the synagogue to prevent its spread, prove that it retained this position.   There was specially one practical argument in favour of Christianity which appealed to the experience of all.   We refer to the miraculous cures performed in the name of Jesus.   As intercourse between the two parties had not at first been strictly prohibited, this mode of appeal was for some time practicable, and probably the capability ceased with the opportunity of employing it.   The New Testament record

---

[1] Comp. Hort, *Judaistic Christianity*, pp. 174–180, 196–200.
[2] *Vide* Orig. *Contra Cels.* vi. 27 ; Just. *c. Tryph.* 10, 108.

offers many instances of converts whose domestic relations with their unconverted friends were not apparently immediately interrupted. Some Christians obtained considerable influence by their character, or by an attestation of their divine mission in their ability to perform miracles. Thus Jewish authors mention a certain Hebrew-Christian physician, James, with whom one of the most exclusive and bigoted Rabbins [1] maintained for a time a friendly intercourse. When the nephew of another teacher [2] had been bitten by a serpent, we are informed that he intended to apply to that disciple for a miraculous cure.[3] Another young man,[4] connected with the leading Jewish sages, joined the Church at Capernaum, and was removed by his friends to Babylon, in order to withdraw him from Christian influences.[5] But gradually, as Christian Jews understood more, and perhaps felt less, ignominious epithets were applied to the Jews. The latter retaliated by calling the Christians " Minim,"[6] or heretics. So great became at last the enmity, that a celebrated Jewish sage [7] declared that, although the Gospels and the other writings of the " Minim " contained the sacred names of the Deity, they ought to be burnt ; that heathenism was less dangerous than Christianity ; that heathens offended from ignorance, while Christians did so with full knowledge ; and that he would prefer seeking shelter in a heathen temple rather than in a meeting-place of the " Minim." [8] Another and more moderate Rabbi [9] also recommends the burning of every copy of the Gospels, as in his opinion inciting to rebellion against God, and to hatred against the commonwealth of Israel.[10] By and by all friendly relations between the two parties entirely ceased. Religious discussions were interdicted as tending to weaken the faith ; Jewish Christians were anathematised as

---

[1] Rabbi Eleazar ; Mid. Kohel. i. 8 ; Ab. Sar. 17a.

[2] Ben Dama, nephew of Rabbi Ishmael.   [3] Ab. Sar. 27b ; jer. ib. ii. 40d.

[4] A nephew of Rabbi Joshua.   [5] Mid. Kohel. i. 8.

[6] [The term " Minim " was applied to apostates in general, and not only to Jewish Christians. In many passages of the Talmud, however, it is clear that Christians are meant.]

[7] Rabbi Tarphon.   [8] Shab. 116a ; jer. ib. xvi. 15c.   [9] Rabbi Ishmael.

[10] Shab. 116a ; Eisenmenger, *Entdecktes Judenth.* i. 493.

worse than heathens or Samaritans ; and Christian books placed in the same category with works on magic. Such was the mutual estrangement, that the ordinary civilities of life were not to be exchanged, and the bread, wine, oil, and meat used by Christians declared polluted. Especially, all miraculous cures in the name of Jesus were strictly proscribed. At last a form of imprecation against the " Minim " was introduced into the daily prayers of the synagogue. As all these ordinances were communicated by letters to the different congregations out of Palestine, a simultaneous and combined effort was thus made by the synagogue to resist the progress of the gospel. These measures, which were well known to the Christians,[1] naturally increased their animosity.[2]

If Christianity made rapid strides in Palestine before the destruction of Jerusalem, it will readily be inferred what an impulse the latter event must have given to its spread. Judaism, as a sacrificial system, had now become an impossibility, and many pious Jews must have felt the want of the temple, with its sin-cleansing sacrifices,—a want which nothing but a substitute, in the truest sense of the term, could have met. The Jewish national and religious hopes were now also, to all appearance, for ever blasted. Under these circumstances, some Jews resolved to lead a life of continual penance. They renounced all pleasures, abstained from meat and wine,[3] and would not even have their houses, the dwellings of mourners, whitewashed. The zeal of Christians soon discovered many who were prepared to listen to their tidings of " the Lamb of God, which taketh away the sin of the world." Another of the secondary causes which power-

---

[1] Comp. Just. *Dialog. cum Tryphone*, c. 17.

[2] However bitter the enmity between Jews and Christians, we believe that writers such as Eisenmenger and others misrepresent the former. It will not do to quote as instances of Jewish hatred the writings of *later* Rabbins, after a long series of relentless persecutions had taught the Jews to consider Christians as their natural and uncompromising enemies. When read along with the *history* of those ages, we have sometimes felt as if the expressions employed by the Jews were not wholly unjust or misapplied. Even the language of the Jews, however bitter, does not contrast unfavourably with the expressions which professing Christians applied to the Jews.

[3] B. Bath. 60*b* ; comp. M. Sot. ix. 14.

fully contributed to the spread of the gospel, was the entire and felt want of real religious provision in the synagogue for unlettered Jews, and the contempt in which they were held by the learned. From the very nature of the case, as their religion was very much a system of casuistry, and individual religious duties became in the classrooms of the teachers matters of dispute, which often depended for decision on the most ingenious sophistry, the unlettered became by and by estranged from the synagogue. Add to this the self-complacency and hauteur which sought merit, connected temporal and spiritual greatness with a mere knowledge of the law and of traditions, and excluded from all honours, and even from the kingdom of heaven, those who were ignorant;[1] and think of the hatred which this exclusiveness must have engendered in those classes which are, at any rate, suspicious and envious of their superiors, and their mutual relations will be readily understood. Thus, according to the statement of the Pharisees, there is scarcely any crime of which the country people,[2] the peasants, or unlearned, are not guilty. They are described as dishonest in their transactions, indelicate in their families, without honour or self-respect, as observant of only so much of the law as suited their convenience, along with other similar charges. The patrician Hebrews abstained from all intercourse with them, forbore from eating at their tables,[3] and even avoided touching their garments from fear of being thereby polluted.[4] Marriages between the two classes were deemed misalliances, and compared to throwing one's daughter to a lion, or coupling one's son with cattle.[5] The illiterate were not to be allowed to bear witness, to be curators of orphans, or to discharge any office connected with the synagogue. Journeying in company with them was to be avoided. Indeed, almost any treatment of, or crime against, them was deemed allowable. It will readily be understood that such conduct evoked the hatred of the lower classes. One Rabbi[6] goes so far as to declare his belief that the illiterate would murder all the sages if they could get on

---

[1] Keth. 111*b*.   [2] The " Am ha-arez."   [3] Demai ii. 3.   [4] Chag. ii. 7.
[5] For this and the following statements, see Pes. 49*b*.   [6] Rabbi Eleazar.

without them. Another sage,[1] who had sprung from the lower classes, confesses that formerly he had often wished to have an opportunity of injuring any of the patricians.

But while the synagogue despised and neglected the lower classes, Christianity addressed itself to them, and broke down the middle wall of partition between learned and unlearned. To this benignant influence of the gospel we may add, as another argument in its favour, that the general conduct and bearing of many Jewish Christians were such as to constrain the respectful attention of the Jews to their message. We have already recorded an instance of this in the intercourse between the physician James and a Jewish Rabbi. We add, as another illustration, the circumstances which attended the death of the Apostle James, of which Hegesippus gives us a more or less legendary account.[2] The care of the Church in Judea had probably at first devolved on James the Just. For a period of thirty years he had watched over the flock at Jerusalem, when (62 A.D.) his enemies succeeded in silencing his testimony. He was generally and deservedly respected, not only by Christians, but also by Jews. His influence, which was uniformly employed for the spread of the gospel, was felt to be great. Making use of this circumstance, the Pharisees took him to an elevation in the temple which over-looked the worshippers, and called on him to warn the assembled multitude against the doctrines of the gospel. James, however, availed himself of the opportunity for giving a decided and distinct testimony for the Lord Jesus Christ. A tumult was now raised, in which James was thrown down amongst the people, and stoned by some of those who had come together. While he yet breathed to pray for his murderers, a person in the crowd dashed out his brains with a fuller's club.

If the Church Catholic exercised such influence upon the synagogue, the latter made itself felt in the way of inspiring the views of many of the heretical sects. Some of these

[1] Rabbi Akiba.
[2] Euseb. *Hist. Eccl.* ii. 23 ; comp. Lightfoot, *Galatians*, p. 366 f.; Schürer, I. ii. 186–188.

were purely Jewish. To this number belonged those who observed the Law (in whole or in part), and the various sects who rejected the doctrines of the Trinity and of the Incarnation of the Son of God. But even Gnosticism derived its principal elements from the synagogue. The tendency of that heresy, as a whole, was, as its name indicates, after " gnosis," or knowledge. The various speculative difficulties connected with the creation of the world, its government, and the relation of the Supreme God to it, were objects of inquiry to the various Gnostic sects. [Like the later Jewish mysticism, Gnosticism sprang from the contact of Judaism with the religious speculations of the farther East. Probably the mystical tendency found in Essenism a soil favourable to its growth and development. As the system itself was Jewish in origin, so the earliest representatives whose names have been handed down to us were Palestinians by birth. Thus the traditional founder of Gnosticism was a Samaritan, Simon of Gitta, who—since the time of Justin Martyr [1]—has commonly, but perhaps erroneously, been identified with the Simon Magus mentioned in Acts viii.[2]] Christian legends describe Simon as equally corrupt in practice and in doctrine, and mention Rome as the field of his labours. It seems not unlikely in itself that the impostor should have resorted to the capital, the more so as, according to the statements of contemporaries, all religious adventurers flocked to it to make religious capital of the corruption and superstition of the degenerate Romans.

The second heresiarch and leader of the Gnostics, to whom ecclesiastical history refers, was Menander, like Simon a Samaritan by birth. Under his auspices, and those of his successors, Gnosticism assumed more and more its definite shape. In general, that system had two great branches,—the one, in which the doctrine of emanation played an important part, and derived from Persian elements ; the other, more dualistic (an attempt to combine theology with Platonism), and bearing traces of Alexandrian culture. In

[1] Comp. Justin, *Apol.* i. 26 ; *Dial. c. Tryph.* 120.
[2] Comp. *Dict. Chr. Biog.* iv. "Simon Magus."

like manner we may also, from a practical point of view,
distinguish between the two branches of Gnosticism, which
more or less enjoined or else opposed an observance of the
law.   This distinction led in turn to different modes of
conduct, according as their knowledge (gnosis) of "the deep
things" (the "depths" of the Book of Revelation) led them
either into asceticism or into licentiousness, agreeably to their
views of the character and authority of the law, and of the
relation subsisting between a true Gnostic and the world
around him.   The ascetic sects found a point of internal
connection, and gradually gave a peculiar shading to the
whole system of theology.   The licentious sects necessarily
soon passed away, though not without inflicting serious
injury.   As the ascetic, so the licentious sects had their
counterparts in Judaism.   The latter, happily, were rare, and
almost foreign excrescences, which manifested themselves
more prominently in distant places, as in Persia and Arabia.
However, the licentious Gnostics seem to have entangled
some Jewish youths, partly by their peculiar mode of interpreting Scripture (which in many particulars resembled the
Rabbinical), and still more, perhaps, by ministering to lust
under the cloak 'of religion.   Jewish history [1] records an
instance of this kind, details the Gnostic perversion of
Scripture for the purpose of justifying their licentious
practices, and adds the appropriate exclamation of horror on
the part of a Rabbi when called to witness such a scene—
" And is it possible that such deeds are enacted by Jews ! "

We shall, in conclusion, rapidly glance at the spread of
the gospel amongst Jews and proselytes *out of* Palestine.
History and legend are here unfortunately so frequently and
closely intertwined, that it is next to impossible to indicate
where the one ends or the other commences.   Thus much
only can be affirmed with confidence, that while St. Paul
pursued his missionary labours, the other disciples were also
engaged in the same blessed work.   Mark is said to have
carried the gospel to Egypt, Thomas to Parthia, and Andrew
to Scythia, while Bartholomew planted the cross in India, by

[1] Mid. Kohel. i. 8 ; comp. Grätz, iv. 100.

which, perhaps, the ancient Yemen may be meant. More trustworthy traditions speak of Philip in Phrygia. At the same time, other Jewish heralds brought the glad tidings to the benighted heathens, and with the simplicity and earnestness of a realising faith went forth to the ends of the then known world, with their lives in their hands. While multitudes of Jews and proselytes became obedient unto the faith, the needs of the dispersed of Israel were not forgotten by the apostles, and James addressed himself particularly to them in his Epistle. Little if any impression, indeed, appears to have been made on the Jews in Babylonia (meaning by this term the country between the Euphrates and Tigris). We have, however, abundant evidence that Osrhoëne and Armenia—countries in which the Jews were numerous—received the Gospel at a very early period. Some of the churches in these lands date almost from the earliest periods of Christianity, and doubtless there were many of Jewish descent among the earliest converts. Thus even when the synagogue rejected Christianity and persecuted its disciples, the Lord left not Himself without witness among His ancient people.

CHAPTER V

THE return from Babylon marked a new period in the history
of the Jews. Many important changes had taken place in
the political and religious condition of the nation. When
Ezra attempted to reform the Jewish polity, he found
his countrymen both ignorant and careless in religious
matters. Elements were also at work within the community
which did not give promise of good to the people generally.
It was Ezra's first care, when undertaking the religious
reformation of his brethren, to cause the whole of the Book
of the Law to be read and expounded to the people. It was
his desire that the restored Jewish commonwealth should
rest upon a scriptural foundation. To enable him the more
readily to carry out the needful measures, tradition affirms
that he associated with himself in the spiritual government of
the people a council of 120, consisting of prophets, elders,
and scribes, or men learned in the law, which is known
as the Great Synagogue. Considerable diversity of opinion
exists as to the nature of this body, and the Talmudic notices
about it are often inconsistent.[1] Here it will be sufficient to
say that probably this assembly represents rather a succession
of men than one synod, the ingenuity of later times filling
in with fictitious names a period of history which was in
reality almost a blank. But the most important fact under-
lying these vague traditions is the growing influence of the
scribes in the period extending from the days of Nehemiah

---

[1] Comp. *Life and Times*, i. 94 f. [The very existence of the Great Synagogue
has been disputed by some scholars ; see Appendix II.]

to the troublous times of the Maccabees. How far they were at this time organised as a regular teaching body, we are unable to say.

Under the guidance of the scribes (*Soferim*), the traditions to which value was attached increased in number and authority. Hence numerous purely ceremonial ordinances were afterwards traced to this period. A few of them are even ascribed to the authority of Ezra himself,[1] although their character scarcely bears out these pretensions.

An important part of the functions of the scribes was that which concerned the study, arrangement, and interpretation of the sacred text. The duties connected with the public reading and exposition of the Scriptures naturally devolved upon the more learned, who, in any case, at a later period were regularly set apart for this purpose; and they appear to have delivered lectures or exhortations on stated days in the various synagogues which speedily sprang up throughout the length and breadth of the land. As the readers had mostly to translate the original text into the dialect of the people, to which they probably often added a brief exposition, the religious education of the people was almost entirely committed to them. The influence which they thus gained, the fact that, from the paucity of books and the general ignorance, the people depended *entirely* on this religious aristocracy, together with the growing tendencies of the age in that direction, contributed not a little to place religious eminence in mere knowledge and outward observances, without spiritual experience or love. It also laid the foundation of the exaggerated notions which both teachers and taught afterwards formed of the dignity of the Rabbi or teacher. Ordinarily, the various congregations met on Sabbaths, on Mondays, and Thursdays; on the latter occasions for the adjudication of causes according to the law of Moses, as well as for the reading and interpretation of the Bible. The principal teachers have left behind them one or more theological commonplaces, which are chiefly valuable as indicating the bearing of their theology and the direction of

[1] Baba Kama 82*a*.

their teaching. They were afterwards collected into one of the treatises of which the " Mishna " or traditional law is composed, and which bears the name of " Pirke Aboth," or Sayings of the Fathers.

The first of these Fathers is *Simon the Just*, who is described as belonging to " the remnants of the Great Synagogue." From Josephus[1] we learn that this was Simon I., who was the high priest in the beginning of the third century B.C. His motto is recorded[2] to have been, " The world is based upon three things : on the Law, on worship, and on works of righteousness." This sentiment sufficiently indicates that Simon belonged to the Pharisaical party; and his title of " the Just " was probably given by them on account of his strict observance of the Law. A long interval separates Simon the Just from *Antigonus of Socho*, the first of the Sopherim who bears a *Greek* name. He lived in the terrible time of Antiochus Epiphanes and the great Syrian persecution, and his recorded saying sounds like an echo of the political state of the country. It was,[3] " Be not like servants who serve their master for the sake of reward, but be like servants who serve their master without a view to the getting of reward ; and let the fear of heaven be upon you." The attempt of Antiochus to force Grecian culture and idolatry upon the Jews, led to the popular rising under the Maccabees. The independence of Israel was secured for a time, and the Maccabees ascended the Jewish throne as the *Asmonean* princes.

A late Jewish legend traces the origin of the sect of the Sadducees to Zadok, a disciple of Antigonus of Socho.[4] We are told that the distinctive tenets of this sect were due to a misunderstanding of the saying of Antigonus just recorded. In reality, however, the Sadducees were primarily a political, and only secondarily a religious party; and their theology, which was rather negative than positive, was due in a large measure

---

[1] Jos. *Ant.* xii. 2. 5 ; 4. 1. [Several scholars, however, in opposition to Josephus, maintain that Simon the Just is Simon II., high priest at the *close* of the third century]

[2] Pirke Aboth, i. 2.   [3] *Ut supra*, i. 3.   [4] Aboth di R. Nathan 5.

to their political position. For the Sadducees represent the party which supported the Maccabees, not only in their struggle for religious liberty, but also in their later national and political aspirations. Their adherents were drawn mainly from the noble and wealthy classes, and especially from the party of the priestly aristocracy.[1] The progress of events gave them more and more influence, and in the reign of John Hyrcanus, as has been related in a previous chapter,[2] the Sadducees obtained for a time political supremacy.

It is in the same reign that we should probably place the establishment or reconstruction of the Jewish tribunal known as the Sanhedrin. At an earlier period we hear of a Senate,[3] in the time of Antiochus the Great (223–187 B.C.). This, as the title shows, must have been an aristocratic body, and was doubtless presided over by the high priest. Under the earlier Maccabees reference is frequently made to a Senate or "eldership,"[4] called in the Talmud the "Tribunal of the Asmoneans";[5] and there are reasons for supposing that this body was reorganised by Hyrcanus. Yet it is only in the reign of Hyrcanus II. that we find the name of "Sanhedrin" actually given to the supreme council at Jerusalem.[6] [According to the analogy of the later Rabbinical courts of justice, Jewish tradition constantly represents the Sanhedrin as merely a body of scribes and learned men. This, however, was not strictly the case. Till the fall of Jerusalem, the priestly aristocracy generally took a leading part in it; although the influence of the Pharisees and of the scribes belonging to this party was considerable, not only under Queen Alexandra, but also in Herodian and Roman times.] The power of the Sanhedrin would, of course, vary with political circumstances.

---

[1] [It is not to be supposed that the Sadducees were merely the party of the priests. The Pharisees always recognised and maintained the rights of the priesthood, and both before and after the destruction of the temple we hear of many priests who were themselves Pharisees. On the two parties generally, see *Life and Times*, i. 310–324 ; Schürer, II. ii. 1–43 ; also Derenbourg, pp. 76 ff., 119 ff., 452 ff.]

[2] See p. 15 f.

[3] Jos. *Ant.* xii. 3. 3.

[4] 1 Macc. xi. 23, xii. 6, xiii. 36 ; 2 Macc. i. 10, iv. 44, etc.

[5] *E.g.* San. 82*a* ; Ab. Sar. 36*b*.

[6] Jos. *Ant.* xiv. 9. 3–5.

The somewhat indefinite accounts of their spiritual activity become more distinct as we approach the period of the Saviour's advent.   The Sanhedrin was the supreme court. All juridical and theological questions were, in the last instance, to be submitted to its decision.   It consisted of seventy-one members, with two clerks.   Their first meeting-place (for the necessities of the times obliged them to remove to different localities) was one of the spacious apartments connected with the temple-buildings, which was termed the "Hall of Hewn Stones."   The members of that court were not necessarily professional men in the sense of devoting their whole time to their peculiar avocation, or deriving their livelihood from it.   A truly devoted or Pharisaical Jew was, according to the current notions of the time, expected chiefly to devote himself to theological studies, and to follow his worldly calling only in order to support himself, or to minister to other students of the Law.   Hence, as the honour of being a member of the Sanhedrin was not reserved for the priestly order (although a considerable proportion of its members probably belonged to it), so the members of any trade, except those which were supposed to be degrading, or to have a tendency to harden, might aspire to this distinction.

The members of the Sanhedrin were chosen for life, and regularly ordained by the imposition of hands (the " *Semicha* "). Every description of their arrangements and order of procedure necessarily dates from a later period, and we cannot be certain how far it will apply to the first century B.C.   It was said that the members sat in a semicircle with the *Nasi* (prince) or president in the middle, the *Ab-beth-din* (the father or head of the juridical college) or vice-president at his right, and the *Chacham* (wise man, whose special duties are not precisely known) at his left.   The other members occupied places according to their rank in the college, so that the fourth, the sixth, etc., in dignity sat to the Nasi's right hand, and the fifth, the seventh, etc., to his left.   At a still later period a certain punctilious etiquette (originating in the pride of some of the Nasis) prevailed.   Thus, when the Nasi entered, all the members were expected to rise, and to remain standing till he had invited them to resume their places. When the Ab-beth-din entered, the first row had to rise, but was allowed again to sit down without intimation to that effect ; while the Chacham was only saluted by each individual member rising as he passed, and immediately sitting down again. It is, however, right to add that the more independent Rabbins resisted regulations like these. Twenty-three members were necessary to form a quorum.[1]

In the Mishnic treatise Aboth, after the names of Simon the Just and Antigonus of Socho, come the names of the five so-called *Zugoth* or " Couples," of whom Hillel and Shammai are the last. [Later tradition has represented these successive couples as respectively the president and vice-president of the Sanhedrin ; but several of them appear to have been merely distinguished scribes, and the heads of the Rabbinic schools. It was the men of this class who devoted themselves to theo-logical pursuits ;] whereas a large number of the priests seem to have been almost entirely engaged in the services of the sanctuary. Even the occupation of the high-priestly office required no knowledge-qualification. This is shown by the fact that the traditional law contemplates and makes pro-vision for cases when the high priest might be unacquainted with the meaning of the rites, and the laws concerning them.[2]

Opposite to the judges, in three rows (each row contain-ing twenty-three), sat the students, arranged according to their merit. Another body of hearers were ranged all around the hall. There were thus two orders, the members of which expected promotion. The hearers might be elevated to the rank of regular students, and the students might advance from row to row, and finally become members either of any of the provincial colleges, or of the Sanhedrin itself. [In view, however, of the influence possessed by the powerful priestly families, and of the political condition of the country

---

[1] [On the question who was the President of the Sanhedrin, see Appendix III.]

[2] Thus in the laws referring to the Day of Atonement, members of Sanhedrin are appointed to instruct the high priest ; and, in general, it is evidently con-templated that he may be an ignorant person. Comp. Joma (Mishn.).

during the last century of the Jewish State, we cannot
suppose that Rabbinic learning formed the only qualification
of membership.]   In order to understand the position of the
Sanhedrin, and its relation to other colleges, we must remember that in the Jewish State the spiritual and secular
administration were in reality not separated.   The authorities
of the synagogues were at the same time the ministers of
justice.   Thus every considerable synagogue had its Sanhedrin, or college of justice, consisting of twenty-three ordained
members, who were entitled to pronounce sentence even in
capital cases.   The smaller synagogues, or those in towns with
fewer than 120 heads of families and ten men of leisure,
possessed an inferior college of justice, which was only
allowed to adjudicate on civil cases, and which consisted
probably of three members.[1]   From the local court or college
an appeal might be taken to the nearest college of twenty-
three, and from the latter to the Great Sanhedrin in Jerusalem.   The priests seem to have been to a certain extent
independent, for they decided on all matters purely relating
to them or to the temple police.

If certain judicial duties devolved on the members of the
various colleges throughout the land, it was theirs also to
provide for the spiritual instruction and edification of the
people.   Hence, on Sabbaths and feast days, lectures were
delivered in the synagogues, and at a later period in the
various schoolhouses also, at which all were invited to attend.
Men and women sat separately, and listened respectfully to
the lecture or address delivered by a Rabbi or distinguished
stranger, the *Darshan* (preacher), as he was designated.   But
in case the preacher should use language too abstruse, or fail
to adapt himself to the weaker capacities of his hearers, an
arrangement was made by which the preacher communicated
his discourse in a low tone to an " interpreter " (the *Metur-*

---

[1] [It is nowhere precisely stated that the local courts were composed of only
three persons, but we find (Sanh. i. 1–3) enumerated a number of small cases,
which three judges were permitted to decide.   There are some reasons for supposing that the local courts consisted of seven members ;   comp. Schürer, II. i.
151–153 ; Derenbourg, pp. 88–90.]

geman), or " speaker " (*Emora*), who in turn rehearsed it to the audience in a plain and popular form.

After these few explanatory remarks, we turn to the history of the Sanhedrin. The first president and vice-president of the Sanhedrin are said to have been Joses ben (the son of) Joeser, from Zereda, and Joseph ben Jochanan, from Jerusalem. There is considerable doubt about the real date of this " couple." Probably they flourished about 150 B.C.; but some historians place them half a generation earlier, and suppose that Joses fell a martyr to his faith during the Syrian persecution. Little is known of their peculiar teaching. Their fundamental principles are somewhat vague, but point in the direction of increasing Rabbinical influence and pretensions. The Nasi said : " Let thine abode be a meeting-place for sages ; cover thyself with the dust of their feet, and eagerly (with thirst) drink in their words." [1] The vice-president said : " Let thy house be wide open, and let the poor be the children of thy house. Do not multiply speech with a woman. If this applies to one's own wife, how much more to that of another man ! Hence the sages say, that the man who multiplies speech with a woman brings evil upon himself, swerves from the words of the law, and will finally inherit destruction." [2] The vice-president differed from the Nasi as to the necessity of the imposition of hands on the head of a sacrifice. [3] Such was the esteem in which both sages were held, that at their decease it was said, " those in whom every excellency was found had now departed." [4]

The next couple was Joshua ben Perachia, said to have been Nasi, and Nithai, who is called Ab-beth-din. Their sayings may here be recorded. Nithai of Arbela said : " Depart from an evil neighbour, and associate not with the wicked, and grow not thoughtless of retribution." The motto of Joshua, which is very characteristic of the Pharisaism of the time, was : " Have a teacher, procure an associate, and judge every man as favourably as possible." [5] These two men lived in troublous times. The throne and priestly office

---

[1] Pirke Ab. i. 4.   [2] *Ut supra*, i. 5.   [3] Chagiga ii. 2.
[4] Sota ix. 9.   [5] Pirke Ab. i. 6.

were conjointly occupied by John Hyrcanus, one of the Maccabees, who, justly or unjustly, was supposed by the Pharisees
to have been derived from a mother who at one time had
been a captive.   In their view this incapacitated him for
being high priest.   Whether this was a pretence to hide their
general opposition or not, their enmity soon manifested itself.
At a banquet, an imprudent Pharisee ventured to call upon
John to resign the mitre on the ground above mentioned.
The king, who had hitherto belonged to the Pharisaical party,
perhaps glad of the pretext, interpreted this demand as an
avowal of the views of the party, and immediately joined
the Sadducees.[1]   The statement of the Talmud about the
slaughter of the leading Pharisees is incorrect; but there can
be no doubt that they were removed from power and exposed
to persecution.   Joshua is said to have escaped to Alexandria.
By a strange anachronism, some Jewish authorities declare this
Joshua to have been the teacher of Jesus of Nazareth.[2]

In the year 105 B.C., Hyrcanus was succeeded in the government by Judas Aristobulus, and, after the brief reign of that
prince, by Alexander Jannai.   The latter also belonged to the
sect of the Sadducees.   This circumstance, together with the
despotism of his reign and the many sanguinary wars in which
he engaged, rendered his administration more than ordinarily
unpopular.   The feeling of the masses displayed itself unmistakably, when, on the Feast of Tabernacles, the worshippers
threw at Alexander, who officiated as high priest, the citrons
(*ethrogs*) which at that feast they always carried in their
hands, and loudly reproached him with his descent from a
captive.   Alexander Jannai took fearful revenge, and his
bodyguard slew not less than 6000 of the rebels.[3]   A
series of insurrections broke out during the next six years,
and a party of the Jews even called in the aid of the Syrians
against the king.   At length, however, Alexander gained the
upper hand, and treated his opponents with such cruelty that
a general flight of the Pharisees ensued, some taking refuge
in Syria and others in Egypt ; nor during the lifetime of the

[1] Comp. Jos. *Ant.* xiii. 10. 5, 6 ; Kidd. 66*a*.   [2] San. 107*a* ; Sot. 47*a*.
[3] Jos. *Ant.* xiii. 13. 5 ; *Wars*, i. 4. 3 ; cf. Succa 48*b*.

king did they again return to the land of Judea.[1] Only one
man of note seems to have found shelter in Palestine. This
was Simeon ben Shetach, who is said to have been the brother
of the Queen Salome.[2] The most distinguished Rabbi among
the refugees in Egypt was Judah ben Tabbai, who, like
Joshua before him, took up his abode in Alexandria. [Joshua
and Judah are, indeed, sometimes confused in the Rabbinic
legends, and certain stories told of Judah in the Jerusalem
Talmud are in the later Babylonian Talmud transferred to
Joshua ben Perachia].[3]

Simeon ben Shetach was soon recalled to Jerusalem, probably at the instigation of the queen, and, after the death of
Alexander Jannai, he exerted himself to procure also the recall
of his friend Judah ben Tabbai, who was still in Egypt. The
following enigmatical letter was accordingly written and despatched in the name of the people of Jerusalem :—

"Jerusalem the Great to Alexandria the Little. How
long shall my betrothed still remain with you, whilst I dwell
forsaken ?"[4]

Judah readily understood the purport of this message,
and immediately returned to Jerusalem, where, together
with Simeon, he now exercised in matters of faith an
influence almost unbounded. The next move of Simeon was
to remodel the Sanhedrin. The story which is told of his
plan for expelling his opponents from the council[5] deserves
mention, [as it affords evidence of the ideas with regard to the
character of the Sanhedrin, which were current in the times
of the Talmud]. It is related that on one occasion, when the
king and queen honoured the Sanhedrin with their presence,
Simeon prevailed upon that body to resolve that in future
every theological or juridical discussion should be supported
by an appeal to Scripture. An occasion soon offered for
putting this resolution in force. As usual, questions were
proposed and answered by the Sadducees after their own

---

[1] Jos. *Ant.* xiii. 14. 2 ; *Wars*, i. 4. 5–6.   [2] Ber. 48*a*.
[3] Comp. Derenbourg, pp. 94, 102.   [4] Jer. Chag. ii. 77*d*.
[5] Megil. Taan 24 [where, however, the remodelling of the Sanhedrin is referred to the reign of King Jannai. Comp. Derenb. p. 102 f. ; Grätz, iii. 137 f., 567].

manner. Simeon insisted on the requisite proofs. One of the senators promised, indeed, to bring them forward at the next sederunt; but, being unable to do so, he felt obliged to resign. His place was filled by one of Simeon's students. By similar measures, the benches formerly occupied by the Sadducees were gradually filled by Simeon's adherents. Judah ben Tabbai is said to have now become Nasi, while Simeon ben Shetach contented himself with the office of Ab-beth-din.

The first victory over the Sadducees was followed by the repeal of a number of ordinances which were not in harmony with the Pharisaical views, and by the substitution of others in their stead. One of the most marked differences between the Sadducees and the Pharisees, was the scrupulous mode in which the latter adjudicated in criminal cases, giving every benefit to the accused. However excellent the motive of diminishing the number and severity of punishments, it was carried by them to a most dangerous excess, and the ends of justice were sometimes defeated by their punctilious adherence to the letter of certain rules. Thus the accordant testimony of at least two witnesses was always necessary,— the evidence required to be clear and decisive, while merely circumstantial evidence, however plain, was not admitted, at least in capital cases. Again, the witnesses were to be scrupulously cross-questioned; every particular favourable to the accused was to be brought forward, while every consideration adverse to him required to be narrowly sifted. Hence it must be allowed that in criminal cases the judges too often acted rather as pleaders for the accused. This is well illustrated in a case related by Simeon.[1] " As I hope for consolation! I saw a man pursuing another into a ruined building. I ran after him, and beheld the sword yet in his hand. It was reeking with blood, and the murdered man lay wallowing on the ground. I exclaimed, Thou wicked man, who has committed this murder—I or thou? Alas! thy life is not in my power, for two witnesses are requisite for conviction before sentence of death can be pronounced. But He who knoweth

[1] Jer. Sanh. iv, 22*b*.

man's thoughts will recompense the murderer of his neighbour." It is added that divine vengeance speedily overtook the malefactor, and that a viper bit him, so that he died.

The importance attached to these differences on legal questions is sufficiently evidenced by the frequent references made to them. On such points Judah and his colleague Simeon frequently differed, though both were Pharisees, and strenuous opponents of the Sadducean party. One instance of this is recorded, in which the scrupulosity of Judah is said to have given his colleague a great ascendancy over him. On one point the Sadducees were more lenient than the Pharisees. They deemed it unlawful to punish a false witness with death, unless the victim of his false testimony had actually been executed,—thus rather avenging the injury inflicted than punishing the crime committed. In his excess of anti-Sadducean zeal, Judah had on one occasion, under the above-mentioned circumstances, gone to the opposite extreme, and actually ordered the execution of a false witness. On relating it to Simeon, the latter allowed, indeed, the soundness of Judah's principle of procedure, but, by a characteristic quibble, demurred to its application in this case, and charged his friend with having shed innocent blood. Henceforth the conscience of Judah gave him no rest, and day by day he would resort to the grave of the victim of his orthodoxy to bewail his sinful rigour. At last the congregated multitude would have proceeded to acts of violence, under the impression that the wailing proceeded from the murdered person, had not the matter been explained to them. It is added, that after this occurrence Judah resolved never to pronounce a decision in the absence of Simeon.[1] [To this circumstance may perhaps be attributed the fact that the Talmud expresses an uncertainty whether Simeon or Judah occupied the foremost place in the Sanhedrin].[2]

We may infer the importance attached by all parties to the mode of administering justice, from the mottoes or maxims

---

[1] Jer. Sanh. vi. 23*b* ; Chag. 16*b* ; Macc. 5*b*.   In Mechilta on Ex. xxiii. 7 the parts taken by the two Rabbins are inverted.   Comp. Derenbourg, p. 105 f.

[2] Jer. Chag. ii. 77*d* ; Chag. 16*b*.

of various Rabbins. Thus the recorded principle of Judah
was: " Make not thyself like those that predispose the judges
(to favour one party against the other). When parties are
before thee, treat them as if they were guilty; and when
sentence is pronounced and they depart, act towards them as
if they were innocent."[1] On the other hand, it was the
principle of Simeon: " Be extremely careful in examining
witnesses; and beware lest from thy mode of questioning they
should learn how to give false testimony."[2]

But Simeon himself did not always exhibit that leniency
which his avowed principles or his remonstrance to his friend
might lead us to express. Indeed,'the assertion of the Talmud,
that he had " hot hands," points to his readiness to adopt extreme
measures when the circumstances of the case seemed to require
it. One instance of this deserves a place as illustrating the
superstition of the period; [but since Ashkelon, where the
scene of the story is laid, was at that time an independent
town, and not in Jewish territory, we can hardly regard the
narrative as having a historical foundation]. We are told[3]
that a celebrated sage had died at Ashkelon. The funeral
was, of course, attended by the principal Jewish inhabitants of
the place. At the same time another procession carried the
body of a publican to the same cemetery. When both parties
had reached the place of interment, but before the last rites
could be performed, a troop of hostile strangers surprised and
quickly dispersed the mourners. Only one friend of the
departed sage lingered behind, and anxiously watched all
night by the body of the Rabbi. Next morning the funeral
attendants returned to finish their sad offices. But, notwithstanding every remonstrance, the coffins, which were similar
in appearance, were exchanged, and the Rabbi descended into
the publican's grave, while the latter reaped all the Rabbi's
honours. This mistake had deeply grieved the faithful friend,
when in a vision the departed Rabbi appeared to console him
by a description of the happy mansions in which he now
resided, and of the tortures which the publican suffered.

[1] Pirke Aboth i. 8.   [2] *Ut supra*, i. 9.
[3] Rashi on Sanh. 44*b*; Jer. Chag. ii. 77*d*; Sanh. vi. 23*c*.

At the same time, he gave such explanations of certain events in their lives as satisfactorily to account for the permission on the part of God of the deplored mistake in the burial. Satisfied on this subject, inquiry was next made as to the period at which the publican's torments were to end. The heavenly visitor simply replied: When Simeon ben Shetach comes to take his place. Naturally enough the astonished sage asked of what crime the Ab-beth-din were guilty. He was then informed that, before his elevation, Simeon had vowed that if he should ever be advanced to the high dignity which he now occupied, he would exterminate all witches in the land. But he had failed to perform this promise, and no less then eighty of these women were at that moment practising the black art unmolested in a cave near Ashkelon. At last the anxious sage obtained leave to warn Simeon of his impending danger.

Simeon at once resolved to put an immediate stop to witchcraft. The only difficulty anticipated was, that the witches might, by the aid of magic, resist if not altogether elude capture. But it was believed that magic could only be practised on "*terra firma*," and Simeon resolved to avail himself of this fact. Accompanied by eighty youths, of whom each had a white garment concealed about his person, he went on a rainy day to the "cave of the witches." While the youths concealed themselves, ready, at the first call, to throw on their white garments, and, at the second, to enter the cave and act their preconcerted part, Simeon entered alone, representing himself as a magician. In his account of this expedition, he pretended that he had seen the witches practising their magic art, producing viands, wine, etc. At last they had asked him to display his powers. "I undertake," said he, "when I call twice, to produce eighty youths who, in spite of the rain, will appear dressed in white, and with whom ye may dance and enjoy yourselves." "Be it so," exclaimed the witches. The Rabbi now gave the preconcerted signals, and the young men appeared. While dancing, each youth lifted his partner from the ground. Having thus deprived them of their magic powers, the witches were dragged out, and, without further investigation, immediately executed. This summary proceeding was contrary to the course of ordinary justice, and only excusable on account of the supposed difficulties of the case. In general, the Jewish law did not allow capital sentence to be pronounced on more than one criminal in one day.

The rigour of Simeon naturally roused the hatred of his opponents, and, according to tradition, some of them vowed vengeance against him.[1] They concocted a false accusation against Simeon's son; and so concurrent were their testimonies, that the youth was wrongfully sentenced to death. On his way to the place of execution, he emphatically declared his innocence, and called God to witness against his accusers. So convincing were his assertions, that the witnesses confessed the falseness of their accusations, and the judges wished to arrest the sentence. But the prisoner himself protested that if the witnesses were allowed to withdraw their testimony, no further credence could be given to them. Simeon admitted the truth of this protest, and the unhappy youth died a victim of judicial formalism. The same inflexible rigour is said to have induced Simeon, in another instance, to summon even the king Jannai before the Sanhedrin. The king appeared; but the divine displeasure was so signally manifested in consequence, that a law was enacted to this effect: " The king neither judges nor is he judged." [2]

The " days of Simeon ben Shetach and Queen Salome " were naturally regarded by the Pharisees in later times as a golden age, and tradition describes in extravagant language the fertility of the land during this reign.[3] But the Pharisees did not know how to use with moderation the influence which they enjoyed. They put to death several of the counsellors of the late king; and such was their persecuting spirit; that at last a revolt broke out, and the Sadducees,

[1] Jer. Sanh. vi. 5 ; comp. Grätz, iii. 147.
[2] M. Sanh. ii. 2 ; bab. *ib.* 19*ab.* [The story is doubtless a confused version of the trial of Herod before Hyrcanus. See p. 117 f., and comp. Derenbourg, p. 146 ff.]
[3] Taan 23*a.* Comp. Derenbourg, p. 111 ; *Life and Times,* ii. 677.

headed by Aristobulus, the younger son of the queen, occupied
many of the strongest fortresses in the country.[1]   Before any
measures could be taken against them, Salome herself died
(69 B.C.).

Her eldest son Hyrcanus was now proclaimed king; but
Aristobulus, his more energetic brother, put himself at the
head of the Sadducean malcontents, and forced the weak
Hyrcanus to abdicate.   But, as before related, the Idumean,
Antipater, the father of Herod, whose ambition, vigour, and
talent were equally great, sensible that the exaltation of a
weak prince was the surest means of promoting his own
schemes, persuaded Hyrcanus, after his abdication, to flee to
Aretas, king of Arabia.   Antipater gained Aretas for the
cause of the fugitive prince.   No sooner was the irresolute
Hyrcanus made aware that he could depend for assistance on
the Arabs, than he broke the compact with his brother, and,
at the head of a Jewish and Arab force, advanced upon
Jerusalem.   Aristobulus went out to meet Aretas, and was
defeated in battle.   A large portion of Aristobulus' army
now deserted to Hyrcanus, and indeed most of the people
were disposed to accept their old king once more.   Aristobulus with his few remaining adherents was obliged precipitately to flee to Jerusalem, where he defended himself behind
the temple walls.

It was at that stage that recourse was had to the celebrated Honias, termed Hammeaggel, a man of high repute
among his contemporaries for his piety and power of working
miracles.   We are told that once, when a season of unusual
drought threatened the land with famine, a deputation came
to Honias to bespeak his prayers.   At their request he
entered the magic circle; nor did he leave it till, in answer
to his prayers, rain descended; at first in drops, but afterwards
in such quantity that he had again to intercede for its cessation.   Thereupon Simeon, who disapproved of the embassy,
and of Honias' conduct, sent the following characteristic
message: "If thou hadst not been Honias, I would have
excommunicated thee; for it would have been better for us

---

[1] Jos. *Ant.* xiii. 16. 2–6; *Wars*, i. 5. 3–4.

to have suffered famine as in the days of Elias, than that the name of the Lord should have been profaned by thee. But what can I do? Thou sinnest against God, and yet He yieldeth to thee even as a father to a spoiled child. If it says, Lead me to a *warm* bath, the parent obeys; if it demands to be bathed in *cold* water, he still yields; if it asks for nuts, almonds, peaches, or pomegranates, it obtains its request. Holy writ refers to thee in the passage, 'Father and mother rejoice over him, and she that bare him exults over him.'"[1]

On the present occasion Honias was brought to the superstitious army of Hyrcanus and urged to pronounce some magical curse against the defenders of the temple. Unable to obey, he is recorded, instead of the desired curse, to have uttered the following beautiful prayer: "Lord God of heaven, and King of the world, since those that now stand with me are Thy people, and those that are besieged are also Thy priests, I beseech Thee that Thou wilt not hear their prayers against each other for evil." It is added that Honias was immediately stoned by the disappointed claimants of his aid. During the protracted siege which now followed, another plan, if possible more absurd and superstitious, was resorted to, in order to gain possession of the temple. Hitherto a regard for the temple and its services had induced the besiegers to furnish the priests besieged in the temple with the animals required for the daily sacrifices. One of the Grecian Jews in the army of Hyrcanus now suggested, as the most likely means of success, that this supply should be discontinued. The advice was acted upon, and although a high price was taken from the defenders of the temple, yet when the vessel was lowered over the wall, instead of the lamb destined for the altar usually placed in it, an unclean animal was sent up. It is said that this profanation was the occasion of an earthquake throughout the land. To mark the national horror of this blasphemous scheme of the Grecian, an anathema was pronounced against all who kept unclean animals, and against the study of Grecian science

[1] M. Taan iii. 9–12; bab. *ib.* 23*a*. Cf. Jos. *Ant.* xiv. 2. 1.

generally.[1] None of these devices succeeded, and Aristobulus obtained temporary safety by securing the protection of the Romans.

We pass over the different events which at last deprived Aristobulus of the favour of Rome, and induced Pompey to recognise Hyrcanus as high priest, but without the title of king. During the political disturbances which followed, the Sanhedrin was at one time reduced by Gabinius to the position of a judicial council for one-third of Judea (56 B.C.);[2] but under the administration of Cæsar its former jurisdiction was restored (47–44 B.C.).[3] During part at least of the reign of Hyrcanus, two of the leading men in the Sanhedrin were Shemaja and Abtalion, who are regarded by tradition as respectively the president and vice-president of the assembly. These should probably be identified with the Sameas and Pollio of Josephus,[4] who appear more than once in the council after the restoration of its authority by Cæsar.

That the political relations subsisting between Palestine and the Romans prevented anything like independent action on the part of that tribunal, requires no proof. At the same time, Herod, the son of Antipater, was not disposed to tolerate any independent authority co-ordinate with his own. His first appearance before the Sanhedrin, even during the lifetime of Hyrcanus, when he occupied only a subordinate position, had already proved that he did not acknowledge its sacred character; for, when summoned to answer for some arbitrary acts, he appeared at the head of a considerable force before the overawed Senate, not in the garb of a culprit, but armed from head to foot, and more like an accuser than one accused. Of all the senators only Shemaja ventured to protest against this presumption. He reprobated energetically the insolent conduct of the youth, and Herod had to flee, but

---

[1] Sota 49*b*; Baba Kama 82*b*. [Comp. Derenbourg, p. 112 f. According to Josephus (*Ant.* xiv. 2. 2), the besiegers kept the money, and sent back the vessel empty. In consequence a violent storm broke out, and destroyed the fruits of the field.]

[2] Jos. *Ant.* xiv. 5. 4 ; *Wars,* i. 8. 5.   [3] Comp. Schürer, I. i. 378 ff.

[4] Jos. *Ant.* xiv. 9. 4 ; xv. 1. 1 ; 10. 4. [Comp. Schürer, II. i. 358 f.; for a somewhat different view, Derenbourg, pp. 148 f., 463 ff. See also Appendix III.]

soon returned again at the head of an army to take vengeance.   From the execution of this purpose he was only
diverted by the entreaties of his father and brother.[1]

We are told that, on the occasion when the youthful
Herod was summoned before the Sanhedrin for trial, Shemaja
predicted that on account of their cowardice the members of
that council would yet fall victims to Herod's vengeance.
Ten years later this prophecy was fulfilled.   Herod inaugurated his reign by putting to death all the principal adherents
of Antigonus, including many members of the Sanhedrin.
The vacancies in the council were filled by men who were
disposed to submit to the new king, many of them belonging
to the party of the Pharisees.   The Sanhedrin must now
have lost all real power, and one consequence of their lack of
independence was an increase of legislation on purely religious questions, or rather on the civil institutions connected
with religion, consisting not so much in an elaboration of a
system of doctrines or dogmatics, as in a kind of *jus canoni-
cum* (canon law).   Accordingly, we find that subsequent
teachers appeal with more than ordinary frequency to Shemaja
and Abtalion as authorities for their own juridical decisions
in these matters.   Perhaps the recorded principles of these
two doctors contain a reference to this change in the
Synagogue.[2]   Of Shemaja few distinct notices are left besides
the principle: "Love labour, hate lordship, and do not press
forward to the authorities."   Of his colleague Abtalion,
tradition has chronicled more particulars.[3]   Jewish legend-
aries, who love the wonderful, and delight to connect their
names with an ancestry inimical to the Jews, so as to show
the triumphs of their faith, state that his father was a
heathen, and had descended from Sennacherib.   His learning
and authority were very great.   The principle to which he
gave utterance was: "Be cautious, ye sages, in your words,
lest ye be condemned to captivity, and led into exile, to
places of noxious waters, from which, if your pupils drink,
they will die, whereby the name of God would be dis-

[1] Jos. *Ant.* xiv. 9. 2–5 ; *Wars*, i. 10. 5–9.
[2] Pirke Aboth i. 10.   [3] Gitt. 57*b*.

honoured." [1] The second consequence of the change in the position of the Sanhedrin was the increase of colleges, instituted for the purpose of initiating the youth in the traditions of the elders, and in theological casuistry. [In the Sanhedrin the real authority fell more and more into the hands of the priestly families whom Herod raised to power. But in the schools the great Rabbins were still able to gather their disciples round them, and to take part freely in the discussion of religious controversies.]

Three sages of this time—Menachem, Shammai, and Hillel—deserve special notice. Menachem has been identified with an Essene of that name who foretold Herod's accession to the throne.[2] According to one Jewish tradition, he forsook the schools and retired to the court of Herod, accompanied by a large number of his disciples.[3] Of all persons mentioned in the literary and religious history of the Hebrew nation, few, if any, equal Hillel in fame. He may well be singled out as the man who gave its peculiar tone to the religious thinking, not only of his own period, but to that of Jewish theology in general. This period was the golden age of Talmudism. The personal history of Hillel is exceedingly interesting. Born in Babylon about the year 70 B.C., of poor parents, although, it is said, descended in the female line from the house of David,[4] he married when twenty years of age. His son was called Simeon, and was, according to some authorities, the first to bear the title of Rabban. It is, however, remarkable that there is not a single allusion to him in the Mishna.[5]

Jewish legend extends the life of Hillel much beyond the usual period. It is said that at forty years of age he emigrated into Palestine, where he studied and taught for forty years, at the termination of which period he was elevated to the rank of Nasi, which he is supposed to have filled for other forty years. Like many other sages, he was poor, and obliged to support himself by the labour of his

[1] Pirke Aboth i. 11.
[2] Jos. *Ant.* xv. 10. 5.
[3] Chag. 16*b*.
[4] Jer. Taan iv. 68*a* ; Gen. Rab. 98.
[5] He is first mentioned Shab. 15*a*.

hands.[1]   It is asserted that he earned daily a very small
sum, the half of which he gave to the doorkeeper of the
college in order to be admitted to the lectures of Abtalion
and Shemaja, and that with the rest he supported himself
and his family.   The mode in which he attracted notice is
curious.   One day his supply of money had failed, and the
janitor would not admit him into the lecture-room.   Although
in the depth of winter, the zealous scholar, rather than lose
the day's instruction, climbed from the outside up to the
window, where he sat till he was completely covered with
snow, and rendered insensible by the cold.   Sabbath morning
dawned, and the teachers wondered why the light remained
excluded from the schoolhouse.   On examining the window,
they discovered their zealous hearer.   Glad for the sake of
so promising a student even to break through the sanctity of
the Sabbath, the requisite remedies were applied, and, to the
joy of all present, Hillel was restored to life.   From that
time his fame increased, and the following account is given
of his appointment as president of the Sanhedrin.   Once an
important question was laid before the sons of Bethera—
[perhaps the members of a priestly family which had been
placed in office by Herod].   The difficulty which had arisen
was,[2] whether, as the Passover occurred that year on the
Sabbath day, the solemnities of the feast were to take
precedence of those of the Sabbath or not ?   The question
does not seem to have been discussed at any previous period,
and the sons of Bethera confessed their inability to decide it.
Hillel was now sent for, as having been a distinguished pupil
of Abtalion.   His arguments failed, indeed, to convince the
members of the college, but his appeal to the authority
of Shemaja and Abtalion settled the question.   The sons of
Bethera resigned their office, and Hillel was elevated to the
presidency of the Sanhedrin.[3]

   The learning of Hillel, whom tradition places side by
side with Ezra, was celebrated in hyperbolical language.   It

---

[1] Joma 35*b*.   [2] Jer. Pes. vi. 1 ; bab. *ib*. 66*a*.

[3] [Whether, during the reign of Herod, Hillel can really have held such an
office, seems at least doubtful.   Comp. Derenbourg, pp. 177–181, 189.]

was said to have embraced, not only Scripture and tradition, but languages, geography, natural history,—in fact, all sciences, human and superhuman. To show the extent of his influence upon the rising generation, it is asserted that Hillel had eighty pupils. Of these,[1] thirty were, in the language of the time, described as worthy that the divine glory should rest upon them, as it did upon Moses; thirty, that at their command the sun should stand still in the firmament, as in the case of Joshua; while only twenty were less noted. Amongst them Jonathan the son of Uzziel was the most distinguished, while Jochanan the son of Saccai, who afterwards sustained so important a part in Jewish history, was the least celebrated. Statements like these are meant to impress posterity with a sense of the greatness of Hillel. [The fact that he is never spoken of as Rabbi Hillel proves clearly that this term had not yet been introduced as a distinctive title; and his grandson, Gamaliel I., is the first to whom the Mishna applies the title of Rabban.[2]]

The following are amongst the theological principles of this sage, as handed down to us :[3] " Be thou of the disciples of Aaron, a lover and follower of peace, a lover of mankind, and one who binds them to the Law." He was also wont to say : "Whoever aims after fame shall only lose his name. Whoever does not increase in learning, decreases. Whoever will not acquire knowledge becomes guilty of death. Whoever tries to make gain of the crown (of the study of the Law) shall perish." He also said : " If *I* am not to be for myself, who then shall be for me ? and as long as I only am for myself, what am I ; and if not now, when then ? " We subjoin a few other choice sayings of this father of the synagogue ; they will indicate the direction of theology at the period of our Lord's advent, when Hillel flourished :[4] " Do not separate thyself from the congregation ; and do not put confidence in thyself till the day of thy death. Judge not thy neighbour until thou art in his situation. . . . Say not, When I shall have leisure I will study ; for perhaps thou

---

[1] Succ. 28*a*.
[3] Pirke Aboth i. 12 ff.
[2] Comp. Schürer, II. i. 315.
[4] *Ut supra*, ii. 4*b*, 5 ff.

mayest never have that leisure." He also said : " An ignorant man cannot properly abhor sin ; a peasant cannot be pious ; a bashful person cannot become learned ; an irascible man cannot become a teacher, nor he who engages much in business a sage ; and where there are no right men, see to it that *thou* prove thyself such a one." " He who has gotten a good name has gotten it for himself. He who has gotten to himself words of the Law, has gotten to himself the life of the world to come." From these various maxims we can see that, like the other Rabbins, he ascribed the highest merit to, and connected the kingdom of heaven with, the study of the Law. Although his learning was so great that it had procured for him the place formerly occupied by the sons of Bethera, yet in the multitude of traditions even he is said on one occasion to have forgotten a certain ordinance.[1] Hillel was extremely simple in his mode of living, modest, meek, patient, and kind. To him the merit is due of having laid down definite rules for guidance in deducing Halachoth or laws of custom from the written law. Of these rules, which were seven in number, more will be said in another place. But the most prominent, though perhaps the least tangible consequence of his teaching, was the peculiarly speculative direction which he gave to Jewish theology, to which he may be said to have given its peculiar form, as he imparted to it that bias which it ever since preserved. The voice from heaven,[2] to which the Rabbins in the last instance appealed for decision, declared indeed at first that the principles of the school of Shammai, which were opposed to those of Hillel, were equally correct with those professed by their opponents. But while the teaching of both schools was declared to be " the words of the living God," the views of Hillel were adjudged to be authoritative or Halacha.[3]

Although agreeing with Hillel in all essentials,[4] a greater contrast could scarcely be conceived, both in method of teaching and in manner of life, than that between Hillel and

---

[1] Jost. iii. 114.   [2] Termed the Bath-Kol.   [3] Jer. Ber. i. 3b.
[4] Hardly any of the points in controversy between the two schools are of real importance ; comp. Schürer, II. i. 361 f.

his great contemporary, Shammai. If the former was poor, frugal, and mild to laxity, the latter was rich, irascible, intolerant, given to the pleasures of the table, and yet towards other offenders severe to harshness. As the speculative principles of the former were liberal, so those of the latter were strictly traditional ; and as the method of Hillel was that of free development of thought, so that of Shammai consisted in a rigid adherence to the letter. It would, however, be a mistake to suppose that the ordinances of Hillel were always the more mild and liberal,[1] [and even the strictness of Shammai could be made a means of showing generosity. Thus we are told[2] that Jonathan ben Uzziel, reputed as the ablest of Hillel's scholars, was disinherited by his father. Uzziel left his property to Shammai, who thereupon sold one-third of this bequest for his own behoof, gave another part to the temple treasury, and returned the remaining portion to the legitimate heir. He bade anyone who protested against this conduct to recover the first two portions before he could touch the third.] Of the learning of Jonathan, fabulous accounts are left. When he busied himself in the study of the Law, it was said the birds which flew over his head were burnt up.[3] Jonathan is best known as the author of a Targum, or paraphrastic translation of the Prophets, which bears his name. According to the tradition, when he brought out this work, a voice from heaven was heard to say : " Who is it that has revealed my secrets to men ? "[4] The existing Targum, however, which must be distinguished from the Targum of a pseudo-Jonathan on the Pentateuch, is a work of a later date, and must be regarded as a Babylonian recension of the old Palestinian Targum.[5]

Shammai was very wealthy. He was said to have carried his punctiliousness so far as to have " daily eaten in honour of the Sabbath." [6] Deeming it meritorious to reserve

---

[1] Comp. Eduj. iv. 1–12, v. 1–5.

[2] Jer. Nedar. v. 39*b*. [This version of the story seems preferable to that found in the Babylonian Talmud (Baba Bath. 133*b*), according to which some unnamed man disinherited his son in favour of Jonathan.]

[3] Succa 28*a*.   [4] Megill. 3*a*.   [5] See p. 400 f.   [6] Beza 16*a*.

the best food for the Sabbath, he was wont to purchase for that purpose any fine animal exposed in the market. This process he is said to have repeated daily, until at length he always dined on what had originally been selected for the Sabbath meal. His recorded theological principle is characteristic both of his scrupulosity and his peculiar method. He said: " Let the study of the Law be a fixed occupation; say little and do much; and receive all men with a frank and respectful countenance." Both he and the teachers who followed in his wake were strict traditionalists in matter and method, in opposition to the school of Hillel, which adhered indeed to traditions, but freely applied and developed them. Although the starting principles of these two teachers seem almost identical, their application and continual development would gradually bring to light and continually increase any real differences which obtained between them. Ultimately the difference became such, that it was said that, by the opposing teaching of Hillel and Shammai, the one Thora (law) had become two.[1] Political differences helped to increase the enmity between the rival schools, and on one occasion, probably about four years before the destruction of the temple, when the parties met, blood was actually shed.[2] Altogether, such was the authority enjoyed by these two teachers, that a Christian Father[3] reports Jewish Christians were wont to apply the prediction (in Isa. viii.), that Christ should be a stumbling-block to both the houses of Israel, to these two schools; nor does this estimate of their influence upon the theological thinking of their own and the following generations seem extravagant.

Among the other prominent sages of that and the next period, we may mention Rabbi Jochanan ben Hachorani, a disciple of Hillel, who was the son of a proselyte mother from the district of Hauran; Ben Bagh Bagh,[4] also a disciple of Hillel and a proselyte, who had, during his life, earnestly

[1] Sanh. 88*b*.

[2] Shab. i. 7 ; jer. *ib*. p. 3*c*; bab. *ib*. 17*a*.   Comp. *Life and Times*, i. p. 239 ; Derenbourg, pp. 272-276.

[3] Hieron. *In Isa*. c. viii. 11 ff.   [4] Pirke Aboth v. 22.

sought the advancement of the study of the Law; and Rabbi Chananja ben Chiskia ben Garon, a person well known in Jerusalem, whose dwelling was the scene of the bitter quarrel between the adherents of Hillel and of Shammai. Amongst other things, Chananja was said to have written a Commentary on the prophecies of Ezekiel, by which he restored to the Jewish Church the use of the writings of that prophet which the Rabbins had interdicted, from an apprehension that it contradicted, on the subject of sacrifices, the law of Moses.[1] Baba ben Bota is mentioned as a disciple of Shammai, who was consulted by Herod on the rebuilding of the temple.[2] Rabbi Nahum Halliblar (Libellarius) had been one of the secretaries of the temple Sanhedrin. Rabbi Papias, who survived the destruction of the temple, was a witness whose evidence was afterwards adduced to decide the legal practice of earlier times.[3]

Chanin Hanachba and Abba Chilkia, both grandsons of the noted Honias Hammeaggel, were reputed to have inherited from their grandfather the faculty of working miracles. The latter was equally distinguished for scrup-u losity in legal observances. A story which is told of an incident in the life of this sage will sufficiently illustrate both qualities.[4] Want of rain induced the Rabbins to send a deputation to Abba Chilkia, to bespeak his prayers for relief. The sages found him busy working in the fields. To their salutation, "Peace to you!" he returned no answer, deeming it dishonest to his employer to interrupt himself in the work for which he was to be paid by him. The sages remained beside him till even, when, after having collected a bundle of sticks, and laid an upper garment which he had borrowed over his shoulder in order to save it, he led the way home with the same punctiliousness which had throughout marked his conduct, taking care neither to waste his

---

[1] Chag. 13*a*. [According to Grätz, iii. 473, 809 f., and Derenbourg, p. 295 f., the defence of Ezekiel was written by Eleazar the son of Hanania.]

[2] Baba Bath. 3*b*.   [3] Eduj. vii. 5–7.

[4] Taan 23. Comp. *Menor. Ham.* iii. 7. 2, 11*c*. We have largely availed ourselves of the mass of Rabbinical information scattered over the pages of that work. 3 vols. ed. Krotoschin, 1848.

shoes nor to injure his feet.   At the entrance of his house, his pious wife, clean, and beautifully arrayed, so that her husband might always fix his regards only on her, awaited his return.   Chilkia made her enter first, as he did not know his guests sufficiently to allow them to remain alone in her company.   He did not invite the strangers to partake of supper with him, as there was scarcely sufficient for all, and he felt unwilling to accept thanks for what was not sufficient. After the meal, Chilkia communicated to his wife the errand of the strangers, but asked her to ascend with him to the roof, in order to pray there, so that the strangers might not know that the rain had descended in answer to their prayers. While engaged in that exercise the desired refreshment came, the clouds first gathering over the spot where Chilkia's wife stood.   For this circumstance Chilkia accounted on the ground that his wife, who was always at home, was able, by an immediate supply, to gladden the poor, while he could only give them money, which could not procure instantaneous relief of their wants.   In connection with this anecdote, and as an illustration of the duty of charity, the author of the book from which we quote it relates an ordinance (ascribed to Ezra),[1] which enjoins housewives to bake bread every Friday morning, so as to be able to distribute it amongst the poor for their use on the Sabbath while fresh and palatable, and to accompany the gift with kind and encouraging words, that the recipients of the charity might, if possible, for a time forget their misery.

Such were the most prominent among the sages whom their theological attainments, personal character, or reputation for sanctity, placed at the head of Jewish religious society. We have faithfully traced their portraits, and purposely dwelt at some length on incidents in their history, that the reader may be enabled to judge for himself of the state of religion amongst the people, and of the direction which theology, piety, and religious ardour assumed at that period. The age of Hillel was, in many respects, the most distinguished.   It was also that in which Jesus Christ appeared.

[1] Baba Kama 82*a*.

Several of the Rabbins whom we have named must have witnessed His advent, and have taught during His lifetime, even if they did not have a more or less direct share in His rejection and death. Considering the state of the synagogue, can we still wonder at this? Could their pride and exclusiveness, their wrangling and learning, their religious zeal and ardour, have found satisfaction in the life, the work, or the teaching of Jesus of Nazareth?

Hillel is said to have been succeeded by his son Simeon as president of the Sanhedrin.[1] [This tradition perhaps really relates to the headship of the Rabbinic school;] but very little is recorded in the writings of the Jews about this Simeon. The grandson of Hillel was Gamaliel I. (the elder), the same who gave the temperate advice which led to the suspension of the persecution of the early Church. His learning and high character gained for him not only the universal respect of the people, but also a position of great authority in the Sanhedrin. [The common Jewish tradition, indeed, represents him as president of that body; but this representation does not accord with the language used of him in the Acts (v. 34).] Deeply versed as he was in the current theological lore, he seems to have attempted to moderate the discussions between the rival schools of Hillel and Shammai. Like Hillel, who had throughout supported the government of Herod, he also abstained from political agitation; and unlike the school of Shammai, who were ardent nationalists, was not opposed to Roman supremacy. We can only briefly allude to his measures for the regulation of the Jewish calendar. The appearance of the new moon was of the greatest importance for the computation of the Jewish feasts. It had been the practice for those who first observed its appearance to hasten to Jerusalem and intimate this to the Sanhedrin, by whom they were closely questioned on the subject. To secure more certainty, and to be less dependent on unsatis-

---

[1] Shab. 15a. He is not named in the Mishna. Some have suggested that in Pirke Aboth i. a section should be transposed, and a saying assigned to Simeon ben Hillel which is now attributed to Simeon ben Gamaliel. Cf. Derenbourg, p. 271, note.

factory reports, Gamaliel laid down certain astronomical rules by which the accuracy of the witnesses might be tested and doubtful cases decided.[1]

The tradition that Gamaliel became a Christian rests upon no solid foundation. In reality he remained to the end firmly attached to the traditions of the fathers. At his decease, about eighteen years before the destruction of Jerusalem, it was said in the magniloquent language of the period, and perhaps not without reference to subsequent events, that the glory of the Law had departed, and that general wickedness had seized men. The recorded[2] principle of Gamaliel expresses his adherence to traditionalism, and his abhorrence of wrangling and over-scrupulousness. It is: "Procure thyself a teacher; avoid being in doubt; and do not accustom thyself to give tithes by guess." In the Christian world Gamaliel is known as the teacher of the Apostle Paul.

Of Simeon the Second, the son of Gamaliel, little is known, save that he took an active part in the defence of Jerusalem, and that he opposed the wild fanaticism of the Zealots.[3] The principle to which he gave utterance was: "All my life have I been brought up among sages, nor have I found anything better than to keep silence,—for, to act and not to explain, is the principle and basis of all; but he who multiplieth words only induceth sin."[4]

We shall, in conclusion, make mention of a contemporary of these Rabbins, who has sometimes been identified with a Jewish ruler who appears in the New Testament, we mean Nicodemus, who came to Jesus by night. A Naqdimon, or Nicodemus ben Gorion, is described in the Talmud as one of the three wealthiest men of Jerusalem (Ben Zizith and Ben Kalba Shabua being named as the other two).[5] His name, Nicodemus, is derived by Talmudists from a miracle which is reported to have taken place in answer to his prayers. His

---

[1] Rosh ha-Sh. 25a.   [2] Pirke Aboth i. 16.

[3] Jos. *Wars*, iv. 3. 9 ; *Life*, 38. [Of Simeon's death nothing is known. It may be observed that the language used about him by Josephus renders it almost impossible to suppose that he was ever *president* of the Sanhedrin. Comp. Derenbourg, pp. 270–272.]

[4] Pirke Aboth i. 17.   [5] Gitt. 56a ; Mid. Kohel. on vii. 12.

former name is recorded to have been Bonai, and a certain Bonai is expressly named in the Talmud as one of the disciples of Jesus.[1] But in spite of this coincidence, we can hardly doubt that this somewhat legendary Nicodemus was *not* the Nicodemus of the Gospel. After the fall of Jerusalem, it is said, the daughter of Nicodemus ben Gorion was exposed to such want as to be obliged to pick up from the ground grains of barley. Then passed by Rabbi Jochanan ben Saccai, who had signed her marriage contract, in which her father had promised her a dowry of a million pieces of gold. "Unhappy nation," he exclaimed, "you could not serve God, and therefore you must serve foreign nations; you would not offer half a shekel for the temple, therefore you must pay thirty times as much to your enemies."[2]

[1] For the origin of the name Naqdimon, see Taan 20*a*; Gitt. 56*a*; for Bonai as a disciple of Jesus, see Sanh. 43*a*.

[2] Mechilta, Jethro, c. 2; Kethub. 66*b*.

CHAPTER VI

THE destruction of Jerusalem and its sanctuary, which shook
the Hebrew commonwealth to its foundation, and removed the
last remainder of national independence, while it destroyed the
old Sanhedrin, produced few marked changes in the synagogue.
It is true that the temple rites, and those sacrifices which
constituted the central point of the Old Testament economy,
had now become impossible, and in consequence the priesthood gradually receded from public life ; but the sacrifices
had already lost much of their interest and importance. In
point of fact, the religious views of Israel had undergone a
gradual modification, to which the destruction of the temple,
and the cessation of its ritual, served only as the completion.
The people clung, indeed, with passionate tenacity, to the
sanctuary and its ordinances; but what of that attachment
was not purely national, belonged to the form and letter, not to
the spirit and meaning, of these rites. We cannot recall a single
instance in which the latter were in any proper sense discussed,
or even referred to, in the religious teaching of the Rabbins.
Throughout, it was the outward observance, and not the
spiritual effects of any ordinance, which were made the subject
of study and discussion in the Jewish colleges. Dogmatics,
or any system of *doctrines*, were not professed in the synagogue. The doctrinal views of the sages were indeed of a
loose and undefined character, and can only be gathered in an
indirect manner from a consideration of their religious poetry,
of their prayers, etc., to which we shall have occasion to refer
more fully in the sequel.

It was on grounds such as those above indicated that, however much the loss of the temple was deplored by the people, its want was in reality little felt from the first. The worshippers had clung to it only as they clung to the letter of the law; and as in the latter case the traditional took the place of the written law, so in the former the synagogue, with its prayers and ordinances, took the place of the temple with its rites and sacrifices. In the present instance the change had been fully prepared. For more than two centuries the influence of the Rabbins had been steadily increasing. The synagogues had long been the proper centres of religious life to the masses, and one set of ordinances might now be substituted for another, in agreement with the wants of the times. We would even go farther, and say that in the existing state of the synagogue such a change had become necessary, and the detachment of the sole remaining member of the old economy could only promote the development of traditionalism. In reality, then, so far from being affected by the cessation of the Mosaic economy, and the removal of the Sanhedrin from the capital, Judaism afterwards not only grew, but rapidly attained its full maturity.

Twice before, we are told, had the Sanhedrin been obliged to change their place of meeting.[1] Forty years before the destruction of Jerusalem they removed from the Chamber of Hewn Stones to the Bazaars, and subsequently from the Bazaars to Jerusalem. These Bazaars are usually identified with the Bazaars of the Sons of Hanan,[2] which are said to have been destroyed three years before the temple, and may perhaps denote the temple market, where victims for the sacrifices were sold. [It must, however, be admitted that our authorities do not enable us to determine the site with certainty,[3] and one passage just cited suggests that these shops were outside the city proper. The Mishna never mentions them, and indeed always speaks as though the Sanhedrin had continued to meet in the Chamber of Hewn Stones

---

[1] Rosh ha-Shanah 31*a*, *b*.   [2] Jer. Peah i. 6.
[3] Comp. *Life and Times*, i. 371 ; Schürer, II. i. 191 ff.; Derenbourg, pp. 465–468.

(Gazith) down till the time of the destruction of the temple.]

Even before the fall of Jerusalem, Jochanan ben Saccai, who had escaped from the besieged city, had founded a school at Jamnia or Jabne, a city near the shores of the Mediterranean, and between the ancient cities of Joppa and Ashdod. According to tradition, as we have already mentioned, Jochanan was the least amongst Hillel's eighty students. To this Rabbi now fell the honour of becoming the first Nasi or President of the new Sanhedrin, [a body which combined the characters of a tribunal and a college of learned men. It can hardly have obtained as yet any formal recognition from Rome, but it was regarded unhesitatingly by Israel as the supreme court of law, and in course of time even usurped the right of exercising criminal jurisdiction]. Jochanan owed his position partly to the influence he formerly possessed in the old Sanhedrin, and partly to his own political and religious moderation.

[Unless we accept the age of 120 years which legend assigns to Jochanan ben Saccai, it seems at least doubtful whether he can ever have actually heard the great Hillel; but he may truly be spoken of as one of his disciples.[1] We know but little about his earlier years.] According to one tradition, for the first forty years of his life Jochanan had been engaged in business; after that he wholly devoted himself to the law. Besides giving glowing descriptions of his learning, which, as usually, is said to have comprised the whole cycle of the knowable, Jewish legends furnish abundant notices of his life and teaching. He is represented as scrupulously observant of the traditions, as entirely engaged with the study of the law, and as surrounded by a numerous and intelligent class of hearers. His virtues were afterwards summed up in the following characteristic catalogue. It was said,[2] he had never been known to engage in any profane conversation; he had always been the first to enter the academy; he had never wittingly or unwittingly allowed himself to be overtaken by sleep while in the

---

[1] Comp. Derenbourg, p. 276.   [2] Succ. 28a.

academy ; he had never gone abroad a distance of four cubits
without carrying about his person a copy of the Law and the
phylacteries ; he had never been found idle, but had always
been occupied with the study of the law; he had always
in person lectured to his pupils ; and he had never taught
anything which he had not received from his teachers. To
complete the sum of his excellences, he had never been heard
to say that it was time to leave the college. Contemporaries
also celebrated his longevity,[1] which he himself ascribed to
scrupulous observance of the traditions, and to diligent study
of the law. He afterwards recommended these measures to
others as the surest means of prolonging life. No doubt
Jochanan's fame was in great measure due to the influence
which he afterwards exercised at Jamnia. But even before
the destruction of Jerusalem he had been a member—according to some, one of the leaders—of the sacred college.
Tradition reports the arguments with which he contended
with the Sadducees on four points, partly religious and partly
juridical, which they controverted. These were: Whether the
Feast of Weeks (Pentecost) required always to be celebrated
exactly on the first day of the week ?[2] What was the
precise portion of the sacrifices due to the priests ?[3] Whether
the daughters of the original testator had a claim to an equal
share in the inheritance if the male heir-at-law had died
leaving only female successors (a point asserted by the
Sadducees and denied by the Pharisees)?[4] and lastly, Whether
the restrictions imposed by the school of Shammai upon the
use of the Scriptures, the handling of which they declared
levitically defiled the hands, were binding,[5]—an ordinance
this which must have greatly restricted their use? The
grounds on which the orthodox opinions were defended by
Jochanan, however powerful they may have appeared to a
Rabbinist, are in themselves not very convincing.

In some respects Rabban Jochanan may be designated
rather as the representative of all the various tendencies in
the synagogue, than as member of any party or as an inde-

[1] Rosh ha-Shanah 31*b*.   [2] Menach 65*a*.
[3] Meg. Taan. 19.   [4] Baba Bath. 115*b*.   [5] Jadaim iv. 6.

pendent thinker.   He employed and developed Hillel's
method.   Like Hillel, he was also liberal in his general views.
Thus he seems to have frequently engaged in discussions with
heathens ; and such was his general affability and courtesy to
all, that no man was ever known to have anticipated his
salutation.[1]   On the other hand, like the school of Shammai,
he was tenaciously attached to the traditions of the elders.
To complete the cycle, he also busily occupied himself with
the study of mystical theology.[2]   Thus, from his peculiar cast
of mind, Rabban Jochanan was exactly the man for the times,
and his deficiency in independence did important service in
the way of consolidating parties and preserving peace at a
very critical period.   Another trait in his character was a
love of peace, which inclined him to favour Roman domination.
During the siege of Jerusalem he had often besought the
Zealots and leaders of the revolution not to bring certain
destruction upon the city and the sanctuary.[3]   He went even
further, and from some evil omens ventured to predict the
impending desolation.[4]   Such declarations, no doubt reported
to the Roman general, afterwards secured for him a favourable
reception in the camp of the enemy.

But the suspicion of the Zealots had been roused, and
Jochanan had to flee.   It is said that, having obtained the
assurance of personal safety from the Romans, he forthwith
prepared to leave Jerusalem ; but the accomplishment of this
was matter of considerable difficulty, as the Zealots guarded
the city gates and prevented all egress.   At last he caused
tidings of his decease to be spread.   It was proposed to elude
their vigilance by carrying the Rabbi in a bier out of the
city.   One of Jochanan's relatives was captain of a company
of Zealots in charge of the gate through which the party was
to pass.   Although the precaution had been taken to put a
piece of putrid flesh into the bier, some of the Zealots had
almost insisted on examining it; but their leader, who was privy
to the plan, restrained them by protesting against a profanation of the obsequies of so great a teacher.   Ultimately the

[1] Ber. 17*a*.   [2] Comp. Bacher, *Tannait.* i. 43 f.
[3] Ab. di R. Nathan 4 ; Gitt. 56*a*.   [4] Joma 39*b*.

procession was allowed to pass, and safely reached the Roman camp, where Vespasian welcomed his arrival, and allowed him to proffer a request. Rabbi Jochanan is said to have first conciliated the general's favour by predicting his future accession to the purple, on the ground that the temple could only be taken by a monarch (Isa. x. 34). Then, instead of asking any personal favour, he only requested permission to continue at Jamnia those schools which had hitherto flourished in the capital. This request was granted ; and he now settled with his disciples in Jamnia, there to await the issue of events.[1]

When tidings of the destruction of the temple arrived, the assembled scholars rent their garments, and mourned as for the death of a relative ; but their master comforted them by reminding them that Judaism still existed, and that works of beneficence might now be substituted for sacrifices, as it was written : " I have chosen mercy, and not sacrifice," [2]—an interpretation (be it observed) in perfect agreement with the spirit of traditionalism. The next step taken by Jochanan and his friends was to convoke a Sanhedrin at Jamnia, of which he was chosen president, the more readily that Gamaliel ben Simeon, the representative of the house of Hillel, was probably a minor, and had only escaped the vengeance of the Romans through Jochanan's special intercession. Besides, Simeon's share in the defence of Jerusalem would have excited suspicion against the Sanhedrin of Jamnia, if any of his immediate descendants had been named its president. In the hands of this council the work of transforming and adapting Judaism to the altered political circumstances proved a task of little difficulty. Jamnia had only to be substituted for Jerusalem, a few ordinances to be discontinued or slightly altered, and certain prayers or good works to be substituted for the sacrifices ; and the change was effected without leaving any trace of violent revolution.

From what has been stated, it will not be difficult to form a correct estimate of Rabbi Jochanan's character and activity. Although destitute of originality or brilliant talents, he was specially the man for the circumstances of the

---

[1] Gitt. 56*a*, *b* ; Mid. Lam. on i. 5. [2] Ab. di R. Nathan 4.

synagogue. With considerable learning stored up in a faithful memory, he combined an earnest assiduity to do all in
his power to recommend himself to the favour of the Deity.
Besides, he served as a channel for communicating traditional
lore to more independent thinkers. The absence of independence in his religious teaching secured for him the support
of all parties, while it enabled him to furnish from his pupils
Rabbins belonging to all the different tendencies of Rabbinism.
The most notable act of his public administration was to
secure the full recognition of the rights and privileges of
the assembly at Jamnia, which was now authorised to fix
definitely the commencement of the new month even in the
absence of the Patriarch.[1]   In principle, the Nasi was a
Hillelite.   His liberality induced him, for example, to admit
that even heathens, if deserving of it by acts of beneficence,
might inherit the kingdom of heaven.[2]   In strange contrast
with a liberality so unusual in those days, was Jochanan's
strict practice, in which he followed the school of Shammai.
The branch of theology in which the Nasi really excelled was
that known as the Hagada.

In general, traditionalism may be divided into two
portions, which respectively treat of the Halacha, the legislative enactments of the Fathers, or engage in the Hagada,
or free interpretation.   While the latter expressed for the
most part the varying views of the times, the former was
strictly traditional, though earlier enactments might be
extended and developed to almost any extent.   Both seem
to be referred to in Scripture, and characterised, the one in
1 Tim. vi. 4, as " questions and strifes of words "; the other
as "fables and genealogies " (1 Tim. i. 4).[3]   The body of
traditional ordinances forms the subject of the Mishna or
Second Law; but it must not be supposed that Halacha
and Hagada formed entirely distinct branches of study.
Indeed, one tract of the existing Mishna consists wholly of
Hagada, and many Hagadic passages are to be found also in
other tracts.   In time the Mishna itself came to require

[1] M. Rosh ha-Shanah iv. 4.   [2] Baba Bath. 10*b*.
[3] Comp. Hort, *Judaistic Christianity*, pp. 135–143.

interpretation, hence the origin of the Gemara or Talmud, which contains the explanation and application of the Halacha to certain cases in dispute. A third discipline, which formed in some respects a transition from the Halacha to the Hagada, was the Midrash. It consisted in explanations of Scripture according to certain defined rules, and was meant to derive the various Halachas from the sacred text, or at least to connect them with it.

The Hagada was a peculiarly fascinating branch of study. Attractive to the hearers by brilliant sallies, by displays of ingenuity, or by wonderful stories, it gave special scope for the cleverness or the imagination of the Rabbins. By it a Halacha might be illustrated, or more frequently a passage of Scripture commented upon in a novel fashion. Without binding himself to any strict or even rational exegetical principles, the Hagadist would bring almost anything out of the text, and interweave his comment with curious legends. A sign or a particle in the verse under consideration, would be twisted so as to convey a special meaning,—in short, it was an ingenious play upon the Scriptures. At the same time, the Hagada remained only the personal saying of the individual teacher, and its value depended upon his learning and reputation, or upon the names which he could quote in support of his statements. Hence the Hagada, which contained the main body of Jewish moral and dogmatic theology, possessed no absolute authority. Probably it was considered that the various Rabbinical principles enunciated or defended by the Hagadists were correct, and that their interpretations, or rather illustrations of Scripture, were of comparatively secondary importance. Nor should it be overlooked that the student of mystical theology derived considerable assistance from the Hagadic method of interpreting Scripture. It enabled him, although according to certain defined exegetical principles, to elicit the hidden meaning of the text. We shall have an opportunity of dwelling on these points in the sequel.[1]

To return : Jochanan excelled principally in Hagadic and

[1] See Chapter XI.

mystical studies ; and some rather ingenious Rabbinical comments, which bear his name, have descended to us.   It was
his fundamental principle: " If thou hast much learned in the
law, claim not merit to thyself, seeing thou hast been created
for that very purpose."[1]   Among the pupils of Jochanan
were five men[2] who afterwards attained to considerable
eminence in the synagogue.   They were Eleazar the son of
Hyrcanus, whom, on account of his tenacious memory, and
attachment to the Halacha, Jochanan compared to a well-
plastered cistern, which does not let out a single drop ;
Joshua the son of Chananja, whose mother he declared a
happy woman ; Joses, whom he termed " the pious priest ";
Simeon the son of Nathaniel, " who feared sin " ; and Eleazar
the son of Arach, who is described as " a fountain whose
waters continually increased."   Among these five youths,
Eleazar ben Arach, Eleazar the son of Hyrcanus, and Joshua
were the most prominent.   The former was famed for the
study of Jewish mysticism.   To such a degree did he excel
in this, that on one occasion the divine glory was said to have
shone around him, and his delighted teacher pronounced
Abraham happy to have had such a descendant.[3]   On the
other hand, his colleague, Eleazar ben Hyrcanus, was a faithful
representative of strict and simple traditionalism.   Rabbi
Jochanan's peculiar mode of instruction, in its most favourable aspect, is illustrated in certain questions which he is said
to have put to his five favourite pupils.   They were to
determine respectively the most desirable and the most
undesirable object.   Among the various replies offered,
Jochanan assented to that of Ben Arach, who found the most
desirable object to be a *good*, and the most grievous an *evil*
heart.[4]

Of the sages who had gathered round the Nasi in Jamnia,
there were many who had seen the temple in its glory.
Amongst these, several deserve particular notice.   Rabbi
Chananiah was one of the few who prayed for the Roman
Empire : [he was probably the last to hold the office of prefect

[1] Pirke Aboth ii. 8*a*.   [2] *Ut supra*, ii. 8*b*.
[3] Chag. 14*b*.   [4] Pirke Aboth ii. 9.

of the priests in the temple.[1]] Upon Rabbi Nahum the Mede had devolved the sad duty of absolving from their vows some who only reached Jerusalem in time to find the sanctuary desolate. Admon and Chanan were celebrated jurists, whose sometimes diverging legal decisions are recorded.[2] Rabbi Zadok was a pupil of Shammai's. Foreseeing the destruction of the temple, he had, in grief for the anticipated event, fasted for forty years. In consequence of these privations, his health had become so shattered that it never afterwards became completely restored.[3] Rabbi Dosa ben Harchinas was a man of great wealth (able to accommodate his guests on golden chairs), and a bitter partisan of the school of Hillel. He did not hesitate to warn others against the insidious opinions of his own brother, who belonged to the school of Shammai.[4] But his views were not always homologated by his contemporaries. Abba Saul ben Botnith had been a wine merchant in Jerusalem, and was noted for his conscientious honesty in business transactions. It was said that he had not retained for himself even the dregs of the wine, deeming them the rightful property of his customers. On his deathbed he extended his right hand, and declared that it had always been scrupulously exact in its dealings.[5] The more noted Abba was for uncompromising honesty, the more painfully truthful appears the sad picture which he drew of the general corruption prevailing amongst the noble priestly families before the destruction of the sanctuary.[6] Another sage who deserves a passing notice, was Chanina ben Dosa. It was said that his worth had been such, that a voice from heaven had daily declared that the whole world was only preserved for the sake of Chanina.[7] His fundamental principle is remarkable as being more practical than those of many others. " The wisdom of a man will be abiding if his fear of sin precedes his desire after wisdom ; but where search

---

[1] Pirke Aboth iii. 2. [On the prefect or *Sagan,* comp. Schürer, II. i. 257–259. He was probably the officer described in the New Testament and Josephus as the " captain of the temple."]

[2] Kethub. xiii. 1, etc.

[3] Gitt. 56*a.*

[4] Jeb. 16*a.*

[5] Jer. Beza iii. 62*b.*

[6] Pes. 57*a* ; comp. Grätz, iv. 20f. ; Derenb. 232 f.

[7] Taan. 24*b.*

after wisdom precedes the fear of sin, wisdom will only prove a temporary possession." In the same sense he used to say: "The man whose works exceed his wisdom really possesses firm and lasting wisdom; but he whose wisdom excels his works, will find that the former also will prove unstable."[1] Many anecdotes are related to show this Rabbi's power. It was supposed that when praying for the sick, he felt, by his liberty of utterance, or by the want of it, whether the person prayed for would recover or die.[2] Thus, when Rabban Gamaliel sent to entreat Chanina's intercession for his son, who lay dangerously ill, after complying with the request, Chanina communicated to the messengers that the lad was restored,—a fact which he gathered from his liberty in interceding for him. It is added, that the event proved the correctness of his assertion.

But the two most remarkable Rabbins at Jamnia were Nahum from Gimso (the present Jimzu near Lydda) and Nechunjah ben Hakanah. The former of these sages was severely tried. With Rabbinical resignation he viewed his trials as so many consequences of his own harshness and unkindness. It is said that on one occasion he had carried to the house of his father-in-law some valuable presents. A poor person had asked him for assistance while he was engaged unloading the beasts which had carried the rich burden. Nahum bade him wait. But before he was at leisure to attend to him, the person who had asked his help had sunk from want and exhaustion. In grief for an unkindness which had caused the poor man's death, he invoked blindness upon his eyes and paralysis upon his hands and feet. These imprecations were soon verified, and Nahum gladly suffered in order to expiate his sin. Accordingly, when his pupils, at the sight of his sufferings, exclaimed, "Alas! that we see thee in such suffering," he replied, "Nay rather, alas! if ye did not see me so suffering."[3] Rabbi Nahum was distinguished in theology as an original thinker; he followed Hillel's method of biblical interpretation. The latter had

---

[1] Pirke Aboth iii. 9.   [2] Jer. Ber. v. 9*a*; Ber. 34*b*.
[3] Taan. 21*a*; jer. Peah (end).

laid down a number of rules, according to which the meaning of the text was to be ascertained. To these exegetical principles (which we shall mention by and by) Nahum added another canon, important in the development of Rabbinism. Certain articles and prepositions in the text were now stated to serve not only a grammatical purpose, but also to indicate that the obvious meaning of the text required either to be enlarged or else restricted.[1] It will readily be conceived what a wide door this canon opened to fanciful interpretation, particularly when afterwards carried to all its consequences.

To this exegetical innovation Rabbi Nechunjah was, on the other hand, decidedly opposed. Untrustworthy tradition, later than the Talmudic age, represents this teacher as occupied chiefly with mystical theology, and ascribes the composition of the oldest cabalistic works to him or to his father. Naturally of a mild and kindly disposition, Nechunjah, who obtained the title of *the Great*, attained to a very old age, which he ascribed to the fact that he had never sought honour in the disgrace of his neighbour, or gone to rest with evil thoughts against anyone; that he had always been liberal, and never accepted a bribe.[2] Himself a living protest against the supposed worldliness of some of his contemporaries, he was heard to declare that the person who submitted himself to the yoke of the law would find exemption from the burdens of this world, while an opposite course would entail corresponding burdens.[3] It is interesting to notice that Nechunjah was one of the few who were wont to ejaculate a short prayer, both when entering the college and again when leaving it. He assigned the following reasons for this unusual practice[4]:—" When I enter," he said, " I pray that I may not be the occasion of error ; and when I leave I bless the Lord for my calling."

Rabbi Jochanan the Nasi died as he had lived. Before his decease he manifested,[5] to the astonishment of his dis-

---

[1] Comp. Grätz, iv. 22 ; Bacher, *Tannait.* i. 61–64.
[2] Megil. 28*a*.   [3] Pirke Aboth iii. 5.
[4] Jer. Ber. iv. 2 ; Ber. 28*b*.   [5] Ber. 28*b*.

ciples, deep spiritual anguish, in the prospect of meeting, as he expressed it, not an earthly king who might be appeased, but the righteous Judge, who punishes sinners with everlasting destruction. He dreaded to be called in question for his manifold iniquities, and wept in the uncertainty whether heaven or hell would become his portion. Before expiring, he expressed to his friends the wish, that the fear of God might as much influence their conduct as the fear of man.[1] Thus in his life and death the Nasi was made to feel and to exemplify, that " by the deeds of the law there shall no flesh be justified."

His successor in the sacred office was Rabban Gamaliel II., the great-grandson of Simeon, Hillel's son. He obtained the dignity of president, both in virtue of his extraction and of his merits. [A man of undoubted energy and ability, always ready to adapt himself to circumstances, and possessed of unfaltering faith in the future of Judaism, he was in many ways admirably fitted for the position now conferred upon him.] Unfortunately his was an imperious disposition. Unable to brook contradiction, he exercised the prerogatives of his office in a despotic manner, silencing by excommunication those whom he could not convince by argument. This attempt at spiritual tyranny, however, ultimately issued in his own humiliation. Gamaliel was surrounded by his former class-fellows who had now become Rabbins, by some of the colleagues of his own teacher, and by their pupils. But jealousies were not wanting among these theologians. At the very outset, and immediately after Jochanan's death, Eleazar ben Arach withdrew to Emmaus, probably in the expectation that the sages would feel his presence indispensable, and that the Sanhedrin would thus become virtually dependent on him. If such had been his hope, he was doomed to disappointment. It is said that, living at such a distance from the Sanhedrin, and cut off from intercourse with the

---

[1] Ber. *ut supra.* [Rabbi Jochanan seems to have died at Berur Chail, in the neighbourhood of Jamnia. Hence it appears not improbable that Gamaliel had become president of the Beth-Din, or Sanhedrin, at Jamnia even before the death of his predecessor. Comp. Derenbourg, pp. 306–311 ; Bacher, *Tann.* i. 76, 79.]

other Rabbins, the man whom Jochanan had at one time declared to outweigh all the sages of Israel put together, came at last to be ridiculed for his ignorance of the law.[1]

Rabban Gamaliel was a close imitator of his predecessors of the house of Hillel. His character exhibited a curious, though not unusual, combination of different elements. On the one hand, he was kind to his inferiors, readily moved to pity, well versed in traditional law and the cognate sciences, and of such liberal principles as even to cultivate intercourse with Gentiles. Indeed, Gamaliel felt himself at liberty to do things which would have been denounced in any other as little less than apostasy. Trifling as it may appear to us, such indulgences as having a figure carved upon his seal, bathing at Ptolemais in a place where a statue of Venus had been placed,[2] and in general displaying a taste for the beautiful in nature and art, were serious innovations to a Pharisaical Jew. But his virtues were, on the other hand, marred by stubbornness, by ambition, and a determination to carry his own views, if necessary, by violence. Perhaps delicate health may have added a degree of nervous irritability to his natural disposition. His public and private conduct (if impartially viewed) bear out this view of his character. His extensive properties he let to farmers, demanding in return only a share in the harvest; and so scrupulous was he in his dealings with them, that when they repaid the seed-corn which he had supplied, he would only compute its value at the lowest figure at which it sold in the market, so as to avoid even the appearance of usury.[3] The Nasi had a favourite slave, Tabi, distinguished for his Rabbinical lore. His master would willingly have restored him to liberty, but some Rabbinical ordinance prevented it. When at last poor Tabi died, the Nasi's feelings overcame his scruples, and he mourned for him as for a relative.[4]

We have already indicated that jealousies prevailed between the sages at Jamnia. The first question which caused

---

[1] Mid. Qoh. on vii. 7 ; Ab. di R. Nathan, c. 14 ; Shab. 147*b*. Comp. Grätz, iv. 28 f. ; Bacher, *ut supra*.

[2] Ab. Sar. iii. 4.   [3] B. Mez. 74*b*.   [4] Jer. Ber. ii. 7.

serious disagreement was an attempt to settle the controversies
long pending between the schools of Hillel and of Shammai.
During the short term (probably extending only over a few
years) of Rabbi Jochanan's presidency, these controversies
had remained in abeyance, not more from the necessities of
the times, which required combined action, than from the
peculiar disposition of the Nasi. But the greater the inactivity of parties during that interval, the more violent was
the shock of the collision, when a direct descendant of Hillel's,
of the disposition of Gamaliel, led the ranks of a party whose
opinions were, at any rate, in the ascendant amongst Jewish
theologians. But there were men of note and influence among
the Shammaites also. Accordingly, an attempt was first
made to reconcile both parties. For three years were the
discussions continued which bore on the fundamental principles
of the two schools. At last, as might have been expected,
compromise was found impossible. To settle the dispute, it
was now asserted by the Hillelites that a voice from heaven
(the Bath-Kol, literally, daughter of the voice) had declared
that the principles of both parties were the words of God,
but that the Halacha,[1] or traditional law, was to be fixed in
accordance with the teaching of the school of Hillel.

Naturally enough, not only the Shammaites, but others
also, and especially Rabbis Joshua and Eleazar, were unwilling
to yield to so summary a mode of settling controverted points ;
but their opposition was vain, and they were at last obliged
to submit. Rabbi Joshua gave vent both to his scepticism and
his dissatisfaction, by observing that such miraculous solutions
of difficulties must always prove unsatisfactory, as the law
was designed for those on earth, and not for those in heaven,[2]
adding, that he attached authority to the decision of the
majority of sages, but not to supernatural interpositions. To
allay the general dissatisfaction, it was felt necessary to pass
a bye-law, which left both parties at liberty to follow in
practice their own theological convictions.[3] But one important consequence of this discussion was, that both parties

---

[1] Erub. 13b ; jer. Ber. i. 3b.   Comp. Grätz, iv. 32, 33, 424.
[2] B. Mez. 59b.   [3] Toseph. Eduj. 2.

became sensible of the necessity of having some independent and ultimate basis for, and criterion of, traditional law, instead of the mere assertions of rival schools and authorities. By common consent, this was sought in a more general reference to, and interpretation of, Scripture, according to certain fixed exegetical canons. In this particular branch of theological science Rabbi Akiba became specially distinguished; but any hope of good which the prospect of recurring more frequently to the sacred text might have opened, was soon disappointed by the fanciful method and the ingenious devices which the various doctors employed in their attempts at Scripture interpretation.

Meantime Gamaliel was resolved to follow up the victory of his party. In the prosecution of his plans he adopted peculiar tactics. To prevent any popular declaration against himself, and at the same time the increase of the opposite party, he stationed a door-keeper at the entrance of the college, whose duty it was to prevent the admission of parties who might prove dangerous or disagreeable.[1] At the same time, he assumed a more dictatorial tone in the college, putting down all contradiction with a strong hand. When his authority failed to ensure submission, he laid an interdict upon the refractory individual. Two, or rather three kinds of spiritual censures are named in Talmudic writings. The first of these,[2] rather a reproof than a punishment, was adjudged for trifling offences. During its continuance, persons so visited had to stay at home and to abstain not only from amusements, but even from needless intercourse with others. The second, a kind of interdict which always lasted for at least thirty days, was inflicted for graver offences, especially for contempt of the law, of recognised traditions, of the person of any of the sages, or for any other breach of religious statutes, of which a later Rabbi instances twenty-four. If the person thus punished showed no signs of repentance within that month, this ban was confirmed, and along with it the nature of the offence published. A person under the ban was deserted by all except the members of his

[1] Ber. 28*a*.   [2] Möed Katan 16*a*.   Comp. Selden, *De Synedriis.*

family, or those who resorted to him for strictly necessary purposes.   He was not allowed to change his garments, and had to share in many of the observances of those who were in deep mourning.   If he died while under this ban, a stone was laid on his coffin.[1]   The last and highest censure was excommunication, which was, however, but rarely pronounced.   The individual upon whom this sentence rested, was neither allowed to expound the Law nor even to listen to its exposition.   The Patriarch or Nasi arrogated to himself the power of pronouncing these sentences, and Gamaliel was not sparing in the exercise of his spiritual prerogative.   Thus an unfortunate sage, Rabbi Joses ben Tadai of Tiberias, who had ventured to demur to a Rabbinical conclusion (an application of the conclusion *a minori ad majus* to ritual questions), and to exhibit its fallacy in a somewhat sarcastic manner, was amongst the first to be punished for his temerity.   His ingenuity was visited by the Nasi with excommunication.[2]   The same punishment was inflicted on Rabbi Eleazar ben Chanoch for venturing to doubt the necessity of washing one's hands before partaking of bread.[3]   Even Rabbi Akiba, one of the most influential men in the synagogue, barely escaped excommunication, which the Nasi at length hurled against his own brother-in-law, the celebrated Eleazar ben Hyrcanus, on occasion of a trifling dispute between them.[4]

This arrogance of one who in age was inferior to many of his opponents, naturally evoked strong opposition.   For, besides doing violence to the convictions of others, he paid no regard to their personal feelings when attempting to carry his point.   Foremost in the ranks of his enemies, as their most able, determined, and therefore most dangerous representative, was Rabbi Joshua ben Chananja.   By extraction a Levite, he had enjoyed the honour of assisting, along with his brethren, in the solemn services of the temple.   Since its destruction he had lived in great poverty, supporting himself and his family by the manufacture of needles, or, as others assert, by working as a blacksmith.   Probably Joshua

---

[1] Eduj. v. 6 ; jer. Möed Katan iii. 81*d*.   [2] Derek Erez R. c. 1.
[3] Eduj. v. 6.   [4] B. Mez. 59*b* ; jer. Möed Katan iii. 81*c*.

had felt the hauteur and pride of the Patriarch the more, that the latter and his friends lived in affluence, while he and other deserving men were exposed to want. Treatment like that to which the Rabbins were now exposed on so many occasions, Joshua, in spite of his gentle and yielding disposition, could ill brook. Their mutual ill-will could not long remain concealed. The occasion only was wanting for open rupture, and this was soon afforded. The question had privately been proposed to Rabbi Joshua, whether an animal accidentally wounded in the lip might afterwards lawfully be presented in sacrifice by a priest learned in the Law, who could not be suspected of having intentionally injured the animal in order to render it unfit for sacred use ? It will be observed that this question was not one of any possible practical importance, and it presents a fair specimen of the subjects commonly chosen for theological discussion. At any rate, Joshua gave it as his opinion that such an animal might be offered in sacrifice. The question was next proposed to the Nasi, who decided in an opposite sense from Joshua. Gamaliel resolved to bring the matter before the Sanhedrin. Here Joshua, without regard to his former opinion, pronounced a sentence in agreement with Rabban Gamaliel's views. The Nasi now charged his opponent, in presence of the whole college, with prevarication. Not satisfied even with this public humiliation, Gamaliel did not invite Joshua to resume his seat, while he himself complacently entered on a long disquisition of the subject, until the indignant exclamations of the sages interrupted him.[1]

Nor was this the only manifestation of his enmity towards Joshua. On another occasion, Rabban Gamaliel, who was proud of his lunar observations,—a subject of considerable importance, it will be remembered,—had rashly given credit to insufficient testimony about the appearance of the new moon, and had, contrary to the opinions of Rabbis Joshua and Dosa, fixed the Day of Atonement accordingly. Rabbi Joshua's astronomical knowledge was superior to that of the Nasi ; and, besides, the observations of others had

[1] Bechor 36*a*.

shown the erroneousness of Rabban Gamaliel's reckoning. Still it was in vain that Joshua proposed to lay the matter before the sacred college. The Nasi refused, and not only insisted on carrying out his own views, but, to humble his opponent, ordered him to appear on the day on which Joshua had calculated the solemn fast should fall, as arrayed for a journey with scrip, staff, and purse,—an injunction which, besides doing violence to his convictions, could not be viewed otherwise than as a studied public affront. Rabbi Akiba, one of Joshua's disciples, was selected to deliver the Nasi's message. At first Joshua determined to resist; but, at the earnest request of his pupils, and of Rabbi Dosa, he yielded. When the aged sage appeared before the haughty Nasi, obedient to his arbitrary command, even he could not repress a generous emotion, and embraced him with these words: "Welcome, thou, my teacher in wisdom, and my pupil in obedience. Happy the age in which the greater obey the less!" [1]

But this fit of humility, and the reconciliation which ensued, were alike temporary. Bent on maintaining his authority over his opponents, the number of whom daily increased, Gamaliel omitted no opportunity of publicly humbling them. At last his tyranny became intolerable, and led to a general resistance. Once more a question had been privately put to Rabbi Joshua. This time it was, whether the recital of the customary evening prayers were absolute duty or only a matter of choice? Joshua took the latter, the Nasi the former view. The above described scene, of prevarication on the part of Rabbi Joshua, and of public humiliation, was now re-enacted. Recriminations between the sages ensued. At last the whole college, incensed at the treatment to which one of their number was systematically exposed, rose against the president, and on the spot deposed him from the sacred office. The choice of his successor was a matter of some difficulty. Joshua did not possess sufficient means properly to sustain the dignity of Nasi; nor would it have been delicate to place in the president's chair the

[1] Rosh ha-Shanah 25a b.

opponent of Gamaliel. Rabbi Akiba's rising fame would have qualified him for the honour, had his reputation been established. Ultimately the choice of the sages fell on Eleazar ben Azariah, the wealthy representative of a noble priestly family. The Nasi elect was scarcely the person to preside over the college. He was too young, and withal too modest, to command the submission of the angry theologians at Jamnia. It had been well had he followed the advice of his wife, and declined the post. But the offer of the highest dignity was too tempting. Eleazar accepted it, and was installed on the day of his election.[1]

The Sanhedrin immediately entered upon a course of reforms. The first measure was to dispense with the services of the door-keeper whom Gamaliel had employed, and to give free admission to all who chose to attend the sittings of the Sanhedrin; the next, to reopen the questions in dispute between the schools of Hillel and of Shammai, which had formerly been so summarily settled by the Bath-Kol. The various Halachas were re-examined, and as their reception depended only on the weight of the authorities from which they had been derived, witnesses were summoned and examined on these points. Their statements were carefully considered and taken down. On some subjects the sages took a middle course between the opposing schools; on others the decision leant rather towards the school of Shammai. The depositions of the various witnesses (termed Edujoth) constituted probably the basis of the most ancient collection of Halachas. In many respects the discussions of that day, in which the ex-Nasi also took part, were interesting. The reader must not, however, suppose that they were conducted altogether in an impartial spirit. Thus, amongst other witnesses, Akabja ben Mahalaleel, a man of learning and probity, had deponed in regard to four Halachas in a manner unpalatable to the sages. As nothing could shake his testimony, an attempt was made to bribe him into compliance with the theological wishes of the Rabbins, by the tempting offer of raising him to the office of Ab-beth-din.

[1] Ber. 27b.

But the old man remained firm. "Rather," exclaimed he, "may I be termed a fool all my life, than for one hour stand as a transgressor before God."[1]   It was in vain that a decision of Shemaja and Abtalion was quoted against him; Akabja would not yield. Argument failing, he was excommunicated; and in the conviction of the righteousness of his cause, he patiently bore this sentence to the day of his death. But before his decease Akabja admonished his son to submit to the Sanhedrin. He could not have done so, as he had received the traditions from more than one Rabbi; but his son had only heard them from the lips of his father, whose solitary testimony should not be set in opposition to that of all the other sages. Before expiring, the Rabbi also directed his son not to seek the patronage of men, but the recommendation of deeds which would deserve the praise of others. It was the maxim[2] of Akabja: "Ponder on three things, and thou wilt be kept from committing sin. Consider whence thou comest, whither thou goest, and in whose presence thou must shortly render an account."[3]

All the questions discussed in the Sanhedrin on the day of Eleazar's election were not of a purely ceremonial or speculative character. Amongst them were some of general importance to the synagogue, and even to the world. One of these concerned the inspiration of some of the books of Scripture. Even at that period doubts were raised as to the claims of the Books of Ecclesiastes and the Song of Solomon to be received into the number of canonical writings. The school of Hillel defended, that of Shammai opposed, their claims to inspiration.[4] Ultimately the Sanhedrin decided in favour of the views of the Hillelites. Rabbi Akiba especially vindicated the Song in very energetic terms, amongst other arguments declaring that if all Scripture were "holy," the Song was "the holy of holies." Another point of some

---

[1] Eduj. v. 6, 7.   [2] Pirke Aboth iii. 1.

[3] [There has been considerable difference of opinion as to the period at which Akabja lived. Frankel (Darke Mishna) and Hamburger place him some eighty years earlier; but see Grätz, iv. 39 ; Derenbourg, pp. 371 ff., 483 f.]

[4] Jad. iii. 5 ; Eduj. v. 3.

importance was that raised by the request of a descendant of
Ammon, a proselyte, to be allowed to "enter the congregation
of the Lord." It will be remembered that the law of Moses
expressly forbade such admissions. But whether from
liberality, or from a sense that the synagogue required in
measure to relax its strictness, the temper of the majority of
the sages was in favour of the admission of the proselyte.
However, the ex-Nasi as violently opposed as Rabbi Joshua
advocated this measure. Both parties appealed to the law
of Moses, and tried to defend their views by scriptural
arguments. The discussion affords so fair a specimen of the
method employed, that we give it in an abbreviated form.[1]

The ex-Nasi urged against the admission of the proselyte
the Scripture injunction (Deut. xxiii. 3) : " An Ammonite or
Moabite shall not enter into the congregation of the Lord,
even to their tenth generation shall they not enter," etc.
Rabbi Joshua replied by quoting Isa. x. 13 : " I have
removed the bounds of the people, and have robbed their
treasures ; and I have put down the inhabitants like a valiant
man." From this passage he inferred the removal and the
mixture of all these nations under Sennacherib, and argued
that the passage in the Book of Deuteronomy no longer
applied to them. The ex-Nasi retorted by quoting Jer.
xlix. 6 : " And afterward I will bring again the captivity of
the children of Ammon " ; from which he concluded that they
must have been again restored. To prove that this prediction was yet unfulfilled, Joshua quoted the analogous promise,
Jer. xxx. 3 : " I will bring again the captivity of my people
Israel and Judah." At last the Sanhedrin decided in favour
of the proselyte,—whether convinced by Rabbi Joshua's
arguments, or because they wished to support his authority
against the ex-Nasi, we will not attempt to decide.

It will have been noticed that Rabban Gamaliel, though
deposed from the presidency, continued in the Sanhedrin and
took part in its deliberations. Indeed, the ambitious prelate
had no intention readily to relinquish the office which he had
so long held. However, that day's discussions had taught

[1] Jad. iv. 4 ; Ber. 28*a*.

him at least the necessity of abating his pretensions, and
conciliating those whom he had hitherto only sought to
control.   He was now as ready to make concessions as he
had formerly been overbearing.   Accordingly, on the day
after his deposition he waited on the leading members of the
opposition to ask their forgiveness for his former harshness,
and to secure their support.   The most humiliating part of
this duty was the necessity which it involved of condescend-
ing to appear as suppliant before Rabbi Joshua.   He found
the latter engaged at his trade.   The Nasi expressed his
surprise and concern when he entered the humble dwelling of
the sage, the blackened walls and empty rooms of which
testified to the laborious occupation and to the difficulties of
its inmates.   But Joshua was not mollified, and bitterly
reproached Gamaliel for his want of interest in the sages.
" Alas ! " exclaimed he, " for the age of which thou art the
leader ; thou art equally ignorant of the cares of the sages
and of their difficulties." [1]   Nothing daunted by this reception, Rabban Gamaliel tried all the arts of persuasion to
conciliate Joshua ; but in vain.   At last he implored his
pardon, appealing at the same time to the sacred memory of
his ancestor, Hillel the Great.   To this plea Joshua yielded,
and even promised to use all his influence to restore Gamaliel
to the lost dignity.

In the execution of this promise, which may partly be
accounted for by the manifest incongruity of elevating a
youth like Eleazar to the presidential chair, Joshua
immediately despatched a message to the college.   Indeed, it
must soon have occurred to the sages, that as the proceedings
had altogether been somewhat irregular, being prompted by
the feelings of the moment, so the choice of a mere youth as
their Nasi, and the deposition of a descendant of Hillel, was,
to say the least, undignified.   The senators had now had
time to consider all this, and their feelings were changed
with the humiliation of Gamaliel.   When, now, even his old

[1] Ber. 28a ; comp. Grätz, iv. 35–42.   [In the Jerusalem Talmud (Ber. iv. 7d)
the story is told in a somewhat simpler, and probably earlier form ; comp.
Derenbourg, pp. 325–329.]

opponent appeared in the council to plead *for* him with as much zeal as he had erst pleaded *against* him, a perfect revulsion of feeling ensued. The sages resolved to reinstate Gamaliel in his former dignity. But the difficulty was to set aside their nominee of yesterday. The delicate task of inducing Eleazar to resign was entrusted to one specially qualified for its discharge, and who had formerly been selected by Gamaliel to convey an equally disagreeable message to his friend and teacher Joshua. But the noble youth had anticipated the deliberations of the council. No sooner had Eleazar heard of the reconciliation between Gamaliel and his former opponents, than, of his own accord, he proposed to reinstate him, and in token of homage, on the following morning, to wait, together with the whole college, upon Rabban Gamaliel. This unexpected act of generosity met with acknowledgment from the sages, and it was ruled that, in future, Gamaliel should preside for three weeks in the Sanhedrin, and Eleazar take the chair during the fourth week.[1] After this occurrence, peace and order seem to have been preserved in the sacred college. Little definite is known of the activity of Eleazar. Throughout he seems to have been distinguished for uprightness, and to have enjoyed general esteem. Great as was his learning, his recorded axiom shows that he preferred practice to mere knowledge of the Law.[2]

Altogether, Rabban Gamaliel occupied the presidential chair about thirty years. He must have died before the beginning of the troubles which arose in the reign of the Emperor Hadrian, but the year of his death is unknown.[3] His colleague Eleazar ben Azariah still survived; but the administration of spiritual affairs devolved on Rabbi Joshua, who now occupied the post of Nasi, either on account of the youthfulness of Gamaliel's son and eventual successor, or of

---

[1] Ber. 28*a*. [According to jer. Ber. iv. 1, when Gamaliel was restored to his position as Nasi, Eleazar was made Ab-beth-din.]

[2] Pirke Aboth iii. 17.

[3] Comp. Grätz, iv. 143, 480 ; Derenbourg, pp. 346, 366 ; Strack, *Einleitung in den Thalmud,* p. 79 (where Gamaliel's death is dated about 110 A.D.).

the political necessities of Palestine.   Rabbi Joshua and his
pupils honoured the memory of the Nasi by a public
mourning.   So great was the respect in which he was held
at the time, that the celebrated proselyte Akylas, well known
as translator of the Bible into Greek, burnt, in honour of
his memory, effects to the value of about twenty guineas,
according to a custom usual on the decease of kings.[1]   But
Rabban Gamaliel was useful, not only during his life, but even
at his death.   Hitherto the foolish practice had obtained
among the Jews of burying the dead in costly garments,—a
custom which involved the surviving relatives in great and
needless expense.   To do away with this, Rabban Gamaliel
expressly requested that he might be buried in plain white
raiment.[2]   To mark the public sense of this seasonable
reform, it was enacted that in future, at funeral meals, an
additional cup should be emptied to the memory of Gamaliel.
The Nasi left at least one son, during whose minority Joshua
presided in the college.[3]

We have before referred to the vicissitudes of Eleazar
ben Hyrcanus, who distinguished himself so much, both as a
student and as Rabbi, for his knowledge of traditions, but
who afterwards incurred the Nasi's ban.   We add a few
particulars connected with the history of that remarkable
man.[4]   The son of a wealthy farmer, he was for more than
twenty years engaged in agricultural pursuits.   It is said
that some domestic disagreement then induced him to leave
his father's house, and resort for employment to Jerusalem.
Here he conceived the somewhat romantic idea of giving
himself wholly to religious and literary pursuits.   With
characteristic ardour and energy he attended the college of
Rabbi Jochanan ben Saccai, who, under his uncouth appearance, soon recognised the peculiar talents of his rustic pupil.
By diligence and perseverance he secured the affection and
respect of his master.   In course of time, Eleazar's father,
who had remained ignorant of the fate of his son, came to

---

[1] Ab. Sar. 11*a*.   [2] Keth. 8*b*.
[3] Comp. the above-quoted authorities, specially Grätz, iv. 143.
[4] Grätz, iv. 43–50, 425

the capital for the purpose of formally disinheriting the fugitive. Jochanan, to whose knowledge the intention of the old farmer had come, resolved to bring about a reconciliation. Without acquainting either party with it, he invited the old man into the college, and commissioned Eleazar to deliver a theological discourse. That his modest pupil might not be confused, Jochanan himself withdrew, but listened unobserved. At the close he came forward, and publicly honoured Eleazar by declaring " that Abraham, Isaac, and Jacob were blessed indeed, since Eleazar had sprung from them." [1] The feelings of the astonished parent, on recognising in the honoured student his long-lost son, may be imagined. When Eleazar left his paternal home, so ignorant was he, that with difficulty he had mastered even the customary prayers; but by piety, frequent fastings, and diligence, he had now become so distinguished as to be deemed by his teacher even worthy of being initiated into the deepest mysteries of theology. The rude peasant had now become a master in Israel. It would scarcely be possible more strongly to indicate the honour which the Rabbins enjoyed at the time, than by the occurrence which is said now to have taken place. Contrary to all established custom, when his father recognised him, he rose before him in token of respect, and now proposed to disinherit in his favour his other children; but the devoted student would not allow either the one or the other mark of distinction. Indeed, such was the general esteem in which Eleazar was held, that he could aspire to the highest connections, and obtained the hand of Emma-Shalom, the sister of Rabban Gamaliel. [2]

On the death of his teacher, Rabbi Jochanan, Eleazar opened an academy in Lydda. Here, seated on a large block of stone, in a place shaped like a race-course, he expounded to numerous and devoted hearers the traditions which he himself had received from his teachers. [3] Not a word would he either add to or diminish from them. Rather than develop traditionalism, he would plead ignorance. The opinion enter-

---

[1] Ab. di R. Nathan. 6; Gen. Rab. 42.   [2] Shab. 116*a*.
[3] Mid. Cant. on i. 3.

tained of him by his contemporaries may be gathered from the fact that Rabbi Joshua, his former class-fellow, compared the stone on which he was wont to sit to Mount Sinai, and Eleazar himself to the Ark of the Covenant.[1] We have already mentioned that his master had characterised the peculiar merits of Eleazar by comparing him to a well-plastered cistern, which would not let out a single drop. Most tenacious of the teaching of the elders, which his faithful memory had treasured up in all its fulness,—honest, strict, and conscientious,—he refused to answer questions when he had no authority to quote in support of his sentiments, or to avail himself of Hillel's principles for the further development of traditionalism. In fact, Eleazar belonged rather to the school of Shammai than to that of Hillel. He was wont to warn others "to keep their children from speculation, and rather to train them up on the knees of the sages." [2]

His acquaintance with the traditions of the elders, more extensive and accurate than that of any of his contemporaries, would have made him invaluable in the deliberations of the Sanhedrin, had not the ban pronounced by his brother-in-law excluded him from its meetings. The immediate cause of the rupture between them was a trifling question in theological casuistry, in which both parties strongly insisted on opposite decisions. On this occasion also Rabbi Akiba was commissioned to intimate the sentence to Eleazar. Dressed in mourning, he presented himself in Lydda, and announced his message in the following delicate manner: "It seems to me as if thine associates had separated themselves from thee!" [3] Rabbi Eleazar understood the hint, and retired to Cæsarea, where he spent the remainder of his days. During his stay in that city he associated with some Jewish Christians, and, at one time, incurred the suspicion of having joined the Church.

---

[1] *Ut supra.*

[2] Ber. 28*b*. [On the meaning of this warning, comp. Bacher, *Tannait.* i. 102 ; Levy, *Neuhebr. Wörterb.* i. 450*b*.]

[3] B. Mez. 59*b* ; cf. jer. Möed Katan iii. 81*c*.

He was in consequence summoned before the magistrate to recant his supposed profession of the Gospel. The explanations which he offered satisfied the authorities that he had never belonged to the hated sect. But Eleazar was not so easily satisfied as the Roman governor. He bitterly reproached himself for having given any ground for such suspicion by holding intercourse with heretics.[1]

It has already been noted that he meekly submitted to the Nasi's sentence of excommunication; but he felt it not the less that he bore it patiently. Indeed, it seems to have embittered his life and spirits. Thus he used to say, perhaps not without reason : " Warm thyself at the fire of the sages ; but beware of their coals, lest thou burn thyself with them. Their bite is as the bite of jackals, their prick as that of scorpions, their tongue as that of serpents, and their words are like burning coals." [2]   At last his health broke down, and the most learned and conscientious man in Israel was about to descend into the grave, laden with the ban of his brethren. When tidings of his approaching decease reached Jamnia, Rabbi Joshua and his colleagues hastened to his side. Eleazar received them with reproaches for their past neglect, which had not only embittered his own existence, but operated so detrimentally on theological science. However, there was little time now left for recrimination. In the conversation which ensued, Eleazar communicated to his visitors valuable information on a number of Halachas. The presence of his former friends, and the long-desired but forbidden theological discussion, seemed to have revived the dying Rabbi. Alike forgetful of the past and present, he continued expounding on his deathbed as he had been wont to do on the stone bench at Lydda, and died while replying to an inquiry addressed to him. The last word he was heard to utter was " pure," a circumstance which the Rabbins present took as a certain indication that Eleazar's soul had departed in purity. On his death, those present rent their garments, and Joshua solemnly removed the ban from him who had been summoned to the bar of another judge. It was the eve

[1] Mid. Qoh. on i. 8; Ab. Sar. 16*b*.   [2] Pirke Aboth ii. 10.

of the Sabbath when Eleazar died, in the midst of those
engagements to which he had given his mind and heart
during life.   The sages remained at Cæsarea during that day,
and at the expiration of its rest the body was conveyed to
Lydda, where it was buried, attended by a vast concourse of
students and people.   The funeral oration on the occasion
was delivered by Akiba, who chose for his text : " My father,
my father—the chariot of Israel, and the horsemen thereof."
In the exaggerated language usual on such occasions, the
preacher declared that the book of knowledge had now been
buried, adding for himself that " he had many coins to change
(theological difficulties to solve), but that the money-changer
was gone." [1]

The merits of Rabbi Eleazar were as extravagantly extolled after his decease, which took place about 117 A.D., as
they had been overlooked during his lifetime.   In hyperbolical language it was said that " if the expanse of the
heavens had been parchment, the trees of Lebanon pens, and
the waters of the sea ink, all would not have sufficed to
write down what Eleazar knew." [2]   Chiefly engaged as he
was with the committal and exposition of the traditions
which he had received from his predecessors, and to which he
would suffer no addition to be made, he alone of the pupils
of Rabbi Jochanan ben Saccai is not stated to have engaged
in mystical studies.[3]   Of the various works ascribed to him,
the best known is one which bears the name of *Pirke di Rabbi
Eleazar*, containing a scientific and theological medley on
subjects connected with Jewish dogmatics, mysticism, and
astronomy ; [but the work is not earlier than the eighth
century of our era [4]].   Eleazar had trained, at least in part,
numerous pupils.   Although he imparted to them much of his
own solid learning, he had, strictly speaking, no successor,—
he rather closed and completed an epoch than originated a
school.   Amongst the students who attended his teaching, we

[1] Sanh. 68*a*. [Again the Jerusalem Talmud (Shab. ii. 6) recounts the story
in a simpler and earlier form ; comp. Derenbourg, p. 366 f.]

[2] Juchasin 32*b* ; cf. Bacher, *Tannait.* i. 28.   [3] Bacher, *Tannait.* i. 126.

[4] Hamb. *Real-Encycl.* Suppl. i. 122 f.

only mention at present Mathiah ben Charash, who ultimately
settled at Rome, where he is said to have presided over a
theological academy.[1]

The other leading Rabbi of that age was Rabbi Joshua
ben Chananja, to whom we have already frequently referred,
as first the opponent, and then the successor of Rabban
Gamaliel. Properly speaking, this sage was rather distinguished for readiness and ingenuity than for depth and
accuracy of learning. It has already been stated that in his
youth he had, as Levite, assisted in the ritual services of the
temple. After the destruction of the sanctuary, Joshua was
thrown entirely upon his own resources, and with difficulty
supported himself by his trade. In spite of the privations to
which he was exposed, his disposition was gentle and con-
ciliatory, but his outward appearance was certainly far from
attractive. But the contorted and emaciated little figure,
and the blackened face, concealed a vivacious intellect, ready
to grapple with intricate questions or to give a telling re-
partee. So distinguished was Joshua for the latter quality,
that after his decease some entertained serious apprehensions
for the cause of Judaism, from the want of one who had
always been ready to give an apt reply.[2] Various anecdotes
are related to illustrate this feature in our Rabbi. The best
known of these refers to an interview at Rome, during
Joshua's presence in that capital on an embassy, which took
place between the Rabbi and the emperor's daughter. It is
said that the young lady had been equally struck with the
Rabbi's mental attractions and his repulsive exterior, and she
had rallied Joshua with the question, " How so much wisdom
could lodge in so ugly a body ? " In reply, the sage advised
her in future to keep her best wine, not in earthen, but in
golden vessels. The lady took the advice literally, and when
afterwards the Rabbi was challenged for offering a suggestion
which had spoiled good wine, he retorted by showing her how
it might be necessary to preserve the most precious substances in the most worthless vessels.[3] Gradually, perhaps
together with his growing political importance, of which

---

[1] Bacher, *Tannait.* i. 385–389.   [2] Chag. 5*b*.   [3] Taan. 7*a*.

more hereafter, Rabbi Joshua's position in Jamnia became more commanding, till after the death of Gamaliel, when he presided over the Sanhedrin.

Joshua's poverty had formerly been relieved by Gamaliel, who assigned to him the produce of his own rich estates. He had also been able, by means of an ingenious device of some of his pupils, to regain the tithes to which he was entitled by virtue of his Levitical descent. Eleazar ben Azariah (Gamaliel's colleague in the presidency) had, after the destruction of the sanctuary, claimed the tithes for the priests alone, denying to the Levites any share in these offerings of the faithful. But a Jewish ordinance prevented the defilement of a descendant of Aaron by touching anything connected with the dead. Accordingly, in order to oblige Eleazar to make some arrangement with Joshua, a number of students agreed in future to deposit their tithes in a garden which could only be approached through a cemetery, while they refused to allow them to be collected through a third party. It is related that this practical argument speedily convinced Eleazar, and he forthwith restored the tithes to his brethren of the tribe of Levi.[1]

The theological and literary activity of Joshua was very considerable. After the decease of Rabbi Jochanan, his teacher, he had opened a college at Bekiin,[2] between Jabne and Lydda. There he trained a number of most intelligent pupils, of whom some became distinguished for attainments in the Halacha, others for their mystical pursuits. Some also became famous for their attainments in mathematics. In the latter branch Rabbi Joshua himself attained considerable celebrity. An anecdote is related of him which, if true, would display an acquaintance with mathematics and astronomy far beyond that of the age in which he flourished. It is related that, when on a long sea voyage, in company with Rabban Gamaliel, perhaps on their journey to Rome, the provisions of all on board began to fail, with the exception of those of Joshua, who could even supply the wants of his

[1] Jer. Maas. Sheni v. 56*b*.   Comp. Jost, iii. 204.
[2] Jer. Chag. i. 75*d* ; b. Sanh. 32*b*.

less provident colleague. In fact, the journey had lasted far
beyond its anticipated duration, and Joshua had foreseen this
by calculating that about that time a comet, visible once in
seventy years, would appear, which the ignorant sailors would
mistake for a star, and alter the direction of the vessel
accordingly.[1] The calculation of the course of comets was at
that time wholly unknown.

Another particular which claims our special attention,
was the influence which Joshua possessed with the Roman
authorities. Frequent allusions have already been made to
his journey to Rome, where, as in Palestine, he is represented
as living on terms of intimate intercourse with those high in
power. Indeed, he was probably the only Jewish doctor who
not only enjoyed the full confidence of the Roman authorities,
but who also employed his influence for the advantage both
of his countrymen and of their rulers. This relationship was
the result of his mild and liberal views on all theological and
general questions, and of an unhesitating adoption of the
political principles of Jochanan and of the great Hillel. In
opposition to his former associate, Rabbi Eleazar, Joshua conceded to virtuous heathens a share in the world to come.[2]
In a similar spirit of liberality, when, after the destruction
of the temple, some zealous Jews mentioned their scruples
about partaking in future of flesh or wine, since these could
no longer be presented upon the altar, he showed the
absurdity of these views, by reminding them that on the same
ground it might be deemed improper to eat bread or to
drink water.[3] In general, Joshua was opposed to the unnecessary imposition of legal burdens. He declared himself
dissatisfied with certain measures which, some four years
before the fall of Jerusalem, the school of Shammai had
carried (known by the name of the eighteen enactments),
and which were designed to prevent as much as possible
all intercourse with Gentiles. "On that day," said he,
"the school of Shammai in reality diminished the measure
of doctrine : just as when water is poured into a vessel

[1] Hor. 10*a*.   [2] Tosef. Sanh. 13 ; b. Sanh. 105*a*.
[3] Tosef. Sota 15 ; Baba Bath. 60*b*.

filled with oil, the more water is poured in, the more oil will run over."[1] In fact, he went even further, and viewed with suspicion the indefinite multiplication of Halachas, some of which, he thought, referred to subjects on which Scripture contained little, if any, information. He expressed his scepticism in figurative language : " One pair of tongs," said he, " may indeed be made by means of another, but how are the first to be made ? "[2] The same sceptical tendency we have previously noticed in his opposition to decisions by the Bath-Kol.

Amongst the many pupils of Joshua, none was more justly renowned than Akiba ben Joseph.[3] Indeed, it may well be doubted whether in some respects he did not surpass even Hillel the Great. Combining originality and even genius with moral earnestness and integrity, he could not have played a secondary part in any community. If to these natural qualifications we add delicacy of feeling, a glowing enthusiasm which invested with a halo every conviction, and made it as much matter of the heart as of the intellect, and finally, the necessary condition in his circumstances,— extensive and thorough erudition, the picture is complete. His early history is almost as romantic as his end was tragic. Tradition makes him a proselyte, and derives him ultimately from no less a personage than Sisera. Born[4] in humble circumstances, and nurtured in ignorance, we first meet the youth as a shepherd in the service of the celebrated Kalba Shabua, one of the richest men (of the three rich men) of Jerusalem, who had undertaken to keep the city in provisions during a siege of many years' duration. His beauty, if not his mental qualities, attracted here the attention, and at last secured for the young shepherd the affections, of Kalba's daughter, the beautiful and accomplished Rachel. It was in vain that her father opposed a union apparently so unsuitable, and at last disowned his child with a vow. Rachel gave her hand to Akiba. Only one condition did she attach to it, that

---

[1] Shab. 153b ; jer. Shab. i. 3c.   [2] Tosef. Chag. 1.
[3] Comp. the above-quoted authorities, and Ganz's *Zemach David*.
[4] See esp. Ned. 50a ; Keth. 62b, 63a.

he should in future devote himself to theological studies.
Akiba had formerly equally hated theology and theologians.[1]
His proud spirit could ill brook their pretensions, or the contempt which they heaped on him and others, whom circumstances alone had prevented from attaining to equal, if not
greater distinction.   According to his own statement, he could
have killed them; but now everything was changed.   Akiba
departed immediately after his marriage, by desire of his wife,
for the college, determined to show himself worthy of her
he loved; and poor Rachel had to leave her father's abode.
And now began a period of unexampled devotion on the part
of the faithful bride.   Twelve years, it had been agreed between them, was Akiba to stay away.   Meantime Rachel
lived in a wretched hovel, in extreme poverty.   She had
been delivered of her eldest and only child on a straw litter.
Such was her destitution, that she had even to cut off and
sell her beautiful tresses to procure a miserable subsistence.
Meantime her father, bound by his vow, was unable to assist
her unless she renounced her husband.   The twelve years of
separation had elapsed, and Akiba was hastening to his beloved Rachel.   He had reached her abode, when he overheard
a conversation, in which Rachel replied to the objections of
her father, by expressing a desire that her husband should
remain with the sages other twelve years.   Without entering
the cottage, Akiba immediately returned to his studies.   At
the close of the second period, he returned the most famed
amongst the sages.

At the head of an immense number of followers,—some
state them at 24,000,—Akiba approached the place where
his devoted Rachel lived in wretchedness, and the people
flocked from all parts to see the celebrated teacher.   The
procession moved on, when one whose haggard face was lit
up with a more than ordinary glow pressed through the
wondering crowd, and, unable to control her feelings, fell at
his feet, which she embraced.   Already his followers were
preparing to push aside the forward intruder, but the Rabbi
stayed them.   " Let her alone," said he, " for what I am, and

[1] Pes. 49*b*.

what you are, we owe it all to her." The poor sufferer was
none other than his faithful Rachel, who from that day shared
her husband's honours and wealth.   It is said that her
neighbours had offered to lend her new garments to go and
meet her husband, but the devoted woman preferred meeting
Akiba in the rags she had worn for his sake.   Tradition adds
that Kalba Shabua was freed from his vow as applying to
ignorant and not to learned Akiba, and that he left his ample
fortune to his celebrated son-in-law.   Akiba's affection towards Rachel manifested itself in every possible way.   It is
said that on one occasion he presented her with a golden
head-dress, representing Jerusalem in its beauty.[1]   So
gorgeous was the ornament, that Rabban Gamaliel's wife,
jealous of Rachel's distinction, would fain have had her
husband interdict its use.   But the Nasi refused, remarking
that she who for Akiba's sake had parted with her own hair,
might well wear any ornament on her head.

It would indeed have been very difficult seriously to
disagree with Akiba.   Better than any other, he knew how
to overcome prejudices, to disarm suspicion, and to conquer
envy and jealousy.   He could whisper comfort into the heart
of the mourner, or stimulate the languishing into energetic
action.   Equally beloved and respected by his teachers and
his pupils, by the learned and illiterate, his devotion to his
country and its cause was only equalled by his readiness to
act and to suffer for it.   Withal, he was so modest, that
during the lives of Rabban Gamaliel and of Joshua, he only
filled a subordinate post, although his extensive learning and
influence might long before have raised him to the highest
dignity.   Ever ready to perform a delicate or a disagreeable
duty, from which others might shrink, it will be remembered
that he was selected to announce to his former teacher, Rabbi
Eleazar, the sentence of excommunication, and on another
occasion to request Eleazar ben Azariah to resign the presidency
in favour of Rabban Gamaliel.   These and similar difficult
tasks he performed with admirable tact and grace.   The
noisy " *odium theologicum* " of Jamnia left Rabbi Akiba alone

[1] Jer. Shab. vi. 7*d*.

in the peaceful enjoyment of his honours. Alas, that his end should present so sad a contrast to his prosperity! Happily the loving Rachel was taken away before Akiba's martyrdom. [We need not attempt to separate solid fact from poetic legend in the account of Akiba's early history. It is enough to say that a large historical basis for the traditions about this Rabbi is implied by the constant allusions which are made to them in Talmudic literature.]

Rabbi Akiba had studied under three different doctors, and derived from each a claim to peculiar distinction. From Nahum of Gimso he had learned those exegetical principles which attached such celebrity to the name of that theologian. Eleazar ben Hyrcanus had probably laid the foundation of his more solid learning, while Rabbi Joshua ben Chananjah initiated him in the secrets of mystical theology. In these various departments he seems almost equally to have distinguished himself, and to have outshone his teachers. Rabbi Eleazar had, indeed, for a long time been doubtful of the spirit and tendencies of his quick, inquisitive pupil. His was not the disposition immediately to gain upon Eleazar. For thirteen years, tradition asserts, would Eleazar not condescend upon one single thorough explanation in answer to the questions with which Akiba overwhelmed him.[1] Nor can we wonder at this, when we remember, on the one hand, Eleazar's strict adherence to pure traditionalism, and, on the other, that Akiba's exegetical principles must have led him in an almost opposite direction from his teacher. But in theological controversy Rabbi Eleazar was not the peer of his pupil. Notwithstanding the contrast between them, Rabbi Akiba was probably indebted to Eleazar for that thorough acquaintance with the Halacha which enabled him afterwards to introduce a new arrangement into that science, known as the Mishna of Rabbi Akiba. Before that period considerable difficulty had been felt in the study of the various Halachas, which were neither written down nor properly arranged upon an intelligible plan; hence it required enormous labour and a very faithful memory to retain this mass of traditions.

[1] Jer. Pes. vi. 33*b*.

[Now for the first time the traditional law was codified and committed to writing.[1]]   Rabbi Akiba arranged the Halachas first after their contents : as, for example, into those concerning Sabbath days, marriage questions, etc., and then enumerated them in such a manner as to assist the memory of the student.   Thus, for example, *thirty-six* kinds of crime were designated by Scripture as deserving of the punishment of being " cut off " : *fifteen* degrees of relationship constituted valid obstacles to marriage with a deceased brother's widow, etc.   Besides this arrangement of the Mishna, he also grounded its text upon Scripture, or at least made the first systematic and consistent attempt towards it.   By the ingenuity of his interpretations, and the authority which he enjoyed, he secured a general reception of this method, and frequently even succeeded in substituting his own decisions for older ones.[2]

A teacher of the reputation and originality of Akiba could scarcely fail to attract numerous students.   But more than the enumeration or exposition of the Halacha did his peculiar and novel method of expounding the Scriptures fascinate the hearers.   It was something new,—it opened ways for the exercise of ingenuity, and its results were made subservient to the interests of traditionalism.   Not that this method was entirely new ; it had been originated by Hillel the Great, who had proposed seven exegetical rules.   It had been further developed by Nahum of Gimso, under whom Akiba had in part studied.   According to the view of Nahum, certain defined particles employed in the text were to be looked upon as so many indications of a hidden meaning in the words.   Rabbi Akiba not only adopted this principle, but went much beyond it.   Starting with an erroneous notion of the character of inspiration, he refused to submit the sacred text to the same critical rules as other writings.   He main-

---

[1] [Against the mistaken belief that it was at this time forbidden to write down the traditional law, see especially Strack, *Einleitung in den Thalmud*, pp. 46-55. Some scholars maintain that written collections of Halachas existed at a still earlier period ; cf. Strack, *ut sup.* p. 61.]

[2] Comp. Grätz, iv. 57 f. ; Derenbourg, pp. 396-401.

tained that *every sentence, word, and particle* in the Bible must
have its use and meaning. He denied that mere rhetorical
figures, repetitions, or accumulations occurred in the Bible.
Every word, syllable, and letter which was not absolutely
requisite to express the meaning which it was desired to
convey, must, he maintained, serve some ulterior purpose, and
be intended to indicate a special meaning.

Akiba reduced his views to a system. The seven
exegetical principles of Hillel were extended and developed,
and they were now strictly applied to every possible case,
irrespective of the consequences of such conclusions. Contrary to former practice, he applied these principles not only
in hagadic interpretations, but in the study of the Halacha,
in the highest judicial procedures, and even as groundwork
for fresh inferences. The adoption of views apparently so
dangerous will in part be accounted for, when we remember
the increase of traditions, and the felt necessity of finding
some support for them in the Scriptures, if the written and
the oral law were not to be placed in irreconcilable antagonism
to each other. Sometimes, however, these principles were
put to a severe test. Thus, on one occasion they were to be
applied to the text, " Thou shalt honour the Lord thy God,"
in which a particle not absolutely requisite was discovered.
One of Akiba's pupils objected that it might be inferred that
someone else besides God was to be supremely reverenced;
but Akiba removed his doubts by replying that the particle
in question was intended to point to the Law, which ought to
be honoured next to the Lord.[1]

In fact, this method of interpretation had in reality
become necessary, and met the deepest wants of traditionalism.
Owing to the number of Halachas, to the controversies which
they elicited, and the difficulty which attached to their application in the different circumstances which the ingenuity of
the sages conceived, or the changes of time brought to light,
it was feared that these unwritten traditions, which depended
on the authority of individuals, would either be forgotten, fall

---

[1] Jer. Sot. v. 7 ; [cf. Pes. 22*b* ; Kidd. 57*a*, where the same particle is interpreted as pointing to the doctors of the Law].

into disrepute, or by and by prove insufficient.   On the other hand, while Akiba's method dazzled the sages by its ingenuity and speciousness, it also promised to elevate tradition above passing opinions, and to place it on an immovable basis.   We need scarce point out the groundlessness of this hope ; but meantime the synagogue indulged in happy anticipations of the future.   Akiba's method was hailed as the commencement of a new period.   His contemporaries yielded to the most extravagant transports of delight.   Thus Rabbi Tarphon,— possibly the Rabbi Tryphon who afterwards disputed with the Christian philosopher, Justin Martyr,—who had formerly been looked upon as Akiba's superior in lore, now yielded this place to him with these words: " He that forsakes thee, forsakes life : what tradition had forgotten thou hast restored by thy method of interpretation." [1]   Rabbi Joshua, Akiba's former teacher, although wary on these subjects, could not repress a wish that Jochanan ben Saccai had been alive to witness the firm establishment of the Halacha.[2]   In their extravagance, later Rabbis went so far as to assert that Akiba had discovered many things of which even Moses had been ignorant.   After the manner of the time,[3] a legend related that Moses had at one time inquired of the Lord as to the meaning and purpose of the marks which He had added to the Hebrew letters in the Bible, and had in reply been informed, that after many generations Rabbi Akiba was to make them the basis of the Halacha.   It was added that Moses had requested to be allowed to see this great teacher, but that he had to sit eight rows behind Rabbi Akiba (in token of his inferiority), and felt unable to comprehend the meaning of his interpretations.

From statements like these, it will be easy to infer what amount of authority Rabbi Akiba enjoyed in the Sanhedrin. Indeed, such was his influence, that in his absence the sages would not decide on any important question.   It was held that " when Rabbi Akiba was absent, the Law was away." [4] But it must not be inferred that his principles met with no

[1] Zebach 13a.
[2] M. Sota v. 2.
[3] Menach. 29b; quoted in Men. Ham. i. 178.
[4] Mid. Cant. on i. 3.

opposition from any of the eminent men of that age. Amongst them none was more distinguished by birth, personal character, or learning, than Rabbi Ishmael ben Elisa, the descendant of a priestly family, the pupil of Rabbi Joshua and of Nechunjah ben Hakanah. Tradition represents his father as a high priest ;[1] and a legend relates how Ishmael was at one time a captive at Rome, where Rabbi Joshua had seen him, and procured his liberation by a large ransom.[2] From that Rabbi he derived much of that sobriety of judgment which was his distinguishing characteristic. Afterwards Ishmael retired to his ancestral possessions in the south of Palestine, where he employed his ample means in bestowing dowries on Jewish maidens whom the late disasters of his country had impoverished.[3] Like his teacher, he refused to acknowledge the validity of any Halacha which was not directly based upon the Word, and only acknowledged the existence of three exceptions to that rule.[4] As formerly Nechunjah ben Hakanah had opposed the exegetical principles of Nahum of Gimso, so now Rabbi Ishmael rejected those of Rabbi Akiba, and kept by the rules of Hillel, which he somewhat altered by rejecting one, revising another, and subdividing a third into eight parts. These principles of Rabbi Ishmael are known as his thirteen exegetical canons. The fundamental difference between these two sages consisted in this, that Ishmael always retained the natural sense of a passage, and held that superfluous words or syllables in a text were not meant to indicate something foreign to the obvious meaning of the passage. [It is, however, only in a comparative sense that we can speak of Rabbi Ishmael as upholding the literal meaning of Scripture.] In opposition to Akiba, he refused to apply mere logical deductions from biblical texts in criminal procedure, and he opposed the practice of employing one deduction from the Law as basis for other deductions. The story of his martyrdom will by and by engage our attention.

---

[1] [According to Grätz, iv. 60, he was a descendant of the priestly family of the Fabi ; but see Derenbourg, p. 387.]

[2] Gitt. 58*a*. [3] Nedar. 66*a*. [4] Jer. Kid. i. 59*d*.

Besides his merits in connection with the Halacha, and his peculiar method of Scripture interpretation, Rabbi Akiba distinguished himself by acquaintanceship with the mystical theology of his day.   This science, which was only to be communicated to a few initiated, treated especially of the history of the creation, of the glory and attributes of the Deity, and of His connection with His creatures, as described by the Prophet Isaiah, and specially by Ezekiel in his vision of the chariot.   [The first chapter of Genesis and the first chapter of Ezekiel were the favourite starting-points for an elaborate system of theosophic speculation, and the strange fancies which were thus formed concerning the spiritual world, developed ultimately into the Kabalah of the Middle Ages.] It was thought that an acquaintance with such mysteries bestowed peculiar powers on the initiated.   Flames of fire, it was said, played round their heads while engaged in studying the Law; and, when necessary, even miracles could be performed by them.   But, in some cases, this knowledge also endangered its possessors.   But Rabbi Akiba had engaged in this study only with profit to himself.   Before him Rabbi Joshua, and after him Chananja Chachinai, were distinguished mystics.   Still such pursuits were always deemed dangerous, and, on one occasion, even Rabbi Akiba was admonished rather to devote his time to the study of the Halacha, and to beware of profaning the name of the Deity.[1]   These apprehensions are illustrated in a parabolic account of the fate of four sages who entered " the enclosed garden," *i.e.* engaged in theosophical studies.   One of them, it was said, had looked round and died; another had looked round and lost his reason; a third eventually tried to destroy the garden; while the fourth alone had entered and returned in safety.[2]

This parable was meant to illustrate the history of three contemporaries of Akiba, and of the latter sage.   The first of these four, Simon ben Asai, died at an early age.   From a desire to give himself wholly to study, he had abstained from a marriage which would have closely connected him with

[1] Chag. 14*a*; San. 38*b*.   Comp. Ersch, *Encycl.* xxvii. 42, etc.   [2] Chag. 14*b*.

Akiba.[1]   In the public orations which this doctor delivered in the market-place of Tiberias, he dwelt especially on the unity of God.   So deep and earnest was his study of the Law, that it was asserted flames of heavenly fire were frequently seen to play round his head.   Such was his moral and ceremonial strictness, that his contemporaries gave him the title " Chasid," the pious.   In popular opinion it was thought to presage piety if a person dreamt of him.[2]

The second of the four theosophic students was Simon ben Soma, renowned for his deep investigations into the meaning of Scripture, which procured for him the appellation of " the sage."   Particularly, he endeavoured to explain in a mystical sense the history of the creation.   One of his inferences, which at the time caused great indignation, is specially remarkable, and in some respects interesting.   From the expression, " God *made* the firmament," he seems to have inferred that its *matter* had not been created at that particular period, but had previously existed,[3]—an inference which, in his case, was probably connected with views of the eternity of matter.   In other respects, also, his teaching sometimes bordered on heresy, so that Rabbi Joshua formally pronounced : " Ben Soma has gone wrong."   The Scripture saying was applied to him : " Hast thou found honey ? eat so much as is sufficient for thee, lest thou be filled therewith and vomit it." [4]

The third of the students in the parable was Elisa the son of Abuja, a wealthy citizen of Jerusalem.   He was early initiated in the study of the Law, but afterwards apostatised from Judaism, and became a bitter persecutor of his brethren. To account for this anomaly in one of the sacred order of Rabbis, Jewish legend has it that Abuja, Elisa's father, had one day invited to his house all the learned in Jerusalem, and amongst them both Eleazar and Joshua.   While these two

---

[1] Comp. Gen. Rab. 34 ; Keth. 63*a*.

[2] Ber. 57*b*.

[3] Gen. Rab. 4.   On this passage comp. Bacher, *Tannait.* i. 425 ; Hamb. *Real-Encycl.* Suppl. " Ben Soma."

[4] Chag. 14*b* ; jer. Chag. ii. 77*b*.

sages conversed about the Law, flames played around their
heads.   The ambitious Abuja immediately resolved to train
his own son to the study of the Law, so that he also might
obtain similar distinction.   The motives which had influenced
Abuja in devoting his son to the Law being impure, the latter
was afterwards so far left to himself.[1]   Of his conduct and
death we shall have occasion to treat in the sequel.   It was
said that the proximate cause of his fall was the study of
mystical theology, which, improperly understood, upset his
religious and even his moral principles.   However, the change
had long been preparing.   At a later period, his former class-
fellows would relate, that even while attending the Jewish
college, he had often been noticed to carry with him writings
of the " Minim " (probably of Gnostics), and that he had even
been in the habit of quoting Greek poetry.[2]   The apprehensions thus excited were realised by his apostasy, on
account of which he bare the name of Acher (the other, the
apostate).   In popular belief, it was supposed to be an evil
augury to dream of him.   However, even after his apostasy
he was frequently consulted by his former pupil, the celebrated Rabbi Mëir, of whom more in the sequel.   The fourth
and only unscathed visitor of " the enclosed garden " was
Rabbi Akiba, whose interpretations often bear traces of his
favourite study.

Though naturally of an ardent and even enthusiastic
temperament, Akiba knew better than his contemporaries how
to console them in sorrows, which he felt even more keenly
than they, and how for a time to bear with patience the
burden of his nation's oppression.   He would always cheerfully express his conviction that whatever happened was sent
from heaven for good.   This principle he was wont, after his
own fashion, to illustrate by two occurrences in his history.[3]
It happened, so he related, that on a journey night overtook him
in a place whose inhospitable inhabitants refused him shelter ;
accordingly he had to spend the night at some distance from
that village in the open air.   He had with him a lighted

[1] Jer. Chag. ii. 77b.   [2] B. Chag. 15b.
[3] Ber. 60b.   Comp. also Jost, iii. 206 etc.

torch, a donkey to carry his baggage, and a cock to awaken him at an early hour for devotions and study. To complete the catalogue of his miseries, the wind extinguished the torch, a lion devoured his donkey, and a fox killed the cock. But what was the astonishment and gratitude of our Rabbi for his escape, when he learned that on the same night the inhospitable place which had refused him shelter had been taken by enemies and completely destroyed! On another occasion Akiba was travelling with some of his companions to Jerusalem.[1] At the sight of it his friends could not refrain from tears, and their grief deepened when they saw a jackal running across the mountain on which the temple had once stood. Akiba alone preserved his equanimity, and comforted his friends by reminding them that if prophecy had so literally been fulfilled in the desolation of the temple, they might also anticipate an equal accomplishment of the promised blessings.

Alas! that erroneous views and too ardent anticipations should have so far misled him as afterwards to become the principal supporter of a leader such as Bar Cochba. When at last he was roused from his dreams of hope, deep disappointment and bitterness seized him, if we may judge from the following misanthropic advice which he is said to have given to his son Joshua: "Teach not in the most elevated place in the city; live not in a town where the teachers of the Law have the management of affairs; enter not suddenly into thy house, far less into that of thy neighbour (to avoid seeing any mischief); keep always shoes on thy feet; eat early in summer, lest the heat rob thee of the enjoyment—in winter, lest the cold benumb thee (enjoy thy comforts before any deprive thee of them); convert thy holidays into work days, in order not to become dependent on others; and take care to choose as thy companions those on whom fortune smiles."[2] We close this sketch by quoting a few of the most remarkable of Akiba's recorded sayings.[3] "Man is loved of God, for He created him in His own image; but the love which made this fact

---

[1] Macc. 24*b*.   [2] Pes. 112*a*.   [3] Pirke Aboth iii. 14 ff.

known to man was even greater than that which so created him. . . . Beloved are Israel in that they are called the children of God, but greater still was the love which acquainted them with the fact of their being called the children of God. . . . Everything is foreseen of God, but freedom of choice is granted to man; the world is judged in mercy, but everything depends on the quantity of work done by man." He was also wont to say: " Everything is given to man on trust; a net is spread for all living; the shop is opened and the merchant gives credit, but a book is open, and his hand records every transaction."

Besides those already mentioned, other eminent sages filled up the circle of teachers and scholars congregated in Jamnia. Some there were amongst them who had seen the temple in its glory—some belonged to another generation. In general, we may name as the five principal teachers of this period, Rabban Gamaliel, and Rabbis Eleazar, Joshua, Akiba, and Ishmael. Less distinguished sages are sometimes described as " judging in the presence of the wise." Of these, Simon ben Soma, Simon ben Asai, Chananja Chachinai, Chanina the Egyptian, and Simon the Temanite, are specially named; but there is considerable variety in the lists which are given of the " judges."

To complete our picture of the Sanhedrin, we add a short sketch of other notable personages in the sacred college. Rabbi Tarphon or Tryphon, to whom we formerly referred, was a friend of Rabbi Akiba, and afterwards the Ab-beth-din. He was very rich, and latterly dispensed much of his wealth to the poor. Noted as a bitter enemy of Christianity, he inclined towards the principles of the school of Shammai. The recorded sayings of this doctor prove how intimately that class of theologians had learned to connect a heavenly reward with the study of the Law, and how largely the element of merit bulked in their personal piety. Rabbi Eleazar of Modin was deeply versed in the Hagada, and afterwards occupied a prominent position in the last Jewish war, in which his death formed one of the saddest episodes. Rabbi Joses the Galilean was well known. His two sons also distinguished themselves in the theological world. An incident in the life of Joses is related to illustrate his almost proverbial kindness and forbearance.[1] It is said that his wife had been so imperious and quarrelsome, that he was ultimately obliged to divorce her. After her separation, she disposed of her hand to the watchman of the city. In course of time, when her second husband grew blind, and was consequently unable to follow his former occupation, she had to lead him about the streets to seek alms. Carefully had the now humbled woman hitherto avoided the street in which her former husband lived. However, the blind man at last, by continued ill-usage, forced her to knock as beggar at the door of the house of which she had once been the mistress. The sound of her well-known voice attracted Rabbi Joses. He took her and her husband into his house, and from that time provided for them.

Of the other sages, Rabbi Ishbab was employed as secretary to the council, and at a later period fell a martyr after the suppression of Bar Cochba's rebellion. Rabbi Chuzpith had been public interpreter to Rabban Gamaliel. Rabbi Juda ben Baba afterwards nobly sacrificed his life in the endeavour to perpetuate the profession of Rabbi; and Rabbi Chananja ben Teradion was throughout a zealous student. Tradition relates that he was afterwards burnt alive in the roll from which he had so often taught. His spirit and disposition may be gathered from the remark, that if two persons could sit together without discoursing of the Law, theirs was " the council of the ungodly " (Ps. i. 1); but if two, when in company, spake of these things one with another, the glory of the Lord was amongst them (Mal. iii. 16).[2] Rabbi Jochanan ben Nuri was a warm friend of the Nasi Gamaliel, although sometimes his opponent in theological discussion. When, after the decease of Gamaliel, his successor and former antagonist, Rabbi Joshua, proposed to abolish many of the ordinances which he had passed, Rabbi Jochanan successfully opposed this petty act of vindictiveness. He remarked at the time that it was scarcely proper " to

---

[1] Jer. Keth. xi. 34*b* ; Levit. Rab. 34. [2] Pirke Aboth iii. 2.

fight the lion after he was dead." [1]   On some subjects, however, the views of this Rabbi were neither sound nor in
agreement with those of his colleagues.   Thus, along with
others, he opposed [2] the doctrine of the eternity of punishments.   It is remarkable how different were the views of the
Rabbins generally on this subject.   Thus Rabbi Akiba
supposed that the punishments of the future world only
lasted for one year, supporting this view by an appeal to
Isa. lxvi. 23 ; while from the same passage Rabbi Jochanan
inferred that they only lasted " from the Feast of Unleavened
Bread to that of Weeks."   Lastly, amongst these sages
Rabbi Joses ben Kisma was known as a warm supporter
of Roman authority, and at the same time so zealous
a student of the Law, that he refused the most tempting
offers to settle in a place where there was no regular
college of sages. [3]

Two other names deserve to be mentioned, as celebrated
even beyond Jewish circles.   They are those of Samuel the
Less, and of Onkelos or Akylas, the translator of the Bible.
The origin of the title " the Less," borne by the former Rabbi,
is unknown.   His mild and gentle character is shown by his
favourite maxim : " Rejoice not when thine adversary falleth ;
and let not thine heart be glad when he stumbleth " (Prov.
xxiv. 17). [4]   On his deathbed he is said to have uttered a
prophecy about the troublous times which were so soon to
come upon his countrymen. [5]   Samuel the Less was a bitter
enemy of Christianity.   At the request of the Nasi, he composed a formula of excommunication against the " Christian
heretics," which was ordered to be inserted as part of the
daily prayers. [6]   Samuel was also famed amongst his contemporaries for modesty.   As an instance of this quality, it
was related that when Rabban Gamaliel II. had on one
occasion summoned a council of seven sages to deliberate on

---

[1] Erub. 41a. [In jer. Gitt. ix. 1 the same saying is attributed to Rabbi
Joshua himself in defence of a certain decision of Rabbi Eleazar ben Azariah.
Comp. Derenbourg, p. 368.]

[2] Eduj. ii. 10.   [3] Pirke Aboth vi. 9.   [4] *Ut supra*, iv. 19.

[5] Tosef. Sota 13 ; jer. *ib.* ix. 24b ; b. *ib.* 48b.

[6] Ber. 28b.   Comp. Chap. X. ; also Derenbourg, p. 345 f.

the insertion of an additional month into the Jewish calendar, —instead of seven, eight Rabbins had appeared. The Nasi, indignant at the intrusion, without naming him, ordered the individual who had come uninvited to withdraw. To spare another the affront, Samuel immediately .rose, and declared that he had been the uninvited assessor, pleading as excuse that he had only come to gain information. Rabban Gamaliel understood the motive of Samuel, and bade him stay as being in every way worthy to. act as member of such an assemblage. This conduct, more accommodating than truthful, insured him general commendation.[1] According to popular opinion, a voice from heaven pronounced him to be " the worthiest of his age." At his death the Nasi himself delivered a funeral discourse.

A difficult and intricate question in Jewish history is that which refers to the identity or diversity of Onkelos (whose name is attached to a paraphrase in Aramaic) and Akylas or Aquila, who has left a Greek translation of the Old Testament. There is, however, now a general agreement among scholars that the two personages are identical, and that the Aramaic Targum of Onkelos is really a translation in the manner of Aquila, made perhaps in the third century, but based on materials of considerably earlier date. Recent Jewish writers [2] have, on most insufficient grounds, sought to identify this Akylas with Aquila, the husband of Priscilla, who was so eminent an ornament of Christianity. Of the life of Akylas, or Onkelos, we know but little, for much that is told about him is certainly fabulous. The stories connected with his history, as recorded by the Fathers,[3] and in the writings of the Rabbins, however, are, that Akylas was originally a noble heathen, a native of Sinope, in Pontus, and related to the Emperor Hadrian ; [4] that at the time of the return of the Christians from Pella, he had, on seeing certain miracles performed by them, adopted Christianity, but never wholly given up mystical studies; that he had finally been

---

[1] Jer. Sanh. i. 18*c* ; comp. b. Sanh. 11*a*.   [2] Grätz, iv. 437 ff.
[3] Hieron. *Ep. ad Pam.* 57 ; Epiph. *de Mens. et Ponder.* 14 f.
[4] Tanchuma, Mishpatim ; comp. Exod. Rab. 30, and Epiph. *ut supra.*

expelled from the Church, and then adopted Judaism.   Other
authorities ascribe his apostasy to love of a Jewish maiden.
Be this as it may, Akylas became at last a most zealous
traditionalist, and, by his learning and influence, materially
assisted the Jewish cause.   He seems to have been acquainted
with the Nasi Gamaliel II., in honour of whom he celebrated
costly and even royal funeral solemnities.   He is described
as even more strict in his observance of the Law than the
Patriarch himself.[1]   After his father's death he received his
share of the inheritance due to him, but would not consent
to take an equivalent for the idols which his brothers had
retained.   In fact, he threw the compensation sent him into
the Dead Sea.[2]

Akylas was a friend of Rabbins Eleazar and Joshua, but
especially of the celebrated Akiba, by whose instructions he
chiefly profited.   His translation of the Bible was almost
painfully literal.   The expressions which in the original
admit of a doubtful or double interpretation, are rendered
into Greek in a manner analogous.[3]   In biblical interpretation
he followed the method of his teacher, and adapted his
version to the purposes of Akiba's exegesis.   At a later
period Akylas recast his translation,[4] when it became, if
possible, still more in agreement with the comments of his
master.   This version he submitted to Rabbins Eleazar,
Joshua, and Akiba, who highly approved of it, and applied
to it the Scripture prediction, according to which Japhet (the
type of Grecianism) should dwell in the tents of Shem.[5]   It
may here be remarked, that the version of the LXX. had
formerly been used everywhere by the Jews in the Dispersion,
and perhaps also in Palestine.   But, owing to the fuller
recognition of the deficiencies of the Septuagint, and still
more to the use made of it by Christians, this version fell
into disfavour.   Later Rabbins compared the day on which
it had been finished to that on which the golden calf had

---

[1] Tosef. Chag. iii.   [2] Jerus. Demai vi. 25*d*.
[3] Grätz, iv. 114.   Aquila also attempted to reproduce Hebrew etymologies
in Greek.
[4] Hieron. in Ezek. c. iv.   [5] Megilla 9*b*.

been worshipped.[1]   On the other hand, the Rabbinistic translation of Akylas was pronounced faultless, declared of equal
sanctity with the Hebrew original, and its public use was
recommended.

We shall afterwards have occasion to recur to this
subject, and meantime return to the political events which
befell Israel at this period.

[1] Mass. Soferim i. 7.

CHAPTER VII

THE LAST JEWISH WAR UNDER BAR COCHBA

It will be remembered that the aged Nerva had felt obliged to associate Ulpius Trajanus with himself in the empire. He did not long survive this event. Nerva died in January 98, and left to Trajan the sole direction of the empire. The new emperor was popular with the legions, strong enough to repress the licentious mob, and dreaded by foreign enemies, so that his accession seemed to bode nothing but prosperity to Rome. Nor were the expectations of his subjects deceived. Trajan's administration showed that he was actuated by principles of moderation and justice, and he alone of the Roman emperors received the title of "the Best."[1] Nevertheless, his reign was not to be one of peace. [It would be unjust to Trajan to suppose that his wars were due solely to a desire of conquest; but he was by training and habit a soldier, and it was natural that he should prefer to solve the difficulties which arose on the frontiers, rather by recourse to arms than by the arts of diplomacy. Accustomed to life in the camp, he must have found it irksome to live in the constraints of society at Rome. The army had now, through his reforms, been brought to a high state of efficiency, and a statesman like Trajan could see the advantages to be gained by readjusting the boundaries of the empire.[2]] But it was also needful to consider whether the circumstances of the State rendered fresh conquests expedient. The case is different with a young nation which enters on the career of military grandeur and overruns older empires, and a vast empire

---

[1] Pliny, *Paneg.* c. 88 ; Dio Cassius, lxviii. 23.
[2] Comp. Mommsen, *Provinces,* ii. 70 f.

which has already begun to exhibit signs of decay, and whose boundaries only touch upon barbarous tribes. In general, the latter will rarely be permanently subdued, unless they are conquered by the civilisation as well as by the arms of their opponents, or unless their territory can be readily occupied. These conditions could be carried out only to a limited extent in the wars waged by Trajan. Consequently, his campaigns led only to endless contests, alike fruitless and weakening to the empire.

About three years after his accession, Trajan led his legions against the barbarians who inhabited the northern bank of the Danube (the present Roumania), with whom Domitian had formerly concluded a dishonourable peace, by which he had even consented to become tributary to them. Trajan was more successful, but it was not till the year 107 that Dacia was fully converted into a Roman province. On his return to Rome, Trajan celebrated his victories by splendid popular entertainments, which lasted for 123 days in succession, and perpetuated their memory by a column on which these exploits were represented, and a colossal figure of himself was placed. But it was principally the East which engaged his attention. [Here his presence was urgently demanded by the somewhat dubious state of relations between the empire and the Parthians. The Parthian king had presumed to nominate a successor to the throne of Armenia, although that State was vassal to Rome. It is true that King Chosroes and his nominee, alarmed by the threats of Trajan, expressed themselves ready to submit to the emperor's wishes; but Trajan had resolved to avoid such troubles in future by reducing Armenia to the form of a province, and as a necessary consequence to extend the frontier line of the empire to the Tigris. All overtures for peace were summarily rejected.] In the spring of 118 A.D., the old emperor, now in his sixty-third year, put himself at the head of his legions, and overran the Parthian dominions. Hampered by dissensions within his realm, King Chosroes could not resist his victorious progress. The occupant of the Armenian throne was deposed, and his country converted into a province of

the empire.   Penetrating still farther, Trajan subjugated
Mesopotamia, and took a number of fenced cities, amongst
which we specially name Nisibis as having been almost exclusively held by Jews.   Nowhere did he encounter serious
resistance.   Abgar, the ruler of Edessa, acknowledged the
supremacy of the emperor, and Mesopotamia became a Roman
province.   At the end of the summer Trajan withdrew, and
passed the winter in Antioch.

In the spring of the year 116, Trajan entered on a
second Parthian campaign.[1]   He advanced beyond Nisibis,
crossed the Tigris, and overran Adiabene.   His progress was
not unopposed, but everywhere victory followed in his wake.
[A third province, bearing the name of Assyria, was added to
the Roman Empire.   Trajan, who had received from the
Senate the well-earned title of Parthicus, now continued his
march down the Tigris to Babylonia, where both Ctesiphon,
the Parthian capital, and Seleuceia, on the opposite bank of
the Tigris, fell into his hands.   The victor's desire for conquest seemed to have been stimulated by success, and when
at length he reached the shore of the Persian Gulf, he is said
to have wished for youth, that he might rival the conquests
of Alexander.[2]]   But his difficulties were really now beginning,
and Trajan was soon made to feel how unsubstantial his
conquests were.   The countries over which he asserted the
supremacy of his arms could only be held by the presence of
the victorious legions.   As these disappeared, the barbarians
rose once more against their new masters.   Even while he
was lingering at the north of the Tigris, his newly-conquered
provinces had revolted. Seleuceia, Edessa, and Nisibis had
all attacked their Roman garrisons, and either expelled them
put them to death.   Meanwhile, by the fatigues of this
or expedition and the vexation occasioned by its fruitlessness,
the emperor had contracted a disease which forced him to
resign the command.   In these new risings the Jews bore a
conspicuous part; nor was their resistance to the Roman
dominion now confined to the Parthian Empire.   It had
already begun to make itself felt in various provinces.

[1] Mommsen, *Provinces*, ii. 68 ff.   [2] Dio Cassius, lxviii. 29.

Jewish authorities, ignoring all political movements, relate fanciful stories to account for the disasters which befell their nation during the "wicked" Trajan's reign. One legend informs us that a national feast, celebrating the birth of a son to the emperor, had fallen on the 9th of Ab, when the Jews, instead of joining in the general mirth, had mourned, as was their wont, in commemoration of the anniversary of the destruction of Jerusalem, and that this had been charged against them as a want of loyalty. On another occasion, while the imperial family were plunged in grief at the death of a daughter of Trajan, the Jews had, as usual at the Feast of Dedication, lighted up their windows,—a procedure which was misinterpreted into a demonstration of joy on their part.[1] But it is not difficult to assign real motives for this renewed attempt at liberation. Although the Romans had warm friends even among the teachers of the Law, yet, as their contempt and insolence vented themselves in various acts of petty persecution, so the Jews, whose religious and national prejudices were at all times easily roused, would retaliate as opportunity offered. And now the Parthians were again risen against their formidable enemies, the victories of the Roman legions in the East had led to no lasting result. Accordingly, while Trajan was engaged in his Parthian campaigns (about the year 115), the Jewish rebellion broke out almost at the same time in Africa, in the island of Cyprus, and in Mesopotamia. [It appears, however, very doubtful whether Palestine took on this occasion any active part in the revolt.[2]] The hostile standard seems first to have been raised in Cyrene, where, as formerly stated, the Jews had for a long period enjoyed great privileges.[3] The leaders of the insurgents in this province were Andreas and Lucuas (or perhaps only one individual who may have borne these two names). At first the movement had only the appearance of

---

[1] Jer. Succa v. 55*b*; Mid. Lam. on i. 16.

[2] [A rebellion in Palestine is denied by Schürer, I. ii. 286 f; Derenbourg, p. 404 ff.; but it is maintained by Grätz, iv. 125 f., 439 ff.; comp. Mommsen, *Provinces*, ii. 221–223.]

[3] For the description of this war, compare Eusebius, *Hist. Eccl.* iv. 2; Dio Cassius, lxviii. 32.

a common revolt. The Jews rose against their Greek and Roman neighbours, and killed all on whom they could lay hands. As the people were wholly unprepared, and the choice Roman troops had accompanied Trajan on his Eastern expedition, the rising became daily more formidable as the number of the rebels increased with their successes. Gradually the insurrection assumed the appearance of a civil war. It spread, and the Jews of Egypt now made common cause with their victorious brethren. Then commenced a series of the most shocking cruelties against the heathens, such as only deep-rooted hatred could have suggested, or long-restrained vengeance perpetrated. The mixed multitude which follows in the wake of every religious movement, destitute of principle, has only passions. If these are no longer restrained, the result must always be terrible. In the present instance, these passions had long only awaited an occasion for their outburst. Now that the Jews were victorious, they fell upon the Greeks and Romans. According to the account of Dio, they literally tore them in pieces, they sawed them asunder, they ate their flesh, they wallowed in their blood, they wound themselves round with their entrails, and dressed themselves in their skins. It was comparatively a mild fate awarded to some of the heathen captives to fight against each other, or with wild beasts in the arena. Though some Jewish historians have attempted to cavil at these details, none has ventured to deny their substantial accuracy. However we may shrink in horror from such deeds, we need scarcely wonder at these manifestations of the savage in man.

The success of the Jews called into the field the Roman garrison under the governor Lupus. But the few and dispirited soldiers were not able to make a stand against the wild enthusiasm of the insurgents. Retreating, the Romans threw themselves into Alexandria, on whose Jewish inhabitants they took terrible vengeance. The Jews requited cruelty for cruelty. They now overran the whole country, killing all heathens, whether found in arms or defenceless, and spread even as far as Thebais. [The regular Roman garrison in

Egypt numbered less than 10,000 men,[1] and at the present time the greater part of the troops had probably been called away to the war in the East. The governor of Cyrene had no army, since this was a senatorial province. In both districts, therefore, the insurgents could easily hold their own until reinforcements arrived.]

While the flame of civil war was thus kindled in Africa, it also burst forth from the island of Cyprus. Considering its proximity to Asia Minor and Syria, Cyprus promised to become the most suitable headquarters of the rebels. This island had long been frequented and partly inhabited by Jews. Its commercial position, its important copper mines, which already Herod I. had rented from Augustus,[2] and its flourishing traffic, offered many attractions to Jewish emigrants. The number of these settlers increased as domestic disasters drove so many to seek a voluntary exile. Accordingly, as the Book of Acts also attests, synagogues were scattered over the whole island. Probably there was no immediate occasion for the outbreak in Cyprus. From the temper of the heathens and the circumstances of the Jews, we may indeed infer that provocations had not been wanting. At a given signal, the Jews now rose all over the island. They marched on Salamis, the capital of Cyprus. They took and destroyed it. Here also acts of barbarity, similar to those perpetrated in Africa, stained the insurrection. Altogether, not less than 240,000 Greeks are said to have been slaughtered.

The news of this unexpected and threatening war must have considerably affected Trajan, whose position in the face of an enemy, conquered but unsubdued, was in itself sufficiently dangerous. At the same time there was a terrible war raging in Africa and Cyprus; Palestine was heaving with the underground fire of general discontent; and the Jews on the banks of the Euphrates and Tigris were taking up arms and inciting the natives to renew the contest against Rome. But Trajan showed himself equal to the emergency.

---

[1] Comp. Marquardt, *Röm. Staatsverwaltung*, i. 285, ii. 433.
[2] Jos. *Ant.* xvi. 4. 5.

He immediately detached one of his ablest generals, Martius Turbo, at the head of a considerable force of infantry and cavalry, to quell the rising in Africa.[1]   The task was one of no slight difficulty ; but, in the end, Roman discipline, and especially the services of the cavalry, of which the Jews were wholly destitute, decided in favour of the Roman soldiery, in spite of the desperation with which the insurgents fought. The Jews yielded only after protracted defence and many bloody affrays.   It was now the turn of the victorious legions to avenge the wrongs of the heathens and the disasters of their comrades in arms.   There is a Jewish legend which relates to the suppression of this revolt.   We are told that Trajan was urged by his wife to punish the Jews for their rebellion, before he made war on the barbarians.   A favourable wind brought him in five days to the scene of the war.   The Jews were surrounded by the Roman legions, the men were at once cut down, and their wives had the alternative offered them of yielding to the lusts of the soldiery, or of sharing the fate of their husbands.   None would accept such a mode of self-preservation.   With one accord they desired the soldiers " to do to them who were above ground as they had done to those who now lay beneath it." [2]   For many years the desolation of whole districts deprived of their inhabitants, and the ruined and blackened cottages, bore testimony to the horrors of this war.   Even Alexandria suffered considerably, and it was only after the lapse of a long time that the traces of Roman revenge were effaced.[3]   Probably at this period the celebrated synagogue of Alexandria was levelled with the ground.[4]

With equal severity the Romans crushed the revolt in Cyprus, where the Jews were commanded by one Artemion. Without recording the particulars of this campaign, which no doubt in all essentials resembled that of Lybia, history has only chronicled the fact that every Jew on the island was

[1] Euseb. *Hist. Eccl.* iv. 2.
[2] Jer. Succa v. 55*b* ;   Mid. Lam. on i. 16.   Comp. Grätz, iv. 128 f.
[3] Euseb. *Chron.* (ed. Schœne) ii. 164 f., on the first year of Hadrian.
[4] Jer. Succa v. 55*b*.

killed. Indeed, such was the bitterness of the inhabitants against that wretched race, that ever afterwards Israelites were prevented from setting foot on their inhospitable shores. Even those who might have been obliged by shipwreck to seek a shelter there, did not meet with the sympathy which barbarians would not have withheld, but fell sacrifices to popular fury.[1] However, after this campaign the commerce and influence of Cyprus decreased. The flourishing mart of Asia became impoverished; while, to adopt the graphic language of Jewish chroniclers, the blood of the slain in Africa passed through the sea and mingled with that of the victims in Cyprus.[2]

Trajan was still unsuccessfully engaged in the attempt to subdue the Parthians, when the Jews of Mesopotamia rose in the rear of the Roman army. The emperor despatched against this new foe his favourite general, Lusius Quietus, a Mauritanian by birth, whom, so a later rumour declared, he intended as his successor to the purple. Such was the indignation of the emperor against these Jews, that Quietus was ordered, not only to overcome, but wholly to exterminate, or at least to expel them from these districts. If it was impossible to carry out literally such commands, Quietus at least put down the revolt with relentless cruelty. Nisibis and Edessa were recovered, and thousands of Jews were put to death.[3] Immediately afterwards Lusius Quietus was appointed governor of Judea, [where it was necessary to keep the inhabitants in check with a strong hand].

While his legions were making way amongst the Jewish insurgents, Trajan himself was less successful against his antagonists. His troops had in vain besieged Atra, a small well-defended fortress situated in a desert district.[4] Leaving Ctesiphon, the emperor advanced against it in person; but, after an ineffectual attempt, in which his life was endangered, he was at last obliged to raise the siege. This event put an end to his long-cherished plans of Eastern conquest.

[1] Dio, lxviii. 32.   [2] Jer. Succa, *ut supra*.
[3] Euseb. *ut supra*, 18th year of Trajan ; *Hist. Eccl.* iv. 2.
[4] Dio, lxviii. 31.

Shattered in body and broken in spirit, Trajan returned towards Rome. He had only reached Antioch, in Syria, when illness prevented his further progress. Here he appointed Hadrian governor of Syria. At last he seemed sufficiently recovered again to embark, but he had to be landed at Selinus, a port of Cilicia, where he died, A.D. 117.

Many rumours were current as to the intentions of the late emperor in regard to his successor ; [1] [but there is little reason to doubt that Trajan had intended Hadrian to succeed him, even if he did not live to formally complete his adoption. We cannot suppose that at this period a Moorish captain like Lusius Quietus could have been designed as the future emperor ; and Novatius Priscus, the favourite of the Senate, could only support his claims upon his fame as a jurist. Hadrian was a relative of Trajan, and also connected with him by his marriage to Sabina, the granddaughter of the emperor's sister. In spite of the scandals circulated about Hadrian, and the odium which he excited in Rome during the closing years of his reign, we may unhesitatingly assert that he was well qualified for a ruler. He had already shown himself an able officer both in war and peace, and a skilful administrator in matters military and civil. The different stories, which assert that his adoption was supposititious, vary considerably in their details]. According to one account, in the bed of a darkened room adjoining that of Trajan, lay one of Plotina's accomplices, who, apparently in the broken accents of the dying emperor, formally adopted Hadrian as his successor in the hearing of a large number of witnesses ; while at the same time the empress despatched letters to the Senate to notify the adoption of Hadrian. [Doubtless Plotina used her influence to secure the purple for her favourite, yet she may have acted throughout in perfect good faith.] Be this as it may, we know that on the 11th August Hadrian was acknowledged by the legions of Syria.

Hadrian came to the throne at a difficult time. From all parts of the Roman world tidings of a disastrous nature

---

[1] Comp. Dio, lxix. 1 ; Aurel. Victor, *Cæsar.* 13 ; Spart. *Hadr.* 4. [For my account of Hadrian I am largely indebted to an unpublished essay of a friend.—ED.]

arrived.[1]   The Britons refused any longer to bear the yoke of
Rome ; Mauritania and Sarmatia were in arms ; Egypt and
Cyrene were still agitated by sedition, while Lybia and
Palestine seemed ready to renew a war of independence.   [But
the chief danger lay on the eastern frontier, where Trajan's
conquests had already melted away.   In spite of the warlike
enthusiasm which Trajan had aroused, the course which
Hadrian adopted was imperatively demanded by the interests
of the State.   The new provinces in this quarter were
abandoned, the Euphrates once more became the boundary of
the empire, and Armenia returned to the position of a vassal
State.   Hadrian's next efforts were directed to the restoration
of peace on the other frontiers, and nowhere were the wars
of a serious character.   Meanwhile the emperor had written
to the Senate, asking for their confirmation of his title, and as
soon as he was able he himself appeared in Rome.   Here he
secured the support of the Senate by a judicious show of
deference.   He refused to accept all the imperial titles at
once ; he preferred that they should be voted to him one by
one as he deserved them.   Nevertheless, the government of
the empire became under Hadrian more autocratic than it had
ever been before, since the administration of all departments
of state became centralised in his hands.   In the year
119 A.D., Hadrian left Rome for a tour through all the provinces of his empire.   Wherever he went, he seems to have
made himself acquainted with the smallest details of the
administration.   His visits were always gratefully remembered
on account of bounties distributed and benefits conferred.]

Meantime Lusius Quietus had administered the affairs of
Palestine in a very different spirit.   [He had already incurred
the enmity of the Jews through the severity with which he
had crushed the rising in Mesopotamia,—probably the war
which is known in Jewish history as the war of Quietus.]   It
was said that the synagogue had commemorated the Jewish
defeat by certain ordinances, such as the injunction on brides
no longer to wear crowns at their marriage, and an interdict
on the study of Greek.[2]   [That there was at this time an

---

[1] Spartian. *Hadr.* 5.   [2] Sota ix. 14.

actual outbreak of war in Palestine appears improbable.   The
silence of our authorities seems conclusive on this point.[1]
But the country was undoubtedly in a disturbed state, and
Quietus was not likely to employ gentle measures for the
preservation of order.   Jewish tradition[2] relates that at some
period the Sanhedrin or sacred college removed from Jamnia
to Usha, again from Usha to Jamnia, and once more again to
Usha.   These migrations may be referred with probability
to the disturbed period which followed the death of Trajan.
Perhaps, in anticipation of an outbreak of war, the Rabbins
withdrew to Usha for greater security, returning to Jamnia
when peace seemed assured.   They may have removed again
to Usha on the outbreak of the war of Bar Cochba.]   The new
governor of Judea was not long allowed to enjoy his honours,
Hadrian, soon after his accession, deeming it prudent to recall
his powerful general.   A Jewish legend[3] preserves a confused reminiscence of the recall and subsequent execution of
the hated Quietus.   We are told that Trajan obtained possession of the persons of two Jewish brothers, Julianus and
Pappus, and was about to sentence them to be executed at
Laodicea.   In the height of his confidence he addressed to
the Jewish warriors the impious taunt that their God should
now deliver them out of his hand, even as He had delivered
Hananiah, Mishael, and Azariah.   The brothers replied that
neither he nor they were worthy of having a miracle performed, yet God would surely require their blood at his hand,
if he slew them.   Before the two Hebrews were led to execution, a decree arrived from Rome, and Trajan was put to
death.   This story is told to explain the celebration of
" Trajan's Day," which was observed annually on the 12th of
Adar,—about the beginning of March.   [Now Trajan, as we
have seen, died early in August, and the real origin of the
anniversary remains a matter of conjecture.]   Quietus after
his recall was sent to Mauritania, and did not long survive.
In the second year of Hadrian's reign a conspiracy against

---

[1] [See p. 183, note ; but comp. also Spartian. *Hadr.* 5 : "Libya denique ac
Palæstina rebelles animos efferebant."]

[2] Rosh ha-Shanah 31*a b* ; comp. Derenbourg, p. 425 f.   [3] Meg. Taanith 29.

the life of the emperor was discovered, and Quietus, with three other men of consular dignity, fell victims to imperial suspicions.[1]

[Little is known of the history of Judea during the first years of the Emperor Hadrian. One untrustworthy authority[2] relates that Hadrian visited Palestine at the beginning of his reign, and proceeded to found the new city of Aelia Capitolina. It is, however, hardly possible for Hadrian to have been at this time in Palestine ; while on independent grounds it is not probable that Aelia was founded so early. It was not till the year 130 A.D. that Hadrian passed through Palestine on his way to Egypt. Coins and medals were struck to commemorate the visit of the emperor to Judea, and to record the good understanding between him and his subjects. One of these represents Judea as a female whom Hadrian is lifting from a kneeling position, while three youths stand by her side.[3] There can be but little doubt that this was the year of the original founding of Aelia Capitolina. Wherever Hadrian went in his dominions, he left behind him traces of his presence in the numerous useful and handsome buildings which he either erected or restored. Many provinces hailed him as *restitutor*, and several cities of Palestine have recorded their gratitude for his beneficence. It was but natural that he should wish to restore to its former splendour a city as famous as Jerusalem.[4] The new city was to bear the name of its benefactor, and to the title Aelia was added the title of the deity to whom the principal temple was to be dedicated, the Capitolian Jupiter. That the foundation of Aelia was intended as a deliberate insult to the Jews, is highly improbable. It is doubtful whether Hadrian was even aware that in this matter he was offending against their strongest prejudices.

A story relating to the rebuilding of Jerusalem is found in a late Jewish authority, and on the strength of this] it has

[1] Spart. *Hadr.* 7 ; Dio, lxix. 2.   [2] Epiph. *Mens. et Pond.* 14.
[3] See Cohen, *Médailles Imp.* ii. p. 179. [On the medals in question Hadrian bears the title of P(ater) P(atriæ), which was not conferred till 126 or 128 A.D.]
[4] Comp. Schürer, I. ii. 295 ff.

been supposed that Hadrian, in the beginning of his reign,
made to the Jews some promises of allowing them to rebuild
the city and temple of Jerusalem.   Hadrian, it is said, afterwards withdrew this permission, and thus occasioned the
Jewish war.[1] [Nowhere, however, do Jewish authorities directly
assert that this was the cause of the war ; nor does the theory
in question receive any confirmation from Christian or heathen
writers, independent reasons being assigned for the revolt.
The story alluded to is as follows] :—A decree had been published by the heathen government authorising the rebuilding
of the temple.   Both in and out of Palestine collections were
made for this purpose.   Julianus and Pappus established
places throughout Galilee where the foreign money of the
pious contributors to the temple was exchanged for the current
coin of the country.   But the envy of the Samaritans was
now aroused, and they represented the danger to Roman
supremacy if the temple were allowed to be rebuilt.   In consequence of these representations, the building of the temple
was not absolutely interdicted, only it was not to be raised
upon its old site.   But the Jews were in no way deceived by
Hadrian's conditions ; they readily understood the real import
of the emperor's exceptions.   Stung to the quick, they resolved
to try the chances of war.   An armed assemblage deliberated
in the valley of Rimmon on the steps which required to be
taken.   When the multitudes assembled in Rimmon heard
the emperor's letter read to them, they burst into passionate
tears.   But while the people only remembered their wrongs
and disappointment, there were not wanting some who dreaded
the consequences of a Jewish rising.   The most influential
among them was Rabbi Joshua, who since Rabban Gamaliel's
death had presided over the Sanhedrin, and was well known
as a friend to the Romans and a lover of peace.   No sooner
had he heard of the proposed assemblage in Rimmon, than he
hastened to the spot to persuade his countrymen to desist
from the hopeless attempt.   Well knowing the character of
popular assemblies, which are swayed rather by the impulse

[1] Comp. Derenbourg, p. 412 ff.; Grätz, iv. 138 ff., 442 ff., against Schürer,
I. ii. 289 ff.

of the moment than by principle, he presented to his audience·
the dangerous character of the undertaking in a well-known
fable.[1]   Once upon a time, commenced the Rabbi, it happened
that, as a lion devoured his prey, a bone stuck in his throat.
There it stuck immovable.   The lion coughed, he swallowed
and wrought, but no effort could dislodge the troublesome
intruder.   His danger became extreme ; it was a question of
life or death.   Then the king of the forest issued a proclamation, offering a large reward to any of his liege subjects who
would succeed in extracting the bone.   The offer was tempting, but the danger of thrusting one's head into a lion's mouth,
and, if unsuccessful, probably leaving it there, was too great
for the daring of most animals.   At last, and just in time
to save him, forth steps a venturous crane to perform the
hazardous operation.   Cautiously he puts in his head, which
his long neck enables him to thrust down deep into the
monarch's throat ; and oh, happiness, out comes the bone in
the crane's bill !   Then came the question of the promised
reward.   But, alas for royal gratitude !   The relieved lion
bade the crane go home, and bless his stars that he had got
his head safely out of the jaws of a lion.   It was the first,
and, added he, it might prove the last time.   So much, then,
for experiments upon a lion's throat.   The application of
Joshua's fable is easy, [and the story rightly represents Joshua
as an advocate of peace ; but it must remain uncertain
whether any historical foundation underlies the narrative.   Of
Christian writers who have been appealed to on this question,
Epiphanius expressly excludes the temple from the intended
restorations of Hadrian, while others regard the attempt of
the Jews to rebuild as itself an act of rebellion [2]].

Rabbi Joshua's political activity was indeed paramount
at that time.   His influence with his countrymen was always
exerted for the preservation of peace, and to him may belong
the merit of retarding a catastrophe which he could not
wholly avert.   These pacific sentiments of our Rabbi seem

---

[1] Gen. Rab. 64.

[2] Epiph. *Mens. et Pond.* 14 ; Chrysostom, *Orat. adv. Jud.* v. 11 ; Cedrenus
(Bekker), i. 437 ; Niceph. Callixtus, *Hist. Eccl.* iii. 24.

to have been well known to the emperor. The Talmud illustrates this by recording many friendly interviews which were said to have taken place between the Rabbi and Hadrian. There may well have been some foundation in fact for these accounts, although the details (such as Rabbi Joshua's argument for the resurrection of the body from the indestructible nature of a bone in the human body called "luz")[1] are often evidently fabulous. Converse with the Rabbi accords well with the emperor's philosophical pretensions. In character inquisitive and versatile, Hadrian seems to have alternated at different times between superstition and scepticism. The same disposition which induced him to lend an ear to the pleas of Christian apologists, would incline him also to learn something of Judaism. The Imperial eclectic, who wished to be initiated in all mysteries, would readily enter into discussions with one so learned and so liberal as our Ab-beth-din. It scarcely requires an illustration to show the superficiality of Hadrian's eclecticism. His satirical judgments and hasty scoffing conclusions are well illustrated in a letter which about that time he addressed from Alexandria to his brother-in-law Servianus. Pretending to portray the religious features of that frivolous capital, he writes with more of oratorical flourish than of truth: "No president of Jewish synagogue, no Samaritan, no Christian presbyter, adores aught else but Serapis. Even that Patriarch who came to Egypt was forced by some to worship Serapis, by others to adore Christ."[2] We only add, that the Patriarch here referred to was none else than our Joshua, who visited the capital of Egypt, and to whom the Alexandrians on that occasion proposed twelve questions, of which three referred to the Hagada.[3] However, so long as Joshua lived, peace was preserved in Judea. At his demise (130–132 A.D.), his contemporaries rightly observed, prudence and counsel had now become lost in Israel.[4]

---

[1] Kohel. Rab. on xii. 5 ; Gen. Rab. 28. On that bone compare Eisenmenger, ii. 932.

[2] Vopisc. In Saturn. c. viii.

[3] Nidda 69b ; comp. Menor. Ham. i. 16.   [4] Sota 49b.

We have already mentioned the transference of the Sanhedrin, after the abandonment of Jamnia, to Usha, a place situated between Akka (St. Jean d'Acre, or Ptolemais) and Sepphoris.[1] Amidst the political agitation of Palestine, we cannot expect that purely religious questions should have principally engrossed public attention. While, therefore, the study of the Law was no doubt continued, the active preparations for the impending war, the general discontent of the people, and the eager jealousy of the Romans, combined to make the theological discussions of the Sanhedrin less interesting than they had been before or became after this period. Only very few of the decrees of Usha are of any importance. Amongst them are an ordinance, which limits the sentence of excommunication (in the case of Rabbins) to the crimes of blasphemy and apostasy; another, which renders it obligatory on parents to maintain their sons until their twelfth year, and their daughters until the period of their marriage; a third, which provides that, if a parent had during his lifetime given his property to his son, the latter should be bound to support him; and a fourth, which restricts charitable donations to one-fifth of a person's estate. It is said that Rabbi Ishbab, the secretary of the Sanhedrin, had, in virtue of the latter ordinance, been prevented from impoverishing himself.[2] These decrees afford painful indications of the state of society at the time. Such are frequently exhibited on the eve of some great national crisis, when the bonds of society appear to give way at both extremes, and unbridled selfishness and all-surrendering fanaticism meet face to face.

The Jews were powerfully incited by one with whose theological activity we have already acquainted our readers. The Rabbi to whom we refer was none other than Akiba, one of those men who leave the impress of their character, not only on the theology and literature, but also on the political events of their times. However limited the number

---

[1] Comp. Neubauer, *Géogr. du Talm.* p. 199.

[2] See Grätz, iv. 144. [Hamburger (*Real-Encycl.* ii. "Hadr. Verfolgungsedikte") places the decrees of Usha after the cessation of Hadrian's persecution. Comp. Derenbourg, p. 426.]

of such persons, at every national crisis they always exercise
a lasting influence, acting, as they do, upon the inmost centre
of society, and consistently carrying out their principles to
all the consequences which their comprehensive minds deduce
from them.   Rabbi Akiba's firm faith, both in God's providence and in the speedy fulfilment of His promises to Israel,
has already been illustrated in a former chapter.   In his
ardent soul every conviction became a passion, every hope a
conviction, and every possibility a hope.   With his whole heart
did he cling to his country and to its faith, and his calm and
believing gaze into a brighter future for liberated Israel
animated him with a vigour and a determination rarely
equalled.   It also nerved him with a patience in sufferings
and provocations under which less ardent souls might have
sunk, or against which they might have risen in the madness
of despair.   Not so Akiba.   More deeply than others did he
feel his country's sufferings.   Thus he was wont to exclaim
that no Israelite could expect any blessing unless he habitually
devoted the whole of the fatal Tisha-be-Ab to solemn meditation.[1]   Not that he meant to waste in empty sorrow the
energy of his people.   No !—it was his hope to kindle, not
an isolated rising only, but, if possible, at a given signal, to
combine the dispersed of Israel in all countries in a holy war.
For this purpose he undertook frequent and distant journeys
to visit his brethren.   [At least it seems natural to connect
his travels, which are often alluded to, with preparations for
another struggle against the power of Rome.]   We hear of
Akiba visiting Rome, and travelling through Galatia and
Phrygia, Babylonia, Media, and Arabia.   Hence it was said
of him, and not without justice, that "his fame had extended
from one end of the world to the other."   Only few indications of this activity have been handed down, but the
simultaneous outbreak of disturbances among the Jews in
many parts of the world,[2] the part which Akiba himself afterwards took in the rising in Palestine, and some direct notices,
confirm the supposition that his visits to other lands were
made to serve political ends, and that everywhere he had

[1] Comp. Ersch, *Enc.* xxvii. 13.   [2] Dio Cassius, lxix. 13.

preached a religious war on a terrible scale. It may indeed be doubted whether he set out with a settled plan of proclaiming such a general rising, and his resolution to employ the opportunity for bringing about a general insurrection may have been formed gradually, as circumstances seemed favourable. Certainly the emotions which he is said to have evoked were of that peculiar character which, if turned into a warlike channel, lead to the most terrible energy. To multitudes of weeping hearers in Media he preached about the sufferings of Job, whom the Lord had meant thereby to prepare for better things, just as He now dealt with His beloved people. At other times his addresses bore the character of direct political harangues,—if we may draw any inference from an incidental statement, in which he recommends to his hearers the practice of the Medes, who, "when they took counsel, assembled in the fields," where their deliberations were less liable to be betrayed.[1] Notwithstanding the severity with which the Jewish revolt had been suppressed in the last reign, there was still a widespread desire in the nation to shake off the yoke of Rome. This disaffection Akiba now endeavoured to foster, both in Palestine and in other countries besides.

If such was Akiba's mission, its eventual success was chiefly due to the circumstances of the Jewish people and of their Roman masters. At this time the government of Judea was in the hands of Tineius Rufus, termed by Jewish authorities Tyrannus Rufus, a man who has become notorious for his cruel and oppressive rule. A fresh instrument of tyranny was placed in his hands, when an Imperial edict was published which forbade circumcision.[2] [It is not certain that this measure was aimed specially against the Jews, or that it was designed for the purpose of rooting out Judaism. It seems rather that the old penalties against castration were extended to circumcision, and that no exception was made in favour of the Jews, with whom this custom was practised as a religious rite.[3] None the less the ordinance threatened the

---

[1] Ber. 8*b* ; Ersch, *ut supra.*   [2] Spartian. *Hadr.* 14.
[3] Comp. Schürer, I. ii. 291 ff.; Mommsen, *Provinces*, ii. 224, 228.

continued existence of the Jewish nation.] It was a fresh insult in their eyes, when it was resolved to erect a new city on the ruins of Jerusalem. [As we have seen, it is not probable that Hadrian was here animated by direct hostility to the Jews. A city built by him was, of course, to be in every respect a heathen city, with a heathen temple in room of the Jewish sanctuary.] But to the Jews this was nothing less than profanation, and, following closely upon the edict against circumcision, was an outrage not to be endured. To see all their hopes not only blasted, but to have in the new Jerusalem a standing insult—to have sacrifices offered to Jupiter, where they hoped again to offer incense to Jehovah —to be forbidden even the initiatory rite of their Heaven-given religion—was a bondage too grevious to be borne. The political and religious existence of the nation was now threatened with utter extinction, and it only remained to contend for it to the last. Even those who had formerly been undecided now saw the necessity of resistance, and the national party was wound up to the highest pitch of excitement. In their preparations for the struggle one of the first objects of the Jews was to procure arms. This was not difficult, as they appeared to have supplied the Roman legions in the East, either as merchants or as armourers.[1] It is said that the earliest indication of the coming contest appeared in the inferior description of arms which the Jews supplied to the legions, either because they reserved the better weapons for themselves, or from a wish to deceive and to impede the Romans. The next care of the national party was to prepare subterranean places for meeting or for retreat, where the military stores were laid up. To complete the whole, they quietly fortified and barricaded, as well as they could, certain important positions.

These preparations had been partly kept in abeyance during Hadrian's presence in Egypt and Syria, when the watchful attention of the Romans was fixed on the East. But no sooner had the emperor departed for the West (about 132 A.D.), than they were resumed with an energy which

[1] Comp. for the following, especially Dio Cassius, lxix. 12, 13.

increased as the course of events hastened on the crisis. Soon the contest actually began, as usual, in the shape of a guerilla war. The danger was at first underestimated by the Romans, and it was expected that Rufus with the troops already at his disposal would be able to put down the rising. The first successes of the insurgents naturally encouraged the Jews. We must not omit here to mention a circumstance which, however trival in itself, was considered a favourable omen. It had been formerly observed that the rise of the city of Cæsarea, renowned in a former war, had dated from the downfall of Jerusalem. The Rabbins had applied to this the passage in Ezek. xxvi. 2 : " I shall be replenished now she is laid waste." But now an earthquake had suddenly destroyed the grandeur of Cæsarea, and the Hagadists predicted to the excited multitude that the downfall of her hostile rival indicated the approaching deliverance of Jerusalem.[1] A circumstance like this would probably have had considerable influence anywhere, but especially amongst the Jews. Only one thing was wanting to transform the guerilla war into a regular and organised contest,—the presence of one recognised leader. This difficulty was removed by the appearance of Bar Cochba.

The real name of the Jewish leader has been lost. His designation as Bar Cochba (the son of a star) dates from his claims to be the long-promised Messiah, and the application to him of the prophetic message in Num. xxiv. 17. The idea of making the Jewish leader the Messiah, was one well calculated to secure its objects—to give the stamp of heavenly approbation to the undertaking—to rally round him all believing Jews—to invest the war with the character of the highest religious duty, and to inspire the warriors with the confidence of assured success. It may well be doubted whether all the Rabbins believed in his pretensions. Some, indeed, openly objected. One Rabbi, Jochanan ben Torta, declared that " grass would sooner sprout on Akiba's cheeks than the Messiah appear."[2] But Akiba himself not only joined the party of the deceiver, but carried his standard,

---

[1] Euseb. *Chron.* (11th year of Hadrian); Megil. 6*a* ; comp. Grätz, iv. 149.
[2] Jer. Taan. iv. 68*d* ; Mid. Lam. on ii. 2.

proclaimed him the Messiah, and applied to him passages such as the prophecy of Haggai (ch. ii. 6–21). [It is, indeed, a probable conjecture that the Simon whose name appears on many of the Jewish coins struck during this rebellion, is none other than Bar Cochba.[1] In this case the coins will have preserved the real name, which has been lost to tradition. Rabbinic writers usually designate the national leader Bar Cosiba, a title derived either from his father's name, or from the name of his native place. It was only at a later period, in allusion to the failure of the rebellion, that some writers gave a new interpretation to the title, and called the unfortunate warrior Bar Cosab, the son of a lie.[2]] What a difference between the Old Testament promises and this reality— what a contrast between Israel's true Messiah and the " son of a lie"! They would not have the meek and lowly Jesus and His rest—they took to themselves a king after their own hearts. He was to be a mighty giant-warrior, and it became one like Bar Cochba. The true Messiah was of God's giving; Bar Cochba was of Israel's making.

We do not know what other claims Bar Cochba had to be a leader in Israel, beyond those of bodily strength and indomitable courage. Still the great majority of the sages and of the people adhered to him, and flocked round his standard, perhaps more incited by the example and influence of Akiba than by personal conviction. It does not appear by what means the new Messiah upheld his claims. He does not seem to have attempted to work miracles. Only one authority,[3] and that of a person equally credulous and hostile to the Jews, records a solitary instance of it, which is too transparent even for a Bar Cochba to have practised. It is said that he pretended to spit fire by blowing burning flax out of his mouth. But though unsupported by such evidence, the report that the Messiah had at last appeared and been acknowledged by the Sanhedrin, was sufficient to attract crowds of eager combatants round his standard. Jews from

---

[1] So Schürer, I. ii. 298 f.; Madden, *Coins of the Jews*, p. 233 f.; Mommsen, *Provinces*, ii. 224.

[2] Mid. Lam. on ii. 1.   [3] Hieron. *Apol. adv. Rufin.* iii. 31.

Palestine and from other provinces daily came to head-quarters. A general insurrection of the Jews in every pro-vince seemed to be imminent; while in Palestine even non-Israelites joined the ranks of the national army, many being induced by the hope of gain to take part in the rebellion.[1] Historians record a number of particulars connected with this army, which seem exaggerated if not fabulous. Thus the number of combatants is put down as 400,000; the strength of Bar Cochba is described as such, that with his knees he could hurl back the immense stones which the Roman war-machines projected;[2] and various fabulous tests are men-tioned by which he tried the fitness and power of endurance of his followers. Whatever deductions we may have to make from those accounts of the national army, without doubt the danger to Rome was sufficiently formidable. The character of the undertaking and of its leader, as well as their confident anticipations of success, appear in the following presumptuous prayer which Bar Cochba is said to have ejaculated: " Lord, if Thou art not willing to assist *us*, at least do not assist *our enemies*, and then we shall prevail."

Such was the Messiah of Israel's choice, whom they now prepared to support. Only one party in the land opposed a passive resistance to the " son of a lie." The small and de-spised number of Jewish Christians neither could nor would own the deceiver's claims. They resisted his overtures, and refused to fight under such colours even for national inde-pendence. They aided not the Romans, but they would not join Bar Cosiba. On this ground they were exposed on the part of the Jews to shocking cruelties;[3] for the reality of their faith in Christ made them specially obnoxious to Bar Cochba and his warriors. Success seemed at first largely to attend the arms of the new Messiah. Tineius Rufus was unable to cope with his opponent, notwithstanding an increase to the Roman army. At one period the Jews held 50 fortified cities and 935 open villages.[4] It was in vain

---

[1] Dio Cassius, lxix. 13. [2] Jer. Taan. iv. 68*d*; Mid. Lam. *ut supra.*

[3] Just. *Apol.* i. 31; Euseb. *Chron.* (ed. Schœne) ii. p. 168 f.

[4] Dio Cassius, *ut supra.*

that Hadrian sent legion after legion, and general after general, to Palestine. They were obliged to yield to or retreat before the Jews. These results alarmed the emperor, and increased the confidence of the Hebrew warriors. As in former wars, so now, those who had formerly sided with the enemy of their country, now deserted the Romans ; some who, during the supremacy of the "tyrant" Rufus, had even submitted to a painful operation in order to conceal their descent, were now circumcised a second time.[1] Jerusalem was, no doubt, in the hands of the Jews, but amidst the engagements of the war there was no leisure to rebuild its sanctuary, or to restore the city to its former importance.[2] Meantime Bar Cochba seems to have proclaimed himself Prince of Israel. To indicate the liberation of his country, he changed the coinage, and not unfrequently restamped the current Roman coins. Some of these coins are still extant, in which above the former Roman mark of Trajan or Hadrian, which is still slightly discernible, we read the name of "Simon," and the number of the year of "the liberation of Jerusalem," or "of Israel." The coins are stamped with Jewish symbols, one side bearing usually the emblem of the temple, a palm tree, or a bunch of grapes ; while on the reverse is seen a vase, two trumpets, or a lyre.[3] Bar Cosiba's reign had now lasted two years, and the danger had become increasingly great. To bring this threatening war to a termination, Hadrian despatched to Judea from Britain, on the uttermost limits of the empire, his ablest general, Julius Severus. Severus felt he was engaged in a war which taxed all his energies as a commander, and called for all the bravery of his legions. Following the usual tactics of the Romans, he endeavoured to avoid regular engagements. By hovering about the Jews, and continually threatening them

[1] Tosef. Shab. xvi.; jer. Jeb. viii. 9*a*; comp. Levy, *Neuhebr. Wörterb.* iii. 276.

[2] Comp. Appian, *Syr.* 50 ; see also Schürer, I. ii. 300 f.; Mommsen, *Provinces*, ii. 224 ; Schiller, *Gesch. der Römischen Kaiserzeit*, i. 612.

[3] [There is much difference of opinion regarding the coins issued during this war, and the Simon whose name appears upon them. Comp. Madden, *Coins of the Jews*, pp. 192 ff., 230 ff.; Schürer, I. ii. 378–392 ; Derenbourg, p. 424 ; Grätz, iii. 819–841.]

with an attack, he wearied them out, while he drew his own troops round them in an ever closer circle. As his own rear rested on Syria, he could always draw reinforcements and supplies ; while the Jews, shut up in their mountain fortresses, were cut off from help, and unable to obtain provisions. Thus at last Severus succeeded in starving and harrying the rebels, and in slowly driving them out of one stronghold after another.

[We know very little about the progress of the war. It has been supposed [1] that a first line of defence was established along a mountain range which extends through Upper Galilee from the Mediterranean to the Lake of Tiberias, and that it was protected by the three forts of Cabul, Sichin, and Magdala. It seems, however, more probable that these places were destroyed during the war with Vespasian.[2] The main scene of the struggle is termed in Jewish writings Tur-Malka, or the Royal Mountain, and should probably be identified with the mountain country of Judea.[3]]

Legend relates how in Tur-Simon, or Tur-Malka, as it is also called, commanded one Bar Droma. Yielding to a fatal security, the inhabitants were in the midst of festive enjoyments, when a Roman army to the number of 300,000 appeared before its walls, and even penetrated into its streets. The dance and rioting was now interrupted by the cries of those who, themselves defenceless, fell under the swords of the enemy. Before the soldiers could be collected, the Romans had occupied the principal parts of the town, and a general massacre continued for three days and three nights. In fact, such was the extent of Tur-Simon, that when the carnage had already commenced in one quarter of the city, the inhabitants of the other, ignorant of their impending fate, were still enjoying the pleasures of wine and of the dance.[4] Jewish historians

---

[1] So Grätz, iv. 157. Comp. jer. Taan. iv. 8.

[2] Comp. Derenbourg, p. 429 ; Hamburger, ii. 89 ; somewhat differently Neubauer, p. 202.

[3] [So Der. p. 428 (S. of Jerusalem) ; Hamb. *ut supra* ; Neubauer, pp. 41, 267 (? N. of Jerusalem) ; Grätz, iv. 158, 459, identifies the Tur-Malka with Mount Ephraim, the northern continuation of the same chain.]

[4] Gitt. 57*a*.

describe, in their own peculiar way, the importance and extent of the towns which had now fallen into the hands of the Romans. Thus they have it, that King Jannai possessed in the Royal Mountain 600,000 cities, each containing as many inhabitants as the number of Israelites who had come out of Egypt; while at Tur-Simon 300 large baskets of bread were distributed every Friday amongst the paupers of its large population. It is also said that the first signal of the war had been given in Tur-Simon. Some lawless Roman soldiers had insulted a bridal procession, and forcibly taken from it the pair of fowls which, according to custom, was carried before the newly married couple. It is added that the infuriated mob had in turn fallen upon and destroyed the Roman garrison, an event which had formed the first act of open hostility between the two parties.

The war lasted for nearly three years and a half (132–135 A.D.). [Jerusalem was taken by assault, and again destroyed;[1] but the fortifications cannot have been important, and the city did not form the centre of the war.] The last Jewish fortress to hold out was the stronghold of Bethar, where the garrison was commanded by Bar Cochba in person. Tradition, as usual, gives a fabulous description of the armies and of the inhabitants of that city, [which, however, do not enable us to form any safe inference as to its size or the number of its defenders]. Thus it was said that the army attacking Bethar had no less than 80,000 trumpeters. Again, so numerous were the theological students there assembled, that there were in the city 400 synagogues, to each of which were attached 400 teachers, while each teacher was attended by 400 students. It is vauntingly added, that with the points of their writing materials the students might have repelled any hostile attack; and that after the destruction of Bethar no less than forty chests, each containing three measures of old phylacteries, were discovered.[2]

Bethar was doubtless a very strong place, but it is not

---

[1] Appian, *Syr.* 50.

[2] Gitt. 58*a*. Different numbers are given in jer. Taan. iv. 69*a*.

mentioned in earlier times. Tradition relates that it used to be visited by many travellers, and among others by wandering Jewish impostors, who played upon the credulity of the inhabitants. It is said that on this ground the inhabitants of Bethar rejoiced over the fall of Jerusalem.[1] [Bethar was situated not very far from the holy city,[2] According to the Talmud, it lay forty miles from the sea ;[3] and its site has been identified, with considerable probability, with the modern Bettir, three hours south-west of Jerusalem.[4]] The defence of the fortress was long and stubborn, and the defenders were reduced to the greatest distress through want of food and water, but history has preserved no details of the progress of the siege. On the authority of a Samaritan history,[5] [which is quite untrustworthy,] it is stated that treason effected what the arms of the enemy could not have accomplished. The hostile agency is here also traced to the ancient jealousy of the Samaritans. It is said that the latter discovered to the Romans some of the secret passages by which victuals were conveyed into the besieged city.

A Jewish tradition relating to the siege also speaks of the treachery of the Samaritans.[6] Three years and a half, we are told, did Hadrian besiege Bethar. The Jews were hardly pressed on every side ; but, still clinging firmly to the hope of heavenly deliverance, the soldiers prepared for a desperate resistance. Amongst those who stimulated the religious energy and encouraged the hopes of the defenders of Bethar, none was more conspicuous than Rabbi Eleazar of Modin. Weighed down by years and emaciated by fasts, the aged ascetic was daily to be seen on the ramparts, where, clad in sackcloth and covered with ashes, he would, in the sight of all, implore heavenly aid with tears and by continual fastings. As long as the defenders

---

[1] Compare the narrative in Lightfoot's *Cent. Chorogr.* c. lii.

[2] Euseb. *Hist. Eccl.* iv. 6.   [3] Jer. Taan. *ut supra.*

[4] Comp. Williams, *Holy City*, i. 209–213. See also Appendix IV.

[5] *Chronicon Samaritanum, Liber Josuæ*, ed. Juynboll, 1848. [This book gives a legendary account of the conquest of *Jerusalem* by Hadrian.]

[6] Jer. Taan. iv. 68*d* ; Mid. Lam. on ii. 1.

of Bethar saw Eleazar at his post, they felt secure under the canopy of his piety, and in the assurance of Divine aid. Even the treacherous Samaritans felt the awe of his presence, and were wont to say that Bethar could not be taken " so long as this cock remained to crow in ashes." At last one of their number undertook to get rid of the object of their fears. For this purpose he entered Bethar by a secret passage.[1] He then managed to approach Eleazar, while the latter, engaged as usual at his devotions on the ramparts, remained unconscious of the presence of the intruder. But the soldiers around, who wondered what the Samaritan stranger had to whisper to the Rabbi, seized him the more eagerly that he feigned an anxiety to escape. He was brought before Bar Cochba and questioned about his communication with Eleazar. The Samaritan played his part but too well. At first apparently unwilling to disclose anything, he at last declared that, since he must die,—by the hand of those who had sent him if he told the truth, by the hand of his captors if he refused to do so,—he would choose rather to perish now than to disclose the secret message which had been entrusted to him for Eleazar. Bar Cochba immediately went to Eleazar and bade him disclose his treasonable designs. In vain the old Rabbi pleaded utter ignorance, even of the presence of the Samaritan. Bar Cochba, who in all this saw only a piece of acting, enraged at his denial, rudely pushed the old man aside with his foot. Eleazar fell to the ground a corpse. It is added that a voice from heaven was heard to declare that, as Bar Cochba had in the person of the sage paralysed the arm and extinguished the eye of Israel, so it should be done to himself.

There could be but one issue to the long and desperate siege. At last came the day of assault, and Bethar was sacked and destroyed. The loss of life on both sides during the war must have been enormous. [Our most reliable authority, the historian Dio Cassius,[2] referring apparently only to the losses of the Jews, asserts that as many as 580,000 men

[1] Comp. Grätz, iv. 162, 461 f.   [2] Dio, lxix. 14.

fell in battle ; while the number of those who perished through sickness, fire, or famine was never reckoned.] Jewish legend describes in extravagant terms the horrors of the massacre after the fall of Bethar.[1] Thus tradition has it, that the horses waded in blood up to the bridles, and that the bed of the river became filled with gore, which was carried in a stream to the sea. Again, the atrocities of the soldiers were not confined to those who had borne arms against them. Young and old were indiscriminately slaughtered. Of all the young men in Bethar, only Simon, the son of Rabban Gamaliel, the former Nasi, escaped. Under one stone alone, it is said, the brains of 300 children were dashed out. An immense vineyard was completely covered with dead bodies. According to tradition, a burial was not even conceded to the Jewish slain, and the cruelty of the victors manifested itself in piling up the dead bodies like a hedge. Altogether, such was the number of persons who had fallen in this sanguinary war, that it was observed the widows of the slain found it almost impossible afterwards to procure, according to the custom of the synagogue, the necessary witnesses to depone to the death of their husbands.

The chief actor in the terrible drama, Bar Cochba, fell in this last engagement. We are told that his head was brought in triumph into the Roman camp—round his body a serpent had twisted itself. When Hadrian saw the corpse, he exclaimed, " If God had not smitten him, what man could have smitten him ? " According to Rabbinic calculation, it was again the fatal 9th of the month Ab on which Bethar was completely destroyed by the Romans.[2] With the fall of the headquarters of the insurrection, and the death of the false Messiah, the war was virtually at an end. But the victory had not been achieved without considerable loss to the Roman army. [Hadrian had returned to Palestine, and was probably with the army during the most critical part of the war.[3]] When now sending to the Senate a report of the

---

[1] Comp. jer. Taan. iv. 69*a* ; Mid. Lam. ii. 1 ; Gitt. 57*a*-58*a*.
[2] M. Taan. iv. 6.
[3] Comp. Schiller, *Gesch. der Römischen Kaiserzeit*, i. 613 f.

close of the campaign, he somewhat altered the usual phraseology of such documents, and instead of informing the assembled fathers of his own welfare and of that of the army, he omitted the customary clause.[1]   In truth, the army had been terribly shattered.   The Senate acknowledged their services by the usual rewards to officers and men, and decreed to Severus the triumphal decorations.   Thus closed the second Jewish war of liberation ; and so perished the false Messiah, and the unhappy victims of this rebellion.

[1] Dio Cassius, lxix. 14.

CHAPTER VIII

STATE OF THE SYNAGOGUE AFTER THE LAST JEWISH WAR

IT appears that, after the fall of Bethar, as formerly after the destruction of Jerusalem, the contest did not immediately terminate. Armed bands of Jews still occupied some posts in the mountain fastnesses, which they prepared to defend. Especially in the mountainous district around the neighbourhood of the lake of Galilee, we hear of two brothers who held command, and for some time successfully resisted or eluded the Romans. It was comparatively easy for resolute leaders, in these inaccessible retreats, to escape the vigilance of a hostile force. It is said that they had gathered adherents, and even proposed to proclaim themselves successors of Bar Cochba, when they fell into the hands of the Romans.[1] The latter are said to have established a threefold line of posts, by which they surrounded the fugitives in the mountains, and thus either forced them to surrender, or at least prevented their escape across the Jordan. A military station at Bethel commanded the approach to the mountains of Ephraim and the neighbourhood of Jerusalem ; another post at Chamoth, or Emmaus, near Tiberias, watched the mountains of Upper Galilee ; while an intermediate station was established at Kephar Lekitaja.[2]

Our authorities tell many stories of the dangers and sufferings of the unfortunate people, and of the cruelties practised upon them by the enraged Romans. In continual apprehension of being surprised by the enemy, they hid themselves in caves and among rocks, and even there scarcely felt secure. Thus it is related that on a certain Sabbath, a large

---

[1] Jer. Taan. iv. 69a.   [2] Mid. Lam. on i. 16.

party had assembled in the interior of a cave.   Of a sudden
they heard heavy footsteps as of their approaching enemies.
In terror they fled further into the cave, the intruders following them.   From overcrowding, from being trampled under
foot in the precipitate flight, and from terror, many of the
wretched fugitives perished.   It afterwards appeared that
those from whom they had fled as Romans were only companions of their misery, whose sandals happened to be armed
with heavy nails.   The unfortunate mistake was commemorated
by the Synagogue in an ordinance, which forbade the use of
such sandals on Sabbath days.[1]   But it was not chiefly from
vague apprehensions that these homeless wanderers suffered.
To all their other calamities that of pinching want was added.
At last, we are told, such were their necessities that they fed
upon the dead bodies of their friends and comrades.   The
horrors of this state of matters are represented in the account
which is given of one of these parties.   It is said that, in
turn, a young man had been sent to provide the unnatural
aliment for his friends.   Unable to discover any other corpse
than that of his own father, he had returned empty-handed.
Another less scrupulous messenger was despatched, and the
youth had, with his companions, completed the unnatural
meal before he learned that he had feasted on the remains of
his parent.[2]   But, besides recounting the privations and sufferings of the fugitives, tradition loved also to dwell on the
cruelty of the Romans, which was only equalled by their
faithlessness.   Thus, on one occasion, so the story runs, when
a body of Roman troops were wearied with waiting for their
prey, they promised a free pardon to all who would lay down
their weapons and surrender ; but those who, trusting their
word, had come down, were speedily undeceived.   They were
marched into the fatal valley of Rimmon, and surrounded by
the soldiery.   In cruel sport the Roman emperor insisted that
they should be slaughtered during the time that he took to
regale himself with part of a fowl.[3]

Such of the captives in this war as escaped death were to

[1] Shab. 60*a* ; jer. Shab. vi. 8*a*.   [2] Mid. Lam. on i. 16.
[3] *Ut-supra*; comp. Derenbourg, p. 436, n.

be sold into slavery. Two great bazaars were held for this purpose, the one at Gaza, the other in Hebron, the place where Abraham of old had pitched his tent.[1] Such was the number of the wretched human chattels, that a great part of them remained unsold, and were afterwards conveyed into Egypt. On the passage many of them were mercifully released from their sufferings by death. However, a large number of Jews contrived to escape to Babylon and Arabia, where their sympathising countrymen gave them a ready welcome. The tragical termination of this war was another added to the monuments of national judgments. To preserve it in the minds of the faithful, the Synagogue abolished another of the tokens of joy formerly customary at marriages. In future, when the bride was conducted to her husband's house, she was no more, as in happier days, to be carried through the streets in a splendidly ornamented chair.[2] Such demonstrations no longer befitted their circumstances, or the descendants of those who had thus suffered.

It is, indeed, almost impossible to realise the desolation of the land. To the Roman legions it had from the first probably been a war of extermination against the Jews of Palestine, and all subsequent measures taken by the government were in accordance with this view. Everywhere the country had been laid waste, and with a ruthlessness for which no plea can be assigned but that of exasperation ; not only were cities razed, and hamlets burned down, but even the fruit trees and vines were destroyed. Galilee, once so renowned for its production of oil, had at the termination of the war scarcely an olive tree left.[3] It was now possible to proceed with the project which had led to the immediate outbreak of the war, the erection of a Roman colony on the site of Jerusalem. [To symbolise the foundation of a new city, a plough was driven across the temple mount, according to the Mishna, on the 9th of Ab.[4]] The buildings erected before the

---

[1] Comp. Hieron. in Jer. xxxi. 15, and specially also in Zech. xi. 5.
[2] Sotah 49*a*. [3] Jer. Peah vii. 1.
[4] Taan. iv. 6 ; comp. Grätz, iv. 167; somewhat differently Schürer, I. ii. 308.

outbreak had probably been destroyed during the war.[1] These were now restored, and in the place of the holy city of the Jews, a heathen city, laid out after Grecian models, and provided with market-places, theatres, and heathen fanes, was reared. Jewish feeling regarded it as an intentional outrage, when a statue of Hadrian was placed where the altar of Jehovah had once stood, and in room of the temple a fane for the Roman Jupiter was built.[2] Over the Bethlehem gate the figure of a pig's head was wrought in relief,[3] [probably the symbol of the Tenth Legion, which still formed the garrison of Jerusalem]. Even the Samaritans, who had taken no part in the war, did not escape unmolested. They had to witness the erection of a temple of Jupiter on their holy mount Gerizim ; but it is not known whether this was actually built by Hadrian. The very name of the province was changed from Judea to Syria Palestina, and, as before the war, the new city built on the site of Jerusalem was called " Ælia Capitolina." Coins of the reign of Hadrian and of later emperors bear that name, and on the reverse the representations of the various heathen deities which under one or other of the emperors were principally worshipped at Jerusalem. A century and a half later, the revulsion was so complete, that when on a certain occasion a Christian convert, in his examination before the governor, referred to Jerusalem, the latter did not know Ælia Capitolina by that name.[4]

To complete the change, and to make it for ever impossible to restore Jerusalem to its former position, all Jews were, on pain of death, forbidden to approach the city, even within such distance as to catch a glimpse of it.[5] At a later period, however, the Jews were again allowed, upon payment of a certain sum to the Roman guards, on the anniversary of the fatal Tisha-be-Ab, to enjoy the melancholy privilege of visiting Jerusalem to weep over the broken walls of their city and temple. The scene which Jerusalem presented on such

[1] Comp. Appian, *Syr.* 50.   [2] Hieron. in Jes. ii. 9 ; Matt. xxiv. 15.
[3] Euseb. *Chron.* (ed. Schœne) ii. 169.   [4] *Ibid. De Mart. Pal.* xi.
[5] *Ibid. Hist. Eccl.* iv. 6 ; Justin, *Apol.* i. 47. Comp. Münter's *Letzter Jüd. Krieg*, p. 92, etc.

occasions has been described by an ecclesiastical contemporary
in terms as unfeeling as they are unbecoming. We quote
them chiefly to exhibit the alienation from the original
relations between the Church and the Synagogue, and the
departure from the spirit of primitive Christianity. " Those
who once bought the blood of Christ," exultingly writes
Jerome, " must now buy their tears ; and even to weep is not
freely conceded them.   On the anniversary of the capture and
destruction of Jerusalem, you may descry a mourning crowd
approaching.   Behold here decrepit women, and aged men
weighed down with grief and years, hastening to bewail the
desolation of their sanctuary.   Their very bearing betokens
that the wrath of God is upon them.   But, while tears are
streaming down their cheeks,—while in their bitterness of
spirit they stand with arms outstretched and hair dishevelled,
—lo ! the Roman soldier rudely accosts them to demand money
that they may longer enjoy the liberty and the privilege of
weeping." [1]   So far the theologian.   We may add, that the
leave accorded to Jews to dwell undisturbed in Jerusalem dates
from the period of Mohammedan rule, [although during the
third century the edict of expulsion was rarely put in force].

As Hadrian had now succeeded in making Jerusalem a
heathen city, so would his other measures, if completely
carried out, have rendered the profession of Judaism in
Palestine impossible.   The edict against circumcision, published even before the war, was still maintained ; and so strictly
was this interdict enforced, that certain parties expressed
doubts in how far it was lawful in present circumstances to
contract marriages.[2]   Jewish tradition affirms further, that it
was interdicted to read in the Law, to put on phylacteries, to
affix the customary legal mark to the doorposts, to eat unleavened bread, on certain festivals to use the customary nose-
gay, to write letters of divorce, and to solemnise the marriages
of spinsters on Wednesdays.[3]   [Whether this be true or not,
to many Jews the prohibition of circumcision meant a pro-

[1] Hieron. in Zeph. i. 15 f.   [2] B. Bath. 60*b*.
[3] Shab. 21*b*, 49*a* ; Erub. 97*a* ; Tos. Meg. iii., etc.   Comp. Grätz, iv. 463 ff. ;
Hamb. *Real-Encycl.* ii. 328 ff. " Hadr. Verfolgungsedikte."

hibition of all Jewish practices ;] and Judaism had so thoroughly intertwined itself with common life, that at every turn a man would be reminded of the tyrannical edict, and made to feel his hopeless bondage.   But there is one instance to be mentioned of Roman brutality, compared with which, if indeed it be a historical fact, all other acts must almost shrink into insignificance.   It is asserted that a Roman decree claimed for the governor the "*jus primæ noctis,*" or right of violating the bride on the first night of her marriage.[1]   The Babylonian Talmud, indeed, explains that this was only awarded as punishment when the order not to marry on Wednesdays had been infringed.   But even this limitation would scarcely alter the character of the base offence.

[It seems that even before the fall of Bethar, a persecution, mainly directed against the Rabbins and teachers, had broken out in Galilee ; after the capture of the last important stronghold, the persecution extended over the whole of Palestine.[2]   In Jewish tradition, the years that passed between the fall of Bethar and the death of Hadrian are known as the "Time of Danger."   We have, however, hardly any means of determining whether the martyrdoms of certain distinguished Rabbins occurred before or after the fall of Bethar.   It is equally difficult to fix the dates of some important meetings of the Rabbins which took place during this period.]   Our Jewish authorities name Tyrannus Rufus[3] as the most active persecutor, and of the severities practised against the unfortunate Jews terrible accounts are given.   We are told that the offenders against the Imperial edicts were no longer punished in the usual modes.   As if to behead, to hang, or to burn alive were insufficient, Roman ingenuity devised new modes of punishment.[4]   Red-hot balls were placed in their armpits, pointed canes were thrust under their nails, the skin was torn off their bodies, and similar cruelties inflicted, and

---

[1] Jer. Keth. i. 5 ; b. *ib.* 3*b*.

[2] Comp. Derenbourg, pp. 429–436 ; Grätz, iv. 167–179.

[3] [Julius Severus seems to have succeeded Rufus as legate about the year 135 A.D.   Comp. Schürer, I. ii. 263 f.]

[4] Mid. Cant. on ii. 7.

that often where not even the excuse of having taken part in the former rebellion existed.   Spies and denouncers were always ready to hunt out the refractory.   Amongst these spies, the most notorious and dangerous were apostate Jews, who, being acquainted with the habits and practices of their countrymen, were capable of inflicting on them more serious damage than strangers.   Especially did Elisa ben Abuja, from his apostasy called Acher (the other), who, himself once a distinguished theologian, had through mystical studies made shipwreck, first of his faith and then of every principle, distinguish himself by a hostile activity.   He well knew how his brethren would attempt to evade the law, and at the same time observe parts of the Jewish ritual, and his ingenuity was exerted in rendering these sorry devices impossible.   If the authorities directed their edicts against all distinctively Jewish practices, it seems to have been their special desire to see the theological schools closed, and the functions of the Rabbins abolished.   Indeed, had they succeeded in this attempt, the hated observances would necessarily soon have ceased of themselves.   The Rabbins were strictly enjoined neither to study the Law themselves nor to teach it to others, and special care was taken to watch over the enforcements of these edicts. Here also Elisa was chief actor.   Perhaps, however, his conduct may indicate some sympathy with his former colleagues, as he is represented as only breaking up and dispersing, but not strictly denouncing, the theological assemblies.   It is said that he would unexpectedly appear at a secret meeting of the academy, and, naming those present and mentioning their trades (the Rabbins being obliged each to learn some trade), call upon them to disperse and go to their proper work.[1]

The sages felt that the most critical period for the Synagogue had now arrived.   It was, of course, impossible to assemble a Sanhedrin to deliberate on the measures requisite, but some of the leading theologians met secretly in the upper room of one Nitsah, at Lydda.[2]   In that assembly were Akiba, [who, without holding any official position, was the most

---

[1] Jer. Chag. ii. 77b.
[2] Jer. Sheb. iv. 35a ; Jer. Sanh. iii. 21b ; b. Sanh. 74a.

prominent Rabbi of his time,[1]] Tarphon or Tryphon the Ab-
beth-din, Joses of Galilee, and perhaps also Ishmael the son
of Elisa, the celebrated compiler of the thirteen exegetical
canons which we have formerly mentioned. The first question
which the Rabbins discussed was that of the comparative importance of the study and of the observance of the Jewish
Law. Under other circumstances such a subject would
scarcely have been mooted, now it had become a grave
question. Manifestly they could not expect the people to
continue the ritual observances, and it was a point of importance to agree whether they themselves should take their stand
and endure martyrdom for these practices, or only in defence
of their professional studies. Naturally, differences of opinion
found expression in this council with reference to a stricter or
laxer observance of the Law. The main question, however,
was decided with little hesitation. It may, indeed, be a fair
question how far practices can be absolutely and religiously
binding, which under any pressure from without can be wholly
cast aside. But with reference to the present circumstances
there was little room for such difficulties. The general
principle being settled by the Rabbins, that as the study of
the Law led to its practice, the former was the more important,
the inference was easy. While the theologians, therefore,
resolved to continue their teaching, they at the same time
granted a general dispensation to the faithful in the meantime
only to observe so much of Jewish practices as they could do
with safety, or in case of danger even wholly to intermit
them. The only exceptions were those made on the three
points of murder, uncleanness, and idolatry. But even on
these points some latitude was given, and Rabbi Ishmael
declared it lawful in cases of extreme necessity even to
simulate compliance with heathen practices.[2]

[From the traditions relating to Hadrian's persecution, it
appears that, while some of the Rabbins set the example of
observing the "decrees of Lydda," there was also a stricter
party which refused, even at the peril of death, to neglect any
of the traditional observances. Among these was Akiba, who

---

[1] Comp. Derenbourg, p. 421, n.   [2] Comp. Ab. Sar. 27*b*.

had been ready to grant to others dispensations which he would not himself use.] The rigour of the Romans seems to have been primarily directed against the teaching and the teachers rather than against the observances and the observers. It is said that, to enlist popular assistance in enforcing the decrees against the Rabbins, it was further enacted, that not only should refractory theologians be punished, but that the towns and districts in which the law was set at defiance should be held responsible for such offences.[1] This applied specially to the ordination of candidates for the Rabbinate. It was hoped that by these means the succession of qualified teachers would be rendered impossible. The effects of these measures were, at least for a time, very extensive. Some apostatised from fear, or were bribed by promises; others, amongst them, perhaps, Rabbi Tarphon,[2] left the country; others openly denied that they continued teaching the Law. Thus, Eleazar ben Parta,[3] when summoned before the judges, simply bore false testimony, satisfying his conscience by a reference to the decrees of Lydda. But while some of the Rabbins intermitted their usual occupation, whether from favour for the Romans or from apprehensions for their personal safety, others, and amongst them the leading men of the Synagogue, prepared to suffer in a cause which to them appeared the most sacred of all.

[Legend has adorned the deaths of the Jewish martyrs of this period with many additions and exaggerations. At a much later period, after the completion of the Talmud, we find references to the Ten Martyrs, who suffered during the persecution of Hadrian,[4] the names of the ten being variously given.[5] The earlier literature only refers casually to the martyr death of one Rabbi or another; and even these accounts are no more trustworthy than many similar Christian legends. The circumstances of Rabbi Akiba's death seem better attested than those relating to many of the other Rabbins. Here we can only repeat the stories of martyrdom as they are given

---

[1] Sanh. 14a.   [2] Comp. Justin, *Dial. c. Tryph.* 1.
[3] Ab. Sar. 17b.   [4] Comp. Mid. Lam. on ii. 1.
[5] Comp. Hamb., *Real-Enc.* Suppl. "Zehn Martyrer"; Schürer, I. ii. 312 f.

in the Talmud and elsewhere.] If we remember the leading part taken by Akiba and his companions in stirring up the late rebellion, it is difficult to understand how they can have so long escaped the vengeance of the Romans. In the absence of historical documents, the actual course of events cannot be determined with certainty. Some have supposed that, as the Rabbins had not been discovered in arms, they for a while escaped. [Others suppose that the persecution raged during the later years of the war, but that Akiba was for a long while kept in prison by Rufus, waiting for Hadrian's triumph.[1]] According to tradition, the first to suffer in the cause of Rabbinism were Simon and Ishmael ben Elisa, the learned priest. Besides his other claims to distinction, so beautiful was the latter, that legend records the emperor's daughter had caused his head to be carried to Rome.[2] When in prison, and while led forth to execution, these two Rabbins consoled each other by conversing about the Divine holiness and justice. Not daunted by his imminent danger, the noble-minded Akiba prepared to follow in their wake. He delivered a funeral oration on the occasion of their martyrdom, in which he called on his hearers to imitate the example of those who had gone before, to whom he declared the honour had fallen of being the first to suffer.[3] It was his turn closely to follow them. The crime of which he was now accused was that of continuing to teach the Law. He had first been warned by friends of his impending danger; but Akiba knew that such an accusation could only be a pretext to enemies whose vengeance he could not hope to escape. Besides, the time of his departure had come, and he was willing to suffer in what he conscientiously believed to be the cause of God. To his well-meaning friends, especially to one of them, Pappus, who had himself submitted to the decrees of the Roman authorities, he replied in a parable, designed to show that theological study was his proper heaven-appointed element, and that if he were not safe in the element for which God had adapted him, he could not

---

[1] Derenbourg, p. 421 ; comp. Sanh. 12*a*.
[2] Ab. Sar. 11*b*, and Rashi, *ad loc.*
[3] Mechilta on Ex. xxii. 22.

expect security in any other. It is said that, by a curious co-incidence, the cautious Pappus had been consigned, for some other imaginary offence, to the same prison with Akiba. He now deplored his cowardice, which, without attaining its object, had made him a sufferer in a less noble cause.[1] At the time of his imprisonment Akiba had attained an advanced age ; tradition assigns to him, as to some other great Rabbins, a length of life equal to that of Moses, namely 120 years.[2] He was in the zenith of his fame and influence, and his sun went down in a noonday splendour.

Tidings of this new calamity seem to have over-whelmed the people and the theologians. Akiba was closely guarded, and prevented from holding intercourse with his friends. The removal of their chief authority had come so suddenly upon the sages, who had never accustomed their minds to the idea of his loss, that when it had become a reality, they felt as if they had not made proper use of his presence even during the long period in which it had been granted to them. A number of knotty questions now occurred to them, on which they wished to have his decision. Partly by bribing the warders, and partly by clever manœuvres, they are said to have succeeded in ascertaining his opinion. Thus, one of his favourite students, Jochanan from Alexandria, would disguise himself as a hawker, and, passing under the windows of Akiba's prison, while pretending to praise his wares, managed to slip in theological questions. In this manner, to the call, " Needles, forks—who will buy my good needles ? What about marriage with a deceased brother's wife ? " Akiba, who readily understood his pupil, would reply, " Have you any thread ?—lawful." [3] On another occasion, we are told, the sum of 400 denarii was given to a messenger who succeeded in holding intercourse with him.[4] Even in prison the authority of Akiba was more than once appealed to for the regulation of the calendar.[5] Rufus himself is said to have become interested in his victim, and to have had frequent interviews with him.

[1] Ber. 61*b*.
[2] Ab. di R. Nathan, 6.
[3] Jer. Jeb. xii. 12*d*.
[4] Jeb. 108*b*.
[5] Sanh. 12*a*.

Jewish legend has recorded, in fabulous language, the particulars of these conversations,[1] which appear to have been almost wholly connected with religious controversy.

Although in prison, and about to suffer, Akiba would omit none of his former ritual observances. Indeed, he is related to have exhibited an increased ardour and punctiliousness. Thus he used the greater portion of his stinted daily allowance of water for the required ceremonial ablutions.[2] In reality, Akiba prepared to die in a manner worthy of his life. As if the leading sage of the nation was to be distinguished by novel and more than usually terrible tortures, Rufus is said to have ordered that the flesh of Akiba should be torn off with pointed iron combs. While undergoing this agony, the suffering patriarch remembered that the hour for customary prayer had arrived. In the midst of his tortures he could fix his mind on these subjects, and began reciting his last prayer. He had reached the closing word in the distinguishing formula of the Old Testament religion—" Hear, O Israel ! the Lord thy God is *one*—" when death came to his relief ,and in the accents of that confession he breathed his last. His constancy had been matter of astonishment even to his tormentors.[3] We need scarcely wonder that Jewish legend represented that on his decease a voice from heaven had been heard to announce his beatification. Some of his faithful disciples contrived to gain possession of his body, which they secretly interred. Akiba left one son and all Israel to mourn his loss.

The next sufferer whom tradition names was that devoted student of the Law, Rabbi Chananja ben Teradion, whose application of such passages as Ps. i. 1 and Mal. iii. 16, to neglect of, or occupation with, theological questions, we have formerly mentioned. As in the case of Akiba, Joses, a devoted friend of the Romans, had warned Chananja of his

---

[1] Such as the three arguments by which he attempted to prove the obligation and the sanctity of the Sabbath, recorded in Sanh. 65b.

[2] Comp. Relandii Notæ in H. Othonis, *Hist. Doct. Mishnic*, p. 134.

[3] Ber. 61b ; jer. Ber. ix. 14b ; jer. Sot. v. 20c.

danger. But, unlike the cautious Joses, who basked in the sunshine of Roman favour, the zealous sage continued his sacred employment. The Roman spies caught him engaged in the perusal of a roll of the Law. To the question how he had ventured to defy the Imperial edict, he replied by appealing to the higher duty of unconditional obedience to the laws of his God. Rabbi Chananja was sentenced to be wrapt in the roll in which he had been studying, and thus to be bound to the stake. To prolong his sufferings, the faggots by which he was to be consumed were to be fresh wood, and damp wool was to be put upon the region of his heart. The scrupulous Chananja refused to do anything which would abbreviate the period of his existence, lest he should incur the guilt of suicide. It is said that the executioner, more humane than the judge, subsequently removed the wool and so cut short his sufferings, and then, overcome by what he had seen, precipitated himself into the flames which encircled Chananja.[1] The heroic wife of our Rabbi fell likewise a victim to her faith. They left two daughters, of whom one was married to a celebrated theologian, Rabbi Meir; the other was sent to Rome, there to be devoted to prostitution. We shall by and by allude to the story of her wonderful escape. Another sufferer was Rabbi Chuzpith, who had formerly officiated as public interpreter to the Nasi. He is said to have been executed after having had his tongue cut out.[2] The martyr death of Rabbi Ishbab, the scribe, is alluded to, but no details about it are recorded.

The seventh of the martyrs of Lydda was Judah ben Baba, designated by his contemporaries the Pious. The death of so many teachers had excited in Judah apprehensions for the preservation of a succession of Rabbins, authorised and capable to administer the spiritual affairs of Israel. Accordingly, he resolved on the dangerous experiment of ordaining some candidates. To evade the threat of destruction which had been decreed against the city in which an ordination of Rabbins should take place, he betook himself

---

[1] Ab. Sar. 18*a*.   [2] Kid. 39*b*.

to a valley between Usha and Shafram, where he formally set apart six students to the sacred office. But no sooner was the solemnity past than they were overtaken by a band of Roman soldiers, who had got notice of Judah's intention. They came too late to disturb the proceedings. On their approach the aged Rabbi insisted on his unwilling young colleagues, for the sake of the common cause, abandoning him, and seeking safety in flight. He himself calmly met his fate, and fell pierced by 300 lances, or, as tradition has it, pierced by them like a sieve.[1]

A series of persecutions like these would have roused the hatred of any nation; nor can we wonder that Hadrian's memory was execrated by the Jews even more than that of Vespasian or of Titus. It sufficiently indicates the popular hatred of Hadrian, that whenever any Jew mentioned his name, he added to it the characteristic imprecation, " May the Lord break his bones !" Indeed, at no previous period had the Roman government adopted such severe repressive measures against the Jewish nation, and they retaliated in the only possible manner, by cursing his memory. The Rabbins who escaped the slaughter in Palestine fled mostly to Babylon, where so many of their brethren enjoyed liberty of conscience and prosperity. Among these fugitives were the newly-ordained teachers. This exodus gave a new impulse to the study of traditionalism in the provinces beyond the Euphrates. Not that the Jewish inhabitants of these districts had ever neglected it, but that the dependence of the Babylonian Jews on the Sanhedrin in Palestine, and the supremacy claimed by the colleges and Rabbins in the Holy Land, necessarily assigned only a secondary position to those in the lands of the Dispersion. Several celebrated teachers resided in Babylonia. Amongst them Juda ben Bethera, perhaps a descendant of the family of the Sons of Bethera, of the time of Hillel, taught in Nisibis.[2] In Nahardea lived Nehemia from Beth-Deli, who consulted Rabbi Akiba when he visited this city to settle the arrangement of the Jewish calendar.[3] Rabbi Chanina, whom, as

---

[1] Sanh. 14a.   [2] Jeb. 108b; Sanh. 32b.   [3] Jeb. 122a.

formerly stated, his uncle Joshua had sent to Babylon in order
to withdraw him from Christian influences, taught in Nahar-
Pacor, or Nahar-Pacod, a city not far from Nahardea.[1] The
influence of Babylon was subsequently felt in Palestine ; and,
had the persecution continued, no doubt Babylon would, even
at that time, have risen to the eminence which it afterwards
occupied.

Before detailing the events which led to the removal of
the obnoxious edicts of Hadrian, and to the restoration of
the Sanhedrin, we glance in passing at the state of Jewish
Christians during this period, and at the progress of the
Gospel amongst the Hebrews. Under the dominion of Trajan,
the edicts against Christians were not of so stringent a
character as necessarily to expose them to persecution.
That emperor had not enjoined any formal procedure against
them, and only ordered Christians to be punished if, when
brought before the magistrates and called upon to recant,
they refused to do so. This left them very much dependent
on the personal feelings of the governors of the different
provinces, and also on the passions of the populace. Under
his reign Christianity not only continued to spread throughout
the limits of the empire, but especially in Palestine, where
the period of national calamity proved also one of religious
inquiry to many Israelites.[2] We have already hinted that,
previous to the transformation of Jerusalem into the heathen
city Ælia, it had, partially at least, risen from its ruins.
We are also able to infer that Christians lived and laboured
there in the cause of their Master.

If the reign of Trajan was not marked by any general
or systematic persecution of the Christians, and if that of
Hadrian was even more favourable to the spread of the
Gospel, the Jewish disciples had, at least in part, to share the
troubles which befell their nation. We have already seen
that, unable to support the claims of the false Messiah, the
inoffensive and non-resisting Christians were selected as the
only victims of the deceiver's vengeance. But the conquest

---

[1] Jer. Ned. vi. 40*a* ; jer. Sanh. i. 19*a*.
[2] Comp. Euseb. *Hist. Eccl.* iii. 35.

of the land by the Romans, and the suppression of the
revolution, in more than one respect effectually improved
their circumstances.   No direct persecution thinned their
ranks, while their decided separation from the national
party procured for them the permission, together with
heathens, to live in Ælia Capitolina, the approach to which
had been interdicted to the Jews.   It may be true, as
Christian tradition asserts, that a sanctuary of Aphrodite was
built where the sepulchre of Christ had been;[1] or, according
to another account, that a statue of Jupiter was erected in
the place that had witnessed the resurrection of the Saviour,
and a temple of Venus was reared on Golgotha to profane
that place of solemn and sad recollections.[2]   It is said that
Bethlehem had to undergo a similar transformation, and that
the very cave in which, according to pious legend, Jesus had
been born, was set apart to the service of Adonis; so that
the spots which Christians so much revered became the
scenes of idolatrous and degrading feasts.[3]   [Nevertheless,
we may be sure that the profanation was accidental; Hadrian
had no wish to injure the Christians, and it was quite
gratuitous for them to see in these shrines intentional
insults to their faith.]   Meantime the separation between the
Church and the Synagogue had been completed, and bishops of
Gentile extraction henceforth presided over the believers in
Judea.   However, we cannot omit noticing the painfully
altered tone which Christian doctors assumed towards Israel,
and the manner in which the bitterness of carnal zeal took
the place of their former meekness.

Such, then, was the state of Judea at the termination of
a war which had exhausted its resources, wasted its treasures,
depopulated and destroyed its cities, and entailed upon the
surviving inhabitants a series of unwonted persecutions.   The
fall of Bethar was, as we have seen, succeeded by a short
guerilla war, after which the members of the national party
either fell or escaped into exile.   At last, when complete
tranquillity had for some time been restored to the land, the

---

[1] Euseb. *Vit. Const.* iii. 26 ; Sozom. *Hist. Eccl.* ii. 1.
[2] Hieron. *Ep.* 58 *ad Paul.*   [3] Hieron. *l.c.*

edicts which had proved so obnoxious to the people were also gradually removed. It is matter of doubt whether any measure of relief reached Palestine before the death of Hadrian. In fact, that emperor became more cruel and oppressive as he drew near his end. Ultimately, such was the popular feeling against him, that on his death the Senate intended to rescind all the ordinances passed towards the close of his reign, and even to deprive him of the title "divus" (or divine), which since the time of Augustus had been invariably decreed to the different emperors. But his successor, Antoninus, resisted this manifestation of ill-will, and perhaps for this devotedness to the memory of the departed, earned the title Pius.[1] Hadrian at first designated Lucius Commodus Verus as his successor to the empire. On his decease, Antoninus Pius was substituted, although on the express condition that he should in turn be succeeded by the son of Lucius Commodus Verus and by Marcus Aurelius as joint emperors.[2]

Under the mild reign of Antoninus Pius, who succeeded Hadrian in 138, about three years after the fall of Bethar, the Jews experienced considerable relief. A proclamation ascribed to this emperor represents him as preventing the superstitious populace of Asia from destroying the Christians by way of propitiating the offended gods, who were supposed to have manifested their displeasure in the earthquakes and other public calamities with which the Roman Empire was at the time visited.[3] This rescript cannot be genuine ; but it is true that Antoninus discouraged irregular persecutions of the Christians, and he showed himself equally tolerant towards the Jews. A story is told of the measures taken by them to obtain a repeal of the obnoxious edicts. A Jewish deputation applied, in the first instance, to a noble lady who was known to feel an interest in the cause of the persecuted. By her advice, this deputation, with Rabbi Judah ben Shamua at their head, passed at night under the windows of the governor's palace, complaining in dolorous accents, "Are we not children of the same parents ? why then are we treated so differently

---

[1] Capitol. *Ant. Pius*, 2.   [2] Spartian. *Hadr.* **24** ; *Ver.* **7**.
[3] Euseb. *Hist. Eccl.* iv. 13.

from other nations, or why are such fearful sufferings inflicted upon us ? " This appeal produced the desired effect, [and we are told, on weak authority, that it was in consequence of the withdrawal of Hadrian's edicts that the 28th of Adar (March) was observed as a feast day [1]]. It is said that the first measure of relief was granted on the 15th of Ab (August), when an edict arrived allowing the interment of the victims of the last war, whom, according to Jewish legend, a miraculous inter-position had preserved from putrefaction. Small and tardy as this concession may appear, such was the bondage under which the Synagogue had groaned, that in commemoration of it a special thanksgiving was ordered to be inserted into the customary prayers.[2] From a different source we learn that Antoninus allowed the Jews to circumcise their children.[3] After this no hindrance was set to the exercise and the teaching of Judaism. Only the approach to Jerusalem was still interdicted, and it was specially enjoined that no Gentile was to be admitted by circumcision into the Synagogue.

Tidings of this happy change rapidly spread, and from their various hiding-places the fugitive teachers retraced their steps towards the land of their affections and their hopes. One of their first meetings took place in the ever-memorable plain of Rimmon, and characteristically the subject of their deliberation was the intercalation of a month to restore order into the Jewish calendar, which had been neglected during the late troubles. Amongst the sages who met in Rimmon were those whose ordination had led to the martyrdom of Judah ben Baba. The most prominent personages in that assembly were two favour-ite pupils of Akiba, Rabbins Meir and Jochanan of Alexandria. But this long-desired meeting had almost proved fatal to the prospects of the new Sanhedrin. The council in Rimmon had assembled by stealth. It consisted of a few fugitives who, on their return, bore unmistakable evidence of their past suffer-

---

[1] Rosh ha-Shanah 19*a* ; Taan. 18*a* ; Megil. Taan. 35. [Comp. Derenbourg, p. 59, n., who gives a different explanation of the origin of the festival.]

[2] Taan. 31*a*,

[3] Modestinus, *Digest*, xlviii. 8. 11.

ings and privations. Yet even under such circumstances the spirit of ambition and of discord manifested itself amongst them. Rabbi Jochanan claimed pre-eminence, declaring that he had listened longer to Akiba standing (*i.e.* as a fully qualified student) than Rabbi Meir sitting (*i.e.* as mere hearer). On the other hand, Rabbi Meir retorted by reminding Jochanan that, as an Alexandrian, his authority was not entitled to much weight. The dispute threatened to become serious, when happily a reconciliation was effected.[1] Rabbi Juda ben Ilai was one of the most influential of these refugees, and at the same time favourably known to the authorities as a friend of the Roman government. He now invited the assembled sages to betake themselves to Usha,[2] where he resided, and where the Sanhedrin had met at a former period. Thither also the Jewish sages flocked from all parts of the country, and Simon the son of Gamaliel II., likewise returned from exile, became Nasi of the new Sanhedrin.

In many respects the circumstances in which the sacred college resumed its sittings had materially changed. The diligence of its predecessors had left few unsolved theological problems, while the method of Akiba had developed traditionalism to its utmost limits. The text of the oral Law, and the peculiar method of Jewish theology, had been almost completed. Any attempt to extend the latter could, with succeeding Rabbins who possessed neither the learning nor the intelligence of Akiba, only degenerate into sophistry and quibbling. Thus theologians would undertake, with an amount of speciousness and an air of sincerity and conscientiousness, to argue and defend both a proposition and its contrary. It became an exercise of logical ingenuity not unlike that of the sophists of Greece. The only thing which still remained to be done was, thoroughly to compile the text of traditionalism, and to introduce method and order into the collection. This was done by the next generation. While the schools declined in importance and influence, the patriarchal dignity proportionally rose for a time as a dignity or post of honour. But it soon sank to rise no more, while at the same time the

---

[1] Jer. Chag. iii. 78*d.*   [2] Mid. Cant. on ii. 5.

religious state of the nation generally was affected in a corresponding manner.

Rabbi Simon ben Gamaliel II. had been almost miraculously preserved during the persecution which followed the war under Bar Cochba. It was said that the party who had been despatched to capture the son of the Patriarch had given a hint of their errand, and that by their connivance the youth had escaped.[1] It is sad, but instructive, to notice how little Simon had profited by his early disasters. In exile he had neither learned wisdom nor humility. When he now came to occupy the highest post in the college, it seemed his chief endeavour to extend his own sway. The necessity may well have been felt of strengthening the central authority, but Simon attempted to do so by means only too likely to arouse jealousies. As frequently happens where offices which depend on mental superiority are connected with birth and station, the successors of Hillel had gradually increased in their pretensions. One of the sources of greatest danger which threatened the supremacy of the Patriarch during the incumbency of Simon, lay in the importance which the rival schools of Babylon had obtained during the late disasters. Not only had many theologians found a refuge there, but the closing of the colleges in Palestine gave a fresh impulse to those of Babylon.

In particular, the famed Rabbi Chanina had formed a Sanhedrin in Nahar-Pacor, near Nahardea, of which he was the president, and another great theologian, Nechunja, the Ab-beth-din. This Sanhedrin now arrogated to itself some of the functions of the patriarchate, more especially in regulating the calendar and the period of the feast days. The college in Usha, or rather the Nasi, resolved to make an end of this schism,—a purpose which was executed in their own peculiar way. Simon despatched to Nahar-Pacor two sages, Rabbins Isaac and Nathan, and furnished them with three different letters, of which they were successively to make use. In the first, Chanina was addressed as the Nasi's colleague and equal, and as "His Holiness Chanina." It

[1] Taan. 29*a*; comp. Grätz, iv. 467 f.

contained a simple recommendation of the bearers.   The ruse
succeeded.   As the two Rabbins, with unusual modesty,
professed to have come in order to learn rather than to teach,
the unsuspecting Chanina, flattered by the letter of the Nasi,
received them graciously.   Soon he gave them licence to
teach, and recommended them to the people as men of learning and authority.   But no sooner had the two doctors
secured a position, than, by perplexing cross questions and
continual contradiction, they sought to lower in public
estimation the authority of the Babylonian Nasi.   It was too
late for Chanina now to recall their licence ; they defied him in
public assembly.   At last, when he expostulated with them
on their conduct, they assigned as its ground Chanina's
assumption of functions which of right belonged only to the
Sanhedrin of Palestine.   An altercation ensued, in which the
Babylonian chiefly pleaded as excuse the closing of the
colleges of Palestine.   The deputies now produced their
second letter, in which the establishment of the Sanhedrin
at Usha was announced.   While Chanina still hesitated,
undecided how to act, the deputies ascended the tribune from
which the Bible was read and addresses delivered.   To show
the people the impropriety of supporting any rival Nasi,
one of the deputies read the ordinary lesson for the day in
Lev. xxiii. 4, etc., introducting certain alterations to describe
their position.   If the multitude had been indignant when
they heard the first deputy reading, "These are the feasts of
Chanina," instead of "the feasts of the *Lord*," loud murmurs
interrupted the second deputy as he paraphrased Isa. ii. 3
in the following manner: "Out of *Babylon* shall go forth
the law, and the word of the Lord from *Nahar-Pacor*."   But
the popular excitement was speedily turned into a different
channel, when the deputies produced their third letter of
instruction, and read the decree of the Sanhedrin at Usha,
which, in the case of continued schism, formally excommunicated Chanina, and declared the Jews of Babylon cut off
from all part or lot in the God of Israel.   The popular
assembly immediately decided in favour of submission.
Chanina still hesitated, and went to consult his friend Juda

ben Bethera at Nisibis.   By his advice he at last yielded, and the new arrangements were communicated to the various congregations in Babylonia.[1]

But although successful in suppressing, at least for a time, the rival Sanhedrin, the imperious disposition of Simon almost led to an outbreak in Usha similar to that which had ended in the deposition of his father Gamaliel. Inferior to several of his colleagues in talent and learning, Simon was jealous of the abler members of the sacred college, and anxious even in trifles to assert his superiority, and to assume a position different from that which they occupied.   As formerly noticed, the patriarchate had ceased to be regarded simply as an office accorded to learning and merit, and had become now a post of honour and hereditary dignity.   However, a man more prudent than Simon might, at any rate, have executed his ambitious designs with more tact.   But the Patriarch's vanity and lack of judgment led him more than once needlessly to offend those who were mentally his superiors.   Thus it was he who introduced the peculiar distinctions in the official salutation of the various college dignitaries, to which we have alluded in another place.

Amongst the Nasi's personal opponents, none was more dangerous than Rabbi Meir, of whom more anon.   This theologian, who held the post of Chacham in the college, persuaded the Ab-beth-din, Nathan, to conspire with him against the Nasi.   Nathan had been gained by the promise of being elevated to the presidental chair, to which he seemed the more entitled as being the son of the " Prince of the Captivity," or temporal chief of the Babylonian Jews. Everything had been preconcerted.   The two Rabbins were on a given occasion to overwhelm the Nasi with difficult questions, to perplex and silence him, and then to get him deposed.   But, unfortunately, their deliberations had been overheard by a zealous friend of the Patriarch, who, without in the first place disclosing the plot, effectually called his attention to the subjects on which the Rabbins were to

[1] Jer. Ned. vi. 40*a* ; jer. Sanh. i. 19*a* ; b. Ber. 63*a b.*

question him, by frequently repeating them in a neighbouring room in his hearing. Simon, whose attention was now called to the points to be debated, had mastered them before the day of trial arrived. The idea of his friend proved excellent, for, while the Patriarch displayed before his abashed opponents his lore, he could triumphantly confront them, detail the particulars of the foul conspiracy against himself, and obtain the exclusion of his opponents from the meetings of the sacred college. But their removal was only temporary. While the Sanhedrin daily felt the want of these two sages, they managed to puzzle their colleagues by sending in written questions, which the " assembled fathers " found difficult to discuss in their absence. At last a theologian, Joses, moved their readmission, with the remark, that "although he and his brethren were within the walls of the house of learning, learning itself remained outside that building." The Patriarch could not resist the general feeling ; but, to avenge himself to some extent, he would not in future allow the names of the rebellious Rabbins to appear in connection with the legal decisions which they had pronounced.[1]

Rabbi Nathan soon afterwards made his peace with the Patriarch ; but Meir persisted in his opposition, and that to such an extent that Simon would have excommunicated him, had it not been for a former decree of the Sanhedrin which protected the sages from the vengeance of their chiefs.[2] After what we have said, it will scarcely be expected that Simon had, during his incumbency, done much to advance Jewish theology. He felt it safest simply to adhere to what had been handed down by former teachers. So strictly did he observe this rule, that he would even confirm decisions which had been arrived at upon erroneous premisses.[3] Tradition reports under his name a number of decisions, of which only three were reversed by his successors. The maxim ascribed to him was that " the continuance of the world depended upon three things, upon truth, righteousness, and peace." [4] Rabban Simon was succeeded by his son, afterwards the

---

[1] Hor. 13*b* ; jer. Bik. iii. 65*c*.   [2] J. Moed Kat. iii. 81*c*.
[3] Comp. Grätz, iv. 188.   [4] Pirke Aboth i. 18.

celebrated Jehuda the Holy, who even during the lifetime of his father had attained a distinguished position amongst the members of the sacred college.

Of Nathan, the Ab-beth-din at Usha, we have already spoken. He seems to have occupied an honourable place amongst the sages of Palestine. His literary activity was chiefly distinguished by a collection of ordinances and statements which no longer exist in their original form. The work ascribed to Rabbi Nathan, bearing the name of the forty-nine " Middoth " or rules,—a work mainly treating of the study of mathematics and geometry,—belongs to a much later period, [and should perhaps be assigned to the ninth century [1]].

The most distinguished personage at Usha was Rabbi Meir, who derived his name (Meir, the enlightener) from the estimate which his contemporaries had formed of his merits. He was a man of undoubted talent and originality, and in spite of all his faults deserved to be " easily chief " in the Sanhedrin.[2] A native of Asia Minor, he shared in the versatility and lightness which constituted the marked characteristics of its inhabitants. Legend traces his origin to the Emperor Nero, in whose death the Orientals were so loath to believe.[3] His quickness early distinguished him amongst the students who crowded the classrooms of Rabbins Ishmael, Akiba, and Elisa ben Abuja. If he principally admired Akiba, whom he seems to have chosen for his theological model, he was by mental affinity specially drawn towards Elisa, with whom he remained on terms of intimacy even after his apostasy and subserviency to the Romans. Although not equal to Akiba, his power of intellect and freshness of imagination recalled the great gifts of that teacher. [Many sayings of Meir reveal the noble motives and depth of purpose with which he devoted himself to the study of the Law. Generous and forbearing, he was for the most part an ardent lover of peace.[4] Unhappily his vanity and ambition involved him in many

[1] Comp. Zunz, *Gottesd. Vortr.* (ed. 2) p. 95 ff. ; Bacher, *Tannait.* ii. 439.
[2] Comp. Grätz, iv. 188–195 ; Hamburger, *Enc.* ii. 705 ff.   [3] Gitt. 56a.
[4] [Comp. the stories told of Rabbi Meir, Gitt. 52a; Sanh. 11a; jer. Sot. i. 16a.]

disputes with the other Rabbins ; while, through the brilliance
of his mental gifts, he was often led to employ methods of
argument which belong rather to a man anxious for display
than to an earnest seeker after truth.] He was even accused
of trifling with the dearest interests of his own family or
of the Synagogue. His wife was Beruria, the talented and
accomplished daughter of Chananja ben Teradion, who, it will
be remembered, was burnt wrapped in the roll which he had
been discovered studying. Meir supported himself by making
copies of the Scriptures.[1] This occupation required not only
considerable learning, but specially scrupulous attention and
carefulness. His teacher, the conscientious Ishmael, anxiously
set these things before him, representing the danger which
must result from any neglect on his part. But Meir, who
felt no peculiar scruples, and was vain of his excellent
memory, which on one occasion had enabled him to copy from
memory the whole Book of Esther,[2] set these prudent counsels
aside. It was the practice of Jewish copyists to use an ink
which, in case of any mistake, could easily be obliterated. On
the other hand, Meir, confident of his accuracy, used an
indelible ink prepared from sulphate of copper (Chalcanthon).[3]
His manuscripts, indeed, were not free from errors, [but he was
always ready to apply some novel and striking interpretation
to any passage where a mistake was found[4]].

We cannot wonder that Meir's talents had early procured
him ordination from Akiba, of whom he was a favourite pupil.
His ingenuity led him to develop Akiba's method even beyond
its intended limits. While his cleverness dazzled, or at least
for the moment staggered, the sages as to the opinions which
he defended, his conclusions were frequently too artificial to
obtain the lasting approval of his colleagues. Owing to this,
and to his strained relations with the Nasi, Rabbi Meir's
reputation was never so great among his contemporaries as it
subsequently became after his death. His peculiar method,
rightly designated as the Dialectics of the Talmud,[5] had been
originated by Akiba, it was developed by himself, and, in

[1] Mid. Koh. on ii. 18.   [2] Tos. Megil. ii.   [3] Erub. 13a.
[4] Comp. Gen. Rab. 9.   [5] Grätz, iv. 194.

the hands of his successors, became the peculiar characteristic of later Rabbinical teaching. His pupils carried it afterwards to such excess, that even the Synagogue felt constrained to interpose, and at length ordered their exclusion from the college, as their object seemed rather to dispute than to elicit truth. It was, in fact, not unlike the Hagada, only applied to the oral as the former had been to the written Law. The quick mind of Meir would discover points which might be capable of advocacy, not only in one view of a question, but also in its direct contrary. He would bring them forward, and, without hesitation, defend the *pro* and the *contra* of a subject till the astonished hearer became bewildered, uncertain where or whether the truth lay anywhere, and what, after all, were the Rabbi's real sentiments. His own contemporaries were unable to say whether these sophistic arguments were to be taken seriously. Where more sober-minded men would have felt no difficulty, Meir could, with an air of sincerity, raise a host of difficulties, answer, again retort, and so on till the mind became giddy, and at last the sense of personal conviction and duty was in danger of disappearing before an unlimited exercise of logical ingenuity. With Meir no theological principle was treated as settled. He would anew investigate every question, and with marvellous ease rattle over all that could be said for and against it, till nothing was left but to choose between what seemed the more rational of two views, or deciding in accordance with the preponderance of conflicting authorities. It would, indeed, be unfair to lay the blame of this peculiar method wholly on Meir. It was inherent in Talmudism, and it had originated with his predecessors ; but probably it was he more than any other who, by developing it fully, cast Jewish theological thinking into that peculiar mould which substituted for depth and earnestness a showy attractiveness and a superficial ingenuity.

It will scarcely be wondered that, in the peculiar state of the Synagogue, Meir attracted around him numerous and devoted students. If his talents were brilliant, and his method such as to flatter the vanity of the Jewish sophists, he knew also how to relieve the dulness of theological teaching by interspersing it with Hagadic stories, sallies, puns, and especially with fables. He was particularly famed for aptness in the latter species of composition, and is said, for example, to have indited no less than 300 fables on subjects connected with the habits of the fox.[1] The most lasting merit of Rabbi Meir was his continuation of the labours of Akiba in the arrangement of the Halacha.[2] This he carried a stage further, by dividing, according to their contents, the traditions which had hitherto been only strung together according to their number. In this respect the Patriarch's son Jehuda was much indebted to his tuition.

The domestic history of Meir is in many respects touching, as describing first the mutual attachment, and then the dangerous trifling, of which a man of Meir's character was capable. It has already been stated that our Rabbi was married to Beruria, so famed for her talents and Rabbinical lore, as, in the opinion of contemporaries, to occupy a high place amongst the sages of the time. It is said that her sister had, after the martyrdom of their parents, been carried to Rome for the purpose of public prostitution, and that Providence had there watched over her honour. When the persecutions ceased, Beruria found no rest till Meir went to Rome to rescue his sister-in-law from infamy. Before entering on the dangerous undertaking, he resolved to try whether her principles had remained unshaken. Disguising himself as a Roman, he approached her, and, having satisfactorily ascertained her steadfastness, he bribed the attendants and procured her escape, though in the attempt himself escaped capture only by disguise and feigning to eat forbidden meat.[3]

Beruria throughout proved herself not only an attached but a devoted wife. She had shared his trials when during the persecutions Meir had fled from Palestine. On his return she cheered and encouraged him, and by her conduct softened the afflictions with which he was visited in providence. For example, while on a certain Sabbath the Rabbi was engaged

---

[1] Sot. 49*a* ; Sanh. 38*b*. [2] Comp. Sanh. 86*a*.
[3] Ab. Sar. 18*a b*.

in the college, his two sons had suddenly taken ill and died. To spare her husband some hours of grief, and especially not to commute the festivities of the Sabbath into a season of mourning, the mother carefully repressed her own feelings and concealed the sad tidings. The Sabbath had been spent as usually, and its holy exercises and stillness were ended with the evening, when Beruria asked her husband whether it were not duty readily and cheerfully to restore to its owner any property, however pleasant, which had been entrusted for safe keeping. When the astonished Rabbi answered the strange inquiry in the affirmative, his weeping wife took him by the hand and led him to the bed on which the lifeless remains of their two children were stretched, reminding him that He whose these two children rightly were, had taken back what for a time He had entrusted to their keeping.[1] At a later time a tragic account was given of Beruria's death. It is said that she had resented the harsh judgment passed upon women by a former Rabbi. To convince her of the truth of the saying, Meir agreed with one of his pupils that the latter should attempt her honour. Accustomed by her Rabbinical discussions to treat of subjects and to converse with the other sex in a manner which would have been deemed improper in other Hebrew females, it is said that Beruria yielded to the fascinations of her seducer. But when the guilty appointment was to take place, instead of her expected lover the outraged husband himself appeared. Shame and vexation so preyed upon the mind of the unhappy woman, that she committed suicide ; and it was felt necessary in future to restrict women from Rabbinical studies, which might throw them into unbecoming if not dangerous circumstances. [According to some authorities, it was on account of this painful occurrence that Rabbi Meir withdrew for a time to Babylon.[2]]

We have already alluded to the relation between Meir and the other sages. He seemed specially attached to Elisa the Apostate, with whom he always remained on intimate terms. Their minds seem to have been very similarly constituted, and doubtless their studies formed a strong bond of union. His

---

[1] Mid. Prov. (end).   [2] Ab. Sar. 18*b* ; Rashi, *ad loc.*

contemporaries, who ascribed their intercourse rather to Meir's laxity than to high-toned principle, objected to this intimacy; but the sage accounted for it from a desire on his part to profit by Elisa's Talmudical learning, which, strangely enough, the latter seems to have cultivated even after his apostasy, thus showing that these studies might easily constitute a mental rather than a religious discipline. Our Rabbi was wont to say that he had found an excellent pomegranate, and that after using what was good he could throw away the rind. However, the forbearance of the two seems to have been mutual. Thus it is related that on a certain Sabbath they had gone together for a little while — Meir on foot, and Elisa on horseback —discussing theological questions. In the eagerness of the engagement, Meir had almost forgotten the day of rest, and walked beyond the usual mark which indicated the boundaries of a Sabbath-day's journey; but Elisa stopped to remind him of it. Astonished at this, Meir seized the opportunity to invite his friend to return into the bosom of the Synagogue,— a proposition to which the latter refused to accede, as repentance could not be granted to one who had so wantonly abused the gifts granted him.[1] Again, when Acher lay on his deathbed, his faithful pupil hastened to his side, and renewed, this time effectually, his solicitations on this subject. Legend has it that Meir spread his cloak over the grave of Acher: a cloud of smoke rose from it, and Meir turned away with the somewhat blasphemous application of Ruth iii. 13: "Tarry this night (of time), and it shall be in the morning (of immortality) that He the All-merciful will deliver and ransom thee; but if He be unwilling, then I will redeem thee."[2]

Besides cultivating intercourse with the most noted theologians of his own nation, Meir was also on friendly and even intimate terms with heathen sages, whose scientific inquiries were neither foreign nor distasteful to his mind. Perhaps his friend Elisa may have called his attention to such subjects. Meir not only admitted that heathens, if virtuous, might have part in the world to come, grounding this concession on the fact that the Scriptures did not limit

---

[1] Chag. 15a. [2] Jer. Chag. ii. 77c.

eternal life to the *Israelite*, but to the *man* who observed the
commandments of the Lord,[1] but placed the heathen who
engaged in the study of the Law, from the peculiar difficulties
which he had to overcome, on the same footing of merit with
a high priest in Israel. [Amongst the heathen philosophers
of that time, none was so intimately known in Jewish circles
as Oenomaus of Gadara, the Cynic.[2] He was celebrated as a
writer, his most famous work being a book which he wrote to
expose the deceits and tricks of oracles.[3] Among the Jews
it was said that Balaam and Oenomaus were the two great
philosophers of heathendom by whom God willed to teach
His wisdom to the nations.[4] Between this philosopher and
Rabbi Meir a close friendship existed, and on the death of
Oenomaus' parents, Meir visited his friend to console him.[5]]

The most noted, if not the most sophistical, amongst
Meir's numerous pupils was Symmachos ben Joseph.[6] He
had attended Meir's prelections, and thoroughly imbibed his
method. It is said that this dialectician, on one occasion,
undertook by forty-nine arguments to prove that the touch
of a certain dead reptile could not defile a person. It was
opprobriously said of Symmachos by his contemporaries, that
his ancestors could not have heard the Law on Mount Sinai;
and after his teacher's death Symmachos was excluded from
the school, together with most of his fellow-pupils.[7] [This
Symmachos must not be confused with the Ebionite Symmachos, who is known as the author of a Greek version of
the Scriptures. The pupil of Meir may have been acquainted
with Greek, but he is never spoken of as a translator of the
Bible.[8]]

Rabbi Meir's teaching, in so far as practice was concerned,
went much in the direction of accommodating the Law to the
necessities of life, and hence of making its yoke lighter, or at
least distributing its burden more equably. This tendency is,
of course, closely connected with his general aim and views;

---

[1] Ab. Sar. 3*a*; Sifra, Lev. xviii. 5.
[2] Comp. Grätz, iv. 192, 469.
[3] Euseb. *Præp. Evan.* v. 18, vi. 7.
[4] Gen. Rab. 65.
[5] Ruth. Rab. on i. 8.
[6] Grätz, iv. 193 f., 470.
[7] Erub. 13*b*; Kid. 52*b*.
[8] Comp. *Dict. Chr. Biog.* iii. p. 20.

but although lenient where others were concerned, he himself refused to take advantage of such provisions. Thus, when on one occasion he had given permission to prepare on the Sabbath a mixture of oil and wine for sick or delicate persons, himself refused to make use of this concession, lest, as he said, selfish motives should be thought to have influenced him in granting the permission.[1] Although Meir's method was, after his decease, and in its full development, disowned by the Synagogue, it was too much in agreement with the spirit of traditionalism not to have added greatly to his fame and influence as a teacher; and the reputation in which he was held by his contemporaries was altogether surpassed by that which he attained in later generations. His ingenuity was extolled in the hyperbolical language of the time. To see Rabbi Meir disputing in the college, was like seeing " great mountains torn up from their base, and rubbed against each other to dust." His pupils would have it that " even to touch the staff of this modern Elijah would impart some wisdom." [2] Meir had frequently changed his residence. After his accession to power he had lived mostly at Tiberias and Ardiscus.[3] But his continual disagreements with the Nasi induced him at last to leave Palestine for Asia Minor, where he died, bequeathing to his countrymen the following proud and characteristic message : " Tell the children of the Holy Land that their Messiah has died in a strange country." According to his expressed wish, the tabernacle of his unquiet spirit found its last resting-place by the seashore, where his grave was washed by the waves, and looked into wide, storm-tossed ocean.[4]

A very different personage from the clever, vain, and versatile Meir was one of his contemporaries, Simon ben Jochai, in cold rationality, exclusiveness, and pride, a genuine Jewish Stoic. His father had been an adherent of the Romans ; [5] but Simon's religious and political views led him to an opposite extreme, and became the source of political troubles, to which we shall refer in the sequel. All his characteristics were peculiarities, and all his peculiarities were so marked as to

---

[1] Shab. 134a.　　[2] Jer. Ned. ix. 41b.　　[3] Nasir 56b ; jer. Sot. i. 16d.
[4] Jer. Kil. ix. 32c.　　　　　　　　　　[5] Pes. 112a.

become noticeable, and to leave an impression upon his period and nation.   Not easily excited, his emotions were, when roused, of the deepest character.   He was pre-eminently a man of conviction, who would unshrinkingly carry his principles, without compromise, to their utmost consequences, however repugnant, such consequences might in themselves appear. There is indeed a fallacy which persons of his disposition are apt to overlook.   Every action should not only be the consequence of a logical deduction from certain absolute principles, but in itself, and without reference to its ultimate principle, be capable of standing the test of moral investigation.   Where logic alone is the prompter, it so happens that, as it sometimes may be falsely applied, a man may, with the best intentions and the most conscientious convictions, act erroneously, if not wrongfully, while in general a cold heartlessness will characterise such rationality.   Such was the case with Simon.   It need scarcely be said that in his study of the Scriptures he repudiated not only the principles of Meir, but even their much more moderate original, those of Akiba.   Even the canons of Ishmael, although he approved of them, were not the guide of his investigations.   Unlike Akiba, he did not endeavour to investigate the hidden meaning of Scripture in order to elaborate and to apply it, nor did he, with Ishmael, read the Bible like any ordinary book, but busied himself to find out its *rational* principles,—the grounds upon which its injunctions were based.[1]

One or two instances of this will exhibit this novel tendency in the Synagogue.   Taking, for example, the injunction not to cut down the harvest along the corners of fields, Simon based it on the following four reasons, which, according to his system, were so many general scriptural principles :[2]—To protect the interests of the poor ; to save their time ; to spare their feelings ; and to protect the farmer from exaction or calumny. Again, having, according to his system, ascertained that the only traces of true worship were to be found amongst Israel,

---

[1] Nid. 31*b*. Comp. Grätz, iv. 198 f., 475 ; Hamb. *Enc.* ii. 1124 ff.; Bacher, *Tannait.* ii. 103 ff.

[2] Sifra on Lev. xix. 9 ; jer. Peah iv. 18*b* ; Shab. 23*a*.

he unhesitatingly avowed the most intolerant principles. He consigned all other nations to future destruction, and declared even the most pious among the heathen to be worthy of death.[1] Similarly, he inferred from the statement which forbade all connection with the seven Canaanitish nations, the exclusiveness of Judaism, and in application of this principle interdicted all close intercourse with heathens. The same inexorable logic he carried into every principle of his conduct. Thus even his contempt of the unlearned was that of conviction and of principle. Similar views induced him to assert more fully the rights of Rabbinism. He was the first amongst the sages to claim support, not from manual labour, but from his profession as a theologian, for he urged that it was impossible for a Rabbi to devote his whole time to the study of the Law if he had to earn his own living.[2]

It is scarcely matter of wonder that a stern, unbending spirit like that of Simon should have gathered numerous students in Upper Galilee (where he resided),[3] who were attached almost to idolatry, and devoted almost to servility, to their master. His sternness was not, as so often is the case, the counterfeit for true merit, or the offspring of narrow-minded bigotry; it was the result of calm conviction, although purely rational and unfeeling, almost to heartlessness. With him the rationalistic school, which attained its high point in Ishmael, was fully developed, just as Meir carried the allegorising tendencies of Akiba to and almost beyond their utmost limits. Henceforth the more calm and trustworthy of the Rabbins followed more and more in this direction. To Simon the drawing of logical conclusions from rational principles was more attractive than the mere learning of traditional Halacha. He used to assert that the study which bore the special name of Talmud was more meritorious than the study of the Mishna, or of the Scriptures themselves.[4] At a later period Simon was regarded as a celebrated mystic; and in the Middle Ages tradition ascribed to him the authorship of the

---

[1] Jer. Kid. iv. 66c ; Mechilt. on Ex. xiv. 7.
[2] Sifre on Deut. xi. 14 ; Shab. 11a.
[3] Shab. 147b. Comp. Grätz, iv. 476.   [4] Jer. Shab, xvi. 15c ; jer. Ber. i. 3b.

great text-book of the Kabalah, the "Sohar." [But, as we
have seen, the real tendency of his mind was practical and
rational; only the slightest traces of mysticism can be found
in any of his sayings.[1]]

Similar in his exegetical principles, but different in his
application of them, was Rabbi Joses ben Halephta.[2] Although
by trade a tanner, he was ardently attached to learned pursuits. Calmly rational in all he said and did, there was a
certain grandeur about this sage, which, as it did not take the
direction of Simon's sternness, but the opposite, that of mildness and liberality, made him an object of attachment rather
than of admiration. While he himself towered far above
those to whom he endeavoured to condescend, he desired to
lighten the burden of the Law, and to introduce such changes
as might make the profession of Judaism more easy. Like
Simon, he sought to apprehend the rational principles which
underlie Judaism; but if we may infer from his conduct, he
seems to have considered these principles alone necessary, and
to have dispensed with the logical deductions which his colleague would draw from them. It will be evident that these
two theologians, starting with the same fundamental views,
would arrive at almost opposite conclusions. While Simon's
logic was too wide, that of Joses was too narrow in its application. Hence, if the former fell into the dangerous error of
excessive sternness, the latter committed sometimes mistakes
arising from an excessive laxity; a tendency which induced
him to lighten the ordinances relating to vows,[3] to advocate
the temporary suspension of certain laws,[4] and sometimes to
act contrary even to his own pronounced principles. Still
there was a quiet but attractive dignity about our Rabbi.
Having never acted precipitately, or taught what was extravagant or ultra-strict, he was not only confident in the
correctness of his principles, but could, although in the pride
of Rabbinism, boast that he had never been obliged to retract
anything.[5] For the most part, indeed, his maxims are worthy

---

[1] Comp. Bacher, *Tann.* ii. 79.
[2] Hamb. *Enc.* ii. 493–498 ; Bacher, *Tann.* ii. 150–190.
[3] Nedar. 21*b*, 23*a*.   [4] M. Peah vii. 1 ; jer. *ib.*   [5] Shab. 118*b*.

of his position. Unlike his proud colleagues, he acknowledged merit wherever he found it, and distinguished it in proportion as it was rare in the circumstances. Thus he would have instituted mourning for slaves who deserved it by their character and worth.[1] He set a high value on learning, especially on the study of the Law in the Holy Land; yet he declared that it was an idle pursuit to learn without teaching others.[2] Careless of honours which conferred responsibility, and of ease which was due to a neglect of duty or an impropriety of conduct, he would admonish his pupils[3] rather to seek the duty of collecting *for* than of distributing *to* the poor; rather to go beyond than to fall short in the way of duty; rather to suffer than to inflict injury.

Joses' claims to scientific distinction in the Synagogue were twofold: he was both a theologian and a historian. [His thorough mastery of the traditional ordinances gave rise to the almost proverbial saying: "The knowledge of the Law is with him."[4]] A remarkable historical work which has been preserved, and is possessed of lasting interest, is commonly ascribed to Joses—the "Seder Olam," Annals or Chronicle of the World. In thirty chapters it professes to give the history of Israel up to the time of the author, or rather to the termination of the last Jewish war under Bar Cochba. But manifestly the later portions of the work have been tampered with by subsequent editors, and all notices of the events subsequent to the return of Israel from Babylon are of the scantiest character. [Since Joses is nine times appealed to in this work as an authority, he should, perhaps, be regarded rather as the author of the main sources of this book than of the book itself, unless, indeed, the passages are later insertions.[5]] The omissions at the close of the work are in part compensated by another historical work which bears the same title, but in contradistinction to the older "Seder Olam," or the "Seder Olam

---

[1] Comp. Ber. 16*b*.   [2] Koh. Rab. on v. 9.   [3] Shab. 118*b*.

[4] Gitt. 67*a*. [The view of Grätz (iv. 200), that this saying referred to a Legal Code (Nomicon) drawn up by R. Joses, is unsupported. Comp. Bacher, *Tann.* ii. 155; Levy, *Neuhebr. Wörterb.* iii. 388*a*.]

[5] Comp. Bacher, *Tann.* ii. 156; Hamb. *Enc.* Suppl. 132.

Rabba" (the larger Chronicle of the World), is designated the "Seder Olam Suta" (or smaller). It seems to have been written at a later period, and with the totally different purpose of advocating the claims of the Babylonian Jews, and the descent of the "Princes of the Captivity" from the family of David. A number of passages in the "Seder Olam Suta" are manifestly culled from the "Rabba," while others are as evidently contrary to historical facts.[1] Up to the fifth century of our era no reliance can be placed upon the list of princes given in this work. It is striking how the historical information becomes more accurate as the period of the author's lifetime is approached; and how, in almost the same proportion, the tendency to garnish his narrative with miraculous stories increases. The closing passages of the "Suta" are probably a later addition, and date from the eleventh century, the body of that work from the eighth or ninth. Rabbi Joses, the reputed author of the original Seder Olam, left five sons, all of whom became more or less celebrated in the Synagogue.[2]

This brief sketch of the Synagogue would scarcely be complete did we not add a notice of another Rabbinical authority, distinguished for his conscientious punctiliousness, and a type of the old school which had nearly become extinct. Rabbi Juda ben Ilai, who, as the reader will remember, invited his colleagues to join him at Usha, was by trade a cooper. He was not only himself industrious, but endeavoured to impress on his hearers the necessity of engaging in manual labour, which, so far from degrading, elevated those who were employed in it. To enforce his teaching by example, he was wont to lecture to his numerous students seated on a kind of cask of his own manufacture.[3] He had, during the troubles in Palestine, experienced the benefits of an honourable independence, and was anxious that, by being masters of some trade, all others should, if needful, enjoy the same advantage. That, however, he did not neglect the study of the Law, is evident, even from the designations by which he was known amongst his contemporaries. He was

---

[1] Comp. Hamb. *ut supra*, p. 133 ; Zunz, *Gottesd. Vortr.* p. 142 ff.
[2] Shab. 118*b* ; jer. Jeb. i. 2*b*.　　　　[3] Nedar. 49*b*.

called "the prudent," "the orator," and "the pious."[1] The
first of these titles he earned by his cautious political conduct,
which procured for him the confidence and favour of the
authorities, and by his domestic habits. It has already been
mentioned that he was most anxious to remain independent
of strangers. To such an excess did he carry this determination, that he was content to possess only one upper garment,
which he and his wife would wear alternately. On one occasion, it is said, he was unable to appear at a public fast,
because his wife had gone with their one robe to the market.[2]
On account of his peculiar rhetorical talent, which secured
for him a distinguished place amongst his colleagues, he was
called "the orator." His claims to the title "pious" rested
on a scrupulous observance of religious duties, and on the
perfect mastery which he had attained over his feelings. The
latter was such that the tidings of the death of his son
could not interrupt him when engaged in a prelection.[3] To
Juda is ascribed a large part of a commentary on the Book of
Leviticus which bears the name of "*Sifra.*"[4]

We can only name some of the other sages in the
college at Usha. Chanina ben Chachinai had, from love of
study, left his young wife and children. After twelve
years' absence, he returned so changed in appearance that
he was not recognised by his nearest relatives.[5] Eleazar
ben Jacob was famous as having rehearsed some interesting
traditions connected with the temple. Besides, Jochanan of
Alexandria, Nehemia, Eleazar ben Shamua, and others,
occupied distinguished places in the Sanhedrin. In reviewing
this period, we become sensible of a considerable change in
the tendency of Jewish theology. Pharisaism, in the sense
in which it obtained distinction at the time of our Lord, had
entirely passed away. The ignorant Pharisee, he whose
religion consisted primarily in ritual observances and long
prayers, had now become only an object of scorn and

---

[1] B. Kam. 103*b*.   [2] Nedar. 49*b*.   [3] Moed Kat. 21*a*.
[4] Sanh. 86*a*.   Comp. Hamburger, *Enc.* ii. 1166 f.; Strack, *Einl.* p. 56;
Weber, *Lehren des Talmud*, p. xx.
[5] Keth. 62*b*.

contempt.[1] But the allegorical method was also passing away. In its room the dialectic had appeared. However, the direction followed by the ablest Rabbins was different, and gradually became more and more rationalistic. Along with this tendency, an attempt was also made to remove a number of ordinances, which were felt to be needless or irksome burdens. At the same time, the theological thinking of Palestine had almost exhausted itself, as its theology had reached its furthest boundaries. If the text of the traditional Law were once perfectly arranged, nothing further remained to be done by the colleges of Palestine. Thus was the decline of these colleges, which could at best experience only a temporary revival, prepared. The office of Nasi had also changed into the dignity of a temporal prince as the colleges declined and their authorities became less capable for their duties. Once more did the academies appear to flourish—once more did the Rabbins and the people experience a storm of persecution—and then the colleges of Palestine closed, and its sages were scattered into other lands. But before describing these events, we invite the reader to follow us through the cities, villages, and homes of Judea, there to observe the manners and habits, and to inquire into the social, intellectual, moral, and religious state of its inhabitants.

[1] Comp. jer. Ber. ix. 14*b* ; b. Sot. 22*b*.

CHAPTER IX

I. SOCIAL CONDITION OF PALESTINE

THE geographical position of Palestine gave it a political importance greater than that to which its extent and population would otherwise have entitled it. Situated between Syria, Egypt, and Assyria, and on the highway to Persia, Arabia, and India, it became in turn the object of the cupidity of its neighbours, and the battle-ground on which their contests were decided. Consequently, except during the reigns of David and Solomon, the inhabitants of Palestine had always more or less to act on the defensive. From the circumstances of the people and of their rulers—from the division of the land into two rival monarchies—and from the uncertain, shuffling, and short-sighted policy which was prosecuted by their kings, it was even found impossible to defend for any length of time the boundaries of Palestine. So far from occupying the position of political importance to which their situation, and the possession of so much seaboard, might have entitled the Hebrews, they gradually became dependent upon, and finally subject to, their neighbours. After the return from Babylon and the brief period of national independence under the Maccabees, the sceptre entirely and finally departed from Judah, and every attempt to regain it proved unsuccessful.

At the time when the Saviour appeared on earth, Palestine had undergone a fourth division and arrangement. The allocation amongst the tribes had given place to a monarchy. The latter had in turn been divided into the rival kingdoms of Judah and Israel. Now, Jew and Gentile had forgotten both tribes and kingdoms, and only spoke of Galilee, Samaria, Judea, and Peræa. The first of these provinces, Galilee, commonly divided into two districts, Upper and Lower, to which Jewish authorities added the district around Tiberias as a third,[1] extended from near the river Leontes, in Syria,[2] to Scythopolis, on the Jordan, and from the borders of Tyre to Mount Carmel. Its western boundary consisted of a narrow strip of land along the sea-shore,[3] and of Phœnicia. Eastward, it extended to the Jordan and the Lake of Gennesaret. Upper Galilee was mountainous, and inhabited in great part by Gentiles (hence the name, Galilee of the Gentiles); Lower Galilee was more level, and exceedingly fruitful.[4] The people were brave and warlike. From their commixture with Gentiles, they were less addicted to the study of Jewish traditions or the observance of ceremonial injunctions, and hence despised by their brethren of the south. This remark applies chiefly to the inhabitants of Upper Galilee. The prosperity of this province is sufficiently indicated by the large number of its towns, which at the commencement of the Jewish war are said to have amounted to 240,[5] of which, according to Josephus, the smallest contained not less than 15,000 inhabitants.[6] Although this computation is evidently exaggerated, some idea of its populousness may be gathered from the fact that in the war with the Romans, Josephus was able to raise in Galilee alone an army of no less than 100,000 men.[7] Galilee covered the ancient possessions of the tribes of Issachar, Zebulon, Asher, and Naphtali. Its most fertile and beautiful district was that around the Lake of Gennesaret, where, along with the products of cooler zones, in certain situations, those of tropical climates also adorned and enriched the landscape during many months;

---

[1] Sheb. ix. 2. Comp. Neubauer, *Geog. du Talm.* p. 178 f.

[2] Comp. Schwartz, *Das heil. Land*, pp. 10 f., 43 f.

[3] According to Josephus (*Wars*, iii. 3. 1), Mount Carmel and the territory of Ptolemais were not included in Galilee.

[4] Jos. *ut sup.* iii. 3. 2. [5] Jos. *Life*, c. 45.

[6] Jos. *Wars*, iii. 3. 2. [7] *Ut supra*, ii. 20. 6.

and a rich soil was assiduously cultivated by a diligent and enterprising population.[1]

Samaria, which covered the ancient inheritances of Ephraim and the half tribe of Manasseh, bordered to the north on Galilee, and was smaller than either of the other provinces of Palestine. It formed nearly a square, as the western strip of land along the Mediterranean, and almost as far as Mount Carmel, was reckoned part of the province of Judea. The soil was fertile, and although the watercourses were not abundant, frequent showers compensated for their want. The water of Samaria was said to be peculiarly sweet. This, together with the quantity of aromatic herbs which grew in the country, gave the Samaritan agriculturists a more than ordinarily large and good supply of milk. The inhabitants, who formed a numerous and prosperous community,[2] lived for the most part at enmity with the Jews ever since the time of the building of the second temple. The occasions when common hopes or misfortunes joined the two classes were rare and of short duration. In general, a mutual distrust and bitterness characterised their relations. The Jews accused the Samaritans of being the lineal descendants of heathens, of practising idolatry, of deceitfulness, etc. ; and the Samaritans retorted by such acts of vengeance and malice as opportunity afforded. Commonly the two parties avoided each other, the Jews preferring to take the longer road to Jerusalem beyond the Jordan to passing through Samaria, by which the capital might have been reached from Galilee in three days.[3] The opinions as to the lawfulness of intercourse with the Samaritans differed with circumstances and Rabbins. Some went even so far as to forbid the purchase of uncooked animal food from them, or the sojourning under the same roof ; but usually a clear distinction was drawn between the Samaritans and heathens or idolaters.[4]

The third province of Palestine was Judea, which extended southwards to the borders of Arabia, and westwards along the seashore for a considerable distance. In every

---

[1] Comp. also *Life and Times*, i. 223 ff. [2] Jos. *Wars*, iii. 3. 4.
[3] Jos. *Life*, c. 52. [4] Comp. *Life and Times*, i. 400 ff.

respect the most important province of the country, it was in part mountainous, and the neighbourhood of the sea was specially adapted for pasturage. From the time of the Maccabees, Idumea was joined to Judea, but retained its peculiar name. The Talmud[1] distinguishes in Judea, as in Galilee, three districts: the mountains, the plain, and the south. For civil purposes it was divided into eleven top-archies or districts;[2] geographically it may be distinguished into Eastern and Western Judea.

The district on the other side of the Jordan, known by the name of Peræa, was divided into three smaller portions, varying in size, fertility, and populousness. This province also was in part mountainous and in part desert. The history of Peræa was not of great importance: within its limits lay the greater part of the Decapolis (or ten cities), so well known to the readers of the New Testament.

Palestine had more towns and villages than might have been expected, considering the agricultural pursuits of the majority of its inhabitants. At first, towns had chiefly served for protection to the agricultural population. But as the wants of the people, so the number of cities also increased. Jewish authorities distinguished between cities or fortified places and common towns, which were reputed large if they could produce ten men whose wealth relieved them from the necessity of manual labour,[3] and small if their number were less. The defence of cities consisted of thick walls, whose gates were often covered with iron, and strongly barred. Above the gates rose watchtowers, and along the walls other works of defence. Outside the walls ran a ditch, and beyond it a low wall. The streets were in general narrow, as those of modern Eastern towns. The shadowy retreat of the gates, with the distant prospect and the busy throng around, formed the place of public resort, where the elders of the city commonly assembled, and the concerns of the town or public affairs were discussed. Sometimes the Rabbins taught in the streets, although this practice was soon interdicted in the

[1] Sheb. ix. 2.   [2] Jos. *Wars*, iii. 3. 5.   Comp. Schürer, II. i. 157 ff.
[3] Megill. i. 3.

spirit of Jewish aristocracy.[1]   Our Lord, however, seems to
have availed Himself of the opportunity of addressing in the
streets those who would not otherwise have heard Him.
Jerusalem itself was paved with white stones,[2] and Antioch
enjoyed the same convenience through the liberality of Herod
the Great.[3]   From the nature of the soil, most of the other
cities, built on high and rocky ground, scarcely required pavement.   The streets and markets had names attached to them,
which were generally derived from the shops or bazaars in
them.[4]   In Cæsarea the sewerage was well attended to,[5] and
generally nothing that could contribute to comfort or ornament was neglected.[6]   The supply of water was derived
either from aqueducts, from wells and fountains, or most
commonly from cisterns.

[A whole treatise of the Mishna deals with municipal
regulations.   Many of these can hardly have been carried out
in practice, but the account of them shows us at least what
was the theory of the Rabbins on this subject, and throws
light on many details of social life.]   In the towns, watchmen
patrolled the streets at night.   Still, the darkness of the
streets at night, though comparatively little felt where
engagements commenced and ended with the day, rendered
it unsafe to go abroad after sunset, especially if the police
regulations were not strictly enforced.   In general, these
regulations were strict, and provided for all possible emer-
gencies.   Larger houses were often occupied by more than
one family, and still more frequently two or more smaller
dwellings opened into one common court, a convenience felt
indispensable by the Jews.[7]   House watchers, like the porters
in most continental cities, watched over the safety and
attended to the general wants of these houses.   To obviate
occasion of dispute, neighbours were prevented from opening
windows which looked into the courts or rooms of others, or
shops to which the entrance led through a common court.[8]

---

[1] Moed Kat. 16*a b.*   [2] Jos. *Ant.* xx. 9. 7.   [3] *Ut supra*, xvi. 5. 3.
[4] Jos. *Wars*, v. 8. 1.   [5] Jos. *Ant.* xv. 9. 6.
[6] Comp. Keth. 110 ; Jos. *Wars*, i. 21. 5-8.   [7] Baba Bathra i. 4, etc.
[8] *Ut supra*, iii. 7, ii. 3.

Attention was likewise paid to the appearance of the streets, and proprietors were not allowed to build beyond the line, or to make any projection on their houses.[1]   Not only were the inhabitants of towns guarded from intrusion or inconvenience, but sanitary regulations, which outstrip those of our own cities, protected them from the carelessness, selfishness, or folly of their fellow-citizens.   Thus a certain space had to intervene between the dwelling of a neighbour and what could occasion annoyance to him ; while cemeteries, tanneries, and similar places which might endanger the health or prevent the comfort of the citizens, had to be removed at least fifty cubits from towns.[2]   So careful in this matter were the authorities, that bakers' or dyers' shops, stables, etc., were not tolerated under the dwelling of another person.[3]   A year's residence, or the purchase of property, constituted residence, and imposed on the citizen the obligation of contributing to the common expenditure or city taxation.   Of the courts of law in the different towns, we may observe that in every city there were civic authorities ; [but in those parts of Palestine in which there was a more or less influential Gentile population, the constitution of the towns varied considerably.   In the strictly Jewish territory all civic business was doubtless in the hands of the local college of elders.   The position of these authorities must have been greatly affected by the two Jewish revolts ; but, even after the total loss of national independence, the Jews were for the most part allowed to decide questions of civil law among themselves, while their courts sometimes usurped also criminal jurisdiction [4]].

The town houses varied in extent and splendour with the condition of their inhabitants, from the humble cottage to the larger dwellings of the patricians.   The walls were built of bricks, of half-bricks, of dressed and undressed stones,[5] and even of white marble or large hewn stones.[6]   These stones were cemented together with mortar, gypsum, and even

[1] Baba Bathra iii. 8.   [2] *Ut supra*, ii. 1 ff., 9.
[3] *Ut supra*, ii. 3.   [4] Comp. Schürer, I. ii. 273 ff. ; II. ii. 55 ff.
[5] Baba Bathra i. 1.
[6] Comp. Jos. *Ant.* viii. 5. 2, and many passages of Scripture.

asphalt. Sometimes they were, besides, riveted with iron or lead, but in such a manner as to be imperceptible. The walls were covered with a kind of whitewash, and palaces were painted with delicate colours, such as vermilion, etc. (Jer. xxii. 14). The woodwork was constructed of sycamore (the most common tree in Palestine), of olive and almond trees, or even of cedar, and adorned or inlaid with ivory or gold. Richer dwellings were distinguished by rows of pillars and other architectural ornaments. The houses of the better classes consisted generally of two or more storeys, to which a stair (often costly) conducted from the outside. From the various uses made of the court, which also served as a kind of ante-chamber to visitors, it was felt to be a most important part of the building. It varied in size with the circumstances of tenants, being sometimes divided into an outer and inner court; at others, shared by several tenants. The inner court, whence the porter opened to callers on mentioning their names (Acts xii. 14; Rev. iii. 20), often led into a large and splendid reception-room, whence other apartments passed to the interior of the house. The upper rooms were not used for common purposes; inner rooms were inhabited chiefly in winter. The apartments were frequently richly decorated, sometimes painted or covered with pictures.[1] The reception-room and the inner court properly formed together but one apartment.

The inner court was paved, surrounded by galleries, and sometimes had fountains and baths. Some outer courts of a peculiar construction, and for special purposes, were termed Tyrian.[2] The roofs, although flat, were somewhat sloping, to allow the rain water to flow into the channels and cisterns, paved with stones or earth beaten hard, and surrounded by a protecting balustrade. The roof was used when great privacy was sought, as in prayer, especially when upper rooms were

---

[1] Jos. *ut supra*. The quotations would necessarily be so many that we have generally omitted them. Our sources of information were, the Scriptures, Josephus, the Mishna, commentators, and Winer's admirable *Encyclopædia*, whose quotations have been carefully revised and verified.

[2] Maaser. iii. 5.

wanting, and in the cool of the evening as the place of resort.
It was also employed for domestic purposes, such as drying
fruits, etc.   The floors of the rooms were of gypsum, and
even of marble ; the doors were of stone, as in the Hauran,
or more frequently of wood, and moved on hinges let into
sockets above and below.   They were barred by wooden bolts,
which could be withdrawn by check keys from the outside.
The dining apartment was very spacious, and often employed
for assemblies.   Instead of glass panes, the windows had
gratings or lattices.   They mostly looked into the streets,
and were distinguished as Tyrian windows, probably large,
and Egyptian, which are supposed to have been small,[1] sometimes only two feet square.   In the houses of the wealthy,
the window-frames were carved, as in general their furniture,
such as tables, couches, chairs, lamps, candlesticks, etc., were
exceedingly costly.   Amongst the articles of luxury, we only
notice soft cushions, destined to be placed under the head or
arms.

The different cities of Palestine were connected together
by roads (denominated field-roads if four, and highways
if sixteen cubits broad).[2]   Some of these highways were
paved, and provided with milestones.[3]   In general, only
the frequented thoroughfares, used for commercial or military purposes, on which toll-money was levied, were well
kept.   The reader will find the principal roads traced on the
map.[4]   One of them conducted from Ptolemais eastward
among the hills to Tiberias, and along the Lake of Galilee to
Capernaum, whence, passing over the Jordan, it continued to
Damascus.   On that road sat Matthew at the receipt of
custom when our Lord called him.   Another highway
went along the seashore from Tyrus (whence a road passed
by Cæsarea Philippi to Damascus) by Ptolemais, Cæsarea,
Jamnia, Gaza, etc., to Egypt.[5]   Travellers to the capital took

---

[1] Baba Bathra iii. 6.   [2] *Ut supra*, vi. 7.
[3] Comp. H. Reland's *Palæstina*, p. 401, etc. [Such roads were mainly due
to Roman enterprise.]
[4] Comp. G. A. Smith, *Historical Geography of the Holy Land*, p. 425 ff.
[5] *Ut supra*, p. 153 ff.

this way, and then journeyed by Antipatris, Lydda (Diospolis), and either by Emmaus (Nicopolis) or by Beth-horon to Jerusalem. A third highway passed from Galilee through Samaria to the Jewish capital, by way of Jezreel, Ginæa, Samaria, and Sichem. Although short, it was rarely taken, on account of the hostility of the Samaritans. At Sichem a road turned north-eastwards to Scythopolis, and again from that place westwards to Cæsarea, or eastwards by Gadara and Capitolias to Damascus. From Jerusalem, a road led by Bethany to Jericho, where the Jordan was forded, and thence passed to Gilead. This road was frequently taken by Jews who came from Galilee. From Gilead other roads led southwards. Finally, another highway conducted from the capital by Bethlehem to Hebron and southwards, while the road from Jerusalem by Beth-horon to Lydda continued as far as Joppa, one of the few seaports of Judea.

Such were the roads along which travellers passed. Their number was at first small, except when large bodies of pilgrims, at the annual feasts, resorted to the capital. Gradually, as commerce increased, more distant journeys were undertaken, and as the Jews spread over the face of the known world, their relations extended, and travelling became more common. Journeys were performed on foot, upon asses, or in carriages (Acts viii.), of which three kinds are enumerated.[1] The round carriage (perhaps like our gig), the elongated, like a bed, and the cart, chiefly used for the conveyance of goods. From the robbers who infested various districts, from the nature of the country, the bad state of the roads, and the want of proper inns and public conveyances, travelling was always difficult and dangerous. These circumstances exercised a reciprocal influence. Of course, where the roads were bad or even dangerous,—where, in case of need, it would have been found difficult to procure shelter for man or beast, and almost impossible to communicate with friends at a distance,—few would, except in cases of necessity, and then generally in company with others, undertake a journey. It was otherwise with the travelling hawker, who,

[1] Kelim xxiv. 2.

well acquainted with the roads, was welcomed in every
district as a friend who could communicate news, or at least
exchange the products of one district for those of another, or
for the still more rare articles of luxury imported from abroad.
Those who went up to the feasts, generally in company, and
often singing the praises of the Lord, were, of course, welcomed
and entertained as became their holy errand. At a later
period, all brethren in misfortune would meet a ready reception ; and, as the wants of the country made hospitality
a more than usually sacred duty, so the paucity of travellers
would continue its practice longer than might otherwise
have been expected. But generally a person who was about
to undertake a journey prepared himself as if for a change of
residence. He would carry with him his tent, sufficient provisions, in the shape of corn and preserved fruit, and clothing.
Equally great were the preparations of those who expected a
guest. The host went to meet him at a considerable distance ;
and again, when he left, escorted and provided him with the
necessaries of life. On solitary roads, or where villages were
thinly scattered, wayside inns, which, in the Talmud,[1] bear
the same name as in the New Testament, provided, for payment, lodging and food for strangers. These inns were
generally kept and resorted to by non-Israelites. Jews preferred to pitch their tents, or even to seek hospitality from
Samaritans, rather than trust themselves to what often
proved lurking places for the ill-disposed. It may be added
that, in the larger towns at any rate, there existed for the
convenience of the inhabitants numerous restaurants and
wineshops, where food and drink could be supplied in great
variety.

The Jews early took part in the extensive trade of the
Phœnicians, and the possession of the seaports on the Red Sea
gave them at one time the command of the Indian trade.
In Roman times the commerce of Palestine became very
extensive. Many of the natural products and manufactures
of the country were exported to distant lands, where some
of them gained a high reputation. The foreign wares

[1] For example, Jebam. xvi. 7.

imported were, with the exception of woods and metals, principally articles of luxury. Fish from Spain, apples from Crete, cheese from Bithynia; lentils, beans, and gourds from Egypt and Greece; plates from Babylon, wine from Italy, beer from Media, household vessels from Sidon, baskets from Egypt, dresses from India, sandals from Laodicea, shirts from Cilicia, veils from Arabia,—such were some of the goods imported from abroad. On the other hand, the Jews exported wheat, oil, honey, figs, balsam, as well as linen and woollen goods.[1] Some idea of the diversity of Jewish trade may be gathered from the fact that in the Talmudic literature about ninety different home products or manufactures are mentioned, and 120 foreign imports; and this cannot be regarded as an exhaustive list of the articles of commerce in Palestine.[2]

The currency varied with the circumstances of the people. After the return from Babylon, first Persian, then Syrian coinage was chiefly in use. When Simon the Maccabee attained power, he issued Hebrew coins, which were in turn superseded by Grecian and Roman currency. Amidst this variety, it is more than usually difficult to ascertain the exact value of coins. [According to later Rabbinic tradition, the Sacred Shekel was computed at double the ordinary; but this statement is not borne out by any extant coins.[3]] The smallest coin was the half-quadrans, or (Jewish) perutah, equal to about one-sixteenth of a penny. Four quadrans, or eight lepta, made an *as*, or about a halfpenny—two and four as-pieces being also in use. The denarius, or drachm (the penny of the New Testament), was worth about $7\frac{1}{2}$d. The *stater*, worth 4 drachms, was approximately equivalent to a shekel; [but the annual temple tribute of a half-shekel was made according to the Tyrian valuation, with which the Jewish exactly corresponded. As the Tyrian drachm or *sela* was rather lighter than the Attic drachm, the Jewish half-shekel, about 1s. 3d. of our money, was a trifle less than the Greek didrachm. The latter coin had fallen out of use in the first

[1] Comp. Schürer, II. i. 41–46; Hamb. *Enc.* ii. 1270–1276, "Welthandel."
[2] Comp. Herzfeld, *Handelsgeschichte der Juden*, p. 129.
[3] Madden, *Coins of the Jews*, pp. 285, 322.

century A.D.   Larger sums of money were reckoned by *minas*
worth 100, and talents worth 6000 drachms.   The usual
gold coin was the Roman *aureus*, worth 25 denarii, and the
difference between the value of gold and silver varied from
1–10 to 1–15 [1]].

While the smallness of the coins in circulation may be
taken as in itself an index of the cheapness of living in the
country, their variety early necessitated a class of merchants,
known as bankers or money-changers.   The readers of the
New Testament are familiar with both these facts.   They
will remember that, if a labourer received for a day's work in
the field or vineyard a denar (7½d.), Matt. xx. 2, while the kind
Samaritan only paid two denars (1s. 3d.) for the charge of the
sick person in the inn, labour must have brought a high price
in comparison to the expense of provisions.   They will also
recall the existence and duties of the money-changers.   These
were necessary, not only from the different currencies in use,
or to accommodate the merchant and the traveller, but
principally to change the various coins in which Jewish
residents at home, or settlers abroad, paid the statutory half-
shekel as temple-tribute.   From all parts of the world did
the contributions of the faithful flow to Jerusalem, which,
wherever scattered, they still regarded as their religious home.
Custom had it, that nothing but the recognised equivalent of
a half-shekel could be received at the treasury.   Every other
kind of coin had therefore to be changed for half-shekels, and
this constituted one of the principal employments of the
regular bankers.   For this purpose they opened stalls throughout the country between the 15th and the 25th of Adar,
the period when also the public roads, market-places, and
baths were yearly repaired, corresponding to our month of
March.   On the 25th of Adar business was only transacted
within the precincts of the city and of the temple ; and after
that date those who had refused to pay the impost could be
proceeded against at law, and their goods distrained.[2]   The
money-changers charged a silver meah, or about one-sixth of a

---

[1] Comp. Herzfeld, *Handelsgesch.* pp. 178–182.
[2] Shek. i. 1–3.

denar [1] (1½d.) as discount from everyone who procured from
them the temple coin.[2] The rate of discount was fixed by law,
perhaps in order to obviate all suspicion of, or temptation to,
usury,—a sin deemed by the Hebrews as amongst the most
heinous of civil offences. The sums which used to flow into
the temple treasury must have been immense. The whole of
the annual contributions to the temple have been computed at
about £75,000.[3] [We are told that on one occasion 800 talents
of Jewish money was deposited at Cos.[4] Flaccus intercepted
100 pounds of gold at Apamea, and 20 pounds more at
Laodicea.[5] The largest contributions came to Jerusalem from
Babylon and the regions beyond the Euphrates. We need not
therefore wonder when we are told that the triumvir Crassus
took from the temple treasure worth more than £2,000,000.[6]]

It need scarcely be stated that the Jews were designed to
be an agricultural people. However, as the agricultural
labourer had neither leisure nor opportunity for studying
the Law, or distinguishing himself in the practice of ritual
observances, he was held in contempt by the Rabbins. It
was otherwise with the large proprietors who let their fields
to farmers, either for money or for part of the produce, or
who employed land-stewards, and also with the small proprietors who resided in the many villages and towns with
which Palestine was studded. These enjoyed the privileges
which a town residence conferred. In their husbandry the
Hebrews used simple implements. In all ordinary cases the
natural fertility of the soil served to the humble farmer in
room of the appliances of the modern agriculturist. The
plough with which he loosely turned up the dry ground was
fragile and comparatively inefficient. The harrow was employed both before and after committing the seed to the
ground, and manure was not altogether unknown. In these
climates the character of the crop chiefly depends on the

---

[1] It is difficult to fix the exact equivalent of the meah. Winer (*Real-
Lexicon*) computes it at one-fourth, Cassel (Ersch, *Encycl.* xxvii. p. 31) at one-
fifth, Herzfeld (*Handelsgesch.* p. 181 f.) at one-sixth of a denar.

[2] Shek. i. 7.   [3] Winer, ii. 589.   [4] Jos. *Ant.* xiv. 7. 1, 2.

[5] Cicero, *Pro Flacco*, 28.   [6] Jos. *l.c.*

supply of water, which was provided by digging canals, and by a rude kind of machinery, which conveyed and helped to pour the water over the fields.   The seed was sown either in October and November, or in January and February.   The " early rain" was expected about the middle of October, the " latter rain " about the end of March or the beginning of April.   Between these periods the ground mainly depended upon the copious and refreshing dew, which fell nightly.   The harvest began in April, the vintage in September.   A considerable diversity of climate, and hence of produce, obtained in different parts of the country.   The neighbourhood of Jericho was probably the hottest, and its produce almost approached that of tropical latitudes.   The Jewish law required the agriculturist to take care that in the varieties of grain and fruit there should be no mixing of different seeds, or engrafting of various kinds.   It also provided that, besides the regular tithes, one-sixtieth of all the produce should be left on the fields, being the portion computed as growing on the borders of fields, and which was to be left for the poor.[1] Whatever was forgotten, or had accidentally dropped from the hand of the shearer, who generally used the common hand-sickle, also belonged to them, and whatever grew of itself during the Sabbatic year.

The grain was threshed with sticks or flails, or trodden out by cattle, not muzzled.   Peculiar threshing machines, which were dragged over the sheaves, were also in use.   After being threshed and winnowed, the corn was laid up in store-houses.   Where the soil was very light, a kind of hoe was used instead of the plough.   Palestine was peculiarly rich in all kinds of fruit.   Ripe figs might be had during ten months of the year; grapes were much cultivated throughout the land.   The vines were pruned and dug about, and the wine used both before and after fermentation.   It was always first filtered, and for common beverage diluted with water;[2] the luxurious prepared it with spices.[3] However, drunkenness was not one of the national sins.   Among other alcoholic liquors we may mention one made from barley, saflor, and

[1] Peah i. 2, 3.   [2] Pes. vii. 13.   [3] Maas. Sheni ii. 1.

salt ;[1] another sweet or honey-wine ;[2] and specially date-
wine, a highly nutritive and agreeable, but very intoxicating
beverage, made by first squeezing out the juice of dates, and
then macerating the residue in water. The fructification of
the date palms was artificial,[3] and their culture required some
care. Another source of wealth to the agriculturist was the
juice which certain plants and trees yielded,—specially the
balsam-plant, which grew in Gilead and in the neighbourhood of Jericho.[4] It rose to the height of about five feet, and
resembled the vine. The juice; which was obtained by small
incisions, was preserved in new earthen vessels. At first thin
and white, it gradually became thick and red. An inferior
kind of balsam was pressed out from the seeds and young
twigs. By a similar process the myrrh tree yielded its myrrh,
the storax tree its storax, etc.

In the gardens, orchards, and even by the wayside, the
more common fruits, such as the apple, the pear, the pomegranate, the mulberry, and the almond, grew in abundance.[5]
In high situations, or very sandy soil, the ground was cultivated in terraces, which were surrounded by stone walls. The
law carefully protected agricultural property and pursuits.
Watchmen in regular lodges guarded the ripe fruit, but were
not allowed to prevent passers-by from taking so much corn
or fruit as was requisite for immediate personal use. The
best grain was got from the neighbourhood of Michmash[6] in
the inheritance of Benjamin, to the north-east of Jerusalem,
and from Chorazim and Kefar Achim in Galilee.[7] The treasurer
of the temple tested the quality of the flour by thrusting his
hand into it ; if any adhered, the flour had to be again sifted.
The inheritance of the tribe of Asher produced the greatest
quantity, and Tekoa, two hours south of Bethlehem, the finest
quality of oil. Next to it was that of Regab[8] on the eastern
bank of Jordan, almost in a line with Shechem. There were
three kinds, and of each kind three qualities of oil, according

---

[1] Pes. iii. 1.   Comp. Levy, *Neuhebr. Wörterb.* i. 533*b*.
[2] Shab. xx. 2.   [3] Pes. iv. 8.   [4] Comp. Schürer, I. i. 423 ff.
[5] Comp. Hamburger, *Enc.* ii. 230 f., "Früchte."
[6] Menach. viii. 1, 2.   [7] *Ib.* 85*a*.   [8] *Ib.* viii. 3.

as it was extracted from the first ripe olives, from those which grew about the middle of the tree, or from those which were indiscriminately gathered and allowed to lie till they were nearly putrid, and prepared either by mere pressure of the hand or under boards and stones, or by macerating machines.[1] The best wine came from Kerochim, situated perhaps in the mountainous country of Judea, and from Hetolim, probably north of Gilgal.   The next best came from Beth-Rimah and from Beth-Laban, also situated in the mountainous district. Kephar Signah in the valley, perhaps a village to the north of Joppa, furnished also an excellent vintage.[2]

A large proportion of a farmer's wealth consisted in his herds and flocks. While, from the character of the soil, certain kinds of cattle were more generally reared in some districts, others, such as unclean animals, were entirely interdicted. Fowls were not allowed to be kept in Jerusalem, or in general by priests, on account of certain laws connected with purification.   On the same ground they were generally kept at a distance from towns.   The dog was a despised animal, "only to be kept on a chain."[3]   Small cattle were reared chiefly in Syria, and on those extensive plains or steppes which constituted a great part of what were termed the "wildernesses" of Palestine, such as the neighbourhood of Engedi, of Tekoa, of Beersheba, of Jericho, of Gibeon, of Bethsaida, etc.   Although these districts were not cultivated, they afforded excellent pasturage to the large flocks which browsed there all summer, being at night sheltered in the folds.   Watch-towers, occupied by armed men, protected them from the predatory incursions of hostile neighbours ; and large cisterns or wells, which became filled in the rainy season, supplied them with water. In the beginning of November the flocks were driven to their stabling, and kept there till the spring months.[4]   On the western side of Jordan the plains of Sharon afforded the best fodder.   The uses to which oxen were put were manifold.

---

[1] Menach. viii. 4.

[2] [Neubauer, *Géog. du Talm.* p. 82 ff. Schwarz, *Das heilige Land*, p. 151, places all these towns n Galilee.]

[3] Baba Kama vii.   [4] Lightfoot, *Horæ Hebr.* on Luke ii. 8.

Besides serving for sacrifices and for food, they were employed
in ploughing, for carriage, and in threshing, etc. Instead of
the whip, a pointed stick or goad (sometimes armed with iron)
was used. The milk of cows, goats, sheep, and camels was
either used sweet or allowed to sour. Butter and cheese were
articles in common use. The cattle were fed on grass and
herbs, and in winter on dried grass and chopped straw mixed
with other ingredients, and a small quantity of salt. The
wool of sheep was either immediately spun in the family of
the farmer, or sold to the merchant. The dung was generally
dried and used for fuel. Horses and mules were mostly imported from abroad.

It has already been stated that, besides the capital, numerous
cities had sprung up throughout the land.[1] South of Jerusalem,
which was called " the navel of the land," [2] and supposed to lie
exactly in the middle of it, lay Bene Berak, a town to the
north-east of Ashdod, where Akiba had often taught. Travelling southwards we reach Beth Gubrin, or Eleutheropolis,
plentifully watered by the dew from heaven, and east of it
Beth Netufah, famed for its oil. Gaza lay near the sea, with
its port at a distance of twenty stades. It had once been a
very flourishing city, and was still reputed as possessing one
of the three finest market-places in the land. Its fair was
much resorted to. A number of small towns studded the
country all round as far south as Osa and Kephar Darom.
Ashkelon, [a city which was never subject either to Jannæus or
Herod,] was mostly inhabited by heathens, who had a splendid
temple there, but also by some wealthy, pious, and influential
Jews.[3] Amongst the natural products of that neighbourhood,
corn and onions, and, amongst its manufactures, large wooden
handles for wells, and packing-straps, were noted.[4] There was
an annual fair at the Terebinth near Hebron, where Hadrian
caused so many captured Jews to be sold into slavery ; but
the most famous market was at Botnah across the Jordan.[5]

[1] Comp. Ersch's *Encycl.* vol. xxvii. p. 25, etc.; and Lightfoot's *Hor.*
Hebr. passim.
[2] Jos. *Wars*, iii. 3. 5.   [3] Comp. Schürer, II. i. 74 ff.
[4] Kel. xiii. 7, xxiii. 2.   [5] Jer. Ab. Sar. i. 39*d*.

Jabne had a strongly Jewish population. In the vicinity
of the latter place many little towns seem to have sprung
up. Lydda was the scene of much that is interesting in
Jewish history. The plain of Sharon extended along the
sea-coast from Carmel to Lydda. Bricks made from the
earth found in this neighbourhood would not stand wind and
rain ; hence on the Day of Atonement the high priest was
wont to pray for the inhabitants of that district, that
their houses might not become their graves.[1] It was also
reputed for the excellence of its vintage. Kephar Loddim,
which was sometimes reckoned outside of Palestine, lay
probably on the coast.[2] Emmaus, about twenty miles from
Jerusalem, had once a celebrated cattle market. The
priests who lived here were less esteemed ; but there were
two families in the town who used to supply flute-players
for the temple.[3]

Travelling eastwards we reach Jericho, situated in a broad
plain shut in by hills, and fruitful amid a desert neighbourhood. Its riches, and the costly produce of its balsam, procured for it the title of the royal district and paradise of
balsam ; but its inhabitants incurred for three reasons the
censure of the doctors of the Law.[4] Not far from Jericho lay
Naarath, whose inhabitants were in constant dispute with
those of Jericho. The Talmud records that the stones deposited
by Joshua were still visible in that neighbourhood.[5] Gophnith
was celebrated for its vines ; Gimso was known as the home
of Rabbi Nahum, and Ono as maintaining the same relation
to Lydda as Naarath to Jericho. Bethel is well known, as
also Beth-horon, with its narrow defile, where the legions of
Cestius were routed.[6] The range of mountains which stretches
from Idumea to Samaria sustained an important part in the
last war. On the boundaries of Samaria lay Bethar, [not to
be confused with Bar Cochba's stronghold,] and Antipatris,
which was reckoned one of the extreme points of Judea, and
supposed to have been the place where Alexander the Great

---

[1] Jer. Joma v. 3.   [2] Comp. Neubauer, *Géog. du Talm.* p. 80.
[3] Arach. ii. 3, 4.   [4] Pes. iv. 8.
[5] Sota 34*b* ; Tosefta Sot. viii.   [6] Jos. *Wars*, ii. 19. 7-9.

had been met by Simon the Just.[1] Cæsarea has also been formerly mentioned. At a later period it became renowned by the learning of the Rabbins who resided and taught in it. Scythopolis, or Beth Shean, termed, on account of the excellence and sweetness of its fruits, the entrance of paradise, and compared with Damascus, had celebrated linen manufactories.[2] Its inhabitants were partly Jews, partly heathens.

Galilee was fully as populous, if not more so, than Judea. Nazareth was a station of priests. Usha and Shafram, towns in the neighbourhood, are familiar to the reader; so are Cabul, Magdala, and Sichin, which are said to have been destroyed, through the moral corruption of the inhabitants, in the former Jewish war. Tiberias was fast growing into importance. The inhabitants of Sepphoris were noted as having been opposed to the national cause. Capernaum had a Christian congregation. Kephar Chanina was the border city between Upper and Lower Galilee, beyond which no sycamores grew.[3] Arbel was known for its linen; Beth-meron and other cities for their oil. Cæsarea Philippi, and the cities of the Decapolis, situated on both sides of the Jordan, are familiar to readers of the New Testament. Amongst the seaports we reckon Acco, or Ptolemais, a city partly Jewish and partly heathen; and Joppa, celebrated for its harbours, its markets, its baths, etc. Between these two ports a brisk coasting trade was carried on; nor was the passage from the one to the other reckoned properly a sea voyage.[4] The finest harbour, and that which commanded the foreign trade, was that of the rich and splendid Cæsarea. It was, however, mostly resorted to by non-Israelites. At that period the rigging out of ships was much more costly than it is at present. Distant sea voyages were undertaken in large ships, from the masts and decks of which, as in our days, the monotonous song of sailors at work might be heard. In the different ports harbour-dues were commonly levied.

[1] Joma 69a; the high priest was really Jaddua, comp. Jos. *Ant.* xi. 8. 4, 5.
[2] Jer. Kid. ii. 6.   [3] Sheb. ix. 2.   [4] Nedar. iii. 6.

II. THE LIFE OF THE PEOPLE

Such of the townspeople as were not in independent circumstances, earned their livelihood generally by some trade. It was deemed the duty of parents to have their children instructed in some light and healthy occupation. Most of the Jewish sages supported themselves by such means. Only a few crafts were despised, either on account of their supposed tendency to harden, or as affording indications of, or assistance to luxury; amongst them were those of weavers, tanners, perfumers, surgeons, and barbers.[1] In general, the rule seems to have been, that the worldly profession should be such as not to unfit for the study of the Law, being only intended to procure the means necessary for carrying on this, the great business of life. The ordinary wants of a household, in the way of cookery and dress, were generally supplied by the labours of its inmates. Hebrew women knew well how to spin, to weave, and to work curiously with the needle.[2] They were also famed for their cookery, specially in pastry, of which various kinds are enumerated and described in Jewish writings. However, the help of the regular baker was often required,—that of the weaver, the pastry-cook, the perfumer, or hairdresser was considered a disgraceful indication of foreign luxury. Amongst the craftsmen, we find artificers in wood and all kinds of metal,—the precious metals being fused with lead or some of the alkalis,—tentmakers, masons, tanners, tailors, shoemakers, jewellers, coachbuilders, etc., who busily and successfully plied their trades, although with tools much inferior to those now in use. The potters and glass-workers produced flat and deep plates, cups, spoons, tumblers (holes in which were covered with pitch or tin), bottles, and smelling-bottles, which were filled with scented oil.[3] Some, as tailors and copy-writers, would go about to procure work, or do it in the houses of their customers. Hats, caps, shirts, napkins, towels, handkerchiefs, veils, and many other articles which we could scarcely have expected to find in Palestine,

[1] Comp. Kidd. 82a.   [2] Comp. Keth. 59b.   [3] Comp. Kelim xxx.

seem to have been in common use. The washers were properly fullers, who first cleaned the clothes with water, and then took out the stains by various chemical agents, such as alum, chalk, potash, etc.[1] Dyeing and ornamental work of various kinds, whether with the brush, the needle, or in wood, ivory, stucco, and metal, were also known and practised.

The Hebrews arranged their year into lunar months, of which twelve, or 354 days, 8 hours, 48' 38", constituted one year. The month consisted of either twenty-nine or thirty days, and was to begin with the appearance of the new moon. If the latter was intimated to the Sanhedrin by credible witnesses on the 30th day of a month, the preceding month was declared to have consisted of only twenty-nine days, otherwise of thirty days, and the day following was always reckoned the beginning of the new month.[2] In order to test the accuracy of the witnesses, some Rabbins attempted the construction of lunar representations and tables. But as, on account of the inclemency of the weather, the first appearance of the new moon might not be observed for many months together, it was ruled that a year should neither have less than four, nor more than eight, full months (each of thirty days).[3] In the Old Testament the months are simply distinguished by numerals, as the 1st, 2nd, 3rd, etc.; but names also occur connected with the agricultural pursuits carried on, such as the month of Abib, or of corn-ears (the 1st), Ex. xiii. 4, xxiii. 15; Deut. xvi. 1; the month of Ziv, or of splendour, of flowering (the 2nd), 1 Kings vi. 1; the month of Bul, or of rain (the 8th), 1 Kings vi. 38; and the month of Ethanim, or of the flowing rivers (the 7th), 1 Kings viii. 2. After the deportation to Babylon fresh names were attached to the various months. [These are proved by the cuneiform inscriptions to be of Assyrian-Babylonish origin.]

[1] Comp. Kil. ix. 10; Shab. ix. 5; Nid. ix. 6.
[2] Comp. Ideler's *Chronologie*, i. 537, etc.; also Hamburger, *Enc.* ii. 608, etc., ' Kalender."
[3] Arach. ii. 2.

The Jewish year was computed in a twofold manner, as civil and ecclesiastical.[1] The ecclesiastical year began with the vernal, the civil with the autumnal equinox. The difference between the length of the lunar and the solar year necessitated an adjustment, which, however unscientific, effected its object. [It had been determined, as early as the second century before our era, that the Passover must always be celebrated after the vernal equinox.[2]] If the calendar had become much disordered, this would plainly be impossible. Hence, during the preceding month (that of Adar), even after the Feast of Purim, the authorities might, if necessary, decree the insertion of an additional (13th) month between Adar and Nisan, which was designated as Ve-Adar, or Adar Sheni. In such a leap year Ve-Adar occupied to all intents the place of Adar. In determining whether the insertion of an intercalary month was required, regard was also had to the state of the crops and of the fruit trees. [We even hear of an additional month being added on account of the feeble condition of the pigeons and young lambs.[3]] In leap years Adar had always thirty, and Ve-Adar twenty-nine days. Every seventh year was a Sabbatical, and every fiftieth a year of Jubilee; [but there is no evidence of the observance of the Jubilee after the Exile]. In the Sabbatical year the ground remained wholly untilled. A Sabbatical could not be a leap year, but the year preceding it usually was such. Sometimes two, but never three leap years, succeeded each other. Commonly every third year required the addition of a month. The mean duration of the Jewish month being 29 days, 12 hours, $44'$ $3\frac{1}{3}''$, it required, during a period of nineteen years, the insertion of seven months in order to bring the lunar era in accordance with the Julian. These insertions are now made in the 3rd, 6th, 8th, 11th, 14th, 17th, and 19th years. Hence, in order to find what Jewish year is a leap year, we have only to divide its number by 19; if the residue be 3, 6, 8, 11, 14,

---

[1] For a short calendar, see Appendix I.

[2] Comp. Schürer, I. ii. 370 f.

[3] Comp. Tosef. Sanh. ii.; jer. *ib.* i. 2; b. *ib.* 11a–12a.

17, or 0, it is a leap year. The somewhat vague and un-satisfactory arrangements of the Jewish calendar were greatly improved by the mathematical labours of various Rabbins, especially by those of Samuel and Adda, two sages of Babylon ; [and the adoption of the nineteen-year cycle is attributed to the Patriarch Hillel, about the middle of the fourth century].

The era adopted in the Old Testament is that which was reckoned to commence with the deliverance from Egypt. After their return from exile the Jews dated their years according to the Seleucidic era, which began 312 B.C., or 3450 from the creation of the world. For a short time after the recognition of the independence of Simon the Maccabee, it became customary to reckon dates from the year of the liberation of Palestine. However, for a very long period after the destruction of Jerusalem (probably till the fifteenth century A.D.), the Seleucidic era remained in common use, when it finally gave place to the present mode of reckoning among the Jews, which dates from the creation of the world. To commute the Jewish year into that of our common era, we have to add to the latter 3761, always bearing in mind, however, that the common or civil Jewish year commences in the month of Tishri, *i.e.* in autumn.

The week was divided into seven days, of which, how-ever, only the seventh—the Sabbath—had a name assigned to it, the rest being merely noted by numerals. The day was computed from sunset to sunset. Before the Babylonish captivity, it was divided into morning, midday, evening, and night, but after the residence in Babylon the Hebrews adopted the division of the day into twelve hours, whose duration varied with the length of the day. The longest day consisted of 14 hours and 12 minutes, the shortest of 9 hours 48 minutes,—the difference between the two being thus more than four hours. On an average the first hour of the day corresponded nearly to our 6 A.M. ; the third hour (when, according to Matt. xx. 3, the market-place was full) to our 9 A.M. ; the close of the sixth hour to our midday ; while at the eleventh the day neared its close. The night was divided by the Romans into four, by the Jews into three

watches.   Later Jews subdivided the hour into 1080 parts
(Chlakim), and again each part into 76 moments.   As the
appearance of the new moon, or the beginning of a month,
was of vast importance for fixing the feast days during the
month, it was customary to telegraph it by fire-signals lit
upon the mountains, and at a later period to intimate it by
special messengers.[1]   As these modes of communication
proved insufficient for Jews who lived in distant countries,
it was ruled that every 30th day should be called the day of
the new moon.   If the month had really consisted of twenty-
nine days, the day of the new moon represented correctly the
beginning of the new month.   If the month consisted of thirty
days, it was provided that both the last day of the preceding
and the first day of the next month should be designated in
Palestine as the days of the new moon.   In connection with
this arrangement, all the more important feasts, as the first
and last days of the Passover, the Feast of Pentecost, New
Year's Day, and the first and last days of the Feast of Tabernacles, were ordered to be doubled, so that on one day at
least they should be kept simultaneously in all places.[2]

It was the general practice to rise with the sun.   The
first duty of the Hebrews was to perform the prescribed devotions.   After that, in towns probably between nine and ten
o'clock (Acts ii. 15), a breakfast was taken, consisting of
bread and fruit, and sometimes of fish or meat (John xxi. 9)
with wine.   Dinner was commonly served towards evening,
though before dark, but sometimes in the middle of the day.
It was preceded by careful lustrations, and the pronouncing
of separate blessings over the different kinds of fruit provided.[3]   The dinner parties of the rich, and feasts, were
generally held in the afternoon or evening.[4]   The guests sat
round a low table.   At a later period, the rich adopted the
practice of reclining on couches, which generally afforded

---

[1] Rosh ha-Shanah ii. 1–3, i. 4.
[2] Comp. Rosh ha-Shanah 21*a*.   This arrangement still subsists, although
its cause has ceased.
[3] *Vide* Chapter X., and comp., generally, *Life and Times*, ii. 205 ff.
[4] Jos. *Life*, c. 44.

accommodation for three persons.[1]   As at present in many
Eastern countries, it was customary to begin the meal with
something pickled,—perhaps to whet the appetite.   Besides
the principal dishes, side dishes were served.   The ordinary
fare consisted of fish, meat, vegetables, farinaceous food, and
fruits.   The wine used during dinner was drunk diluted, two
or three parts of water being added.[2]   The poor dined on
vegetables.   After the meal, prayers were again offered, and
then the apartment was swept and perfumed.[3]   It was
deemed unwholesome to go in the morning fasting about one's
ordinary business.   The rules about the divers washings, and
the prayers which had to be offered, were exceedingly minute ;
the principle in this kindred matter being, that to derive
advantage from anything in the world without returning
thanks, was to rob from the Lord.[4]

The observances at table were very punctilious.   Moderation was recommended, and special care bestowed on the use
of bread, which was neither to be wasted nor spoiled.[5]   Even
the crumbs were to be carefully gathered up.   Legend had it
that demons would sit upon any waste bread which was not
swept away after the meal.   The conversation at table was
to be sparing, and upon edifying subjects.   When a feast
was given, slaves were sent to invite the guests, and generally
a master of ceremonies appointed to take charge of all the
arrangements.   At table they were seated according to their
rank.[6]   Music, dancing, and other amusements engaged the
time of the party often to a very late or early hour.   The
laws of Jewish etiquette, and female decorum, did not allow
ladies, who, on ordinary occasions, dined with the gentlemen,
to appear at promiscuous feasts ; but at more homely entertainments the duty of attending to the guests devolved upon
them.   The most agreeable, as the most thoroughly Jewish
domestic feasts, were betrothals, marriages, the weaning of
children, etc.   Although, in general, the Jews were very
moderate, the bounds of temperance were on festive occasions

---

[1] Comp. Ber. vi. 6 ; bab. *ib.* 46*b.*
[2] Nid. ii. 7 ; Pes. 108*b.*
[3] Ber. vi. 6, 7, viii. 4.
[4] Ber. 35*b.*
[5] Derek Erez 9.
[6] Ber. 46*b.*

sometimes sadly transgressed even by celebrated Rabbins. It need scarcely be remarked that the ancient Hebrews dispensed with knives and forks, and served themselves, or were served, with the hand, out of plates, on which the meat, previously cut in pieces, had been placed.

The position assigned by the Hebrews to the female sex has been frequently misunderstood.   From the permission of polygamy, from its supposed general practice, and from isolated expressions by some Rabbins, it has been hastily inferred to have been low.   To arrive at correct views on this subject, we ought to compare the position of the Hebrew female, not only with the elevated place which Christianity, in acknowledgment of her real vocation, has assigned to her, but chiefly with that which she then occupied, and even at the present time holds, among other Eastern nations.   The readers of the New Testament cannot but feel that the relations there indicated proceed upon the assumption that monogamy was the rule, and polygamy the exception.   The permission of polygamy, and the comparative facility of obtaining a divorce, may seem to militate against the fundamental idea of the marriage relation.   But against these drawbacks we have to put the two indubitable facts, that generally men were only united in wedlock to one wife, and that Jewish females occupied not only a comparatively but an absolutely high position.   The law throughout recognised and protected the rights of women, and discouraged the practice of polygamy. An impartial reader cannot rise from the perusal, not of a few isolated passages, but of the sections of the Mishna bearing upon this subject, without being impressed with this conviction.

According to the Rabbins, to the age of twelve years females were reckoned minors (boys to thirteen years and one day),[1] during which period they were absolutely in the power of their father, who might betroth or give them in marriage, and who derived the benefit of what they might earn by their personal exertions.[2]   Marriage was preceded by a betrothal,

---

[1] Nid. v. 6 ; cf. vi. 11.

[2] Kethub. iv. 4.   In general we have collated here from Kethuboth, Gittin, and Kiddushin.

which, in the province of Judea, was celebrated by a feast.[1]
The conditions of the marriage were then very precisely fixed,
the dowry brought by the wife, and the sum of money to be
paid to her in case of divorce or of widowhood, settled. Only
a *bonâ fide* breach of these arrangements was deemed a valid
ground for dissolving the bond thus formed. From the
moment of this formal betrothal the couple were looked upon
as married, and the relation could only be dissolved by a
regular divorce. A betrothal might be entered into by the
parties personally, or by delegates ; but in order to be valid it
was necessary for the bridegroom to hand to the bride, either
in money or otherwise, the value of at least a perutah.[2]
From the period of the betrothal, twelve months were allowed
to either party (if the bride was a maid, and thirty days if a
widow) to prepare for the marriage. In cases of longer delay,
the bridegroom was bound to maintain his betrothed.[3] If the
bride was divorced before marriage, she received the sum
settled at the betrothal, which, in the case of a maid, was by
statute not less than 200, and in that of a widow 100 dinars,
but might be augmented to any extent according to previous
agreement.[4] But it is doubtful whether, in the case of
divorce before marriage, the bride could sue for any very considerable increase of the statutory sum. On the marriage
day, the bridegroom, with his friends, went to bring home his
espoused wife, who was accompanied by her companions.
Festivities, lasting for some days, inaugurated the happy
event.[5] Maidens were generally married on the fourth day
of the week (Wednesday),[6] to allow three free days to prepare
for the marriage, and to enable the bridegroom without delay
to bring any complaint as to the past chastity of his bride
before the tribunals, which met every Thursday. Widows
were generally married on the fifth day of the week. At
their marriage, maidens wore garlands of myrtles, or a

[1] Keth. i. 5.
[2] Kidd. ii. 1.
[3] Keth. v. 2.
[4] *Ut supra*, i. 2, v. 1.
[5] Comp. also the curious work of Hartmann, *Die Hebräerinn am Putztische*,
3 vols. Amst. 1810.
[6] Keth. i. 1.

peculiar kind of veil covering the eyes; sometimes their hair hung loosely down. It was a common practice to distribute among the company dried seeds,[1] and, in some parts of the country, to carry before the newly-married couple a pair of fowls, probably to indicate a wish for their fruitfulness.[2]

Legally speaking, marriage was concluded by the handing of the money, by a written contract, or by cohabitation;[3] and it was again dissolved by a divorce, or by the death of either party. While the law, no doubt, afforded considerable facilities for obtaining a divorce, it also protected the rights of women, and generally gave a preference to their testimony in cases of dispute. On the legitimate grounds of divorce, the two theological schools differed materially. The Shammaites restricted them to the commission of an iniquitous action by the wife (probably adultery); the Hillelites going to an opposite extreme, and playing upon the original of the text (Deut. xxiv. 1) quoted by Shammai, inferred that a divorce was warranted even when the wife had only spoiled her husband's dinner. Rabbi Akiba endeavoured, in the same manner, to prove that a man might lawfully dismiss his wife if he found another more attractive.[4] Passing over such exceptional extravagances, it was held lawful to dismiss a wife without paying her the legally-secured portion if she transgressed the law of Moses and of the Jews, which was applied not only to sin, but to acts of impropriety, such as going about with loose hair, spinning in the street, familiarly talking with men, ill-treating her husband's parents in his presence, and brawling, *i.e.* "speaking with her husband so loudly, that her neighbours could hear her voice in the adjoining houses";[5] a general bad reputation in the place,[6] or the discovery of damaging circumstances which had been concealed before marriage. On the other hand, the wife could insist on being divorced from her husband if he was a leper, if he was affected with polypus (cancer?), or if his trade obliged him to perform either dirty or disagreeable manipulations, as in the case of tanners and coppersmelters.

[1] Keth. ii. 1.   [2] Gitt. 57a.   [3] Kidd. i. 1.
[4] Gitt. ix. 10.   [5] Keth. vii. 6.   [6] Gitt. iv. 7.

However, the sages generally limited this concession to the first-mentioned disease.[1] To discourage a plurality of wives, it was enjoined that, in her claims, the first married wife should always take precedence of the second, the second of the third,[2] etc. The ordinances with reference to divorces by absent husbands were, as all legislation on this subject, very punctilious.

The law specified the mutual duties and rights. The husband was bound to love and cherish his wife, comfortably to support her, to redeem her if she had been sold into slavery, and to bury her. On these occasions, the poorest Israelite was bound to provide, at least, two mourning fifes and one mourning woman.[3] On the other hand, the wife was " to grind the meal, to bake, to wash, to cook, to suckle her children, to make her husband's bed, and to work in wool." These regulations were modified if she was wealthy. " If she had brought with her one slave, she was not required to grind the meal, to bake, or to wash; if two slaves, she was also free from cooking and suckling the children; if three slaves, she was not required to make the bed, or to work in wool; if four slaves (it is added), she might sit in her easy-chair."[4] However, this indulgence was limited, and, under all circumstances, the wife expected, at least, to work in wool. If, by a rash vow, a husband had forsworn himself not to allow his wife to work, he was bound immediately to divorce her, as it was thought that idleness induced insanity.

The whole of the personal property of, or the income derived by, the wife belonged to her husband. On the other hand, he was bound to make over to her one-half more than her dowry, if it consisted of ready money, and one-fifth less, if it consisted in any other property. Besides, the bride-groom was to allow his wife one-tenth of her dowry for pin-money. If a father gave away his daughter without making any distinct statement about her dowry, he was bound to allow her, at least, fifty sus; if it had expressly been

---

[1] Keth. vii. 10.
[2] *Ut supra*, x.
[3] *Ut supra*, iv. 4.
[4] *Ut supra*, v. 5.

provided that the bride was to receive no dowry, it was
delicately enjoined that the bridegroom should furnish her,
before the marriage, with the necessary outfit. Even an
orphan, who was given away by her natural guardians, the
parochial authorities, was to receive, from the common funds,
at least, fifty sus as dowry.[1] A husband could not oblige his
wife to leave the Holy Land or the city of Jerusalem, or to
exchange a country for a town residence, and *vice versâ*; or a
good for a bad house, and *vice versâ*.[2] A widow might insist on
being maintained in her husband's house, or, if the surviving
relations and she herself were young, in her father's house.
If she had lived in her father's house, she was at all times
at liberty to claim her legal portion; but if she had spent
twenty-five years with the heirs of her late husband, her
money was forfeited, as it was considered that during that
period she must have received from the heirs for her
maintenance a sum equal to that to which she was legally
entitled.[3] The period of suckling is variously stated. The
Mishna fixes it at two years, or, at least, eighteen months.[4]
The education of daughters was almost entirely confided to
their mother, and even in that of sons she sustained an
important part.[5] Besides their peculiar domestic duties,
daughters were to be taught the written, but not the oral,
law, as such studies might lead to undue familiarity with
the other sex.[6] As mothers should admonish their sons to
apply themselves to study, so wives were to encourage their
husbands to the same.

Ordinarily, every male child was circumcised on the
eighth day, even though it fell on the Sabbath, the duties
attendant on circumcision superseding even the sanctity of
the day of rest.[7] On certain defined occasions it was delayed
two or three days; when the child was weakly, or if two of
its brothers had died in consequence of the operation, it was
deferred to the restoration of health, or till a more mature
age promised immunity from danger. It was performed in a

[1] Keth. vi.   [2] *Ut supra*, xiii. 10.   [3] *Ut supra*, xii. 3, 4.
[4] Gitt. vii. 6.   [5] Sota *apud* Wagenseil, p. 490.
[6] *Ut supra*, p. 496, etc.   [7] Comp. Shab. xix. 1–5.

manner somewhat different from that customary amongst
other Eastern nations.[1] As the ceremony was of the greatest
importance, strict attention to the prescribed rules was
necessary, if the ordinance was to be valid. The only
difference in the mode of it, which obtains at present, lies
in the substitution of better instruments for those formerly
in use. Any Israelite—in case of necessity, even a woman
—might perform the operation, although surgeons were
latterly employed. At circumcision the child obtained its
name.

Every parent had personally to instruct his sons up
to the sixth year of their age. After that they might be
sent to the public elementary schools.[2] The study of the
Bible was begun when the child was five years old.[3] If no
progress was made during a period of three or five years'
instruction, little hope was entertained of future eminence.
Wealthy Jews probably employed private tutors, who were
often slaves. The institution of elementary schools was
ascribed to the high priest Joshua ben Gamla, who fell by
the hands of the Zealots during the siege of Jerusalem. He
is said to have established a school in every province and in
every town.[4] A Jewish legend states that at its destruction,
Jerusalem possessed no fewer than 480 schools, each consisting of three classes. This account is evidently exaggerated;
and, indeed, another authority ascribes the fall of the city to
the neglect of the education of the young.[5] The schoolmaster
was generally a regular officer of the Synagogue,[6] paid from
the treasury of that synagogue to which he was attached,

---

[1] The following pretty accurate description of the rite is taken from Othonis,
Lex Rabb. p. 133 : "Circumcisor imponit mentulæ bacillum et præputium
quantum potest super illum extendit, deinde forcipe partem ejus prehendit et
novacula præcidit. Deinde duobus pollicis unguibus præputium arripit et
devolvit, donec glans tota denudatur, quo facto sanguinem exsugit, donec
advenerit sanguis e remotioribus corporis partibus, vulnerique emplastrum
imponit." This plaster consisted in part of bruised aniseed (Shab. xix. 2) ;
oil and wine were also used, and the child bathed.

[2] Comp. Ehrmann's pamphlet on this subject, Prague, 1846 ; also Hamburger, *Enc.* ii. "Lehrer," "Schule," "Schüler," "Unterricht."

[3] Pirke Ab. v. 21.   [4] B. Bath. 21*a*.

[5] Shab. 119*b* ; comp. Ehrmann, p. 10.   [6] Shab. i. 3.

and within the precincts of which the children usually met. He was allowed in certain cases to take fees from his pupils,[1] but he was not on that account to show undue favour to the children of the rich.[2] To discourage an unwholesome rivalry, parents were interdicted from sending their children to schools in other towns. The number of children committed to one individual was not to exceed twenty-five; for any greater number (short of fifty) an assistant was to be provided. The teacher was to endeavour to secure the confidence, the respect, and the affection, both of parents and children. The latter he was to treat rather with kindness than with rigour. Beating, if necessary, with a strap,[3] never with a rod, was to be the principal means of correction; but a teacher could not be deposed merely upon complaints of too great severity. The alphabet was taught by drawing the letters on a board till the children remembered them. In reading, well-corrected books were to be used, and the child was to point to the words as he spelt them. In teaching the Bible, the schoolmaster was to begin with the Book of Leviticus, and after the Pentateuch to take up the Prophets, and then the Hagiographa.[4] In the case of more advanced pupils, the day was divided into three portions, one of which was set apart for the study of the Bible, and the other two for the Mishna and the Talmud.[5] The Mishna was begun at ten years of age, the Talmud at fifteen. At thirteen, a young man became major; at eighteen, it was deemed his duty to enter into wedlock.[6] The study of foreign languages was not a branch of education, and, indeed, since the war of Quietus it had been declared unlawful. Gymnastic exercises were also interdicted, as leading to dangerous contact and assimilation with heathens.[7]

The number of hours during which junior classes were to be kept in school was limited. As the close air of the schoolroom might prove detrimental during the heat of the day, schools were closed between ten o'clock A.M. and three

---

[1] Nedar. 37*a*.　　　[2] Taan. 24*a*.　　　[3] B. Bath. 21*a*.
[4] Lev. Rab. 7; Deut. Rab. 8.　　　[5] Kidd. 30*a*.
[6] Pirke Ab. v. 21.　　　[7] Comp. Ab. Sar. i. 7.

P.M.   For similar reasons, school hours were limited to four hours a day during the period from the 17th Tammuz to the 9th Ab, and the teacher forbidden to chastise his pupils during these months.   [Many of these regulations date probably from the beginning of the fourth century.]   The schoolmaster was to make the lesson as plain as possible, and not to lose patience if it was not immediately understood.   Want of knowledge or of method were sufficient causes for removing a teacher,[1] but experience was always deemed a better qualification than mere acquirements.   It was one of the principal duties of an instructor of youth to impress upon their minds and hearts the lessons of morality and chastity.   The latter virtue was peculiarly esteemed by the Hebrews; and the teacher, who was always a married man, was required carefully to avoid anything calculated to call up disagreeable or indelicate associations.   The office of teacher was very highly esteemed, and the pupil expected to show him greater respect, and to entertain for him a warmer attachment, than for his own father.[2]   On the other hand, the teacher was, both by word and example, to incite his pupils to everything good and noble.   In tuition, care was also to be bestowed on the choice of elegant language.   The inhabitants of Judea excelled in this respect.   To acquire fluency, pupils were to read aloud, and certain mnemonic rules were devised to facilitate the committing to memory.[3]

Of the higher schools, or colleges, we have already spoken.   They gained a peculiar importance when the Jewish Sanhedrin was shorn of its executive power, and its discussions turned on purely religious questions.   Although the mutual jealousy between the Jews of Palestine and of Babylon would induce us to receive with caution the opinions of rival teachers as to the state of learning in their respective countries, we can readily conceive that the character of the purely theological teaching of Babylon developed much more rapidly and smoothly than it did in Palestine.   Other sciences besides theology were, however,

---

[1] B. Bath. 21*b*; comp. Chul. 107*b*.   [2] B. Mez. ii. 11.   [3] Erub. 54*b*.

cultivated in Babylon, and in these the Eastern Jews seem at an early period considerably to have outstripped their brethren in Judea. Celebrated theologians attracted pupils from great distances, and although the number of students who are stated to have attended the lectures of certain sages is certainly fabulous, no reasonable doubt can obtain that, owing to the merit attaching to such studies, and the fact that students and Rabbins carried on their various trades, the classes were much more fully attended than, judging according to modern notions, we might have anticipated. Students were encouraged to put questions, and even to urge objections, provided they were stated respectfully, and for the purpose of gaining information. Some teachers endeavoured to make their lectures attractive by varying them with riddles, fables, allegories, and even witticisms. Besides the colleges of Palestine and of Babylon, there were similar institutions in some foreign cities inhabited by Jews, as, for example, in Rome. The respect shown by the pupils to the Rabbins, amounting almost to idolatry, and the extravagant claims put forth by them, and often supported by a perversion of Scripture passages, almost pass credence.[1] Any man might become an expounder of Hagada, but a regular teacher required ordination, which was bestowed by three ordained persons, or, in later times, by one Rabbi with two assessors.[2]

The religious cast of Jewish social life became apparent in the general mildness of their laws, and in an urbanity equally distant from the verbosity of modern Orientals and the cool stiffness of Occidentals. With the various modes of salutation between superiors and inferiors, or between equals, every Bible reader is sufficiently familiar. The common mode of it was, "Peace to you," or "Good luck to you,"[3] the latter phrase being addressed especially to labouring men.[4] The fanaticism of pharisaical Jews manifested itself

---

[1] Comp. Weber, p. 122 ff.   [2] Comp. *Life and Times*, ii. 382.
[3] Lightfoot, *Hor. Hebr.* on Matt. xxviii. 9.
[4] Comp. the elaborate chapter on salutations in Zunz, *Zur Gesch. u. Literat.* p 304, etc.

also in their refusal to exchange the ordinary civilities of
life with heathens or Samaritans. [On the other hand, it
was generally maintained that greetings should always be
exchanged with the heathen for the sake of peace, and that
a Jew might wish them good success in their work, even in
the Sabbatical year.[1]] The place of honour was always on
the right hand, and strangers were dismissed with a blessing.
The same urbanity characterised all the different social
relations. Friendship, faithfulness, affection, and devotedness
are eminent traits in Jewish life. No crime was more
reprobated than a breach of the fifth commandment.
Children were bound to provide for the wants, even for the
comforts, of their parents; if necessary, to wait upon, and
even to beg for them.[2] On the other hand, the parental tie
was peculiarly strong. Parents are represented as fondly
watching over their children, and children as requiting
their care by readily bearing with their foibles, and even
with the trials arising from the caprices of old age and
infirmity. Crimes such as the murder of parents or of
children were happily unknown. No doubt the above
virtues are in great measure traceable to the sanctity of the
marriage relation, and the absence, or at least the great
rarity, of prostitution, which in turn, specially in times so
dissolute as those to which we refer, were due to the
leavening influence of the Old Testament, notwithstanding
its various corruptions by tradition.

From the peculiar political relations of Palestine, slavery,
in a modified form, was common from the earliest times.
However, the safety and rights of the slave were amply
protected, and he was kindly treated. It is plainly impossible
to draw from the modified slavery of Palestine a warrant for
the antichristian practice which so long disgraced Christian
countries. In Palestine, where the land was so equally
divided amongst the inhabitants, and hired labour so rare,
slavery was almost necessary. Besides, Judaism found slavery
as a social institution intimately connected with the habits

---

[1] Sheb. iv. 3, v. 9 ; Gitt. v. 9.
[2] Jer. Kid. i. 61*b* ; Lightfoot on Matt. xv. 5.

and war-rights of the ancient world.   To have isolated
the Jews from this practice would have been almost impossible; but Judaism busied itself to mitigate, and, as much
as possible, to abolish it.   Besides slaves, day-labourers were
also occasionally, though not regularly, employed.   Hebrew
slaves were acquired by purchase or by contract.[1]   Jewish
female slaves were exceedingly rare.   All slaves of foreign
origin were designated as "Canaanites."   They might be
acquired by purchase, by letter of sale, or by right of war,
and again obtained their liberty by redemption or by letter
of manumission.   They were not set free on the Sabbatical or
the Jubilee year, nor were they allowed to redeem themselves
with their own money,[2] as they and all theirs were considered
the absolute property of their masters, which was not the case
with Hebrew slaves.   It was deemed meritorious to have one's
heathen slaves circumcised.[3]   If they refused to submit to
this, they were to be sold as speedily as possible.   Opinions
were divided about the duty and expediency of manumitting
foreign slaves, the majority entertaining views unfavourable
to them.[4]   Their treatment was in general very mild, being
considered rather as members of the family than as strangers.
Any act of cruelty at once set the slave free.   We hear of
Egyptian slaves sold for as much as one talent,[5] [but in the
Talmud 100 denarii, or about £3, seems to be regarded as a
common price for a slave[6]].   Besides the common duties of the
household, slaves had to do all the menial work, such as
dressing and undressing their masters, tying, loosing, and
carrying their shoes, anointing them, turning the hand-
mill,[7] etc.

It is well known that in early times the precious metals
were weighed; hence the names of weights and of coins are
identical.   As the current value of coins afterwards varied, it
is difficult to ascertain the real value, either of the different
pieces of money or of the weights.   The lowest weight was
the *Gera*, of which twenty formed a *shekel*; [but in later times

---

[1] Kidd. i. 2.   [2] *Ut supra*, i. 3.   [3] Lightfoot on Matt. iii. 6.
[4] Sot. 3*b*; comp. Lightfoot on Acts vi. 9.   [5] Jos. *Ant.* xii. 4. 9.
[6] B. Bath. 127*b*.   [7] Lightfoot on Matt. iii. 11.

there was considerable divergence of opinion as to the original value of a shekel. When the Greek currency became common in Palestine, the gera was identified with the Greek *obol* (about 11 grains), and a shekel was therefore equivalent to $3\frac{1}{3}$ Attic drachms.[1] This was just the weight of the Tyrian *sela* of nearly 224 grains. Accordingly, when Simon the Maccabee received the right of coinage, he adopted the *sela* as his standard. The average weight of the silver shekels of Simon has been found to be about 220 grains.[2] Subsequently the Attic drachm was reduced, so that it weighed only one-fourth of the Jewish shekel].

It is equally difficult exactly to fix the capacity of measures. Leaving vague expressions, such as a handful, a mouthful, the size of a druggist's spoon, or of an olive, etc., we find the following definite measures :—In fluids, the log was the smallest measurement, twelve logs were a hin, six hins a bath, and ten baths a homer or cor. Dry substances were measured as follows :—The homer contained 10 ephahs, or 30 seahs (3 seahs to an ephah), or 100 omers (10 omers to an ephah), or 180 cabs (6 cabs to a seah). Now we learn from the Talmud that there were three standards of measurement in use.[3] The smallest was the so-called " wilderness " measure, which is explained to be the same as the " Italian." The Jerusalem measure was one-fifth larger ;[4] and that of Sepphoris, which was probably used in Galilee, again one-fifth larger than that of Jerusalem. The size of a log in the common or " wilderness " measure is fixed by the Rabbins at six eggs.[5] [This quantity has been calculated to amount to about ·079 of a gallon, or two-thirds of a Roman *sextarius*. The seah, accordingly, was equal to a *Modius*, or nearly a quarter of a bushel, while the bath or ephah contained about $5\frac{3}{4}$ gallons. In the Sepphoris measure, on the other hand, the log was nearly equal to a sextarius. This agrees with the statement of Josephus, who identifies the Hebrew bath with the Greek *metrêtes* of 72 *xestæ*.[6]] We add the measure-

---

[1] Comp. Herzfeld, *Handelsgesch.* pp. 181–185.
[2] Comp. Madden, *Coins of the Jews*, p. 285 ff.
[4] Men. viii. 1.   [5] Maimon. in Kel. xvii. 6.
[3] Comp. Herzfeld, *ut supra*.
[6] *Ant.* viii. 2. 9.

ment of lengths and distances. The former were computed by finger-breadths; hand-breadths (= four finger-breadths); spans (= twelve finger-breadths); cubits, reaching from the elbow to the tip of the third finger (= two spans, or six-hand-breadths), and rods (= six cubits). The Roman cubit, which was in common use, amounted to about $17\frac{1}{2}$ inches. Distances were generally reckoned according to Roman miles, which were 1000 geometrical paces, or 142 yards less than the English statute mile. Eight Greek stadia, or furlongs, constituted a Roman mile, and thirty stadia a Persian or Syrian parasang.

It will scarcely appear strange that in a country where commerce was not the chief occupation of the people, and where the virtues inculcated in the Bible were extended and applied by Rabbinical punctiliousness to every possible circumstance, the laws regulating trade should have been exceedingly strict and minute, and that to such an extent as even to prescribe the time when the merchant was statedly to cleanse his weights and scales.[1] A bargain was not considered closed until *both* parties had taken possession of their respective properties; but after one party had received the money it was deemed dishonourable and sinful[2] for the other to draw back. It was declared downright imposition, no matter what the state of the market, to charge 20 per cent. of profit on any article. In such cases the purchaser had the right of returning the article, or of claiming the balance of the money, provided he applied for it after an interval sufficient to show his purchase to another merchant, or to a relative. Similarly the rights of the merchant were protected. The money-changer was allowed to charge a fixed discount for light money, or to return it within a certain period if below the weight at which he had taken it. A merchant might not be pressed to name the lowest price of an article which the questioner had no serious intention of purchasing; nor might he, by way of inducing him to lower his prices, be reminded of any former

[1] Baba Bathra v. 10.
[2] Baba Mezia iv. 1, 2. Consult this section generally for the following particulars.

overcharge. Different qualities of goods might not be mixed, even though the articles added were equal or superior in value to those originally exposed for sale. For the protection of the retailer and of the public, the agriculturist was interdicted from selling wine diluted with water to the dealers in any of the cities of Palestine where such was not in general use. Such are some of the ordinances by which the scrupulosity of Rabbinism sought to elevate trade and to protect all parties. One of the theologians went so far as to declare it improper for merchants to distribute little presents amongst the children in the various villages through which they passed, by way of gaining them, and thereby, as he thought improperly, attracting customers. He also deemed it wrong to lower the customary price of articles. However, his colleagues allowed the latter, but united in reprobating, as a species of deceit, the practice of endeavouring to give a better appearance to any article which was to be exposed for sale.[1] Purchases of corn could not be concluded until the market price had been fixed.[2]

Greater precautions, if possible, were adopted against the very appearance of taking interest or usury. The latter term was apparently equivalent to every kind of speculation.[3] So delicate were the provisions for guarding the interests and sparing the feelings of debtors, that creditors were expressly interdicted from using anything belonging to the debtor without paying for it, from sending him on an errand, or even accepting a present from a party who had solicited an advance.[4] So punctilious were the Rabbins, that they would have a woman who borrowed a loaf from her neighbour immediately fix its value at the time, lest a sudden rise in flour should make the loaf returned of more value than that borrowed. When a house or field was rented, it was deemed lawful to charge a somewhat higher rental where prepayment was not made ; but such increase was interdicted when a field was purchased. It was declared of the nature of an improper speculation to promise a merchant one-half of the profits on any sales which he effected, or to advance him money, and

[1] Baba Mezia iv. 11, 12.   [2] *Ut supra*, v. 7.
[3] *Ut supra*, v. 1.   [4] *Ut supra*, 2, 10.

allow one-half of the profits on the speculations which had been undertaken with it.[1]   In either case the merchant was exposed to undue temptations; by law he was only entitled to a commission in payment of the services he had performed, and as compensation for his time and trouble.

When Jewish commerce became more extensive, creditors were in the habit of getting regular documents drawn out at the expense of the debtor, and signed before witnesses.   For any part-payment the creditor granted a separate discharge. In all dubious cases the law decided in favour of the debtor. To prevent any mistake, the sum lent was written at the top as well as in the body of the document, and minute directions were given about the signatures of witnesses.   A third party was not considered to have become security for the borrower if he had only come forward after the loan had actually been contracted.[2]   It is well known that in reference to taking interest or pledges, and in dealing with insolvent creditors, the mildness of the Hebrew law is almost unparalleled, compared not only with that of ancient, but even of modern nations.   Under certain restrictions, it was, indeed, lawful to take pledges, and in the event of non-payment to sell them; but wearing apparel, bedding, the ploughshare, and any articles requisite in the preparation of food, were excepted, and were to be restored whenever required for use.   Similarly, under any circumstances, pledges which belonged to a widow could neither be taken nor sold.[3]   In no case could the creditor claim a pledge till he had obtained permission from a court of law.   Tradesmen or labourers were bound to perform their contracts, and all complaints about having been taken advantage of were to be left for after-adjudication.[4] But while on these and similar points the law which protected Israelites was exceedingly strict and minute, it must be allowed that the interests of Gentiles were not always so well watched over.[5]   The Rabbins seem frequently to have considered that what applied to the chosen race could not

---

[1] Baba Mezia v. 2–4.   [2] Comp. Baba Bathra x.
[3] Baba Mezia ix. 13.   [4] *Ut supra*, ix. 1–9.
[5] Comp. B. Kam. iv. 3, and contrast B. Mez. ix. 12.

regulate intercourse with those whom they contemplated with feelings similar to those entertained by strict Mohammedans towards all " infidels."

Intercourse with parties at a distance was kept up by letters, which were either conveyed by travellers or despatched by special letter-carriers.[1] These letters were sealed with red clay, or with a kind of sealing-wax.[2] The art of writing seems to have been extensively known in Palestine, even during the reign of David. Unlettered Hebrews employed writers or scribes, denominated in the Mishna " Liblar " (Libellarius). Their reed or pen was called " kolemos " (the Greek calamos).[3] At a later period the duties of the Liblar were chiefly connected with drawing out contracts, sales, marriage settlements, etc., in short, different kinds of legal documents in civil and juridical cases.[4] Some appear to have been in possession of particular secrets connected with the mechanical part of their profession, which they kept as a sort of patent (although with general disapprobation), just as others possessed similar secrets in the preparation of perfumes and of the shewbread.[5] A single letter or word affixed to an article indicated that it was set apart for the sanctuary, or was part of the tithes.[6] The writing materials in use were pens or reeds, ink of different colours, and paper or parchment. Among the various kinds of ink we may mention a sympathetic ink, prepared from the bark of the ash ; another chiefly made up of vitriol, and specially noted for its indelibility ;[7] and a powder made of lamp black, mixed with oil or honey, and dried, which was dissolved when required for use. A kind of paper was much in use, as well as writing tables, *rough* or unprepared leather, and *parchment*, or prepared leather. Sometimes tables of wax or of wood, and pointed pens, were employed. We even read of writing upon the leaves of olive trees, the horn of a cow, or the hand of a slave.[8] Among the various alphabets handed down to us,

---

[1] Shab. x. 4.
[2] *Ut supra*, viii. 5.
[3] For example, Shab. i. 3.
[4] Moed Katan iii. 3.
[5] Comp. Joma iii. 11.
[6] Maas. Sheni iv. 9–11.
[7] Megill. ii. 2 ; Gitt. ii. 3 ; Sota ii. 4.
[8] Gitt. *ut supra*.

without doubt what is known as " the Phœnician " is the most
ancient.   By caligraphical improvements it first became what
is now designated as the Samaritan alphabet.   [The transition
to the square character, which first appears in Aramaic
inscriptions, seems to have been completed in Palestine shortly
before the Christian era, but the old alphabet was retained on
all Hebrew coins.[1]]   The Rabbins ascribe the alteration by
which our modern square Hebrew letters have arisen, to the
period of Ezra.[2]   What are now known as the vowel-points
and diacritical signs, date from a comparatively late period,
[perhaps the sixth or seventh century after Christ.   The
custom of representing long vowels in Hebrew by means of
the letters *vau* and *yod* had been gradually introduced, but it
was not in regular use at the time when the Septuagint
version was made [3]].

Legend had it that there were seventy nations, and as
many languages in the world,[4] amongst which, of course,
Hebrew was the only one which deserved or ought to be
studied.   But in course of time, and specially after the
Babylonish captivity, the " sacred language " underwent considerable modifications.   Although the Hebrews at the time
of their return had not forgotten their former peculiar dialect,
it gradually became transformed into the Palestinian or West
Aramean dialect, which, at the time of our Saviour, and afterwards, constituted the spoken and written language of Palestine.   It was spoken in greatest purity in Judea.   In Galilee
it approached more to the Syrian, and the gutturals were
indistinctly pronounced.[5]   Of course, the more learned the
speaker, the more pure was his dialect.   The ancient Hebrew,
however, was always retained for sacred purposes and extensively studied.   Although the study of foreign languages,
more probably of their literature, was interdicted, yet, from
the necessity of their circumstances, the Greek, and soon
afterwards the Latin, were in common use in Palestine.   As

---

[1] Driver, *Notes on Samuel*, Introd. § 1, esp. p. xvii.
[2] Sanh. 21*b*.   [3] Driver, *ut supra*, p. xxxiii ff.
[4] Lightfoot on John xii. 31.
[5] Meg. 24*b* ; comp. Neubauer, *Géog. du Talm.* p. 184 f.

the knowledge of many things had been acquired from these foreigners, many Greek and Latin words with Hebrew terminations became current, and found their way into the Talmud.[1] However, the Synagogue was liberal towards unlettered Hebrews, and recognised the use of Greek not only in legal documents, such as letters of divorce, although drawn up in Palestine,[2] but even allowed to Israelites who had settled in foreign countries the use of foreign languages in their prayers.[3]

Jewish law fully protected both persons and property. Where property was even accidentally injured, the party who had occasioned it was held responsible, if every precaution had not been used, or distinct intimation of the danger given.[4] If a person had been hurt, damages might be claimed for actual injury (calculated by a valuation of the party both before and after the hurt), for pain (calculated by an estimate of what the injured party would have been willing to pay rather than suffer), for medical expenses, for loss of time, and for the affront (the latter in cases of intentional injury). A Hebrew slave possessed in this respect the same rights as a free man, only that, if the injury had been inflicted by his master, he could not, of course, claim compensation for loss of time. Even foreign slaves might sue for damages, although not on the ground of affront. Damages could not be claimed from a married woman or from a slave, as neither could, in law, possess any property of their own. But they might be sued for at any later period when the offending party had either been divorced or manumitted. The damages for a blow with the fist were fixed at 100 sus or denars ; at 200 for a box on the face, or 400 if given with the back of the hand, and the excuse of provocation was not held valid.[5]

If mildness and kindness characterised the social intercourse of the Hebrews, another virtue, that of charity, was still more inculcated and prized. Passion for gain or lust of wealth was not one of the national sins, till centuries of

---

[1] Comp. examples in Ersch's *Encycl.* xxvii. p. 28, etc.; Schürer, II. i. 31–47.
[2] Gitt. ix. 8. [3] Sot. vii. 1.
[4] Comp. specially Baba Kama iii. [5] Comp. Baba Kama viii.

the most relentless persecution had made the possession of riches their only means of influence or hope of safety. The stated annual contributions for religious and charitable purposes were very considerable. Beside the customary sacrifices, the first-fruits of all fields and cattle and the heave-offerings belonged to the priests, from whom the firstborn had likewise to be redeemed. The amount of the heave-offering was generally computed at one-fortieth, one-fiftieth, or at least at one-sixtieth of the whole produce.[1] Besides, a tithe of everything was contributed for sacred purposes. A second tithe was levied, but not devoted to the priests. Heads of families were expected to bring these second tithes or their full value with them to Jerusalem (to the annual feasts), where the learned or the poor were to be entertained with them during the festivities, which made the capital a grand religious banqueting-house, and all Israel a joyful religious brotherhood. Every third and sixth year a third tithe was collected for the poor, and distributed, not at Jerusalem, but among those who lived in the neighbourhood of the farmer or landholder.[2] The laws connected with the Sabbatical year are well known. Besides these religious imposts, a half-shekel was annually contributed to the treasury,—all these imposts being paid by every Israelite in Palestine and Syria, and probably for the most part also by the Jews of the Dispersion.[3]

It was enjoined to show kindness to all who were employed. The farm-servant was allowed to partake of the fruits of the ground, and the day-labourer, besides his hire, shared in the meals of the family.[4] During the harvest, at morning, noon, and even, the poor assembled to receive their gifts.[5] At other times of the year, officers specially appointed for the purpose went about every day to collect victuals, and on Fridays money for the poor.[6] Besides these statutory contributions, the opinion generally entertained of

---

[1] Ter. iv. 3 ; comp. specially the treatises Peah, Maaseroth, and Maaser Sheni.

[2] Maas. Sh. v. 6.   Comp. Schürer, II. i. 241.

[3] Ut supra, II. i. 247 f.   [4] B. Mez. vii. ; Maas. iii. 1, 2.

[5] Peah iv. 5.   [6] Jer. Peah viii. 7.

the peculiar merits of private charity led to such profusion, that it had at last to be limited to giving away one-fifth of one's property. However, poor relatives might receive part of the legal contributions destined for the poor generally. The vagrant poor were to get food and lodging, and on Sabbaths not less than three meals,[1] so as to feel at least the material joy of that day. Equally liberal was the law in determining who were proper recipients of charity. Given as a religious contribution, and as to brethren, the law had rather to encourage than discourage applicants for relief. There were three degrees of parochial relief, according as the recipient obtained a share of the harvest only, or also of the money and of the victuals collected for the poor. Any person who possessed less than 200 sus was a pauper, and hence had a claim upon part of the harvest ; nor was he obliged to sell his house or furniture in order to make up the sum fixed as the statutory limit of charity. Persons engaged in trade or business were very properly excepted from a rule which was only meant to apply to women, or aged and infirm persons. Any party who had not sufficient to purchase food for fourteen meals, was to apply to the authorities for money ; while, if sufficient for two meals was not in the house, the pauper received a share of the victuals which were daily collected for the poor. To seek assistance where it was not needed, was looked upon as a sin, exposing to divine judgments. All moneys for the poor were collected by two, and distributed by three parochial officers. Relief to the brethren was not to be doled out grudgingly, nor were the indigent treated with contempt or indifference. On the contrary, as will by and by appear, they were treated with the greatest delicacy and deference. What they received had either been first offered to the Lord, and was in turn given them by their heavenly Father, or they partook of it together with the rich donors (often at their table), and as members of the same family. The wealthy landholder was a spiritual chief, and the poor of the district members of a holy family, for which he was the divinely appointed

[1] Peah viii. 7-9.

steward. Beggars, properly speaking, with the exception of such as were afflicted with diseases or infirmities, were unknown in Palestine, and to a great extent are still unknown amongst the Jews.

The civil taxes varied considerably with the circumstances of the country. Under Persian domination, road-money, duty on provisions, and a property and income-tax were paid, besides the exactions to which a conquered province would always be subject. Under Egyptian rule, the taxes of Palestine, including Phœnicia and Cœle-Syria, were farmed for eight thousand talents.[1] Under Syrian government the taxation was exceedingly vexatious, including a tax on salt, the crown-money (the "aurum coronarium"), and an impost of a third of all that was sown, and of a half of the fruits of trees; head-money or poll-tax, some tax on cattle, and custom duties, were also levied. When the Romans first interfered in the affairs of Judea, they did not at once levy the usual taxes; but the descendants of Antipater derived a large income from crown lands (*Ant.* xiv. 10. 6); from a tax upon land and its produce (xv. 9. 1); from a house-tax (xix. 6. 3); from export duties (xiv. 10. 22); and from a market-tax upon everything that was bought or sold (xvii. 8. 4, xviii. 4. 3). The last-mentioned tax was specially galling. From all these sources the income of Herod the Great is estimated to have amounted to more than a thousand talents, or £240,000.[2] With the death of Herod the last shadow of Jewish independence passed away. Each "free-born Jew" had now to pay to his heathen master property-tax, poll-tax, and specially custom and duties, levied by the publicans on the different highways and in the seaport towns.[3] This amounted to large sums, chiefly derived from balsam and other valuable exports. A superior excise officer (chief of the publicans) was located in Jericho, which was the centre of the balsam district. The tax on all articles bought and sold was continued till 36 A.D., when it was abolished by Vitellius, and, after the

[1] Jos. *Ant.* xii. 4. 4.   [2] *Ut supra*, xvii. 11. 4, 5 ; *Wars*, ii. 6. 3.
[3] Comp. Schürer, I. ii. 65–71, 109–111.

destruction of the temple, the customary half-shekel had to be
paid to Rome. If we bear in mind that the customs were
farmed, as a mercantile speculation, by lessees who employed publicans, while the latter, in turn, sought to profit as
much as possible by the unpopular occupation in which they
were engaged, it will be understood how a taxation, oppressive in itself, became most odious and grinding. True, the
law gave a right of appeal against improper exactions, but
it will readily be understood that such appeals were always
difficult and expensive, and rarely led to satisfactory results.
As the agriculturist passed to town or market, the hated
publican sat by the wayside to examine every conveyance,—
often to violate the secrecy of letters,—to demand or to
furnish a receipt for payment of dues. Every ass or beast
of burden that carried the rich produce of the land towards
Ptolemais or Cæsarea was stopped, each package opened and
tumbled about, and new and vexatious exactions hampered
every branch of industry. No wonder, then, that the publicans were hated and despised, nor even admitted to bear
witness in Jewish courts, and in general treated like heathens
or harlots. It was not even allowed to receive charity from
them.[1] They were unworthy of this privilege, nor could
they have given what too often had been unjustly acquired.
However, there were honourable exceptions,—amongst them
Zacchæus, who is mentioned in the Gospel.

Under these circumstances, the separation between Jews
and Gentiles became daily greater. Since the Exile, and
especially from the time of the Maccabees, there had been a
strong separatist party among the Jews; still for the most
part strangers were treated with a kindness and justice which
Israelites did not meet with in return. Many of the foreign
settlers in Palestine became proselytes, of whom two classes
are mentioned. Those of the first class, termed in the
Talmud "resident strangers" or "proselytes,"[2] were only

[1] B. Kam. x. 1.
[2] [*Ger tôshab.* The expression Proselyte of the Gate, frequently used to
denote this class of aliens, does not occur till considerably later than the period
of the Talmud ; comp. Schürer, II. ii. 316 ff.]

naturalised aliens, bound to obey the seven Noachic ordinances [1] (as they were termed), which interdicted blasphemy, idolatry, murder, incest, robbery, resistance of the magistrates, the eating of blood, all of which were necessary for the protection of the State and of the established religion. Proselytes of Righteousness were, besides, converts to Judaism, and admitted by circumcision, baptism, and a sacrifice. Some authorities suppose, although on insufficient grounds, that baptism was only introduced after sacrifices had become impossible. [2] [This classification, however, was little more than a theory of the Rabbins. The real distinction was between foreigners who adopted monotheism and the principal Jewish observances, and proselytes in the narrower sense of the term, who became essentially Jews.] The foreigner admitted into the Synagogue was considered to have left his country, family, and friends, to whom he was now so completely a stranger, that, theoretically, he might even have married his heathen sister or mother. [3] By his entrance into the Synogogue he became a new man, and in every respect equal to a native Israelite. [4] Although later Jewish writers have professed carelessness as to proselytism, —a profession which reflects credit neither on Judaism nor on their own religious convictions,—extraordinary zeal was at times displayed by the Synagogue to gain proselytes. But the later converts to Judaism were mostly of an inferior caste, who had joined the Synagogue either as slaves of Jews, or in order to marry into Jewish families. It is to such proselytes that the contemptuous expressions used by later Rabbins, who designate them as "the leprosy of Israel," [5] must apply. Pious, or rather bigoted ritualists, dreaded their influx as likely to bring in a set of unlearned persons not zealous for the rites, while the proud sages despised them for their origin and their ignorance of Rabbinical lore.

In some respects the etiquette of the Hebrews led to a more simple, in others to a more complicated ceremonial,

[1] Ab. Sar. 64b ; Sanh. 56a.   [2] Comp. *Life and Times*, ii. 745 ff.
[3] Comp. Jeb. 22a.   [4] Comp. Schürer, II. ii. 325 f.
[5] Jeb. 47b.

than that of modern nations. If the articles of dress in use were less subject to the alterations of fashion, the rules of good society and the climate necessitated a larger number of them than with us. At a later period, contact with foreigners led to a conformity with their manners, once unknown in Palestine, and the leaders of fashion imported from abroad articles of luxury, the use of which a former generation would have repudiated. The Talmud [1] enumerates eighteen articles, which might form parts of an elegant toilet. Commonly [2] it consisted of one or, in the case of rich persons and travellers, two under garments, which reached to the ankles, and were kept close to the body by a girdle. The upper robe, which was variously arranged according to taste or fashion, was also used by the poor at night for a covering. This was a square garment, with borders or fringes of blue or white attached to the four corners. Of course the shape and material varied with the rank and manners of the wearer. Amongst the finest were the white, the embroidered, and the purple garments. On particular occasions, as in mourning at court or in travelling, a different style of clothing was adopted. At a later period, travelling-cloaks with hoods attached to them were worn. The head-dress consisted of a pointed cap or of a kind of turban. The dresses of females were distinguished by their shape, the fineness of their texture, and their ornaments. In the latter class we may include the nets which they wore over their hair [3] and their frontlets. Of the veils, which were laid aside in the house, and while going about the usual avocations, there were various kinds. The Arabian veil hung down from the head and covered the face, but left the eyes free; [4] the veil-dress was a kind of cloak or mantilla thrown over the whole person and covering the head; the Egyptian veil, like that still used in the East, covered the breast, neck, chin, and face, leaving only the eyes free. Jewish

---

[1] Shab. 120*a*.
[2] Comp. Derek Erez x. ; also *Life and Times*, i. 621 ff.
[3] Kel. xxviii. 9, 10.
[4] Shab. vi. 6 ; comp. Levy, *NHWB.* iv. 460*a* ; Tertul. *De vel. Virgin.* 17.

ladies wore not only sandals, which consisted merely of soles strapped to the foot, but also more or less costly slippers, sometimes embroidered and bestudded with gems.[1] Thus, both in veils and shoes, necessity gave place to luxury.

Still more manifest was the love of splendour, which, indeed, is one of the natural characteristics of Orientals, in the ornaments worn by both sexes. Gentlemen generally wore a seal either on the ring-finger or suspended round the neck, which, together with the staff, were almost in universal use. The barbarous practice of shaving had not as yet banished the natural ornament of man, and the fashionable Jews carefully trimmed, anointed, and perfumed their beards. The hair was considered another of the chief points of beauty, and a bald person was held unfit to discharge the priestly functions. Young people and females wore their hair long, but in men such would have been regarded as a token of effeminacy. Peasant girls tied their hair in a simple knot, but the rich patrician ladies were wont to curl and plait it, and to adorn its tresses with gold ornaments and pearls. Indeed, hair-plaiting and curling was a special, although not a respectable business.[2] Some dandies had their hair dressed, and the Talmud mentions both hairpins and combs. A lady's hair was anointed, perfumed, and sprinkled either with gold-dust,[3] or dyed so as to appear reddish, this colour being the favourite in climates where it is rare. Even false hair seems to have been used.[4]

In general, anointing was usually combined with washing, as tending to comfort and refreshment. The hair, the beard, the clothes, the forehead and face, even the garlands worn at feasts, were anointed. Ointments were prepared of oil and home or foreign perfumes, and, if very costly, preserved in alabaster flasks. Perfumers, however, were generally despised, even amongst heathen nations. Some Jewesses used also cosmetics. They painted their cheeks, and especially blackened their eyelids with a mixture of antimony and oil, which

---

[1] On this and the following, see Hartmann's *Hebräerinn am Putztische.*
[2] Shab. 94*b*, 104*b*.　　　[3] Jos. *Ant.* viii. 7. 3.　　　[4] Shab. vi. 5.

at the same time acted as a preventive against inflammation of the eyes, a disease common in the East.[1] Of the other ornaments worn by ladies, we may mention gold head-dresses, nose-rings, finger-rings, necklaces, bracelets, and ankle-rings. Girls had also their ears bored, a thread or small piece of wood being kept in the hole till the wound was healed,[2] when either a plain ring or a drop or pendant was inserted. Besides their head-dresses and gold ornaments, frontlets and ear-rings, Hebrew ladies also wore nose-rings, which the law ordered to be put aside on the Sabbath.[3] In the East these rings are now either fastened in one of the nostrils, or in the septum between the nares, and made so as gracefully to hang over the mouth, without, however, interfering with the salute of the privileged friend. Two kinds of necklaces were worn, the one closely fitting, the other loose and like a chain, frequently consisting of stones and pearls strung together, which depended over the chest, and even to the girdle. Fashionable ladies wore two or three such chains, to which smelling-bottles, perfumeries, and even small heathenish ornaments, as crescents, suns, snakes, etc., were fastened. From the frontlet, or the head ornament, which was frequently in the shape of a snail,[4] gold pendants descended. The bracelets, sometimes worn even by gentlemen, were fastened above the wrist, and were made of ivory, gold, or of precious stones strung together. The girdle worn by ladies was fastened lower and more loosely than that of gentlemen, who wore it round the loins. It was frequently made of very costly fabric, and adorned with precious stones. The rings round the ankles were generally so wrought, as in walking to make a noise like the tinkling of little bells. Besides, ladies wore gold or diamond pins in their clothes, rings on their fingers, and, when needful, even false teeth in their mouths.[5]

However luxurious in their dress, the Hebrews were much more simple in their domestic arrangements than the neighbouring nations. The places on which they rested at night varied with the rank and circumstances of their owners, from

---

[1] Comp. Shab. 64*b*, 80*a* ; Levy, *NHWB.* ii. 313 f.
[2] Shab. vi. 6.   [3] *Ut supra*, 1.   [4] *Ut supra*, 3.   [5] *Ut supra*, 5.

the stone pillow and the covering of the upper garment, or the more or less simple couch, to beds, the posts of which were hung with gay and costly fabrics. The middle classes, no doubt, used low couches, similar to the modern divans of the East, which served as sofa by day and as bed by night. Baths, partly for refreshment, partly as means of preserving or restoring health, and partly for Levitical purifications, were very common. The laws with reference to purification were punctilious in determining where, when, and how lustrations were to be performed.[1]   Some were in the habit of daily resorting to these plunge-baths. In general, the houses of the better classes had bathing-rooms, or else a bathing apparatus attached to the court. Public baths in and near towns were provided for the poor, in which a kind of bran seems to have been used for removing impurities.[2] Palestine possessed several mineral springs which were used internally and as baths, but their use was generally restricted to invalids. During the summer season a retreat was indeed sought in the cooler parts of the country,—especially in the neighbourhood of the Lake of Gennesaret,[3]—where the wealthy and the noble had their villas. The most famed mineral baths were those of Tiberias or Emmaus, of Gadara, and of Callirrhoë. Tiberias lay at a distance of 200 stadia from Scythopolis, and about twenty English miles from Nazareth. Close beside it, at the village of Emmaus, are hot springs (about 144° Fahr.), which contain sulphur and salts of soda and of iron. About fifteen miles from Tiberias, and at no great distance from the south-east corner of the Lake of Gennesaret, lay Gadara, the modern Om-keis, situate upon the mountains, at the foot of which hot sulphurous streams flowed towards the Jordan.[4] The waters of Gadara were specially resorted to by lepers, and famous even outside of Palestine. Callirrhoë lay on the east of the Dead Sea.[5]

The Hebrews presented also a favourable contrast in the

---

[1] Compare specially Mishna, Mikwaoth.   [2] Pesach. ii. 7.

[3] In Gen. Rab. 98 the name "Gennesaret" is fancifully explained as "Gene Sarim," the gardens of the nobility.

[4] Relandi *Palœstina*, p. 773, etc.   Comp. Schürer, II. i. 100 ff.

[5] *Ut supra*, p. 679.

simplicity of their amusements when compared with the barbarous sports of heathen nations. While in the streets and markets children engaged in amusements with which we are familiar,[1] young persons exercised themselves in athletic games, by lifting, swinging, and throwing great weights. Games of chance, such as dice, and a kind of racing, not with horses, but with doves, are mentioned,[2] but always in terms of unqualified disapprobation. The chase was not resorted to as an amusement, and snares were laid for game and fowls simply in order to get possession of them. Public popular amusements were unknown till the period of Syrian domination and Jewish decadence. With the exception of religious festivals, all such amusements were contrary to the Jewish idea of proper individual and family life. The exercises of the gymnasium only led to close intercourse with Gentiles, and engendered a dangerous familiarity with heathen practices, which ultimately even originated the idea of effacing the peculiar bodily mark of Judaism.

The first verses of the first Psalm were held to apply equally to the amusements of the theatre or amphitheatre, to frequenting the ring, and to witnessing the performances of jugglers.[3] It was well known that such indulgences would operate detrimentally upon the piety and morality of the people. Under the rule of the Herodians, theatres and amphitheatres were indeed reared in various cities of Palestine, in imitation and in honour of the Romans.[4] But as the games there celebrated were essentially foreign, they were discountenanced and even interdicted by the Rabbins. With equal zeal did the Rabbins warn against all contamination with idolatry. Anything that could directly or indirectly be connected with idolatry, such as heathen ornaments, etc., might not be lawfully used by a Hebrew, who was in no way to compromise himself with countenancing anti-Jewish practices. To throw down a stone in honour of Mercury,[5] or to touch

---

[1] For example, Kelim xvii. 15.　　　[2] Shab. xxiii. 2 ; Sanh. 25*a*.
[3] Ab. Sar. 18*b*.　　　[4] Comp. Schürer, II. i. 23 ff., 32 f.
[5] Ab. Sar. iv. 1. On this and the following particulars, comp. the treatise Aboda Sara.

those which had so been thrown down, to enter into business relations with heathens three days before or after their feasts,[1] to make purchases in shops decorated with garlands in honour of idols, even to celebrate the first of January (the new year), or any other calends (first of the month), the saturnalia, the birth or the coronation day of a heathen emperor, was strictly interdicted.[2]   Sometimes these views took the direction of intolerance and persecution.   Thus it was not lawful to assist at the birth of, or to suckle, a heathen infant.[3]   Sad experience daily corroborated the Biblical testimony of the character of heathenism, and although the manifestations of Jewish abhorrence were sometimes wrong, we can scarcely wonder at the repugnance of the Synagogue.

III. JEWISH MORAL PHILOSOPHY

Before closing this account of the state of society amongst the Hebrews, it may be well to present the popular ideas on various subjects, as these are scattered over the pages of the Talmud.[4]   Although at the risk of going back upon our record, or of anticipating to some extent what is to follow, they will afford a more faithful portraiture of the popular mind than any other description could have done.

The Divine word, which was the framework of Jewish society, admitted, in popular opinion, a variety of interpretations.   " Every line and stroke in the Bible is of vast importance, "[5] was the fruitful principle of this view, to which a great part of traditionalism owed its origin.   It was held that the oral law had been received by Moses from God, and communicated first to Aaron, then to his sons, and finally to the elders of Israel.   In point of fact, these studies were preferred to the Bible.   The Talmud [6] (in application of Isa. iii. 1) compares the Halacha to bread, and the Hagada to water.

---

[1] Ab. Sar. i. 1, 2.   [2] *Ut supra*, i. 3.   [3] *Ut supra*, ii. 1.
[4] This sketch of moral philosophy is a condensation of *Menorath Hammaor*, by Isaac Aboab, a celebrated Spanish Rabbi (1433–1493).   The edition before us is in 3 vols. Krotoschin, 1848.
[5] Erubin 21*b*.   [6] Chag. 14*a*.

A Midrash [1] explains Deut. xxxii. 13, 14, respectively of the Pentateuch, and of the other portions of Scripture ; of the Mishna, of the Talmud, of the various exegetical rules, of the Halacha and of the Hagada,—an interpretation which, however extravagant, sufficiently indicates the state of feeling. As the law of God, both written and oral, was the source of happiness and delight, so from lust and ambition all wretchedness flowed. Thus, while Korah, Dathan, and Abiram suffered in consequence of their envy, lust, and ambition, Aaron received as reward of opposite virtues, the honour of wearing the breast-plate and the Urim and Thummim.[2]   Satisfied with little, the pious ought not to take care for the morrow, not knowing what a day may bring forth,[3] and thus to imitate the Rabbins, who laboured with their hands in order to acquire the means for those studies which are the grand end of life. Hillel, the rich Eleazar ben Charsom, and the Patriarch Joseph, were instanced to show that neither poverty, riches, nor temptation should prevent from engaging in such occupations.[4]

In general, it was thought that punishments and rewards stood in exact correspondence with man's actions. Thus, Samson was blinded for letting his eyes stray, Absalom's vanity led to his being hung by the hair ; while, on the other hand, as Miriam had waited on Moses when he lay in the ark of bulrushes, so Israel waited for her seven days in the wilderness during her leprosy.[5]   Similarly,[6] unchastity would induce dropsy ; groundless hatred, jaundice ; pride, poverty ; calumny, diseases of the respiratory organs, etc.   Some sins, as blasphemy, a denial of the truth of Scripture, and especially of the resurrection, entailed not only temporal, but eternal destruction.[7]   Broken vows entail the loss of one's wife ; non-payment of tithes causes famine (Mal. iii. 10) ; robbery brings locusts (Amos iv. 1, 9) ; mal-administration of justice leads to war, pestilence, etc. (Jer. xxxiii. 23, 24). As these calamities fall on the whole nation, every person ought, as far as possible, to prevent his neighbour from sinning, or at least reprove

[1] Sifre, *ad loc.*
[2] Shab. 139*a*.
[3] Sota 48*b*.
[4] Joma 35*b*.
[5] Sot. i. 8, 9.
[6] Shab. 33*a*.
[7] Sanh. 91*b*.

him. Neglect of this duty (to which Lev. xix. 17 referred)
brought punishment even on the righteous (Ezek. ix. 6).[1]
However, a reproof should be administered delicately and in
private. Rabbi Tarphon thought that in his age nöne was
worthy to reprove ; for, to the admonition, " Remove the mote
from thine eye," it might be replied, " Remove first the *beam*
out of thine own eye " ;[2] whilst Rabbi Akiba doubted if any
would be found willing to listen to reproof. It was deemed
an unfavourable sign if the inhabitants of a place loved a
Rabbi, as indicating unfaithfulness on his part.[3]

True riches were not to be sought in the possession of
wealth, but in contentment with one's estate.[4] A different
spirit could only lead to theft, which was more culpable even
than robbery, as manifesting a greater fear of *man* than of
God ;[5] hence theft and not robbery was mentioned in the
eighth commandment. Upon the same principle the use of
false measures and weights was considered a greater sin than
theft.[6] Robbery, however, was the iniquity which filled up
the measure of the antediluvian world (Gen. vi. 13).[7] In
point of principle, the robbery of a penny was as culpable as
that of a life ;[8] and forced sales, damaging one's neighbour,
or the keeping back of wages, were of the same stamp.[9] Comparatively speaking, it was more culpable to rob an individual
than even to abstract from that which had been dedicated for
the temple.[10] Usury was a heinous offence, entailing poverty
here and wretchedness hereafter. So carefully was it to be
avoided, that a debtor was not even to bow to his creditor,
unless he had formerly been in the habit of so doing. But a
penitent usurer was to be encouraged ; the parties wronged
were to forgive him as God forgave them, and not to press the
offending brother for restitution.[11] Bribery was compared to
the small hook by which large fishes were caught. Judges
were warned against the bribery of flattery, and even the offer
of a gift to him incapacitated a judge from deciding in a

[1] Ab. Sar. 4.   [2] Arach. 16.   [3] Keth. 105.
[4] Shab. 25.   [5] Baba Kama 79.   [6] Baba Bathra 85, 88.
[7] Sanh. 108.   [8] Baba Kama 119.   [9] Baba Mezia 111.
[10] Baba Bathra 88.   [11] *Ut supra*, 90, 94.

cause.[1] Every appearance of covetousness was to be avoided. An article should not be purchased below its fair value, and parties were interdicted from buying anything at less than five-sixths of its real value, or selling it at more than one-sixth above its value.

Gluttony and wine-bibbing (Prov. xxiii. 20, etc.), which "made red here and pale hereafter," entailed sorrow and led to sin.[2] On the other hand, chastity was one of the principal virtues. All needless conversation with females, looking at them, at their hair, dress, etc., was improper. According to the not inapt mode of speaking at the time, it was said that to preserve chastity in the midst of temptations conferred merit equal to that of a *poor* man who restored what he had found, or of a *rich* man who gave his tithes in *secret*.[3] Assiduous study of the Law was recommended as the most likely help to this virtue.[4] All the curses (in Deut. xxvii. 15 ff.) applied to adultery.[5] Self-confidence was here specially out of place. Legend had it that the fall of David was due to this cause. It was said that he had presumed to expostulate with God because He was not called the God of David as well as of Abraham, Isaac, and Jacob. The folly of his challenge to be submitted to a trial similar to theirs was shown in his fall [6] (Ps. xxvi. 2). Indeed, every person had a good and an evil inclination; the latter, at first slender like a thread, became by and by strong as a cart-rope.[7] In 2 Sam. xii. 4 this evil inclination was represented as first a *pilgrim*, then a *guest*, and, finally, a *lord*. To overcome this evil concupiscence [8] was equal in merit to offering all the sacrifices prescribed by the law.

Ambition was another dangerous enemy, which had brought Joseph into an earlier grave than his brethren.[9] All honours came from God, who bestowed them not only on an individual, but on his latest posterity (Job xxxvi. 7), who are only deprived of them if they become proud.[10] That pride might not be fostered, parochial offices should only be

---

[1] Keth. 105.   [2] Sanh. 70.   [3] Pesach. 113.   [4] Ab. Sar. 20.
[5] Sota 37.   [6] Sanh. 107.   [7] Succa 52.   [8] Sanh. 43.
[9] Sota 13.   [10] Meg. 13.

conferred with the express sanction of the congregation
(Ex. xxxv. 30), and administered with meekness.[1]   To this
virtue Deut. xxx. 12 referred, while the expression, " The
commandment is not in heaven," indicated that observance
of the law was not with the proud.[2]   God only establishes
man in the way which he himself chooses, and the sinner
is ultimately left like Balaam ; while he that seeks the Lord
is assisted, protected, and sanctified from on high.[3]   It was
thought comparatively easy to observe the law which only
consisted in loving one's neighbour as one's self.   Thus
Hillel the Great had summed up Judaism in the one
command, " Do not that to thy neighbour which would be
displeasing to thyself." [4]   Circumstances could not palliate
any of these three sins,—idolatry, incest, and murder.   All
other transgressions of positive injunctions were thought
to be expiated by penitence ; those of negative commandments, by penitence and the Day of Atonement ; those of
which the breach entailed the threat of " being cut of," by
penitence, the Day of Atonement, and sufferings ; while only
death could set free from the guilt of sins connected with
a profanation of the Divine name.[5]   Trifling offences, if
committed by sages, may bring dishonour upon the name of
the Lord.   The command, " To love the Lord our God," was
generally interpreted as referring to the duty of making His
name beloved.   An excessive anxiety on this subject, however, induced a relaxation of rigour when sins were committed in secret.[6]

The tongue, which God had given only to praise Him, had
become a dangerous member,—a circumstance which even
its position within the twofold walls of cheeks and teeth[7]
indicated.   Every word of God, whether embodied in the
written or the oral law, was to be implicitly believed and
carefully studied.[8]   Legend had it [9] that when Moses ascended
into heaven he found God making strokes at the letters of
the law.   " Is it not customary in thy city to salute ? "

[1] Ber. 55.   [2] Erub. 55.   [3] Macc. 10 ; Joma 38.
[4] Shab. 31.   [5] Joma 86.   [6] Sanh. 74.
[7] Arach. 15.   [8] Sanh. 99.   [9] Shab. 89 ; Menach 29.

asked the Lord. " Lord of the world," replied Moses, " may the servant salute his master ? " " Then thou shouldst at least assist Me," rejoined the Lord. These were the strokes from which Rabbi Akiba and his successors elicited the Halacha. Even apparently incredible statements of Rabbins, such as that God would in the last days make the gates of Jerusalem of jewels, each thirty cubits square, that women would conceive and bear in one day, etc.,[1] were to be implicitly believed. On the other hand, all untruth, even by way of joke, was to be avoided,[2] except when spoken " for the sake of peace," when it was not only lawful, but even duty.[3] Thus, an ugly and disagreeable bride might be praised before her intended as being beautiful, clever, pious, etc. Falsehood, for the sake of gain, was like idolatry.[4] Promises were to be inviolable, and all oaths were to be made in the sense in which others were likely to understand them.[5] As vows, however rashly made, were strictly binding, all vowing was disapproved.[6] The term *Amen* indicated either an oath, an assent, or a confirmation. . Flattery was one of the greatest and most dangerous sins.[7] To punish a want of faithfulness, God, in answer to the expostulations of justice, recalled the merciful passing by of His people in Ezek. ix. 4, and ordered the work of destruction to begin at IIis saints (ver. 6).[8] To deceive even a heathen by word or deed was strictly forbidden.[9] So far was scrupulosity here carried, that it was held to be wrong to invite to dinner, or to offer a present, where it was known that it would not be accepted.

One witness could only give private information against a person, and even then incurred a danger similar to that of Joseph, who had accused his brethren both of having eaten flesh cut out of living animals, of having reproached the sons of Bilhah and of Zilpah, and also of having sinned with the heathen maids of the country. For these denunciations he himself afterwards suffered analogous punishments.[10]

[1] Shab. 30 ; Baba Bathra 75.   [2] *Ut supra*, 88.   [3] Jebam. 65.
[4] Sanh. 92.   [5] Shebuoth 39.   [6] Nedar. 20.
[7] Sota 41.   [8] Shab. 55.   [9] Chul. 94.
[10] Gen. Rab. 84.

It was thought [1] that people generally accused their
neighbours of the faults of which they themselves were
guilty, while regular gossips spake evil of every person.
Secrets were always to be respected.[2] Calumny was not
even excusable in a student or sage, such as Doeg the
Edomite, the calumniator of David, supposed to have been
very learned, to whom Ps. l. 16 and lii. 1, 5 were thought to
apply.[3] The party who had formed a habit of this kind was
in danger of being cut off from the people of God. The
Talmud speaks also of "the dust of calumny," [4] or conduct
which leads to calumny. The danger of this sin, which
stands next to murder, incest, and idolatry, may be gathered
from the fate of the spies whom Moses sent into Palestine.[5]
God generally punished it with leprosy, as in the case of
Moses' sister. Those who listen to calumny are equally
guilty (Ex. xxii. 31, xxiii. 1), as fingers and earlaps are
provided to enable us to shut our ears against backbiters.[6]
Jeroboam had been admitted to parity with the kings of
Judah (Hos. i. 1),[7] because he had not listened to calumnies
about Amos (Amos vii. 10, 11), while the kingdom of David
was divided in consequence of this sin (2 Sam. xix. 29).
It was, of course, more heinous if committed against the
sages, who ought to be praised by every person.[8]

Light or indecent conversation led to various trials [9]
(Isa. ix. 17), as, for example, the loss of children while they
were still young. Even the most trivial conversation will
form subject of inquiry in the day of judgment (Amos
iv. 13).[10] Delicacy and kindliness were amongst the most
sacred duties. To affront another was almost equal to the
sin of murdering him. It was one of the three sins—
adultery, using hard words to our neighbour, and offending
him—which entailed the punishment of hell, and which in
such cases will never cease.[11] An eminent example of
delicacy was Tamar, who, not to put her father-in-law to

[1] Kidd. 70.   [2] Sanh. 31.   [3] *Ut supra*, 106.
[4] For example, Baba B. 164.   [5] Arach. 15.   [6] Keth. 5 ; Pes. 118.
[7] *Ut supra*, 87.   [8] Baba M. 84.   [9] Keth. 8.
[10] Chag. 5.   [11] Baba M. 59.

shame, only sent him his staff and ring.[1] In general, talkativeness was a sign of low breeding. As all conversation was either wholly detrimental, or partly useful and partly detrimental, or neither useful nor detrimental, or wholly useful, three-fourths of all common talk ought to be wholly dispensed with. " When two persons quarrel, one of them at least is of low origin," [2] was a common and not untrue saying. Besides actual ill-usage, all hatred, cursing, revenge, and bearing of grudges were interdicted. It was declared to be better to suffer persecution than to persecute.[3] Excessive merriment also might lead to sin, and even on joyous occasions mirth should be tempered; hence, when at a marriage one of the sages was asked to sing, he complied only by reminding the company of death; while another Rabbi, on a similar occasion, purposely broke a splendid vase.[4] Especially when going to prayer or to study, all talk and laughter should be avoided. These exercises required a composed and happy frame of spirit. On feast days half the time was to be spent in study, and the other half in prayer and amusements.

God hath in His law given Israel 613 commandments (365 *commandments*, according to the number of days in a solar year, and 248 *forbids*, according to the number of the members of the body) in order to make them happy.[5] These laws David had reduced to eleven (Ps. xv.), Isaiah to six (Isa. xxxiii. 15), Micah to three (Mic. vi. 8), again Isaiah to two (Isa. lvi. 1), and Amos and Habakkuk each to one (Amos v. 4 ; Hab. ii. 4). The different ordinances had not always a reason attached to them, as [6] such specifications might have led even good men to break them, under the impression that the grounds of the law did not apply to them. From such views Solomon had neglected two warnings in Deut. xvii. 16, 17. If only the letter of the law were obeyed, the motives were of smaller importance, as continued practice would at last lead to proper motives.[7] A pietism intended merely to gain

[1] Sota 10.   [2] Kidd. 71.   [3] Baba K. 93.
[4] Berach. 30, 31.   [5] Macc. 23.   [6] Sanh. 21.
[7] Nazir 23.

the esteem of *men* was despicable. In this respect the revulsion of feeling from the overweening estimate attached in the days of the Saviour, to the utter contempt of the Pharisees manifested at a later period, is remarkable. The Talmud caricatures seven kinds of Pharisees:[1] the Pharisee "like the inhabitants of Sychem," for filthy lucre; the Pharisee who walked slowly by way of looking grave; the Pharisee who knocked his head against the wall through walking with his eyes closed; the Pharisee with the drooping head, as if he were not to see what was going on in the world; the Pharisee who sounded his own merits; the Pharisee from a desire for future rewards; and the Pharisee from fear of future punishments.

The possession of children being looked upon as one of the most desirable blessings, it was considered that matrimony without issue should be dissolved; but male descendants were the great object of desire. It was said that the Bible had employed different expressions (1 Kings xi. 21) to intimate the death of David and that of Joab, because the one left sons and the other not.[2] Unmitigated indulgence towards children could only have evil consequences, as in the case of Ishmael, who, in his fifteenth year, had brought an idol into Abraham's house, so that Sarah had to insist on the removal of so dangerous a companion to Isaac.[3] On the other hand, learning was to be encouraged, not only on its own account, but as conferring merit on those who had taken part in the upbringing of a sage.[4] Neither trouble nor sacrifices were spared to attain the desired result. The duties of children towards their parents were of no less importance than those towards God, provided obedience involved no sin; hence the fifth commandment was placed on the first table, which detailed the duties towards God. During the first year after a parent's death, the children were to pray, "Let all the punishments due to him come upon me." Afterwards the deceased should be spoken of as "of blessed memory." Even heathens received reward for this virtue. Any injury should

[1] Sota 22. Comp. Levy, *NHWB.* iv. 143. [2] B. Bath, 116.
[3] Gen. Rab. 53. Comp. Gen. xxi. 9; Ex. xxxii. 6. [4] Kidd. 30, 31.

be borne by children with patience and meekness, and every respect shown to parents. A Rabbi distinguished himself by serving every morning as footstool to his aged mother; another is mentioned as having agreed successively to her various extravagant demands.

Marriages were supposed to be arranged in heaven; and forty days before the birth of a child it was there announced to whom he or she was to be wedded.[1] The marriage relation should be entered between eighteen and twenty; but these ties did not prevent the zealous student from prosecuting his studies. The policy of second marriages was considered doubtful. An unmarried person was without any *good* (Gen. ii. 18), without *joy* (Deut. xiv. 26), without *blessing* (Ezek. xliv. 30), without *protection* (Jer. xxxi. 22), without *peace* (Job v. 24), and could not properly be called a man (Gen. v. 2).[2] In the choice of a wife regard should be paid to her family, as daughters generally imitated their fathers, and sons their maternal uncles. The most prized connection was that with the family of a sage, or at least with that of a ruler of a synagogue, of the president of a poor's board, or of a teacher of youth.[3] Connection with the unlettered could only be allowed if the wealth so acquired were to be devoted to assist the sage in his studies. It was observed that God formed women neither out of the head, lest she should become proud; nor out of the eye, lest she should lust; nor out of the ear, lest she should be curious; nor out of the mouth, lest she should be talkative; nor out of the heart, least she should be jealous; nor out of the hand, lest she should be covetous; nor out of the foot, lest she should gad about: but out of the rib, which was always covered.[4] Improper marriages—from lust, for beauty, or for money—were strongly condemned, and described as leading to wretchedness. The husband is bound not only to honour and love, but to treat his wife with courtesy: her tears call down Divine vengeance. In general, he is to spend less than his means warrant for food, up to his means for his own clothing, and beyond that limit for that of

[1] Sanh. 22. [2] Jeb. 62, 63.
[3] Pes. 49. [4] Gen. Rab. 18.

his wife and children.[1]   As woman is formed from a rib, and
man from the ground, man seeks a wife, and not *vice versâ ;*
he only seeks what he has lost.   This also explains why man
is more easily reconciled than woman ; he is made of soft
earth, and she of hard bone.[2]   A woman should abstain from
all appearance of evil, immodesty or impropriety ; she should
always meet her husband cheerfully, cleanly, and kindly,
receive his friends with politeness and affability, and be
obedient and respectful.

Hospitality was a duty much prized amongst the Hebrews.
It was thought that Abraham had planted the tamarisk at
Beersheba for the reception of pilgrims,[3] and that, while partaking of the refreshment set before them, he had taught
them to call upon the Lord.   Strangers were to be kindly
received and provided with all necessaries, both while under
the roof of their host and when departing.   Next to hospitality was charity,—a virtue incumbent even on those who
themselves were the recipients of it.   The relief of the poor
conferred rewards in this life and in that which is to come.
Thus when Rabbi Akiba had spent four thousand pieces of
gold belonging to Rabbi Tarphon, which he had taken on pretence of buying a piece of ground for him, for behoof of the
poor, he replied to his expostulations by reminding him of
Ps. cxii. 9.[4]   In illustration of this duty, it was said that,
as the proprietor who let his fields to farmers expected at
least part of the produce, so God also expected a return from
us, whom He for a time had entrusted with what properly
belonged to Him.   In giving charity, relatives were, of course,
to be first remembered.   Poor persons were to be assisted
according to their former stations.   Hence Hillel once provided
a horse for a pauper, while another Rabbi, under similar circumstances, sent fowls and old wine.[5]   To provide for orphans,
and especially for orphan girls, was an important duty, which
even in this life often met with deserved reward.   Thus
Eleazar of Bartotha, who was so liberal that the parochial
officers used to avoid him, as he distributed beyond his means,

[1] Chul. 84*b*.   [2] Nid. 31*b*.   [3] Sot. 10*a b*.
[4] Mas. Kallah.   [5] Keth. 67*b*.

had given away the whole of his daughter's portion, except
one measure of wheat, when his barn was again miraculously
filled.[1] Great delicacy should characterise every act of
charity, lest the feelings of the recipients be wounded.
Money should be lent to those who would not accept of it
otherwise, and even untruths might be resorted to in order
to overcome the scruples of the poor. A duty of greater
importance than even the bestowal of charity, was that of the
redemption of captive Jews.

To visit the sick was to imitate the Lord, who had Himself
visited Abraham and buried Moses.[2] This duty was the more
obligatory as each visitor was supposed to carry away a small
part of the disease. Thus Akiba personally tended a neglected
sage, and thereby contributed to his recovery. It was thought
the Divine Majesty rested at the head of the sickbed.[3] A
kindred duty was to bury the dead, to accompany them to
their last resting-place, and, if they had not left male issue,
to act as mourner. So sacred was this as to take precedence
of all the other commandments.[4] It should be performed in
a manner respectful to the dead, the more so as the body
retained consciousness until it had become wholly putrid.
Some added that the bodies of sages crumbled to dust only
one hour before God again raised them.[5] Death, which set
free from the ills of life, was not to be dreaded as a calamity.
All the acquaintances of the deceased were to take part in
the mourning, especially if he had been a sage, whose loss was
felt by his whole generation. Funeral orations were commonly
delivered by some Rabbi, who dilated on the good qualities of
the departed, who was supposed to listen to the oration, and
to notice its effects upon the hearers. Examples of such
addresses, or at least an abstract of them, are left us. The
following may be taken as a specimen, probably, of the
peroration : " The palm-trees bend their tops for the departure of the godly ; for he was like one of them. Let us
mourn for him both by day and by night, even as his days
and his nights were solely devoted to study." At the funeral
of R. Chanan, who, on the day of his decease, became for the

---

[1] Taan. 24*a*.   [2] Sot. 14*a*.   [3] Nedar. 40*a*.   [4] Meg. 29*a*.   [5] Shab. 152*b*.

first time father, it was said, "The day of joy became one of
sorrow. Delight and grief went hand in hand. Sighing came
in the season of his joy, and he departed on the day of
receiving the favour for which he had longed." It was
thought that certain portents accompanied the death of
eminent sages. Legend had it, that on one occasion the gates
of a city shed tears ; that on another blood flowed from the
pipes of a city, or that the stars became visible in the day-
time ; that trees were rooted up, red-hot stones fell from
heaven, the statues in the streets broke in pieces, thorns grew
upon date-trees, the walls on opposite banks of a river bent
over and met, etc.[1]

In Galilee the mourners were wont to walk before the bier,
announcing the good deeds of the departed ; in Judea they
followed it.[2] A roll of the Law was also carried before the
bier or laid upon the coffin, to indicate that the departed had
obeyed its behests, and that study had been his chief occupation.[3] As Joseph had fulfilled the last offices to the patriarch
Jacob, his bones were allowed to accompany the ark into the
Land of Promise. The Hagadists related that Joseph's coffin
had been lowered by the superstitious Egyptians into the
Nile, to ensure its yearly overflow, but that at the command
of Moses the coffin had risen of its own accord.[4] While the
regular funeral orations for sages were sometimes delivered in
the synagogues, the lecture-rooms remained closed for some
days, and orations were delivered at the grave.[5] To die
without having become very emaciated, without weeping, or
looking to heaven or into the room (not to the wall), on a
Friday (not Saturday), immediately after the Day of Atonement
(not before it), were all deemed favourable indications. After
death every person was supposed to be welcomed by three
divisions of angels.[6] Mourners were to be comforted, not by
pointing out the *necessity* of submitting, but by referring to the
fact that all the Lord's dealings were for good, and that too
much sorrow could only entail upon the mourner other trials.
Mourners were not to be first accosted by their visitors, who

[1] Moed K. 25b.   [2] Shab. 153a.   [3] B. Kam. 17a; Moed K. 25a.
[4] Sota 13a.   [5] Meg. 28b; Moed K. 22b.   [6] Keth. 104a.

were to sit in silence, from time to time making such Hagadic applications of Scripture as seemed suitable.[1]

The Torah, or Divine Law, had existed before creation, and had served as the plan and model upon which God had framed His world. Seven things (the last five only ideally) existed before the world,—the Torah, the throne of God, penitence, paradise, hell, the temple, and the name of the Messiah.[2] As the world was only created for the sake of the Torah, it was, of course, the most important object, and Israel, as its recipients, the noblest and most favoured of nations. The most suitable time for study was the night, specially in its last watch. It was thought that David, whose harp was placed against his bed towards the north, so that the north wind at midnight might wake its sounds, rose at that time, and, having first played sweet melodies, betook himself to the study of the Torah, and that his subjects followed his example.[3] A reward was promised to those wives who encouraged their husbands in such occupations. For the sake of study, it was duty even to leave one's family, to expose one's self to privations, difficulties, and even disease, for all which the Lord would compensate in the world to come. Worldly callings were, however, not to be neglected, lest students should be cast upon the charity of others; and if only all the spare time was dedicated to the Law, it was considered as if the *whole time* had been set apart for that purpose.[4] A person might indeed, by worldly motives, be induced to *enter* on sacred studies; but if a *sage* used his acquirements "as a crown wherewith to shine, or as a spade wherewith to dig," he not only lost his reward in the world to come, but injured his happiness on earth.[5] Accordingly, when on one occasion the disclosure of his name had saved Rabbi Tarphon from imminent death, he mourned that he had made use of his reputation for such a purpose.[6] The study of the Law was of greater importance than the preservation of a man, than the building of the temple, than the honouring of parents, and conferred

---

[1] Moed K. 28*b*. [2] Pes. 54*a*; Nedar. 39*b*. Comp. Gen. Rab. 1.
[3] Sanh. 16*a*. [4] Comp. Chag. 5*b*; Pirke Ab. ii. 2.
[5] Pirke Ab. iv. 5. [6] Nedar. 62*a*.

greater honour than even the mitre of the high priest.   There were three crowns, that of study, that of the priesthood, and that of worldly dominion, of which the first was the most glorious.[1]   It was duty to converse about theological subjects, and disputation was of the greatest importance.   As occupation with theological subjects procured freedom from disease, so the neglect or forgetting of what had been acquired involved various evil consequences.[2]   Hence, also, the merit of training pupils, and the corresponding sin of shutting up knowledge.

As the Torah was eternal as the tree of life,[3] so Israel also were never to be destroyed, and their days to be like those of the tree of life.   Various illustrations of the value of learning were given.   It could even deliver from the grasp of the angel of death.   When David knew that his last day had come, he continued studying without interruption.   At last the angel of death succeeded in diverting his attention by rustling among the trees of the garden, and then seized the happy moment to remove the pious sage.[4]   Study was not to be neglected for the sake of prayer, as the latter was an application for things temporal, while the former was directed towards things eternal.[5]   The unlettered, who by the produce of their labour assisted the sages, would reap an eternal reward.   Every honour was to be shown to sages.   They were to be chosen for the highest congregational posts,—their cause was to be first heard in court,—they were free from parochial burdens, and had a claim upon the services of their fellow-citizens.[6]   Study delivered also from future punishments ; and if a sage could not enter into joy, he was at least in no danger of the pangs of hell.   Thus, when Acher died, the ministering angels declared him, on account of his learning, free from punishment.[7]   In the other world, the pious— and an ignorant person could not be pious—had mansions assigned to them varying with the amount of their merit. God would crown them with refulgent crowns, and prepare for them a splendid feast.   " The spirit returning to Him

[1] Joma 72b.   [2] Comp. Ber. 5a ; Joma 38b ; Pirke Ab. iii. 8.
[3] Mechilt. on Ex. xv. 25.   [4] Shab. 30b.   [5] Ut supra, 10a.
[6] Shab. 114a ; Nedar. 62b.   [7] Chag. 15b.

who has given it," should return pure and without spot to
mingle again with the eternal source from which it had at
first issued.[1] Looking upon this life as a preparation for the
future, Rabbi Jochanan ben Saccai compared it to the preparation for a royal banquet. The wise made haste and
waited at the entrance of the palace for the summons to
appear, while fools, deeming the time far off, delayed and continued at their usual avocations. Suddenly the summons
would be heard, when those who were dressed for the feast
would sit down, while the rest would have to look on, a prey
to hunger and want.[2] All this, however, only referred to
Messianic times, beyond which no prophet's eye had ever
pierced. Some pious persons obtained even in this world a
glimpse of the eternal rewards. Thus it had been ascertained
that Rabbi Chija, whose peculiar merit lay in having improved
the education of the young, stood highest in heaven, and was
so well acquainted with it, that, unlike its other inhabitants,
he was able to find his way without the guidance of angels. His
glory was so great that, when a beholder, despite the warning of
Elijah, looked at him, he lost his sight, which, at the intercession of Chija, was again granted him during the daytime, to
enable him to continue his studies.[3] Another of the sages
had prevailed on Eliezer, Abraham's servant, to announce his
visit to the patriarch, who reposed in the lap of Sarah. It
was, however, found impossible to bear a sight of Adam, but
his heels were declared to have resembled two suns. All the
beauty of earth combined appeared like the face of an ape
when compared with that of Sarah. The same comparison
applied to the respective beauty of Sarah and of Eve, and
again to that of Eve and Adam.[4] Sometimes the spirits of
the departed acquired knowledge of what was to befall men,
and information of it might be gathered by overhearing their
conversations, or by direct communications from them.[5]

The Lord reserved to Himself three wondrous works :—
To open the womb of the barren, to send the latter rain, and
to raise the dead.[6] Disbelief in the latter doctrine excluded

---

[1] Shab. 152*b* ; Meg. 15*b*.   [2] Shab. 153*a*.   [3] B. Mez. 85*b*.
[4] B. Bath. 58*a*.   [5] Ber. 18*b*.   [6] Taan. 2*a*.

from all share in future bliss. The arguments in favour of a resurrection were either derived from Scripture, as from passages in which an action of the departed is in the original mentioned in the future, and not in the past tense, as, " Then *shall* Moses and the children of Israel sing," etc. ; or from direct statements of the prophets. But the argument upon which most reliance was placed, and which, in the mouth of Rabbi Gamaliel, was supposed to have silenced the Sadducees, was from such unfulfilled promises as Deut. i. 8, xi. 9, wherein the Lord had promised to give the patriarchs (*to them*) the land of Canaan, — a line of argument, it will be observed, which bears some resemblance to that adopted by our Lord Himself. It was also argued by analogy, that if the Lord quickened the seed of corn buried in the ground, He would in due time deal similarly with His people.[1] It was held that men would rise with the same infirmities and diseases to which they had been subject on earth, which, however, the hand of the Lord would immediately remove. In proof, 1 Sam. xxviii. 14 was quoted. On the same principle of essential identity in the risen saints, it was even thought that the departed would reappear in the same dress which they had worn on earth.[2]

As God had created the world only in order to be known and reverenced, it was inferred that the fear of the Lord was the fundamental requirement. Without this fear, even a sage was only like a person who had got the keys of all the apartments in the house, but not that of the house itself.[3] In the prosecution of studies a certain amount of caution was requisite. Only very few, and these under the guidance of a pious and experienced teacher, were to be initiated in the mysteries of the " Chariot " (Ezek. i.) ;[4] and even then every such student was to be at least forty years of age. The same age was requisite to warrant an attempt at settling questions concerning the ritual.[5] The study of Scripture without the assistance of the traditional commentaries was wholly interdicted to youth.[6] Repentance removed guilt, and con-

---

[1] San. 90*b*, 91*b*.   [2] Jer. Keth. xii. 35*a*.   [3] Shab. 31*a b*.
[4] Chag. ii. 1; comp. b. *ib.* 13*a*.   [5] Sota 22*a b*.
[6] Ber. 28*b*; comp. Levy, *NHWB.* i. 450.

verted sins committed willingly into " sins of ignorance." It
even elevated the penitent to a higher position than that
occupied by continued piety.[1] Reuben returned to look
for Joseph in the pit into which his brethren had cast him,
after he had spent the interval at home in the exercise of
repentance, having fasted in sackcloth and ashes ; hence the
prophet Hosea had sprung from the tribe of Reuben.[2] In
the same sense, the passage in Job xxxiii. 23, 24, was accom-
modated to penitence ; and it was argued that the intercession
of *one* angel, thus propitiated, would silence the accusations of
a thousand adversaries.[3] Open confession was required in the
case of public offences. To pardon injuries procured the
pardon of sins, because it indicated a humble mind ; hence
efforts, some say three times, should be made to bring about a
reconciliation with our enemies. If the person offended had
departed this life, a confession of the wrong should be made
at his grave in the presence of ten persons.[4] In illustration
of the value of self-humiliation, Ahab's delayed punishment
was mentioned, and it was said that Cain " went out from the
presence of the Lord " with a joyful heart,[5] the half of his
punishment having been remitted upon making a confession
of his crime. Likewise Pharaoh, when almost perishing in
the Red Sea, had made the profession (Ex. xv. 11), " Who
is like unto thee, O Lord, among the gods ? " and was hence
preserved and sent to Nineveh, where he became king, in confirmation of Ex. ix. 16, " For this cause have I raised thee
up, for to show in thee My power ; and that My name may
be declared throughout the earth." Hence, when Jonah
arrived in that city, Pharaoh and the inhabitants of Nineveh
were ready to humble themselves before the Lord.[6]

Fasting was an essential element in humiliation ;[7] but
in course of time, as the anti-pharisaical tendency, to which
we have alluded, was developed, it became more rare, until
at last it was almost wholly relegated amongst the exercises
prescribed to penitent sinners, while sages were warned

[1] Joma 86*b* ; Sanh. 99*a*.   [2] Gen. Rab. 84.   [3] Shab. 32*a*.
[4] Joma 87*a*.   [5] Gen. Rab. 22.   [6] Pirke R. Eliezer, 43.
[7] B. Mez. 85*a*.

against its frequent practice.[1] It was, however, in use as an expiation for sins,[2] and as "a feast of sadness" on the anniversary of national calamities. When any public calamity, as famine or pestilence, threatened the land, an extraordinary fast was proclaimed. Then the ark containing the roll of the Law was carried to the street and ashes put upon it, the head of the Synagogue and all the sages fasted in sackcloth and ashes, whilst one of their number, in an oration suited to the occasion, called to repentance. Then an old man, the father of a family, recited the daily prayers, with special intercessions and selections from the Psalms.[3] Many stories were told of the power of famous Rabbins to obtain rain in answer to their prayers. To absent one's self from such solemnities involved exclusion from the consolation of Israel. As penitence produced such mighty effects, and the door to it was open to all, none need despair. It was even suggested that Israel had made the golden calf, and that David had sinned with Bathsheba, merely in order to show that return to God was open to every sinner.[4]

Some Rabbins held that the Lord judged men every day and every hour; but the general opinion was that on the Feast of the Passover (the 15th of Nisan) the Lord settled about the harvest for the ensuing year; on the Feast of Pentecost, about the produce of fruit; on New Year's Day (the 1st of Tishri), about the fate of men; and on the Feast of Tabernacles, about the quantity of rain during the year.[5] The judgment of the New Year's Day commenced immediately after the Jewish Sanhedrin had settled that the new moon of Tishri had actually appeared.[6] Then the fate of Israel was first sealed, afterwards that of the other nations. In Tishri the world had been created; in that month Abraham and Jacob were born and died, having thus lived out their full years. Others held that these events took place in Nisan, but it was agreed that the 1st of Tishri was a memorable day. Sarah, Rachel, and Hannah had been visited on that day; and on it Joseph and the children of

---

[1] Taan. 11*b*.   [2] Comp. Ber. 17*a*.   [3] M. Taan. ii.
[4] Ab. Sar. 4*b*.   [5] Rosh ha-Sh. 16*a*.   [6] *Ib.* 8*b*; Pesikta 53 f.

Israel were respectively delivered from their trials in Egypt. In the month of Nisan, Isaac had been born, and Israel led out of Egypt; the future deliverance of the world was to take place in the same month.[1] To return, on the 1st of Tishri, three books were opened in heaven, in which respectively the deeds of perfect saints, of perfect sinners, and doubtful cases were chronicled. Immediate judgment was then passed for the year on the two first-named classes, while the final sentence of the third was delayed till the Day of Atonement.[2] During that interval, penance and penitence might be of special avail. Hence the ten days between New Year's Day and the Day of Atonement should be well improved.[3] The Day of Atonement, which was the anniversary of the second gift of the tables of the Law, was the most solemn in the year.[4] All sins committed during the past year and repented of, were forgiven on that day.

Sufferings were sent partly to remind man of his sins, partly to invite to repentance, and to expiate guilt. They were also meant to try the godly. Under all circumstances they should be meekly borne. Rabbi Jehuda suffered from illness for twelve years because he refused protection to a calf which had sought it at his feet. For a corresponding act of kindness, he was afterwards restored. It was remarked that, during the whole time of Rabbi Eleazar's sufferings, every person had attained a good old age, and that the rain had never been withheld during Jehuda's illness,[5]—such was the value of the sufferings of the pious sages, for whose sake alone God had created the world. The humiliation of pious Hezekiah, and of Israel, had led to the destruction of the vast host of Sennacherib, which had marched ten days' journey in one day in order to surprise Jerusalem. It was laid low in one night; it is variously asserted by the hand of the Lord, by His finger, by the sword, or by the breath of Gabriel; by terror occasioned on hearing the clapping of his hands, or the song of the living creatures in heaven. The Hagadists related curious stories about this deliverance, and

---

[1] Rosh ha-Sh. 10*b*, 11. [2] *Ib.* 16*b*. [3] Pesikta 156.
[4] Taan. 30*b*. [5] B. Mez. 85*a*.

about Sennacherib and Nebuchadnezzar. It was asserted that of all the host only five escaped,—Nebuzar-Adan, Nebuchadnezzar, and Sennacherib, with his two sons. In order to disguise himself, and so to escape the vengeance of the princes whose relatives had fallen, Sennacherib cut off his hair and beard. But when on the water a terrible storm overtook the party, the sight of a floating board then reminded Sennacherib of the ark of Noah, on whose God he now called, vowing, if delivered, to sacrifice one of his sons. The lad overheard his father, and accordingly resolved on the death of his parent (2 Kings xix. 37).[1] Nebuchadnezzar obtained the throne for having walked four steps for the glory of the God of Israel. When godless Ahaz died, the day was shortened by ten hours to prevent any mourning for him, while ten hours had been added to the day of Hezekiah's restoration to health. Wondering at this marvellous prolongation of a day, King Merodach-Baladan, who had been informed of its occasion, sent to congratulate Hezekiah in a letter, which commenced, "Peace to King Hezekiah, peace to the city of Jerusalem, and peace to the great God," etc. The king's secretary, Nebuchadnezzar, had been absent when the letter was written and despatched, but afterwards successfully remonstrated with his master because the name of the Lord had not been put foremost. Nebuchadnezzar was sent to bring back the letter, but he had only gone four steps when the messenger, who had been stopped by Gabriel, returned. It was also said that when Nebuzar-Adan entered the temple, he saw the blood of the murdered prophet Zacharias continually boiling. To propitiate the manes of the departed, he successively killed the members of the Sanhedrin and the noblest Jews. But by and by he became conscious of the magnitude of his own guilt, who had slaughtered so many Jews, and immediately became a proselyte. Had not the ministering angels expostulated, some of Nebuchadnezzar's posterity would have become ornaments of the religion which their ancestor sought to destroy.[2]

[1] Sanh. 94*b*–96*a*.   [2] Sanh. 96*a b*.

Wherever Israel's lot was cast, if they were only faithful to their God, they would be protected against their enemies; while, on the other hand, their sin would quickly find them out. Thus, when the spies sent by Moses into the land on the 29th of Sivan, returned after forty days' absence on the 8th of Ab with their false report, Israel wept all night to the 9th of Ab; accordingly that day became ever afterwards a fatal day in their history.[1] If the sins which led to the destruction of the first temple were fearful, they had at least been acknowledged. Hence the first captivity was limited to seventy years; but as the sins which induced the ruin of the second temple are not mentioned, so Israel's captivity also is indefinite.[2] However, the Lord, it was thought, had been very reluctant to destroy the temple, and comforted the patriarch Abraham, who interceded for his children, by the promise (Jer. xi. 16) that Israel was to be "a green olive tree, fair and of goodly fruit."[3] From Isa. xxxiii. 7 it was inferred that even the angels wept over the desolation of the sanctuary; and from Isa. xlii. 14, that the Lord Himself had ever since mourned, and only engaged in teaching children who had died in infancy (Isa. xxviii. 9).[4]

But dark as any former period may have been to Israel, the darkest was yet to come, in the days which are to precede the advent of the Messiah. Then there would be a famine of the Word; for three successive years wretchedness would follow wretchedness, and at last truth and righteousness would perish from the earth; the daughter would rise against her mother, the son against his father, and infidelity would occupy the thrones of the world and spread amongst its nations. It was thought that Rome would fall and be raised, then fall again to rise no more. Then would Messiah come. But in those days the very coffins in Palestine would be dug up to serve for mangers to the horses of the Persian army, and the palm-trees would not be sufficient for posts to the horses of the Medes.[5] The period of Messiah's coming may be hastened by Israel's return unto the Lord,

---

[1] Taan. 29a.   [2] Joma 9b.   [3] Menach. 53b.
[4] Ab. Sar. 3b.   [5] Sanh. 97a.

according to the Scripture statement, "To-day, if ye will hear
My voice." After the troubles of the latter day, God will
recall His banished; earth will be renovated, many of the
heathen be converted, and Israel be at peace with God. On
the morning of the day of Israel's deliverance, God will
prepare a great feast for all the pious departed, and after it
the cup will be offered to Abraham to pronounce over it the
customary blessing. But Abraham will return it, as having
begotten wicked Ishmael, so will Isaac on account of Esau,
Jacob on account of his marriage with two sisters, Moses on
account of his sin, and Joshua as not having left a male
descendant; but David will take it and say, " I will take the
cup of salvation, and call upon the name of the Lord." [1]

A number of vague superstitions were afloat amongst the
people. Thus superstitious views were entertained about the
influence of outward things upon the mind. Thus, that to
eat of that which mice had touched, or of the heart of an ox,
or too many olives; to drink of that which had been left
from the ablution of the hands; or to wash the feet with the
one foot crossing the other; or to place the garments under
the head at night, was thought to impair the memory. On
the other hand, to eat wheaten bread, soft-boiled eggs without
salt, to drink pure oil, well-spiced wine, water left from that
which had been destined for kneading dough; or to dip one's
finger first in water, then in salt, tended to strengthen the
memory.[2] Again, the number two was under the special rule
of Ashmedai the prince of spirits, and consequently highly
dangerous. To drink two or four cups, to eat two eggs, etc.,
was deemed unlucky. Some persons could exercise supernatural powers, which were to be again counteracted by
magical formulas. It was deemed unlucky to pass between
dogs, between date-trees, pigs, serpents, and women, or to
eat under the shadow of a tree, especially of a date-tree.
Evil spirits dwelt amongst caper bushes, but as these spirits
were blind, it was comparatively easy to eschew them. Other
spirits frequented waste places and ruined houses. To comb
one's hair without having first dried it, to drink the drops

[1] Pes. 119a b.   [2] Hor. 13a b.

from a bucket, and to put on shoes without having properly dried the feet; to cut the nails or the hair, or to be bled without washing after it, were supposed dangerous.[1] However, evil spirits which did mischief might be cited before the Jewish tribunals, and forced to give compensation.[2] It was thought dangerous to go into an empty lecture-room, because the angel of death kept his armoury there.

In outward demeanour the sages were to be distinguished from the common people. They were neither to go forth perfumed, nor with patched shoes, nor alone at night; they were not to talk with women in the street, nor to appear late in a lecture-room, nor to hold intercourse with ignorant people.[3] They were to be cleanly and neatly attired, and to walk slowly and modestly, avoiding, however, the mock pietism which had at one time constituted the distinguishing mark of spiritual superiority. A sage was allowed full discretion when to speak the truth and when to tell a lie. He was in every respect to conduct himself in a manner becoming his dignity, and to be treated by others accordingly.

To yield to passion, or to indulge in anger, deprived a sage of his wisdom (as in the cases of Moses and Elisha), and involved grievous punishments. It was on this ground that David's elder brother Eliab, who had been angry with David, was deprived of the throne, which otherwise he and not David would have occupied.[4] For the sake of peace, Gentile paupers were to be allowed to share with the Jews in the charities of the harvest season;[5] and in order to promote mutual goodwill, it was right to inform the recipient of a gift of the name of the donor.[6] Examples of the exercise of charity are very numerous among the Jewish sages. Another virtue of great merit was humility, which conciliated the favour of God and men. However, a little pride was not only allowable, but even necessary in a Rabbi.[7]

In the full and faithful picture of Jewish life which we have attempted to present, amidst much punctiliousness and externality, many things truly good, noble, and great will

[1] Pes. 109*b*–112*a*. [2] Chul. 105*b*. [3] Ber. 43*b*. [4] Pes. 66*b*.
[5] Gitt. 61*a*. [6] Ber. 10*b*. [7] Sot. 5*a*.

have been observed.   In truth, the spirit of the Old Testament had pervaded the nation, and cast Jewish social life in its mould.   What was spiritual in that economy—what referred to things unseen and eternal—had become bedimmed. But what was external and all the relations between man and man were preserved.   Only that here also the externality of Rabbinism confined the life-blood till it almost stood still. The impulse of the heart of Judaism was feeble,—its arteries had almost become ossified.   The blood improperly propelled, returned sluggishly through the social system to its fountainhead.   Still it circulated.   What a contrast is that presented by the social state and the virtues of the Hebrew race, and the dissoluteness and moral disorganisation of all other nations at the time !

It will also have been noticed that often the views and even the words of the Rabbins closely approach those enunciated in the pages of the New Testament.   The reverent and careful student of history will not hastily infer from this that either party had borrowed from the other.   He will rather conclude that both had drawn from the same source, and gathered up the gems of Divine truth with which the Jewish commonwealth was even in its most degenerate times so richly bestudded.   Only we must be allowed to add that the one polished and presented them in their proper setting as a crown of glory, while the others buried them amidst a mass of rubbish, from which only the search of the antiquarian, or the restlessness of spiritual traffic in merit, could rescue them.

CHAPTER X

PROGRESS OF ARTS AND SCIENCES AMONG THE HEBREWS

I. *Poetry and Music*

THE religious tendency which gave to Jewish social life its peculiar aspect, exercised a marked influence upon the progress of literature and art in Palestine. [It was impossible to resist the continuous advance of Greek culture; and in order to preserve their national religion and character, the Rabbins were compelled to raise artificial barriers between themselves and their Gentile neighbours. The principal means to the desired end was the multiplication of legal regulations and restrictions, which formed a constant hindrance to free intercourse with the heathen. Even familiarity with the writings of the great poets and thinkers of antiquity was regarded with suspicion, and literature and art were left to develop themselves on purely national lines. But the same religious earnestness which despised the attractions of Hellenistic learning, were unfavourable to a real interest in literature and culture for their own sakes. Zeal for religion was the primary motive for the Palestinian writers of our period, and we find that nearly all the literary productions which survive are made to serve some moral or religious purpose.[1]]

Unfortunately our materials are more scanty than could have been wished. In the pages of the Talmud we can only look for incidental notices, which require to be connected, arranged, and interpreted. Yet sufficient may be gathered to form a tolerably correct notion of the intellectual life of the period over which our record extends.

[1] Comp. Schürer, II. i. 51-56, iii. 1-6.

It is remarkable that Palestine has never produced any distinguished painters or sculptors. Whether the genius of the Old Testament was averse to the development of arts, which might so readily be engaged in the service of idolatry or of lust, or whether the prejudices of the Rabbins operated against all attempts at representation, certain it is, that not only at that period, but even to our own days, painting and sculpture have not been cultivated amongst the Jews. The dwellings of the rich were indeed decorated with works of art,[1] but their introduction was one of those foreign innovations which indicated an assimilation with heathen manners and modes of thinking. It was otherwise with those arts which more especially are the exponents of thought and feeling. Poetry and music have always been favourite engagements with Israel; and from the period of biblical times to our own days, Jews have distinguished themselves by a depth and originality peculiarly their own, and peculiarly expressive of their national mental characteristics. Even when the dry logic and the theological wrangling of the schools seemed to have absorbed the intellectual efforts of the nation, the poetic sentiments found an utterance in their songs of praise, in their prayers, and in the unfettered compositions of the Hagadists.

The poetry of popular common sense is embodied in the peculiar proverbs current in a country. Every nation has more or less of these, indicating both the aspects of common life and the popular mode of viewing them. Sometimes these proverbs are more scientifically elaborated into similes, collections, sententious sayings or maxims, parallels, and fables. The latter form the point of transition into more regular poetry. An abstraction from common life, clad in poetic and concise language,—such is the proverb. Of these the Hebrews, who united dry humour, the faculty of viewing and presenting things as they are, with readiness of expression, possessed a large number.[2] Some of them are similar to Arabic

---

[1] Jos. *Ant.* xv. 2. 6, xix. 9. 1.

[2] Dukes (*Rabbin. Blumenlese*) collects 665, but does not arrange them in any scientific manner.

proverbs, others occur in the New Testament. We mention a few on which the reader may make his own comments :— " Sell your goods as long as the dust is on your feet." " People say to a wasp : We neither want your honey nor your sting." " Have you poured out water, add to it meal." " All kinds of wood give no peculiar sound in burning, except thorns, which in crackling say : We also are wood." " Even if a peasant becomes a king he will carry the basket on his back." " A handful does not satisfy a lion, and a hole cannot be filled up with the earth dug out of it." " The fox does not die in his lair." " If you have not made preparation on the eve of the Sabbath, on what will you dine during the Sabbath ? " " Physician, heal thyself." " A cure without fee is generally worth no fee." " A little coin in an empty bottle makes a great noise." " Do not throw a stone into the well from which you have drunk." " With the measure with which a man metes shall others mete to him." " In three ways you may learn to know a man, at the cup, in money transactions, and when he is angry." " Let the lord of the vineyard come and root up his thorns." " Everyone who humbleth himself is exalted by God, and he that exalteth himself is humbled." " To make an elephant go through the eye of a needle."

Of the regular collections of proverbs and sententious sayings, we mention the work of Jesus ben Sirach, a treatise in the Mishna, entitled " The Sayings of the Fathers," and the sayings of Rabbi Nathan. The " Wisdom of Jesus the son of Sirach " (about 190 B.C.) is a collection of proverbial sayings, originally written in Hebrew, but soon translated into Aramean, and so largely interpolated that Jewish authorities distinguished between the good and the worthless in the Babylonian collection. In its Greek translation (made by the grandson of Ben Sira) the work is still extant—at least in part—amongst the Old Testament Apocrypha. One of the most interesting passages in it is the hymn, probably the writer's own composition, which he represents as being sung at the close of the Day of Atonement, after the high priest's blessing had been pronounced (ch. l. 22–24).

" Now, therefore, bless ye the God of all,
Who alone doeth wondrous works everywhere ;
Who exalteth our days from the womb,
And dealeth with us according to His mercy.
He grant us joyfulness of heart,
And that peace may be in Israel in our days for ever !
That He would confirm His mercy to us,
And deliver us in His own time."

From their antiquity and contents, the proverbs of Ben Sira are amongst the most precious relics handed down to us. The Talmud contains frequent quotations from them, which do not generally agree exactly with those in our Greek version ; [1] it also states that certain Rabbins interdicted the use of the work, [2] but this prohibition does not seem ever to have been really observed. The " alphabet of Ben Sira " is a small production of much less interest, and of a later date.

Besides the proverb in the stricter sense, the *Mashal*, or proverbial poetry, included all sententious sayings, parables, and fables. If the symbol was given without the morale, it was a " Chidda," or riddle ; if the morale only, it was a maxim ; if introduced or followed by an imaginary narrative, it was either a fable or a Hagadic tale. The Talmudists tried to connect their Meshalim with scriptural expressions or texts. Sometimes a definite number of subjects were grouped under a common attribute. " Three persons the Lord—blessed be His name !—loves :—him who gives not place to anger, who avoids intoxication, and who does not persist in his own will." " Three persons He hates :—him who utters one thing with his mouth, and another in his heart ; him who, being able to do so, forbears to testify in favour of his neighbour ; and him who, perceiving something improper in his friend, is the only one to bear testimony of it." [3]   " Three things are bad in abundance, but good in moderation : — leaven, salt, and obstinacy." [4] At other times the sentences are more antithetic, as—

---

[1] Comp. Zunz, *Gottesd. Vortr.* (ed. 2) p. 106 ff. ; Delitzsch, *Gesch. d. jüd. Poesie*, *passim*, and Dukes, *Rabbin. Blumenlese.*   [A collection of the proverbs of Ben Sira which occur in Talmudical writings, may be found in the *Jewish Quarterly Review*, July and October 1891 (No. 12, pp. 682–706, by S. Schechter ; No. 13, p. 162 ff., by Dr. Neubauer).]

[2] Jer. Sanh. x. 28*a* ; Mid. Qoh. on xii. 12.   [3] Pes. 113*b*.   [4] Ber. 34*a*.

> " The more flesh, the more worms ;
> The more riches, the more care ;
> The more wives, the more witchcraft," etc.[1]

In other proverbs, by a series of comparative grada-
tions, a climax was ultimately reached, as—" It is beautiful
that one be learned, it is doubly beautiful if he be learned
and of good descent ; but if of good descent and unlearned, let
the fire devour him." [2] Sometimes the point of the Mashal
lay in punning upon the words, or in antithetic lines in
rhymes, as—

TO A SKULL FLOATING ON THE WATER.

> " Because thou madest float,
> They made thee float—
> In turn who made thee float
> Shall also float." [3]

or—

> " Each one who seeks a name
> Shall only lose his fame ;
> Who adds not to his lore
> Shall lose it more and more ;
> Each one deserves to perish
> Who study does not cherish ;
> That man shall surely fade
> Who with his crown does trade." [4]

It has already been indicated that both proverbs and
maxims were frequently introduced by the sages into their
lectures by way of illustration, and to enliven the monotony
of logical abstraction. Specially telling were the parables
and fables, which Hagadists intertwined with their comments.
Thus it was said that when Noah came to plant his vineyard, Satan joined him, and asked, " What are you planting ? "
He replied, " A vineyard." " For what purpose ? " rejoined
Satan. " Its fruits," answered the patriarch, " are sweet,
whether used fresh or dried, and wine is made from them,
which rejoices the heart " (Ps. civ. 15). " Then shall we two
work at it together," observed the enemy. Noah consented ;
but the wily deceiver now brought a lamb, a lion, a pig, and a

---

[1] Pirke Ab. ii. 7.   [2] Menach. 53*a*.   [3] Pirke Ab. ii. 6.
[4] Pirke Ab. i. 13.   The crown of learning or of the Law.

monkey, successively killed them, and caused the vineyard to be saturated with their blood. And now before a man commences to drink, he is simple like a lamb; when he has drunk in measure, he becomes like a lion, and says, "Who is like me in all the world?" If he continues to drink, he becomes like a pig, wallowing in all manner of filth; and ultimately like an ape, jumping about, garrulous, full of uncleanness, and not knowing what he does.[1] We can only select one or two of the smaller fables by way of illustration.[2] "A cock and an owl awaited the dawn in company. Said the cock, 'The light is of use to me, but what can it profit thee?'"[3] "The tail of the serpent had reproved the head because it always took precedence. 'Let me have it for once,' demanded the tail. The wish was no sooner uttered than granted. But, alas! the new guide successively precipitated the serpent into the water, into the fire, and into thorns. Whence all these accidents, but because the head took its direction from the tail? So, as long as the small take their direction from the great, God grants them their desires; whenever this process is reversed, they fall backwards."[4] "When the iron was created, the trees all trembled. 'Why tremble?' asked the iron: 'let no wood from you join itself to me, and none of you will suffer any damage.'"[5] Rabbi Meir was peculiarly distinguished for his apt fables.[6] As amongst the contemporary theologians were two Indian proselytes, his three hundred fables about the fox may have been somewhat akin to similar Indian compositions. We hear also of the proverbs of Eleazar and of Rabbi bar Mare, and of Palestinian proverbs and songs quoted by Rab Dime. In the Meshalic class of compositions we may also rank some of the Old Testament Apocrypha, and a work entitled "The Book of Secrets," or "of the Pious," apparently containing the sayings of R. Isa ben Jehuda, of which only

---

[1] Tanchuma, Noah 14*b*.

[2] We have necessarily left out specimens of longer fables, some of which Herder has beautifully rendered into German.

[3] Sanh. 98*b*.   [4] Deut. Rab. 80*a*.   [5] Gen. Rab. c. 5.

[6] Sota ix. 15; Sanh. 38*b*.

a few fragments are preserved. The "Aboth" of Rabbi
Nathan is followed in the ordinary editions of the Babylonian
Talmud by three small treatises, of which the first
("Derek Erez") contains rules for ordinary conduct; the
second ("Derek Erez Suta"), ethics for sages; and the third
("Perek ha-Shalom), a laudation of peace.

Passing from the didactic to lyrical poetry, the Shir,
song, claims our special attention. Of the profane or secular
song hardly any fragments remain, but various allusions in
Jewish literature prove that at weddings and other occasions
the song formed part of the entertainment; but if the
common Shir was less known amongst the Hebrews, the
sacred song or hymn had, under the guidance of scriptural
example, early attained a place of eminence. Not only the
hymn of praise, but many portions of the regular prayers of
the synagogue breathe the spirit of the purest, truest, and
most elevated poetry. The songs of praise in general use in
the synagogue were those poetic portions of Scripture which
have always formed the groundwork of this exercise to the
Church. But the Hebrew festivals were festivals in the
truest sense. Not confined to certain ceremonies in the
temple or synagogue, the day or week was spent in festive
enjoyment and festive communication with God and Israel.
Each individual or family confined not its religious enjoyments to the hours of worship, or even to the narrow circle
of the family. It was enlarged so as to embrace all who
shared the same hopes, and unmingled joy characterised the
intercourse. On occasions like these the hymn found its
proper place, and few as these relics of temple times are,
they sufficiently indicate the relation to which we have
referred. We will not expect them to breathe a purely
devotional spirit. They are rather the social songs of a
happy brotherhood congregated on festive occasions.

One of the happiest seasons was the Feast of Tabernacles,
which occurred five days after the Day of Atonement, and
lasted uninterruptedly for a full week, and was followed by
an eighth-day of special solemnity, which, indeed, was often
regarded as a separate festival. On this occasion, which

equally commemorated Israel's stay in the wilderness, and
the goodness of the Lord in granting year by year of the
fruits of the land, which had newly been ingathered, the
people lived in booths, constructed generally of branches of
fruit-trees, from many of which their rich clusters still
depended.   The worshippers, lately purified from sin, kept
this as a feast of thanksgiving.   Arrayed in festive garments,
carrying in one hand a citron,[1] and in the other the
" lulabh," or palm-branch, intertwined with willows and
myrtle, the worshippers appeared daily in the temple.
Every morning, before the customary sacrifice, a priest drew
from the pool of Siloam water into a golden pitcher, capable
of containing three logs.   Amidst the sound of trumpets he
entered the temple through the water-gate, and poured the
water into one of the two silver bowls by the side of the
altar of burnt-offering.   Into the other bowl, at the same
time, another priest poured the wine of the drink-offering,
which, like the water, flowed into a receptacle under the
altar, destined to receive drink-offerings.   Louder than the
sound of the Levites' instruments was the voice of praise, or
the call for mercy and deliverance.   In the evening of the
first day a religious feast was celebrated.[2]   After the evening
sacrifice, announced by the customary nine blasts from the
trumpets of the priests, the people congregated in the court
of the women, the men below, the women upon balconies
all around.   Immense golden candelabra, each with four
branches, gave their light ; and on four ladders, one beside
each branch to feed the flame, youthful priests were placed.
The glare of that light shed its brightness over the city
beneath, and every court in Jerusalem was lit up by the
flame in the temple.   The worthiest and most pious (called
" the men of deed ") danced before the people, and swung and
threw up the torches in their hands.   The music of the harp,

---

[1] On the Feast of Tabernacles, comp. *Life and Times*, ii. 148 ff., 156 ff.   No
water was poured on the eighth day ; [but it is disputed whether " the great
day of the feast " (John vii. 37) is to be understood of the seventh or of the
eighth day.]

[2] Succa v. and bab. *ib.* 51*b.*

of the cymbal, and of the psaltery, of flutes and of trumpets, resounded from the courts of the sanctuary. On the fifteen steps which led to the court of the women, stood Levites, who, with their instruments, accompanied those hymns, of which the following is a fragment :—

THE PIOUS AND THE MEN OF RENOWN.

"O happy youth, devoted, sage—
Which does not put to shame our age ! "

THE PENITENTS.

"O happy, also, is our age,
Which now atones for youth, not sage ! "

BOTH IN CHOIR.

"O happy he on whom no guilt does rest,
And he who sinn'd with pardon shall be blest." [1]

At the upper gate, which led from the court of the people to that of the women, stood two priests with trumpets. As soon as the crowing of the cock announced the approach of dawn, with blast of trumpets they descended into the court and passed on to the eastern gate, when, facing round towards the temple, they sang—

"Our fathers here establish'd by Thy grace,
Had turn'd their back upon Thy holy place,
And to the rising sun they set their face ;
But we will turn to Thee, Jehovah God,
Our eyes are set on Thee, Jehovah God."

Another happy day was the 15th of Ab, when the collection of wood, required in the sanctuary, was finished. Then the maidens all went forth arrayed in white garments, specially lent them, that so rich and poor might be on an equality, into the vineyards round Jerusalem, where they danced and sang. The following fragment of a song has been preserved :—

"Around in circle gay the Hebrew maidens see,
From them the happy youths their partners choose.
Remember beauty soon its charms must lose,
And seek to win a maid of fair degree.

---

[1] Succa 53*a*.

When fading grace and beauty low are laid,
Yet her who fears the Lord shall praise await;
God blessed her handiwork, and, in the gate,
'Her works have followed her,' it shall be said."[1]

Such are some of the interesting relics of temple-days and temple-usages which have been preserved. It is scarcely necessary to state that, as in Scripture, so in early Jewish poetry, neither definite and continued metre, nor regular and premeditated rhyme, must be sought. As it was composed for song, a certain metre no doubt must have been observed, but it was rather that of thought, the unfettered, immediate outpouring of the soul, than the measured step to which we have been accustomed. [It is true that Josephus[2] and some of the Fathers[3] assert that the poetry of the Old Testament is written in metres similar to those employed by the poets of Greece and Rome. But we cannot accept their testimony without reservation; and in some cases, at any rate, it seems clear that the writer was thinking merely of general resemblances, and did not intend his words to be understood too literally. Nor have the attempts of various modern scholars, to find in the Psalms and in some old post-biblical poetry a fully developed metrical system, been hitherto regarded as successful. No doubt in the Hebrew fragments of Ben Sira we find several examples of couplets where the lines end in rhymes or contain an equal number of syllables. A similar transition to the use of rhyme and metre is found in Pseudo-Sirach and many Rabbinic proverbs. Yet the Talmud does not contain a single metrical poem, and regular metres first appear in the poetry of the tenth century.[4]]

From the Shir we naturally pass to the Tefilla or prayer. Properly, prayer was considered the spontaneous effusion of the soul, called forth by a sense of immediate wants or experienced blessings. The measures taken, perhaps soon after the time of Ezra, for the celebration of public worship

---

[1] Jer. Taan. iv. (end).　　[2] Jos. *Ant.* ii. 16. 4, iv. 8. 44, vii. 12. 3.

[3] *E.g.* Euseb. *de Præp. Evang.* xi. 5; Jerome, *Præf. in Hiob; in Chron. Euseb.*, etc.

[4] Comp. Delitzsch, *Jüd. Poesie*, pp. 131–138.

throughout the land, and the regulation of the temple-service, were the first steps towards a liturgy, which at first consisted probably in traditionally preserved prayers of sages and leaders of congregational devotions (the " Sheliach," " angelos," or messenger of the congregation). They were afterwards committed to writing, and gradually became the nucleus of the present Jewish prayer-book. In this liturgy about fifty fragments belonging to the Talmudical period are incorporated. The oldest, which certainly date from before the Christian era, comprise the confessions of the high priest on the Day of Atonement, the arrangement of the " Shema," its three accompanying prayers, and six of what are called the eighteen eulogies. The high-priestly confessions on the great fast were successively for himself, for his household, for the priests, and for the people.[1] Turning towards the most holy place, and laying his hands on the bullock which stood between the altar and the porch of the temple, he pronounced the first, which in substance is similar to all others. " Alas, O Jehovah! I have committed iniquity, I have transgressed, I have sinned before Thee, I and my house. Alas, Jehovah! atone for the iniquities, the transgressions and the sins which I have committed and sinned before Thee, I and my house, as it is written in the law of Moses Thy servant: For on that day will he atone for you to make you clean, from all your transgressions shall ye before Jehovah be cleansed." [2]

Again, after he had tied a strip of red wool round the head of the scape-goat, and another round the neck of the goat to be sacrificed, he turned the former towards the east gate, whence it was to be led forth, and laid his hands upon the head of the bullock, confessing the sins of the sons of Aaron. Legend had it that the voice of confession was heard even as far as Jericho.[3] In response there rose the praises of the people, who, when the high priest pronounced the ineffable name of Jehovah, fell on their faces and exclaimed, " Blessed be the name of the glory of His kingdom for ever and ever." Though pronounced ten times on that solemn day, yet the voice of praise and the sound of priests' instruments concealed

---

[1] Comp. generally, Mishna, Joma.   [2] Joma iii. 8.   [3] *Ut supra*, 39*b*.

the mysterious name from priest and layman. Then the high priest slew the bullock, caught its blood in a vase, and caused it to be stirred by an attendant. Having put fire into a golden censer, and incense into a spoon, he rapidly advanced to the Ark of the Covenant,[1] placing the censer between its staves, and put the incense on the coals. A second and a third time he entered with the blood of the bullock, and then with that of the goat, and sprinkled the Ark once above and seven times below. In the same manner he sprinkled the curtain, and then, mingling the blood of the sacrifices, the Golden Altar and its horns. He then confessed over the scape-goat the sins of the people. At the close of the service he prayed, " May it please Thee, O Lord our God, and the God of our fathers, that neither this day nor during this year any captivity come upon us ; yet if captivity befall us this day or this year, let it be to a place where the Law is culti-vated. May it please Thee, O Lord our God, and the God of our fathers, that no want come upon us either this day or this year ; but if want visit us this day or this year, let it be due to the liberality of our charitable deeds. May it please Thee, O Lord our God, and the God of our fathers, that this year may become a year of cheapness, of fulness, of inter-course, and of trade, a year with abundance of rain, of sun-shine and of dew ; one in which Thy people Israel shall not require assistance one from another. And listen not to the prayers of those who go forth on a journey.[2] And as to Thy people Israel, may no enemy exalt himself against them. May it please Thee, O Lord our God, and the God of our fathers, that the houses of the men of Sharon may not become their graves." [3]

The only really fixed form of daily prayer was a collection of passages constituting a kind of confession of faith (termed the " Shema " from the first word occurring in it), which every Israelite was to repeat morning and evening. It con-

---

[1] *Ut supra*, v. 1, 2. There was, of course, no Ark in the second temple.

[2] Who might pray against the fall of rain.

[3] Jer. Joma v. 42c. There are other versions of this prayer, but the above is the most simple.

sisted of Deut. vi. 4–9, xi. 13–21, Num. xv. 37–41, and
was in the morning preceded by two and succeeded by one,
and in the evening both preceded and succeeded by two
prayers, which, although considerably enlarged, are still in use.
We quote them, omitting all later additions as probably in
use at the time of our Lord.[1]

[*Before the Shema morn and evening*]—"Blessed art Thou,
O Lord, King of the world, Who formest the light and
createst darkness, Who makest peace and createst everything;
Who in mercy givest light to the earth and to those who
dwell upon it, and in Thy goodness renewest day by day, and
continually, the works of creation. Blessed be the Lord our
God for the glory of His handiworks, and for the light-giving
lights which He hath made for His praise. Selah! Blessed
be the Lord, Who hath formed the lights!"

Subjecting the second prayer to the same criticism, we
read it: "With great love hast Thou loved us, O Lord our
God, and with much overflowing pity hast Thou pitied us.
Our Father and our King, for the sake of our fathers who
trusted in Thee, and Thou taughtest them the statutes of life,
have mercy upon us, and enlighten our eyes in Thy Law;
cause our hearts to cleave to Thy commandments; unite our
hearts to love and fear Thy name, and we shall not be put
to shame, world without end. For Thou art a God who
preparest salvation, and us hast Thou chosen from amongst all
nations and tongues, and hast in truth brought us near to Thy
great name, Selah, in order that we in love may praise Thee
and Thy unity. Blessed be the Lord who in love chose His
people Israel." Then follows the "Shema": "Hear, O Israel,
the Lord thy God is one Lord," etc. The morning prayers
concluded with the following portions of the prayer now in
use: "True it is that Thou art Jehovah our God and the
God of our fathers, our King and the King of our fathers,
our Saviour and the Saviour of our fathers, our Creator, the
Rock of our salvation, our Help and our Deliverer. Thy
name is from everlasting, and there is no God besides Thee.
A new song did they that were delivered sing to Thy name

[1] Compare the criticism in Zunz, *Gottesd. Vortr.* p. 382 ff.

by the seashore, together did all praise and own Thee King, and say, Jehovah shall reign world without end! Blessed be the Lord Who saveth Israel." An addition, dating from the second century, inserts before the words " A new song," etc., a particular record of God's past dealings. The additional prayer for the evening is as follows : " O Lord our God ! cause us to lie down in peace, and raise us up again to life, O our King ! spread over us the tabernacle (covering) of Thy peace ; strengthen us before Thee in Thy good counsel, and deliver us for Thy name's sake. Be Thou for protection round about us ; keep far from us the enemy, the pestilence, the sword, famine, and affliction. Keep Satan from before and from behind us, and hide us in the shadow of Thy wings, for Thou art a God Who keepest and deliverest us ; and Thou, O God, art a gracious and merciful King. Keep Thou our going out and our coming in, for life and for peace, from henceforth and for ever ! "

Although these prayers were sometimes lengthened or shortened,[1] they were, at a very early period, in general use amongst the Hebrews. Among the other forms of prayer then in use, we reckon portions of the grace at meat, various thanksgivings, supplications, and confessions. For a long time, however, the Psalms of David continued the only regular prayer, as well as hymn-book. This inspired collection was arranged into certain divisions adapted to various festivities, of which indications are even found in the LXX. and the writings of Philo. Thus the 23rd, the 47th, the 93rd, the 92nd, and the 91st [2] are expressly set down for five days of the week, and the 28th for the last day of the Feast of Tabernacles ; two hallelujahs are spoken of—the larger embracing Ps. cxiii. to cxviii., and the smaller in which Ps. cxv. 1–11 and Ps. cxvi. 1–11 are omitted, etc. On the Feast of Tabernacles, priests and people sang Ps. cxviii. 25, while the priests marched round the altar of burnt-offering. There is a tradition that, in times of public calamity, the Levites, standing at their oratories, to which every morning the herald summoned them, the priests and the people used

---

[1] Ber. i. 4.
[2] According to the enumeration of the LXX.   Comp. Tamid vii. 4.

to plead daily from Ps. xliv. 23 ; and it is said that John Hyrcanus abolished this custom, saying, " Doth God sleep ? He that keepeth Israel shall neither slumber nor sleep " (Ps. cxxi. 4).[1] The collection of Psalms designated as the Great Hallel is variously supposed to commence with Ps. cxviii., with Ps. cxx., or even cxxxv., and to end with Ps. cxxxvi.[2] Were this the place for it, we might, from an analysis of the prayers of that period, gather interesting information as to the theological views and spiritual tendencies of the Synagogue. However solemn, and often sublime, their conceptions of the Divine greatness, goodness, and power, and strong the expressions of the confidence and submission of the chosen people, they are throughout characterised by a certain deficiency of a sense of spiritual wants. Part of the ritual, still in use, for Sabbaths, fast-days, the new years, and Day of Atonement, the feasts of Esther, and of the temple-dedication, date from, and previous to, the first centuries of our era. However, the Synagogue had not at that period adopted any regular prayer-book.

Besides the ordinary devotions, which seem to have taken place three times a day, and after the destruction of the temple as far as possible to have been substituted for the sacrifices, another class of devotional exercises was general, and apparently became much sooner liturgical than the proper Tefilla,—we mean the blessings, eulogies, or " berakas." Besides generally concluding other prayers, they were used before partaking of food or drink, in prospect of danger, etc. As every beraka contained a recognition of the Lord, it was reckoned a merit to pronounce every day a large number of them. These eulogies became sooner liturgical than congregational prayers, as the wants of a congregation are much more apparent, and there is always sufficient cause for entreaty and thanksgiving, even where the mind is not alive to deeper spiritual necessities. Certain expressions, as " Blessed be the Lord our God, and the God of our fathers," " the Lord, the great, the mighty, the terrible," " from everlasting to everlasting,"—the latter said to be a

---

[1] Sota ix. 10 ; bab. *ib.* 48*a*.　　　　[2] Comp. Buxtorf and Levy, *in verb.*

testimony against Sadduceeism,[1]—recur frequently in these eulogies. The most remarkable collection of them are the Eighteen Berakas, which were to be repeated every day, at least in part or summary.[2]   They were as follows :—

THE EIGHTEEN BERAKAS

I. " Blessed be the Lord our God and the God of our fathers, the God of Abraham, the God of Isaac, and the God of Jacob, the Lord, the great, the mighty, and the terrible One ; the eternal God, Who showeth mercy and kindness, to Whom belongeth everything, Who remembereth the piety of our fathers, and in love for His own name's sake sendeth a Redeemer to their children's children,—King, Helper, Deliverer, and Shield !   Blessed be the Lord, Abraham's Shield ! "

II. " Thou, Lord, art mighty to all eternity, Thou raisest the dead, Thou art mighty to save.   In kindness He satisfieth the living, in great pity He raiseth the dead ; He upholdeth those that fall ; He healeth the sick, and setteth free them that are bound ; He will manifest His faithfulness to those who sleep in the dust.   Who is like the Lord of might, and who is like Thee, Thou King, Who killest and makest alive, and causest salvation to spring forth ?   Faithful art Thou to restore life to the dead ; blessed be the Lord Who restoreth life to the dead."

III. " Holy art Thou, and Thy name is holy, and Thy saints shall praise Thee every day, Selah !   Blessed be the Lord, the Holy God !   (We will sanctify Thy name in the world as those do who sanctify it in the heights of heaven, as it is written by Thy prophets, 'And they called one to another, Holy, holy, holy is the Lord of hosts ! the whole earth is full of His glory.'   Together do they sing praise ! blessed be the glory of the Lord from His habitation.   And in Thy holy word it is written, 'The Lord shall reign for ever; Thy God, O Zion, from generation to generation,'—Hallelujah ![3])   From genera-

---

[1] Ber. ix. 8.   [2] *Ut supra*, iv. 3.

[3] These words form the reply of the people to the leader of the congregation. The words which follow are his reply to them.

tion to generation will we declare Thy greatness, and for ever and ever we will sanctify Thy holiness; and Thy praise, O our God, shall not pass from our lips, world without end, for Thou, Lord, art a great and holy King; blessed be the Lord, the great and holy One."

IV. "Thou grantest knowledge to man, and teachest him understanding. (Thou hast granted to us the knowledge of Thy law, and hast taught us to do the statutes of Thy good pleasure. Thou, O Lord our God, makest a separation between the holy and the profane, between light and darkness, between Israel and the nations, between the seventh day and the six work-days. Our Father, our King, cause the days that are before us to begin in peace to us, deliver from all sin, and clear from all iniquity, and uphold us in Thy fear.)[1] Grant us from Thyself knowledge, understanding, and wisdom; blessed be the Lord Who granteth knowledge."

V. "Bring us back again, O our Father! to Thy law; bring us near, O our King! to Thy service; and cause us to return with a perfect repentance before Thy face; blessed be the Lord Who taketh pleasure in repentance."

VI. "Forgive us, our Father, for we have sinned; pardon us, our King, for we have transgressed, for Thou pardonest and forgivest; blessed be the gracious Lord Who multiplieth forgiveness."

VII. "Behold our misery, and plead our cause, and redeem us quickly for Thy name's sake, for Thou art a strong Redeemer; blessed be the Lord, the Redeemer of Israel."

VIII. "Heal us, O Lord, and we shall be healed; save us, and we shall be saved, for Thou art our praise. And grant us a perfect remedy for all our ills, for Thou, Lord and King, art a physician, faithful and merciful; blessed be the Lord Who healeth the sick amongst His people Israel."

IX. "Bless to us, O Lord, this year, and all kinds of produce in it, for good; grant a blessing upon the land; satisfy us by Thy goodness, and bless our years even as the good years; blessed be the Lord Who blesseth the years."

X. "Blow Thy great trumpet to announce our liberty,

[1] These words were inserted on the evening of the Sabbath.

and lift up the standard to gather our banished; yea, gather us together from the four corners of the earth; blessed be the Lord Who gathereth the outcasts of His people Israel."

XI. " Restore our sages as at first, and our counsellors as at the beginning; remove from us sorrow and sighing, and reign Thou alone, O Lord, over us in mercy and in pity, and justify us in the judgment; blessed be the Lord the King, Who loveth righteousness and judgment."

XII. " And let there be no hope for the heretics,[1] and let all workers of wickedness perish as in a moment; and let all of them speedily be cut off, and lay them low speedily, in our days; blessed be the Lord Who breaketh down the enemies, and layeth low the wicked." [2]

" Let Thy tender mercies, O Lord our God, abound to the pious, to the elders of Thy people, the house of Israel, to the remnant of their scribes, to the proselytes of righteousness, and to us, and grant a good reward to all who in truth trust in Thy name. Let our portion be with them for ever, and we shall not be put to shame, for we trust in Thee; blessed be the Lord, the Support and the Hope of the pious."

XIII. " And return in pity to Jerusalem Thy city, and dwell in the midst of it, as Thou hast spoken, and build it speedily, even in our days, with an everlasting building, and establish speedily in the midst of it the throne of David; blessed be the Lord Who buildeth Jerusalem."

XIV. " Speedily cause Thou the branch of David, Thy servant, to shoot forth and exalt his horn by Thy salvation, for in Thy salvation do we trust all the day; blessed be the Lord Who causeth the horn of salvation to shoot forth."

XV. " Hear our voice, O Lord our God, and spare us, and show mercy upon us, and accept in mercy and in grace our prayer, for Thou art a God Who hearest prayer and supplication. Let us not return empty, O our King, from before Thy face, for Thou, Lord, in mercy hearest the prayers of Thy people Israel; blessed be the Lord Who heareth prayer."

---

[1] [Heretics (*Minim*), not calumniators (*Meloshenim*), is the original reading. The later addition of this prayer raises the number of berakas to nineteen.]

[2] This prayer is altered in most editions of the prayer-book.

XVI. " Be gracious, O Lord our God, to Thy people Israel, and to their prayers, and restore the service to the halls of Thy house, and accept the men of Israel in grace, and their prayers in love, and let the services of Thy people Israel be well-pleasing for ever. Cause our eyes to see it, when Thou in mercy returnest to Zion ; blessed be the Lord Who bringeth again His Shechinah to Zion."

XVII. " We bow down before Thee, because Thou art Jehovah our God, and the God of our fathers for ever and ever. The Rock of our lives, the Shield of our salvation art Thou, from generation to generation. We will bless Thee, and show forth Thy praises for these our lives, which are in Thy hand, and for our souls, which we commit to Thee, and for Thy wondrous works, which we witness every day ; for Thy marvellous doings and Thy mercies at all times,— evening, morning, and noon. Gracious God ! because Thy mercies are without bounds ; merciful Lord ! because Thy kindnesses are never done,—we trust in Thee to all eternity. For all these things shall Thy name, O our King, be blessed and exalted for ever, world without end ; and all living shall praise Thee, Selah, and shall in truth bless Thy name, O Lord, our Salvation and our Help, Selah. Blessed be the Lord, Thy name is ' The Merciful,' and to praise Thee is comely."

XVIII. " O bestow on Thy people Israel great peace for ever. For Thou art King and Lord of all peace ; and it is good in Thine eyes to bless Thy people Israel at all times and at every hour with Thy peace. Blessed art Thou, Jehovah, Who blessest Thy people Israel with peace."

It will be observed that affection and trust in the Lord and His word, longing for the coming of a Deliverer, confidence in their privileges as Hebrews, and a desire after and respect for knowledge of the Law, constitute the chief burden of these prayers. The first three and the last three eulogies are probably the earliest. Between them private prayers were inserted on various occasions, according to the felt wants of individuals or of the times. Eulogies IV., V.,

VI., VIII., IX., XV. stand next in the order of composition ; VII. dates probably from a period of national calamity,— perhaps the time of Pompey. Eulogies X., XI., XII., XIII., XIV. were composed about the time of the final dissolution of the Jewish commonwealth, when certain changes were also introduced in Eulogy XVI., such as the addition, "Restore the service to the halls of Thy house." The prayer against the Minim, beginning, "And let there be no hope," etc., was composed by Samuel the Less, and prefixed to Eulogy XII.[1] The sect of the Essenes, described by Josephus, but apparently not mentioned in Jewish writings, had peculiar hymns and prayers suited to their mystical tendencies. We shall refer to these when treating of the peculiar doctrines of Jewish mysticism ; suffice it meantime to say, that the rising sun found them each morning finishing their old traditional prayers with their faces towards the east.[2]

There is much in the poetry of the East that has been derived from the paraphrastic translations of the Bible (the Targumim), Hagadic commentaries, and current legends. The Talmud has sometimes poetical descriptions, of which the following is a specimen : "If anyone should wish to form an idea of Rabbi Jochanan's beauty, let him take a silver cup as it comes glowing from the mould, and fill it with the purple seeds of the pomegranate, then encircle its brim with a garland of purple roses, and place it between light and shadow. The rays which it emits are but faint emblems of the beauty of R. Jochanan."[3]

We present three other specimens of early Hebrew poetry, as expressed in legends, comments, and even Halachic opinions[4]—

"Upon that burning pile the sun has set,
With slaughter weary, Babel's warriors sleep,
And with them misery and death do rest ;

---

[1] Comp. Zunz, *ut supra.*   [2] Jos. *Wars*, ii. 8. 5.   [3] B. Mez. 84*a*.
[4] They are rendered from the free paraphrastic version of M. Ch. Sachs and M. Veit, in their *Stimmen vom Jordan and Euphrat*, Berlin, 1853 ; and are taken respectively from Aboth di Rabbi Nathan, from Tanch. Ex. xxvii., and Sanh. 22.

Yet, as the frame from that dread hour recoils,
In which the spirit leaves its house of clay,
So shrank Jerusalem from Babel's sword—
It fell, but left Jerusalem unharm'd.

In Zion's streets unbroken silence reigns,
The temple-roof presents a vision strange :
The priests, array'd in robes of white come forth.
One bears the incense, one the harp of praise,
The knife a third, a fourth the trumpet holds.
Each brings what he for sacred service used,
Yet without sacrifice. No incense mounts ;
No sound of harp or horn the stillness breaks.
And now from out the ranks of priests forth comes
Their venerable chief. His form is wrapt
In garments worn on that most solemn day,
When, with atoning blood, the ark he nears.
Now slowly he approach'd the building's verge,
And, looking upwards, spake : 'Thou Lord of all,
None other hand but Thine could light these flames ;
Yet, Lord, we bless Thy name, that Babel's rites
Will ne'er profane where once the ark had stood ;
But we no longer are required. Lo ! here,
The badge of office which I held from Thee,
I now return it to Thy hands.' Then he
From out his garment takes the golden key
Which shut the temple-gates. He lifts it high :
It shone so bright as from the temple now
The light did mingle with the sheen of stars.
And lo ! a hand from heaven has seized the key,
And from the roof the high priest and the priests
Precipitate themselves into the flames :
The temple falls,—their grave and monument."

In the second specimen Israel is compared to a dove—

"A dove art thou, my people dear,
And well may'st thou a dove be call'd,—
As faithful to her chosen mate,
No other friend the dove doth know.
So faithful thou to Him, thy Lord,
Remembering still the solemn vow.
As calm the dove bows down her neck
To the destroyer's cutting knife,
So thou, when for thy vow of love,
Thou bear'st the torture and the death.
As when the flood, in judgment dire
All living men had swept away,

> The dove brought first the olive-leaf,
> A sign of coming peace and life ;
> So Israel goes forth abroad
> A herald of His word and love."

We give yet another specimen—

> " If death has snatch'd from thee the wife of youth,
> It is as if the sacred city were,
> And e'en the temple in thy pilgrim days,
> Defiled, laid low, and levelled with the dust.
> The man who harshly sends away from him
> His first-woo'd bride, the loving wife of youth,
> For him the very altar of the Lord
> Sheds forth its tears of bitter agony."

Among this class of composition many of the apocryphal writings must be included, of which some have erroneously been supposed to have originally been dramatic compositions.[1]

Among the poetic contributions of Jews in foreign countries, those of Alexandria were specially distinguished. The peculiar philosophy with which Judaism was brought into contact in that city so tended to develop the mystical element, that a complete separation was made between the uninitiated, to whom the Law applied in its literality, and adepts, who, through it, penetrated to a deeper philosophy.[2] This tendency gradually induced the belief that the initiated of other times and nations had substantially held the same principles. In order to prove this statement, the fragments of unknown authors were published as the compositions of Orpheus, Linus, Homer, Hesiod, Pindar, etc. By and by Jewish writers ascribed, by a " pious fraud," their own compositions to these classical writers. Some of these pieces will be found in the work of Eusebius, *On the Preparation for the Gospel*, lib. xiii. 12–14, and other passages. Whether the writers whose compositions are there cited had in reality been all Jews may be doubted, but these extracts were either written under Jewish influence or interpolated for such purposes. From internal evidence, we would infer that

---

[1] For example, by Luther; comp. Schudt, *Jüd. Denkwürdig.* vol. iv. Cont. ii.

[2] Euseb. *Præp. Evang.* viii. 10, p. 378.

Theodotus the poet was a Samaritan, and Philo the elder (not Philo Judæus) a Jew, although Josephus ranks them [1] both amongst heathen writers. Theodotus recorded in verse part of the history of Jacob, Philo sings of Jerusalem.[2] Among Jewish compositions we also include some of the oracles of Apollo recorded by Eusebius. The frequent contact with Alexandrian Jews, whose religion had assumed the peculiar philosophical cast of the time and place, must have exercised a considerable influence upon the heathens. It gave to some more correct notions of Jewish history, which had already begun to attract attention. [The genuine fragments of Hecatæus of Abdera (about 350 B.C.) show that he wrote on the origin, laws, and manners of the Jews;[3] while Clearchus, a disciple of Aristotle, describes the meeting of his master with a Jew in Asia Minor.[4]] Even before the translation of the Bible into Greek, portions of Scripture history were known to heathens. The LXX. gave a new impulse to the Judaising tendency of philosophers, and again stimulated Jewish philosophers to bring their peculiar system more into harmony with current opinions. Judaism, as represented by Philo, however distasteful to the bigoted idolater and hateful to a suspicious and zealous people, would present many attractions to Grecian philosophers.

Two chapters of the thirteenth Book of the above-quoted work of Eusebius are devoted to extracts from the works of Aristobulus, the Jewish peripatetic, and of Clement, one of the Christian Fathers, professedly containing extracts from ancient heathen poets corroborative of Jewish doctrines. Many of these are doubtlessly Jewish interpolations. One specimen will suffice. After an introduction of nine verses, in which Orpheus is represented as calling on all to forsake former errors, and to enter on the road which alone preserves from destruction, as revealed in ancient writings, he says of God—

> " One and self-existent ! Though all be formed by Him,
> And He pervadeth all, yet none of mortals e'er

---

[1] Jos. *Against Apion*, i. 23.   [2] Comp. Schürer. II. iii. 222–225.
[3] *Ut supra*, p. 305 ff.   [4] Jos. *Against Apion*, i. 22.

Beholds His face ; the soul alone perceiveth Him.
The source of good, He sends no ill to mortal men.
Though favour follow Him, and with it also strife,
And war and pestilence, and weeping sorrow, too,
Beside Him is no other God. If thou on earth
Him first discern, 'tis easy *all* the rest to learn.
His mighty hand, His goings, as they shine,
Reveal, my son, the mighty Being there divine.
Himself I cannot see ; for mist enshrouds from me,
And tenfold covering envelopes Him from men.
The God who ruleth mortals none has e'er beheld,
Save one alone of yore, who sprung from Chaldee race."

Then follows a sublime description of this God as revealed to the inspired seer. We quote the following line to show the Hebrew cast of its theology—

"And in Himself He has beginning, middle, end."

Various readings of this fragment are extant,[1] showing that whoever may have been the author of this bold forgery, it had at least been recast by later editors. Among confessedly Jewish compositions, we reckon also a tragedy by a Jewish Alexandrian poet, entitled "The Exodus from Egypt," of which the theology, the poetry, and versification are all second-rate;[2] and a poem bearing the name of Phocylides (in 230 hexameters), which, having successively been described as the production of a heathen, and of a Christian, is now generally assigned to Jewish authorship.[3]

Although some Alexandrian Jews distinguished themselves by Talmudical lore, their theological tendencies generally took a different direction. They were rather mystical and rationalistic than traditional. The religious intercourse between Egypt and Palestine was not confined to the transmission of sums of money to the temple. In spite of the existence of

[1] Clem. Alex. *Strom.* v. 14, p. 259 ; Justin [?], *De Monarchia*, 2.

[2] For specimens, see Appendix V.

[3] The poem of Phocylides was used as a class-book amongst the schoolmen, on account of its elegant Greek and Biblical sentiments. Scaliger, in 1606, ascribed it to a Christian author, but since the elaborate treatise of Bernays (1856) the Jewish origin of the work has been generally accepted. [Recently Harnack has again maintained the Christian authorship. Comp. Schürer, II. iii. 313–316, and the literature there quoted.]

the rival temple at Heliopolis, the Alexandrians, like other
Jews, were accustomed to make pilgrimages to Jerusalem.
The best-known representative of Alexandrian Jewish literature
was Philo Judæus. In comparing the imaginative poetry of
antiquity with that of inspiration, he finds in the former
metre, rhyme, and songs, which merely delighted the ear ; in
the latter, the Divine poetry of God's works, while all nature
constituted a hymn of eternal truth, harmoniously executed.
In Divine poetry truth takes the place of myths, and the
harmony of nature that of metre and rhyme.[1] In another
passage he somewhat similarly contrasts the myths of the
ancients with the types and allegories of the Bible.[2] Still it
may be mentioned, as an instance of the essential difference
between the Judaism of Philo and that of the Rabbins, that
the former never scrupled to attend heathenish theatrical
representations, the Circensian games, and athletic contests,
and records with approbation passages which, to say the least,
are essentially Grecian.[3]

The facts to which we have already called attention, that
extra-Palestinian Jews used in their prayers the languages to
which they were accustomed, is in itself a proof that a regular
liturgy was unknown at that time. Even the Shema seems
to have been recited in Greek.[4] Of the prayers of the Egyptian Jews, only two thanksgivings uttered on their delivery
from the cruel governor Flaccus are preserved. These compositions are, however, rather those of Philo than of the
Egyptian Jews, and accordingly contain the un-Jewish
address to the Deity,—" Father of mortals and of immortals."[5]
The Therapeutæ, an Egyptian Jewish sect called into existence
by a tendency akin to that which produced monasticism,
resembled in many of their principles and practices that of
the Essenes in Palestine. In their devotions they used hymns
and prayers of a mystical character, but all have unfortunately been lost.

To the above brief sketch of strictly Jewish poetry, we

[1] Philo, *Quod deter. potiori* (ed. Mangey), i. 215.
[2] *De Mundi Opificio*, i. 38.   [3] *Quod omnis probus*, ii. 449, 469.
[4] Comp. Sota vii. 1.   [5] *In Flaccum*, ii. 535.

may add that, notwithstanding the disapprobation of the more exclusive Rabbins, a certain acquaintance with classical literature seems to have been common even in Palestine. This is implied by the interdict which was laid on the study of Greek after the war of Quietus.[1] In the Mishna there is possibly a reference to the Homeric writings (*Siphré Homeros*),[2] and elsewhere we hear of the Greek songs which flowed from the mouth of Acher, even before his avowed apostasy.[3]

Music and poetry were at first almost inseparably united. The poet generally sang his productions, or accompanied them on an instrument. This arrangement accounts in part for the simplicity in the forms of both arts, and for the absence of artificial arrangements in both. Music, poetry, and dancing were resorted to under very different circumstances. Whenever the soul was full, it poured forth its feelings in the language of poetry, and in harmonious accents. At feasts, marches, in triumphal entries, and even on mournful occasions, but specially in the services of the sanctuary, music and poetry were prominent features. The melodies were very simple, and, as such strains generally are, expressive and touching. They embodied, or carried home the poetic thought, and were not separate from it. The production of one mind and heart, the melody modulated with the feelings of the poet,—it harmonised with the hymn, and *accompanied* it. Notes were not known, and, of course, compositions unwritten ; nor was there any artificial harmony, although the arrangement of the voices must early have led to a natural harmony. Ordinarily, the performance consisted of a simple, sweet melody, sung in unison, and often supported by instrumental music, which also filled up the intervals between the stanzas. Different divisions of time must necessarily have been observed. Thus we find, that on the Feast of the New Year, which was pre-eminently designated as "The Feast of Blowing the Horn," the different sounds emitted were regulated by time. A *tekiah* was a blast of thrice the duration of a *teruah*,

---

[1] Sota ix. 14. [2] Jad. iv. 6 ; comp. Levy, *NHWB.* i. 476.
[3] Chag. 15*b*.

while an interval of one-third the duration of a *teruah* is
also mentioned.[1]

In the temple, an elevated place was occupied by those
Levites who sang the praises of the Lord. Their number
amounted at least to twelve, but might be indefinitely
increased. Beneath them stood the young Levites, whose
voices were agreeably to harmonise with those of the adult
performers.[2] Daily, as the priest bent over the altar to pour
out the drink-offering, an official gave the signal, and the
song of praise commenced with the sound of cymbals. The
Levites then took up the hymn. At every paragraph they
stopped, the trumpets sounded, and the people fell in adoration on the ground. The Psalms were sung in the following
order in the temple. On the first day of the week the 24th
Psalm was recited; on the second, the 48th; on the third,
the 82nd; on the fourth, the 94th; on the fifth, the 81st;
on the sixth, the 93rd; and on the seventh or Sabbath, the
92nd Psalm, which was ascribed to Adam, and supposed to
refer to the happiness of the eternal Sabbath.[3] The instruments in use amongst the Hebrews have been arranged as
stringed, wind, and instruments of percussion. Those most
common were the cymbal, the flute or pipe, with its mouth-
piece of reed to sound softer, the trumpet (of silver or brass),
and the horn (bent or straight), the lyre and the harp;—some
add to these a kind of organ. In a flute-solo one performer
concluded the piece, in order to make the melody more soft.
For the same purpose not more than one pair of cymbals were
sounded in the temple, nor less than two trumpets and nine
lyres.[4] The performers are by some supposed to have been
subordinate priests; by others, members of the noble families
of Emmaus, Phegorim, and Zipparja; others suppose that
they were Levites.[5] At the time of Ezra women sang in the
temple (Ezra ii. 65), but at a later period all public singing of
females was deemed improper, and indeed confined to wandering foreign prostitutes. Popular opinion on the subject is
indicated in the following expression: " If men sing and

---

[1] Rosh ha-Shan. iv. 9.   [2] Arach. ii. 6.   [3] Comp. Tamid vii. 3, 4.
[4] Arach. ii. 3–6. Comp. the above Mishnic treatises.   [5] *Ut supra*, 3, 4.

women respond, it is indecent; if women sing and men respond, it is like fire amongst stubble." [1]   The dance, as the expression of the highest stage of mental excitement, when all the members of the body sympathised with the emotions, was generally connected either with religious or idolatrous festivities. In the first class we also reckon the dances which welcomed the heroes of the nation, or took place at public festivals; in the second class, the dancing festivities which intercourse with other nations introduced.   The dance consisted of rotatory, semi-rotatory, or saltatory motions, arranged according to the fancy of the moment, or pantomimically representing any event.   In either case the steps were accompanied with music by the dancer, or by an orchestra.

II. *Scientific Knowledge*

It would be idle and ungrateful to enter on the various erroneous opinions current amongst the Jews on scientific subjects.   In as far as the natural sciences were based on speculation, and not simply a record of observed facts, and of deductions from them, they could only lead to unfounded and often extravagant results.   The classical student knows that philosophical investigation among the heathens frequently fell far short of truth.   The study of the exact sciences was more cultivated in Babylon than in Palestine, and Chaldean and Persian elements found their way amongst the Rabbins.   The speculative parts of many sciences were often theosophic and mystical.   Various speculations were propounded as to the size of the earth and its place in the universe, and the different ways in which first the centre and then the sides of it were formed; while in one passage the earth surrounded by the sea is compared to a ball in a dish.[2]   The thickness of the crust of the earth was computed by some at 1000 cubits.[3]   The idea of *pure* creation out of nothing, in opposition to formation or emanation, was by no means so general and firm an article of faith as might be supposed.[4]

---

[1] Sota 48a.   [2] Jer. Ab. Sar. iii. 42c.
[3] Succa 53b.   [4] Comp. Gen. Rab. 2 and 10.

The geographical allusions in the writings of the Jews are of interest as throwing light on the extent of their knowledge, and on the countries visited by them.[1] The dispersed of Israel were doubtless to be found in the greatest numbers in the seats of the Captivity in Babylon, but we have already spoken of the importance of the Jewish settlements in Egypt and in Asia Minor. Moreover, from an early period, the stream of Hebrew emigration flowed westwards, and before the second century of our era most of the countries along the Mediterranean seem to have been known to and visited by the Jews. [The Septuagint speaks of Carthage for Tarshish (*e.g.* Isaiah xxiii. 1), and of Miletus (Ezek. xxvii. 18). In the Talmud [2] many of the provinces of Asia Minor are mentioned, including Cilicia, Phrygia, Lydia, Cappadocia, and probably Galatia.] There are allusions to the islands of Rodos (Rhodes) and of Kipris (Cyprus). Of places in Africa, naturally Mizraim (Egypt) and Alexandria occur. Further, we read of "Cartigna" for Carthage [of "Berberia" or "Mortania" for Mauritania, and of Africa for the Roman province of that name. The last-named country is regarded as a distant and little-known part of the earth.[3]] In Europe we read of "Athuna" for Athens, of "the great city of Rome," of "Perandisin" for Brundisium, of "Grecian Italy" for the southern portion of the Italian peninsula, and of "Aspamia" for Spain. It is somewhat uncertain whether by "Galia" we should understand Gaul or Galatia, but the name was probably applied to both countries. [Certainly the former is meant in a passage which speaks of ships trading between "Galia" and Spain.[4]]

Mathematics, geometry, and astronomy were looked upon as the peculiar study of the Jews, to which such passages as Deut. iv. 5, 6, were applied. These were considered as a natural sequel to sacred study, and even formed part of theological lore. To ignorance in these respects, Isa. v. 12

[1] For a brief abstract of the geographical notions of the Rabbins, compare App. VI.

[2] Comp. Neubauer, *Géographie du Talmud*, esp. pp. 289–319, 400–419.

[3] Comp. Sanh. 91*a* ; Tamid 32*a*.　　　　[4] Jebam. 63*a*.

was applied, and it was said, "Woe to men who see, but know not what they see; who stand, but know not on what they stand."[1]   Such studies were supposed to lead the student to a more perfect knowledge of the Creator.   Nor were the attainments of the Hebrews inconsiderable.   The Talmud recounts the planets by name, as Cochab (the star) for Mercury; Nogah (splendour) for Venus; Maadim (red) for Mars; Zedek (righteousness) for Jupiter; Sabbatai (Sabbath star) for Saturn.   [Other names for some of the planets are also found.   The periods of their revolutions are roughly given.   Jupiter is said to complete its course in 12 years, Saturn in 30 years, Venus in 10 months, Mars in 18 months.[2]]   Besides the seven circles of the planets, other two were enumerated, of which one is called that of the stars, being the sphere which contains the stars, the other that which contains the whole universe.   The twelve constellations of the Zodiac were in the ninth orbit of stars.[3]   These constellations are enumerated and partly described.   The Milky Way was called "the fiery stream," or "the heavenly path," and the tail of the Scorpion was described as lying to the west of it.   It was asserted that if a comet passed beyond Orion, it would destroy the world. The heat of Orion and the cold of the Pleiades maintain the equilibrium of proper temperature, and if the tail of the Scorpion were not close to the Milky Way, "no creature could endure the bite of the Scorpion."[4]   It was suggested, that at the time of the flood, God had taken two stars from the Pleiades, and when the waters were to subside, two from the opposite constellation.[5]   Rabbi Samuel was popularly called the "Moon-gazer,"[6] and said to be as well acquainted with the motion of the stars as with the streets of Nahardea.

The details connected with the equalisation of the

---

[1] Chag. 12b.

[2] Gen. Rab. 10.   [More exactly, the respective periods are 11½ years, 29½ years, 7½ months, and 23 months.]

[3] Ber. 32b; Pes. 94b.   [4] Ber. 58b.   [5] Ber. 59a.

[6] B. Mez. 85b.

calendar and the changes of the seasons are very elaborate, and exhibit both original investigation and acquaintance with the studies of Gentile philosophers. A cycle of nineteen years was adopted in the fourth century A.D., and the change of seasons (Tekupha) and the appearance of the new moon (Moled) were exactly calculated. Between one Tekupha and another 91 days 7½ hours intervened. According to Jewish calculations, the world was created in Moled Tishri, in the year of the Julian period 953, being Monday, 5 hours and 204 Chlakim (*i.e.* under the meridian of Jerusalem), or Monday the 7th October, 5 hours 204 Chlakim; and, according to our division of hours, on the 6th October, at 11 minutes past 11 o'clock of the year 3761 B.C.[1] Tradition also records the existence of works on the structure of the world, on the sun and moon, the stars, the seasons and the causes of their changes, the laws of nature, etc. Nor is it impossible that the following quotation may indicate some acquaintanceship with the principles of electricity.[2] "To lay iron between newly-hatched chickens is superstitious (literally, according to heathen ways); to do so on account of thunder and lightning is lawful." [To the magnet, under the name of *eben shoëbeth* (attracting stone), we find more than one allusion. It is said that by this means Gehazi caused the golden calves of Jeroboam to ascend into the air,[3] and the crown of the Ammonite king was held suspended over the head of David.[4]]

In Egypt, where medicine and surgery were not only known, but where every physician confined himself to the treatment of only one species of disease, these sciences must have reached a considerably more advanced stage than in Israel. Among the Jews, partly from the circumstances of the nation, and partly from ignorance, surgical manipulations, outward applications, and assistance at child-birth, were at first the principal departments of. medical lore. But gradually the study of medicine became enlarged, and at the time of our

---

[1] For details, compare Ideler's *Chronologie*, i. p. 537 to the end.
[2] Compare Schwartz, *das Heil. Land*, p. 325.   [3] Ab. Sar. 44*a*.
[4] Sanh. 107*b*; Sot. 47*a*.

Lord physicians seem to have resided not only in larger towns, but even in the country.[1] Certain diseases (specially those of the abdominal viscera) are described as peculiar to students, and a special physician was employed for the priests who served in the temple, and whose constant exposure must have rendered them peculiarly liable to various distempers.[2] The frequency of sacrifices and the laws concerning clean animals, etc., must have early led to an acquaintanceship with anatomy. In common opinion, there were 248 bones in the body,[3] of which 30 belonged to each foot and hand (120 in all), 10 to each ankle, 2 to each leg, 5 to each knee, 1 to each thigh, 3 to each haunch, 2 to each forearm, 2 to each elbow, 1 to each arm, 4 to the shoulder, 11 ribs on each side, 18 bones to the spine, 9 to the skull, 8 to the neck, 6 to the breast, and 5 to the various outlets of the body.[4] Much attention seems to have been paid to the art of preserving life and health. As purely physical means of prolonging life, long-protracted sitting at table, attention to regularity of secretions, and proper diet—wheaten bread to youths, and oil to the aged, together with wine—are recommended.[5] The first requisite for the preservation of health was *purity of air*, and the sanitary police regulations were very strict. From its geographical position, the climate of Palestine was very salubrious ; and it is almost more than a figure of speech when the Talmud maintained that the very air of Palestine made its inhabitants wise. The Hebrews recommended a moderate temperature, and looked upon the cooling north wind as restoring its balance. The hot southerly or easterly winds were deemed exceedingly dangerous, and during their prevalence no surgical operation was ordinarily performed.[6] The divers washings, however useless in a religious point of view, were important as sanitary regulations. Besides the

---

[1] Jos. *Life*, 72.   [2] Compare Lightfoot, *Horæ Hebr*. i. 904.

[3] M. Ohal. i. 8.

[4] M. Ohal. i. 8 ; comp. Rabbinowicz, *Médecine du Thalmud*, p. 104.

[5] For what follows, compare [with caution] R. J. Wunderbar, *Bibl. talmud. Medizin*, Riga, 1851.

[6] Jebam. 72*a*.

use of baths in private dwellings or public establishments, bathing in rivers, the use of warm or of medicated baths— either in the mineral waters of Tiberias, etc., or in warmed oil [1]—and vapour baths, were recommended. In the latter it was the practice to inhale vapour (though this was supposed to be detrimental for the teeth [2]), to drink hot water, and to have the body rubbed with ointments and perfumeries. Immediately after the vapour bath, cold water was poured over the whole body, and a mixture of wine, oil, and water rubbed on.[3] Cleanliness was felt to be of such importance, that parties on a journey, in the wilderness, or in the country, were pitied, as being far from bathing establishments.[4] Students whose garments were filthy deserved to die, nor were they to settle in any place where either police or bathing establishments were defective.[5]

After every meal some *exercise* was deemed requisite to promote digestion, but excessive exercise was thought dangerous. Equally noxious were all *violent emotions.* " Even one sigh destroys half the body," [6] while " anxiety, the discomforts of travelling, and sin, consume all the strength of man." [7] The night is destined for *sleep ;* [8] and if a person vows that he is not to sleep for three consecutive days (and nights), he is to be punished with stripes (for perjury), and to be immediately sent to bed." [9] Sleep early in the morning was refreshing, but to remain too long in bed, or to sleep during the day for more than 60 breaths, was unwholesome. To sleep on the ground was unsafe. Particular attention was also paid to *diet.* Milk and honey, the latter specially for children and old people, wheaten bread, meat boiled, roasted, or fried, and of vegetables, lentils, beans, and onions, constituted the chief articles of food. Hunger or thirst were to be the immediate indications for seeking supply ; [10] and at every meal a proper quantity of fluids was to be used.[11] To eat early in the morning

[1] Jos. *Wars*, i. 33. 5.   [2] Jer. Ab. Sar. iii. 42*d.*
[3] Ab. Sar. 30*a.*   [4] Erub. 55*b.*   [5] Sanh. 17*b.*
[6] Ber. 58*b.*   [7] Gitt. 70*a.*   [8] Erub. 65*a.*
[9] Shebu. 25*a.*   [10] Ber. 62*b.*   [11] Gitt. 70*a* ; Shab. 41*a* ; Ber. 40*a.*

imparted strength, and dinner was to be taken with daylight. Between supper and bedtime three or four hours were to intervene. Proper attention to mastication was conducive to health, nor should eating be continued to satiety. Particular directions were given as to the diet of pregnant women and suckling mothers. Directions for the treatment of new-born infants occur already in Ezek. xvi. 4.

The Talmud distinguishes between indisposition and dangerous diseases, and allows that the latter may be attended to even on Sabbaths.[1] The proximate causes of diseases were noxious winds or insufficient wind; deficiency of heat;—hence moderate fever was deemed to contribute to the healing process;[2]—and the state of the bile, which was thought to induce eighty-three different kinds of disease. A disease commenced with different premonitory symptoms, such as a rash, yawning, pains, etc., and if terminating favourably, passed through different stages to convalescence. The crisis of the disease was anxiously watched for on certain days, and appeared by sternutation, perspiration, abdominal secretions, sleep, or dreams.[3] Certain hours brought relief to the patients. They felt most easy during the three first hours of the day, and most uneasy during the three last hours.[4] Summer was more favourable for effecting cures than winter. Changes of diet might entail disease, and one ailment led to another. Thus croup began in the abdomen and terminated in the throat.[5] As some of the ailments which seem to have been common among the Hebrews, we may mention fevers, inflammations, diseases of the heart, malignant ulcers, dyspepsia, dysentery, poisons introduced by bites, and gout. Of surgical operations, the most frequent, important, and most accurately described is that of circumcision. The help of art for obstetric purposes was early called in. Midwives are mentioned in the oldest Hebrew records. Inability to suckle on the part of the infant was thought to be due to chill, and was to be remedied by the application of heat.[6] Of the obstetrical

[1] Comp. Joma viii. 6.   [2] Nedar. 41*b*.   [3] Ber. 57*b*.
[4] Nedar. 40*a*.   [5] Shab. 33*b*.   [6] Shab. 134*a*.

operations, we may mention the gastrotomia or *side*-operation,[1] and the Cæsarean, the latter only practised when the mother was dying, the partition of the infant,[2] and in certain cases the introduction of a tube.[3]

Blood-letting, practised in Greece at a much earlier period, was frequently resorted to in the first centuries, not only in actual disease, but by way of prevention. Up to the fiftieth year, venesection was recommended once a month ; after that period, gradually, more rarely. To touch the wound, to expose oneself to cold, to go about, to bathe, or to commit an error in diet after the operation, was deemed dangerous.[4] Blood-letting was also resorted to under certain astrological combinations.[5] The operation was, according to circumstances, performed on the upper or the lower part of the body, either by scarificators (in a manner analogous to our cupping), by opening a vein,[6] or as arteriotomy by a lancet.[7] One surgeon devised a special mantle to wear during the visits of female patients.[8] An unskilful surgeon was amenable to justice ;[9] a skilful one bore the designation of Doctor.[10] Students of the Law and divines were not expected to pay any fee, and the poor were rather to be assisted than hardly dealt with by pious medical advisers.[11] A variety of surgical operations are referred to in the Talmud, and in cases of amputation the deficiency was, if possible, supplied by artificial limbs.[12] In fractures of bones, splints of wood or metal plates were employed.[13] The excision of tumours and cancerous swellings was practised ;[14] and, in Alexandria, the excision of the ovarium in cows and swine, which were to be sold into other countries, seems to have been resorted to.[15] Dislocations were treated by cold-water bandages ;[16] other wounds by the application of vinegar and wine,[17] or by surgeons' lint, soft

---

[1] Bechor. 47*b* ; Nid. 40*a*.   [2] Nid. 28*a*.   [3] Nid. 21*b*.   [4] Shab. 129*b*.
[5] A practice adopted much later in Germany. Comp. Fr. Rapaldi's *Mag. and Perpet. Alman.* for it. Antwerp, 1551.
[6] Taan. 21*b* ; comp. Ohal. ii. 3.   [7] Kerith. 22*a*.   [8] Taan. *ib.*
[9] B. Bath. 21*b*.   [10] *Ut supra*, 21*a*.   [11] Taan. 21*b*.
[12] Shab. 65*b* ; Jeb. 102*b*.   [13] Shab. 53*a*, 147*a*.   [14] Ab. Sar. 26*b*; Jeb. 75*b*.
[15] Bechor. 28*b*.   [16] Shab. 147*a*.   [17] Shab. 109*a*.

cotton, etc. Operations are recorded for reducing a dislocation of the neck,[1] and for healing a swelling in the throat of a child.[2]

The remedies employed in the cure of disease were either sympathetic and supernatural, or scientific. Supernatural influences were often brought into requisition, and people born under the same constellation were supposed to stand in "rapport" with each other. But above these superstitions—the offspring of a false philosophy, and of unacquaintance with the laws of nature—towered a firm confidence in a special overruling providence, preventing the consequences which might otherwise have resulted. The Essenes and other mystical sects performed cures, partly by the application of herbs and roots,[3] and partly by supernatural means. Amulets, consisting of small pieces of parchment, on which verses of Scripture or mystical formulas were inscribed, were worn as preventives, and deemed probate if they had performed three cures, or been executed by an adept. In their scientific treatment the Hebrews placed more confidence in dietetic and preventive than in remedial agency. However, as in Europe some centuries ago, the rarity, the costliness, and the oddity of a remedy often invested it, in the opinion of the people and of doctors, with extraordinary powers. The next step in the progress of the science was the adoption of very composite formulas. As a general rule, however, minerals were not much resorted to, and, whether consciously or unconsciously, the principle seems to have been acted upon that nature provided remedies for the diseases peculiar to a district, in the products of that district. It was a principle, that too much drugging was hurtful.[4] Mineral waters and purgatives were, unless absolutely requisite, only to be used in spring.[5] Among them the juice of the date-palm, derived by incision into the tree;[6] Babylonian beer; an Egyptian decoction, prepared from equal portions of barley, saflor, and common salt;[7]

---

[1] Shab. 66*b*. [2] *Ut supra*, 123*a*. [3] Jos. *Wars*, ii. 8. 6.
[4] Pes. 113*a*, and Rashi, *ad loc*. [5] Shab. 110*a*, 147*b*. [6] *Ut supra*, 110*a*.
[7] Pes. 42*b* ; Ber. 38*a*.

mechanical means; and what was known as the trometon egg, or one prepared in a very peculiar manner,—were in common use.[1] Certain articles of diet, as hard-boiled eggs, roasted meat, liver, etc., were interdicted; others, as spinach, honey, the stomach and the lungs of geese, etc., were recommended to convalescents.[2] Along with much that is absurd, some of the remedies prescribed in the Talmud indicate that experience and extensive observation had characterised the medical practice of the Hebrews.

III. *Jewish Law*

Following the analogy of the law of Scotland,[3] we may arrange the code of the Hebrews into *Statutory* or *Written* (meaning by this the law of Moses) and *Customary* or *Unwritten* law (referring to the traditionary law of the Mishna). It is with the latter exclusively that we have at present to do. All jurisdiction was either civil, criminal, or ecclesiastical, according as questions of private right, public morality, or religious duty were to be decided. It requires, however, to be borne in mind, that by the peculiar constitution of the Jewish courts, and by the institutions of the country, a complete separation between these different branches could not be effected. Besides the above, a number of police, sanitary, and public regulations were also enacted by the Rabbins, which we shall notice as occasion offers.[4]

The Jewish law acknowledged rights in every individual, and, with few exceptions, placed all on a footing of equality. We have already referred to some of the rights of women, and shall only supplement our statements. Though a mother could not claim equal [5] respect, she was on the same footing towards her children as the father, and biblical examples of her influence will readily occur. All the forbids of the law applied equally to both sexes, but all those *commands* whose

---

[1] Nedar. 50*b*; comp. Levy, *NHWB.* ii. 193.   [2] Ber. 57*b*.
[3] *Vide* Erskine's *Principles of the Law of Scotland*, p. 6, etc.
[4] Comp. Saalschütz, *d. Mos. Recht*, Berlin, 1853.
[5] Kerith. vi. 9.

execution was confined to certain definite periods (for example, the day-time, etc.), were only binding on males.[1]　Legal exceptions to the validity of marriages entailed the disqualification of the offspring.　In all ordinary circumstances the child inherited the rank of the father.　If the mothers had been incapable of contracting marriage, as in the case of female slaves, the children ranked with the mother.　Thus the family of a bastard might become legitimate, if the bastard (father) married a slave (mother).　Their children were then not bastards, but slaves, and, being emancipated, might become legitimate citizens, and intermarry with Israelites.[2]

Of the different relations of foreigners to Jews we have already spoken.　They were either passing or resident strangers, or naturalised denizens.　An uncircumcised person was allowed to offer sacrifices and tithes (of course according to the Jewish ritual), but not to partake in the Passover, or to marry a Jewess.　Jews were allowed to marry the daughters of heathens, except those of the seven Canaanitish nations, and of the Amalekites.　The grandchildren of Egyptians and Edomites, who had settled in Palestine, might enter the congregation.　The law with reference to the Moabites and Ammonites, as well as to the seven nations and the Amalekites, was, however, repealed by the Rabbins in favour of proselytes, and the sons of all foreigners resident in Palestine, and all proselytes, were allowed to enter into the congregation.[3]　Any intercourse with heathens which might either further their idolatry, or issue to the disadvantage of the Jewish nation, was interdicted.　[We can hardly suppose that foreigners resident in Palestine troubled themselves much about Jewish regulations ; but, according to the theory of the Rabbins,] they were obliged to observe the seven Noachic Commandments which we have formerly specified.[4]　Finally, it is noticeable, that the Mishna confines the term bastards to those begotten in incest, to cases where marriage had been legally impossible, and to the children of harlots.[5]

[1] Kidd. i. 7. 8.　　　　　　　[2] Kidd. iii. 12. 13 ; bab. *ib.* 69*a*.
[3] Jad. iv. 3. 4 ; Jeb. viii. 3.　　[4] Ab. Sar. 64*b* ; *vid. sup.* p. 293 f.
[5] Jeb. iv. 13 ; Kidd. iii. 12.

Every householder shared in all the public burdens, such as the keeping up of roads, baths, city walls, gates, etc. Any party who transferred a public road from one part of his property to another, forfeited his right to both.[1] All obstructions were to be removed from streets and roads, and, where they had been the occasion of damage, the person to whom it was traced was liable for compensation.[2] All property consisting of fields was restored in the jubilee, but the party restoring could claim something for improvements made. Within that period fields could be redeemed by the original proprietor only after a lapse of two years from their disposal. Houses in open (not walled) towns, or in villages, or in fields etc. enclosed within town walls, or built on the city wall itself, were considered as fields, and returned in the jubilee to the original proprietors.[3] Houses in walled or in unwalled towns might be redeemed by the original proprietor within a year after their sale; but after the lapse of a full year, houses in walled towns remained the *perpetual* property of the purchaser.

To our former remarks on servitude, we add, that only one of two grounds could exist for the servitude of a Hebrew, namely, theft, when, in order to discharge the legal pecuniary punishment, the authorities might order the sale of the culprit; or poverty inducing a Jew to sell himself. His servitude lasted till the jubilee or till the death of his master, or he might obtain freedom by paying the amount for which he was sold, after deduction of the value of his services.[4] Hebrew maids obtained freedom in the seventh year; nor could they have their ears bored. If a Hebrew sold his daughter, the law assumed that it was for the purpose of marriage, and forbade her sale by her master. As she could only be sold during her minority, she attained freedom whenever the marks of puberty appeared.[5] A heathen slave might obtain his liberty by redemption, manumission,[6] or in consequence of

---

[1] B. Bath. vi. 7.

[2] B. Bath. ii. 14, iii. 8 ; B. Mez. x. 5 ; B. Kam. iii. 1–3.

[3] Arach. ix. 1–7. [According to a Talmudic tradition, which is probably correct, the jubilee was not observed after the Exile.]

[4] Kidd. i. 2.   [5] *Ut supra.*   [6] Kidd. i. 3.

ill-usage. If a slave was sold to a heathen, or beyond the boundaries of Palestine, he obtained by the very act his legal freedom, and, if fugitive, could not be reclaimed.[1] Heathen slaves, however, did not share all the privileges of Jewish servants. Thus, for example, they could not retain possession of anything found by them.[2] If the slave of a heathen became a proselyte through baptism, he received his freedom when sold to a Jew. The daughters of such proselytes enjoyed the same rights as other Hebrewesses, and, if their mother had been a Jewess, might even be married to priests.[3] If a man left his fortune to his slave, he attained with it his liberty also.[4] Regular letters of manumission were given, in which the essential words were " from this time forth be free," or be " thine own master." These letters, if once written, even though not delivered or despatched, could not again be annulled.[5] Hired servants, if engaged by the day, could claim their wages at night—if during the night, on the following day. But while the law respected the rights of the employed, it also carefully protected the employer.[6]

Properly speaking, marriage was considered a purely civil contract, but it was customary to wed the bride in presence of witnesses, and with the pronunciation of certain blessings, or to wed her " according to the law of Moses and of Israel." A bride descended from the family of Aaron had a double dowry (400 dinars) assigned to her.[7] If a young girl had been married while a minor, she was allowed to repudiate her husband on attaining her majority ; if the marriage had taken place without her consent, it was necessarily void.[8] In all other cases, from the moment the marriage-contract had been signed the union could only be separated by formal divorce. If sufficient funds were on hand, a bride could insist on having a portion assigned to her conformable to her station in life. A second daughter could claim a portion equal to that of her elder sister.[9] A mistaken opinion as to the circumstances of the bride, unless she had wilfully

[1] Gitt. iv. 6.   [2] B. Mez. i. 5.   [3] Bikkur. i. 5.
[4] Peah iii. 8.   [5] Gitt. ix. 3, i. 6.   [6] B. Mez. vii., ix. 11. 12.
[7] Keth. i. 5.   [8] Jeb. xiii. 1. 2.   [9] Keth. vi. 5. 6.

deceived her intended, formed no valid ground for divorce.
If the lady's property had been entered into the marriage-
contract, the bridegroom was bound to assign to his wife
the full value of her portion, and one-half more, or, if it
consisted in jewellery, etc., one-fifth less than their value.[1]
In such cases the property belonged to the husband, either
simply for use—the wife retaining her right of disposal—or
absolutely, the husband being, however, answerable for any
loss.   If a wife inherited property, the husband enjoyed only
the use of it, but a wife could not dispose of any property
without the consent of her husband.[2] If the husband's
rights were attainted by any vow of his wife, he was at
liberty to absolve her from such obligations.   The duties of
both parties, and their mutual rights, have already been
detailed.   We add, that the claims of the wife upon her
dowry, and those of children, did not require to be expressly
mentioned in the marriage-contract.[3]   The husband was the
heir of his wife.   In cases of separation (not divorce) he was
bound to assign her a proper aliment.[4]   In cases of dispute,
the law protected chiefly the interests of wives.   One
witness, even though incapable of giving testimony in other
cases, was sufficient to attest the death of the husband,
i.e. if no suspicion of collusion existed ; but a period of three
months was to elapse between a first and second marriage.[5]
Before receiving her dowry, the wife had to swear that she
had not previously got any portion.   We need not detail
the laws regulating marriage with the wife of a deceased
brother, as even the Mishna recommends that it should not
be performed.   An Israelite was prevented from marrying
within the prescribed degrees of consanguinity, and priests
from uniting themselves with harlots, with divorced or
profane persons, *i.e.* the offspring of marriages forbidden to
priests.   To prevent interdicted marriages, every priest was
to inquire into the family of his bride (up to four degrees,
if she descended from the family of Aaron—in other

[1] Keth. vi. 3.
[2] Keth. vi. 1, viii. 1–5.
[3] Keth. iv. 7–12.
[4] *Ut supra*, v. 8. 9.
[5] Jeb. xv. 1–4, iv. 10.

circumstances, to five degrees), except when the bride's father was a priest in active service, or a member of the Sanhedrin.[1] The daughters of proselytes, provided that one of their parents had been an Israelite, and of the daughters of degraded priests, might be married by priests.[2] In a city taken by an enemy, the priests had to divorce their wives, unless special testimony could be borne to their chastity.[3]

Although divorce was lawful, the various regulations to be observed must, in practice, have considerably limited it, and its practice was generally reprobated. Besides, it was always first sought to bring about a reconciliation. If a wife had transgressed " the law of Moses " (in her duties as wife), " or that of Israel " (by immodesty or forwardness, etc.), and in other exceptional cases, she had no claim on her dowry.[4] A letter of divorce had to be signed by witnesses, and expressly stated that N. N. was now regularly divorced, and free to marry any other.[5] In prospect of a distant journey, or of death, the mere order of the husband to draw up a letter of divorce was deemed sufficient, except when he had specially been solicited to do so.[6] Letters of divorce might be transmitted by messengers, provided they had been delivered by both parties in the presence of witnesses. The messenger was not allowed to marry the divorced party.[7] Where the doubtful fame of a woman was the ground of separation, she could never be taken back again.[8]

The mutual rights and duties of parents and children have been already referred to. While the sons were in measure independent, the father could dispose of his daughters during their minority, either by marrying or by selling them.[9] However, the disposal of a daughter was deemed improper, except in cases of urgent necessity. Although the father was bound to have his son circumcised, redeemed, educated, trained to a trade, and even taught to swim, some maintained

[1] Kidd. iv. 4. 5. [2] *Ut supra*, iv. 6. 7. [3] Keth. ii. 9.
[4] Keth. vii. 6. 7. [5] Gitt. iv. 2, ix. 3–8. [6] Gitt. vi. 5. 6, vii. 2.
[7] Jeb. ii. 9. [8] Gitt. iv. 7. [9] Keth. iii. 8, iv. 4.

that he was under no legal obligation to maintain his daughters.[1]
The first-born son inherited a double portion of the property
actually left by the father (not by the mother), and on hand
at the time of his decease. Sons and their descendants,
though these descendants were females, were considered the
sole heirs, when even the right of primogeniture extended to
the daughters of the deceased eldest son in preference to their
father's brothers.[2] Failing direct heirs, the property passed
to the father of the deceased, and then to his brothers or
sisters, and so on upwards. Bastards, or the offspring of
illicit connexions, with the exception of the children of
heathen or slave mothers, were not excluded from sharing in
the inheritance.[3] Crimes of any kind did not disqualify
from the above rights.[4]

The Rabbinical law makes provision for disposal by
testament (termed after the Greek " Dijathiki "). It
distinguished between the disposition of persons in good
health and of those in prospect of death. The latter might
either leave or dispose of their property, if such disposal did
not run contrary to the law of Moses. Only an inheritance
could never go wholly beyond the circle of the rightful heirs,
nor could any of them be excluded by name, though they
might be tacitly passed by.[5] If a person in good health
gifted away any portion of his property, actual possession on
the part of the recipient was requisite to complete the
transaction. If a patient recovered, he could recall the
donation, provided he had not, by retaining part of his original
property, indicated that he had at the time anticipated
recovery.[6] The claims of the widow have already been
referred to. The duty of burying a widow devolved upon *her*
legal heirs.[7] A widow could only claim payment of her
dowry from what was *actually* left at the time of her
husband's decease. Daughters had to be maintained by their
brothers, even though this would have thrown the latter upon
public charity.[8] Where the father had not chosen tutors or

---

[1] Kidd. i. 7 ; bab. *ib.* 29*a* ; Keth. iv. 6. 11.   [2] B. Bath. viii. 2. 3.
[3] Cf. Kidd. iii. 12.   [4] Sanh. xi. 4.   [5] B. Bath. viii. 5.
[6] *Ut supra*, ix. 6. 7.   [7] Keth. xi. 1.   [8] *Ut supra*, xiii. 3.

curators, such were appointed by the authorities.[1]   The wife
was not heir to her husband, nor a mother to her children.[2]
The husband might formally renounce his right to his wife's
property, whereupon she was at liberty during her lifetime to
dispose of it.[3]

A farmer was obliged to keep the ground in good order,
and to make all customary improvements.   If a crop was
destroyed by locusts, fire, or any public calamity, the
damage was borne by the landlord.   Leases were generally
for seven years, but flax might only be sown or wood cut
during the first year, as the former exhausted the ground, and
the latter took long time to grow.[4]   If any person let his
house to another in winter without fixing a term, he could not
dispossess the occupant between the Feast of Tabernacles and
that of the Passover (the end of autumn and the end of
spring).   In summer, thirty days' notice of removal had to
be given, and, to the occupants of shops or of town-houses, a
full twelvemonth.   The occupants of manufactories and large
works had to receive three years' notice.   The proprietor
was bound to execute any repairs which required a trades-
man.[5]

The law distinguished between movable and immovable
property.   The latter afforded security to creditors even
where such had not formally been stated; the former did
not.   Claims upon movable property could only be sub-
stantiated if such property had actually been delivered, else
neither the fact of payment nor the statement of witnesses
could make the transaction legal.   Immovable property was
acquired by payment, document, or actual possession.[6]   In
cases of exchange of one article for another, actual possession
by *one* of the parties was sufficient.[7]   A deaf and dumb
person might conclude a bargain by signs,[8] and if a transaction had been concluded, no after-agreement could annul it.

The drawing up of documents for various purposes presupposed such minute acquaintance with the forms of law,

[1] Gitt. v. 4.   [2] B. Bath. viii. 1.   [3] Keth. ix. 1.
[4] B. Mez. ix. 1–9.   [5] B. Mez. viii. 6. 7.   [6] Kidd. i. 4. 5.
[7] B. Mez. iv. 1. 2.   [8] Gitt. v. 7.

the smallest neglect of which destroyed their validity, that
professional writers, who bear in the Talmud the name of
Liblars, were soon required. [It was customary for them to
keep the formulas requisite for divorces and other legal
transactions written out and ready for immediate use. Such
a form bore the name of *tōpos*.[1]] Documents were either
plain or *folded*. In plain documents the contents were
recorded consecutively, and the signatures of *two* witnesses
followed at the end. In folded documents a fold succeeded
after every few lines, and was always attested by three
witnesses. Any informality, or the absence of proper signatures of witnesses, rendered the document invalid. A letter of
divorce might be drawn up in the absence of the wife, and
her receipt for the dowry in the husband's absence——an
acknowledgment of debt in the absence of the creditor, and
a letter of purchase in that of the buyer.[2] Documents concerning marriage, farms, arbitration, or judicial findings, could
only be written with the consent of both parties, and the
latter were valid even if drawn up by non-Jewish authorities.
Property professedly bought or received, consisting of houses,
fountains, baths, slaves, fields, and anything else from which
continual profit might be derived, was indisputable if the
original proprietor had not, during three years, objected to
the validity of the rights of the holder of the property. The
holder of the property was not bound after that term to
produce documents to prove his right of tenure, provided he
had, during that period, given the original proprietor sufficient
intimation of his claims. But the burden of proof might
rest on the defender in the case of tradesmen or workmen, of
part - proprietors, farmers who shared in the fruits of the
ground, of curators, or in questions between husband and
wife or father and son.[3] If a property was too small for
division, or such division was inconvenient, neither party
could insist on it unless prepared to purchase the whole.[4]
Where flats belonged to different parties, the proprietor of
the upper storey could, if the house fell, insist on the rebuild-

[1] Jer. B. Bath. x. 17*c* ; *ib.* Git. ii. 44*a*.   [2] B. Bath. x. 1–4.
[3] B. Bath. iii. 1–3.   [4] B. Bath. i. 6.

ing of the lower, or take possession of the ground.[1]   A wall
had to be removed at least four cubits from the windows of
a neighbour, and if broad enough to allow a person to stand
upon it, required to be built either four cubits higher or
lower than such windows.   Where a neighbour's wall was in
danger of being injured by any operation, a distance of three
spans was to intervene, and the wall to be protected.   It was
not allowed to cultivate in a field what might injure the crop
or property of a neighbour—as to cultivate mustard if a
neighbour owned beehives.   Trees had to be removed four
cubits from the property of a neighbour, and the branches, if
they overhung the wall, might be cut off.[2]   If two gardens,
of which the one was higher than the other, bounded, the
declivity belonged in part to both, so that the proprietor of
the higher ground claimed so much as he could reach from
his property with his hand, while all the rest went with the
lower ground.[3]

Sequestration of an insolvent required legal permission.
A curious legal provision, strongly indicative of the altered
times and views, was made by the Rabbins to prevent the
cessation of monetary obligations in the Sabbatical year.   It
was not only declared lawful to accept payment during that
year (if proffered), but such conduct on the part of the debtor
was declared meritorious.   It was also enacted that debts
contracted upon pledges, or secured by written documents
deposited in court, or containing an express reservation of the
right of reclaiming on the part of the creditor, technically
termed *Prosbol*, did not come within the range of the
Sabbatical remission.   The *Prosbol* was introduced by Hillel
as a means of restoring public credit.[4]   If a debtor died, the
claims of heirs took precedence of those of the creditors,
and the claims of the widow upon her dowry were those of
a creditor.[5]   Various provisions were made for the protection
of either party from fraud.   Acknowledgments of debt did not
require to contain the name of the lender, and were payable
to any party who possessed the document.   If a dying person

[1] B. Mez. x. 2. 3.   [2] B. Bath. ii. 1–13.   [3] B. Mez. x. 6.
[4] Shebiith x. 3–9.   [5] Keth. ix. 2. 3.

declared in general terms, that one amongst many outstanding loans had been repaid to him, all obligations to him became thereby invalid (on account of the doubt), but if more than one had been incurred by *one* creditor, only the largest was held to be discharged. In cases of part repayment a special receipt was granted.[1] If a party *wholly* denied a debt, he could not be constrained to swear, as the law assumed his innocence, and the burden of proof rested with the pursuer. It was otherwise when the defender admitted part of the debt. Notices of orders, etc., in a merchant's books, were admitted as partial proofs.[2]

The Jewish law arranged all occasions of damage under four classes, as those by cattle, by pits, by grazing, and by fire.[3] If a person dug a pit ten span deep, he was responsible for deterioration or loss of any animal which had fallen into it; otherwise, only for the former.[4] Anything left or spilt on the street which occasioned damage, involved responsibility. The person last engaged with an object causing damage, was held responsible, and the amount computed by competent judges.[5] If any object had been lost, or received damage, while in the temporary possession of a stranger, the law made several distinctions. If a party had been intrusted with an article, he could not be sued for damages; if he had borrowed it, he was obliged to pay damages; if it had passed out of the proprietor's hands in the way of business, the temporary owner, who had remained within the conditions of the contract, was only responsible if it had been stolen or lost.[6] A party was allowed a certain percentage for waste, if the article intrusted had been wheat ($2\frac{1}{2}$ per cent.), barley (5 per cent.), or flax (10 per cent.). A vessel must not be needlessly removed, nor any money intrusted diminish through negligence. A banker, but not a private party, was allowed to use money intrusted to him.[7] The proprietor or keeper was answerable for damage caused by his cattle, if the party injured had not exposed himself; but where such injury

---

[1] B. Bath. x. 6. 7 ; bab. *ib.* 172*a*.
[2] Shebuoth vi. 1, vii. 5.
[3] B. Kam. i. 1.   [4] *Ut supra*, v. 5.
[5] *Ut supra*, iii. 1–3, i. 2.
[6] Shebu. viii. 1 ; B. Mez. vi. 3–5, vii. 8.
[7] B. Mez. iii. 7–11.

could not have been foreseen, only half the actual damage could be claimed, and that only from the value of the injuring animal.[1] If a flock had been properly secured, the proprietor was not answerable for its breaking loose and causing damage. If a fire originated from the spark of an anvil, the party causing it was answerable. The master was not answerable for any damage caused by his slaves.[2] An article found in a public place, if possessing any value, and characteristic marks by which it might be recognised, was publicly described during three festive occasions, and for seven days after the third of these feasts.[3] But letters of divorce, of manumission, testaments, conveyances, and receipts, were not to be returned, as probably they had been purposely thrown aside.[4]

The criminal law of the Hebrews contrasts favourably, not only with that of heathen, but also of many professedly Christian nations. Much stress was laid by the Rabbins on the removal of ulterior consequences from the criminal, so that the punishment was transformed from a harsh reprobation and haughty exclusion into a kind and parental correction. The death of the criminal or the infliction of forty stripes, which in law took the place of the biblical threat of " being cut off," was supposed to atone for the crime of the penitent criminal, and to remove the crime, both in this world and in that which is to come.[5] The crime ceased with the punishment. Hence the attempt to induce the culprit to confess, the solemn and mournful conduct of the judges, and the beautiful practice, on the part of the relatives of a felon, to wait on the judges and witnesses, in order to show that they harboured no ill-feeling towards them.[6] Another equally peculiar provision of the law was that by which no person could be executed or receive forty stripes, unless the witnesses to the deed had warned the criminal, and he had persevered in his sin.[7] The punishments awarded by the Jewish law were upon the life, body,

---

[1] Gitt. v. 1 ; B. Kam. i. 1-4.   [2] B. Kam. vi. 1. 6, viii. 4.
[3] B. Mez. ii. 1-6.   [4] B. Mez. i. 7.   [5] Macc. iii. 15.
[6] Sanh. vi. 2. 6.   [7] *Ut supra*, v. 1 ; bab. *ib.* 40*b*.

and property of the criminal. Incarceration was not a Jewish mode of punishment.

The law of Moses is explicit in the mention of those crimes to which the punishment of death was to be awarded, but the Rabbinical statutes limited its exeċution in various ways. In fact, every legal device was employed to avoid this unpleasant necessity, and it was expressly stated that the court which inflicted capital punishment more frequently than once in seven, or, according to some, in seventy years, was cruel. Rabbins Tarphon and Akiba declared they would never have consented to such a sentence.[1] The Jewish law recognised four modes of execution. The party to be stoned was cast by one of the witnesses from a height, after which (if he was not dead) a second witness threw the first stone at him. If this punishment had been inflicted for blasphemy or idolatry, the body was hung up till even. There were different places of interment destined for criminals, and their relatives were not to mourn for them.[2] Burning was generally executed by pouring boiling lead into the criminal. Decapitation was performed with the sword. Strangulation was the ordinary punishment, and executed with a cord wrapped in a cloth, and drawn together by two persons.[3] From the punishment threatened in John viii. 5 we gather that the adulteress there accused had not been actually married, but was only a bride. When the criminal was led to the place of execution,—which always took place on the day of his condemnation,—a herald going before him called upon all who might be able to say anything in his favour to appear before the judges, and the criminal was allowed to urge anything in his own behalf. When near to the place of punishment, he was admonished to confess and repent.[4] On Sabbaths or feast-days, and on the days of preparation, capital offences could not be tried.[5] If the punishment of forty stripes had been twice inflicted, the criminal was on a third occasion confined into a narrow prison, and fed first upon very spare diet, then on barley bread, until "his

---

[1] Macc. i. 10.   [2] Sanh. vi. 4. 6.   [3] *Ut supra*, vii. 2. 3.
[4] *Ut supra*, vi. 1. 2.   [5] Beza v. 2 ; Sanh. iv. 1.

bowels gushed out." Spare diet was also used when a murderer escaped capital sentence through non-observance of any legal form.[1]

The different degrees of ecclesiastical censure were called *Neziphah* or reproof, which lasted only for seven days, *Niddui* or *Shammatha*, denoting a temporary excommunication, and *Cherem* or bann, that is, permanent exclusion from the congregation.[2] The punishments executed on the body of the criminal consisted in the infliction of stripes, the largest number being forty, or in practice thirty-nine, from a dread of inflicting one in excess, it being always first ascertained that the culprit was able to bear his sentence. The instrument used was a scourge of leathern thongs. The hands of the criminal, who was in an inclined position, were tied to a pillar, and two-thirds of the stripes inflicted on the shoulders, the rest on the chest. During the infliction, Deut. xxviii. 58 and 59, xxix. 9, and at the close Ps. lxxviii. 38, were read to the criminal.[3] Later Jewish writers recount 207 cases in which forty stripes were to be inflicted. The fines prescribed in the law of Moses were so far modified by the Mishna, that no actual fine (only simple restitution) was required when the criminal confessed his fault of his own accord. However, under no circumstances was an individual incriminated by any statement of his own, nor could such be used against him.[4] As a general principle, severe punishments were only inflicted where amendment, restitution, etc., was in the nature of the thing impossible. The Rabbins recount thirty-four breaches of forbids and two of commands which expose to the threat of "being cut off,"[5] a punishment in their opinion more severe than that of sudden death by the hand of God. Corporal punishments were inflicted by the officers of the various synagogues.[6] In exceptional cases, the law warranted those present at the perpetration of a crime to execute summary vengeance.[7]

---

[1] Sanh. ix. 5.
[2] Comp. Buxtorf, *in verba*, and Schürer, II. ii. 60 f.
[3] Macc. iii. 10–14.   [4] Keth. iii. 9.   [5] Kerith. i. 1. 2.
[6] Macc. iii. 12.   [7] Sanh. ix. 6.

In general, the Jewish law assumed the innocence of every party till actual and intentional guilt had been established, nor, while declaring the rendering of testimony meritorious, did it oblige any person to lay information.[1] The most fearful crime was that of blasphemy, which was only then supposed to have been committed if the ineffable name of Jehovah had been used. That name had originally been generally known, and was, in certain defined circumstances, still pronounced. In cases of accusations of blasphemy all present were removed, and the judges asked the worthiest amongst the witnesses to repeat what they had heard; the others simply assented. The judges then rent their garments in token of mourning, and the convicted party was stoned.[2] The Mosaic law, which ordered the extermination of a city whose inhabitants had become idolators, was limited by the Rabbins to instances in which the *majority* of the inhabitants had been seduced by parties belonging to the same town and tribe.[3] Direct acts of idolatry, witchcraft, or having a familiar spirit, were punished by stoning; intentional profanation of the Sabbath deserved stoning; the breach of other ritual ordinances, forty stripes.[4] A false prophet, *i.e.* one who prophesied without having received a divine message, or who delivered what had been sent by another prophet, or spake in the name of a strange god, was to be strangled.[5]

The Rabbins also distinguished between casual and unintentional homicide; manslaughter, where there had been an intention to hurt but not to destroy; and murder, which implied premeditation and the infliction of blows or wounds in themselves mortal, and from which escape would have been impossible. *Only* in the last-mentioned case was the murderer executed.[6] During the investigation every party accused had a right to go for safety to one of the cities of refuge, under the escort of two Rabbins.[7] If death issued in consequence of a quarrel and fight, the murderer was

---

[1] Sanh. iv. 5. [2] Sanh. vii. 5. [3] *Ut supra*, xi. 4.
[4] *Ut supra*, vii. 4. 6–8 ; Macc. iii. 1–4. [5] Sanh. x. 1. 5–6.
[6] *Ut supra* ix. 1. 2. [7] Macc. ii. 5.

executed if the blow given was in itself sufficient to induce immediate death. Any person about to commit murder, unnatural crimes, or to violate a bride, might lawfully be killed.[1] Where fatal injury had been sustained from an animal, the animal was stoned; and the proprietor, if previously warned of its dangerous character, had to pay the computed value of the party killed, and, in the case of slaves, thirty shekels, whatever might be the real value of the slave.[2] If a murder was committed, and the perpetrator unknown, a deputation, consisting of five members of the Sanhedrin, performed, along with the elders of the township nearest to the place of murder, certain prescribed solemnities, after which the latter were declared free of the blame of official negligence.[3] In cases of suicide the body remained uninterred till even.[4] Persons guilty of men-stealing were strangled, if the party stolen had actually been brought within the domain of the accused.[5]

In cases of theft the punishment was restitution, with the addition of double or five-fold the value of the article stolen. In order to constitute theft, the article must have actually been lifted up or removed from the boundaries of the owner. Thus a thief who killed and then sold an animal on the property of its rightful owner was only bound to make restitution.[6] Nor did the law of compensation apply to the theft of slaves, documents, immovable property, or things dedicated.[7] A thief who voluntarily confessed, under whatever circumstances, was only bound to make restitution.[8] If perjury had been committed to conceal the theft, when the article stolen was restored, it must be accompanied by an addition of one-fifth of its value, and handed to the proprietor in person, and that however trifling the article or distant his place of residence, so that his forgiveness might be obtained.[9] Tradesmen, as tailors, carpenters, etc., were interdicted from retaining any of the material intrusted to

---

[1] Sanh. viii. 7.   [2] B. Kam. iv. 5.   [3] Sota ix. 1–6.
[4] Jos. *Wars*, iii. 8. 5.   [5] Sanh. x. 1.   [6] B. Kam. vii. 5. 6.
[7] B. Mez. iv. 9.   [8] Shebu. viii. 4.
[9] B. Kam. ix. 5; B. Mez. iv. 7.

them. To prevent temptation, it was also forbidden to buy wool, milk, or young animals from a shepherd; fruits or trees from a hired gardener, etc.[1] If the thief had not the means of paying the legal fine, he might be sold, but not beyond the bounds of Palestine. Females could not be sold.[2]

The witnesses who intentionally bare false witness were ordinarily visited with the punishment which would have been awarded to the accused party. In exceptional cases this was converted into a fine or the infliction of forty stripes. Where the charge was capital, and sentence had actually been pronounced, the witnesses were liable to death.[3] The various crimes connected with oaths were arranged into inconsiderate, needless, and criminal swearing—the latter when a party either denied his knowledge of, or refused to mention a favourable circumstance—and perjury; all of which were more or less severely punished. In all these cases a simple " Amen," in answer to adjuration, was deemed an oath.[4]

Rabbinical ordinances, as in all other crimes so in respect of adultery also, tended to lighten the law of Moses. The evidence of two witnesses was requisite to establish the crime.[5] If a woman had married again, after having received false tidings of her husband's death, both her first and second husband had to divorce her with the loss of her dowry, and the offspring of her second marriage was deemed illegitimate.[6] Rabbi Jochanan ben Saccai abolished the practice of administering the waters of jealousy, on account, as he said, of the frequency of adultery.[7] This mode of detection, which was supposed not to act immediately when the woman's merits partly atoned for her guilt, could only be used after the husband had, in the presence of two witnesses, admonished his wife to abstain from intercourse with a suspected party. One witness, even a slave or a maid, was

---

[1] B. Kam. x. 9. 10.

[2] Sota iii. 8. Comp. Jos. *Ant.* xvi. 1. 1. [A law of Herod allowed house-breakers to be sold into foreign countries, and this was regarded as an act of tyranny.]

[3] Macc. i. 1–6.   [4] Shebu. iii.–v., viii.   [5] Sota vi. 3.

[6] Jeb. x. i.   [7] Sota ix. 9.

sufficient evidence in cases of actual adultery after admonition, when a woman might be divorced with the loss of her dowry, except when the witness against her was a near female relative of her husband.[1] In cases of seduction a threefold, in rape a fourfold fine had to be paid. While the seducer was free, the father of the damsel might in the latter case insist also on marriage, which could not again be dissolved.[2] The strict biblical law concerning criminal resistance to parents was almost rendered nugatory by Rabbinical additions. Thus the parents were to be perfectly agreed in their accusation; neither of them was to be decrepit, blind, deaf, lame, etc. The son must once before have been judicially punished by stripes, and have reached the age of puberty; finally, the law could only be applied during a period of about three months.[3] Cursing parents—whether living or dead—was punished by stoning; striking, if traces of the ill-usage had been left, by strangulation. Insubordination to magistrates was severely punished, and, if committed by a judge who had taught or acted against the decision of the Supreme College, he was to be executed in Jerusalem, and at the time of one of the feasts.[4]

The office of judge was generally filled by the learned and doctors of the Law. It had no immediate or necessary connection with the office of teaching, [and probably in small towns the judges were often men who had been chosen through the confidence of their fellow-citizens, but who had never attained the position of a regularly ordained Rabbi]. Nevertheless, from the nature of the case, the ablest teachers were generally selected as judges. [After the fall of the Jewish State the influence of the Rabbins greatly increased; and though there was no external power to enforce their authority, it became more than ever the custom to appeal to their decision in matters of dispute.[5]] The law distinguished three classes of judges, according to the size and importance of the place in which they resided. The lowest court was that of three, or possibly seven judges,[6] the next that of the

---

[1] Sota i. 1. 2, vi. 2. 3. [2] Keth. iii. 4. 5. [3] Sanh. viii. 1–4.
[4] *Ut supra*, x. 1–4. [5] Comp. Schürer, II. i. 326f. [6] *Vid. sup.* p. 106.

Sanhedrin of twenty-three, and the highest that of seventy-one, or the Great Sanhedrin.[1] The judges of the highest court were regularly ordained by the imposition of hands. This solemnity was performed by an ordained Rabbi, in the presence of at least two others.[2] The number of judges in the various colleges of justice was uneven, in case of diversity of opinion.[3] In a capital conviction, which could only be passed by a Sanhedrin, a majority of at least two was requisite, and sentence was only pronounced after a night spent in solemn deliberation had passed.[4] In cases of dubiety assessors might be chosen. Besides these colleges of regular judges, parties might choose three judges or arbiters to decide in cases of dispute.[5] In Jerusalem, besides the Great Sanhedrin, there are said to have been two other Sanhedrins of twenty-three. The power of appealing to higher courts lay with the judges, if they were not sure of their sentence, or in pecuniary matters with the accusing party.[6] The judges were not in receipt of any regular salary, but were compensated for any loss of time.[7] Any communication with the parties, or favouritism, disqualified a judge from pronouncing sentence. The candidates for the senatorial office were required to be of good report, learned, grave, not engaged in any degrading or sinful occupation, to be married and to have children, not to be either too young or too old.[8] Even the high-priest was subject to the jurisdiction of the Sanhedrin, but kings were neither members of the Sanhedrin nor subject to its authority.[9] The regular times for meetings of the local courts were the second and the fifth days of the week, [but it is not known whether this was also the case with the supreme Sanhedrin at Jerusalem [10]]. The ordinary hours for the sitting of the court were from after the morning sacrifice till the time of the meal.[11] The judges were not allowed to communicate to parties on which side they had voted.[12]

---

[1] Sanh. i. 1–6. Consult generally, Selden, *de Synedriis Ebr.*
[2] Sanh. i. 3; bab. *ib.* 13*b*.   [3] Sota ix. 1.   [4] Sanh. iv. 1.
[5] Sanh. iii. 1.   [6] *Ut supra*, xi. 2 ; bab. *ib.* 31 *b*.
[7] Bechor. iv. 6.   [8] Sanh. 17*a*, 36*b*.
[9] Sanh. ii. 1. 2.   [10] Keth. i. 1.
[11] Shab. 10*a*.   [12] Sanh. iii. 7.

Perfectly distinct from ordination to the office of judge was that to the office of Rabbi or teacher, or, as it was expressed, for " loosing and binding." [1]   Sages set apart for one office were indeed generally supposed to be qualified for the other also, but in theory and in practice a distinction was made between the two.   The Rabbi set apart " to loose or bind " might authoritatively declare what was binding on the conscience and what not, and in Talmudical writings the phrase continually recurs by which a teacher or a school is said to *loose* or to *bind, i.e.* to declare something obligatory or non-obligatory—a licence or ordination which was afterwards conferred by the Saviour upon all His disciples, acting under the guidance of His Holy Spirit. [2]

In all criminal, and even in most civil cases, the testimony of at least two witnesses was requisite.   Parties interested, enemies, men or women related to parties, minors, slaves, heathens, robbers, felons, usurers, gamblers, and publicans, as well as idiots, etc., were incapable of bearing witness. [3]   Witnesses were adjured by the parties at the bar ; they were strictly examined concerning the time, place, and circumstances of the crime, and the slightest disagreement between them annulled the whole testimony. [4]   If the judges did not understand the language of any of the witnesses, they were not allowed to engage the services of an interpreter, and, if dubious concerning their veracity, the case had to be heard again before another court. [5]   The law distinguished three kinds of oaths which might be exacted from the parties at the bar,—that according to Biblical, according to Mishnic, and according to Gemaric ordinance. The first was made by a party suspected of unfaithfulness, by a defendant who had admitted a claim in part, and by one against whom only *one* witness had testified.   The second was made by the *pursuer* in a cause where other sufficient proof was wanting.   The third form of oath was introduced at a later period for all other disputed cases, and

---

[1] Comp. Selden, *ut supra,* lib. II. c. 7, ii.
[2] Comp. *Life and Times,* ii. 85.   [3] Sanh. iii. 1. 3–5.
[4] Sanh. v. 1–3.   [5] Macc. i. 9 ; Shebu. 30*b.*

for testing witnesses.[1] Finally, a legal provision denominated
" Miggo," *in consideration of,* declared that a favourable presumption attended the party who admitted a fact, which,
if fraud had been intended, might have been concealed by
him.[2]

We have already hinted that the priests themselves
attended to the duties of temple police, and decided in all
purely priestly questions.[3] Any further details on this
subject would necessarily lead us to an extended sketch of a
former period. We therefore close this account of the state
of the Hebrew nation by a brief exposition of their Theology,
with its kindred sciences.

[It has already been hinted more than once that the law
laid down in the Mishna frequently represents the theories
and speculations of the Jewish doctors of the second century,
and not the actual practice of any given period. Several
of their regulations deal accordingly with obsolete customs,
and have little regard to the actual circumstances of the
time. The truth of this statement may be illustrated by
sundry passages in the above sketch of the traditionary
law, as, for example, the principles laid down respecting the
nations of Canaan and the Noachic Commandments (p. 362),
the jubilee (p. 363), the cities of refuge (p. 375), the king
(p. 379), and the penalty of death. When Judea became a
Roman province, the power of life and death was taken away
from the Jewish courts.]

[1] Ex. xxii. 11 ; Shebu. vi. 1 ff.; *ib.* vii. 1–5 ; bab. *ib.* 40*b*, 41*a*.
[2] Shebu. 42*a*.   [3] Comp. Schürer, II. i. 264 ff.

CHAPTER XI

THEOLOGICAL SCIENCE AND RELIGIOUS BELIEF IN PALESTINE

I. *Interpretation of Scripture*

IF any person conversant only with the inspired writings were to transport his preconceived ideas into the relations which existed at the time of the Saviour's advent, and to expect that the Synagogue had any system of doctrines regularly elaborated into a confession of faith, an examination into the actual state of matters would soon convince him of his mistake. Only on two dogmatic points, directly connected with the Bible, were the Rabbins agreed,—the being and unity of God, and the claims of the Scriptures to implicit belief and obedience. On almost every other article of faith, and on many of the duties incumbent on members of the Synagogue, we have nothing but the isolated and often discordant opinions of the sages. It is, therefore, comparatively easy for friends and enemies of the Synagogue to find in these various statements proofs of what either approaches to gospel teaching, or of what not only contradicts it, but is opposed to sound reason, right feeling, and the acknowledged codes of morality. All such inferences are equally unsatisfactory. It must be borne in mind that the statements of individual Rabbins are not the deliberate verdicts of the Synagogue ; that they were not uttered as the result of professed investigations of the subjects on which they treat ; and are hence at most to be taken as indications of the prevalence of certain tendencies amongst the Rabbins, and of the currency of certain religious ideas amongst the people.[1]

In its general aspect Judaism was a vast system of rationalism, in which the only settled thing was the letter of the Law, the text of the Commandments. The meaning and application of the latter formed subject of inquiry. This rigid adherence to the letter, and the attempt to apply it to all conceivable relations, introduced the principles of traditionalism. At first propounded with a desire to apply the text of the Law in agreement with the wants of the times, and in accordance with the wisdom of the Fathers, this principle rapidly developed. Gradually men sought not so much to elicit from the text, as to introduce into it, the principles of their peculiar schools or the decrees of the Synagogue.

It is a point of great importance in the study of Judaism generally, and of traditionalism in particular, to bear in mind that the outward observances, and not the doctrines of the Bible, formed the subject of authoritative teaching, Every separate traditional legal ordinance was termed a " Halacha." The Halachas, or traditional ordinances, in their scientific arrangement, constituted the Mishna, or Deuterosis (traditional or Second Law), of which the Talmud or Gemara was the commentary, the explanation, illustration, and application. But as traditionalism itself was understood to be not so much an addition to, as a paraphrastic comment on the Bible, it was early felt necessary to connect the Halacha with the text of Scripture. The latter was to remain the basis of all teaching in the Synagogue, from which the Mishna was to be evolved, or with which it was at least to be organically connected. At the same time traditionalism, which, either in its principles or in its ordinances, was traced through the Fathers to God, was declared inspired, or rather of Divine authority, and, as the infallible and authoritative explanation of the requirements

---

[1] Hence, while we repudiate not only the conclusion, but also the spirit of certain enemies of the Jews, such as Eisenmenger, Wagenseil, and their successors, we cannot wholly admit the bearing of the reasonings even of some friends of the Jews, such as Macaulay and Oxlee.

of Scripture, was in some sense superior to them, and at all events required more careful study, and demanded more implicit obedience.

It may at first appear strange that the outward ordinances of the Bible should have exclusively formed the subject of teaching in the Synagogue; but, leaving out of consideration the fact that they frequently formed the distinguishing mark which separated the Jews from the heathen around them, these ordinances, and the books from which they were derived, occupied in the mind of the Hebrews a peculiar position. Although all Scripture was divinely inspired, the Jews distinguished three kinds, or at least degrees, of heavenly teaching. Only to Moses (in the law) had God spoken face to face. The Prophets were indeed under the direction of the Spirit of God, but their inspiration was different in kind from that of Moses. In fact, great teachers and commentators were to some extent subjects of a similar inspiration. The third kind of Divine direction, applying specially to traditionalism, was the " Bath-Kol," " daughter-voice," perhaps the echo of the voice which Moses had heard, to which we have already referred. If the law (the Pentateuch) was thus separated from all other portions of Scripture, as inspired in its letters, sounds, and signs, so that not a stroke, particle, or preposition in it could possibly be in vain, or without special meaning, nor a figure or rhetorical illustration be found in it, a somewhat similar view was taken of the ritual observances contained in it. These were neither symbolic nor temporary, but constituted the substance of religion, were in themselves right, and of eternal obligation. This confusion of the moral with the ceremonial law, which ran through all Judaism, and made it all ceremonial, led to startling and even blasphemous inferences. As legal observances were eternal, and in themselves right and binding, not only had Abraham, Abimelech, and even Adam himself practised them,[1] but they were the

---

[1] Joma 28b; Sanh. 38a. We refer here generally to Dr. Hirschfeld's works on the Halacha and the Hagada, to the classical production of Dr. Zunz, *Gottesd. Vortr. d. Jüden*, [and to F. Weber's *System der Altsynagogalen Palästin. Theologie*].

law of heaven itself. Bound by these legal determinations, God, who, according to the notion of the Rabbins, even wore the phylacteries, had, against His inclination, felt obliged to take the sceptre from Judah. The court of heaven was turned into a Synagogue, and it was thought that God Himself could not improve upon the dicta of the Rabbins, which were eternal truth, but felt bound to decide accordingly. He studied the Bible, consulted the opinions of the Rabbins, and had theological discussions with His angels.[1] [However, the Rabbins did make practical distinctions between their own ordinances and the plain and express injunctions of Scripture. Transgression of the former usually involved less serious consequences to the offender, and it was acknowledged to be a graver offence if a teacher of the Law supported an erroneous doctrine by Scripture, than if he merely appealed to tradition.[2]] It certainly seems unaccountable that, with this adherence to the ordinances of the Pentateuch, the Synagogue could have ever reconciled itself to the abrogation of sacrifices. But it requires to be borne in mind that this was not only a stern necessity, but that, in the course of its complete development, traditionalism had by that time reached the pole opposite to literalism, that of pure rationalism.

To connect the Halacha with the text of Scripture, was the first and principal task of Jewish theologians. That problem once solved, traditionalism rested on a secure basis. Hillel the Great, Nahum of Gimso, Nechunjah, Ishmael ben Elisa, but specially Akiba, had attempted to accomplish this. Unlike the Hagadist, whose teaching had no absolute authority in doctrine or practice, and who, therefore, might be allowed more loosely to import his lessons into, to intertwine them with, or to lean them upon Scripture, the connection between the Halacha and the Bible had to be established on clear and definite exegetical principles, which in turn gave rise to the " Middoth," or exegetical canons of these Rabbins, which are the condensed formulæ of their exegetical methods.

A Halacha might be derived from Scripture in various ways. It was first sought directly to gather it from a plain

---

[1] Gitt. 6*b*.   [2] Gen. Rab. c. 7 ; Para xi. 4. 5.   Comp. Weber, p. 99 f.

and natural interpretation of a text, it being, however, understood that for this purpose it was not necessary to consult a
text in its connection, but that any portion of a verse torn
out of its natural context was sufficient to establish a
Halacha.

In the absence of a simple scriptural proof, logical
inductions or deductions were attempted. If such were
impossible, a superfluous letter, word, or particle, or something unusual in the mode of expression, was laid hold of, or a
transposition, omission, or change of letters attempted, in all
which, however, " wont and custom " formed a chief element
of determination. When all these means failed, Scripture was
used as a *point d'appui*, as a mere means of support to the
Halacha.[1]

In the Hagada, which was the second branch of Jewish
theology, a sage was not fettered by legal determinations. It
allowed an unlimited display of Talmudical ingenuity and wit,
and hence gradually swallowed up other studies. Like the
Halacha, the Hagada took the Bible for its foundation, and
presented commentaries, translations, paraphrases, legends,
moral sayings, philosophical views, sermons, etc., in connection
with it. Here also the Pentateuch was held to be pre-eminently
Divine. As Philo claimed inspiration for the LXX.,[2] so the
Talmud for some of the Targums, or paraphrastic versions.[3]
The theological predilections of the Hagadists, in fact, varied
from the most material and often coarse literalism to a
spiritualism, which is sometimes wholly ideal, at others
introduces the abstractions of heathen philosophy. As the
Hagada was intended to explain and apply the hidden meaning
of the text, two tendencies became manifest in it. It was
either attempted to explain—sometimes to play upon—
merely the words of a passage, or else to elicit the secrets not
of its letter but of its contents,—in short, the doctrines and
spiritual facts which the text either indicated, or to which it
alluded. The former of these tendencies we may distinguish
as the Talmudic, the latter as the Gnostic Hagada. Both

---

[1] For a fuller account of the methods of Rabbinic exegesis, see App. VII.
[2] *De Vita Mosis*, ii. p. 140.   [3] Meg. 3a.

were identical in their fundamental idea, and both spiritualised and ultimately discarded the text of Scripture. It needs no demonstration that the Gnostic Hagada was in reality such only in form. Necessarily, it was the fundamental principle of every Hagadic mode of interpretation that a number of diverse comments might lawfully be attached to one and the same passage of Scripture. Nevertheless the Hagada remained only the personal saying of the individual teacher, whose authority depended upon his learning and reputation, or on the distinguished names which he could quote in his support. [The only checks upon the individual fancy were a kind of exegetical tradition, and the necessity of making the exegesis agree on the whole with accepted Jewish ideas.[1]] The means used by the Hagadist for eliciting the meaning of the text were, simple study of the expressions, of any hint which the text afforded, investigation of the contents of the passage, or an attempt at directly ascertaining its mysterious import. These various methods are together termed *Pardes*, a word formed by the contraction of the initial letters into one word.[2] [The party of the Sadducees, which had been supported by the influence of the priestly nobles, disappeared from history at the fall of Jerusalem. There was, therefore, now no party to offer real resistence to the tendency of the Rabbins, for the differences among the Schools related only to minor points, and not to the general principles of interpretation.]

The student of Scripture was enjoined to begin his studies with prayer, to prosecute them with zeal, and to pay due attention to the guidance of properly authorised teachers.[3] Frequently the Hagada introduced foreign ideas and subjects into the sacred text, by way of illustrating the Scriptures, or of independently establishing the points elicited from the text. Proverbs, fables, and witticisms were brought forward as exegetical auxiliaries, and the scientific notions of the times were freely referred to. Thus it was said that the attraction of the magnet had been taken advantage of by Gehazi, in order to make the idolatrous calves ascend, so as to lead Israel to

---

[1] Comp. Weber, pp. x. f.; 95 f. Erub. 54*b*; Chag. 15*b*.

[2] Comp. Schürer. II. i. 348.

adore them ;[1] or that the firmament was formed by mingling together fire and water. Any historical references were generally grossly erroneous and absurd. Thus it was asserted that Romulus had reigned over the whole world, that Alexander had made an expedition to Carthage,[2] etc. Even with respect to Palestine curious legends were current, such as that at one time it had been 400 miles square, that since the Exile it had shrunk like a deer's skin, etc.[3] Even heathen myths were introduced, and mixed up with biblical histories. Thus, when Esau embraced Jacob, the neck of the latter became marble ; [and in the Midrashim we meet with several stories which are evidently derived from well-known classical legends [4]]. We meet also with other heathen notions. Some Hagadists spoke, like Platonists, of original ideas, prototypes, etc. ; others observed and interpreted numbers, like the Pythagoreans. At the same time all these views were professedly derived from Scripture, and for this purpose figurative expressions were explained literally, and *vice versâ*. By such quotations the exact powers of fire were, for example, described, the nature and progress of the wind defined, geographical names explained, the number of worlds fixed at 18,000, etc.[5] Sometimes the reins were given to imagination, and the appearance, etc., of a leviathan described ; at others, with voluptuousness and even obscenity, passages of Scripture were distorted, and particulars elicited vastly different from those meant by the inspired penman. Historical allusions were frequently enlarged and spiritualised, and allegorical interpretations introduced. Thus in the Targum the Song of Solomon becomes an allegory of Jehovah's dealings with Israel.

Still, as the Halacha had its seven and its thirteen Middoth, so even the Hagada proceeded on defined principles. Certain peculiarities of the Hebrew language admitted different interpretations. Thus, as the second person masculine of the future sounds like the third feminine, the one was exchanged for the other ; and the command to Noah to

---

[1] Sanh. 107*b*.   [2] Levit. Rab. 27.   [3] Gitt. 57*a*.
[4] Comp. Hamburger, *Enc.* Suppl., "Sage," p. 128 f.
[5] Joma 21*b* ; B. Bath. 25*b* ; Ab. Sar. 3*b*.

make the ark was interpreted that the ark made itself.[1] The letter which indicates comparison was made to intimate apparent but not real similarity, as when Israel is compared to Sodom, etc. Where any distinct purpose was to be served, the rules of grammar and construction were directly violated. Again, with no other purpose than that of giving a striking or clever comment, letters were changed. Even the order and shape of the letters themselves gave rise to Hagadic sayings. Ordinarily, the exact meaning of words was determined by sometimes valuable traditions; but if necessary, an unusual application of a term was devised. Words were separated into two, or explained by other and similarly sounding words. Sometimes they were traced to cognate languages, or their meaning elicited from parallel passages. Similarly the slightest hint was eagerly watched, and the proper vowel-points (the Hebrew being written only with the consonants) or the connection set aside. The first letter of the alphabet was exchanged for the last, the second for the one before the last,[2] etc., or the twenty-two letters divided into *two* parts, and the first interchanged with the twelfth, the second with the thirteenth, etc. Still more arbitrary methods were "gematria," by which the numerical value of the letters was ascertained, and the text interpreted accordingly; and "notarikon," by which every letter of a word was made the initial letter of a new word.[3] Everything good and high was always connected with God, the name "Jehovah" indicating His grace—that of "Elohim" His justice. The repetition of a name, a promise, or a blessing was viewed as an omen for good.

Upon principles like these, thirty-two exegetical rules for the Hagada were propounded by Joses ha-Gelili. Without enumerating them, we may say in general, that besides the substance of the thirteen Halachic Middoth, they referred to gematria, notarikon, transposition and exchange of letters, division of words, explanation of particles, rearrangement of sentences, inferences from the context, or from the subjects

---

[1] Gen. Rab. c. 31.   [2] The principle of "Atbash"; comp. Shab. 104*a*.
[3] Comp. Weber, p. 118 ff.

treated in it, general applications of similes employed and of statements made in a particular passage, reference of things to more suitable subjects, selection of most suitable things, application of numbers, etc.

In order to remove difficulties, the text had often to be supplemented, and dialogues between biblical persons, as between Nadab and Abihu, between Joshua and Achan, between Solomon and the Queen of Sheba, and even the riddles which she propounded to him, were introduced.[1] In fact, everything that could possibly be twisted into a difficulty was made subject of lengthened discussion, sometimes at the expense of common decency. Anything marvellous in the text became legendary in the commentary. Thus, the haunch-bone of Og was three miles in extent, and afforded room for hunting deer ;[2] Samson reduced two mountains to powder by rubbing them against each other ;[3] gems fell from heaven along with the manna, etc. Again, ingenious reasons were assigned for certain statements, or an exact analogy was traced between man's conduct and the Divine government. At all times the biblical favourites of the Hagadists were magnified, while their opponents were vilified in the same ratio. Thus Moses was so beautiful, that all the husbands were jealous of him. He was perfect; his face was like the sun, his stature ten cubits, etc.[4] Aaron's sin is excused. Reuben had not really committed incest, but only obliged his father to live with Leah, by depriving him of Bilhah.[5] David did not commit actual adultery with Bath-Sheba, as all soldiers had to divorce their wives, etc. On the other hand, Laban had only embraced Jacob in order to feel about his person whether he had brought any treasures with him. Esau had made only a pretext of disinterestedness with Jacob,[6] etc. Upon the same ground many stories were invented. Remarkable results were obtained by the combination of divers passages and events. Thus, when Jacob kissed Rachel, and wept, it was because he foresaw that they would not

---

[1] Sanh. 43b ; Targ. ii on Esther.   [2] Nidda 24b.
[3] Sota 9b.   [4] Moed K. 18b ; B. Bath. 75a ; Bechor. 44a.
[5] Shab. 55b.   [6] Gen. Rab. ad loca.

rest in the same grave.[1] When Potiphar's wife set her eyes upon Joseph, it was because she foresaw that Ephraim and Manasseh were to descend from her, for Asenath, Joseph's wife, was her daughter. Leah's eyes were weak from weeping, because she thought that, being the elder, she was destined to be the wife of Esau, etc.[2] In the same way the different portions of Scripture were combined, and all religious ordinances were shown to be implicit in the Ten Commandments.

Again, Halachic laws were applied to biblical times and events. Thus, after the death of Methuselah,[1] God waited the seven days of mourning before sending the flood. Abraham Rabbinically examined the knife before proceeding to immolate Isaac. On the other hand, because Jacob rent his garments, every mourner was bound to do the same ; because Job's friends sat on the ground, others must do likewise in similar circumstances. Long before the Law was given on Sinai, choice spirits had prosecuted its study. Shem and Eber had an academy, in which Jacob studied up to his fourteenth year.[3] Elisha, Manasseh, and David were engaged with particular branches of the Halacha, some of them not very edifying.[4] It was in this way that Boaz ascertained that he might wed a Moabitess. Jonathan, the grandchild of Moses, had, by a misunderstanding of a Halacha, been induced to become priest to Micah's idol ; but, being better informed by the sages, he gave it up.[5] When David was fleeing before Absalom, he was uncertain whether he should not worship idols, in order to induce others to suppose his misfortunes a consequence of his apostasy.[6] Haman disputed with Mordecai about the rights of master and slave ; David with Saul about the law of marriage ; and their different views are manifest in their conduct towards Michal.[7]

The Hagadic statements about the Canon of Scripture add little to our knowledge. It was said that Moses wrote the Pentateuch, the book of Balaam (perhaps his Prophecies)

---

[1] Gen. Rab. *ad loca.*
[2] B. Bath. 123*a.*
[3] Gen. Rab. c. 63 ; Mid. Cant. on iv.
[4] Sota 47*a* ; Sanh. 103*b.*
[5] B. Bath. 110*a.*   [6] Sanh. 107*a.*
[7] Sanh. 19*b.*

and Job; Joshua, the work that bears his name, and the last eight verses of Deuteronomy; Samuel, the corresponding books, Judges and Ruth; David, at the direction of the "ten elders," Adam, Melchisedek, Abraham, Moses, Haman, Jeduthun, Asaph, and the three sons of Korah, the book of Psalms; Jeremiah wrote his Prophecies, Lamentations, and Kings; King Hezekiah and his college wrote the Prophecies of Isaiah, Proverbs, the Song, and Ecclesiastes; and the men of the Great Synagogue the Prophecies of Ezekiel, of the Twelve Minor Prophets, and the books of Daniel and Esther; Ezra wrote his book and the genealogies of Chronicles down to his own time, that work being completed by Nehemiah. The last verses of Joshua were written by Eleazar and Phinehas, the last chapters of Samuel by Gad and Nathan.[1]

The discourse or sermon also belonged to the Hagadic productions. Its object was mainly practical: it expounded some difficult Halacha, or enforced some important duty. It frequently contained witticisms, parables, etc., in order to keep up the attention. Such discourses were delivered on solemn or festive occasions. We have elsewhere given specimens of fragments of funeral orations, and now present one on the duty of sobriety from Lev. x. 9: "Do not drink wine or strong drink."[2] Why is wine interdicted? Because those who drink it have wounds, sorrow, and shame; for the Holy Spirit says (Prov. xxiii. 29, etc.), "Who hath woe," etc. The meaning of these verses is as follows: Who hath woe and sorrow? he that is contentious. To whom does this point but to him who has wounds and redness of eyes, who tarries at the wine? Look not upon the wine, for blood comes at last (in our version, it is red). Blood looks bright, but it contains mischief. Do not think that wine is as fair within as it is without, for the toper looks into the cup, but the giver into the purse (a play upon the word "cup" in the original, and a slight change in its translation). He that looks into his neighbour's cup to

---

[1] B. Bath. 14*b*, 15*a*.
[2] Tanchuma viii. p. 154. Compare Hirscheld's *Hagada*, p. 504, etc.

seek wine for himself, covers himself with filth and then goes to law (again a play upon the words of the original); he sells all his gear, remains without children or garments, and with an empty house; he walks in plains (a play upon the word in verse 31, "aright"), he sets himself loose and into the ways of sin. He talks openly with strange women, utters bold speeches, uses bad words, and loses all sense of decency (verse 33). He is confused, and does not know what he does or what he thinks. At the last it biteth like a serpent (verse 32), *i.e.* the lust of the wine bites in that manner, for the bite of an adder also is not felt at once, but when you reach your home the wound will fester. It as certainly bites as a serpent; and as the earth was cursed on account of the serpent, so Canaan on account of wine (Gen. ix. 25),—Canaan, one of the sons of Noah, hence the third part of the world. Thine eye shall behold strangers ("strange women," verse 33); it shall behold strange gods (Ps. lxxxi. 9), for wine is the occasion of idolatry; as it is said (Isa. xxviii. 7), "They also have erred through wine, and through strong drink are out of the way." When did they err? when they said (Ex. xxxii. 8), "These be thy gods, O Israel"; but on that occasion the people ate and drank and rose up to play; it was therefore through wine that they thus erred. Thine heart shall utter perverse things; wine is the occasion of idolatry, incest, and murder, for wine makes a man to transgress (Hab. ii. 5). A word there used is also applied to the proud (Prov. xxi. 24); and the same term, "proud," is in other passages applied to idolaters, incestuous persons, and murderers. Beware, therefore, of wine; if you drink too much of it, you see the world like a bark (verses 34, 35). You are made to lie down in it, they beat you and you feel it not, and yet you say, "When I shall awake I will seek it again." Woe to those who drink wine, says the Lord (Isa. v. 11). Join them not, beware of wine (in Hebrew the letters of the word "wine" are equal to seventy), lest the seventy elders see you, for the drunkard was brought before the Sanhedrin (Deut. xxi. 18, etc.). Wine is called Chomer in Aramaic, the numerical value of which is 248,

which is exactly the number of bones in the body.   For wine
penetrates into every member, weakens the body, and robs us
of consciousness.   Where wine goes *in* the secret goes *out*,
for the numerical value of the words " wine " and " secret "
are the same.   A drunkard does not retain his reason, hence
the Lord issued the command of the text, which is a perpetual
law.   But the Lord tells Israel that wine is only in *this*
world a sign of the curse.   In that which is to come He is
to change the wine into *new* wine (which does not intoxicate),
and " the mountains shall drop down new wine, and the hills
shall flow with milk, and a fountain shall come forth out of
the house of the Lord " (Joel iii. 18).   However absurd it may
appear, the above is rather a favourable specimen of a Hagadic
sermon.   Of the manner of delivery by means of an Emora or
Methurgeman, we have already spoken in another place.[1]

The various versions of, and commentaries on, the Old
Testament are objects of equal interest to the scholar and
the Bible student, as not only expressing the views of the
writers and their contemporaries, but often embodying
valuable traditions of former centuries.   It is interesting and
important to know how certain passages of the Bible were
rendered and explained at, before, or immediately after the
coming of our Lord.   Happily our materials are here not
scarce, and we present them in abstract and in their historical
order.[2]   At first, traditions were simply handed down from
Rabbi to Rabbi.   Akiba was the first to make a collection of
the different Halachoth, but the authoritative arrangement of
the oral law, which is termed Mishna, was the work of the
Nasi, Jehuda the Holy, about 190 after Christ.   It consists
of six separate treatises.   Partly older than that collection
are the following Midrashim or Commentaries : (1) *Sifra*, or
" Torath Kohanim " (the law of the priests), a Midrash on
Leviticus ; (2) *Sifre*, or " Vishalchu," on Numbers and
Deuteronomy ; (3) *Mechilta*, on part of Exodus.   Some
fragments are also still preserved of a second or smaller Sifre

---

[1] See p. 106 f.

[2] Comp. Hirschfeld's *Hagada*, p. 324, etc., and Zunz's classical work, *Die
Gottesd. Vortr. d. Juden*; [also Schürer, I. i. 117–153, 163–166.]

on Numbers. All these contain later additions, but belong in the main to the third century. Next in order came the Baraithas or additional Halachas, not contained in the Mishna, and the Toseftas, or additions to the Mishna. These also date, for the most part, from the period ending 243 after Christ. We then arrive at the Talmuds. The Jerusalem Talmud was finished before the end of the fourth century, the Babylonian about a century and a half later. Both are commentaries upon the Mishna. The Jerusalem Talmud, of which only a part has been handed down, comments on the first four treatises of the Mishna; the Babylonian, on the first section of the first, and the greater part of the following four Mishnic treatises. Of treatise six, one section only is commented upon in either Talmud. The Babylonian is about four times as large as the Jerusalem Talmud, and fills 2947 folio pages, being about ten or eleven times the size of the Mishna. Both enjoy supreme authority to this day.

Amongst the historical Hagadoth, including some of Greek origin, we may mention the additions to the Books of Esther and Daniel found in the LXX., a great part of the Second and Third Books of the Maccabees, Judith, Tobit, and the letter of Aristeas about the Seventy interpreters. Of very ancient date, and indeed older than the Mishna, is the oldest part of the Hagada for the Passover, still in use among the Jews. Megillath Taanith, a kind of almanac recording memorable events which befell the nation, dates from the first and second centuries.

Next in order we have the historical work called Seder Olam, now the Seder Olam Rabba. It gives the history of the Jews to the reign of Alexander the Great, and dates from the second century; and to the same century belongs a Baraitha known as the thirty-two Middoth of Rabbi Eleazar. [In the third century begin collections of legends and stories no longer preserved in their original form, but often alluded to in the Talmud. Of several of these there still remain later editions from the post-Talmudic age, *e.g.* the Book of Antiochus, the Seder Olam Suta, which records the succession of Babylonian-Exile princes, the Midrash Ele

Eskrah relating to the Ten Martyrs, and the Midrash Vajisu and the Chronicle of Moses dealing with biblical times.] The long Hagadic expositions of different parts of the Bible are all apparently later than the Talmud. Probably the oldest are " Bereshith Rabba " on Genesis, and the Midrash on Lamentations. In the course of five or six centuries these were gradually enlarged into a commentary on the whole of the Pentateuch and the other five books prescribed to be read in the synagogues, and the whole collection is known as " Midrash Rabba." [Of the two Pesiktoth, or commentaries on the special lessons read in the synagogues, that of Rab Kehana may be older than Bereshith Rabba ; [1] but the Pesikta Rabbathi dates from the first half of the ninth century.] Jelamdenu or Tanchuma, the oldest continuous Midrash on the Pentateuch, belongs to the same period, while the Pirke di Rabbi Eleazar is perhaps somewhat earlier.

The attempt to make the Scriptures popularly accessible, would probably first lead to versions, then to paraphrastic and more general commentaries. The *Targum* frequently occupied a kind of intermediate position between the translation and the paraphrase. Of translations, strictly so termed, the oldest and best known is the Greek or Septuagint version of the Old Testament. The fables so long and firmly believed about the Seventy sages summoned for that purpose to Alexandria by Ptolemy Philadelphus (B.C. 283–247), their inspiration, etc., may now be dismissed as no longer possessing credence. Although not within the sphere of our present history, we may simply state that this version was made by different authors, and for behoof of extra-Palestinian Jews. The version of the Pentateuch to which alone the Aristeas legend relates, dates no doubt from the third century before our era ; [while the work of translating the remaining books of the Old Testament was probably completed in the course of the next century]. The character of the translation varies greatly in the different books.[2] [The version of the Pentateuch,

---

[1] So Buber, Weber (p. xxii.) ; but Zunz (p. 206 f.) dates the work at about A.D. 700. Comp. Hamburger, *Enc.* Suppl., " Pesikta."

[2] See Driver, *Notes on Samuel*, p. xxxix. ff.

with the exception of a few poetical chapters, is quite the best; on the other hand, many parts of the Minor Prophets are entirely unintelligible.] Leaving out of view the mistakes, additions, or emendations by copyists, it is quite clear that the Hebrew text used by the translators differed widely from that which we now possess. The variations affect in some cases whole paragraphs, [and in the Book of Jeremiah we have virtually another recension]. Important variations are to be found also in the last chapters of Exodus, in 1 Samuel and 1 Kings, and in Job, while to the Books of Esther and Daniel the LXX. makes large additions, to which we have already alluded. When differences of reading occur, in the great majority of cases the Jews have preserved the purer text. [Nevertheless there are many passages in which it is clear that the Massoretic text is corrupt; and in these cases the LXX., which carries us back to a period considerably before the Hebrew text had received its present form, often gives us very valuable assistance. In the Books of Samuel, of Ezekiel, and in parts of Kings, the renderings of the LXX are especially important.]

Some characteristics of the Greek version may here be noticed. " It bears evident marks of its origin in Egypt in its use of Egyptian words and references, and equally evident traces of its Jewish composition. By the side of slavish and false literalism there is great liberty, if not licence, in handling the original; gross mistakes occur, along with happy renderings of very difficult passages, suggesting the aid of some able scholars. Distinct Jewish elements are undeniably there, which can only be explained by reference to Jewish tradition; although they are much fewer than some critics have supposed." [1] References to the Halacha cannot perhaps be traced with certainty in more than six or eight passages. Allusions to the Hagada are probably more frequent. Thus, the Greek of Josh. xiii. 22 has been explained by the Hagada, that Balaam had by magic flown into the air, but that Phinehas had thrown him to the ground and killed him in the *fall*. Again, the reading in 1 Sam. xxviii. 14 depends perhaps upon the legend that

---

[1] *Life and Times*, i. p. 27, cf. pp. 23–30.

apparitions of ghosts were generally in an inverted posture of body, while that of Samuel had come up in the ordinary or straight position. Considerable Hagadic additions also occur. Thus, we have in Prov. vi. 8, praise of the diligence of the ant; in Josh. xxiv. 30, a Hagadic story about the knives with which Joshua circumcised the Jews, in imitation of a similar Palestinian Hagada about Moses; an addition to Hag. ii. 9, etc. Sometimes verses were left out, or even whole passages transposed. Passing over grammatical and other blunders, contractions, amplifications, and attempts at circumlocution, we notice that sometimes words are translated in one, and left untranslated in another place, as the word " plain " (R.V. Arabah) rendered " west " in Josh. xi. 16, and " Araba " in xii. 8 ; or, " the children of Solomon's servants," in Ezra ii. 55 (A), while in verse 58 we read " the children of Abdeselma," etc. Sometimes prepositions are treated as if they formed part of the appellative, while evident traces of the familiarity of the translators with Aramaic are found in Ps. lx. 10, etc.

The Samaritan version is of much less interest. In a large number of passages, which are mostly unimportant, its readings agree with the LXX. against the Hebrew, [pointing to the numerous small changes which the Massoretic text has undergone since these versions were made. On the whole, however, the Greek version bears a much greater affinity to the Hebrew than to the Samaritan.] The Syriac version, or the Peshitto, dates from the second century A.D., and is probably the work of Jewish Christians. [The translation does not come all from the same hand, and the treatment of the text varies considerably in different books. Thus, while Job is literal, in the Books of Chronicles we have almost as many paraphrases and additions as in a Targum. The Psalms show the influence of the Septuagint, the Pentateuch that of Jewish exegesis.[1]]

If Greek versions of the Bible, and specially of the Pentateuch, were at an early period felt requisite for

[1] Comp. Driver, *ut supra*, p. xlii.; Buhl, *Canon and Text of the Old Test.* pp. 185–193.

liturgical purposes, the Jews, who spoke mostly the Aramaic language, must have also been provided with Targums in that tongue.[1] At one time the translations were not written, for fear of usurping the authority of Scripture. At any rate, in the public reading of the Bible, the interpreter gave his rendering orally; and verse by verse in the Pentateuch, and every three verses in the Prophets, were given first in Hebrew, then in the known dialect.[2] [The rendering was not to be too literal, nor were additions to be made to the text;[3]] but, as confessedly certain passages were omitted and others paraphrased, we can readily conceive that the general tendency of these prelections was in favour of traditionalism. Various circumstances, perhaps among them political troubles, combined to break down the prejudice against written Targums. Jewish writings refer to one on Job, apparently dating from the first century of our era; [and it is not improbable that the earliest written Targums were made on books which were not publicly read and interpreted in the synagogues. We are told that Rabbi Gamaliel expressed his strong disapprobation of the Targum on Job;[4] but the Mishna, rather more than a century later, seems to imply that written Targums were then not uncommon.[5]] The most important Targum is that which is still preserved as the Targum Onkelos. Of Akylas, the pupil of Akiba, we have already spoken; and if anything were required to establish his identity with Onkelos, it is found in this, that almost the same statements are made about Akylas in the Jerusalem Talmud and the Midrashim, as in the Babylonian and Tosefta about Onkelos.[6] Certainly the Aramaic of Onkelos is not a translation of the Greek of Aquila, for the two versions frequently differ in rendering and in spirit. [Probably the statement that Onkelos was the author of an Aramaic Targum is simply due to a confusion, for the corresponding passage in the Jerusalem Talmud

---

[1] Comp. Deutsch in *Smith's Dict. of the Bible*, "Targum"; Buhl, *ut supra*, pp. 167–185; Wellhausen-Bleek, *Einleitung in das A. T.*,[5] pp. 560–565; Schürer, I. i. 154–163.

[2] Meg. iv. 4.   [3] Kidd. 49*a*.   [4] Shab. 115*a*; jer. Shab. xvi. 15*c*.
[5] Jad. iv. 5.   [6] Deutsch, *ut supra*, iii. 1642 f.

relates to the Greek translation of Aquila.[1]]   There can be
but little doubt that the Targum Onkelos was written in
Palestine, probably about the end of the second century ; but
it has passed through a later revision in Babylon.   On the
other hand, it doubtless preserves many traditional renderings
of a much earlier date ; [and since it contains many indications
of being an abridgment of a more paraphrastic translation,
it would seem that our existing Targum is the result of a
learned revision and reduction of the oral Targum which had
long been traditional in Palestine.]   The dialect is a late variety
of Palestinian Aramaic, similar to the biblical " Chaldee," but
the language is coloured with Babylonian idioms.   The first
characteristic of this version is that it is a translation, and
not a paraphrase ; [2] indeed, it is often so literal as to reproduce
the difficulties of the original.   Sometimes, however, we have
a comment, and the text of the original is then often altered.[3]
It frequently differs from the Halacha, and only rarely, in
poetical passages, does it introduce the fanciful renderings
of the Hagada.   The Messiah appears as a personage, and
passages such as Gen. xlix. 10, Num. xxiv. 17, are applied to
him.[4]   Passages which contain indelicate allusions (as was
supposed) or anthropomorphisms, are omitted or modified.
In particular, a reference to the Memra or Word is generally
introduced, where the original attributes bodily affections to God,
or represents Him as entering into direct relations with men.[5]

An equally important version was that on the Prophets,
attributed to Jonathan ben Uzziel, the pupil of Hillel, and
supposed to be derived from traditions of the Prophets
Haggai, Zechariah, and Malachi.[6]   It is much less literal
than Onkelos, and in the matter of unfulfilled prophecy
often quite Hagadic.   Traditionary elements and legends
have found their way into it, questions occurring in the text
are answered, difficulties solved, etc.   Anthropomorphisms,

---

[1] Comp. Meg. 3a, jer. *ib.* i. 71c.   [2] Weber, p. xiii.
[3] For example, in Gen. iv. 23.
[4] A list of passages in the Old Testament Messianically applied in ancient
Rabbinical writings will be found in *Life and Times*, ii. App. IX.
[5] See further, p. 426 f.   [6] Meg. 3a.

or anything that might be used against Judaism, are omitted or modified, and the miraculous is garnished. Jonathan's views of inspiration were somewhat peculiar, and the sons of the prophets were converted into Talmudical students. [This Targum is usually supposed to quote from Onkelos, but the similarities may be due to the dependence of both on ancient traditional renderings. Like the Targum on the Law, this also is doubtless a later recension of old oral paraphrases, but it has preserved much more of the old traditions than Onkelos.] The language shows that it has undergone a later revision in Babylon. Targums of various dates exist on all the Hagiographa except Ezra and Nehemiah, but none of them are earlier than the seventh century.[1] Of these, the works on Psalms, Proverbs, and Job are mainly translations, but the versions of the five Megilloth, or books read in the synagogue (the Song of Songs, Ruth, Lamentations, Esther, and Ecclesiastes), partake rather of the nature of paraphrases and commentaries.

Very different from the translations of Onkelos and Jonathan are the Targum Jonathan (falsely so called) on the Pentateuch, and the Jerusalem Targum, containing fragments upon the same portion of Scripture. The Targum Jonathan on the Pentateuch, which probably owes its name to a mere error, is in its present form of quite a late date, and indeed contains notices of historical events which bring it down at least to the beginning of the seventh century.[2] [On the other hand, it still lies before us in an unabridged shape, and seems in this respect to be earlier, and to retain more of its original character, than the two Babylonian Targums. The Jerusalem Targum, which only exists in a fragmentary form, is closely allied to the Pseudo-Jonathan, and like it represents the Palestinian tradition; but it is difficult to determine the relations of the two to one another. It is, in the first place,

---

[1] Comp. Weber, p. xviii.

[2] For example, mention is made of Mohammed's wife and daughter in Gen. xxi. 21; comp. also the six *Seders* of the Mishna in Ex. xxvi. 9; Constantinople and Lombardy in Num. xxiv. 19. 24. On the other hand, the rendering of Deut. xxxiii. 11 seems to date from the time of John Hyrcanus.

uncertain whether the Jerushalmi was ever a continuous translation; and if from the first nothing more than a collection of detached glosses, it is disputed whether it supplemented, or was supplemented by the complete Pseudo-Jonathan.[1]] The difference between the Palestinian Targums and that of Onkelos lies in this, that while the latter generally translates and occasionally interprets, the former generally interpret, and only occasionally translate.[2]   The Targum Pseudo-Jonathan is a Hagadic commentary.   Thus, the words of various texts are compared to elicit a peculiar meaning.   For example, Num. xx. 11, compared with Ps. cv. 41, is made to prove that on the first stroke the rock sent forth a stream of blood.   The text is generally expounded, enlarged, or modified, and brought into agreement with the prevailing theology.   Miraculous additions occur, difficulties are attempted to be removed, and apparent discrepancies reconciled.   Dialogues are also introduced as between God and man into Gen. iii., and there is a decided want of artistic taste about its clumsy attempts at simplicity. The interpretation is often poor and without regard to grammar, meaning, or chronology.   Legends are introduced, and the general characteristics of the Hagada are well exemplified in this Targum.   We refer not only to the many superstitious ideas and views broached, but to the curious views of heaven and hell, the strange attempts at excusing Hagadic favourites, and incriminating others, etc.   The Law naturally is interpreted in the sense of the Halacha.   Historical facts are altered and improved upon, and in general it presents a by no means favourable specimen of Jewish traditionalism.   On the other hand, amongst the mass of rubbish there are also exegetical gems.[3]

The Palestinian tradition is also found in the Targums to the five Megilloth, but these no longer exist in their original form.   All have been largely expanded, and are now even more plainly Hagadic than Targum Pseudo-Jonathan.   Stories are invented, such as that the Angel Gabriel stuck a tail to Queen Vashti's forehead, that she was asked to appear naked, and much

---

[1] Comp. Weber, p. xvii.   [2] Zunz, *Gottesd. Vortr.*[2] p. 75.

[3] For further particulars, see Hirschfeld, Zunz, and Hamburger, *Real-Enc.*, "Targum," etc.

more of low ribaldry and licentiousness. The letters are resolved into their numerical value, words are torn out of the context, letters transposed, words differently pointed, etc. Images are resolved, and the young roes are Moses and Aaron, the breasts are the two Messiahs (the son of David and the son of Joseph); gross anachronisms occur, such as that the Jews had called in the Romans to deliver them from Nebuchadnezzar, but that, instead of this, Titus and Vespasian had taken Jerusalem for themselves, etc. The Song of Solomon appears as an allegory, representing the relation between God and Israel, and is made to embrace the story of the Exodus, the giving of the Law, the Apostasy, the building of the Temple, the miracles of the Prophets, the destruction of the Temple by Nebuchadnezzar, the rebuilding of the Sanctuary, and the wars of the Maccabees. It also contains a good many legends about paradise, the fable about rolling after death under ground, etc. The Targum on the Book of Ruth is much less extravagant, and contains more of historical relations, such as about the various seasons of famine, etc. Allegories occur, as that the six measures which Ruth got were six heroes sprung from her, a defence of monogamy is made, etc. Of similar character are the expositions of Ecclesiastes and Lamentations. Historical events are assigned as the occasion of particular portions of these books, and the former Targum is conceived in a spirit favourable to Rome. The Book of Esther has three Targums, of which one is of a literalistic character, but the other two are sufficiently extravagant. Everything is here Jewish; sometimes the bounds of modesty are passed, and Haman is especially made the subject of all kinds of witticism. The "second" Targum, which is more modern, goes even further than the first. It contains a great many digressions, such as a comparison of the throne of Ahasuerus with that of Solomon, an account of the visit of the Queen of Sheba, etc. Fragments of Targums to some portions of the Prophets are also preserved, and it would scarcely be a bold conjecture to suggest that at one time a complete Palestine Targum existed on all the books of the Bible.

Another view of the same subject might be presented by a critical investigation of the various apocryphal books, but these are generally accessible, and any criticism would necessitate too long digressions. In connection with this, it is interesting to study the views of Bible history as embodied in Josephus' *Antiquities of the Jews.* He quotes Berosus, Hecatæus, and Nicolaus in support of the history of Abraham (i. 7. 2); other heathen writers in confirmation of the Flood (i. 3. 6); a great number of authorities for the longevity of the first inhabitants of the world (*ut supra,* 9); the Tyrian Chronicles and Dius for the fact that Hiram had propounded riddles to Solomon (viii. 5. 3), etc. He also makes additions to the text. Thus, Lamech had seventy-seven children by Zillah and Adah (i. 2. 2); Adam predicted the destruction of the world by fire, and again by water, and the children of Seth engraved this on two pillars (*ut supra,* 3); Abraham conversed with the wise men in Egypt, and introduced them to the study of mathematics and astronomy (i. 8. 2); the practices of the Sodomites (i. 11. 1), the war of Moses with the Ethiopians, his cleverness, and marriage (ii. 10), etc., are described. We find also a number of deviations from the text. Thus, David brings 600 *heads* of the Philistines to Saul (vi. 10. 2). Other things are omitted, or historically rearranged, and speeches and letters are attributed to biblical personages, the chronology is fixed, etc. But, on the whole, the *Antiquities* are the work of a Jewish apologist rather than of a Rabbi. Some very un-Jewish theological views appear (*e.g.* vi. 11. 8; viii. 4. 2). The work on the opinions of his countrymen about God, and on their laws, to which Josephus refers at the close of his *Antiquities,* was probably never written.

II. *Mysticism and Philo*

An interesting and important branch of Jewish theology was that concerned with the mystical views of the Synagogue. The same tendency appeared amongst the Jews both in Palestine and in Egypt, although in each case it was modified by the foreign elements with which it was brought into contact. Mysticism marks usually a period of transition. [In Palestine it represented the reaction of the spirit against the letter, the attempt of minds wearied with the formalism and legal questionings of the Rabbins to penetrate more deeply into the knowledge of the Divine. In Egypt its rise was due to somewhat different causes. Amid the decline of Greek philosophy, and the extinction of free political life, Jewish ideas exercised a powerful influence upon the thinkers of Alexandria. At the same time, the Jew, separated from his own country, gave up much of his former exclusiveness,— and along with this much of the definiteness of his national creed,—and readily embraced the Hellenistic culture, in the midst of which he lived. From this combination of Greek and Jewish thought there was developed a system of dreamy mysticism, which exalted contemplation above active life. In Egypt, Jewish mysticism reached its highest development in the writings of Philo Judæus. In Palestine the system evolved more slowly ; and while abundant traces of it are found in the Talmud, it only reached its culminating point in the Kabbalah of the Middle Ages.

This name was not used to denote a system of theosophic speculation till after the Talmudic age. In the Mishna, the earliest Midrashim, and the Talmud, the Kabbalah (from *Qibbēl,* to hand down) denotes the whole body of Jewish tradition. The name is even applied to the prophetic writings of the Old Testament, and the Hagiographa, in contradistinction to the Pentateuch.[1] The older names for mystic speculations are " the Hidden Things," or " the Secrets of the Law."] There were two subjects about which the Jewish imagination especially busied itself,—the history of the Creation, and the " Merkabah," or the Divine apparition to Ezekiel. Both touch the question of God's original connection with His creatures, and that of His continued intercourse with them. They treat of the mystery of nature and of Providence, especially of Revelation ; and the question how the Infinite God can have any connection or intercourse with finite

[1] See Taylor, *Sayings of the Jewish Fathers,* pp. 120–122.

creatures is attempted to be answered. The greatest dread
was felt of any reckless or irreverent treatment of such
themes, and the same feelings which placed careful restrictions upon the oral teaching or discussion of these subjects,
would also prevent any attempt being made to write down
an exposition of the mysteries. [There is, in fact, no trace of
a literature on the subject till after the completion of the
Talmud. The oldest Cabbalistic text-book which has come
down to us, the Sepher Jezirah, or the Book of Creation, is
not earlier than the ninth century; and the principles here
propounded receive their fullest and most remarkable development in the book "Sohar" (splendour), a work of
the thirteenth century. Doubtless the groundwork of the
system is very old, reaching back probably to a period
before the Christian era; and it is the presence of these
ancient elements which so long supported the belief in the
early origin of the two books just named.

It is difficult to say how far back it is possible to trace
with certainty the Jewish mysticism.[1] Even in Sirach
(Ecclus. xlix. 8), it is the special praise of Ezekiel that he
saw the chariot of the Cherubim; and there is much of a
mystical character in the Book of Enoch and other apocryphal
writings. When we come to the Mishna, we find the existence of a body of esoteric doctrine already presupposed. It
is laid down that "no one ought to expound the history of
Creation (Gen. i.) with two, or the Chariot (Ezek. i.) with one,
unless he be a scholar who has knowledge of his own." [2]
Further allusions to these mysterious doctrines occur in the
Talmud, but any rash investigation of them was discouraged,
as is shown by the story of the Four Sages in the enclosed
Garden, of which we have already spoken.[3] The term
Sephirah is never found here in its later technical sense, nor
have we more than hints of the characteristic Cabbalistic
doctrine of emanation. Nevertheless the *ten things* created
on the first day, and still more the *ten things* by which the

----

[1] For traces of mysticism in Rabbinic literature, see Hamburger, *Real-Enc.* ii., "Geheimlehre."

[2] Chag. ii. 1.   [3] See pp. 170–172.

world was created (viz. wisdom, understanding, knowledge, strength, rebuke, might, righteousness, mercy, judgment, and compassion),[1] remind us of the ten *Sephiroth* of the Kabbalah. Names of God consisting of twelve and of forty-two letters are spoken of,[2] and there are speculations on the import of the letters of the sacred Tetragrammaton similar to those which play such an important part in later mystical writings. The Metatron as an intermediary subsistence occurs even in the Talmud; in the Targums we find also the Memra and the Shechinah. The existence of a belief in the pre-existence of souls and of the plurality of worlds can readily be proved from Rabbinic literature. Some of the Midrashim discuss the question of primeval matter. The Targums of the sixth and seventh centuries in their rendering of the 1st chapter of Genesis, and still more in their angelology, illustrate the further development of Jewish thought. Yet even here we are separated by a considerable interval from the elaborate system of the mediæval mystics.

It is unnecessary to discuss here the theology of the "Sohar," owing to its very late date;[3] but we may perhaps be permitted to give a brief sketch of the doctrine of the earlier work, although even this really lies outside our period.] The "Sepher Jezirah" is properly a monologue on the part of Abraham, in which, by the contemplation of all that is around him, he ultimately arrives at the conviction of the Unity of God.

We distinguish the substance and the form of creation; that which is, and the mode in which it is. We have already indicated that the original of all that exists is Divine. 1st, We have God; 2nd, God manifest, or the Divine *entering* into form; 3rd, That Divine *in* its form, from which in turn all original realities are afterwards derived. In the "Sepher Jezirah," these Divine realities (the substance) are represented by the ten numerals, and their form by the twenty-two letters which constitute the Hebrew alphabet,—language being viewed as the medium of connection between the spiritual and the

---

[1] Chag. 12*a*; comp. Pirke Ab. v. 6.   [2] Kidd. 71*a*.

[3] For an account of Cabbalistic doctrines, see *Dict. Chr. Biog.* i. "Cabbalah."

material; as the form in which the spiritual appears. At the
same time, number and language indicate also the arrangement
and the mode of creation, and, in general, its boundaries.
" By thirty-two wonderful paths," so begins the " Sepher
Jezirah,"—" the Eternal, the Lord of Hosts, the God of Israel,
the living God, the King of the World, the merciful and
gracious God, the glorious One, He that inhabiteth eternity,
Whose name is high and holy,—has created the world." But
these ten numerals are in reality the ten Sefiroth, or Divine
emanations, arranged in triads, each triad consisting of two
opposites (flowing or emanating from a superior triad until
the Divine Unity is reached), and being reconciled in a middle
point of connection. These ten Sefiroth, in the above arrangement, recur everywhere, and the sacred number Ten is that
of perfection. Each of these Sefiroth flows from its predecessor, and in this manner the Divine gradually evolves.
This emanation of the ten Sefiroth then constitutes the
substance of the world; we may add, it constitutes everything
else. In God, in the world, in man, everywhere we meet
these ten Sefiroth, at the head of which is God manifest, or
the *Memra* (*Logos*, the Word). If the ten Sefiroth give the
substance, the twenty-two letters are the form of creation and
of revelation. " By giving them form and shape, and by
interchanging them, God has made the soul of everything
that has been made, or shall be made." " Upon those letters
also has the Holy One, Whose name be praised, founded His
holy and glorious name." These letters are next subdivided,
and their application in all the departments of nature is
shown. In the unit creation, the triad—world, time, and man
—are found. Above all these is the Lord. Such is a very
brief outline of the rational exposition of the creation,
attempted by the " Sepher Jezirah." [1]

The theology of Philo occupies the other extreme in the
chain of Jewish mysticism. Alike the result and the ex-
ponent of the peculiar Alexandrian direction, it influenced the
theological thinking of the Church, and the speculations of
the academy. [The development of Greek philosophy having

---

[1] For a translation of the Sepher Jezirah, see *Life and Times*, ii. pp. 692–697.

ended in eclecticism or scepticism, it was now ready to be modified by the admission of Oriental ideas. But in Alexandria no influence was more powerful than that exerted by the presence of a large body of thinkers belonging to the Jewish faith, chief among whom was Philo.] To gain universal acknowledgment for his creed, and to elevate its mysteries to the highest pinnacle, by showing that what of truth there was in Platonism was derived from Judaism,—such was the object of Philo.·

The Jews of Egypt passed, in general, through a peculiar training.[1] However firmly they clung to their national faith, the more cultured amongst them could not fail to be strongly attracted by Greek thought and speculation. At the same time, they found that their nation and their religion were continually being made the objects of bitter attack by the Greek *literati* of Alexandria. It was therefore necessary for them to learn how best they might reconcile heathen philosophy with the Jewish creed, and defend the latter from the charges brought against it. To retain the truths of Platonism in Judaism, to vindicate them for and to elicit them from the Old Testament, such was the first task of the Alexandrian Jewish apologist. But if the very symbols and letter, the husk of that religion, already placed the Jew on a footing of equality with, or even elevated him above the Platonic philosopher, what a distinguished position was occupied by the Jewish theosophist, whose ecstasy equalled in kind, though not perhaps in degree, the inspiration of the prophets! Hence the study of philology, logic, poetry, rhetoric, and heathen philosophy was highly to be commended, but they served only to prepare for the Divine philosophy of Judaism. They were only the porch before the entrance.[2] Such, it appears, were the fundamental views entertained by Philo.

Though the writings of Philo are the oldest connected

---

[1] Comp. *Dict. Chr. Biog.*, "Philo," iv. 358–362.

[2] *De Prof.* i. 573. [For Philo's system generally, see Zeller, *Philosophie d. Griechen*,[3] iii. 2, pp. 338–418 ; also *Life and Times*, i. 40–57 ; and Dr. Edersheim's article "Philo" in *Dict. Chr. Biog.* iv.]

production breathing the spirit peculiar to the Alexandrian school, he was by no means the first to originate it. He himself appeals to predecessors in these inquiries, and besides the kindred extracts from previous writers, preserved, for example, in Eusebius' *Præparatio Evangelica*,[1] even in the Old Testament version of the so-called Seventy interpreters some indications of a similar theology may probably be traced. Philo, an Alexandrian Jew, by birth connected with the most influential of his countrymen in Egypt, where his brother held the important office of Alabarch,[2] was a man of profound erudition, thoroughly acquainted with Grecian literature and philosophy, but specially of deep moral earnestness.   Often had he retired to the wilderness to lead in solitude and abstinence a more spiritual life ; but as often did the felt plague of his heart convince him " that it was not change of place that brought either evil or good." [3]   Above all, he was devotedly a Jew.   He had visited the Holy City,[4] to offer, after the fashion of extra-Palestinian Jews, prayers and sacrifices ; but there is nothing in his own writings to confirm the statement of Jerome that he was of priestly descent.[5] Notwithstanding the scorn which the bigotry of some of his co-religionists brought upon his creed, he was not ashamed publicly to avow his connection with them.   The persecution which the envious Egyptians sought to raise against the Jews on the occasion of the mad attempt of the Emperor Caius to enforce the universal adoration of his statue, led to the de-spatch of an embassy to Rome, of which Philo was the most prominent member.   He has described the ill-success of that mission in a treatise which throws some light upon the state of the Roman court at that period.[6]

[Many of Philo's writings have evidently been lost, but we still possess the greater part of them, and several fresh fragments have been discovered and published within the

---

[1] To this we have already alluded ; see p. 346 ff.

[2] That is, chief collector of customs on the Arabian side of the Nile ; see Schürer, II. ii. 280.

[3] *Leg. Alleg.* II., i. 81 f.

[4] Euseb. *Præp. Evang.* viii. 14.

[5] Hieron. *De Vir. Illustr.* xi.

[6] *De Legatione ad Caium.*

present century. Yet in spite of the abundance of material, and the fulness with which this celebrated philosopher expounds his doctrines, it is difficult to give a connected account of his system.[1] Many of his views he has merely worked out in the course of an elaborate series of commentaries on portions of the Pentateuch ; while the different elements on which his system was based were too heterogeneous to be combined into a consistent whole.] As to his general views of Scripture, it may be sufficient to indicate that he clings with tenacity to the letter,—in the version of the LXX.,—and that in perfect consistency with his allegorical mode of interpretation, by which not only individual passages bear a profound and mystical meaning, but Scripture, as a whole, becomes one connected allegory. In such a system, clinging to the letter, to which generally the peculiar interpretation strictly attaches itself, was necessary. Where philosophical interests do not demand its rejection, the ordinary historical interpretation is, however, retained, and forms the basis of the mystical. The *doctrinal* views of Philo may briefly be characterised as a mixture of Platonism and Jewish mysticism. In point of *practice,* he advises conformity to the Jewish ritual observances, although mainly, it would seem, on the ground of avoiding scandal.[2] Moral perfection is sought in asceticism, in opposition to the Platonic view of this subject, although the fundamental principles concerning matter are the same in both systems. [However, Philo sometimes applies to matter language borrowed from the Stoic school.[3]]

Like most Jewish theologians, Philo places the authority of Moses above that of the other inspired writers, who are considered rather as his interpreters and followers than as his equals. But even in Moses we have to distinguish what he attained by philosophical acquirement from that which he received from God, either in ecstasy (a state more or less attainable by all initiated), in answer to his inquiries, or by direct communications.[4] The results of all these are laid down in the Scriptures. But all deeper spiritual truths

---

[1] Comp. Schürer, II. iii. 366.
[2] *De Migrat. Abr.* i. 450.
[3] Comp. Zeller, *ut supra*, p. 386 f.
[4] *Vita Mosis*, ii. 163 f.

appear there veiled; the letter conveying comparatively low and carnal views in order to condescend to the gross and carnal notions of the vulgar, so as to bring at least *some* truth to them.[1] It were impossible, it is ridiculous, to interpret literally many scriptural statements, which, so understood, are contrary to reason, and would degrade Judaism below the level of heathen philosophy.[2] In explaining the supposed allegories of Scripture, the Greek text of the LXX. is rigidly adhered to by Philo, though traces of a respectable acquaintance with the Hebrew occur. A good deal was, of course, to be left to the exegetical tact of each interpreter, but the following seem to have been some of the principles of Alexandrian exegetics :—1. The terms in the text may be expanded, and its statements applied to any or all topics to which the same expressions might figuratively be applied. Thus the word " place " might, besides its proper meaning, apply to the Logos, and even to God, Who contains and fills all. 2. The *idea* conveyed in the text may be educed from the *words* by showing a similar etymological derivation, and hence an affinity between the words and the idea. 3. Everything not absolutely requisite in the text was supposed to point to some special and hidden meaning. 4. Attention was to be given to the exegetical traditions of the Fathers. 5. Above all, the commentator may, by reaching the ecstatic state of the inspired writer, sympathise with and gain an immediate view of the same truth. 6. Several differing interpretations may all convey portions of truth.[3]

The *theology* of Philo [is determined by the dualistic standpoint which he adopts; for he] continually dwells upon the antithesis between God and the world, the Infinite and the Finite, and emphasises the absolute transcendency of God.[4] Philo affirms that the Divine nature is in itself without quality, and indefinable. All his definitions on this

---

[1] *Quod Deus immutabilis*, i. 280 f; *de Somniis*, i. 656.

[2] Comp. Zeller, p. 348.

[3] Comp. Siegfried, *Philo von Alexandria*, pp. 160–197. Siegfried gives twenty-three rules of allegorical interpretation.

[4] Comp. Zeller, p. 353 f.

subject are only *negative,* showing that neither thought nor language can approach Him. " He is more indivisible than indivisibility ; " " more good than goodness ; more beautiful than beauty," etc. ;[1] in short, " He is more simple than a monad, or than unity itself." [2] Three inferences are drawn from the absence of all quality in God and His separation from all : 1. That He is free. 2. That He is inaccessible to feelings of every kind, or apathetic. 3. That He is perfectly happy, rejoicing in Himself. Apathy, freedom, and happiness are thus combined, affording a distant view of the origin of Asceticism. Such a God can never be known by mortals,—they can only recognise *that He is,* and that which is *by* Him.[3] But as God is in all and pervading all, His rational creatures may, by virtue of this Divine power in them, rise to Him in ecstatic moments when the fetters of matter are for a time cast aside.[4] No particular name ought to be given to the Deity,—" He Who is," " that which exists," " He Who exists in truth," are His only lawful designations. Names may, however, be given to that inferior Being, " the Logos," God manifest, which stands in contact with the world as its Creator, and to the individual Logoi, the attributes, or rather the active intermediaries of the Deity, which in their totality constitute the Logos. All those passages in Scripture which attribute affections, etc., to God, are only anthropomorphisms, and must be explained allegorically.

In his *Cosmology,* Philo approaches to Plato more closely than to the Kabbalah. This world is to him the gate to the invisible, the first step of the heavenly ladder.[5] The order and adaptation of the world point to a heavenly Architect, while the fact that everything that exists is dependent on higher powers, and subject to change, sufficiently indicates their created origin. However, such proofs for the being of a God are second in rank when compared with the evidence which " the truly pious and holy " obtains by rising, " without any external help," to an immediate contemplation of the

---

[1] *De Præm. et Poen.* ii. 414 ; *De Virt.* ii. 546.
[2] *De Vit. Cont.* ii. 472.   [3] *Qu. De. immut.* i. 282.
[4] *Quis rer. div. h.* i. 508 ff.   [5] *De Somn.* i. 641, 648 f.

Divine.[1]   But we have to distinguish between the form and the matter of this world.   The latter is inert, irrational, and continuous, and must be viewed as a principle coeternal with God, entirely different from, and therefore not produced by Him.   The *forms* of matter alone exhibit design, and are the workmanship of God, Who is the Architect rather than the Creator, the Demiurgos, though also the Father of this world.[2] To complete this part of our sketch, the world was produced by the Divine life pouring itself forth into and pervading matter, in as far as matter was capable of receiving it, and that in a peculiar manner.   When God was about to form the world, He proceeded, like other architects, to form a plan, an invisible, purely intelligible world; of which the visible is the exact counterpart.[3]   These ideas, or the individual Logoi, are again all combined into the one Logos, who contains and comprises in himself that incorporeal world.   The Logos formed the world in a twofold manner, by separating the chaotic mass of the four elements, and dividing them into antagonists until the simplest forms were reached; and by binding them again together into a higher unity.[4]   By the Logos the continued connection between God and the world is also kept up; for, on the one hand, he is the soul of the world, the living and moving force within it; and on the other, he is the Great High Priest, who makes intercession for the world to God.[5]   In these respects the Logos is the Mediator, the connecting link between God and the world, the interpreter of our spirits and of God, the name of God, the vicar of God, the image of God, etc.   In a certain sense he may even be spoken of as God, though, in contrast to the Most High, he is only the *second* God.[6]   The Logos is made to say: "I stand in the middle between God and you," being neither unbegotten as God nor begotten as us, but the middle between these extremes.[7]

---

[1] *De Praem. etc.* ii. 415.   [2] Comp. Zeller, p. 387 ff.
[3] *De Mund. Op.* i. 4 f; comp. Zeller, p. 362 ff.
[4] *Quis rer. div. h.* i. 491, 499, 506 ; comp. Zeller, 377 f.
[5] *De. Prof.* i. 562.   [6] Ap. Euseb. *Præp. Ev.* vii. 13. 1.
[7] *Quis rer. div. h.* i. 502.

The relationships existing between God, the Logos, the potencies, and the world, are described by Philo in different passages, which cannot be entirely reconciled. Generally he speaks of two supreme powers, which are combined by the Divine Logos, while the latter is regarded as the instrument of Creation.[1] "After the only true God there are two supreme and primary potencies, goodness and power, and everything has been made by goodness, and is governed by power. Between them and connecting them is the Logos." "The author of this world is God, by Whom it is made; the matter of the world, the four elements from which it has been prepared; the instrument is the Logos of God, by whom it has been built, and the final cause the goodness of the Demiurgos." [2]

In another passage the potencies are six, symbolised by the six Levitical cities of refuge, and they include, beside the Divine Logos, the *creative*, the *ruling*, the *atoning*, and the *legislative* potencies.[3] This enumeration is, however, really unimportant; other potencies besides these are mentioned; their number is unlimited, for they are indeed the infinite powers of an infinite God.[4] Philo's system required some intermediary beings or powers, whereby his transcendent and absolutely perfect God could be brought into relation with the world and with matter.[5] Two philosophical theories supplied him with what he required, the Platonic doctrine of ideas, and the Stoic doctrine of active causes. These he accordingly combined, so that his potencies are not only archetypal models, but also productive causes. [But, in part, his system is derived from popular notions, for the Jewish teaching about angels and the heathen belief in demons or demi-gods also suggested a pattern for the intermediary beings and messengers of God. And if we ask whether Philo conceived of the potencies as personal or impersonal beings, the only possible answer is that he did not clearly distinguish between the two. Many passages seem to show

[1] Comp. Zeller, p. 369 f.
[3] *De Prof.* i. 560.
[5] Comp. Zeller, pp. 360-365.

[2] *De Cherub.* i. 144. 162.
[4] *De Sacrif.* i. 173.

that they are separate hypostases, but this view cannot be brought into harmony with other equally definite statements. It is said, for example, that the powers or types exist only in the Divine thought.[1] Indeed, it is this very inconsistency, of which Philo himself does not seem to be aware, which enables them to fulfil the part assigned to them in his system.   In so far as they are identical with God, they establish a connection between God and the world : in so far as they are distinct from Him, they allow the Godhead to remain free from all contact with matter.]

The same difficulty meets us again with regard to the Logos.[2] In the earlier portion of this sketch, expressions have been used which point to a personal being ; nevertheless we find the Logos spoken of as the totality of the Divine powers, or reckoned as one of them. [The Logos is for Philo the power of God, the active Divine intelligence ; it is the idea, which contains all other ideas, the suprasensible world.[3]]   In one place it is identified with the wisdom of God ;[4] yet elsewhere it becomes the first-born son of God, born of wisdom, the spouse of the Most High.[5] [The Logos is, in fact, both impersonal and personal, a property of God and a distinct subsistence.   This double character becomes possible, because in Philo's conception of personality there is an indistinctness which is to be found also in other thinkers of antiquity, and the Logos accordingly serves at the same time to unite and to separate the finite world and the infinite God.]

In Philo's *Anthropology* we may notice especially the distinction which he draws in the immaterial part of man, between sensibility and reason.[6] The former of these was connected with the body, and would die with it.   The reasoning part in man was not produced, as all other creatures in the world, by the Divine potencies, but is, like the other high intelligences, of whom it is one, a direct

---

[1] *De Mund. Op.* i. 4 f.   [2] Comp. Zeller, pp. 371, 378–381.
[3] *De Mund. Op.* i. 5.   [4] *Leg. Alleg.* I., i. 56.
[5] *Conf. Ling.* i. 427 ; *De Prof.* i. 562.
[6] *Leg. Alleg.* II., i. 71 ; comp. Zeller, pp. 393–400.

emanation of the Deity, and the very image of the Logos. In fact, man stands on the dividing line between mortal and immortal beings, so that he is the microcosm of which the world is the macrocosm.[1] Hence, in his production, the Divine potencies co-operated with God, as it is written, " Let us make man." Beside our earth the whole universe is peopled. The air is specially the dwelling-place of a higher class of beings, some of whom had descended on earth, and by uniting with the material elements there, originated the human race. These air-spirits (or angels) constitute the Spirit of God. There are no evil spirits or devils, as all sin is connected with and inherent in matter, and depends upon the power of sense. Evil angels are only the disembodied souls of evil men.[2] The body—as the seat and cause of moral evil—is the prison of the soul, and virtue consists in victory over the material. When conquering it, the soul, the air-spirit in us, rises by virtue of its nature to an ecstatic communion with the Divine. If such have been our life, the liberated spirit rises at death to an immediate contemplation of God. A twofold bond connects during our present state the spirit with matter, that of necessity and that of pleasure.[3] The former cannot be loosened, but the latter, in itself the closest and most dangerous, has to be broken. Love of pleasure is the source of all sin, and to its removal the energies of man must be directed.

In his *ethical* disquisitions, Philo has an opportunity of fully developing his peculiar method of Scripture interpretation. The history of the Old Testament, as a whole, is transformed into an allegory.[4] Adam is pure reason unconnected with sense, but which, in order either to act or to be happy in this world, required to assume a form similar to it, or a body. It was not good for Adam to be alone, and God gave him (pure reason) a companion, namely, sensibility. But they were both naked, *i.e.* not properly connected. An end was put to this state of matters by the serpent, or pleasure. The union thus brought about constitutes the fall

---

[1] *Quis. rer. div. h.* i. 494.   [2] *De Gigant.* i. 263 ff. ; *De Somn.* i. 641 ff.
[3] Comp. *De Gigant.* i. 267.   [4] Comp. Zeller, p. 349 ff.

of pure reason, which, however, implies not sin, but imperfection and liability to moral evil. Hence also the child, though fallen, is not corrupt during the first seven years of its life, its soul then being a " tabula rasa." [1] It is only when reason is steadily rejected, and the soul seeks after and loves the sensual, that the dominion of sin is established. The beasts brought before Adam, and over which he was to reign, are the passions. From the connection between Adam and Eve (reason and sensibility) sprang, as first child, pride and presumption, or Cain. For after the union of mind with the senses, the mind at first considered everything as its own, and from this arrogance, or Cain, spring all human ills. The names of the progeny of Cain are therefore expounded as allegorically expressing the various ills of the soul. On the contrary, Abel was natural and untrained piety, —the younger son, because it succeeds the tempest of first-born youthful passion. Cain and Abel enter into contest, in which Abel succumbs, because his piety is uncultivated, and his mind untrained.

In another series of allegories we have the processes described whereby the soul rises from sin and sense to devotion to reason.[2] The desired end might be attained by learning, by discipline (askesis), or by a good natural disposition. In each case there is a lower and a higher stage of advance, the former typified by Enos, Enoch, and Noah, the latter by Abraham, Jacob, and Isaac. Enos represents hope fixed on God ; and Abraham is study, which, leaving the land of sensuousness, passes through the cycle of secular learning, and rises to Divine philosophy. Enoch (repentance) is translated from the world of sin ; Jacob is the type of a soul struggling against things of sense, often nearly failing in the conflict, but conquering at last by the help of God. Noah is rest or righteousness ; he was only perfect in *his* generation, in the ordinary virtues ; but Isaac (joy) symbolises the free unfolding of the innate spiritual life.

Asceticism consists in abstinence from worldly or

[1] *Quis. rer. div. h.* i. 515.
[2] *De Somn.* i. 646 ; comp. Zeller, p. 411 f. ; Siegfried, pp. 256–272.

material pleasures, and patient endurance of all sufferings. However, asceticism does not imply abstinence from the necessaries of life, or the self-infliction of pain for the mortification of the flesh. Its full practice in entire renunciation of the world, and retirement to the wilderness, is only recommended to those of *mature* age and at the close of a *practical* life, in which the principles of asceticism have been studied, defended, and partially exemplified.[1]

We conclude this brief sketch by giving Philo's replies to some questions on which the reader may desire information. Trials and difficulties, the necessary consequences of our connection with matter, are in this respect indeed requisite for the moral education of the ascetic, but absolutely speaking they are hindrances, and even Philo looks forward to a period when such impediments will no longer intervene between the soul and God. The privileges of the Israelites do not consist in their original choice by God, but in possessing an ancestry which, by gradual development, attained in Moses to full communion with God.[2] Their sufferings were due to sin, and were intended as a warning to all men. But a brighter day is yet to dawn upon Israel.[3] Their common return to piety will fill the nations amongst whom they are dispersed with awe; they will be dismissed from the lands of their captivity, and return to Palestine, under the guidance of a Divine superhuman appearance, visible only to themselves.[4] An era of universal holiness, peace, and prosperity will then ensue. Passion will give place to virtue, wild beasts will lose their destructive character, war will cease, or at least its commencement and termination will be almost simultaneous. The harvests will be so plentiful that none will require to collect stores, and the supply of each will be abundant. A numerous family, long life, exemption from disease,—in a word, everything requisite for happiness and comfort will be provided. The Messianic

---

[1] *De Prof.* i. 549 ff. ; *De Joseph, passim* ; comp. also Zeller, p. 406 f.
[2] *De Const. Princip.* ii. 366 ; *De Nobil.* ii. 440 ff.
[3] *De Exsecrat.* ii. 435 f. ; *De Præm. et Poen.* ii. 421-428.
[4] *De Exsecrat.* ii. 436.

king also appears in Philo's ideal future, [in the person of a
man who shall go forth to war and subdue great nations [1]].
This belief in a personal Messiah, which stands in no connection with the doctrine of the Logos, only shows how
fully Philo shared the popular expectation of his countrymen.

Mysticism was represented in Egypt by the sect of the
Therapeutæ, in Palestine by that of the Essenes. The difference between them, according to Philo, was that the
Therapeutæ led a contemplative, the Essenes an active life.
It is not ours to advert in this place to the peculiarities of
climate and natural disposition favourable to the development
of asceticism and monachism,—the embodiment of the spirit
of bondage, which even in nature seems to delight only in
solitude and awe. Egypt, the home of Christian asceticism,
produced also a set of Jewish monks. The Therapeutæ were
men and women [2] who, for ascetic purposes, left their friends
and dwellings, and, having disencumbered themselves of every
worldly care, by giving their substance to their relatives,
retired to desert places, where they lived in communities,
each individual inhabiting a solitary dwelling, yet, for the
purposes of mutual protection, within easy reach of each
other. The neighbourhood of Alexandria, not far from Lake
Mareotis, was the chief resort of these recluses.[3] Their
houses were of the most simple description, so as only to
afford shelter from heat or cold. Meat and drink were only
touched after sunset, as the glorious light of day was not
to witness any bodily indulgence. Sometimes their fasts
were protracted for three or even six days. On the Sabbath,
together with peculiar attention to spiritual wants, those of
the body were also cared for. However, the luxuries of that
day consisted only of bread and salt, or hyssop and water.
Their garments also were of the simplest kind. It is scarce

---

[1] *De Præm. et Poen.* ii. 423.

[2] Comp. Philo, *De Vita Contemplativa*, a treatise which, notwithstanding
many objections raised against it, there are good grounds for regarding as
genuine. See Dr. Edersheim in *Dict. Chr. Biog.*, "Philo," iv. 368 ff. ; also
App. VIII.

[3] *De Vit. Cont.* ii. 474 ff.

necessary to add that they lived in celibacy, longing only for the marriage of the soul with God. In each of their dwellings was a little sanctuary, called " Semneion," or " Monasterion," in which everyone spent the day in meditation, study of the Law, or of the sayings of the saints, and in spiritual songs. Twice daily they prayed. When the sun made his appearance, they entreated for a happy day, *i.e.* one in which their minds might be filled with heavenly light. When the sun set, they prayed that the soul, set free from the encumbrance of everything sensual, might be able to rise to the contemplation of truth.[1] The Law was interpreted according to the rules of an allegorical exegesis, the letter of Scripture being deemed but a symbol. The Therapeutæ professed to possess the writings of the founders of their sect, which served them as models for meditation and the composition of hymns. Every seventh day they met. They sat according to age and dignity, with hands turned inwards, the right between the breast and chin, the left resting on the side. The oldest and best initiated then delivered a discourse, in which, not in studied or persuasive language, but simply and gravely, he referred to some of the mysteries of Scripture. All listened in silence, indicating their assent only by a motion of the head or eyes. In this common sanctuary, women and men sat apart, being separated by a low breast-wall of three or four cubits height. Specially solemn was the seventh Sabbath,[2] when they commemorated the passage of the Red Sea,[3] which was perhaps regarded as a symbol of the passage from the world to asceticism. One of their officers arranged the worshippers, who appeared in white raiment. After prayer they reclined on beds of papyrus round a table (the eldest occupying the places of honour), the men at the right, and the women at the left side of the room. The junior members served, all slavery being repudiated as the iniquitous consequence of injustice and avarice, in consequence of which the stronger lorded it over the

---

[1] In general, it is remarkable that in every form of mysticism the meditative element greatly preponderates over the devotional.

[2] *De Vit. Cont.* ii. 481 ff.   [3] *Ut supra*, 485.

weaker. The viands were those for ordinary Sabbaths. A member then delivered a discourse on some scriptural subject, amidst profound silence, only interrupted by the inquiries of the hearers. Looks and nods indicated that the audience understood the argument; serenity of countenance, or a slight turn of the face, applause; a shake of the head, or a sign with the finger, expressed doubt. At the close all made a joyful noise; then one of the members sang a hymn, composed by himself or by one of their own poets; others followed, the rest joining in chorus. After this exercise, the meal was served, and then the distinctive feast of the evening commenced. Men and women ranged themselves in two bands, and, under the leadership of the most experienced, sang hymns, accompanying them with gesticulations and dances. Then the two bands mixed, "inebriated with Divine love as in the feasts of Bacchus." Thus the night was spent; when morn dawned, they looked to heaven and parted with mutual good wishes, each to his Semneion.

Of the rise and origin of the kindred sect of the Essenes we know hardly anything. We first hear of them in the time of Jonathan Maccabæus, and one Judas, an Essene, is named in the reign of Aristobulus I. (105 B.C.).[1] [Though there is no satisfactory evidence to connect them with the Chasidim, it is not improbable that the sect is the outcome of a similar tendency towards exclusiveness. Their principles and practices are mainly of Jewish origin, but they show unmistakably that they have been modified by external influences, which were probably those of Parseeism or Pythagoreanism.] Gradually the party attained the peculiar organisation described by Josephus,[2] when it consisted of four grades, distinguished by degrees of ceremonial purity, by acquaintanceship with mystical theology, and by varied occupation, from the tilling of the ground through the practice of medicine upwards to the working of miracles. The members of the four classes, amounting in all to about four thousand, kept distinct from

---

[1] Jos. *Ant.* xiii. 5. 9; 11. 2. For the Essenes, comp. Lightfoot, *Colossians*, pp. 80–96, 347–417; Schürer, II. ii. 188–218.

[2] *Wars*, ii. 8. 2–13.

each other, avoiding even the touch of a member of the inferior grades. They lived in the various cities of Palestine, but their chief settlements were near the Dead Sea. They welcomed as brethren all strangers belonging to their order. They despised riches and pleasures, held disparaging views of marriage, but we are not expressly told that they were given to ascetic practices.[1] They threw all their means into a common fund, administered by special officers of their own. A noviciate of one year was requisite to admit the candidate to the first degree of purity, and a further membership of two years before he could be admitted to the common table, or obtain that second degree of purity requisite to allow the brethren to eat with him. Some of the Essenes are said to have obtained a knowledge of the future, and Josephus relates more than one instance of their predictions being fulfilled.[2] The Essenes joined in common meals, prayed at sunrise, repudiated slavery, were under the unlimited control of their officers, etc. From certain scruples connected with ceremonial purity, they abstained from offering sacrifices in the Temple, though sending other gifts there. Probably they regarded the shedding of blood as being itself a pollution. Purifications, the study of mysticism, separation from the uninitiated, and some peculiar doctrines,—for example, with reference to predestination,—distinguished them from the other Jews. Their discipline seems to have been very strict, and an oath of secrecy bound the possessors of the mysteries. The sect became extinct some time after the destruction of Jerusalem.[3]

[Both Neo-Platonism and the Kabbalah present many strong resemblances to that form of Jewish mysticism which is represented by Philo. All three agree in their abstract conception of God, in their theory of intermediary powers or beings whereby God acts in the visible world, in their treat-

---

[1] Their abstinence from flesh and wine is asserted by Lightfoot and Zeller (*Phil. d. Griechen*, iii. 2. 287 f.), but denied by Schürer and Lucius (*Therapeutæ*, p. 38 f.).

[2] Jos. *Ant.* xiii. 11. 2 ; xv. 10. 5 ; xvii. 13. 3.

[3] [The Essenes are apparently not mentioned in Rabbinical literature.]

ment of matter as the seat of evil, and consequently in their
ethical teaching,—that it was necessary to rise superior to the
bondage of the senses. But while Philo subordinated the
systematic treatment of his doctrine to his exposition of the
Jewish Scriptures, the Neo-Platonists gained alike in clearness
and consistency by their adherence to scientific method. It
was on purely philosophical grounds that they sought to
resolve the original dualism between God and matter. Such
a dualism the Kabbalists also, from the standpoint of Jewish
monotheism, rejected far more decidedly than Philo ; this,
however, did not prevent them from forming a definite theory
of emanation, of which we can find nothing more than traces
in the Jewish philosopher.[1]]

III. *Jewish Theology*

In attempting to arrange the doctrinal views of the
Rabbins, we are bewildered by a mass of erroneous, blasphemous, and even contradictory statements. Still, as to
withhold them would interfere with a proper appreciation of
the state of the Synagogue, we now supplement our former
remarks. We have already referred to the extravagant
preference for Moses, which the doctrinal predilections for
the letter of the Pentateuch engendered. If all Israel were
God's favourites, while the Gentiles were cast off, Moses was
worth all Israel put together.[2] His superior knowledge
rendered him but a little lower than the angels ;[3] God
Himself left the higher heavens and came to him; the angels,
as well as the sun, moon, and stars, sang their hymns to him,
and the latter obtained from him permission to enlighten the
world. In the same manner the Talmud [4] relates how Moses
in argumentation silenced the angels, who were jealous of
him ; and the passage, Ps. lxviii. 18, is applied to their
ultimate reconciliation. On the other hand, after the Fall, the
carnal intercourse between the serpent and Eve put sin into
the heart of every one of her descendants. Happily this evil

---

[1] Comp. Zeller, p. 421 ff. ; Siegfried, pp. 289–299.
[2] Mechilt. on *Ex*. xv. § 9.   [3] Rosh ha-Sh. 21*b*.   [4] Shab. 89*a*.

seed has, in the case of Israel, been purged by their presence at Sinai.[1] There also assembled the souls of the prophets yet unborn, and first learned what they were afterwards to proclaim.[2] Among the prophets, Isaiah, Ezekiel, and Daniel seem to have been the most highly esteemed.

The views of the Rabbins concerning the Divine Being are sometimes sublime. His unity is the central truth of the Jewish creed ; His freedom from all human limitation and imperfection is often asserted.[3] He is represented as the Aleph (the first letter, the beginning), the Mem (the middle letter, middle), and the Tav (the last letter, the end) of all,[4] Who created everything for His own glory ; power, wisdom, and goodness are His prominent characteristics. However, His mercy was not to be isolated from His justice.[5] But whenever the Rabbins descend from general to particular statements, we meet with absurdities and even blasphemies. The most general representation of the Divine Being is as the chief Rabbi of heaven ; the angelic host being His assessors.[6] This heavenly Sanhedrin takes the opinion of living sages in cases of dispute. Of the twelve hours of the day, three are spent by God in study, three in the government of the world (or rather in the exercise of mercy), three in providing food for the world, and three in playing with Leviathan. But since the destruction of Jerusalem, all amusements were banished from the courts of heaven, and three hours were employed in the instruction of those who had died in infancy.[7] On every subject, except the giving of life, of rain, and the resurrection of the dead, God deliberated with His Sanhedrin.[8] His properties were, according to Ex. xxxiv. 6, 7, arranged under thirteen particulars.[9] Some Rabbis, however, reduced them to eleven, to ten, and even to three.

[But besides the extremely anthropomorphic conception of God which Jewish writings often present, we find, especially in the earlier literature, a very different, nay, almost an opposite

---

[1] Ab. Sar. 22*b*.
[2] Exod. Rab. 28.
[3] Comp. Weber, p. 146 ff.
[4] Jer. Sanh. i. 18*a*.
[5] Ber. 7*a*.
[6] Gen. Rab. 49.
[7] Ab. Sar. 3*b*.
[8] Taan. 2*ab*.
[9] Rosh ha-Sh. 17*b*.

conception. God is regarded as an exalted and almost
unapproachable Being, Who could have no immediate intercourse with earthly creatures. Jewish theology accordingly
introduces Divine representatives or intermediaries, by means
of which God is brought into relations with man and the
world. Of these, the most important is the " Memra," " the
Word," [1] which is often introduced in the Targums, but never
appears in the Talmud or the Midrashim. Even in the Old
Testament we sometimes find a personification of the Word
of God, which goes forth from His mouth and accomplishes
His will in the world. Such a passage as Isa. lv. 11 will
help us to understand the Memra of the Targums, though
there is one important difference ; for we can hardly doubt
that the Targums present us with a real hypostasis. When
the Old Testament uses anthropomorphisms, or attributes
bodily parts or affections to God, the Targums usually employ
some paraphrase, and often introduce a reference to the
Memra. This, for example, is the case where originally
mention was made of the eyes (*Jn.* Isa. i. 16 ; Ezek. vii. 4),
or the mouth (*Jn.* 1 Kings viii. 15, 24), or the voice of God
(*On.* Gen. iii. 8; *Jn.* Jer. xliv. 23). God repents by His
Memra (*Jn.* 1 Sam. xv. 11, 35), swears by His Memra (*On.*
Ex. xxxii. 13; *Jer.* Gen. xxii. 16; *Jn.* Isa. xlv. 23), and acts
for His Memra's sake (*Jn.* Isa. xlviii. 11). A covenant is
made between the Memra and man (*Jer.* Gen. xvii. 7, 11 ; cf.
On. Ex. xxxi. 13). Again, according to the Targums, the
Memra was actively working throughout Israel's history,
especially when God revealed Himself. The Memra acts as
the protector of the patriarchs (*On.* Gen. xxi. 22, xxvi. 24),
and as the Saviour of Israel (*Jn.* Isa. lxiii. 8; Jer. iii. 23).
He leads the people through the wilderness (*Jer.* i. and ii., Num.
x. 35 ; *Jn.* Isa. lxiii. 14), accepts their service in the Tabernacle
(*Jer.* Lev. ix. 23; cf. *On.* Lev. xxvi. 11), and delivers to the
Prophets their message (*Jn.* Isa. vi. 8, viii. 5). In conclusion,
we may add that the Memra is distinct from the Messiah,
and from the Angel of the Lord. The latter expression is
generally retained in the Targums (*e.g. On.* Gen. xvi. 7 ; *Jn.*

---

[1] Comp. Weber, pp. 172–184, also *Life and Times*, i. 46–48, ii. 660–663.

Jud. vi. 12); and in *Jn.* Isa. xlii. 1 the Memra and the Messiah are mentioned together.[1]

God's active presence in the world is also represented by the Shechinah. This term is found in the Targums, and also in the Talmud and Midrashim; but a certain distinction must be drawn between the earlier and the later usage. In the Targums the Shechinah is the visible token of God's presence, or more strictly of His communion with His people. The Old Testament conception with which it most nearly corresponds is the visible Glory of the Lord. Indeed, the Shechinah is sometimes brought into connection with the Jekara or Glory: thus we read in *Jer.* Ex. xxxiv. 5, "Jehovah revealed Himself in the clouds of the Glory of His Shechinah"; similarly in Ex. xxxiii. 22, 23, the Glory of the Shechinah is spoken of (comp. *v.* 18). The full glory of the Lord rests upon the throne of God in heaven, but a portion of this brightness has been manifested on earth. Thus the Shechinah dwelt on the Tabernacle (*On* Ex. xxv. 8), and on the Temple (*Jn.* Hab. ii. 20), and withdrew to heaven when the people sinned (*Jn.* Hos. v. 6, 15). It can hardly be doubted that the Shechinah was originally conceived of as impersonal; and herein lay the difference between it and the Memra. Men call upon the Memra (*Jer.* Ex. xxxiv. 5), or trust on it (*Jn.* Isa. xxvi. 4; Mic. iii. 11); such expressions would never be applied to the Shechinah. The Memra chose the land of Israel to make the Shechinah of God dwell there (*Jer.* Deut. xii. 5, 11). When God reveals Himself on earth by a visible sign, He does so by means of the Shechinah; by means of the Memra, when the revelation takes the form of a message or a personal activity. But in the Talmud and the later literature, where, as we said before, the Memra never occurs, the term Shechinah is used somewhat differently. It still denotes, as before, the visible token of God's presence;[2] but it sometimes has a more personal reference. It may not be so distinctly hypostatised as the Memra, but it frequently expresses relations of God to the world, which were indicated by the use of that term in the old Targums. Thus, it is by

---

[1] Comp. also *Jn.* Isa. ix. 6. [2] Ber. 17*a*, 64*a*.

means of the Shechinah that God displays His favour to
men.   It withdrew further and further to heaven as sin
increased in the world, but returned to earth in the days of
Moses (Gen. Rab. 19).   There is now no place on earth
where the Shechinah is not (B. Bath. 25*a*), but in a special
sense, wherever the Law is taught and practised, the Shechinah
brings blessing and protection.[1]]

The dogma about angels and fallen spirits presents a
curious mixture of beliefs.   The period of their creation is
variously stated; some of them appear occasionally as per-
sonifications of the affections of the Deity.   Daily does God
create a vast number of angels, who, after having praised
Him, pass away.[2]   There are four classes of angels: the
Ofanim or wheel-angels, the Seraphim, the Living Creatures
who bear the throne of glory, and the ministering angels.[3]
The greatest of all is the Metatron.   Chief among the princes
who stand before the throne, are Michael, Gabriel, Raphael,
and Uriel, and of these Michael, to whom Israel is specially
committed, is the highest.   Each angel can only be sent on
one errand at a time.[4]   Every individual has his protecting
angel.   But the principal among the throne-angels, Samael,
from a desire to gain dominion over man, had come to Eve
as a tempter in the form of the serpent, in consequence of
which he was banished, and became the devil.[5]   There are,
however, two kinds of evil spirits,—those who had originally
been angels, but whom sin had deprived of their high estate,
and their progeny by carnal intercourse with men.   Of the
latter class there are again two subdivisions,—the offspring
of devils and our first parents, and those of devils and the
daughters of men (Gen. vi.).   From Gen. v. 3 it was attempted
to prove that Adam had human children only after he was
130 years old.[6]   During the previous period Adam and Eve
begat each male and female evil spirits.   [St. Augustine mentions

---

[1] [Comp. Ber. 6*a*, "where two men met to pray"; Sot. 17*a*, "where man
and wife live in piety."]

[2] Chag. 14*a*; comp. Weber, 161–168.   [3] Chag. 12*b*.

[4] Targ. Ps.–Jon. in Gen. xviii. 2.   [5] Weber, 211ff.

[6] Erub. 18*b*.

a Jewish tradition that the first man had two wives,[1] and in the later Jewish literature a beautiful woman named Lilith appears as Adam's first wife. Elsewhere, Lilith is the queen of female spirits.[2]] Samael himself committed fornication with Eve. It is to be remarked that early Christian heretics entertained similar notions.[3] Satan himself acted in man as the evil concupiscence, the Jezer ha-Ra, to which seven names were given.[4]

Devils were arranged in various classes.[5] The Shedim, of whom Ashmedai was chief,[6] appeared usually in the form of human beings, but might also assume other shapes. Besides these there were the Lilin or night-hags, which killed young children, and the Ruchin or evil spirits. Devils were supposed to have three things in common with angels, and three things with men. Like angels, they had wings, flew from one end of the world to the other, and knew about the future, having heard the Divine decrees. Like men, they ate and drank, propagated themselves, and died.[7] If the eyes of men were opened to perceive their number, they would be overwhelmed by fear. On our right there are no less than 10,000, and on our left 1000 of these evil spirits. If we wish to convince ourselves of this fact, we have only to strew fine ashes before our beds, and we shall in the morning see their foot-prints as those of cocks; and if we wish to see them, we are to burn the after-birth of a black cat, this cat and its mother having been both pure black and first-borns, and rub our eyes with the ashes.[8] They ruled specially at night, and inhabited desolate and ruined or filthy places, and the branches of certain trees. The devil frequently assumes the appearance of a goat,[9] or dances between the horns of an ox returning from pasture. He seeks in every possible manner to do harm to men. Many diseases, such as epilepsy, violent headaches, hydrophobia, etc., are caused by him. But as he may be conjured by incense and formulas, so he may also be exorcised. The Talmud mentions[10] the following

---

[1] *Cont. advers. legis*, ii. 2.   [2] Nidd. 24*b*.
[3] Comp. Iren. i. 30; Epiphan. *Haeres.* xl. 5.   [4] Joma 69*b*; Succa 52*a*.
[5] Comp. Weber, 245f.; *Life and Times*, ii. 755–763.   [6] Pes. 110*a*.
[7] Chag. 16*a*.   [8] Ber. 6*a*.   [9] *Ut supra*, 62*a*.   [10] Shab. 67*a*.

formula for exorcising the devil from persons possessed by him:—" Burst, burst, curst, dashed, banned art thou, Bar-Tit, Bar-Tema, Bar-Tina " (or, as otherwise read, " Son of clay, son of the unclean, son of dirt "), " in the name of Marigo, Moriphath, and his seal." Many similar spells might be quoted. By power-ful formulas evil spirits may even be rendered serviceable. Thus, King Solomon built the Temple by such means.[1] Josephus speaks also of the havoc made by demons, although his views of their origin differ somewhat from those of the Talmud. Samael, who is to be identified with Satan and the angel of death, stands as the accuser of Israel, opposed to Michael, their advocate. We read also of his gnashing with the teeth, in malicious pleasure at the calamities of men, or in anger when he finds that they are out of his power.[2]

The Talmud speaks [3] of a multitude of worlds (18,000) which God visits every night. The Midrashim also refer to other worlds, which were created and destroyed before our world, a view similar to that held not only by some of the Gnostics, but also by some of the orthodox Christian Fathers. To return, the earthly Jerusalem was only an image of the heavenly,[4] in which everything, the temple, the altar, and Michael, as its minister, are found, only in larger and more glorious proportions. Seven things were created *before* the world, and ten on the first Friday immediately before the darkness which ushered in the rest of the first Sabbath. The former comprise the Law, repentance, the temple, the name of the Messiah, the throne of glory, the garden of Eden, and hell.[5] Several Jewish writings introduce amongst the creatures of the fifth day the male and female leviathan, immense fishes happily kept each alone,[6] as their brood would have destroyed the whole world ; and amongst those of the sixth day, the male and female behemoth, or large oxen, subjected to similar separation, which are to be killed and prepared for the feast of the Messianic days.[7] We learn also that the belief

---

[1] Gitt. 68*ab*.   [2] Jer. Keth. xii. 35*b*.   [3] Ab. Sar. 3*b*.
[4] Taan. 5*a* ; Chag. 12*b*.   [5] Pes. 54*a* ; Nedar. 39*b*.
[6] Pirke El. xi. ; B. Bath. 74*b*.
[7] Comp. also Targ. Ps.-Jon. in Gen. i. 21 ; 4 Esdr. vi. 49.

in the existence of seven heavens was common amongst the Jews.[1] The first heaven, or " Velin " curtain, was drawn every evening and removed every morning ; the second, or " Rakia " firmament, was the place where sun, moon, and stars were fixed ; the third, or " Shechakim " clouds, contained the mill-stones necessary for making the manna for the saints ; the fourth, or " Zebul " place, contained the heavenly Jerusalem, temple, and altar ; the fifth, or " Maon " dwelling, contained the hosts of angels who sing praises during the whole night, the day being assigned to Israel for the same purpose ; the sixth, or " Macon " residence, contained the stores of snow, hail, noxious dews, rains, storms, vapours, etc. ; the seventh, or " Araboth," contained justice, the judgment of mercy, the treasures of life, of peace, and of blessing, the souls of saints, souls before they were clothed with bodies, and the dew by which God was to raise the dead. There also dwelt the Ofanim, the Seraphim, the Living Creatures, the ministering angels, the throne of glory, the eternal King, the living God. Similar views are propounded in some of the Apocrypha.[2] Each of these heavens was so distant from the other, that the journey from one to the other would occupy five hundred years (like the years of Abraham, Isaac, and Jacob).[3]

As to the comparative proportions of heaven and hell, we are informed [4] that the garden of Eden was sixty times as large as the world, and hell sixty times as large as Eden, of which the garden formed a sixtieth part. The joys and torments of heaven and hell are described. When the just reach the two ruby gates of heaven, they are received by the 600,000 ministering angels who keep watch there.[5] They are then arrayed with eight garments, crowned with two crowns, and receive eight myrtle branches. They are next conducted to a place beside rivers, surrounded by eight hundred different kinds of roses and myrtles, and placed

---

[1] Chag. 12b.
[2] Comp. the Testam. Levi in *Fabricii Cod. Pseudepigr.* i. pp. 545–548, although there the objects in each heaven are somewhat differently arranged.
[3] Chag. 13a ; j. Ber. i. 2c.   [4] Taan. 10a.
[5] Jalkut Shim. Ber. 20.

under a canopy.   Four rivers, one of milk, one of wine, one
of balsam, and one of honey, water, and a golden vine with
thirty shining pearls, adorn this place.   During the three
watches of the night every saint is successively transformed
into a child, a youth, and an aged man, in order to enjoy the
pleasures peculiar to every age.   Eden has 800,000 kinds of
trees, and in each corner 600,000 ministering angels.   The
tree of life overshadows the whole garden, and its fruits
have 500,000 various kinds of taste and smell.   Under its
branches the sages sit and expound the Law, each of them
having two canopies, one formed of the stars, and the other
of the sun and moon, and between both a veil woven of the
cloud of glory.   On the other hand, three gates—one from
the wilderness, the other from the sea, the third from
Jerusalem—lead to the abodes of hell.[1]   [To hell seven
names are given, and the older literature makes no distinction
between Sheol and Gehenna.   At a later period] we meet
with the notion that heaven and hell are adjoining, and only
separated by a wall of the thickness of one handbreadth.[2]
Thus the inhabitants of either place know what is going on
in the other.

Man consists of body and soul.[3]   The body comes from
below, and is formed of earth taken from different countries.[4]
The soul, on the other hand, has been in a pre-existent
state, and comes down from above.   Before a soul sees the
light of the world, an angel shows it the glories of heaven
and the torments of hell.   Then the child is beaten and
driven forth into the world,—hence the crying of new-born
babes.[5]   [The soul at the moment of birth is clean, and man
should endeavour so to live that he may restore it to his
Maker in its original purity.[6]   But the body, which is
earthly and the seat of the Jezer ha-Ra, is relatively
unclean.]   In consequence of the fall of Adam, death has not
only passed on all men, as being connected with Adam (their
bodies having as it were been in Adam), but a liability and

---

[1] Erub. 19*a*.   [2] Koh. Rab. on vii. 14 ; comp. Weber, p. 326 ff.
[3] Comp. Weber, pp. 203–207, 217–223.   [4] Sanh. 38*b*.
[5] Tanchuma, Pikkude 3.   [6] Shab. 152*b*.

proneness to sin has become natural to man. This Jezer
ha-Ra is not actual sinfulness, but an inclination to it, or
evil tendency. On the other hand, when men arrive at years
of discretion, at thirteen, a good inclination, Jezer Tob,
makes itself felt. A struggle then ensues, on the issue of
which the future state depends.[1] After death the soul
hovers for a long time round the dead body.[2] Besides the
just who pass immediately to heaven, and sinners who go to
destruction, there is a middle class who are to be purified
by fire in hell during a period of twelve months.[3] Israelites
are not liable to perpetual hell-fire, unless the peculiar bodily
mark of their descent has been effaced. As we have seen,
the Talmud appears to assign a special place in heaven to
the souls of children who have died in infancy. [Some
Rabbins admitted that pious Gentiles might enter heaven.
Thus, Rabbi Jehuda is said to have promised the Emperor
Antoninus a part in the world to come, and Chanina ben
Teradion made a similar promise to his executioner. [4]

The Jezer ha-Ra[5] is in the first place merely a natural
impulse, which is necessary for the continuance of the world.
Without it no man would marry a wife or build a house.[6] It
is called evil, because its dominion would imply the rule of
the body over the soul ; and since the Fall, man's natural
impulses, unless controlled by the Jezer Tob, often lead him
into sin. Hence the Jezer ha-Ra is sometimes spoken of as
altogether evil, and] the prayers of Rabbins for the removal
of the Jezer ha-Ra, or "leaven," [7] as it is sometimes called,
were frequent and earnest, as that evil inclination might
ultimately ruin the soul, or at least expose it to the fire of
purgatory. But in order that any breach of the law might
really become sin, the will must have consented to its
commission. If the Jezer ha-Ra is early and energetically
opposed, it may be kept in subjection. Some have even
completely subdued it. The most efficacious means for this

---

[1] Nedar. 32*b*.   [2] Ber. 18*b*.
[3] Rosh ha-Sh. 16*b*, 17*a* ; comp. Weber, pp. 326–330.
[4] Ab. Sar. 10*b*, 18*a*.   [5] Comp. Weber, pp. 223–231.   [6] Gen. Rab. 9.
[7] For example, Ber. 17*a*.

purpose is study of the Law.[1]   It was said that the evil
inclination was implanted in man, in order that he might
merit a reward by overcoming it;[2] for the Talmudists seem
to have held that God was the author of Adam's Jezer ha-Ra,[3]
or evil inclination (not of his sin), the power and prevalence
of which in his posterity, and their sorrows and death, are
connected with the fall of Adam.

On the doctrine of predestination, the Talmud seems to
have been undecided.   No doubt was entertained that at
certain fixed periods God decreed concerning all events, and
even sealed the judgment of men ;[4] but repentance could
arrest the impending doom, and even reverse the heavenly
decree.   It was a principle[5] almost necessary to Judaism,
that everything was in the power of Heaven except the fear
of God, *i.e.* that man alone had the power to produce in himself true piety; that God only assisted and crowned with
success all sincere endeavours.   At the same time, God
possessed perfect *foreknowledge* of man and his actions.[6]
Certain events, such as the begetting of children, the
duration of life, worldly prosperity, etc., may in part depend
on the constellation under which we are born,[7]—a view this
foreign to Judaism.   To make it fit into Talmudical theology,
it was added that the stars had influence only on Gentiles.[8]
[It is unnecessary to multiply further details, but it is clear
that the problem of freewill and predestination had engaged
the attention of Rabbinic Judaism.   To judge from the
Talmud, the commonly accepted doctrine was that which
asserted a belief alike in Divine providence and in human
freedom and responsibility.[9]]

The moral obligations incumbent upon Israel have
already been detailed.   Entrance into the kingdom of heaven
was made dependent on conformity to them.   Next to the
love of God, an affection which implied a readiness to obey
His commandments and to do good, stood love to one's
neighbour, which, indeed, both Hillel and Akiba declared to

---

[1] Kidd. 30*b*.   [2] Sanh. 64*a*.   [3] Ber. 61*a*.
[4] Rosh ha-Sh. i. 2.   [5] Ber. 33*b*.   [6] Pirke Ab. iii. 15.
[7] Moed K. 28*a*.   [8] Shab. 156*a*.   [9] Comp. Schürer, II. ii. 14–17.

be the highest commandment.[1] On the other hand, to withhold charity—denominated *Zedakah*, righteousness—was a
sin similar to idolatry.[2] Humility or meekness, the study
of the Law, obedience to its peculiar tenets, and prayer,
procured great blessings. It was the humility of Moses
which elevated him to so lofty a position.[3] However, in
another passage,[4] this is attributed to his prayerfulness, and
his example is quoted to prove that even good works are less
effectual than prayer. The beneficial effects of the latter
were not confined to him who prayed, but, in answer to his
entreaty, diseases were removed or public calamities averted.
Thus we are told how the son of Rabbi Gamaliel was healed
of his sickness by the prayer of Chanina ben Doza.[5]
Earnestness was deemed by some Rabbins a necessary
condition of prayer, nor were devotions to be transformed
into daily or formal tasks. To avoid such practices, a Rabbi
recommends a daily variation of the prayers.[6] As to the duration of prayer, opinions were divided, but the usual practice
seems to have been in favour of lengthened exercises. The
praises of God formed the beginning and end of the prayer ;
the expression of personal wants was inserted in the middle.[7]

We have already exhibited specimens of the prayers of
the synagogue. With the exception of the absence of a
sense of personal spiritual wants, the sublime character of
these compositions entitles them to a high place. We quote
two prayers, supposed [8] to approach somewhat to the prayer
which the Lord taught His disciples. R. Samuel prayed : [9]—
" Thanks and praise be to Thy name ! Thine is the greatness,
the power, and the glory. May it please Thee, O Lord our
God, and the God of our fathers, to lift us up when we fall,
and to raise us up when we are bowed down ; for Thou liftest
up those that fall, and raisest up those that are bowed down.
Thou art merciful, and beside Thee there is none. Blessed
be the Lord." Bar Kappara prayed :—" Before Thee do we

[1] Shab. 31*a* ; Sifra iv. 12.
[2] Tos. Peah iv. 13.
[3] Mechilt. on *Ex.* xx. 21.
[4] Ber. 32*b*.
[5] Ber. 34*b*.   [6] Jer. Ber. iv. 8*a*.
[7] Ber. 34*a*.
[8] Gfrörer, *Urchristenthum*, ii. p. 149, etc.
[9] Jer. Ber. i. 3*d*.

bend, before Thee we bow, before Thee we fall down, and Thee alone do we adore.   To Thee every knee shall bend, and every tongue confess.   Thine, O Lord, is the majesty, the power, the glory, the victory, and the praise ; for what is in heaven, and what on earth, is Thine.   Thine, Lord, is the kingdom, and Thou art exalted above all.   Riches and honour are before Thee.   Thou reignest over all, and in Thine hand are power and might.   It is in Thy power to make anyone great or mighty.   We bless Thee, O our God, and praise Thy glorious name.   We adore Thee with all our heart and soul.   All our members say, Who is like Thee, O God, Who deliverest the needy from the mighty, and the poor from the hand of him who doeth violence ? "   [The expressions used in the above prayers, and indeed in the Lord's Prayer itself, are based to a large extent upon the language of the Old Testament ; and to nearly every clause of the Lord's Prayer we might quote parallels from Rabbinical writings.[1]]   Yet the fact of such resemblance only makes the difference the more striking.   As might have been expected, much in the Synagogue reminds us of the Church ; it is the difference of spirit and tendency which brings home to us the conviction that the Gospel presents a *new* creation.

In prayer, care was taken to turn towards the Holy Place. Along with prayer, penitence was a great means of averting the Divine displeasure.   Were all Israel properly to repent but for one day, the Messiah would at once appear.[2]   [Faith, that is, a firm trust in the promises of God, received like any good work its due reward.[3]]   All Israel, except a few notorious sinners and unbelievers, were supposed to have part in the world to come.[4]   [Repentance alone could not atone for the sin of apostasy, which must be expiated by the sinner's death. A heathen's penitence availed him nothing unless he embraced the Jewish faith, and in theory it was right to refuse to save the life of an unbeliever.[5]]   A proper observance of the Sabbath procured the pardon of sins.   The merits of Jews

---

[1] Comp. Taylor, *Sayings of the Jewish Fathers*, pp. 138–145.
[2] Jer. Taan. i. 64*a*.   [3] Comp. Weber, p. 295 f.
[4] Sanh. xi. 1.   [5] Ab. Sar. 17*a*, 26*ab*.

secured their entrance into heaven, and a share in the resurrection of the just, while the good works of the impious and of heathens met their reward only in this world.[1] Sufferings were means of procuring merit and atoning for guilt. Chastisements caused the pardon of sins; but if sent as a dispensation of love, they accompanied or preceded special blessings. Under trials, the pious should examine whether they had been guilty of any special sin, and whether they had sufficiently engaged in the study of the Law. If a satisfactory reply could be given to these two questions, the trials should be gladly taken as marks of God's special favour and gracious designs.[2] All means of grace were available up to death, when the soul appeared before the Judge, who put the good works in one balance, and the evil in another, and adjudged heaven or hell according to the preponderance of good or evil.[3] But when the good and evil works exactly counterbalanced one another, it was generally supposed, though the Rabbins were not quite unanimous, that God pressed down the one side of the balance or raised the other, so that the merits might preponderate.[4] Certain acts of kindness might in themselves prove sufficient to atone for a whole life of sin. On the whole, there was in this respect a great want of moral earnestness in the Synagogue. Some saints were supposed to possess a superfluity of merits, which might be made available to compensate for the deficiencies of others. Thus, amongst others, the celebrated Simon ben Jochai arrogated to himself the power of atoning by his righteousness for the sins of the whole world, from his time to the end.[5] Popularly, the merits of the three fathers, Abraham, Isaac, and Jacob, and of the four mothers, Sarah, Rebecca, Leah, and Rachel, were viewed as procuring favour for their descendants.[6] [It was one of the greatest privileges of a true-born Israelite, that he had a claim upon the treasury of the merits of the patriarchs.[7] Similarly, the son of a good man might

---

[1] Targ. Jer. in Deut. vii. 10.
[2] Ber. 5a.
[3] Jer. Kidd. i. 61d..
[4] Arach. 8b.
[5] Jer. Ber. ix. 13d; Succ. 45a.
[6] Tar. Jer. in Deut. xxxiii. 15.
[7] Comp. Weber, p. 282 ff.

feel more assured that his prayers would be heard, because of his father's merits.[1] The sufferings of righteous men might suffice to atone for the sins of the whole generation in which they lived.[2]] Condemned criminals were, if unwilling to confess, to be admonished at least to exclaim, " May my death be the expiation of my sins." [3] The death of the just might be the means of procuring pardon for all Israel.[4] The cessation of sacrifices induced the Rabbins to substitute in their room the study of the Law, which is exalted above every other merit. Confession, repentance, fasting, and the Day of Atonement, together with personal sufferings and merits, specially the study of the Law and works of kindness, and finally a man's last agony,—such were the means of reconciliation with God to which the Synagogue pointed a sinner, whose conscience the mere fact of his connection with the patriarchs could not satisfy.

We close by briefly sketching the traditions of the Jewish Fathers concerning the Messiah and His kingdom.[5] On no one subject were opinions more divergent than on this. The circumstances of the nation were such as to damp the hopes of the most sanguine, and to contradict the favourite notions of the Rabbins as to the value of Israel, and the sacredness and meritoriousness of their conduct and occupation. All miseries were indeed to be removed by the advent of the Messiah, but this happy event was delayed by some mysterious sin of Israel, which the Rabbins could not name. It was inferred from analogy, that as the world had been created in six days and the seventh been the Sabbath of rest, so it would continue for 6000 years, while the seventh thousand would become the Sabbath of the world. Such seems to have been the opinion pretty generally entertained by all sections of the Synagogue, from which it passed into the early Church.[6] Opinions varied, whether the Messiah was to appear during

---

[1] Jebam. 64*a*.   [2] Comp. Weber, p. 314 f.
[3] Sanh. vi. 2.   [4] Moed K. 28*a*.
[5] Comp. Weber, pp. 333–386 ; Schürer, II. ii. 126–187 ; *Life and Times*, ii. 433–445, etc.
[6] Sanh. 97*a* ; Ep. Barnabas, 15.

the fifth or the seventh millennium. We need scarcely remind the reader that at the time of our Lord the expectation of the coming of a great Deliverer was very general, not only amongst the Jews, but also amongst heathen nations. With the exception of splendour and honour to Israelites individually, a universal Jewish empire, and an ample supply of everything needful or agreeable, the fancy of the Rabbins presented to them little to distinguish the happy Messianic from ordinary times.[1] It must, however, be remembered that a distinction was made between the days of the Messiah and "the world to come," which was to follow them. In the latter the removal of the Jezer ha-Ra and the cessation of everything carnal or terrestrial were placed. The days of the Messiah, on the other hand, were even to witness the profession of arms.[2] In fact, the wars of Gog and Magog, the final judgment, and the creation of new heavens and a new earth, were to intervene between the days of the Messiah and the world to come. [Older writers, however, do not distinguish between the world to come and the Messianic times.]

With reference to the person of the expected Deliverer, [He was commonly thought of as a ruler of human origin, but specially endowed by God with supernatural powers ; but there was also a widespread belief in His premundane existence.[3]] He was derived from the tribe of Judah, from the family of David, and from the city of Bethlehem.[4] As the time apparently passed on, and the promised One did not appear, the opinion began to be entertained that Messiah had indeed already been born, but remained concealed, and would only appear to make an end to the fearful calamities which are termed "the woes" or "the travail" of the Messiah. In the Targum ascribed to Jonathan ben Uzziel it was stated that Messiah was hid on account of the sins of the people, and in the days of our Lord, some of the Jews declared that "when Christ cometh, no man knoweth whence He is" (John vii. 27). Only constant engagement with sacred studies and in good works, would procure exemption

---

[1] Ber. 34*b*; Pes. 68*a*   [2] Shab. 63*a*.
[3] Comp. Schürer, II. ii. 160 ff.   [4] Tar. Jon. in Zech. x.; Isa. xi.; Mic. v.

from the latter-day tribulations.[1] The Messiah was to be preceded by Elias, whose mission is variously stated,[2] as the expelling of those who had wrongfully intruded into the Synagogue, the receiving of those who had wrongfully been expelled, or even the settling of the controversies of the Rabbins. Meantime Elias was engaged in chronicling the history of the world.[3]

When the Messiah had at last appeared, it was thought that He would hide Himself for forty-five days, and then appear again.[4] His coming would be the occasion for a last struggle on the part of the world-power of Rome under the leadership of Armilus—[the name is probably a form of Romulus]. This chief enemy of Israel the Messiah Himself would slay, and the last of the four great world-empires would be destroyed. Then would the deliverance of Israel be accomplished. Those who were dispersed in all parts of the earth were to be miraculously gathered together and restored to the Holy Land. The dead Israelites were to rise again to share the blessings of the Messianic kingdom. It was thought that one bone in the body was never destroyed, but served as the basis for the new man, who in his grave-clothes would roll underground till he reached Palestine.[5] The question of the return of the ten tribes was disputed. Rabbi Akiba declared that they would never come back,[6] but the majority of opinions seems to have been favourable to a belief in their return. Those heathens who had not oppressed Israel, were to come and bring gifts to the Messiah, and to become converts to Judaism. Another and more intolerant party, however, supposed that these proselytes would speedily fall away and join the armies of Gog in the last struggle.[7] Rabbins differed as to the duration of the Messianic reign, computing it variously (from analogy) at 40, 70, 90, 365, 400, 1000, 2000, and even 7000 years.[8] After that period the hosts of Gog and Magog were to come up to

[1] Sanh. 98b.
[2] Eduj. viii. 7.
[3] Seder Ol. R. c. xvii.
[4] Pesikta 49b ; comp. Weber, p. 348 ff.
[5] Jer. Kil. ix. 32c.
[6] Sanh. xi. 3.
[7] Ab. Sar. 3b.
[8] Sanh. 97a–99a ; comp. *Life and Times*, ii. 737–741.

battle, but the Messiah would destroy them with the breath of His mouth.

[On the subject of a *general* resurrection a great variety of belief prevailed. The older view asserted only the resurrection of the righteous; then there grew up a belief in a general resurrection to judgment, and as the Messianic age ceased to be regarded as the consummation of all things, it was thought that this would take place at the end of the Messiah's reign.] All were to rise to be judged except some notorious sinners, who had already in their lifetime received their condemnation.[1] The heathen, who had been offered the Law on Sinai, but had refused to accept it,[2] would then receive their sentence. For some of the ungodly at any rate the punishment of Gehenna was regarded as everlasting.[3] After the last judgment the renewal of heaven and earth would inaugurate the period of the world to come, and in that future world there would be neither darkness nor evil desire. Opinions differed, however, on the manner of life of the blessed. According to some, in the future world there is to be neither eating, nor drinking, nor marrying, nor envy, nor hatred, nor strife, but the righteous will sit with crowns on their heads, and enjoy the brightness of the Shechinah.[4] But others held more materialistic views, and spoke of the banquet to be prepared for the righteous from the flesh of Leviathan.[5]

In one passage of the Talmud,[6] and frequently in later writings, we meet with a second Messiah, the son of Joseph, who is, however, always regarded . as subordinate to the Son of David. His work is to fight against the powers of the ungodly; and, after he is slain in the conflict, the Messiah, the Son of David, appears to triumph over his enemies, and to reign in glory. [This late view is probably unconnected with the belief in the sufferings of the Son of David, to which some Jewish writings allude.[7]] It was commonly supposed that the deliverance by the Messiah would

---

[1] Sanh. xi. 1–4.   [2] Ab. Sar. 2*a*–3*a*.   [3] Rosh ha-Sh. 17*a*.
[4] Ber. 17*a*.   [5] B. Bath. 75*a*.   [6] Succ. 52*a*.
[7] Comp. Weber, p. 346 f; Schürer, II. ii. 167 f., 184 ff.

take place in Nisan,[1] the month of the Exodus, and this idea soon found its way into the Church.[2]

The purely religious assemblies of the Jews were held in the synagogues.[3]   According to a Rabbinic injunction, these buildings were to be reared on the highest point in the town ;[4] but it cannot be shown that in Palestine this was ever carried out.   In fact, the synagogues were frequently built outside the towns, and preference seems to have been given to sites near to rivers or to the seashore, so that water might be at hand for the various purifications.   [It is, more-over, very difficult to say wherein lay the difference between a synagogue and a *proseuche ;* for while a distinction between the two is implied in Acts xvi. 13,[5] Philo certainly uses the latter term to denote the regular synagogues.[6]]   In Palestine there was probably at least one synagogue in every town, and even in the larger villages.   Large towns would contain several synagogues, according to the number of the inhabit-ants.   In Jerusalem, where with characteristic exaggeration the Talmud asserts that there were 480 synagogues,[7] we know that the different nationalities, and indeed the different trades, had their own places of worship.   An assembly for public service had to consist of ten men at the least, and a large town was defined as one in which there were ten men whose business did not prevent them from attending the synagogues even on week-days.[8]   [At a later time it became customary to pay a small fee to ten men, whose duty it was to attend daily at the public services; but it is not clear that this custom had been introduced in the Talmudic period.]

The origin of the synagogues is involved in some difficul-ties.   Their want must have been felt by the exiles in Babylon, who were shut out from the Temple and its services. The measures adopted by Ezra and Nehemiah for public religious instruction doubtless encouraged their establishment

---

[1] Rosh ha-Sh. 11*a*.   [2] Hieron. in Matt. xxv. 6 ; Lact. *Inst.* vii. 19.
[3] Comp. Schürer, II. ii. 62–83.   [4] Tos. Meg. iv. 23.
[5] Hort, *Judaistic Christianity*, p. 89.

[6] Hence Schürer, *l.c.* p. 73, denies that there was any difference between the two terms.

[7] Jer. Meg. iii. 73*d*.   [8] Meg. i. 3.

in Palestine; and during the times of the Maccabees they seem to have existed throughout the country, and amongst the Jews scattered abroad. The officers employed in the synagogue were the ruler or president, to whom was entrusted the superintendence of Divine service; the elders, who, in a purely Jewish locality, would be also the elders of the community; and the servant or attendant.[1] Everything connected with the public worship and the membership of the synagogue was under the management of the president and elders. The beadle or servant generally inflicted the punishment of stripes on refractory members. Sometimes the beadle or Chazzan was also employed as teacher of the youngest class of children.[2] To these officials we may add those who collected for and distributed relief to the poor. The Messenger, or delegate of the congregation, whose duty it was to lead the devotions, was not a permanent official; but any member of the congregation might be called upon by the ruler of the synagogue to perform this function. The interior of the synagogue was simple. A Rabbinic ordinance prescribes that the entrance should be toward the east,[3] but nearly all the ruined synagogues of Galilee have their entrances on the south. At the opposite end was a kind of ark containing copies of the Law. There was a special place for the leader of the devotions, and a raised platform for those members of the congregation who were invited to read aloud a portion of the Law, or to expound it. The latter duty was discharged by the Rabbins, or any other notable person, with the consent and under the direction of the elders.

Though the synagogues were open daily, a prolonged and more solemn service was celebrated on Mondays and Thursdays,[4] as well as on Sabbaths and feast days. Every Monday and Thursday three persons were called to the platform to read in the Law, on feast days five, and on Sabbaths seven.[5] Besides the portions of the Law, selections from the Prophets were also read. The origin of this practice is unknown, but

---

[1] Comp. Schürer, *ut supra; Life and Times*, i. 434–445.
[2] Macc. iii. 12; Shab. i. 3.   [3] Tos. Meg. iii. 3.   [4] Meg. iii. 6; iv. 1.
[5] Meg. iv. 1. 2.

it dates from before the Christian era. The choice of the passage was probably left to the reader himself; [certainly in the time of the Mishna the cycle of lessons for feast days had not been definitely settled [1]]. The reading of the Law was accompanied by a version into the known dialects, to which the origin of the Targums may be traced. In course of time various feasts were added to the calendar, and restrictions and rules defined the biblical festivals. Thus thirty-nine occupations were specified as illegal on the Sabbath ;[2] various practices, such as the solemn blessing pronounced over the cup on the evening which ushered in the Sabbath, etc., were enjoined.[3] The solemnities observed on the various feasts were, as closely as possible, imitations of the services of the Temple, but there were inevitably many divergencies from the stately ritual which had there been practised. The practice of wearing coverings with fringes upon their corners, phylacteries, containing passages of Scripture, on the forehead and left arm, and of affixing them on the door-posts, all in fancied observance of the law of Moses, are known to the readers of the New Testament. The phylacteries were generally put on only during morning prayer, [and were not worn on Sabbaths or on feast days.[4] We hear, however, of Rabbins who, from scrupulous piety or from love of ostentation, wore their phylacteries at other than the stated times.] In the synagogue, the spiritual aristocracy occupied the foremost seats. Men and women were separated from each other, and, except the responses of the people, nothing interrupted the public devotions. The five books of Moses were read through once in three, or, as others suppose, in three and a half years. The present arrangement, by which the Pentateuch is divided into fifty-four sections (read through once every year), originated amongst the Babylonian Jews.[5]

---

[1] Comp. Meg. iv. 4; and see Hamburger, *Real-Enc.* ii. 336, "Haftara."
[2] Shab. vii. 2.   [3] Comp. Pes. 101a.
[4] Comp. Hamburger, ii. 1203 ff., "Tephillin."
[5] *Ut supra*, pp. 1263–1268, "Vorlesung aus der Thora."

CHAPTER XII

THE attempts at shaking off the foreign yoke made during the reign of Hadrian, were, in part at least, renewed in the time of his successor, Antoninus Pius.[1] We are not informed of the occasion of this fresh rising, nor of its prospects; [nor do we know whether it took place before or after the removal of the obnoxious edicts which followed the unhappy termination of the war under Bar-Cochba. Possibly it was connected with the disturbances in Parthia and Armenia, which broke out at the end of the reign of Antoninus.[2] That the hopes of some of the Jews were turned towards Parthia, we may probably infer from the expectation, which even the cautious Juda ben Ilai cherished, that the Roman Empire would one day fall by the hands of the Persians or Parthians.[3] But Simon ben Jochai seems to have been less sanguine, for he exclaimed, "When thou seest a Parthian horse tied to an Israelite gravestone, then canst thou believe in the coming of the Messiah."[4]] In any case the, rebellion could not have been widespread, as the forces at the disposal of the Roman governor in Judea were sufficient speedily to suppress it.

[Some vague recollections of these fresh troubles have been preserved in Jewish writings. The Nasi, Simon ben Gamaliel, complained of the suffering and oppression which he continually witnessed. "Our forefathers," he would say, "only scented troubles from afar, we have long suffered from them; we have much more right than our forefathers to be impatient. If we wished to inscribe our troubles and

---

[1] Capitolinus, *Ant. Pius*, 5. [2] Comp. Schiller, *Röm. Kaiserzeit*, i. 632.
[3] Joma 10a. [4] Mid. Lam. on i. 13.

temporary relief on a scroll, we should not find room enough." [1]   One consequence of the recent revolt would seem to have been the loss of jurisdiction in civil and pecuniary matters, which the Jewish courts or Jewish judges had still retained.[2]   Simon ben Jochai, indeed, is said to have rejoiced in this limitation of power, as it set him free from a difficult and painful duty, for which he declared himself unfit. But another account shows that this Rabbi bore in reality no friendly feelings to the Roman Government.

On a certain occasion,[3] so the story runs, during a public discussion of Jewish sages, Rabbi Juda, known as a friend of the Romans, took an opportunity of extolling their power and activity,—calling attention to the market-places, bridges, and public baths which they had constructed in the various towns of Palestine.   This was the signal of a more public expression of their feelings.   Rabbi Joses silently listened to praises which he could not reciprocate, and which he dared not contradict.   Not so Simon ben Jochai.   He broke forth in an indignant rebuke, which showed his deep hatred and contempt for the oppressors of his people.   A proselyte present reported the episode,—and while Juda was rewarded, Joses was banished to his native city Sepphoris, and Simon condemned to death.   Flight alone prevented the execution of this sentence.   Rabbi Simon and his son hid themselves in a cave near Gadara, where they subsisted for thirteen years upon fruits, nor was their retreat known even to their nearest relatives.   At last, one day, on leaving his cave, Simon noticed a bird suddenly escaping from the net of the fowler.   Rabbi Simon remembered that, if even a bird could not be caught without Divine permission, he might with still greater confidence anticipate the extension of the same care to himself.   Accordingly he left his retreat, and soon learned that his persecutors were dead or gone, and that he might return to his colleagues and friends.

Later   tradition   adorned   this   story   with   miraculous

---

[1] Mid. Cant. on iii. 4 ; Shab. 13*b*; comp. Grätz, iv. 205 f.

[2] Jer. Sanh. vii. 24*b* ; comp. Grätz, iv. 471.

[3] Jer. Sheb. ix. 38*d* ; Gen. Rab. 79; Shab. 33*b*, 34*a*.

additions. Miraculously did those trees which afforded sustenance to Simon and his son spring up—miraculously a fountain was opened for them. Meanwhile the two had spent their whole time in the study of the Law, sitting naked in the sand to preserve their garments for the stated seasons of prayer. At last, after twelve years, Elijah had appeared to intimate to them the death of the emperor, upon which they left their cave. But the worldliness with which, on their return, they were brought into contact, so filled them with indignation, that they killed many by their look, and at the command of a voice from heaven (the Bath-kol), they returned for another year to the cave. At the end of it, the occurrence of the escape of the bird, together with a voice from heaven explaining it, induced them again to come forth. It was also said that Simon composed the "Sohar" during that period of retirement.

The privations to which Simon had been exposed, had shattered his health, and he repaired to the warm baths of Tiberias, which proved instrumental in restoring him. In gratitude, he removed a reproach which had hitherto prevented many Jews from residing at Tiberias. Built 120 years previous to this period by Herod Antipas, on a site which had been a cemetery, Tiberias was, notwithstanding its advantages of situation and climate, eschewed by the pious, as residence on a cemetery entailed Levitical impurity. Simon undertook to mark those parts of the town which had been built over graves, and so to separate them from pure quarters. For this purpose he put a certain kind of bean into the ground. The places where they failed to take root were marked as graves,—the rest of the town was declared clean. Tradition has adorned this also with wonders. The jealous inhabitants of the neighbouring town of Magdala endeavoured to ridicule the decision of Simon. But the sudden demise of Dinkai, their leading sage, in consequence (it was said) of his opposition, silenced all further objections, and Tiberias was henceforth not only levitically pure, but soon became the centre of Jewish life and the residence of the Sanhedrin. But the political troubles of the time and the compulsory retirement of the

leading men in the Sanhedrin at Usha apparently put an end
to that assembly.   Most of the doctors seem to have retired
to the neighbouring town of Shefaram,[1] but no trace has been
left of their activity.

Antoninus Pius was succeeded on the throne by Marcus
Aurelius and Ælius Verus in 161.   The first-named of these
rulers endeavoured to combine the philosophical principles and
the simplicity of a Stoic philosopher with the dignity of a ruler
of the Roman world.   No one acquainted with the history of
that emperor can doubt his deep moral earnestness, which
most favourably distinguished his reign from that of the
majority of those who had worn the purple.   He was at the
same time devoted to the "ancient religion," and embodied in
acts of persecution the contempt or hatred which he felt for
those who, in this respect, would not or could not share his
views.   War broke out almost immediately on several of the
frontiers, but only in the East was the danger sufficiently
threatening to require the presence of a Roman emperor.
Aurelius committed the campaign against the Parthians to
Verus, in the vain hope that the prospects of military glory
might rouse the energies of that imperial debauchee.   But
Verus contented himself with entrusting the conduct of this
war to some of his generals, while he spent his time at Antioch
in unbridled self-indulgence, until peace was restored in 166.
During the progress of the war, the Roman generals captured
Nisibis, Ctesiphon, and other cities where there was a large
Jewish population.[2]   Doubtless the Jews took part in the
resistance to the Roman arms, [but we are nowhere told that
their brethren in Palestine suffered on this account.   A
Jewish legend,[3] however, which hardly seems to apply to the
time of Hadrian, relates that] edicts were once issued
prohibiting circumcision, and certain other Jewish rites.
Under these circumstances, it is said, a Jew, in the disguise
of a Roman, procured admission into the Roman Councils, in
order to induce that assembly to rescind these decrees, on
pretence that their tendency was only advantageous to the

[1] Rosh ha-Sh. 31*b*.   [2] Comp. Schiller, *ut supra*, p. 641.
[3] Meila 17*ab*.

Jews. But the device was discovered. A Jewish deputation was then despatched to Rome to entreat toleration from the emperor. The members of that embassy were Simon ben Jochai, and, at his special request, the youthful Eleazar, the son of Joses. It was with doubt and hesitation, and only after distinct promises of moderation on the part of Simon, that Eleazar agreed to accompany him. The embassy attained its object, and its success was ascribed to the miraculous cure of the emperor's daughter by Simon, who had cast out an evil spirit which had possessed her. [Whatever be the real value of this story, Eleazar's visit to Rome seems to be historical.] He could afterwards assert that he had seen in Rome those spoils from the Temple which Titus had carried to the capital.[1]

Uncertain though the exact succession of these events be, it seems that the Patriarch Simon closed his career about the year 165.[2] He was succeeded by his son, Rabbi Jehuda, by far the most distinguished of that race since Hillel the Great. From the celebrity for sanctity and learning which that patriarch obtained, he is generally designated simply as "*the Rabbi*," as Jehuda-ha-Nasi (the Prince, *par excellence*), and as Jehuda the Holy. Whether his lore and influence, or else his authorship of the Mishna, or the fact that he was the most truly distinguished Jewish Patriarch of Palestine, procured for him these distinctions, certain it is that few, if any, are placed by tradition on a higher eminence. Divesting his history of the fabulous, we have enough left to distinguish the characteristics of this celebrated personage. Born about the year 136, as tradition has it, on the very day on which Rabbi Akiba died a martyr's death,[3] he attracted attention at an early age, and excited the hopes of the college by the ingenuity of his questions, and the diligence with which he applied himself to study. Accordingly he occupied, at a comparatively tender age, the foremost bench amongst the students, indicating (as we have seen) that he stood nearest in knowledge and claims to the regularly ordained teachers.[4]

---

[1] Meila 17*b* ; Jer. Joma iv. 41*c*.
[2] Comp. Hamburger, *Enc.* ii. 1121 ff., "Simon ben Gamaliel ii."
[3] Gen. Rab. 58.   [4] B. Mez. 84*b*.

Like other distinguished Rabbins, he profited by the instructions of various teachers representing different theological tendencies. The most celebrated of these were the famous Simon ben Jochai, Eleazar ben Shamua, the most popular lecturer of his day, and Jacob ben Karshai, the Rabbi whose assistance rendered the plans of Nathan and Meir against the late Patriarch Simon nugatory. Jehuda inherited, to a remarkable extent, the two qualities of his predecessors, acuteness and ambition. The vast riches which his family had accumulated, and the learning and originality which far surpassed the attainments of his father Simon, enabled him to carry out the hierarchical designs of the latter, which had now almost become the traditional policy of the family of Hillel.

In spite of the vast wealth which he had inherited, Rabbi Jehuda lived very simply, and devoted to the support of theological students a large part of his revenues.[1] His stables, it was said, contained more cattle than the Persian treasury could have purchased,[2] an exaggeration which at least affords an insight into the fame which he enjoyed. The Patriarch kept a sort of court, of which his students and dependents were the officers. All divines were there maintained at the expense of the Patriarch ; and when, at a later period, a famine in the land deprived many of the means of existence, he ministered to the wants of all who applied to him.[3] But even in the exercise of this charity he manifested his peculiar disposition. At first it was ruled that none ignorant of the Law (no uneducated person) should be admitted to enjoy its benefits ; at another time the daughters of the apostate Acher were excluded, and only admitted in consideration of their father's learning.[4] But these restrictions soon gave way to a more liberal policy. In fact, Jehuda scarcely required to resort to such means for the establishment of his authority. However, the most decisive step towards obtaining the supreme dignity was the regulation which he enforced, according to which the right of ordination was exclusively reserved to the Patriarch.[5] The Sanhedrin

---

[1] Erub. 53b ; Shab. 113b.   [2] B. Mez. 85a.   [3] B. Bath. 8a.
[4] Chag. 15b.   [5] Jer. Sanh. i. 19a ; comp. Grätz, iv. 487.

had formerly exercised that authority, but even the supreme college now required for it the Nasi's sanction. Generally, to extend his sway, it was also enacted that none but regularly ordained teachers were in future to pronounce on any religious question,—a rule which, as will easily be inferred, excluded all but those who possessed the Patriarch's confidence from places of influence or authority. The residence of Rabbi Jehuda and of the Sanhedrin was at first Beth-Shearim (now Esh-Shayerah),[1] and afterwards Sepphoris. The latter place was chosen for its salubrious air, which, together with the appliances of art, restored the Patriarch from a disease of thirteen years' standing.[2]

A brief account must be given of the character and teaching of this remarkable man. Kind, benevolent, and a devoted patron of Jewish learning, [he strove in every way to set forth the Divine claims of Judaism. He warned his hearers against neglecting even the minor precepts of the Law, and bade them remember that they were ever in the presence of an all-seeing eye.[3] By a later generation he was regarded as an eminent example of a humble and God-fearing man ; and it was asserted that "from the days of Moses to Rabbi we have not found in one man such a union of possession of authority and knowledge of the Law."[4] Yet it must be admitted that] the Nasi often manifested an irritable and imperious disposition; he seemed unable or unwilling to distinguish personal, intentional enmity from opposition on principle, or even from unintentional slights. Perhaps his bodily weakness may have contributed to sour his temper. Yet rarely did anyone venture to express publicly his dissatisfaction with one so influential, so popular, so learned, and, let us add, so determined as Rabbi Jehuda.

The fame of the Patriarch's teaching attracted students from all quarters. Rabbi Jehuda stimulated their ambition and rewarded their diligence. In Sepphoris, strangers, Jews from Babylon, filled the highest ranks, and outshone

---

[1] Rosh ha-Sh. 31*b* ; comp. Neubauer, *Géog. du Tal.* p. 200.
[2] Keth. 103*b* ; jer. Kil. ix. 32*b*.   [3] Pirke Ab. ii. 1.
[4] Gitt. 59*a* ; Sanh. 36*a*.

the native theologians. We refer only at present to Rabbi bar Chana, and to Abba Areka, to Rabbins Chanina, Achija, Samuel, and other Babylonians, of whom more in another place. [Incidentally we obtain an interesting account of the qualifications required for a Jewish teacher.[1] The community of Simonias, a village to the south of Sepphoris, requested the Patriarch to send them a man who could deliver public discourses, decide questions of law, superintend the synagogue, draw up legal documents, instruct the youth, and attend to all the higher interests of the community.]

To enforce his rule, the Patriarch was in the habit of administering spiritual and even temporal punishments upon offenders, and that without consulting the Sanhedrin. A few instances will show the absoluteness of his administration. His friend and favourite, Rabbi Chija or Achija, was distinguished by the Patriarch as "the man of his counsel."[2] In familiar conversations Jehuda had extolled to him his own high position, and added, as one of the claims of the patriarchate, that the family of Hillel had, in the maternal line, sprung from David. At the same time, he owned the superior claims of the Babylonian Jewish Prince of the Captivity, who claimed descent from David in the male line. When the Babylonian Prince died, and his body was brought to be buried in Palestine, Achija, by way of a practical joke upon the Patriarch, tried to excite his fears by announcing the approaching arrival of the Babylonian Prince. The Patriarch changed colour at the announcement, and when he found that Achija had only meant playfully to call up his fears, he punished the jest by banishing him from his presence for thirty days.[3] Another Babylonian sage, Chanina, ventured to take exception to Jehuda's pronunciation of a word, and appealed to a Babylonian authority.[4] The angry Patriarch punished the contradiction by a refusal to ordain Chanina,—an injustice which Jehuda himself felt so keenly, that, on his deathbed, he commissioned his son and successor to bestow the Rabbinical office, in the first place, on the long-neglected

[1] Jer. Jeb. xii. 13a.
[3] Jer. Kil. ix. 32b.
[2] Menach. 88b.
[4] Jer. Taan. iv. 68a.

Chanina.[1] Another sage was suspended for venturing to propound sophistical questions.

Fear of taking the Patriarch by unawares, and so bringing him into contempt, restrained Chija from asking unexpected and irrelevant questions. Chija had reproved his nephew, Abba Areka, for neglecting this;[2] but his own submission did not protect him from the imperious hierarch. On one occasion he had discoursed in the street upon Rabbinical subjects, with his learned nephew, contrary to the Patriarch's injunction, who perhaps dreaded that such disquisitions might give rise to persecutions.[3] For this offence he was banished for thirty days. At another time, the Patriarch and Chija observed, on their walk, a scrupulous Rabbinist, who, to preserve the rights of the proprietor, walked with considerable difficulty along the edge of a field. In accordance with the commonly received law, the Patriarch and his friend were pursuing their way, making a footpath within the field. The appearance of greater punctiliousness than his own seemed to Jehuda an affectation of dignity, for which he would have severely punished the unhappy divine, had not Chija's intercession averted his anger.[4]

In general, however, the Patriarch, though soon angry, was easily reconciled where his dignity was not endangered, or where a sufficient apology satisfied him of the humility of the offending party. Thus, at a banquet, the Patriarch, noticing the silence of Chija's sons, Juda and Chizkijah, had freely plied them with wine. The youths, whose tongues were now loosened, declared, among other things, that the Messiah would not come till the patriarchates of Palestine and Babylon had ceased.[5] [In these words they doubtless gave expression to a widespread discontent, which had been aroused by the Nasi's inconsiderate and arbitrary conduct.] Happily the father of the youths overheard the conversation, and, pleading the effects of wine on his children, appeased the wrath of the Nasi. Jealousy for the honour of his family induced him never to mention Rabbi Meir's name even when

[1] *Ibid.* ; Koh. Rab. on vii. 7.   [2] Shab. 3*b*.   [3] Moed K. 16*b*.
[4] B. Kam. 81*b*.   [5] Sanh. 38*a*.

quoting his opinions.   The representations of the Patriarch's son produced only a slight concession in favour of the departed teacher.[1]

One of the Nasi's favourites was Bar Kappara, of Babylonian extraction, and equally distinguished for learning, readiness, and poetical talent.   He was, as far as we know, the only poet of his time, and he possessed a keen satirical humour, which was restrained by no respect for persons, and sometimes degenerated into mere punning and coarse allusions.   Rabbi was sometimes amused by, and at others afraid of, his uncontrollable desire for punning.   A marriage-feast was always a season of merry-making, where amusement was even deemed a religious duty.   Bar Kappara promised the Patriarch's daughter, that at her brother's marriage he would keep the company in continual merriment, and even make the Nasi dance.[2]   Rabbi Jehuda, dreading his friend's humour, resolved, by way of security, not to invite him to the wedding.   Bar Kappara pretended to be so deeply offended at this slight, and took the liberty of expressing his feelings so strongly, that the Patriarch at last yielded, and invited him, on condition that he was for once to control his tongue, promising, in return for his moderation, a present of wheat.   But the temptation was too great for Bar Kappara.   He appeared at the marriage carrying an immense hamper, and demanding from the Patriarch the wheat which he had lent him.   An explanation ensued, and the shouts of laughter, in which the Nasi himself joined, encouraged Bar Kappara to continue.   He proceeded to ask riddling questions on passages of Scripture, and refused to reveal the answers (so the story runs) till his host had been induced to dance.   Finally, he plied the company with so many indelicate jokes, that the Patriarch's daughter, and her husband, Bar Elasa, felt at last constrained to withdraw from the assembly.   Bar Elasa had been chosen by the Patriarch as his son-in-law, only for his wealth, with which, as is too frequently the case, he combined a considerable amount of pretension and an equal measure of ignorance.   On a festive occasion, when all

[1] Hor. 14a.   [2] Nedar. 50b, 51a.

the assembled Rabbins emulated each other in propounding ingenious or learned questions, the mischievous Bar Kappara suggested a witty enigma to Bar Elasa, which he had himself composed.[1] In his simplicity, poor Bar Elasa propounded it as his own ; but the mischievous smile, which Bar Kappara could not suppress, betrayed its real author, who, in punishment, was for ever excluded from obtaining Rabbinical ordination. [The real meaning of the riddle has never been discovered, but it probably contained covert satirical allusions to some member of the Patriarch's family or household.]

The patriarchate of Rabbi Jehuda was marked by important internal modifications and outward changes, but specially by the termination of a work at which many Rabbins had formerly laboured, namely, the collection of the traditions into one work, and their arrangement into the Mishna or Deuterosis, which forms the text of which, as already stated, the Jerusalem and the Babylonian Gemara are the authorised Commentaries. The changes within the Synagogue which the Patriarch inaugurated, were all in the way of lightening the burden which, in the altered circumstances of the nation, was yearly becoming more grievous and intolerable. Thus, he relieved some cities from the payment of tithes, by declaring them beyond the boundaries of Palestine,—an ordinance so distasteful to many of the Patriarch's relatives and colleagues, that he only succeeded in silencing their objections by an appeal to his supreme authority.[2]

Another practical difficulty was felt in observing the sabbatical year, as the many taxes and foreign impositions rendered the cessation of agricultural labour, etc., almost impossible. Accordingly, the Patriarch seriously meditated the total abolition of this institution. But before taking this important step, he wished to secure the support of R. Pinchas ben Jair, the son-in-law of Simon ben Jochai, a zealous upholder of the letter of the law, and a model of austere piety, whose reputation for sanctity might, in case of opposition, easily have roused the superstitious multitude.

---

[1] Jer. Moed K. iii. 81c ; comp. Grätz, iv. 215 f.
[2] Jer. Dem. ii. 22c; Chul. 6b.

But Rabbi Pinchas proved inexorable, and when he saw mules in the Patriarch's court, he left abruptly, horrified at the fact that the head of the Jewish community should keep animals the possession of which was interdicted in the law.[1]

But the most lasting and important measure of the Patriarch was the collection of the Mishna. Jehuda adopted as the basis of his collection the labours of Akiba and Meir. [With the aid of his most learned colleagues, he investigated the most correct form of many Halachoth; he was not ashamed to ask the meaning of words and phrases with which he was unfamiliar, and] in later years he undertook a revision and correction of the whole work.[2] The Babylonian Jews adopted the second; Rabban Simon, Jehuda's son and successor, the first edition of the Patriarch's Mishna. [The view, which has often been maintained,[3] that the Mishna was not committed to writing till after the fourth century, is apparently not warranted by the facts. The opinions expressed by Rabbins Jochanan bar Napacha and Jehuda ben Nachmani, two teachers of the third century, against writing down the oral law, do not seem to have been rules generally recognised. On the contrary, many passages of the Talmud imply the existence of books containing both Hagadic and Halachic traditions, and it is very probable that written collections of Mishnas were compiled even before the time of Rabbi.[4] Nor did the Mishna reach its final form during his lifetime. Not only did some of his disciples, as Chija, Ushaja, and Bar Kappara collect Mishnas, but in the present Mishna passages are found which are as late as the third century.] The text is in the later style of Hebrew, largely intermixed with Aramean, and even Greek and Latin words in Hebraised forms. Without entering on an analysis of its contents, we notice that it embodies not only the legally sanctioned traditions on all theological and juridico-theological questions, but also the leading objections urged against each

---

[1] Jer. Dem. i. 22*a*; Chul. 7*b*.

[2] Comp. Hamburger, *Enc.* ii. 794 ff.   [3] So. Grätz, iv. 221, 494 f.

[4] See Strack, *Einleitung in den Thalmud,*[2] pp. 49–55 ; comp. Schürer, I. i. 130 f.

Halacha. R. Jehuda was an excellent scholar, who cultivated the Hebrew language to such an extent, that, after his death, even a female slave in his family was consulted as to the peculiar meaning attached by her master to certain Hebrew words.[1] He wished that the Syrian dialect should fall into desuetude, so that the Jews in Palestine might either speak Hebrew or Greek.[2]

As far as the external relations of the Jews were concerned, the presidency of Jehuda seems to have fallen in a fairly tranquil though hardly a prosperous period. Palestine shared in the troubles which followed the death of Commodus, but there was no other serious war. It is true that the people were oppressed by taxation; in particular, the "aurum coronarium," the crown-money, was at one time exacted, and we are told that this proved so heavy an impost that the inhabitants of Tiberias fled by common consent, and for a time left the Rabbins sole inhabitants of the city.[3] But as it is by no means certain that Palestine suffered more from this tax than other provinces, it can scarcely be construed into an act of special persecution. Marcus Aurelius indeed does not appear to have shown any decided preference for the Jews. On his visit to Palestine, after the unsuccessful rebellion of Avidius Cassius, he once found himself surrounded by a clamorous crowd of Jews, and the imperial philosopher is reported to have exclaimed that he had at last found a people more contemptible even than the Marcomanni, Quadi, or Sarmati.[4] But, against such expressions, we have the frequent mention in Jewish literature of a friendship which subsisted between Rabbi Jehuda the Holy, and a Roman emperor Antoninus. [There are reasons for identifying this emperor with Marcus Aurelius, but it is difficult to supply these traditions with a definite historical background, or to be certain which emperor is really intended.[5]

In the first place, we must reject the theory that the

[1] Jer. Meg. ii. 73*a*; b. Rosh ha-Sh. 26*b*.　　[2] B. Kam. 83*a*.
[3] B. Bath. 8*a*.　　[4] Am. Marcell. 22, 5.
[5] [See especially the discussion of this point by Dr. D. Hoffmann in *Magazin Berliner* for 1892, pp. 33 ff., 245 ff.]

traditions relate to Rabbi Jehuda II., who, it has been
suggested, may have had friendly intercourse with Alexander
Severus.[1]   Not only are friends of the Rabbi sometimes
introduced, whom we know to have been contemporaries of
Jehuda I., but the oldest stories of Rabbi and the emperor
are found in Mechilta, where Jehuda II. is never mentioned.
In different Rabbinic writings we read of Antoninus the
elder, Asverus the son of Antoninus, Antoninus the son of
Asverus, and Antoninus the younger, the grandson of
Antoninus the elder.[2]   If we are really to distinguish these
different persons, we may with some probability identify the
first with M. Aurelius, and the next with Septimius Severus,
who sought to establish his connection with the family of
the Antonines.   The two last titles may then both be
understood of Antoninus Caracalla, the son of Severus.   It
is chiefly with Antoninus (the elder) that the Nasi is brought
in contact, and some reasons for applying to the virtuous
Aurelius the stories of the Nasi's imperial friend are to be
found in the deference shown him by Rabbi,[3] in his care for
justice and philosophical inquiry,[4] and in the character
assigned to him of a pious heathen, if not a proselyte, to
whom Rabbi even promised a part in the world to come.[5]
It is true that the saying of Aurelius, already referred to,
implies no partiality for the Jews, nor should we have
supposed that the proud Stoic, with his thoroughly Greek
training, and his regard for the old Roman state religion,
would be drawn towards a Jewish Patriarch.   Yet, while the
Jewish traditions in their present form contain much that is
exaggerated and obviously unhistorical, there remains the
possibility that Jehuda and Aurelius met, while the latter
was travelling southwards through Palestine in 175.   It is
noticeable that one of the oldest traditions speaks of an
interview when the emperor was on his way to Alexandria;[6]

---

[1] So. Grätz, iv. 243 f., 485 ff.
[2] Koh. Rab. on x. 5 ; Ab. Sar. 10*a*, Nidd. 45*a* ; Ab. Sar. 10*b*, San. 110*a*.
[3] For example, Jer. Sanh. x. 29*c*; Gen. Rab. 75 ; Ab. Sar. 10*b*.
[4] Mechilt. on *Ex.* xiii. 21 ; Sanh. 91*ab*.   [5] Ab. Sar. 10*b*; jer. Meg. i. 72*b*.
[6] Mechilt. on *Ex.* xv. 7.

another makes Rabbi allude to the emperor's attention to justice, without stating that the two had actually met.[1] The latter stories may well have been built up on a very slight foundation of fact ; or else it is possible to suppose that the distinguished Roman friend of Rabbi Jehuda was not really an emperor at all.[2]]

Marcus Aurelius was succeeded by his infamous son, Commodus, who reigned from 180 to 192. Weak, but not originally devoid of good qualities, the new prince soon surrendered himself to vicious pleasures. A conspiracy which took place three years after his accession, roused his suspicion,[3] and induced him to surround himself with creatures of his own, who served as instruments of his cruelty and lust. It would be almost impossible to describe the course of folly and cruelty through which Commodus passed, and which finally terminated in his assassination. The conspirators chose Pertinax, apparently a man of worth and energy, to succeed him.[4] His very virtues and rigour were, in the eyes of the corrupt Romans, so many faults, and the bribe with which he sought to purchase the fidelity of the imperial bodyguard proved ineffectual. He was killed after a reign of only eighty-seven days. The purple was so attractive, that the father-in-law of Pertinax, not warned by his fate, made an offer for it to the imperial guard, who promised the empire to the highest bidder. Ultimately Julianus, a wealthy old senator, mounted the throne, on condition of paying to each soldier in the bodyguard a sum equivalent to about £200.[5] But the empire revolted against this barter. The three divisions of the Roman army, that in Pannonia under Septimius Severus, that in Britain under Cl. Albinus, and that in Syria under Pescennius Niger, pro-claimed their respective generals emperors. Sept. Severus

---

[1] Mechilt. on *Ex.* xiii. 21.

[2] So Levy, *NHWB.* i. 107 f. See also Hamburger, *Enc.* ii. 63 ff., "Antoninus" ; Bacher, *Tann.* ii. 458 f.

[3] Dio, lxxii. 4 ; Lamprid. *In Commod.* 4 ; Herodian, i. 8.

[4] Herodian, ii. 1 ; Capitolinus (*In Pertin.* 4. 4.) represents Pertinax as acquainted with the plot. Comp. Schiller, *Kaiserzeit*, i. 668.

[5] Herodian, ii. 6 ; Dio, lxxiii. 11.

proved the most energetic and successful of the three. Having secured his rear by adopting Albinus as his colleague, he rapidly advanced to give battle to Pescennius Niger. Meanwhile the time-serving Senate ordered Julianus to be decapitated (June 2, 193). On his entrance into Rome, Severus had first avenged the death of Pertinax upon his murderers, and dispersed the Janissaries of antiquity, the Pretorians or imperial bodyguard. Pescennius Niger, who had meantime wholly surrendered himself to sensual pleasures, was defeated in three battles and killed, although his adherents maintained an obstinate resistance in some parts of the East.

To the Palestinians, including perhaps the Jews, Pescennius Niger was bitterly hostile. When they appealed to him for an alleviation of their burdens, he exclaimed, " You wish to hold your landed property free of taxes ? Would that I were able to tax the very air you breathe." [1] In spite of this reply, Niger had found adherents in Palestine, and Severus after his rival's death showed in various ways his resentment of the opposition of that country to his government. [The punishments fell chiefly on Samaria, and Neapolis was deprived of its civil rights. It was not long, however, before Severus remitted the penalties which he had imposed, and some years later he conferred fresh privileges on various cities of Palestine.[2] What part the Jews took in the civil war is uncertain. Eusebius speaks of a Samaritan and Jewish war ;[3] and after the Parthian campaign] the Senate voted to Bassianus, the son of Severus, a Jewish triumph, in honour of his father's success in Syria.[4] Perhaps this was to celebrate the defeat of a robber chief, Claudius by name, who had overrun Judea and Syria. During the war the rebel captain had the boldness to ride into the Roman camp, and to embrace the emperor ; he escaped before he could be captured.[5]

The Emperor Septimius Severus was of African extraction,

[1] Spart. *In Nigrum*, 7.   [2] Spart. *In Sever*. 9. 14. 17.
[3] Euseb. *Chron*. (ed. Schœne), ii. 177.   [4] Spart. *In Sever*. 16.
[5] Dio, lxxv. 2.

and favourably disposed towards Christians, to the medical skill of one of whose number he owed his life.[1] He was suspicious towards strangers, but unreasonably indulgent towards his two sons, Bassianus and Geta, the offspring of his beautiful and learned but profligate wife Julia. Bassianus, who from a strange dress which he introduced, was also denominated Caracalla, had in early childhood a playmate who had become a convert to Judaism,[2] but this incident proves nothing as to his later attitude toward the Jews. Tertullian asserts, perhaps on insufficient grounds, that as a child Caracalla was surrounded by Christian attendants.[3]

[Judea remained disturbed for some time after the recent political troubles.] Marauding bands of Jewish adventurers traversed the country, ready to act as plunderers, patriots, or insurgents, as circumstances or the necessity of the case might indicate. The Roman troops had to track these guerillas to their mountain fastnesses and hiding-places, in which they were assisted by the experience of some Jews, notably of two celebrated Rabbins, Eleazar the son of the famous Simon ben Jochai, and Ishmael the son of Joses. However necessary for the common good, yet such direct countenancing of the Romans, especially by celebrated theologians, excited the general indignation of their countrymen.[4] In fact, tradition has it that Eleazar afterwards bitterly repented of his sin against his brethren, and that Simon's son had inflicted on himself the severest castigations by way of atoning for his sin. None the less his fame for mystical and Rabbinical lore and sanctity were such, that the inhabitants of the town of Acbara (to the south of Safed),[5] where he died, would not allow his body to be committed to the ground, in the expectation of immunity from the incursions of wild beasts while his body was amongst them. The citizens of the neighbouring town of Biria were obliged secretly to carry it away in order to lay his remains by those of his parent in

---

[1] Tertull. *Ad Scap.* 4.   [2] Spart. *In Caracallam*, 1.
[3] Tertull. *Ad Scap.* 4, "Lacte Christiano educatus."
[4] B. Mez. 83*b* ; j. Maaser. ii. 50*d* ; comp. Grätz, iv. 227.
[5] Comp. Neubauer, *Géog. du Talm.* p. 226.

Meron.[1]   The Nasi, Jehuda the Holy, sought in vain the hand of Eleazar's widow, who disdainfully reminded him " that it was not lawful to profane to the use of the vulgar a vessel which had at one time been destined for holy purposes."

Severus showed himself at first tolerant both towards Jews [2] and Christians, and during his reign humane magistrates extended in some provinces to the followers of Christ the protection of the law against the populace.[3]   But in 202 an edict appeared, which, under severe penalties, forbade conversion either to Judaism or Christianity.[4]   As the Synagogue was protected in the enjoyment of its freedom of worship, this edict could only check the *spread* of Judaism, but entailed no further annoyance upon its professors.   It was otherwise with Christians, whose creed and worship were contrary to law, and over whom, in some provinces, a storm of persecution now burst.   The only fresh burden which Severus imposed upon the inhabitants of Palestine was an order to pay on the seventh or sabbatical, as on other years, the tribute (in kind), a regulation which obliged the Rabbins to repeal, or at least to suspend the Mosaic law, which, during that year, enjoined a rest for the ground.[5]   Up to this period the Jews had been exempt from such tribute in sabbatical years, [by virtue of a special privilege first granted to them by Julius Cæsar [6]].

Severus was succeeded in 211 by his two sons, who during his lifetime had been his colleagues.   Caracalla had once before attempted his father's life, and now aimed at that of his brother.   Geta was murdered in the arms of his mother.   It is said that no less than 20,000 individuals, who either actually were or were suspected to have been his adherents, shared his fate.   Caracalla combined the folly with the cruelty and debauchery of former emperors.   The Alexandrians, who had

---

[1] B. Mez. 84*b* ; Koh. Rab. on xi. 2.

[2] Comp. p. 471.   [3] Tertull. *Ad Scap.* 4.

[4] Spart. *In Sever.* 17 ; Euseb. *Hist. Eccl.* vi. 1.

[5] Comp. Sanh. 26*a* ; jer. Shebi. iv. 35*a*; jer. Sanh. iii. 21*b*.   [Grätz (iv. 231) refers this regulation to the reign of Caracalla.]

[6] Jos. *Ant.* xiv. 10. 6.

probably irritated him by their railleries and their tumults, had to bear his vengeance. A large popular assemblage was surrounded by the soldiers and put to the sword, and the town for some days given up to pillage. During a campaign against the Parthians, Caracalla was murdered near Carrhae,[1] in the year 217.

Macrinus, the chief of the conspirators and one of the prefects of the guard, succeeded him. But he soon disgusted the soldiers by his incapacity and severity. Besides, they began to suspect the part which he had borne in the assassination of Caracalla, who had been a favourite with them. The maternal aunt of Caracalla, Mæsa, who lived in the neighbourhood, availed herself of this disposition of the troops. She had two daughters, Soæmias, whose son was called Bassianus, like his uncle Caracalla, and Mamæa, whose son was called Alexianus. Mæsa and her daughters spread the rumour that Bassianus was in reality the son of Caracalla. What their persuasions did not effect, their gold and the beauty and priestly dignity of Bassianus secured. The young prince acted as Syrian high-priest of the sun, from which office he afterwards obtained the name of Heliogabalus. Macrinus was murdered in 218, and Heliogabalus succeeded to the empire.

Heliogabalus surpassed even his uncle in folly and debauchery. Spoiled by the indulgence of his mother, and accustomed to the abominable excesses connected with the Syrian worship of the sun, that prince seemed anxious to show the world what amount of folly and knavery would be tolerated in an Roman emperor. He walked about on gold-dust, indulged in the wildest excesses, associated with the lowest of the populace: in a word, ran mad in riot. His mother formed a female senate which adjudged on matters of etiquette. In reality women conducted all the affairs of the State. Happily Heliogabalus' cousin, Alexianus, had been differently educated. He was now brought forward, first as the colleague of his cousin, and when dissensions arose between them, Heliogabalus and his mother were killed, and Alexianus

---

[1] Herodian, iv. 13 ; Dio, lxxviii. 5.

or Alexander Severus proclaimed sole emperor in 222. The administration of this excellent emperor, and his equally distinguished mother, forms one of the brightest episodes in Roman history. We only add that, as Heliogabalus intended to make the worship of the sun that of the Roman Empire, he tolerated and protected in the meantime that of the Jews and of the Christians.[1]

If the above short sketch has informed the reader of the *outward* relations of the Synagogue to the Roman power during the patriarchate of Rabbi Jehuda I., it remaineth yet to indicate its *internal* relations with reference to Samaritans and Christians. From reasons which are not accurately ascertained, the relations between the Jews and Samaritans had become much more friendly after the termination of the rebellion under Bar Cochba. Indeed, the intercourse became so cordial that it almost seemed as if the two parties would recognise each other as brethren. But the truce proved only of short duration. During a journey through Samaria, Rabbi Meir had found cause to interdict the use of their wine.[2] Rabbi Eleazar ben Simon pointed out blunders, accidental or intentional, in their copy of the Pentateuch.[3] Rabbi Eleazar ben Joses disputed with their Rabbins about the doctrine of a future resurrection;[4] and finally Rabbi Ishmael ben Joses discovered, or at any rate reproached them with, their idolatrous veneration for Mount Gerizim, a statement which would have cost him his life had he not left Sichem abruptly.[5] Accordingly, the Patriarch Jehuda I. declared that the Samaritans were to be treated as heathens.[6] A short time previously they had been styled "proselytes of truth,"—their conversion to Judaism (as far as it went) was now traced to the fear of wild beasts, and they were designated " proselytes of lions," in allusion to 2 Kings xvii. 25, etc.[7] The candour of some Rabbins constrained them, indeed, to acknowledge that the Samaritans or Cutheans (as they were named) were more

---

[1] Lamprid. *In Heliogab.* 3.   [2] Chul. 6a.
[3] Jer. Sot. vii. 21c.   [4] Sanh. 90b.
[5] Gen. Rab. 81 ; jer. Ab. Sar. v. 44d.   [6] Jer. Keth. iii. 27a.
[7] Sanh. 85b ; Kidd. 75b.

punctual and strict in such observances as they kept than the Jews.[1]

At an early period a considerable number of Samaritans seem to have inhabited Alexandria. [Without entering more particularly into their history, it is worth noticing that a Samaritan community existed in Rome in the fifth century, and frequent reference is made to the Samaritans in the later imperial legislation.[2]] In the war between Pescennius Niger and Severus, they appear to have taken part with the former, and were punished for their resistance by the loss of many of their privileges.[3] The Samaritans retorted the intolerance of the Jews in every possible manner. Amongst other things, they endeavoured to deceive the Jews at a distance as to the appearances of the new moon, by lighting the usual watchfires at improper times.[4] This induced the Patriarch to abolish this mode of telegraphing the commencement of the month, and special messengers were from that time despatched to intimate the event to those at a distance. Various other unimportant alterations were also introduced in the mode of verifying the appearance of the new moon.

The same intolerance which characterised the conduct of the Jews towards the Samaritans may also be traced in their relations to the Church. Although the Jews were still a despised and homeless race, the privileges accorded them by the Roman emperors remained not without their practical effects. They could therefore venture to gratify their enmity against the Church by exciting the prejudices of the heathen against the followers of Christ. Several circumstances combined to convince the Christians of the growing and implacable hatred of the Jews. But the most notable act of persecution was that in which the Jews of Smyrna took a leading part, and which ended with the martyrdom of the venerable Polycarp, the Bishop of Smyrna, in 155. This trial of the Church's faith took place under the reign of Antoninus Pius, and during the administration of a Roman governor who was by no means personally hostile to the Christians.

[1] Kidd. 76a.
[2] Comp. Schürer, II. ii. 241.
[3] Spart. *In Sever.* 9.
[4] Rosh ha-Sh. ii. 2.

The record of the particulars of this fiery ordeal belongs
to a different department of history.   So much only shall we
state :[1] that a persecution having from some unknown cause
broken out againgst the Christians, the fury of the populace
was at last directed against the venerable Polycarp, who had
been a disciple of the Apostle John.   Polycarp yielded so
far to the entreaties of his friends as to withdraw to a
villa in the neighbourhood of Smyrna.   His asylum having
been betrayed, he retreated to another.   But his hour had
come.   When the officers of justice approached his retreat,
Polycarp might have escaped by the flat roof to another
house, but refused to do so, saying, " The will of the Lord be
done."   He only requested an hour for prayer, which in the
fulness of his heart was protracted to two.   In vain did
various magistrates urge the venerable bishop, by entreaties
and threats, to recant, at least in appearance, or to pacify the
multitude by yielding a little.   He replied, " Eighty and six
years have I served Him, and He has done me nothing but
good ; and how could I curse Him, my Lord and Saviour ? "
At last the proconsul proclaimed that Polycarp had confessed
himself a Christian, and, yielding to the shouts of the infuriated
Jewish and heathen mob, condemned him to the stake.   Jews
and pagans hastened to bring from the workshops and baths
wood for the funeral pile.   Before the fire was lighted, he
prayed : " O Lord, Almighty God, Father of Thy beloved Son
Jesus Christ, through Whom we have received knowledge of
Thyself ; the God of angels and of the whole creation ; of the
human race, and of the saints who live in Thy presence ; I
praise Thee that Thou hast judged me worthy, this day and
this hour, to take part among the number of Thy witnesses
in the cup of Thy Christ."   The multitude did not even allow
the Church the privilege of collecting the remains of their
pastor and spiritual father.   Such occurrences must have
embittered the feelings of Christians.   However, although
conversions to Christianity were not so frequent as at first,
the Gospel still continued to gain adherents from amongst the
Jews.   Thus an instance is recorded when a Jew, travelling

[1] See letter of the Smyrneans ; also in Euseb. *Hist. Eccl.* iv. 15.

in company with Christians through the desert, felt so earnest a desire after admission into the Church, that in the absence of water he was baptized with sand.[1] A celebrated teacher of the Church at that time, Hegesippus, was of Jewish descent, [and had originally belonged to the Jewish faith. There seem, however, to be no good grounds for supposing that he belonged to a Judaising party within the Church.[2]]

Rabbi Jehuda I. had raised the patriarchate to its highest point. At no after period did it present so many claims to the universal respect of the Jews. Its power was indeed exceeded under some of the Nasi's successors, but, from their inferiority in personal talent and learning, and from the gradual decline of Jewish theology in Palestine, these patriarchs did not command the same influence. Jehuda's eminent piety, modesty, and learning secured not only the universal respect of his contemporaries, but attached to his name the title "Ha-Kadosh," the Holy, and surrounded him in the Synagogue with a halo of almost superhuman glory. To his collection of traditions or Mishna, his successors added such legal ordinances as had either been omitted or not quite established under Rabbi Jehuda, under the title of "Matnita boraita," or simply "Baraitha," "the External Mishna," in contradistinction to the Mishna itself, or "our Mishna," which had soon gained a sort of canonical authority.

Rabbi Jehuda was surrounded by celebrated contemporaries, among their number being many who were not of Palestinian extraction. One of the most distinguished of their number was Rabbi Chija, whose chief merit seems to have consisted in the fresh impulse he gave to the instruction of youth, for whom he procured a large number of copies of portions of Scripture. He also introduced a system of mutual instruction, by which students, each of whom had mastered a different subject, communicated to one another the knowledge which each had gained.[3] Rabbi Chija's nephew was the

---

[1] Joannes Moschus, *Pratum*, 176.

[2] Euseb. *Hist. Eccl.* iv. 21, 22. Comp. Hort, *Judaistic Christianity*, pp. 164–180.

[3] Keth. 103*b*.

celebrated Abba Areka, or Rab, as he was afterwards denominated in Babylon, in order to indicate his eminence.   Another celebrated authority was Rabbi Chanina, between whom and Abba a good deal of jealousy existed.   Some trifling matter brought the secret dislike to an open rupture.   In vain did Abba afterwards wait upon his colleague year after year, on the eve of the Day of Atonement, to effect a reconciliation.[1] Chanina remained inflexible, and Abba at last, in disgust, left Palestine, to sustain a distinguished part in the rising academies of Babylon.

Rabbi Ishmael ben Joses was an authority much consulted by the Patriarch.   Though Ishmael neither possessed the talent nor attained the eminence of his father, his faithful memory had stored up the statements of his parent, and frequently had the Nasi to submit his personal opinion to the acknowledged authority of the late Rabbi Joses as quoted by his son.[2]   [He had outlived the distrust due to his support of the Roman authorities.]   Chija's two sons were celebrated as Rabbinical interpreters.   Rabbi Ushaja was called the " Father of the Mishna." [3]   Of Bar Kappara's wit and readiness we have already spoken.   Samuel was attached as physician to the patriarchal court, where he also became a theological celebrity.   For some unascertained reason the Patriarch, however, refused to ordain him ; and when, in conversation, he would have excused himself to the physician, the latter playfully retorted, " that so it was appointed in the Book of Adam that Samuel should be called a sage, but not a Rabbi, and that the Patriarch's disease should be removed by him." [4]   Rabbi Jehuda had for many years been sickly, and specially suffered from neuralgic pains in the face, and from an abdominal disease.   The ingenuity and application of Samuel had, by the blessing of God, indeed removed the distemper, but the Patriarch continued subject to frequent infirmities.   We have already noticed to what causes Jewish tradition ascribed the origin of his ailments, and what beneficial effects it was thought they had on his con-

[1] Joma 87a b.   [2] Comp. Pes. 118b ; Jeb. 105b.
[3] Jer. B. Kam. iv. 4c.   [4] B. Mez. 85b.

temporaries : the Rabbi's sufferings atoning for the sins which
would have brought judgments upon the land.[1] These
legends show at least in what estimation the Nasi was held
by posterity. At last the hand of death was about to snatch
away the great representative of the house of Hillel. During
his last years there had been many disputes amongst the
theologians, which even his authority could not altogether
repress. [Fresh troubles seemed to be in store for the Jewish
nation. "After the death of Simon the son of Gamaliel
came sufferings ; after the death of Rabbi they were re-
doubled," was a saying current in later times.[2] Probably for
some forty years had the Patriarch wielded supreme spiritual
authority,]—he had passed the allotted short period of three-
score and ten,—when the man of iron will and determination,
to whose decision the most wayward theologian had implicitly
to submit, the pride and idol of his people, was descending
into the dark valley. The tenderest care of Samuel seemed
unavailing ; the devoted attention of his favourite servants,
Joses and Simon, who bestowed on their master the
affectionate services of friends, was lavished in vain. The
sages assembled round his couch to hear the Patriarch's last
will.[3] After committing their stepmother to the special
affection of his sons, and minutely enjoining the continuance
of the present household arrangements, he nominated his
eldest son, Gamaliel, his successor ; and his second son, Simon,
Chacham. He gave directions for the ordination of Chanina
ben Chama, and then proceeded to instruct his sons in the
rules to be observed by those who filled the high places to
which they were elevated. Then turning to Rabban Gamaliel,
the Nasi-designate, he said, " My son, use your office with
dignity. Throw gall amongst the theologians."

Meanwhile, on tidings of the Patriarch's danger, the
populace had, in vast numbers, assembled in the streets of
Sepphoris, and before his abode. Jehuda's impending death
had put an end to both business and study. Many a prayer
was offered for his recovery, and the excited multitude went

---

[1] B. Mez. 85*a* ; comp. p. 319.   [2] Sot. 49*b*.
[3] Jer. Taan. iv. 68*a* ; Kil. ix. 32*a b* ; b. Keth. 103, 104*a*.

so far as to threaten with death the bearer of the tidings of the Patriarch's demise. The Nasi had expired, but none ventured to intimate the event to the people. At last Bar Kappara went to the balcony, his head covered and his garments rent, and said to the people—

> "Angels and mortals contended for the ark—
> The angels have conquered—the ark is gone!"

A general outburst of grief followed the announcement. "Is he dead?" asked thousands. "You say it," replied the ever-ready Bar Kappara. The sound of the lamentation was heard, as tradition affirms, at a distance of some miles. His favourite servants prepared the body for the burial, which took place on the day of his death,—a Friday. Rabbi Jehuda had requested that public mourning should not be instituted for him in the various cities, and that the colleges should be reopened after the lapse of thirty days. An immense crowd accompanied his body to its last resting-place in Beth-Shearim, and funeral orations were delivered in no less than eighteen synagogues. Although by law the descendants of Aaron were interdicted from defiling themselves by contact with dead bodies, veneration for the departed Nasi led to the suppression of this ordinance for that day, and even priests took part in the last offices. Tradition had it that the sun remained longer on the horizon, to enable the funeral cortege to reach their homes before the sunset of Friday ushered in the Sabbath of rest and sanctity.

In truth, the general mourning of the Synagogue was not unreasonable. ["After the death of Rabbi," it was said, "humility and the fear of sin ceased from among men."[1] The schools of Palestine had now reached the zenith of their splendour; in the next generation, Babylon would become the chief seat of Jewish learning.] Rabbi Jehuda I. was the last of a particular class of Talmudical teachers, which are denominated as the *Tannaim*, the *traditionaries*. They were succeeded by the *Amoraim*, or *expounders*, whose special task

[1] Sot. 49b.

seemed to be to explain the ordinances settled by their predecessors, rather than to originate new statutes.

[The date of Jehuda's death is difficult to determine, but we may assign it approximately to the year 210.[1] Of the life and doings of Rabban Gamaliel III., his son and successor, history tells us little beyond the fact that he faithfully carried out his father's instructions. His distrust of the Roman authorities is shown by the warning which he addressed to his disciples : "Be cautious of those in authority, for they let not a man approach them except for their own purpose. They appear like friends when it is to their advantage, but they will not stand by a man in his hour of need."[2] Perhaps he regarded with suspicion the increased friendliness of the Roman government; for both the emperors Severus and Antoninus Caracalla issued laws favourable to the Synagogue.] From a legal determination preserved to us,[3] we learn that these emperors allowed Jews to attain civic honours. In one respect the privilege thus accorded offered few attractions to the exclusive Jews, who had no inclination to identify themselves with the Roman government, or to bear the burdens and duties which such honours would necessarily bring with them. Although Jews were expressly set free from all offices which in their discharge offered violence to their religious convictions, it was a current saying in Palestine (showing the general aversion to all such offices), "If you are chosen member of a council, flee to the deserts around Jordan."[4] [Jerome also informs us that a remarkable change took place about this period in the social relations of the Jews, so as to induce them to apply to the times of Severus and Antoninus the passage, Dan. xi. 34, "Now, when they fall, they shall be holpen with a little help."[5]]

Rabban Gamaliel was succeeded by his eldest son, Jehuda II., whose patriarchate is distinguished by certain

---

[1] [Comp. Grätz, iv. 414, 480 f. ; D. Hoffmann (*Magazin Berliner*, 1892, p. 251 ff.) fixes the date at 217 A.D.]

[2] Pirke Ab. ii. 3.   [3] *Dig. de Decur.* L. 50, tit. 2 § 3.

[4] Jer. Moed K. ii. 81*b* ; cf. Gen. Rab. 76.

[5] Hieron. *Comm. in Dan.* xi. 34.

internal and external reforms which indicated striking changes in the views of the Rabbins. Hitherto, although the province of Judea had been almost entirely forsaken by theologians, the custom had still continued of determining the period of the new moon in *that* part of the country. The Patriarch now transferred this function to Tiberias, which he chose as his residence.[1] Gradually the southern part of Palestine, erst the sacred soil to which the memory of Judah had clung so tenderly, lost its Jewish inhabitants, and its few synagogues became disorganised. Galilee, once so despised, now became the Holy Land, and Tiberias its Jerusalem. A degree of jealousy, which seems to have subsisted between the teachers of Galilee and a celebrated theologian of Judea, may have contributed to this result. Greater changes followed. Jehuda II. allowed the use of oil prepared by heathens; and it is certain he would even have granted permission to eat their bread, had he not been afraid of the opposition of some of his contemporaries.[2] The 9th of Ab was no longer to be strictly observed;[3] the decree by which some of the expressions of joy at marriages had been suppressed in consequence of former persecutions, was repealed, and even the marriage with a childless widowed sister-in-law,[4] and many other legal enactments, would have been declared no longer obligatory, had not the sacred college interposed to put a stop to the spirit of innovation. Other and more important changes were, however, introduced. Thus the study of the Greek language was not only allowed, but recommended;[5] intercourse with heathens became frequent and intimate; paintings were admitted into houses;[6] and, in general, Judaism broke down the barriers which it had anon so carefully raised to protect itself against heathenism.

Alexander Severus, who ascended the throne in 223, was very favourable to the Synagogue. That emperor differed greatly from his immediate predecessors, both in his

---

[1] Jer. Sanh. i. 18*c*; comp. Rosh ha-Sh. 31*b*.

[2] Ab. Sar. 35*b*–37*a*; jer. *ib.* ii. 41*d*.   [3] Jer. Meg. i. 70*c*.

[4] Gitt. 76*b*; jer. *ib.* vii. 48*d*.

[5] Jer. Shab. vi. 7*d*; comp. Grätz, iv. 244, 487.   [6] Jer. Ab. Sar. iii. 42*d*.

private and public conduct. For a short time, justice, moderation, and temperance took the place of the unbridled licentiousness and intolerable tyranny of the masters of the world. In matters of religion, Alexander Severus displayed considerable moral earnestness. As in the case of many at the time, it led him, however, into a religious eclecticism which placed the various creeds and their representatives on a footing of equality. In his Lararium, or domestic chapel, he had, amongst others, the statues of Orpheus, of Abraham, and even of Christ.[1] His mother Mamæa, during her stay at Antioch, held intercourse with the celebrated Christian teacher Origen.[2] It will be readily understood how an emperor of such a disposition, and of Syrian descent, should have entertained views peculiarly favourable to the Synagogue. Independent non-Jewish confirmations are not wanting to prove the existence of that favouritism. The Alexandrians gave him, in mockery, the title of "Syrian Head of the Synagogue" (Archisynagogus).[3] [We are told that the emperor publicly commended the care taken by the Jews and Christians in selecting proper persons for ordination, and he desired to introduce the same precautions in the appointment of officers of state.[4]] It was doubtless at this time that the alterations above referred to were made by the Synagogue, with a view to approximating to the Gentiles. It was even allowed to the members of the Patriarch's household to have the hair dressed in a manner similar to the Romans,[5]—a concession which, however trivial in itself, when viewed together with the permission to learn Greek, to decorate the houses with paintings, etc., indicates an altered state of feeling. [Possibly some of the traditions with regard to Antoninus and Asverus contain indistinct recollections of privileges enjoyed under Alexander Severus.]

Remarkable evidence of the favoured position of the Jews is given by Origen,[6] who describes, as the result of personal observation, the almost regal authority exercised in

---

[1] Lamprid. *In Al. Sever.* 29.

[2] Euseb. *Hist. Eccl.* vi. 21.

[3] Lamprid. *ut supra*, 28.

[4] *Ut supra*, 45.

[5] Jer. Shab. vi. 7*d*.

[6] *Ep. ad Africanum*, 14.

his day by the Jewish Patriarch. The court over which he presided administered not only civil but also criminal justice, even putting offenders to death,—and all this with the connivance, at least, of the Roman government. From other sources we learn that the punishment of stripes was frequently administered not only by the authority of the Supreme Court, but in the various synagogues.[1] To enforce their authority, the Patriarchs surrounded themselves with a bodyguard,[2] while their revenues were mostly derived from the religious offerings of the Jews in and out of Palestine, which were collected in all countries by means of regular legates.[3] [The Jews were indeed now far more favoured than the Christians. In the time of Septimius Severus we hear of Christians who had professed Judaism in order to escape from persecution.[4] In the present reign, while the Christians were merely tolerated, the former privileges of the Jews were confirmed, —a distinction which doubtless rested upon the fact that the latter represented a nation, while the former did not.[5]] The intimacy between heathens and Jews, which naturally resulted, operated unfavourably on the Church; and a father of the Church complains[6] of the hostile attempts of the Jews against the Christians, which were apparently countenanced by the heathens.

[In private life, Rabbi Jehuda II. displayed a simplicity of manners and disregard of ceremony which sometimes even called forth the disapproval of his friends.[7] At the same time he showed himself determined to exalt the external power and dignity of the patriarchate. Allusion has already been made to his armed bodyguard, and to the princely state which he assumed.] He also endeavoured to put the Rabbins on the same footing with the laity; and insisted, for example, on their bearing their share in the civic burdens, from which they had hitherto been exempt.[8] This innovation was

---

[1] Euseb. *Hist. Eccl.* v. 16.   [2] Ber. 16*b*, 44*a*.; Gen. Rab. 78.

[3] Euseb. *Comm. in Jes.* xviii. 1 ; Epiph. *Hær.* xxx. 4. 11 ; *Cod. Theod.* xvi 8. 14.

[4] Euseb. *Hist. Eccl.* vi. 12.

[5] Lamprid. *In Al. Sev.* 22 ; comp. Mommsen, *Provinces,* ii. 226.

[6] Orig. *Hom. i. in Ps.* 36.   [7] Jer. Sanh. ii. 20*c*.   [8] B. Bath. 7*b*.

violently resisted by the theologians, and serious disputes
ensued. But still greater dissatisfaction was aroused by the
manner in which the Patriarch exercised his power of conferring ordination. Jehuda II. was covetous, and ready to
admit those to the sacred office who had no other qualification than their wealth to recommend them. This naturally
occasioned some painful scenes, and brought upon the
Patriarch severe practical rebukes. Those on whom the
sacred office was bestowed merely for money, were now
designated as "silver and golden idols," and generally
despised.[1] It was probably at this time that the sacred
college formally deprived the Patriarch of the sole right of
conferring ordination, and made it in future depend upon
the joint consent of the Patriarch and the Sanhedrin.[2]

If this be the true occasion of the change, it must be
allowed that the college had too good reason to interfere.
Thus, on one occasion, a rich but ignorant man had been
ordained, and, according to general custom, had sat down to
deliver a theological dissertation.[3] Beside him stood, as
Methurgeman, the able and ready Juda ben Nachmani, so
well known in his days as a poet and divine. In vain did
Juda bend down his ear for the discourse of the newly-
ordained Rabbi, which, as was his duty, he had to give in a
popular shape to the audience. At last Juda began, with
an evident allusion to the silent preacher : "Woe unto him
that saith to the wood, Awake! to the dumb stone, Arise!
It shall teach! Behold, it is laid over with gold and silver,
and there is no breath (in the Hebrew, *spirit*) at all in the
midst of it" (Hab. ii. 19). The scandal which this occasioned may readily be conceived. Another Rabbi of great
influence, whose prayers the Patriarch had solicited, probably
on account of the troubles which succeeded the death of
Alexander Severus, expostulated, "Take not from others,
and others will not take from thee."[4] Still more severe
was the reproof administered to the Patriarch in a sermon

---

[1] Jer. Bik. iii. 65d.
[2] Jer. Sanh. i. 19a ; comp. Grätz, iv. 249, 487.
[3] Sanh. 7b.   [4] Gen. Rab. 78.

by one Joses from Maon.[1]   Indeed, so sensible was the Nasi
of the affront, that he sent to imprison the preacher.   But
R. Joses had fled.   Two influential Rabbins, to whose advice
the Patriarch generally deferred, interceded for the offender,
and procured for him pardon and an interview.   But when
the Patriarch tried to puzzle the preacher by curious questions, the latter retaliated by replies which plainly indicated
his low estimate of the spiritual head of his nation.   One
of the two Rabbins to whom we have just referred, Rabbi
Jochanan, exercised a remarkable influence over the
Patriarch, and zealously supported him in many of the
reforms which Rabbi Jehuda had determined to introduce.

There are few persons of whom tradition records more
than of Rabbi Jochanan bar Napacha.   Left an orphan at
an early age,[2] he lived a long and happy life, to die amidst
sorrow and misery.   He is described as the most beautiful
man of his age ; and many are the poetic and other allusions
to his bodily attractions,[3] according to which he seems to have
resembled rather a beautiful woman than a fine-looking man.
Combined with his bodily, were rare mental qualities.   At
an early age he had attended the lectures of Jehuda I.,
although without much profit.[4]   His limited means induced
him for a time to engage in commerce.   He entered into
business with one of his colleagues, Rabbi Ilpha.   But a
voice from heaven, which intimated his future greatness,
induced him to sell his small paternal estate, and to devote
himself exclusively to study.[5]   He soon attained eminence
and importance.   Unlike many of his colleagues, he often
deviated from the Mishna to decide certain questions according to the Baraitha, *i.e.*, if the latter had the preponderating
weight of authority.[6]   His lectures attracted students from
all countries, and filled Tiberias with theologians ; and he
became the principal adviser of the Patriarch.   While differing from contemporary sages, chiefly in not simply accepting
the Mishna as such, he kept on friendly terms with all the
other Rabbins.   His pupils diffused his opinions.

[1] Jer. Sanh. ii. 20*d* ; Gen. Rab. 80.   [2] Kidd. 31*b*.   [3] B. Mez. 84*a*.
[4] Chul. 137*b*.   [5] Taan. 21*a*.   [6] Jer. Ter. x. 47*a* ; Bez. i. 60*a*.

Rabbi Jochanan was very liberal in his conduct. To him the ordinances which allowed the study of Greek (to males and females), the alteration in the dress of the Jews, the introduction of paintings, etc., were due. However, as others of similar character, he was a bitter opponent of the Roman power, and of that of Palmyra,—in short, of all foreign domination. To the former he applied the prophecy of Daniel, declaring that the Roman Empire was the fourth beast and the little horn of that vision.[1] The term of his life extended much beyond the usual period. His latter days were saddened by severe family affliction. He successively lost each of his ten sons,—the youngest perished by accidentally falling into a caldron of boiling water. The unhappy parent, who had now but one daughter left to him, is said to have ever afterwards carried about with him a bone of the body of his youngest son, to comfort mourners by exhibiting that memorial of his own severe affliction.[2] Rabbi Jochanan was also distinguished for great moral earnestness. The trials with which he was visited during his latter years induced illness, or temporary insanity.[3]

Ben Lakish was Rabbi Jochanan's personal friend and brother-in-law, but his theological opponent. In his youth he had seen Jehuda I., [and had been trained in the school of his successors. At one time, probably on account of poverty, he accepted an engagement at a circus, where he acted as slaughterer of wild beasts ;[4] and many were the stories told of his enormous bodily strength.] Tradition records that on one occasion Ben Lakish surprised Jochanan while bathing, and, attracted by the beauty of the woman (for which he took Rabbi Jochanan), plunged into the water after him. The conversation and admonitions which then ensued, together with Jochanan's promise of giving his sister in marriage to Ben Lakish, on condition of his devoting himself to Rabbinical pursuits, are said to have induced a complete change in the latter.[5] Certain it is that Ben Lakish left his companions,

[1] Gen. Rab. 76.
[2] Ber. 5*b* ; B. Bath. 116*a*.
[3] B. Mez. 84*a* ; Jer. Meg. i. 72*b*.
[4] Gitt. 47*a*; cf. Grätz, iv. 261.
[5] B. Mez. 84*a*.

married Jochanan's sister, and became as distinguished for his Rabbinical lore as he had formerly been for strength and prowess. His investigations were characterised by acumen and an earnestness which even bordered on austerity. A smile was never seen to play on his features, as unbecoming a member of that nation which groaned under heathen bondage ; [1] nor did he ever associate with any of whose probity he entertained not the fullest conviction. So much was this the case, that, popularly, intimacy with Ben Lakish was looked upon as a sufficient guarantee of character, conduct, or testimony.[2] He did not scruple to rebuke even the Patriarch (although on intimate terms with him) ; and on one occasion actually proposed that in cases of delinquency, the head of the Synagogue should, like other defaulters, be subject to the punishment of stripes.[3] Anticipating that the Patriarch would scarcely tolerate the statement of such doctrines, Ben Lakish fled, just in time to escape the messengers of justice sent by the Nasi. But when, at the public sitting of the college, Jochanan refused to go on in the absence of Ben Lakish, the Patriarch not only waived the point in dispute, but even consented to go and meet the bold Rabbi,—a step which the latter somewhat profanely compared with God's going down to Egypt to deliver His people. However, even on that occasion the language of Ben Lakish was so unconciliatory that the quarrel was almost renewed.

The method of Ben Lakish differed from that of Jochanan : while the latter decided according to the preponderance of authorities, the former raised ingenious questions, and propounded novel and striking theories. Thus he held that the Book of Job was only an allegory,[4] declared that the name of angels dated from the sojourn in Babylon,[5] maintained that former times had not been better than the present,[6] etc. Views such as these brought him into continual theological collision with Rabbi Jochanan. At last a dispute ensued in which Jochanan forgot himself so far

---

[1] Ber. 31a.

[3] Jer. Sanh. ii. 19d.

[5] Jer. Rosh ha-Sh. i. 56d.

[2] Joma 9b.

[4] Jer. Sot. v. 20cd.

[6] Joma 9b.

as to remind his friend of his former mode of life.[1]   Tradition has it that Ben Lakish was killed by a look from Jochanan, who was reputed to possess what is still familiarly known as " the evil eye." Certain it is that the latter used to reproach himself for having been in some way the cause of the death of his friend. Rabbi Jochanan never recovered from the shock of this occurrence. He adopted Ben Lakish's son, and soon afterwards followed his friend into the grave.

The third of a famous trio of Palestinian Amoreans was Rabbi Joshua ben Levi, a sage who, to some extent, represented the mystical tendency in the Synagogue. His father was perhaps Levi bar Sissi, one of the last of the Tannaites.[2] Levi and Rabbi Ephes, the immediate predecessor of Rabbi Joshua in the presidency of the college at Lydda, had both been so distinguished that even the proud R. Chanina had given them Rabbinical precedence.[3] At that time Lydda was almost the only place in Judea proper where traditionalism and theological learning were still cultivated, although the inhabitants of that place were looked down upon by the spiritual aristocracy of Galilee. Rabbi Joshua reorganised the congregations in Judea, at least for a season. He was no less reputed in the Synagogue for his Halachic decisions,[4] than for his power of working miracles. He conversed with Elijah,[5] his prayers brought down rain,[6] the angel of death had no power over him; the Rabbi even deprived him of his sword, and entered Paradise.[7] These legends, which sufficiently indicate in what repute Joshua was held, by and by assumed more definite shape, and increased in proportions with the lapse of time. In the later Midrashic literature we find an account not only of his journey to Paradise, but of his visit to all the regions in the other world, of which he sent an accurate and full description to Gamaliel by the angel of death.[8]

[1] B. Mez. 84*a* ; cf. Taan. 9*a*.   [2] Comp. Bacher, *Pal. Amor.* i. 124.
[3] Keth. 103*b*.   [4] Koh. Rab. on vii. 7.
[5] Macc. 11*a* ; Gen. Rab. 94.   [6] Jer. Taan. iii. 66*c*.
[7] Keth. 77*b*.   [8] Comp. Zunz, *Gottesd. Vortr.*[2] 148f.

We have already referred to Rabbi Chanina, the friend and companion of the elder Jehuda. He presided over the academy of Sepphoris, where he represented the genuine traditional element. Like Eleazar ben Hyrcanus, he taught only what he had heard from his teacher, and had himself proved by experience on at least three separate occasions.[1] His reputation for piety and severity enabled him to expostulate with his contemporaries for their moral laxity, in terms which would scarcely have been tolerated in others. It must be allowed that the conduct of the inhabitants of Sepphoris afforded but too much ground for the Rabbi's reproofs. It was to this moral degeneracy that he ascribed the inefficiency of his prayers in times of public trial.[2] So great was his influence and reputation, that when he appeared on one occasion before the proconsul at Cæsarea, the latter respectfully rose, declaring that Chanina and Joshua " appeared to him like angels." [3]   Rabbi Chanina was the teacher of Rabbi Jochanan. The pupil, it will be remembered, slightly modified the theological system in which he had been trained. The Synagogue was also well represented in Cæsarea. Another sage, Rabbi Simlai, by birth a Palestine Jew, would deserve more full notice, but that he spent the greater part of his days in Babylon, with the history of whose Jewish inhabitants he is more or less identified. Rabbi Simlai had no claims to distinction in the Halacha,—in fact, his decisions were rather distrusted. But he acquired fame in the Hagada, and for his violent opposition to Christianity.[4]

One of the persons engaged in this controversy was possibly the celebrated Origen, who spent considerable time in Palestine, and whose interpretations of Scripture not unfrequently recall the methods of Jewish exegesis. It will readily be conceived that Christian truth was placed at disadvantage when made to depend on isolated portions or texts, and defended by exegetical niceties and subtleties ; instead of resting on the general scope and bearing of the

[1] Jer. Ab. Sar. i. 39d ; Nidd. ii. 50b.   [2] Jer. Taan. iii. 66c.
[3] Jer. Ber. v. 9a.
[4] Jer. Ber. ix. 12d ; Gen. Rab. 8.

Old Testament teaching, and on whole passages, taken in their breadth and fulness, as the individual exponents of general and well-ascertained principles. However, Hagadic studies led sometimes to a spirit of zealous inquiry, and to frequent controversies between Christians and Jews. [Moreover, they proved to Christian scholars the necessity of gaining some knowledge of Hebrew, instead of relying entirely upon the Septuagint.[1]] So general, indeed, became these Old Testament studies, that when Porphyry, a heathen, would attack Christianity, he felt constrained to attempt an exposition of the prophecies of Daniel,[2] in which he accounts for these predictions on the supposition that they were penned by a contemporary of the Maccabees, and with reference to the events of their times. Origen himself was instructed in Hebrew by a Rabbi, whom he designates as the Patriarch Huillus,[3]— probably Hillel, the brother of the Patriarch Jehuda II. Many of his exegetical views he acknowledges to have derived from Jewish sources. One of the results of his studies was the celebrated *Hexapla,* a work in which the Septuagint translation is placed side by side with the original Hebrew, and compared also with the Greek versions of Akylas, Symmachus, Theodotion, and with others which he had discovered at Nicopolis and at Jericho.[4]

---

[1] Comp. *Dict. Chr. Biog.* ii. "Hebrew Learning."

[2] Hieron. *Præf. in Dan.* (Op. v. 617).

[3] Origen, *Selecta in Psalmos* (Op. ii. 514); Hieron. *Apol. adv. Ruf.* I. (Op. i. 469).

[4] Euseb. *Eccl. Hist.* vi. 16.

CHAPTER XIII

EXTINCTION OF THE PATRIARCHATE AND FINAL DISPERSION
OF THE JEWS

THE Jewish schools and the Jewish nation in the Roman
provinces had attained the highest point of prosperity, when
both declined,—the schools to be finally closed, and the nation
to be exposed to a storm of persecution which, in duration
and severity, far surpassed aught that had formerly been
endured. No doubt they had not made proper use of their
brief liberty. Those who had so frequently suffered from the
intolerance of others, had not learned to extend again that
freedom which they had so earnestly claimed for themselves.
More especially their conduct towards Christians exhibited a
degree of bitterness and a desire for extermination, which,
when occasion offered, the latter were but too ready to
retort. In truth, toleration, as distinct from persecution or
indifferentism on the part of a ruling or influential majority,
seems to be a virtue of most difficult attainment, requiring a
thorough conviction not only of the truthfulness, but of the
spirituality of our principles, as independent from and not to
be promoted by material means.

The close of the reign of Alexander Severus is con-
temporaneous with the commencement of those great troubles
which terminated in the destruction of the Roman Empire.
In the trans-Euphratic provinces, to the history of which we
refer at present only so far as absolutely necessary, a new
dynasty, representing the ancient Persian dynasty and religion,
had violently displaced the Parthian rule. [The new king,
Ardashir, declared war against Rome, and invaded Mesopotamia

and Cappadocia (230).[1] Alexander Severus was compelled to march against the invaders. He seems to have gained some advantage, but in the end retired without honour to Antioch.] Another invasion soon called him to the banks of the Rhine (235), where the rude Maximinus, a Thracian by birth, held an important command.[2] Here the disaffection of the army, originally aroused by overtures for peace, ended in the murder of the emperor and of his mother, and the elevation of Maximinus to the imperial dignity; and now a period ensued which, for its confusion and pernicious effects on the commonwealth, is unparalleled. [Of twenty-three emperors who assumed the purple between the years 211 and 284, very few escaped a violent death; while in 237–238, six emperors perished in the course of a few months.[3]] Most of these emperors were nominated by the soldiers from amongst their generals, and speedily gave place to other equally worthless usurpers. It appears strange—almost an irony upon Rome—that at that very period one of these emperors, Philip the Arabian, should have celebrated by great festivities the Roman millennium,—1000 years having elapsed since the foundation of the city.

Amidst these rapid and frequent changes in the tenure of the supreme office in the State, one episode at least deserves to be more particularly recorded, not only from the interest, we might almost call it the romance, attaching to it, but from its connection with our history. The new Persian dynasty had proved everywhere victorious, and the Roman emperor, Valerianus, had fallen into the hands of its representative, Sapor. His weak son, Gallienus, was both unable and unwilling to rescue his father. At that time Odænathus, the husband of Zenobia, was the hereditary chief of Palmyra.[4] This city, known also as Tadmor, was built on an oasis in the midst of a desert, north-east from Damascus, and at about the same distance (sixty miles) south-west from the Euphrates,

---

[1] Comp. Mommsen, *Provinces*, ii. 89 f.; Schiller, *Kaiserzeit*, i. 779 ff.
[2] Herodian, vi. 8, 9; Capitolinus, *In Max. duo*, 5–8.
[3] Comp. Pelham, *Outlines of Roman History*, p. 495 f.
[4] Comp. Mommsen, *Provinces*, ii. 96–112.

on the high road between the Roman and Parthian monarchies. From its advantageous position, beauty, and salubrity, that city had gradually risen to opulence and importance.   Odænathus was soon involved in a quarrel with the Persian monarch.[1] We are told that, while Sapor was prosecuting his successful incursions into the Roman provinces, a train of camels, laden with the richest presents for him, arrived from Odænathus. But Sapor, offended because the Palmyrene chief had not appeared in person, haughtily replied to the embassy, that "if Odænathus entertained a hope of mitigating his punishment, he was to fall prostrate at the foot of his throne with his hands bound behind his back."   Odænathus, repulsed in his friendly advances, threw himself into the Roman cause. He fought with success against Sapor, reduced Nisibis, and twice besieged Ctesiphon, the Persian capital.[2]   During six years Palmyra defended the Roman Empire, and well did Odænathus deserve the honours which Gallienus conferred upon him.

Jewish writings speak of a certain Papa bar Nazar,[3] [who is styled both a king and a robber chief]; and it has been supposed that this individual, who was designated by some of the Jews as "the little horn speaking great things," was none other than Odænathus,[4] [one of whose ancestors bore the name of Nasor [5]].   According to Jewish historians, Papa bar Nazar took and destroyed the Jewish city of Nahardea.[6]   [An obscure passage in the Talmud brings Papa bar Nazar into connection with Zenobia, while Zenobia is represented as in direct conflict with some influential Rabbins.[7]]   The Jews, who were at first adverse to the Persian power, whose fanaticism gave them too much cause for apprehension, had gradually become reconciled to it, and stood in friendly and even intimate relations with the new dynasty.   On the other hand, Palmyra, as the ally of Rome, seems to have shared in the cordial hatred felt by the Jews for the Roman power.

---

[1] Petrus Patricius, in *Patrol. Gr.* cxiii. 676.
[2] *Vita Gallieni*, 10 ;   *Trig. Tyran.* 15.   [3] Keth. 51*b* ; Gen. Rab. 76.
[4] Comp. Grätz, iv. 295, 489 f.   [5] Corp. Insc. Gr. iii. 4507.
[6] *Seder Olam Suta*, ed. Mayer, p. 113.   [7] Jer. Ter. viii. 46*b*.

Thus Rabbi Jochanan declared that "*he* was happy who should witness the fall of Tadmor."[1]

About 267, Odænathus was murdered, perhaps on political grounds, when Zenobia assumed the reins of government, and soon showed that she meant not only to call herself, but to act as the Queen of the East.[2] If only part of the almost fabulous descriptions of Zenobia are true, that queen must have surpassed in beauty Cleopatra, in courage Semiramis, and in energy, coupled with liberality of sentiment, the more recent royal ornaments of her sex, Elizabeth of England and Maria Theresa of Austria. To unrivalled beauty she added equal chastity; to fortitude and courage, fertility of device; to administrative wisdom, the faculty of discerning and availing herself of the talents of others. Nor were arts and sciences less cultivated in Palmyra than statecraft. At her court we find the celebrated philosopher Longinus; [while through her favour and protection Paul of Samosata, the heretical Bishop of Antioch, was able to retain his See, although he had been condemned and deposed by a Council at Antioch for denying the divinity of our Lord[3]]. Jews and Christians have in turn claimed and disclaimed Zenobia as their co-religionist. The truth seems to be, that she belonged neither to one nor other of these parties, but shared the general eclectic views of her intimate friends,—one of whom, for example, Longinus, could not sufficiently express his sense of the sublimity of the command, "Let there be light," in the Mosaic account of Creation.[4] But Zenobia's reign was cut short, in the midst of her conquests, by the victorious advance of the Emperor Aurelian, who at last took and destroyed Palmyra, and brought her queen in chains to Rome (273).

Under the reign of Diocletian, who ascended the throne in 284, the empire became for a time more settled. However rigorous and systematic were the persecutions of that emperor against the Church, which he had resolved wholly to

[1] Jer. Taan. iv. 69*b*.
[2] Comp. *Enc. Brit.* xviii. pp. 198–203, "Palmyra."
[3] Athanasius, *Hist. Arian.* 71; Eus. *Hist. Eccl.* vii. 30.
[4] *De Sublimitate,* ix. 9.

extirpate, or against the Samaritans, whom he is said to have
forced to worship idols,[1] the Synagogue escaped. According
to a Jewish tradition,[2] some suspicion at first existed against
the Synagogue. Enemies had reported that the Patriarch and
his friends had spoken in a disparaging manner of Diocletian's
origin and mode of accession. Tradition asserts that when
the emperor was in Paneas, at some distance from Tiberias,
he suddenly sent a message on a Friday afternoon, ordering
the Patriarch and the principal Jews to appear before him on
Sabbath evening. The order, which seemed to involve the
necessity of Sabbath desecration, reached the Patriarch and
his friends while taking the Friday bath. However, a friendly
demon, the Argonaut, who came to their assistance, undertook
and succeeded in conveying them to Paneas before the Sabbath.
The emperor, in mark of contempt, ordered the Jews to bathe
for several days before appearing in his presence. But at
their interview the Patriarch completely conciliated the
emperor. It is difficult to indicate how much foundation in
truth this story may possess. [The Patriarch referred to was
Jehuda II.,[3] and Diocletian was in Syria three or four times
between the years 288 and 300.[4] Elsewhere it is stated
that this emperor treated the inhabitants of Paneas with such
harshness, that they resolved to leave their homes.[5] Usually,
however, the reign of Diocletian is mentioned with approbation in Jewish writings. Rabbi Chija bar Abba is said even
to have risked Levitical defilement in his desire to see the
emperor during one of his visits to Palestine.[6]]

Meantime the Patriarch Rabbi Jehuda II. and his friends
and coadjutors had, one by one, been gathered to their
fathers. If the first generation of Amoraim exhibited a sad
declinature when compared with the Tannaim of former
generations, their successors proved still more clearly the
decadence of the Synagogue in Palestine. Rabbi Gamaliel IV.,

---

[1] Jer. Ab. Sar. v. 44*d*.   [2] Jer. Ter. viii. 46*bc*; Gen. Rab. 63.

[3] [So Hamb. *Enc.* ii. 150, "Diocletianus"; Bacher, *Pal. Amor.* i. 479—
after Frankel. Grätz, iv. 302 f., calls this Patriarch Jehuda III.]

[4] Marquardt, *Rom. Staatsverwalt.* i. 267.

[5] Jer. Sheb. ix. 38*d*.   [6] Jer. Ber. iii. 6*a*.

son and successor of Rabbi Jehuda II., was openly and
avowedly treated by the teachers of Palestine as an unlearned and ignorant person, to whom, by way of precaution,
it was even necessary to interdict what in itself might be
lawful.[1] He was apparently unable to decide in any case of
dispute, and had to refer all these matters to the sages. At
the same time the study and knowledge of the Scriptures
declined so sadly, that one of the most celebrated Rabbins
confessed that he was (at least exegetically) unacquainted
with the text of the Ten Commandments.[2] Nor was even the
study of the Halacha cultivated. It had gradually given
place to the sophistry and allegorical playing of the Hagada,
a discipline to which the term "rooting up and carrying
away mountains" was applied.[3] The very style of correspondence and the language of that period, with its turgidity
and its meaningless puns and pleonasms, contrasts most unfavourably with that of former days.[4]

[The decline of the spiritual authority of the Patriarch is
evidenced by the absence of his name from an important
decree of the Sanhedrin relating to the Samaritans.[5]] The
temporal power of the Patriarchs, however, rather increased
during these troublous times, and the patriarchate was
treated by the Romans as a civil dignity. Although Rabbi
Jochanan had affected a thorough contempt for the Babylonians (as he called them), those of his successors who
enjoyed any fame, had come from beyond the river, and
ultimately submitted their own decisions for review to the
superior wisdom of the trans-Euphratic teachers. Jochanan
had solemnly ordained, amidst the sound of songs in their
praise, his Babylonian pupils, Rabbins Ami and Asi, as
"judges of the land of Israel." [6] After the death of Jochanan's
successor, the Babylonian Rabbi Eleazar ben Padat, they were
almost the sole, as well as the supreme judicial authorities of
Palestine. [Yet even they, of their own accord, subordinated
themselves to the sages of Babylon. They taught in a

---

[1] Jer. Ab. Sar. i. 39*b*.   [2] B. Kam. 55*a*.

[3] Hor. 14*a*.   [4] Comp. Grätz, iv. 308 f.

[5] Chul. 6*a* ; jer. Ab. Sar. v. 44*d*.   [6] Keth. 17*a* ; Sanh. 17*b*.

colonnade at Tiberias,[1] which may have dated from Herodian times; and it is said to have been their custom to choose suitable places in the sun or the shade, according to the different seasons of the year, so as to consult the comfort of their students.[2]]

The two sons of Abba, Chija and Simon, were equally celebrated for their merits and misfortunes. Both suffered from crushing poverty. Chija had at first been largely assisted by the wealthy family of Silvani in Tiberias, who continued to pay to this Rabbi, as a descendant of Aaron, the regular tithes. But when another sage declared something lawful which Chija had interdicted, and the Silvani gave him to understand that more moderate views were requisite in one who depended on their bounty, he not only declined their assistance in future, but resolved never to receive it again from any other party. To fortify himself in this resolution, he accepted a post which forced him to travel out of Palestine.[3] The Patriarchs now employed "apostles,"[4] as they were termed, to collect in all lands an annual tribute, or religious contribution (mentioned as "aurum coronarium," like that of the Roman emperors,— or as "canon" and "pensio "),[5] a kind of Jewish "Peter's pence." Rabbi Chija was appointed to this post. However, notwithstanding his celebrity, he was so ignorant of the Bible, that, in answer to a Hagadic query, he had to confess he was not aware whether the word "good " occurred in the Decalogue.[6]

Chija's brother Simon was reputed so pious, that his teacher, the celebrated Jochanan, said of him, " He that cannot form a notion of the virtues of our Father Abraham, may become acquainted with them by observing this Simon."[7] Although very poor, he was too independent to accept any assistance, and his friends supplied his wants by putting money in his way, that he might accidentally find it.[8] His difficulties at last compelled him to seek employment out of

---

[1] Ber. 8a.   [2] Keth. 112ab.
[3] Comp. jer. Hor. iii. 48a ; Sheb. iii. 1 ; Maas. Sh. v. 56b.
[4] Epiph. *Hær.* xxx. 11.   [5] *Cod. Theod.* L. xvi. tit. 8, § 29.
[6] B. Kam. 54b, 55a.   [7] Jer. Bik. iii. 65d.   [8] Jer. B. Mez. ii. 8c.

Palestine, which was at first refused, from a desire to retain him in the Holy Land.[1] He afterwards settled in Damascus. In spite of his learning, through lack of a suitable opportunity, he failed to obtain ordination.[2] A similar uprightness and similar sufferings marked his private and his public life. He successively lost his two wives, both of whom he seems to have married mainly from conscientious motives.[3] The two sons of Abba were rigid Talmudists, and interdicted a Grecian education to Jewish maids.

Another highly interesting personage was Rabbi Abbahu, by birth a Palestinian. He was a manufacturer of veils in Cæsarea Augusta, where he also presided over a celebrated academy. Abbahu was very rich, lived gaily, and educated his daughter after the Grecian fashion, to which his more strict colleagues objected.[4] He possessed considerable influence with the Roman proconsul, which he employed in favour of his co-religionists and colleagues.[5] His personal attractions, both of body and mind, and his wealth, secured him a leading position in Cæsarea, and indeed in Palestine. At the same time, he was so modest and retiring as even to be unwilling to become the head of a school. On one occasion he lectured to a crowded audience on the Hagada, while his more learned colleague, Chija bar Abba, could scarcely collect a few to listen to his expositions of the Halacha.[6] In fact, the Halacha had lost its attractions for the Palestinian Jews. An analogous change took place in the mode of delivering public orations, where the Methurgeman, instead of simply interpreting the preacher's language, now arrogated to himself independent powers, and taught according to his own, not according to the preacher's views.[7] Rabbi Abbahu owed a great part of his reputation to his wealth and to a certain amount of acuteness and prudence. He was ignorant of the Halacha, but, in deference to his position, his colleagues did not venture to contradict even his erroneous assertions.[8] By

---

[1] Jer. Moed K. iii. 81c.
[2] Jer. Bik. iii. 65d.
[3] Keth. 23a ; jer. *ib.* ii. 26c.
[4] Jer. Shab. vi. 7d.
[5] Sanh. 14a ; Chag. 14a ; jer. Meg. iii. 74a.
[6] Sot. 40a.
[7] Koh. Rab. on vii. 5.
[8] Joma 73a ; Jeb. 65b.

his patronage, Cæsarea was elevated into an academical city, along with Tiberias. He taught in the Synagogue still known as that "of the revolution," probably the same whence the rising against the Roman power, in the time of Nero, had first issued.[1] Abbahu saw not only his sons, but even his grandchildren ordained.[2]

Meantime Judaism, decaying within, was represented by some of the Gentiles as a species of heathen mysticism, while the vast majority despised and openly ridiculed it. Abbahu complained that the Jew formed the never-failing theme of ridicule in the comedy, the Punch of every provincial theatre.[3] In some respects there was indeed too much ground for the reproach. The state of the Synagogue is well illustrated in the following occurrence:[4]—A season of general drought and scarcity elicited, as usual, the prayers of the congregation. According to custom, the worthiest man was to be chosen to lead these devotions. For this honour a person was recommended who, on account of his infamous avocation, bore the popular designation of "Pente-kaka," or "Five-Sins." In conversation, Abbahu had however elicited from that man, that although he directly or indirectly ministered to almost every vice, he had on one occasion given all his means to an unknown weeping Jewish female, to enable her to redeem her husband from slavery without having to gain the requisite money at the expense of her honour. This good deed of "Pente-kaka" induced Abbahu to appoint him leader of the devotions, as being the worthiest in the land.

The relations between the Church and the Synagogue were now becoming more and more embittered; nevertheless the *religious* controversy between the two parties was zealously, and not unsuccessfully prosecuted. Rabbi Abbahu complained of the spread of Christianity, and frequently disputed about the doctrines of the Gospel, although such of his arguments as have been preserved are not very formidable.[5] But if

---

[1] Jer. Ber. iii. 6a; Naz. vii. 56a. Comp. Grätz, iv. 313, [and contrast Levy, *NHWB*. ii. 360a].

[2] Kidd. 31b.   [3] Mid. Lam. on iii. 14.   [4] Jer. Taan. i. 64b.

[5] Jer. Taan. ii. 65b; Gen. Rab. 25; Ex. Rab. 29.

numerous Jewish converts adopted Christianity, on the other hand, many Gentiles became Jews, while still more adopted Jewish practices. Even within the Church there were not only Judaising sects, who held certain Jewish doctrines, and conformed to many of their practices, but the complaints of ecclesiastical fathers at a later period against evils which must have existed long previously, sufficiently indicate their extent. St. Chrysostom complains of the undue influence of the numerous Jewish physicians, or rather soothsayers, who supplied charms against various diseases.[1] He had even to deliver eight orations for the purpose of warning against Jewish practices. Christians seem to have attended the synagogues at Antioch; to have taken part in the Jewish feasts and fasts; to have preferred administering and taking an oath in the synagogue, as being more solemn,[2] etc. Imperial rescripts[3] refer to intermarriages between Jews and Christians, which frequently ended in the conversion of the latter; the circumcision of Christian slaves; and even to the voluntary submission of causes in dispute to the decision of Jewish tribunals. The enmity of Jews to Christianity manifested itself not only in various calumnies, and acts of violence when they had the power, but even in the despatch of special messengers to all parts of the Roman world to hinder the spread of the Gospel.[4]

The son and successor of Gamaliel IV. was Jehuda III., whose character and learning did not secure for him greater esteem than that enjoyed by his father. [In his time, the monthly examination of witnesses as to the appearance of the new moon sank into a mere formality.[5]] The new Patriarch, however, displayed a deep interest in the cause of education, for he despatched some of the leading Rabbins to inquire into the state of the elementary schools throughout the land, and to supply any deficiencies in this respect. It

---

[1] Chrysost. *Orat. adv. Jud.* viii. 7 (Op. i. p. 938).

[2] Chrysost. *ut supra*, i. 3 (i. p. 847).   [3] Comp. *Cod. Theod.*

[4] Compare the testimony of Justin Martyr in his Dialogue with Tryphon (c. 17), and of Eusebius in his notes on Isaiah xviii. 2.

[5] Rosh ha-Sh. 20*a*; Grätz, iv. 301.

is said that, when in a certain city the deputation found not any scholastic provision for the youth, they inquired of the magistrates for the city guard. When the armed men were paraded, the Rabbins replied, " Nay, these are the destroyers, not the guardians of your city ; its proper guardians are the teachers of youth and the instructors of the people ; for except the Lord keep the city, the watchman waketh but in vain." [1]

Conformity to heathen rites had led to a complete separation between the Samaritans and the Jews. Rabbins Ami, Assi, and Abbahu brought about their formal exclusion from the Synagogue.[2] This was probably the last decree of the Palestinian Sanhedrin. Another Rabbi, belonging to this and partly to the succeeding generation, deserves mention. Seira was a Babylonian by birth, but his theological standpoint, as well as personal inclination, powerfully drew him towards the land of his fathers. So great was his ardour to touch the sacred soil, that when he reached Jordan he did not tarry to seek a bridge, but crossed the stream, to the danger of his life, apprehensive, as he stated, " of delay in entering the Holy Land, which even Moses and Aaron had not been allowed to enter." [3] On his arrival in Tiberias, he was ordained,[4] and held in high repute for that very Babylonian method of teaching which he had formerly disclaimed, and to get rid of which he had earnestly, and with protracted fasting, petitioned Heaven.

The rule of Diocletian and his colleagues, so terrible to the Church, was succeeded by that of Constantine, the first Roman emperor who professed Christianity. It is not our province to do more than indicate the way in which he became sole ruler of the empire, or the mode and the degree in which he embraced Christianity. Diocletian had nominated Maximianus his colleague, and also elevated Galerius and Constantius to the dignity of Cæsars. Galerius was a bitter enemy of the Church, and became the instrument of a fearful persecution. Soon afterwards, Diocletian and

---

[1] Jer. Chag. i. 76c.
[3] Keth. 112a.

[2] Jer. Ab. Sar. v. 44d ; b. Chul. 6a.
[4] Sanh. 14a ; jer. Bikk. iii. 65cd.

Maximianus resigned, while Constantius, who had always shown himself mild and tolerant to the Christians, was succeeded by his son Constantine, afterwards denominated the Great. On the other hand, Galerius had named Severus and Maximinus as his colleagues. Heavy taxation in Italy, and jealousy at Rome, before long led to a rebellion, in which Maxentius, the son of the former Emperor Maximianus, was proclaimed emperor, and Severus was put to death. There were now five rulers of the Roman Empire : Galerius, Maximinus, Constantinus, Maxentius, and Maximianus, the old emperor, who again assumed the purple, and who had united his daughter Fausta to Constantinus. To these must be added, as sixth, Licinius, whom Galerius elevated to that dignity.

The continual intrigues of the old Emperor Maximianus led to his fall. After the death of Galerius, Maxentius attacked Constantine, who conquered, fighting under the standard of the Cross, to which, in a vision which led to his conversion, he had been directed. Maxentius fell in that contest. This victory seems to have elated the young Cæsar, who now allied himself to Licinius, by giving to the latter his sister Constantia in marriage. Their only remaining rival, Maximinus, engaged in war with Licinius, was defeated, and died of the effects of poison which himself had taken (313). Two years afterwards, Constantine and Licinius engaged in hostilities, which were succeeded by a peace of eight years' duration. Constantine distinguished himself during that period by his moderation, wisdom, and protection of the Christians ; Licinius, by the opposite qualities. In 323, another war ensued between them, in which Constantine was victorious. Having killed his brother-in-law, he now attained the sole command of the Roman world.

History has dealt unjustly with the character of Constantine. While his friends have elevated him far beyond his deserts, his opponents have equally detracted from his merits. Constantine was a wise, firm, and able emperor ; [but it cannot be denied that, although free from gross vices, he was wanting in the best heathen and Christian virtues.

He was vain and self-confident, and, under the influence of the passions of the moment, committed numerous acts of cruelty ; yet he was far from being a mere despot. We cannot doubt that his profession of Christianity was sincere ; but he realised very imperfectly the obligations which his new faith laid upon him, and, regarding himself as an instrument of God, manifested no real sense of personal shortcoming.[1]]

The conversion of Constantine greatly swelled at least the numbers of the adherents of Christianity from amongst Jews and Gentiles. Partly many obstacles were now removed, partly Christian zeal found more scope and opportunity of displaying itself, and partly the dominant religion could offer many outward advantages to its professors. On the other hand, it must be allowed that the spirit of toleration which Constantine and his immediate successors displayed was much in advance of the tendency of their times, and contrasts most favourably with later enactments. Without entering on the laws concerning heathenism, no fair representation of history can construe the legislation of the first Christian emperors into intolerance against the Jews. Before Constantine publicly professed his adherence to the Gospel, he had promulgated an edict of general toleration,[2] in which, of course, the Jews were included. Under former emperors they had enjoyed perfect civil equality. The edicts of Severus and Antoninus had admitted them to every civic office, and freed them from such as imposed duties contrary to their religious principles ;[3] while in many other ways their feelings were respected. [Now the Jews were once more forbidden to make proselytes,[4] but their position as citizens was still fully recognised.] The Patriarchs, and other heads of synagogues, were exempt from civic offices,[5] and received even from Christian emperors such titles as were granted only to the nobility or the highest magistracy. The only edicts in this respect which seem to indicate any restraint, are those in which Jewish converts

---

[1] Comp. *Dict. Chr. Biog.* i. 644 f.　　[2] Lact. *de Mort. Pers.* c. 48.
[3] *Digest. (de Decur.)*, L. 50. tit. 2, § 3.　　[4] *Cod. Theod.* L. xvi. tit. 8, § 1.
[5] *Cod. Theod.* L. xvi. tit. 8, § 2 ; cf. §§ 3, 4.

were protected from personal violence and the vengeance of the Synagogue [1] (an edict probably called for by the actual necessities of the case, as will appear by and by), and that by which ultimately the circumcision of their slaves was interdicted.[2] The latter enactment will not appear unjust, when it is remembered that, as slaves were actually the property of their masters, they were exposed to constraint; and the former becomes still more reasonable when it is added that a similar decree protected the Jews from the violent zeal of Christian neophytes. At the same time, the documents extant indicate an amount of general popular irritation and contempt for the Jews. Probably fanatics throughout the empire, perhaps even some of the magistrates, would, under the influence of mistaken zeal, act contrary to the spirit of these moderate laws. Manifestly spurious expressions are put into the mouth of Constantine by ecclesiastical writers, sufficiently indicating at least what spirit animated those who used them. The Council at Nice fixed a regular time for the celebration of Easter, instead of connecting it, as hitherto, with the Passover of the Jews.[3] Some years later, the Council of Laodicea forbade the observance of the Jewish Sabbath, which had in some places in the East been retained along with that of the Christian festival.[4] [At Elvira, in Spain, a more intolerant spirit was shown, and it was forbidden for a landowner to call upon a Jew to bless the crops, or even for a Christian to eat with a Jew.[5]

Jehuda III. was still Patriarch during the earlier years of the reign of Constantine.] The more celebrated sages around him were Rabbins Chaggai, Jonah, Joses, Jacob ben Abon, and especially Jeremiah, a Babylonian by birth. The low state of learning in Palestine will be gathered from the fact that Jeremiah, so celebrated in Palestine, had been censured in Babylon for raising futile discussions, and been dismissed from the colleges of his native country.[6] With a patriarchate

---

[1] *Cod. Theod.* L. xvi. tit. 8, §§ 1, 5. [2] *Ibid.* tit. 9, § 1.
[3] Eus. *Vit. Con.* iii. 18 ; Socr. *Hist. Eccl.* i. 9. [4] Conc. Laod. c. 29.
[5] Conc. Illiber. cc. 49, 50. [6] B. Bath. 23*b* ; comp. Grätz, iv. 331.

subsisting merely in name—with a general decay of learning and influence in Palestine—with the ascendancy of an antagonistic creed, and the many acts of violence which were either committed or threatened—with the fearful pressure of taxation, of which, indeed, bitter complaints were now to be heard in all parts of the empire—lastly, with the daily growing number of those who left their ranks to join those of the Church—the Jews began at last to feel that another period of misery and oppression had begun. Loud are the complaints against the many worldly allurements by which "sinful Rome, the son of thy mother, endeavoured to shake the steadfastness of the faithful." [1]

To this spirit of anxiety and longing many of the discussions and conversions which at that time took place must be ascribed. Later traditions have embellished these records with a number of apocryphal miracles, which, it scarcely requires to be said, are the offspring of monkish imagination, inspired by what they conceived to be for the glory of God, or for the triumph of the Gospel. In this number we reckon the story of the discussion between Pope *Sylvester* and the Jews, under the leadership of one *Sambres*.[2] It is said that the Jews, desirous of converting Constantine to their creed, had applied to the emperor's mother, Helena. Accordingly, a meeting was arranged in presence of the emperor and a distinguished circle. When the Jews were worsted by Sylvester in argument, they appealed to the power of working miracles. Accordingly, Sambres muttered something into the ear of a bullock, which, after violent convulsions, fell dead to the ground. Not to be outdone, Sylvester had now to recall the ox to life, in which, of course, he succeeded, when all the Jews present immediately professed Christianity.

Of a totally different character from such legends is the story of the conversion of no less a personage than the Patriarch himself.[3] The story was related to St. Epiphanius, Bishop of Salamis in Cyprus, by a converted Jew, who was

---

[1] Pes. Rabb. c. 15.　　　　　　　　[2] Zonaras, *Annal.* xiii. 2.
[3] Epiph. *adv. Hær.* xxx. 4–12.

intimately connected with the Patriarch, and who had been an eye-witness of all he related. The account is comparatively free from exaggeration and miraculous additions, [and we can hardly dismiss it as incredible without further consideration. We must, however, remember that the story was told to Epiphanius many years after the event, and was not written down by him till a considerably later time, when, as he admits, he no longer remembered with certainty the names of the Patriarch and his son.[1] In this point, at any rate, our informant seems to be mistaken. He calls the Patriarch Hillel; but Jewish authorities appear only to recognise Hillel II., who was contemporary with Julian, and who is said to have been the son of Jehuda III. It therefore seems probable that the names of father and son have been confused, that the alleged convert was really Jehuda III., and that the son who succeeded to the patriarchate as a young man was Hillel II.[2]]

St. Epiphanius, who, although credulous and blindly zealous for what he deemed truth, was thoroughly honest, earnest in his adherence to Christ, and devout, received his account from Joseph, a convert whom Constantine the Great had elevated to the dignity of " Count." It is interesting to note the circumstances of the narrative. During the reign of the successor of Constantine, Constantius, who had joined the Arian party, the adherents of the orthodox creed were persecuted. Amongst others, Eusebius, an Italian bishop, was exiled, and found an asylum in the princely mansion of Count Joseph. There Epiphanius, with some other Christians, waited on the bishop, and also elicited from Joseph, at that time a man of about seventy years of age, the history of his conversion. Though surrounded by Arians, and alternately cajoled and threatened by them, Joseph not only remained attached to the orthodox faith, receiving and sheltering an exiled bishop and his friends, but another younger Jewish convert, it is recorded, waited secretly (from fear of the violence of the Arians) on the persecuted ecclesiastics. To return : Joseph related that at one time he had occupied a

---

[1] *Ut supra*, xxx. 4.   [2] Comp. Grätz, iv. 483 f.

high post amongst the Jews, being attached to the person of the Patriarch Hillel. When at the point of death, the Patriarch had sent for the Christian bishop, who seems also to have practised medicine. The latter came as physician of the body. When all present had been removed, Joseph, whose suspicions had been excited, lingered behind, and witnessed, through the crevices of the door, an unexpected scene. The dying Patriarch opened his mind to the bishop, and craved baptism at his hands. He obtained it, and felt strengthened in both body and mind. The bishop visited the Patriarch two or three times in the character of a physician, until the converted Jewish dignitary entered into his rest, leaving his trusty friend Joseph, and another sage, guardians of his youthful son and successor, who is called Jehuda.

That the conversion of the Patriarch should he kept secret cannot appear remarkable under the circumstances ; [and the absence of any allusion to this event in Jewish literature does not disprove the truth of the narrative. At the same time, we may doubt whether Joseph rightly understood the nature of the scene which he witnessed, or whether his account has not been coloured by the recollection of his subsequent experiences. We will, however, continue the story.] If Joseph had been deeply impressed by what he had observed in the sick-chamber, his curiosity, as that of others, was roused by noticing a large seal on the treasury-box of the late Patriarch. He secretly opened it, and, to his astonishment, found there, instead of money, what had proved much more precious to the Patriarch :—a Hebrew translation of the Gospel according to St. John, of the Acts of the Apostles, and a copy of the Hebrew of the Gospel of St. Matthew. Though this discovery and the reading of the sacred writings deepened Joseph's impressions of the truth, he still resisted its power. Meantime Jehuda, his young ward, had grown up, and been unfortunately led astray by light companions. According to the practice of those times, when unbridled licentiousness sought its object, and found it impossible otherwise to obtain it, recourse was had to magical means, to incantations and love-potions, a practice which the ancient Church denounced

—correctly in its spirit, though not in its literal meaning—as satanic agency. Possibly the strong belief entertained by all parties as to the efficacy of such means may have contributed to secure their success; while, on the other hand, faith in Christ, and the confidence of safety with which the pronouncing of the name of Jesus, and the sign of the cross, inspired Christians, may help to explain the alleged impotence of magical means against the members of the Church. It is said that the young Patriarch had recourse to such magical means to seduce a Christian female, but without effect. Joseph, aware of these circumstances, looked upon her deliverance as another instance of the miraculous power of Christianity.

While his mind was agitated on these important questions, he dreamt that Christ appeared to him and called upon him to believe. These severe mental struggles induced a dangerous disease. When on the point of death, one of his Jewish friends whispered into his ear some adjuration or formula in the name of Jesus. It is not necessary to resort to the explanation, that as the patient's thoughts were so much engaged with this subject, he might in his febrile excitement have readily misinterpreted the words of his friend, since St. Epiphanius adds, that he had ascertained that many Jews were in the habit, in cases of extreme danger, of attempting a miraculous cure in the name of Jesus. Such practice is quite conceivable not only on the part of believers in the exclusive claims of Christ to the Messiahship, but of superstitious persons generally, and tallies both with an inspired record of a similar occurrence (Acts xix. 13) and the prohibition issued by the Synagogue against all such practices. However, Joseph had on his sickbed another vision, in which health was promised to him, and the command—to believe, reiterated. Such visions—viewing them simply as internal psychological phenomena—are scarcely wonderful in the circumstances, nor does it appear inexplicable how he should have so long and seriously resisted the voice within. Accordingly, on his recovery he relapsed into unbelief; but, in consequence of another vision, attempted the

miraculous cure of a demoniac in the name of the Lord. In
this he succeeded, as the Jews supposed, by means of the
ineffable name of the Lord; mention of which, they con-
jectured, he had found in the Patriarch's sealed treasure-box.

Soon afterwards, the Patriarch sent Joseph, as an apostle,
into Cilicia, to collect the tribute and inquire into the affairs
of its congregations. In a certain city of Cilicia, he lodged
close by the residence of the Christian bishop, whose aquaint-
ance he made, and from whom he borrowed the sacred
writings. The suspicion of the Jews was now aroused, while
his strictness excited the enmity of their officials. They
came suddenly upon him, found him reading the Gospels,
dragged him into the synagogue, and would have beaten him
to death had not the bishop interposed and rescued him.
However, when he would have departed from the city,
another tumult arose, in which he was thrown into the
river Cydnus, and supposed to be drowned. But he escaped
a watery grave, and soon made a public profession of Christianity. Constantine the Great, to whose ears this story had
come, and who may have enacted the edict for the protection
of converts in consequence of this and similar instances of
violence, elevated Joseph to the dignity of Count, and commissioned him to build churches in certain towns of Palestine
where they had not hitherto been reared. At this stage a
somewhat rambling account is given of certain incantations
by which the Jews had tried to prevent the erection of these
buildings, and of the exorcistic means by which Joseph
succeeded in his plans. Probably, were we better acquainted
with the circumstances, we should discover a readier mode of
accounting for these reverses and successes than that of
supernatural agency,—the favourite and general explanation
of those times for all extraordinary cases or points of
difficulty. Besides the interest attaching to this story of
St. Epiphanius, it is of importance to notice that at that
time, apparently, Hebrew translations of the Gospels and of
other parts of the New Testament had circulated, and were
secretly persued by Jews.

The mind of the Jewish nation seems to have been much

agitated about this time, and, while many inquired after the Messiah, others despaired of His coming, or sought a different deliverance. In the spirit of such doubts, Rabbi Hillel is said to have expressed himself at one time, that the Messiah had already come in the days of Hezekiah. However, such interpretations were disavowed by other sages. [Rab Joseph, on hearing of Hillel's assertion, exclaimed, "May God forgive Hillel for this"; and he protested that even Zechariah had prophesied of the Messiah.[1]] St. Chrysostom relates [2] that in the time of Constantine the Great the Jews made a rebellious attempt to repossess themselves of Jerusalem, in consequence of which the emperor took signal vengeance, by cutting off their ears and selling them into slavery. This story, however, [is not confirmed by any reliable Jewish or Christian authority, and it] is discredited by most authors.

Constantine, who was only baptized a short time before his death, was succeeded by his three sons, who divided his dominions between them. Two of them, Constans and Constantine, entered into a war, in which Constantine fell. In 350, Constans was slain by Magnentius, an aspirant to the purple; but the usurper was not able to maintain his position, and *Constantius* became sole emperor. [A pious Christian in his own way, and not without some knowledge of statecraft, Constantius was nevertheless altogether inferior to his father. Weak and suspicious, he allowed himself to be governed by the chamberlains and officials of the court, while he was frequently guilty both of treachery and of cruelty in ridding himself of his enemies.] This reign is marked by a growing spirit of religious intolerance; and the emperor was a bitter persecutor of all opponents of Arianism, to which he himself was attached. At first the aspect of affairs seemed promising for the Jews. While the bitterness of the Arians against the Catholics was naturally grateful to the Synagogue, and held out the prospect of detriment to the Church by internal dissensions, the doctrinal views of the Arians concerning the Lord Jesus agreed much more with those of liberal Jews than did the sentiments of the orthodox

[1] Sanh. 99*a*. [2] *Orat. adv. Jud.* v. 11 (i. 900).

party.   Many Arians who lived in Palestine were in friendly
relations with the Jews.   Accordingly, when, at the removal
of the orthodox Bishop of Alexandria, Athanasius, tumults
broke out, and churches were broken open, ransacked, and
profaned by deeds of violence and licentiousness, the Jews
took, along with the pagans and the Arians, a leading part
in these disgraceful riots.[1]   Such displays of unprovoked
hostility must have increased the bitterness of the Catholics
against the Synagogue, and serve to account not only for
expressions of unmitigated hatred on the part of some from
whom other things might have been expected, but for the
outburst of actual persecution in a party which had lately
pleaded for religious liberty and toleration.

Constantius decreed the supression of paganism, [and his
edicts against the Jews, though not very numerous, are marked
by an increasing severity].   He interdicted the reception of
proselytes into the Synagogue, on pain of the loss of all their
possessions.[2]   [A Jew was forbidden to hold Christian slaves on
pain of forfeiture, while the circumcision of non-Jewish slaves
was an offence to be punished by death.[3]]   Probably the political attitude of the Synagogue may have somewhat incited the
emperor's resentment.   [Some of these edicts were published
after the Jewish revolt, and the Jews may have been suspected of sympathising with the Persians, with whom Constantius was at war.   Sapor II., indeed, had not shown himself
altogether friendly to the Jews ;[4] but the fact that many of
the sages of Palestine emigrated about this time to Babylonia[5]
implies that they preferred Persian to Roman rule.]   On
the other hand, the Christian subjects of Sapor were subjected
to a fearful persecution, [which one writer attributes, probably without much authority, to the instigation of the Jews[6]].

---

[1] Athan. *Hist. Arian.* 71 (i. 305) ; *Encyl.* 3 (i. 89); Lucifer, *Pro S. Athan.*
ii. 16 (*Patrol. Lat.* xiii. 916).

[2] *Cod. Theod.* L. xvi. tit. 8, § 7.   [Comp. § 6, where Jews are forbidden, on
pain of death, to marry Christian women attached to the imperial court (from
the *gynaecea.*)]

[3] *Cod. Theod.* L. xvi. tit. 9, § 2 ; Sozom. *Hist. Eccl.* iii. 17.

[4] Moed K. 26*a*.   [5] Ab. Sar. 73*a* ; Chul. 106*a* ; comp. Grätz, iv. 490.

[6] Sozom. *Hist. Eccl.* ii. 9.

When, in the year 351, after strengthening himself by means of intrigue, Constantius marched against the usurper Magnentius, he had elevated his cousin Gallus to the dignity of Cæsar, and committed to his charge the affairs of the East. If at any previous period, energy and success were now required to maintain the cause of Rome against the growing Persian power. But Gallus, who only occupied himself with amusements, left the conduct of the war in the hands of Ursicinus, [one of the ablest generals of the time. Ursicinus, who bears a twofold character in Jewish history,[1] is usually represented as a cruel oppressor, but elsewhere he appears on friendly terms with certain Rabbins.[2]] Judea had now to suffer from the presence of an army quartered there ; and the Romans probably had the less regard for its inhabitants, as the general tendency of the times was antagonistic to the Jews. Accordingly, no regard was paid to their religious scruples. Jewish bakers had to work for the Romans on Sabbaths as on other days, and, contrary to their religious ordinances, to furnish leavened bread during the Feast of Passover. Unlike their ancestors, who would readily have sacrificed their lives rather than submit to such ordinances, the Rabbins found pretexts for sanctioning these violations of the law. [Thus they justified the baking of bread on the Sabbath on the ground that Ursicinus did not directly wish to compel the people to transgress the law, but only required fresh bread for his army.[3]]

The tyranny and incapacity of Gallus, together with the hopes inspired by the dubious contest in which Constantius was engaged with Magnentius, and by the successes of Sapor II., at last induced a general insurrection of the Jews in Palestine.[4] Simultaneously they rose in various towns, and cut down the Romans on whom they could lay hands, without giving any quarter. The headquarters of the rebellion was the mountain-city *Sepphoris*, or, as it was then

---

[1] Comp. Hamburger, *Enc.* ii. 73 f., "Arsicinus."

[2] Jer. Ber. v. 9*a*.   [3] Jer. Sheb. iv. 35*a*; Bez. i. 60*c*.

[4] Socr. *Hist. Eccl.* ii. 33 ; Sozom. *Hist. Eccl.* iv. 7 ; Hieron. *Chron.* Ol. 283 (355 A.D.). Comp. Pesikta, c. 8.

called, Diocæsarea, well calculated by its situation, its
historical character—having long been the seat of Jewish
learning,—and its almost exclusively Jewish population, to be
the general rendezvous of the rebels. By some the Jewish
leader is called *Patricius*, perhaps a corruption of the word
patriarchus.[1] But the success of the Jews was brief. Gallus
sent fresh legions into Judea—Sepphoris was levelled with
the ground, Tiberias, Lydda, and other cities were partially
destroyed. Fearful atrocities were committed by way of
revenge. Thousands were slain,—neither age nor sex was
spared. The inhabitants of Sepphoris suffered most severely.
[Tradition tells of unavailing attempts to evade death by
disguise[2] or flight, and of fugitives who took refuge in subterranean passages and in caves.[3] A riddling letter, sent
about this time to Babylonia, seems to imply that certain
religious usages had been prohibited in Palestine.[4] The same
may perhaps be inferred also from the statement that
Ursicinus caused a roll of the Law, destined for use in the
synagogue, to be burnt in the neighbourhood of Tiberias.[5]]
Gallus was recalled and put to death in 354, but the condition of the Jews did not improve. In fact, Constantius
seems to have intended imposing new and exorbitant taxes on
the Jewish population of the empire,[6] when death deprived
him of the power of oppression.

Mention has already been made of Epiphanius, Bishop of
Constantia in the isle of Cyprus. This pious ecclesiastic, who
took a leading part in some of the stirring controversies of his
times, was a native of the village of Bezanduca in Palestine.[7] It is said that he was born of Jewish parents, and
converted when about fifteen years of age; [but our only
authority for this statement is a worthless biography, written
in the name of Polybius, who pretends to have been his pupil.
Epiphanius shows no slight knowledge of Jewish customs, and
in his account of various Jewish sects he has preserved

---

[1] Aurelius Victor, *De Caesar*. xlii. 11.

[2] Jer. Jeb. xvi. 15*c*; Sot. ix. 23*c*.   [3] Gen. Rab. 31.

[4] Sanh. 12*a* ; comp. Grätz, iv. 342, 490 f.   [5] Jer. Meg. iii. 74*a*.

[6] Julian. *Epist*. 25.   [7] Sozom. *Hist. Eccl*. vi. 32.

several valuable traditions, together with a remarkable number of mistakes.] He was acquainted with the Hebrew, Syriac, Egyptian, Greek, and Latin languages, and otherwise possessed considerable erudition. But he was exceedingly credulous, and, though his genuine piety generally kept him right, he was ever ready to arrive at sweeping conclusions, or to be betrayed into a course of action which often exhibited more of rashness and enthusiasm than of meekness and wisdom. He closed his earthly career in 403, in the hundredth year of his age.

The Jewish patriarchate in Palestine had continued, in spite of the numerous migrations of Rabbins to Babylon, [but there is some uncertainty about the names and order of the last few Patriarchs.[1] Probably Hillel II., the son of Jehuda III., held the office during the whole of the reign of Constantius, and survived till the reign of Julian the Apostate.] This emperor, the cousin and successor of Constantius, had, during his extended intercourse with heathen philosophers, imbibed their principles, and been long secretly addicted to the ancient superstition. Probably the religious constraint under which he had for a time to live, together with the palpable inconsistencies and the manifest hypocrisy of many who professed Christianity, may have deepened his aversion to the religion of Jesus. After his accession to the empire, he openly renounced the faith, and attempted to substitute in its place a kind of rationalistic heathenism. Had he lived long enough, he might have been driven to persecute openly the creed against which, during the period of his reign, all his influence was indirectly exerted. Julian professed himself a warm friend of the Jews. In a letter, still extant, addressed to them,[2] he repeals and disowns all persecuting or oppressive edicts, and promises the restoration of Jerusalem and its Temple. He also offers advice as to the best means of promoting their cause, and calls upon his " brother, the venerable Patriarch Julos (or Hillel)," to relinquish the oppressive tribute which had hitherto been paid to him by the Jews in all parts of the Roman Empire. In conclusion, he asks the Jews to

---

[1] Comp. Grätz, iv. 484 f.   [2] Julian. *Epist.* 25.

pray for his success in the Persian war upon which he was about to enter.

Julian hastened to perform what he had promised.[1]   He despatched a former governor of Britain, Alypius, to Jerusalem, with commission immediately to rebuild the Temple.   Neither trouble nor expense were to be spared, and the civic authorities of the country were in every way to assist in this good work. It is difficult to understand the emperor's special motives for such an undertaking.   [No doubt he was pleased to depress Christianity by giving encouragement to all other parties, and he had already shown a desire to conciliate the Jews.   He may have wished, in view of his Persian campaign, to gain the support of their brethren in Mesopotamia.]   Possibly the measure was part of his general policy of restoring the old forms of religion, and he would feel sympathy with the sacrificial system of the Jews.   One writer asserts that he wished to gainsay our Lord's prophecy of the desolation of the Temple ;[2] and doubtless a variety of motives combined to influence his conduct.   Although many Jews had emigrated to Babylon, and were hence unable, and perhaps, from peculiar views, unwilling to assist in the undertaking, the vast majority were enthusiastic in their support of this sacred labour.   However, while the workmen were engaged in clearing away the ruins, volumes of fire burst forth from the subterranean vaults. Panic seized those entrusted with the labour, and it was suspended at least till further orders, or Julian's return from the Persian war.   Whatever may have been the proximate cause of these eruptions,—whether purely natural or primarily supernatural,—it proved, in the providence of God, the most effectual answer to the blasphemies of the opponents of Christianity, and the most palpable confirmation of the Lord's prediction.

[Julian's Persian campaign was at first a brilliant success, and he penetrated as far as Ctesiphon.   But the succours which he was expecting from Armenia failed to arrive, and

---

[1] Am. Marcell. xxiii. 1 ; Socr. *Hist. Eccl.* iii. 20 ; Theodoret, *Hist. Eccl.* iii. 15 (Migne).

[2] Philostorgius, *Hist. Eccl.* vii. 9.

the army was forced to retreat along the Tigris, through a country wasted by the enemy. During the retreat,] Julian was killed in a skirmish (363). Legend related that he died with this sentence on his lips: "Thou hast overcome, O Galilean!"[1] Although Julian had interested himself so much in the Jews of Palestine, their brethren of Babylon appear to have sided with his enemies. Perhaps they inferred that this patronage of Judaism would only be temporary. More probably they preferred Persian to Roman domination. Besides, the Babylonian sages had, in the interest of their schools, begun to depreciate the mother country, to claim a superior dignity for their citizens, and even to declare that only the dregs of the population had originally returned with Ezra to Palestine.[2]

With the death of Julian vanished the hopes of the Jews in Palestine. They had looked forward to a speedy national restoration, of which they considered the favours which they enjoyed under Julian as merely the preparation. Already they were threatening to take full revenge upon the Christians,[3] when the unexpected demise of Julian once more put an end to these anticipations. The Roman Empire was now fast approaching its dissolution. [The provinces beyond the Tigris were lost at the death of Julian; in Europe the policy was adopted of allowing large bodies of barbarians to settle within the frontiers.] At Julian's death the soldiers proclaimed Jovian, a Christian, emperor. But he died before reaching Constantinople, and was succeeded by Valentinian I. (elected also by the soldiers) and by Valens,—the former connected with the Catholic, the latter with the Arian party. In spite of his ferocity of temper, Valentinian was, in matters of belief, liberal and tolerant, [but his weaker colleague countenanced many acts of persecution]. The former promulgated an edict which granted full liberty to all parties (364).[4] During the reign of the successors of these princes, the Visigoths, Vandals, and other races successively possessed themselves of portions

---

[1] Theodoret, *Hist. Eccl.* iii. 20.   [2] Comp. Kidd. 69*b*, 71*a*.
[3] Socr. *Hist. Eccl.* iii. 20; comp. Ambrose, *Epist.* 40. 15, 18.
[4] Comp. *Cod. Theod.* L. ix. tit. 16, § 9; Amm. Marcell. xxx. 9.

of the empire, and dictated terms of peace to the feeble emperors. Men of that period, who witnessed the terrible successes of the Goths, declared them to be Gog and Magog spoken of in prophecy,[1] while the Jews contrasted the apparent permanence of Israel with the passing away of other nations.[2] In the meantime, the explanations of the Mishna, and the legal traditions current in the colleges of Palestine, had been collected during the latter half of the fourth century, and immediately after the decline of these colleges. It was natural that, when the living authorities had passed away, such attempts should have been made to preserve their teaching, and thus to perpetuate an influence which could no longer be claimed by their successors. These collections formed the basis of what is now known as the Jerusalem Talmud. It is impossible to ascertain the name of the principal compiler of these collections. Tradition names Rabbi Jochanan, [but we find references to persons who lived many years after his death [3]].

Owing to the increasing troubles of the time, the Patriarch Hillel seems to have felt the necessity of relinquishing the last prerogative of his office,—the arrangement of the calendar, and with it the fixing of the period for the feasts.[4] Instead of the former method of communicating the arrangements of the calendar, a new and scientific method of adjusting the lunar with the solar year had been adopted, the principles of which, although very complicated, have proved so correct that it has not since undergone alteration. However, this act of the Patriarch did not meet with the approbation of all the sages, one of whom wrote to the various congregations exhorting them to continue the observance of *two* feast-days, as had been enacted under different circumstances,[5]—an arrangement which still prevails. [Hillel II. was succeeded in the patriarchate by Gamaliel V., who was

---

[1] Hieron. *Quæst. Hebr. in Gen.* x. 2 ; cf. jer. Meg. i. 71*b*.

[2] Midr. in Ps. 36.

[3] Comp. Strack, *Einleitung in den Thalmud* (ed. 2), p. 62 f.

[4] Comp. Ideler, *Chronologie*, i. 569 ff.; Hamburger, *Enc.* ii. 627 f.; Grätz, iv. 344 f., 491 f.

[5] Jer. Erub. iii. 21*c*.

still living in the reign of Theodosius the Great. He in turn was succeeded by Jehuda IV., of whom nothing further is known.[1]]

Theodosius I., the son of a celebrated general of the same name, was the only one apparently capable of maintaining for a time the dignity and integrity of the empire. He not only tolerated, but as far as possible defended the rights of the Synagogue against the lawlessness of an increasing fanaticism. An edict protected the Synagogue from every interference with its internal administration, and allowed the Jews to choose for themselves judges and magistrates.[2] When the Roman consular Hesychius committed an act of violence against the Patriarch, he decided in favour of the latter, and condemned Hesychius to death.[3] But frequently the fanaticism of the rabble vented itself in acts of violence, which, encouraged and vindicated by eminent prelates, could not easily be put down even by the arm of the law. The first recorded instance of this kind happened during the short occupation of Italy by the rebel Maximus. Some Christians in Rome had set fire to the Jewish synagogue, when Maximus ordered that it should be restored. [We are told that the Christian populace were highly indignant at the support thus given to the enemies of the Church, and that they predicted the speedy downfall of Maximus, who (they said) " had become a Jew." [4]]

A similar occurrence shortly afterwards took place at Callinicum, a town in Northern Mesopotamia, the incendiaries in this case being led by the bishop of the town.[5] Theodosius ordered the bishop to rebuild the synagogue. But here St. Ambrose, the great Bishop of Milan, came forward in defence of the men whose conduct was so little in accordance with the religion which he taught. In a sermon, and in a letter to the emperor,[6] he violently attacked this edict; [and while he expressed his disapproval of outrage, since priests should strive to promote peace, he declared that no Christian bishop could conscientiously assist in building a place of worship for

---

[1] Grätz, iv. 384 f., 484 f.   [2] *Cod. Theod.* L. xvi. tit. 8, § 8.
[3] Hieron. *Ep. ad Pam.* 57. 3.   [4] Ambrose, *Ep.* 40. 23.
[5] *Ut supra*, 41. 1 ; 40. 13.   [6] *Ut supra*, 41. 2-26 ; 40.

unbelieving Jews].   From the fanaticism which animated one
of the most celebrated bishops of his time, it is easy to infer
the general spirit which prevailed among clergy and laity.
Theodosius had to recall his edict, but enjoined the magistrates
to protect the Jews in their worship, and severely to punish
all who offered them any violence.[1]

Theodosius left the empire to his two sons (395).
Honorius reigned in the West, and Arcadius in the East.
The latter was succeeded by Theodosius II.   These emperors
at first extended the same protection as their father to the
Jews.   They went even further.   They wrote expressly to
prevent all interference in the affairs of the Jews, to protect
Jewish dignitaries, and to exempt them from all public burdens.
But in 399, Honorius forbade the payment of tribute to the
Patriarch of Tiberias, and ordered that what had already been
collected should be paid into the imperial treasury.[2]   However, this order seems not to have been issued upon religious
grounds, and was repealed in 404.[3]   Perhaps it arose from
the peculiar relations between the west and the east.   Both
emperors were wholly under the sway of their respective
prime ministers, whose mutual jealousies and intrigues embroiled the empire in much more serious difficulties than
that connected with the Jewish tribute.   In 409, Honorius
issued an edict, conceived in a very tolerant spirit, by which
he exempted Jews on Sabbath and feast-days from attendance
at courts of law.[4]

In the Eastern empire the laws were somewhat less
favourable.   The Jews were interdicted from building new
synagogues,[5] and from possessing Christian slaves ;[6] [but they
were allowed to appoint their own judges in purely Jewish cases,[7]
and existing synagogues were protected from violence[8]].   The
Patriarch Gamaliel v., probably the Gamaliel who was specially
distinguished for his medical lore,[9] received at first some marks

[1] *Cod. Theod.* L. xvi. tit. 8, § 9.   [2] *Ibid.* L. xvi. tit. 8, § 14.
[3] *Ibid.* tit. 8, §§ 15, 17.
[4] *Ibid.* L. ii. tit. 8, § 26 ; L. viii. tit. 8, § 8 ; comp. L. xvi. tit. 8, § 20.
[5] *Ibid.* L. xvi. tit. 8, §§ 25, 27.   [6] *Ibid.* tit. 9, §§ 4, 5 ; t. 8, § 22.
[7] *Ibid.* tit. 8, §§ 13, 15.   [8] *Ibid.* tit. 8, §§ 25-27.
[9] Marcellus Empir. 23. 77 (ed. Helmreich).

of distinction from the emperor, but was speedily reminded
of his real position in the empire. Presuming perhaps on
supposed favours, the Patriarch had broken some of the
imperial edicts, by building synagogues, etc. In consequence
of this he was in 415 deprived of all his honours.[1] With his
death terminated the Palestinian patriarchate, about the year
425. Jews were gradually excluded from holding public
offices; and to increase the pressure which now bore them
down, it was enacted (429) that the tribute formerly paid
to the Patriarch should, according to accurate calculations, be
in future levied on all Jews, and paid into the imperial
treasury.[2] About the same time the Vandal king Genseric
carried, amongst other spoils of his triumph in Italy, the
sacred vessels of the Jewish Temple from Rome to Africa.[3]

It is scarcely necessary to observe that the studies which
had so long been successfully prosecuted in Palestine were
not suddenly relinquished, but gradually ceased. [Even after the
fifth century Palestine was still the chief seat of learning in
matters connected with the text of Scripture.] But the study
of the Hagada, and even that in most fanciful form, had long
taken the place of the more sober pursuits of the Halacha.
Amongst the Hagadic authorities of that time, Rabbi Tanchuma bar Abba is specially named, to whom an elaborate
commentary is ascribed, which, however, dates from a later
period.[4] At the same time the study of the Hebrew began
to be cultivated by many Christian ecclesiastics. In this
they encountered considerable difficulties, as the Synagogue
had interdicted the teaching of the Law to Gentiles.[5]. Thus
Jerome (a celebrated ecclesiastical writer), who was conversant
not only with the Hebrew language, but also with Jewish
traditions and modes of interpretation, could only in secret
procure instructions in Hebrew from Jewish Rabbins.[6] These
studies and aids assisted him in the composition of the Latin
translation of the Bible, well known as the " Vulgate," and

---

[1] *Cod. Theod.* L. xvi. tit. 8, § 22.   [2] *Ibid.* tit. 8, § 29.
[3] *Evagrii fragm.* iv. 17.
[4] Comp. Hamburger, *Enc.* Suppl. p. 154 f.   [5] Chag. 13a.
[6] Hieron. *Ep. ad. Pam.* 84. 3.

still in use. [Where special difficulties arose, Jerome obtained
the assistance of Jewish doctors from Lydda and Tiberias.[1]
From many passages in his writings it is clearly shown that
the elaborate system of vowel points and accents had not yet
been introduced into the Hebrew text. The prejudices of
Christians added to the difficulties of the scholar. Jerome's
adversaries spoke of Bar Chanina, his Hebrew teacher, as
Barabbas,[2] and imagined that a version of the Bible on which
Jewish authority had been consulted must be tainted with
Judaism.] Although the Church owed so much to the Jews,
the state of feeling too general at that period towards them
was probably accurately expressed in a statement of Jerome.
" If it is requisite," says that Father, in self-vindication,
" to hate individuals or a nation, I own that I detest the
Jews with inexpressible hatred ; for to this day they persecute
our Lord in their synagogues." [3]   A strange inference, certainly,
from such premises !

The troubles to which the Jews were increasingly exposed
kept alive their desire for the promised Deliverer, and as
time passed on more of earnest expectation was awakened.
Accordingly, several calculations were made, one of which
fixed the appearance of the Messiah for the year 440.[4]
Several Rabbins felt it indeed a necessary measure of prudence
to add certain cautions, so as to moderate an ardour which
was doomed to continual disappointment. Such a state of
mind encouraged the pretensions of deceivers and false
Messiahs. One of these appeared in the isle of Crete
(in 432), and, after having for a year gone through the
island persuading the Jews that, like Moses, he would lead
them dry-shod through the sea to Palestine, he at last
assembled them to commence the exodus. On a given
signal, the deceived people threw themselves from a promon-
tory into the sea, expecting that its waves would part.
Happily a number of fishermen with boats were at hand,
and succeeded in rescuing most. The deceiver himself dis-

---

[1] Hieron. *Praef. in Job ; ad Domnionem in Chron.*
[2] Hieron. *Apol. adv. Ruf.* i. 13.   [3] *Ep. ad Pam.* 84. 3.
[4] Sanh. 97*b* ; comp. Ab. Sar. 9*b*.

appeared, and the greater number of the Jews in Crete joined the Church.[1]

But scenes of a different character also took place. It seems to have been customary amongst the Jews, during the somewhat riotous festivities of Purim (the Feast of Esther), when their minds were elated, to pour special contempt upon Christianity, and particularly, instead of publicly hanging Haman on a gallows, to nail him to a cross, with a too manifest allusion to the Crucifixion.[2] These blasphemous provocations led often to riot and bloodshed, and required the serious interference of the authorities. Specially had the Jews in the neighbourhood of Antioch carried these provocations so far as (in 415) to affix a Christian child to a cross, and to scourge him to death. A fight now ensued between the Jews and the Christians. The emperor ordered the perpetrators of this murder to be severely punished.[3] However, this did not allay the irritation. Some years after this occurrence, the populace of Antioch deprived the Jews of their synagogue.[4] The governor himself felt so much the injustice and lawlessness of this popular rising, that on his representation the emperor ordered full reparation to be made. But one of those fanatical monks, who at that time stood so high in popular veneration for the supposed superior sanctity connected with their mortification of the flesh, *Simeon*, surnamed *Stylites* from having spent the greater part of his life on the top of a column by way of penance, expressly wrote to the emperor expostulating on the subject. The weak Theodosius not only revoked his edict, but even deposed the governor of Antioch, who had advocated the cause of the Jews.

[Still more stormy scenes were witnessed at Alexandria, where the vehement and impetuous Cyril now occupied the episcopal throne.[5] At all times the population of Alexandria had been notorious for its turbulent and unruly spirit. In addition to constant feuds between Christians, Jews, and

---

[1] Socr. *Hist. Eccl.* vii. 38.
[2] *Cod. Theod.* L. xvi. tit. 8, § 18; cf. § 21.   [3] Socr. *Hist. Eccl.* vii. 16.
[4] Evagrius, *Hist. Eccl.* i. 13.   [5] Socr. *Hist. Eccl.* vii. 13.

pagans, at the present period the city was disturbed by fierce factions, which disputed about the merits of rival dancers at the public entertainments. These contests, which rarely ended without bloodshed, were especially frequent when the performances took place on the Jewish Sabbath.] Accordingly, the governor Orestes felt it necessary to affix some police regulations in a place where public amusements were wont to be held. No sooner did the Jews discover amongst those who read—and perhaps commented on—these regulations, Hierax, one of Cyril's most zealous followers, than they exclaimed that he had only come for the purpose of exciting a tumult. Orestes, who was jealous of the civil power which was usurped by the Archbishops of Alexandria, caused Hierax to be arrested and severely punished. Immediately Cyril summoned the chief of the Jews, and threatened them with fearful vengeance. Driven to desperation, the Jews, in self-defence, leagued against the Christians, agreeing upon some mark by which they might recognise each other. During the night they raised the cry that the principal church was in flames. From all quarters of the town did the unarmed Christians hasten to assist in extinguishing, as they supposed, the flames. The Jews then surrounded them, and a murderous fight ensued. Day separated and revealed the combatants. Cyril then immediately put himself at the head of a band, burnt down the synagogue, pillaged the houses, killed many, and expelled all the Jews from the city. Orestes, indignant at the conduct of Cyril, to whose interference he ascribed the whole tumult, reported the matter to the emperor. But before a reply could arrive, the feud between the governor and Cyril had grown to a greater height. A multitude of frenzied fanatical monks poured into the city, surrounded and insulted, and one of them, Ammonius, severely wounded Orestes in the head. The Alexandrians hastened to the spot. Ammonius was secured and tortured to death. Cyril caused him to be buried in pomp, preached a funeral oration, and extolled Ammonius as a martyr. Finding that the more moderate of his own friends did not approve of his proceedings, he was glad to let the matter be forgotten, and tried to

make peace with Orestes.[1]   When the governor refused, the
incensed followers of Cyril went so far as to wreak their
vengeance on the celebrated, beautiful, and highly accomplished Hypatia, whom they suspected of having prevented a
reconciliation,—actually tore her to pieces, and burnt her
remains.[2]

Another, although happily a different event, which
occurred about the same time, deserves to be recorded.
The Bishop Severus, the principal actor in it, has in his
account so mixed up the fabulous with the true, that it is
almost impossible to relate it without exaggeration.[3]   On the
island of Minorca, of which Severus was the bishop, lived a
small but respectable community of Jews, whose leader was
Theodorus.   The arrival in the island of the supposed relics of
St. Stephen roused the zeal of the bishop, and of the inhabitants of Minorca, who, in the absence of other objects, resolved
on a wholesale conversion of the Jews, partly by the spiritual
means of prayer, of hymns, and of argumentation, but chiefly
by the application of a little temporal force.   The Jews had
indeed prepared for resistance, but were unequal to the
contest.   The synagogue was burnt down, and, partly by
admonitions, partly by threats, partly by promises, partly by
the force of example and of necessity,—a few, perhaps, from
better motives,—all the Jewish inhabitants of the island, 540
in number, professed their adherence to Christianity.   Severus,
in communicating this triumph, takes occasion to admonish
others to follow the same example, and promises them a
similar success.

Thus the dark clouds of persecution were once more
gathering on the horizon.   The storm of heathen violence
had indeed passed away, but the much more terrible and
prolonged tempest of mediæval persecution was impending.
Palestine was now no longer the centre of Jewish life—its
sages were unknown to fame—its colleges were closed—its
synagogues dilapidated or destroyed—its last Patriarch had
deceased.   Henceforth the holy and beautiful land was

---

[1] Socr. *Hist. Eccl.* vii. 14.   [2] *Ut supra*, vii. 15.
[3] Baronius, *Annales Eccles.* v. ad ann. 418.

forgotten, except in the tearful remembrance of past glory, or in the deep and earnest longing for future delivery,— unvisited except by the weary foot of the pilgrim, who loved to kiss the holy ground, or by the armies who vainly contended for its possession. Israel had another Exodus, with its bitter herbs and unleavened bread, and staff of wandering, and wilderness of suffering and death, but without its paschal lamb, its Moses, its pillar of cloud and of fire. But amidst all its untold sufferings, in all the lands of the Dispersion, the song of wailing was still heard on the 9th of Ab from all Israel, and on the night of the Passover still rose the prayer of hope from every heart and dwelling.

APPENDIX

I

JEWISH CALENDAR

1. NISAN.

Spring Equinox, end of March or beginning of April.

1. Beginning of the month.
14. The preparation for the Passover.
15 and 16. Feast of Passover.
21 and 22. Close of the Passover.

2. IJAR

1. Beginning of the month.
18. Lag-be-Omer, or the 33rd day in Omer, *i.e.* from the presentation of the first ripe sheaf offered on the 2nd day of the Passover, or the 16th of Nisan.

3. SIVAN.

1. Beginning of the month.
6 and 7. Feast of Pentecost, or of Weeks—7 weeks or 50 days after the beginning of the Passover, when the first-fruits (specially of wheat) were presented; commemorative also of the giving of the Law on Mount Sinai.

4. TAMMUZ.

1. Beginning of the month.
17. Fast; taking of Jerusalem by Nebuchadnezzar on the 9th, and cessation of the daily offering during the siege of Titus on the 17th. If the 17th occurs on a Sabbath, the Fast is kept on the day following.

5. AB.

1. Beginning of the month.
9. Fast—twofold Destruction of the Temple and fall of Bethar.

6. ELUL.

1. Beginning of the month.

7. TISHRI, beginning of civil year.

1 and 2. New-Year's Feast.
3. Fast for the murder of Gedaliah.
10. Day of Atonement. Great Fast.
15 and 16. Feast of Tabernacles.
22 and 23. Feast of the Eighth Day.
23. Feast on the annual completion of the Reading of the Law in the Synagogue.

8. MARCHESHVAN or CHESHVAN.

1. Beginning of the month.

9. KISLEV.

1. Beginning of the month.
25. Feast of the Dedication of the Temple, or of Candles, in remembrance of the Restoration of the Temple after the victory gained by Judas Maccabæus (B.C. 165) over the Syrians.

10. TEBÊTH.

1. Beginning of the month.
10. Fast on account of the Siege of Jerusalem.

11. SHEBAT.

1. Beginning of the month.

12. ADAR.

1. Beginning of the month.
13. Fast of Esther. If it fall on a Sabbath, kept on the Thursday preceding.
14. Purim, or Feast of Haman.
15. Purim Proper.

II

[THE GREAT SYNAGOGUE [1]]

[MUCH has been written in recent years about the Men of
the Great Synagogue, and it has at least been proved how
slight is the authority for many commonly accepted opinions
upon this subject. Our primary source of information is a
passage in the Mishnic treatise Pirke Aboth (i. 1. 2), where
" the men of the Great Synagogue " are represented as handing on the tradition of the Law, which they had received
from the prophets. We are also told (*ibid.*) that Simon the
Just was " of the remnants of the Great Synagogue." Now
the Mishna was reduced to writing about the end of the
second century of our era: Simon the Just lived probably
about B.C. 300. Our authority is therefore nearly five
centuries later than the time at which the Great Synagogue
is apparently believed to have ceased. Moreover, no mention
of any such body is to be found in the Old Testament or the
Apocrypha, or in the writings of Philo or Josephus; for the
passages which have sometimes been quoted from 1 Maccabees
(vii. 12, xiv. 28) cannot apply to the council to which
Jewish tradition relates. The statements of the Mishna are
indeed supplemented by a number of passages from the
Talmud and later Jewish literature, but these are not
entirely consistent, and cannot be said to add much to the
sum of our real historical information. Here the Great
Synagogue appears as the council which exercised the chief
authority in all religious matters after the return from Exile.
To it is ascribed, among other things, (1) the regulation of
the observance of Purim (Meg. 2*a*; jer. Meg. i. 7); (2) the
writing down of certain books of Scripture (B. Bath. 15*a*);
(3) the arrangement of the Eighteen Berachoth (jer. Ber. ii. 4);
and (4) the restoration of the Law to its ancient authority.
Several traditions connect the Great Synagogue with the
assembly described in Neh. viii.–x. (*e.g.* Gen. Rab. 78,
Ex. Rab. 41, Ruth Rab. on ii. 4); and it is recognised that
many of the statements respecting the number and names of

[1] See p. 100 ; and compare *Life and Times*, i. 94 f.

its members are derived from lists of names in Nehemiah.[1] The period of the activity of this body is especially connected with the time of Ezra; but Simon the Just is said to have been one of its members.

The scantiness of our information has given rise to numerous theories as to the character and composition of the Great Synagogue. Kuenen, following the example of older scholars, has denied that such a body ever existed. He argues, with much probability, that the whole tradition respecting it is merely a legendary version of the historical narrative in Neh. viii.–x.[2] The great assembly, which met to receive the Law and to promise obedience to it, would, according to this view, have been transformed by tradition into a college which transmitted the oral knowledge and interpretation of the Law after the cessation of prophecy. Kuenen's view has been adopted by many recent writers;[3] but even assuming that this is the true account of the Talmudic traditions, it need not follow that it explains the original passage in the Mishna.

Derenbourg,[4] on the other hand, would see in the Great Synagogue a body organised by Ezra to carry on his work, and to provide for the teaching and study of the Law. To its labours he would attribute the undoubted fact that in the time of the Maccabees we find a large portion of the people devoted to the Law, and preferring to die rather than to disobey it. The great objection to this view is the complete absence of definite confirmation of it earlier than A.D. 200. Doubtless many of the traditions recorded in the Mishna are themselves of considerably earlier date, but it must not be forgotten that Jewish tradition is often untrustworthy and unhistorical. In particular, it is clear that the later Jews possessed only slight and inaccurate knowledge of the history

---

[1] The Great Synagogue is said to have consisted of 120 members, or of 85 together with or including 30 prophets. In Neh. x. 1–28, we have 84 (or 85) signatories. 33 or 34 more names are to be obtained from Neh. viii. 4–7, ix. 4, 5.

[2] *Over de mannen der groote Synagoge* (1876); in German, *Gesammelte Abhandlungen*, pp. 125–160.

[3] *E.g.* Schürer, II. i. 354 f.; W. R. Smith, *Old Testament in the Jewish Church* (ed. 2), p. 169 f.   [4] *Histoire de la Palestine*, Ch. II.

of the period succeeding the return from Exile. Thus they do not distinguish the times of Zerubbabel and Ezra, and they allow for the dominion of the Persians in the time of the Second Temple a period of only thirty-four (Ab. Sar. 9*a*), or fifty-two years (Seder Olam).

The suggestion that the Great Synagogue was a council of prophets and scribes called together in the time of Ezra, and lasting only for a single generation, is inconsistent with the Jewish accounts, which represent Simon the Just, as well as Haggai and Zechariah, as members of that body. If, on the other hand, we accept the theory that the name is only a collective term, used to describe a succession of great teachers, it must be acknowledged that we are then abandoning Jewish tradition, and adopting in its place a plausible conjecture. This last theory contains at all events a certain amount of truth. It was owing to the activity of the scribes who carried on Ezra's work that the Law became the standard and guide of life for the Jewish people. We know nothing of the organisation of the scribes, nothing of any formal means taken by Ezra to secure the continuation of his work ; but it was the scribes who carried on the line of Jewish teaching and tradition between the time that Old Testament history closes, and the time of the first " couple " of celebrated teachers whose names have been preserved.

To sum up, the evidence which we possess is not sufficient to *prove* that there ever was such a body as that described by tradition as the Great Synagogue ; but if its existence is altogether legendary, we can account for the rise of the legend. It may have grown out of later traditions based on Neh. viii.–x. ; or it may be due to a natural desire to describe under a collective name the succession of unnamed scribes who filled up the period between the time of Ezra and B.C. 300.

For further discussions on this subject, see especially H. E. Ryle, *The Canon of the Old Testament*, Excursus A. 2, pp. 250–272 ; and, on the other side, C. H. H. Wright, *Ecclesiastes*, pp. 5 ff., 475 ff. Compare also Kuenen, *Religion of Israel* (Eng. Trans.) iii. 5–9 ; C. Taylor, *Sayings of the Jewish Fathers*, Excursus II. p. 124 f.]

III

[THE PRESIDENT OF THE SANHEDRIN[1]]

[IN Rabbinic tradition, the Sanhedrin appears as a council of scribes, with two of the most eminent scribes at its head,—the President, or Nasi, and the Vice-President, or Ab beth Din. It is, however, difficult to reconcile this representation with the statements of our Greek authorities,—the writings of Josephus and the New Testament. The principal evidence on both sides may be briefly summarised :—

(1) In the Mishna the five " couples " are named in the treatise Aboth (i. 4–12); in Chagigah ii. 2 they are introduced in a different connection, and it is stated that the first named of each pair was the Nasi, and the second the Ab beth Din.

(2) In the Talmud (Shab. 15*a*) there is quoted a Baraitha, or statement belonging to the age of the Mishna, to the effect that " Hillel and Simon, Gamaliel and Simon, held the office of Nasi during the existence of the Temple for a hundred years."

(3) In Jer. San. i. 2 (18*d*) we find three letters ascribed to Rabban Gamaliel the elder, in which he writes in a tone of authority to various Jewish communities on matters connected with the tithes and the regulation of the calendar.

(4) The appointment of Hillel as Nasi is named in Tosefta (Pesach. ix.). It is unnecessary to refer to the later Talmudic literature, or to ordinances which bear the names of famous scribes, such as Simon ben Shetach, Hillel, or Gamaliel the elder. The latter do not necessarily prove more than that their authors were the leading Rabbinic authorities of their time.

On the other hand, neither in the New Testament nor in Josephus do we find any allusion to the office of Nasi. In the New Testament the high priest writes letters to distant communites (Acts ix. 1, 2); he presides at the trial of Jesus (Matt. xxvi. 62–65), of the two apostles (Acts v. 17–28),

[1] See p. 105.

and of St. Paul (*ib.* xxiii. 2–5), and elsewhere takes the leading part (*ib.* vii. 1, xxiv. 1; Matt. xxvi. 3).[1] Gamaliel appears simply as one of the Sanhedrin, "a Pharisee, a doctor of the Law, had in honour of all the people" (Acts v. 34). According to Josephus, the high priest is the supreme judge (*Apion* 2. 22), and the head of the nation (*Ant.* xx. 10. 5). It is Hyrcanus II. who presides at the trial of Herod (*Ant.* xiv. 9. 3 – 5), while Sameas (*i.e.* Shemaiah, or possibly Shammai) is an ordinary member of the court. Ananus the younger in A.D. 62 summons a council of judges (συνέδριον κριτῶν, *ib.* xx. 9. 1). Josephus several times mentions Simon the son of Gamaliel, but nowhere hints that he was president of the Sanhedrin (*Life*, 38, 39, 44, 60; *Wars*, iv. 3. 9). The fact that Simon is described as being of very distinguished family (γένους δὲ σφόδρα λαμπροῦ, *Life*, 38) does not prove that Josephus believed Hillel to have held the position of Nasi.

In weighing the divergent evidence, it must be remembered that our Greek authorities are decidedly the earlier. A collection of Halachic decisions was made by Akiba (about A.D. 130), and a still older Mishna is spoken of (*e.g.* San. iii. 4; Naz. vi. 1). Nevertheless, we are not able to separate with certainty between the earlier and later elements in our existing Mishna, which was not committed to writing till about A.D. 200. It is true that the writers of the New Testament need not have been familiar with the details of the constitution and procedure of the Sanhedrin; and that Josephus, in his accounts of the Jewish constitution, often shows a tendency to idealise, or passes over important particulars. But more serious difficulties meet us in dealing with the statements of the Mishna, which was codified under conditions very different from those which prevailed before the fall of Jerusalem. Its descriptions clearly represent in many cases the theory of the Rabbins, and not the actual practice. In earlier times the Sanhedrin was not merely an assembly of doctors, for the "chief priests" were an important

---

[1] Any difficulties arising from the position assigned to the ex-high priest Annas in Acts iv. 5, 6, do not concern us here.

element in the council. Yet the Mishna gives us hardly any hint of the changes which must have taken place within the Sanhedrin between B.C. 140 and A.D. 70. It tells us very little about the position of the powerful priestly families, or the influence of the Sadducean nobility.

It has been attempted to show that there is no real contradiction between our different authorities. It is suggested that under Herod and the Roman procurators the high priests presided in great criminal cases ; or that Christ was brought to trial not before the Great Sanhedrin, but before an informal meeting of Sanhedrists, or before a smaller court of twenty-three. It is urged that Shemaiah may have not yet become president when the youthful Herod was summoned before the court, and that the action of Ananus was irregular. But the language of Josephus respecting Simon the son of Gamaliel remains unexplained, and we have to take into account the actual composition of the Sanhedrin, and the state of political parties, in the time of the Herods and during the period of direct Roman rule. After considering all the circumstances, it is not too much to assert, with Derenbourg (*Historic de la Palestine*, pp. 189, 239, 270), that neither Hillel nor Gamaliel nor Simon can have presided in the Sanhedrin. Indeed, Derenbourg denies that Hillel was ever a member of that body, while, from the tone of authority in the above-named letters of Gamaliel, he is inclined to believe that some confusion has arisen between Gamaliel the elder, and his grandson, Gamaliel of Jabneh. In fact, the supposed patriarchate of the first four members of the house of Hillel rests upon no sufficient evidence, and even tradition is silent as to the persons who were believed to have held the office of vice-president under them.

With respect to the period before Hillel, our information is more scanty ; Josephus is no longer a contemporary authority, and there is nothing to show that the Rabbinic tradition is more trustworthy here than at a later date. Kuenen (*Over de samenstelling van het Sanhedrin*; in German, *Gesammelte Abhandlungen*, pp. 49–81), Wellhausen (*Pharisäer und Sadducäer*, pp. 26–43), and Schürer (*Jewish People*, II. i. 180–184)

reject the whole account of the Nasi and Ab beth Din of the
old Sanhedrin as an attempt to carry back to the last two
centuries of the Jewish State the institutions of a later age.
Derenbourg and Grätz prefer to accept such portions of the
Jewish tradition as seem to be reconcilable with information
derived from other sources; but neither of them receives the
statements of the Mishna in their entirety.   Derenbourg calls
the Talmudic accounts a compromise between the traditions
of different times; but he regards it as certain that the
Sanhedrin was remodelled by John Hyrcanus, with the Nasi
and Ab beth Din at its head (*Hist.* pp. 87–93).   To Grätz it
seems self-evident that, from the time of Simon the Maccabee,
the high priest stood at the head of the council, and exercised
the office of Nasi; he supposes that under Queen Alexandra
two scribes for the first time presided over the Sanhedrin, in
the persons of Juda ben Tabbai and Simon ben Shetach (*Geschichte der Jüden* (ed. 4), iii. pp. 100 f., 137ff.).   But neither
of these theories explains the position occupied by Hyrcanus II.
at the trial of Herod; or follows any real principle in accepting or rejecting the authority of the Mishna.   It is indeed
possible that under Hyrcanus I., or under Queen Alexandra,
when the influence of the Pharisees was all powerful, some
official position was given to the leading Rabbis in the
Sanhedrin.   But even in this case the principal doctor in the
Sanhedrin must have occupied a very different position from
the Nasi of later times.   Indeed, Kuenen seems almost to
do more justice to the statements of the Mishna and Talmud,
when he regards them as preserving an authentic tradition of
the succession of "the heads of the scribes of Jerusalem"
(*Rel. of Israel*, iii. pp. 142, 240, 281–6).   Only after the
destruction of the Temple, when the high priest and the old
aristocracy had disappeared, and the priesthood had lost its
importance, did a college of doctors of the Law become the
supreme authority for Israel.   Then for the first time a
Rabbi, who was chosen to preside over a reconstituted Sanhedrin,
became the head and representative of the Jewish nation.

It should be added that Dr. Edersheim did not accept
the views of Kuenen on the Presidency of the Sanhedrin,

and considered that an adequate reply to them had been made by D. Hoffmann ("Der oberste Gerichtshof in der Stadt des Heiligthums, Jahresbericht des Rabbiner-Seminars für das orthodoxe Judenthum, 1877–78"). Dr. Edersheim acknowledged that the Rabbinic accounts of the Sanhedrin often represent "rather the ideal than the real," and that under the rule of Herod and of the Roman procurators the Sanhedrin was deprived of the power of decision of all matters of real importance. He supposed that the high priest, as the nominee of the ruling powers, presided in all great criminal causes or important investigations, while the presidency of the *Nasi* was confined to legal and ritual discussions. The trial of Christ recorded in the Gospels he regarded as a preliminary examination before an informal assembly of Sanhedrists, and not as a legal trial before a regular meeting of the Sanhedrin. See *Life and Times of Jesus the Messiah* (ed. 6, 1891), ii. 553–562.]

IV

[THE SITE OF BETHAR [1]]

[The story of the Jewish war under Hadrian, as narrated in the text, differs considerably from the account which was given, on the authority of Grätz, in the first edition of this work. One of the most important points of difference concerns the scene of the war and the site of the fortress of Bethar. Our principal authority in this matter is Eusebius, who states (*Hist. Eccl.* iv. 6) that Bethar was not far from Jerusalem; and accordingly, amongst others, G. Williams (*The Holy City*, i. 209–213) has identified the place with the modern Bettir. This village lies about six miles south-west of Jerusalem. Here a steep ridge projecting into the valley forms an admirable position for a stronghold. The hill is surrounded by the valley on three sides; only on the south,

[1] See p. 205.

near the modern village, is it connected with the main mountain range by a narrow isthmus. Traces of an old fortress are still to be seen on this hill, and a deep trench has been cut through the isthmus on the south side. This identification of Bar Cochba's stronghold has now been adopted by many writers, *e.g.* Schürer, I. ii. 309 f. ; Renan, *Les Evangiles*, p. 26 ff. ; Derenbourg, *Mélanges*, 1878, pp. 160–165 ; Conder and Kitchener, *Survey of Western Palestine*, and Memoirs, iii. 20. It is supported also by Neubauer, *Géographie du Talmud*, pp. 103–115, who places Bethar in the neighbourhood of the ancient Beth-Shemesh, and identifies the latter site with the modern Bettir ; and in the main, by Hambürger, *Real - Encyclopädie*, ii. 106 ff., who supposes Bethar to have been somewhere on the mountains of Judea. This view agrees, moreover, with the statement of the Jerusalem Talmud (Taanith, iv. 69*a*), that after the fall of Bethar, the blood of the slain rolled with it masses of rock to the sea, a distance of forty miles. In a straight line Bettir is rather more than thirty miles from the coast. Several writers, on the other hand, have preferred to identify the fortress of Bar Cochba with another Bethar or Betarus which is mentioned in two old itineraries (*Itinerarium Antonini Augusti*, and that of the Bordeaux Pilgrim, *Palaestinæ Descriptiones*, ed. Tobler, p. 9 ; compare Reland's *Palaestina*, pp. 417, 419 f.) as being on the road from Cæsarea to Antipatris. Grätz (*Geschichte*, iv. 156 f., 458 ff.), in support of this view, appeals to the other Rabbinic accounts, which reduce the distance of Bethar from the sea to *one* mile (bab. Gittin, 57*a*), or *four* miles (Midrash on Lam. ii. 1). He quotes also a passage from the Tosefta (Parah, c. 8), which states that "the stream descending from Salmon failed during the war." [1] This he refers to the Bar Cochba war, and identifies the stream from Salmon with the Nahar Arsuf, which runs by the supposed site of Betarus. This view is, however, open to grave objections. The Jerusalem Talmud is here more likely than the other

---

[1] *Yoredath ha-Çalmon* ; but Levy (*NHWB*. ii. 264*b*, 312*a*) reads *Yoredath ha-Çalmin*, the stream of the images.

Jewish authorities to have preserved a true tradition; and the context certainly suggests a longer distance for the stream of blood than one or four miles.[1] It is doubtful whether the passage from Tosefta refers to this war at all. Moreover, the proposed site is in itself improbable. Betarus stood in a region mainly inhabited by heathens; it was at no great distance from the Roman city of Cæsarea; and, being situated in a plain, it could not have been fortified either speedily or secretly. We may add that there are independent grounds for believing that the Tur Malka, mentioned as the seat of the war, was in Judea rather than in Ephraim (comp. p. 203). It will be seen, therefore, that there were strong reasons for adopting the site proposed by Williams in preference to that advocated by Grätz.]

V

ALEXANDRIAN JEWISH POETRY [2]

A FEW specimens from the drama "The Exodus," by Ezekiel, a Jewish poet who flourished the century before Christ, will sufficiently indicate its cast. Both its poetry and versification are second-rate. In the first fifty-nine lines Moses is introduced, describing in a long monologue the fate of Israel in Egypt and his own history. Zipporah enters, and Moses questions her about the virgins whom he sees in her company.

ZIPPORAH.

This country, stranger, all around is Lybia call'd,
The many tribes and families that people it
Are Ethiopians all. But he that rules the land,
Their lord and leader too—yon city owns his sway;
Their holy priest, himself, who settleth all disputes—
He, parent is to me, and parent is to those.

[1] Jer. Taan. *l.c.* "If you think that (Bethar) was near the sea (you are mistaken); it was forty miles distant from the sea." Similarly in b. Gitt. 57*a*.

[2] See p. 348.

Then follows a description of the watering of the flock, of the marriage of Moses and Zipporah, and a fragment of a dialogue between the latter and Choum. In another fragment, Moses relates to his father-in-law a dream.

MOSES.

Upon the highest mountain-top appeared to stand
So vast a throne, it reached to heaven's very vault,
On it a glorious Being seated I beheld,
Array'd with diadem. His left a sceptre held,
And with His right hand stretched out He beckon'd me.
Obedient I advanced before this glorious throne;
The sceptre He held out to me, and on His throne
He bade me sit, Himself descending from its height;
Then on my brow He placed a kingly diadem.
Anon I see around me all the world extend:
Beneath, the earth lies stretch'd; above, the vast expanse,
And now the host of stars lies prostrate at my feet.
When I assay'd to count the number of that host
Before me, lo! like soldiers marshall'd they pass on—
But at this wondrous sight, and filled with fear, I wake.

In another fragment, Moses is introduced as standing before the burning bush.

MOSES.

Ah! what portends to me that sign in yonder bush,
How marvellous it is, and passing credence! Lo!
How suddenly the flames envelop it about,
And yet withal its growth uncheck'd, and fresh and green
It stands. How that? I will advance, and see myself
This greatest wonder, far surpassing all belief.

GOD.

Stand back! oh, bravest man, and hither venture not
Without adoring. Loose the shoes from off thy feet,
The trembling ground on which thou standest, holy is.
The Word Divine sends forth His rays from yonder bush!
Take courage, O My son! and hear the word I speak.
In vain would any mortal seek to see My face,
But thou shalt be allowed to hear what purposes
Divine I have conceived—to tell them I've come down.
Behold, of those thou callest fathers I am Lord,
Of Abraham, of Isaac, and of Jacob, God.
I still remember them, and for My mercy's sake
I come to save the Hebrews, whom I claim as Mine;

My servants they—their ills and sorrow I behold.
But go thou forth, the gracious tidings carry first
To them, declaring to thy brethren what to thee I speak ;
Then tell their king, that I their God commit to thee
Thyself to lead My people forth from yonder land.

Then follow Moses' objections, God's commission to Aaron,
and the gift of the rod, whose wonder-working powers are
described at great length. We close our extracts with a
description of the drowning of Pharaoh's army in the Red
Sea, as given by an escaped Egyptian.

MESSENGER.

When from his palace Egypt's king went proudly forth,
And with him all the host with weapons thousand-fold,
With horsemen grim ; four steeds each heavy chariot drew,
Each party led by captain and subordinate,
How terrible appear'd the army thus led forth !
The centre infantry in phalanx close had form'd,
The parts where en'mies might be near'd with chariots flank'd,
And all around the host of Egypt was array'd
Both to the left and right with horsemen grim.
Would you compute the number of this mighty host ?
An hundred times ten thousand valiant men were there.
We march'd, and soon in front the Hebrew camp appear'd :
Along the beach of th' Erythrean sea we saw,
In groups recumbent some, engaged in converse sweet,
While others, way-worn and exhausted, still supplied
The wants of tender children, or of weary wives ;
The household goods lie scattered here, there cattle graze.
But when unarmed they beheld our marching host
Prepared for battle, they lift up a weeping voice,
Together all to heaven look, and to their God
They loudly cry—How large that Hebrew host !
But joyful confidence fill'd each Egyptian's heart.
Advancing still, we pitch'd our camp against their camp,
Where Beelziphon rears its walls and towers high.
Anon where Titan Helios sheds a fav'ring light,
'Gainst them an early battle we propose to wage,
Confiding in our host with weapons burnished.
But soon portents of origin Divine are seen,
That usher in events more wonderful by far
Than aught yet seen. For suddenly a pillar great
Descended like a cloud, and reach'd unto the earth,
It stood in midst between the Hebrews' camp and ours
Anon their leader Moses, lifting up the rod
Divinely given, with which he had on Egypt's land

So many evils brought, and signs so wonderful,
He smites the Erythrean sea—its waves divide.
No sooner had they seen the pathway made for them,
Than through the deep they quickly pass to yonder shore,
But we to follow them prepare immediately.
Though dark and low'ring be that night, we still pursue
With war-cry loud. But suddenly the chariot-wheels
Refuse to turn, as chains had bound them to the ground ;
And from the skies, like sheets of lightning or of fire
To us appeared. A helping God stretch'd forth His hand
To them. And now they all have pass'd to yonder shore.
But hark ! the rushing wave—the sea returns on us,
The horror-stricken soldier sees and cries aloud,
"In vain is here pursuit, oh, flee ! God's hand to them
Brings help, but death to us." He speaks, but cannot move,
The pathway in the sea is cover'd by the waves—
In them is Egypt's mighty host all swept away !

> (*Translated from Ezekiel's Tragedy, and from Demetrius in
> Eusebius, Præpar. Evangelica,* ix. 28, 29.)

VI

GEOGRAPHICAL NOTIONS OF THE RABBINS [1]

TALMUDICAL and other Jewish writings supply us with the
following explanations of the ethnographical tables in Gen. x.[2]
In the sacred text we read, " The sons of Japhet were Gomer,
and Magog, and Madai, and Javan, and Tubal, and Meshech,
and Tiras." The first name the Targums (Ps.-Jon. and Jer. ;
also Gen. Rab. 37) render by " Africa," meaning perhaps
Phrygia or Iberia, the country south of the Caucasus ; [in
the Talmuds (Joma 10a, jer. Meg. i. 11, f. 71b), however, Gomer
is Germamia, that is, the country of the Garamaei, a tribe
living on the banks of the Lycus in Assyria.] Magog is
applied by the Jerusalem Talmud to the Goths, by Josephus
(*Ant.* i. 6. 1) to Scythia. [It is probably only by error that
in the Targum Pseudo-Jonathan, Magog is rendered by Germania.] Madai (or Media) is explained in some of the

---

[1] See p. 353.
[2] Compare especially Neubauer, *Géoj. du Talm.* pp. 421–429.

Targums as Hamadan, the capital of Media. Javan was considered to be either Ephesus (jer. Meg.) or Macedonia (Targ. Ps.-Jon., Jer.). Tubal is rendered as Vittinia, which must be Bithynia in Anatolia; Josephus explains Tubal as referring to the Iberii, a Caucasian tribe. Meshech is Mosia (so the Talmuds; the Targums have Usia), that is, probably, Mysia. Josephus identifies it with Cappadocia. Tiras or Tarki is generally explained as Thrace; Rabbi Simeon said Persia.

"The sons of Gomer were Ashkenaz, Riphath, and Togarmah," explained by the Targum as Asija (Asia), Parsoi (Persia), and Barbaria. According to Josephus, Riphath is Paphlagonia, but others (jer. Meg. *l.c.*; Gen. Rab. 37) explain the name as Adiabene. Togarmah appears in the Jerusalem Talmud as Germanicia, probably the town of that name in Commagene; [in the Midrash we find Germania, probably the European country of that name]. Barbaria also had been explained of *Germania barbara*, but may well be Barbary in Northern Africa. Saadias fancifully renders Ashkenaz as the Slavonians, Riphath as the Franks, and Togarmah as the Burgundians.

In the same genealogical table we read, "And the sons of Javan; Elishah, and Tarshish, Kittim, and Dodanim," explained by the Targum as Alas, Tarsas, Achia, and Durdenia. [Alas is Aeolis, or perhaps Hellas; Tarsas is Tarsus in Cilicia; Achia, which is misspelt as Achsia (Targ. Ps.-Jon.) and Abija (jer. Meg. *l.c.*), is doubtless Achaea; but] the Midrash and two of the Targums (Jer., Ps.-Jon., in Num. xxiv. 24; comp. Jon. in Ezek. xxvii. 6) render Kittim as Italy. Durdenia is supposed to be the district of Dardania, in which Troy lay.

The genealogical table continues, "And the sons of Ham; Cush, and Mizraim, and Phut, and Canaan," interpreted by the Targum as Arabia, Egypt, Alicheruk, and Canaan. However, in Isa. xi. 11 and Jer. xiii. 23, Cush is rendered by the Targum as India. Alicheruk is supposed to be a part of Egypt, [perhaps the nome of Heracleotes in Middle Egypt]. "And the sons of Cush; Seba, and Havilah, and Sabtah, and Raamah, and Sabtecah: and the sons of Raamah, Sheba, and Dedan," paraphrased by the Targum as Sinerai, Hindeki,

Samdai, Lubiai, Zingai, Zamargad, and Mezag. Seba or Sinerai has been supposed to be the land of Senaar in the Soudan. Havilah or Hindeki was India. [Sabtah or Samdai should probably be Samrai, that is, the Sembritæ, a people living in Ethiopia, south of Meroe. Sabtecah or Zingai is perhaps Zingis, a headland on the east coast of Africa, not far from Cape Gardafui. Dedan or Mezag denotes possibly the Mazyes or Mazices, a Mauretanian tribe; while Sheba or Zemargad is perhaps the emerald district of Mons Smaragdus, near the western shore of the Red Sea.] In the Talmud, Sabtah, Raamah, and Sabtecah are rendered "the inner and outer Sakistan," by which name we should probably understand Scythia.

VII

RABBINICAL EXEGESIS [1]

[WE cannot attempt in this place to give a complete account of the principles of Rabbinical exegesis, or of the rules to be observed in deducing Halachoth from texts of Scripture. It will be enough to give some examples of the methods which were in use, and to refer the reader for fuller details to more extensive works upon this subject.[2]]

It was distinctly asserted, as a fundamental principle, that Scripture employed only such modes of expression as were common in ordinary language, and only rarely was it admitted that mere figures and illustrations were introduced. For clearness' sake, Scripture sometimes repeats or adds, what might otherwise have been inferred, as in Deut. xxiv. 16 ; but if a statement is simply repeated, the repetition indicates that something additional was now meant to be conveyed.

Inferences may be drawn from the juxtaposition of laws on subjects vastly different ; and often a word or verse is explained

---

[1] See p. 386.
[2] Compare Hirschfeld, *Halachische Exegese ;* Hamburger, *Enc.* ii., "Exegese" ; Weber, pp. 106–121.

by a parallel passage in which the same word occurs. Thus, Ex. xii. 19, the word used for *found*—"no leaven shall be found"—occurs in Gen. xliv. 12, as: "he searched and found"; and again, the word used for *searched* occurs in Zeph. i. 12, as: "I will search Jerusalem *with candles.*" Hence leaven (Ex. xii. 19) must be searched for with candles.

Rules were laid down for cases where different provisions of the law came into conflict, and for solving apparent contradictions. If one command ran contrary to another, *i.e.* could not be executed at the same time with the other, the more comprehensive, the more frequently recurring, or the more holy and important, took precedence. Where a command ran contrary to a forbid, the command set aside the forbid, provided it was not necessary to transgress a forbid before the command could be obeyed; nor might it run contrary to two forbids, or to a forbid with a command attached to it, unless the forbid was particular, while the command for which it was to be set aside was general, or else the forbid was one of which the neglect involved the Divine threat of "being cut off." [When two passages of Scripture seemed entirely to contradict one another, it was held that if one of them confirmed the injunction contained in the second, while the second appeared to annul the injunction of the first, the second passage was to be rejected. Thus in Lev. vi. 14 it was inferred that the injunction "before the LORD," *i.e.* before the Holy Place, or on the west, overrode the injunction "before the altar," *i.e.* on the south.] If, however, there was only a partial contradiction between two passages, it was necessary to wait till a third verse was found which reconciled them. So Ex. xl. 35 and Num. vii. 89 are reconciled by means of Ex. xl. 34.

Again, careful distinctions are drawn between the different modes of deducing logical conclusions from one or more passages of Scripture. If a legal determination applies to a less important object or relation, it of course equally applies to a more important cognate object or relation. This mode of conclusion is termed "Kal Ve-Chomer" (light and heavy). A well-known instance of this occurs in Num. xii. 14. By the "Gezerah Shavah," or same class, it is meant that one or more words of the same kind occurring in two texts indicate that they belong to the same class, and hence are subject to the same legal provision. [For example, from the mention of the "right foot" in Lev. xiv. 17, the conclusion was drawn that a widow should draw off the *right* shoe of her brother-in-law, who refused to perform his duty as next-of-kin (Deut. xxv. 9).] However, the application of this mode of inference required the sanction of tradition. The "Hekesh" differed from the Gezerah Shavah in that the latter proceeded upon the analogy of the words, the former upon that of the contents of the two passages. Thus, as in Deut. xv. 12 male and female slaves are placed in the same category, it is inferred that the laws applying to the one apply also to the other. Hence, as a female slave becomes the property of the purchaser merely by payment, a male slave is subject to the same regulation, etc.

In a fourth mode of reasoning, a common quality which was found in one or more clauses was elevated into a general principle, and the legal determinations applicable to one case became in consequence applicable to all analogous cases. Thus in Lev. xv. 4, every bed and every chair of him that has an issue is declared unclean. From the special mention of these two objects, which belong to two different classes of one genus, it is inferred (by a comparison of the two) that the quality common to both is that the party affected rests on them; and the legal inference is, that all things which serve for resting are unclean. This method of combination and deduction is termed "Binjan Av" (the building or structure of the father), and may either be a simple Binjan Av, or a combination from two verses.

Another group of exegetical principles was derived from the pleonastic structure of whole sentences. If in a sentence a general expression occurred, followed by a particular one, or *vice versâ*, one of these was apparently superfluous, as the general naturally included the particular. These expressions were then combined into one sentence, the first expression being the subject, the second the predicate.

The general expression was termed " Kelal," the particular " Perat " ; and the rule was, that the predicate modified the subject, so that the object of the law was general or particular according as the predicate was general or particular. We have thus two exegetical principles, Kelal and Perat, and again Perat and Kelal. We give an illustration of each. In Lev. i. 2 it is commanded to " bring an offering of beasts (in our version, *cattle*), of the herd and of the flock." The expression " beasts " is the Kelal, " herd " and " flock " the Perat ; and the interpretation Kelal and Perat, namely, that only such beasts as belonged to the herd, or to the flock, were to be brought. Again, when in Num. vi. 3, 4, the Nazir is interdicted from partaking of wine, vinegar, etc., and from eating anything made of the vine, we have Perat and Kelal, and accordingly the inference that nothing coming from the vine, not even leaves or stalks, were to be used by the Nazir.

If a sentence consisted of more than two members, various combinations of general and particular terms might occur, but the only one of importance is that termed Kelal, Perat, and Kelal. In this case the Kelal was first absorbed into a Perat, and then again swallowed up into the Kelal. While the Perat was thus generalised, it still retained many of its peculiarities, as its properties were specified, and the legal determination extended to all that shared these properties. Thus in Deut. xiv. 26 we have a Kelal, Perat, Kelal: " Thou shalt bestow that money for *whatsoever* thy soul lusteth after, for oxen, or for sheep, or for wine, or for strong drink, or for *whatsoever* thy soul desireth." In order to generalise the Perat in the above text, its essential qualities, namely, that it is fruit from fruit (" seed from seed "), and produced from the earth, are first selected. Its non-essential quality is, that all these objects were originally formed from the ground, not from water, etc. According to the prevailing opinion, the non-essential qualities determined whether an object came within the range of that legal determination. Thus in the above case it was ruled that birds or fishes were not to be bought with that money. The general exegetical principle was expressed as follows :—

" Kelal, Perat, and Kelal—you can only infer that which is like to the Perat."

Talmudical ingenuity traced many modifications of the general principles. Thus there was " the Kelal which requires the Perat," and " the Perat which requires the Kelal." The rules of Kelal and Perat might also be applied to clauses, or even verses, in their mutual relation. If a general legal determination was followed by a kindred particular, the latter modified the general, either in the way of determining it more particularly, or of limiting it. Thus, when it was in general forbidden to work on the Sabbath, while in Ex. xxxv. 3 it was particularly added that no fire was to be kindled, the latter more clearly determined that not only working in general, but particularly *every* kind of work, was interdicted. On the other hand, as the statement that redemption was not to be taken for a murderer was needless, it was meant to indicate that redemption might be taken in cases of inferior importance, such as in that of an " eye for an eye." [These different methods of drawing inferences from the statements of Scripture were not all of equal value, and some were only to be used with caution. Especially the argument from analogy underwent in the course of time numerous modifications and limitations. Rab, indeed, restricted its use altogether to cases in which the two passages compared dealt with the same subject-matter.

An important distinction was drawn between proof proper and a mere reference. There were numerous Halachoth which, though generally received, rested only on custom and tradition, and could not be proved from Scripture. In such cases the attempt was made to connect the traditional usage with the sacred text, by discovering some hint or support for it in Scripture through methods which often seem to us entirely valueless and arbitrary.] Thus, if an acknowledged Halacha could be established by an alteration of the vowel-points of the text, such a change was unhesitatingly made. Anything unusual in the language indicated a special meaning, since Scripture contained nothing that was not absolutely necessary. Letters might be drawn from the end of one word to the beginning of another, or words thrown out of their natural order, to establish a Halacha. Similarly, sentences and whole sections might be interchanged. In order to reconcile the Halacha with the sacred text, it became necessary to seek in the latter indications for enlarging—technically called "increasing"—and for limiting its provisions. The particles "and, also, that," belonged to the first class; "only, merely," etc., to the second. Some, such as the article, the suffixes, etc., enlarged or limited according to circumstances. But if the connection between a Halacha and a text was deemed certain, almost anything might be employed for proving all the details of the former. Thus the verb "he shall be" was, according to the value of its letters in numerals, made to indicate that a vow, not otherwise limited, extended over thirty days. Naturally, in deductions of this character, great weight was attached to the authority of celebrated Rabbins as warranting certain interpretations, which might again be used for involving other inferences. Thus the Halacha continually increased, in agreement with the principle that "every point was a hill and mountain (of laws)."

This sketch will enable the reader to form a tolerably accurate idea both of the method and of the results of Rabbinical studies. It will also enable him to understand the controversies to which we have partly referred, and to appreciate the extant monuments of Jewish exegetical investigations. When the elders of Bethera confessed their inability to decide the question of the occurrence of the Passover on the Sabbath, it is said that Hillel had endeavoured to prove it by a Hekesh, by a Kal Ve-Chomer, and by a Gezerah Shavah, but that he was unsuccessful until he referred to a tradition from Shemajah and Abtalion. From this we gather that at that time the Middoth or exegetical rules had not yet been received by the Synagogue. To Hillel, Jewish historians ascribe the following seven Middoth : [1]—1. Kal Ve-Chomer, *inductio a minore ad majorem.*

---

[1] Tosefta Sanh. vii.

2. Gezerah Shavah, verbal analogy. 3. Binjan Av from one verse, or deduction by combination from one verse. 4. Binjan Av from two verses. 5. Kelal and Perat, generalisation and particularisation. 6. Hekesh Mah Mazinu, analogy of the contents of a verse, " as it results from one passage." 7. Inference from the context. These Middoth, in their development, gave rise to certain controversies in which Nahum of Gimso and Nechunjah the son of Hakanah distinguished themselves on opposite sides; the former asserting that the particles " only, also," were meant to extend or limit the meaning of the text, the latter denying it. These two sages were followed by Akiba and Ishmael, of whom the former adopted, enlarged, and elaborated the views of Nahum, the latter those of Nechunjah. Akiba carried the principles of Nahum to their utmost consequences, and would even have made his interpretations the basis of other deductions. Ishmael resisted these attempts, and propounded thirteen Middoth, which are only a logical explanation of the seven Middoth of Hillel. Middoth 3, 4, and 6 were contracted into one, Middah 5 was divided into eight separate Middoth, something was added to Middah 7, while Middah 13 is entirely new.

The 13 Middoth of Rabbi Ishmael, whose authority was universally acknowledged by the Synagogue, and which were inserted into the prayer-book, are: 1. Kal Ve-Chomer; 2. Gezerah Shavah; 3. Binjan Av from one, and Binjan Av from two verses; 4. From Kelal and Perat; 5. From Perat and Kelal; 6. Kelal, Perat, and Kelal infer only what is similar to the Perat; 7. Kelal which requires a Perat, and Perat which requires a Kelal; 8. If anything contained in the Kelal is singled out (particularised) for a decrete, this is done not in order to decrete about itself, but about the Kelal; 9. If anything contained in the Kelal is singled out to impose a new obligation which is related to the general obligation of the Kelal, it has been singled out in order to lighten, but not to increase the burden; 10. If anything that is contained in the Kelal is singled out to impose a new obligation which is not related to the general obligation of the Kelal, it has been singled out both in order to lighten and to increase the burden (it is entirely independent of the Kelal); 11. If anything contained in the Kelal is singled out in order that a new matter may be attached to it, the latter may not again be ranged with its Kelal, unless Scripture itself expressly range it again with the Kelal; 12. Something may be learned from the context of a verse and something from its own bearing; 13. When two verses exclude (contradict) each other, we wait till a third verse is adduced which decides between them. The school of Shammai differed from that of Hillel in its refusal to acknowledge the validity of the Middoth. It simply referred the Halachoth to the authority of tradition. But it has to be remembered that while the teaching of Hillel was generally received, that of Shammai was not wholly repudiated.

VIII

[THE TREATISE *DE VITA CONTEMPLATIVA* [1]]

[THE genuineness of the treatise *De Vita Contemplativa*, commonly ascribed to Philo, was first disputed by Grätz in his *Geschichte der Juden* (ed. 2), iii. 463 ff. The view of Grätz was adopted, with various modifications, by Jost, Nicolas, Derenbourg, and Kuenen (comp. *Religion of Israel*, iii. 217 ff.). Opinions were, however, divided on the question whether the writer of the spurious treatise was a Christian, or a Jew, or a member of some Ebionite or Gnostic sect. But the ablest and most thorough examination of the disputed work was that of Lucius (*Die Therapeuten*, 1879), whose principal arguments may be briefly stated:—

1. Neither the *Therapeutæ* nor the *De Vita Contemplativa* are mentioned by any writer before Eusebius,—not even by Josephus or Strabo. Moreover, Philo himself never alludes to this sect in his other writings, but applies the term *Therapeutes* to any pious servant of God.

[1] See p. 420.

2. The writer is far more hostile to heathenism than Philo is.

3. Philo never lays so much stress on asceticism as the writer of this work does; nor would Philo have allowed women and children to be admitted into an ascetic community.

4. In tone and language this treatise differs from the genuine writings of Philo; indeed, several terms are used in a sense which first appears at a later date in Christian writings.

5. The practices of the Therapeutæ manifest a close resemblance to those of Christian ascetics in the third century. Hence Lucius inferred that the author of the work was a Christian, who composed it in the name of Philo about the end of the third century, as a defence of Christian asceticism (comp. Zeller, *Phil. d. Griechen* (ed. 3), iii. 2, p. 307 f.). The views of Lucius were, in the main, accepted by Zeller, Schürer, and Harnack; and for a time many scholars regarded the spuriousness of the treatise to have been finally proved.

More recently, however, the language of the *De Vita Contemplativa* has been carefully analysed by Massebieau, who has compared it with the language of the undoubted works of Philo (*Le Traité de la Vie Contemplative*, Paris, 1888). Massebieau maintains that nowhere is this treatise opposed to the philosophic conceptions of Philo; that there is, indeed, hardly a sentence to which it is not possible to find some parallel in his undisputed writings. But that a Christian writer of the third century should have been able to reproduce so closely the ideas and phraseology of the Alexandrian philosopher seems almost impossible. These conclusions of Massebieau are indorsed by Cohn (*Jewish Quarterly Review*, Oct. 1892, p. 25 ff.), who urges that, although there are several peculiarities in the external life of the Therapeutæ, there is nothing recorded of their doctrines or practices which is inconsistent with Judaism. He points out, moreover, that the argument from the silence of all authorities earlier than Eusebius is somewhat delusive. We do not know how long the Therapeutæ continued to exist; Josephus is little concerned with the Egyptian Jews; while any Father of the Church who regarded the Therapeutæ as a Jewish sect would probably not feel called upon to mention them. Under these circumstances we seem to be justified in still treating the *De Vita Contemplativa* as a genuine work of Philo.

Since the above was written, there has appeared a new work on the *De Vita Contemplativa*, by F. C. Conybeare (Oxford, Clarendon Press, 1895), in which the genuineness of the treatise is defended at considerable length.]

INDEX

Where several References are given for one Subject, the most important are generally distinguished by an Asterisk.

AARON, 300f.
Ab beth Din, 104 f.*, 149, 153 n., 174, 522, 525 f.
Abba Areka = Rab, 452 f., 468*, 537.
Abba Chilkia, 125 f.
Abba Saul, 139.
Abbahu, 489 f., 492.
Abraham, 308, 310 f., 318, 321 f., 384, 391 f., 437 ; in Philo, 418.
Abtalion, 117 f.*, 120, 150, 538.
Abu-Cariba, 65.
Acbara, 461.
Acher = Elisa b. Abuja.
Acco = Ptolemais, 143, 254, 265.
Adiabene, 45, 55–58*, 182, 532.
Admon, 139.
Adultery, 377 f.
Ælia, 191*, 198, 211 f., 224.
Ælius Verus, 448.
Africa, 353, 531.
Agriculture, 259f.
Agrippa I. and II., see Herod ; last Herodian, 82.
Akabja b. Mahalaleel, 149 f.
Akiba, 145 f., 162–174*, 449 ; sent to R. Joshua, 148, and to R. Eleazar, 156–158 ; travels of, 86 f., 196 f., 222 ; his share in Bar Cochba's rebellion, 195 f., 199 f. ; in decrees of Lydda, 215 f. ; imprisonment and death, 217–220. His pupils, Aquila, 178 ; Meir, 232 f. Mystical studies of, 170, 172 ; exegesis of, 145, 166–168*, 385, 539 ; Mishna of, 165 f., 394, 456, 523 ; sayings of, 96, 176, 274, 302, 310 f., 373, 440 ; Akiba compared with Moses, 168, 305.
Akylas = Aquila, 154, 176–178*, 399, 481.

Alabarch, 70, 410*.
Albinus, 23.
Alcimus, 13.
Alexander the Great, 5 f., 264, 388.
„   Jannæus. *See* Jannæus.
„   Severus, 458, 463 f., 472–474*, 482 f.
„   , Tiberius, 71.
Alexandra or Salome, 16, 59, 103, 109, 114 f.*, 525.
Alexandria, Jews in, 6, 67–72*, 109, 184, 186, 513–515 ; Jewish writers, 346–349*, 404 f., 408 f. ; Synagogue of, 67, 186.
Allegory, 388, 403* ; in Philo, 411 f., 417 f.
Am ha-arez, 95 f. ; cf. Unlearned.
Ambition, 301, 303 f.
Ambrose, 509 f.
Ami, 487 f., 492.
Amoraim, 470 f.*, 479, 486.
Andreas, 183.
Angels, 424, 428 f. ; in Philo, 415, 417.
Anileus and Asineus, 51–53.
Antigonus, 6 f. ; Asmoneans, 16, 18 ; of Socho, 102, 105.
Antioch, 7, 54, 60 f.*, 251, 473 ; tumults in, 513.
Antiochus I., 63, 103 ; II., 7 ; III., 8 f.
„   IV., Epiphanes, 9–12*, 60, 102.
„   V., 12 ; VI., Balas, 14 ; VII., 15 ; VIII., 15.
Antipas. *See* Herod Antipas.
Antipater, 16 f., 115.
Antipatris, 255, 264 f.
Antoninus Pius, 225 f.*, 445, 448.
"Antoninus" and Rabbi, 457–459*, 473.

543

twin brooks series BOOKS IN THE SERIES